# ISLAM & BLACKNESS

ALSO BY JONATHAN A.C. BROWN

*Slavery & Islam*
*Misquoting Muhammad*
*Hadith*

---

'A must-read for students and scholars of slavery in historical and contemporary Islam, as well as for anyone interested in slavery and its relationship to religion . . . *Slavery & Islam* is a thoughtful, well-researched, and well-written elucidation of a very difficult problem.'

*Journal of Islamic Ethics* on ***Slavery & Islam***

'. . . written in such an engaging manner that the reader may find it difficult to put it down.'

*Journal of Shi'a Islamic Studies* on ***Misquoting Muhammad***

'Brown's remarkably learned, engaging, and wide-ranging book will certainly find favor with students of all levels, but it is also accessible to educated lay readers and offers a fruitful read for specialists.'

*International Journal of Middle East Studies* on ***Hadith***

# ISLAM & BLACKNESS

Jonathan A.C. Brown

ONEWORLD ACADEMIC

Oneworld Academic

An imprint of Oneworld Publications

Published by Oneworld Academic in 2022


A CIP record for this title is available from the British Library

ISBN 978-0-86154-484-4
eISBN 978-0-86154-485-1

Typeset by Hewer Text UK Ltd, Edinburgh
Printed and bound in Great Britain by Clays Ltd, Elcograf S.p.A.

Oneworld Publications
10 Bloomsbury Street
London WC1B 3SR
England

For Maysam al-Faruqi, who guided me
Haifaa Khalafallah, who taught me
&
Wadad Kadi, who refined me

# Contents

# Preface

Social media is to books before publication what reviews are to them afterward. As I worked on this book, not a few doubts were expressed online regarding my suitability as its author. The most common were 'Who is he to write this book?' and 'What makes him think he's qualified?' Fortunately, among the many blessings bestowed on us is that we need not read everything printed, and anyone is free to compensate for the shortcomings of one publication with the composition of another. Whatever my qualifications, they would yield me little were the finished product wanting. But these preliminary questions do raise a good point. I am not black.

I did not plan to write this book. In one sense, it is a coda to my previous book, *Slavery & Islam* (2019). That monograph ended with an appendix that, put briefly, showed how little slave status meant to a pious Muslim but also how profound and inexplicable Muslim anti-blackness could be. As I discuss in the introduction of the present volume, this paradox perplexed me. The book before you is an answer to that question, among others.

In a more concrete sense, this book grew out of efforts to respond to specific questions proceeding from an academic debate over whether Islam is antiblack. As a Muslim, I take interest, I have interest, in accusations leveled at my faith. Several participants in this discussion forwarded me questions that dealt with topics I'd previously published on, and I set out to answer them. I quickly realized, however, that answering these questions required clarifying related issues, that understanding those related issues meant exploring their larger historical, cultural, or linguistic contexts, and that those contexts could not be understood from a modern, global-Western perspective without addressing other topics, and so on. The horizons of my knowledge loomed quickly. As my research led me into territory well outside my expertise, I drew on that of others and gained enough command of particular topics to find what I needed. What started out as answering a few, very specific questions about Hadiths and Islamic law ballooned into this sizable volume.

Of course, there have been a number of excellent books written on the problematic of 'Islam & Blackness,' but they either did not deal with my questions with sufficient detail or did not address what was entailed contextually and conceptually in enough depth. It is not that these books were lacking. It is that 'Islam & Blackness' looms before scholars like a chimera, a hybrid of what must be uncovered in the distant past, understood in the intervening centuries, and put into perspective in the imperious present. I have done my best to subdue it in this book, merging existing scholarship, addressing unanswered questions, and improving on those answers already given.

One comment on social media, however, stuck with me. A Black Muslim asked me, with the sincerity of a Muslim brother, 'Do you know what it feels like to be considered sub-human?' I do not. Once, in the outskirts of Dakar, as I sat with the family that had raised me there, a toddler came into the yard, saw me and started bawling in fear. That is the one time in my life that I ever felt singled out by my race, and it was more entertaining than anything else. Throughout my life, I have been treated like royalty at home and abroad.

I feel that my knowledge, understanding, analysis, and, most of all, my awareness of my own limitations have served me well in writing this book. I am confident that it has much to offer those interested in the knot of 'Islam & Blackness.' But I have never felt the pain or injustice of discrimination. I have tried to include the voices and perspectives of those who have. But this is an inexorable limitation of this book. Once, while writing it, I took down my father's volume of Léopold Sédar Senghor's poems, which the Senegalese president had gifted him. I spent hours reading it. Whatever the poems' value, I felt no connection to them until I read these lines (my translation):

> I no longer recognize white men, my brothers.
> Like this evening at the cinema,
> Lost as they were past the void made around my skin.

What I connected with in Senghor's words was not the feeling of being disappeared into the darkness. That I could imagine but never feel. It was that I too no longer recognize white men, my brothers, lost as they are. Whatever this means to anyone else, and whatever my failings, more than white I am a Muslim. That might not be enough for some, but I count it a great blessing.

McLean, Virginia, January 2022

# Acknowledgments

Those who deserve profuse thanks for their help on this project merit a slim volume of their own. As I began this book (quite accidentally), I soon realized that answering the questions that struck me as important required ranging far outside my areas of expertise. I was blessed to have friends and colleagues generous enough to help me with their knowledge and also to meet new ones open-minded and charitable enough to guide or assist a stranger looking for help. The prodigious list of their names follows, along with an expression of my great gratitude: Momodou Taal, Ahmad Al-Jallad, Abdullah bin Hamid Ali, Bruce Hall, Omid Safi, Ebony Coletu, Saif Ul Hadi, Saadbouh Cheik, Isma'il AbdulHaqq, Bader Al Saif, Hamza Zafer, Adnan Rashid, Kyle Ismail, Zachary Wright, Bilal Ware, Abdulaziz Aljohani, François Kaboré, Nadia Al-Dayel, Guy Burak, Morshed Khan, Ken Apalo, Alden Young, Flagg Miller, Dmitry Bondarev, Khalil Abdur-Rashid, Mohammad Fadel, Shahid Mathee, Farid Esack, Alex Thurston, Jeremy Dell, Philip Grant, AbdulHakeem Adebogun, Axmed Cabdiweli Salaad Kadare, Jared Sexton, David Drennan, Mohamed Ali, AbdulHaq al-Ashanti, Hisham Aidi, Morgan Robinson, Fiona McLaughlin, Ibrahima Cissé, Daren Ray, Timothy Cleaveland, Andrea Brigaglia, Fareeha Khan, Elliott Colla, Saad Yacoob, Saadia Yacoob, Asim Qureshi, Hasan Alsulami, Suzanne Stetkevych, Cheikh Anta Babou, Ubaydullah Evans, Hamzah Raza, Farid Hafez, Omar Anchassi, Amin Gharad, Sana Jamal, and Chris Haufe.

But there are a few that need special acknowledgment. Muntasir 'The Machine' Zaman has, as always, aided me greatly with his knowledge and exceptional attention to detail. Nathaniel Mathews – poor

Nathaniel Mathews – if only he had known what a drain on his time and mental energy responding to my messages would entail! He has been so giving and patient, despite disagreeing with many of my bizarre ideas. I can only hope to be able to assist him to even a fraction of the degree he has aided me. Lameen Souag is a historical linguist whose intellectual hospitality makes the warm welcome of a Tuareg campfire look like the motel reception in a Tarantino movie. He introduced me to sources I would never have found otherwise and checked my assertions on matters beyond my ken. Oludamini Ogunnaike took me under his capable wing early on in this project, correcting my mistakes and sending me material. He could have left me to err on my own, awash in compound ignorance. Iskander Abbasi also reached out to help me when he could have let me stumble like a night-blind camel. His suggestions for sources and careful reading of chapters were absolutely crucial for the subject matter areas of this book that I had no earthly business writing about. Habeeb Akande read almost the entire manuscript and provided insights I could never have imagined without his help. Ousmane Kane was kindly supportive and indulgent of my questions, helping me as a parent would help a child and always making me feel that my efforts were worthwhile.

Two scholars, however, I must thank with even greater profundity. They had every reason to ignore my work and inquiries. Doing so would have been understandable and spared them time and effort. But, whether out of scholarly integrity, pity, or some surfeit of altruism, they read large parts of this book and gave me detailed and considered feedback. Danielle Widmann Abraham should, by all rights, view me as little better than roadkill. But she took me seriously when I was still in the initial stages of the book, read an early version, and invested her time and energy into improving it substantially. I am just so appreciative of her. Later on, Kristina Richardson read several lengthy chapters and engaged my ideas with the gravitas of a real scholar. Her advice and suggestions have proven invaluable, and I am greatly in her debt. In a time of isolation, Danielle's and Kristina's correspondence provided collegial voices in the silence.

To my wife Laila: I should get you a bumper-sticker that says *Quo usque tandem abutere, marite mi, patientia nostra*? For someone who already sees the ivory tower as too insulated from what matters, you are patient and supportive of my interests in a way that is, for me, the sincerest form of appreciation. To my sons, I am so sorry for my obsessions, that they take me away from you or distract me, my little friends. I promise no more books for a while! Only martial arts movies. To my parents-in-law, Dr. Sidu and Umm Abdullah, thanks for your love and helpful responses to my random questions. To Ali, Leena, Lama, Abdullah, and Shadia, you are all so full of insights. I don't deserve your support. To Kate, Lucinda, and Senem, I love you.

Of my mother, Dr. Ellen Patterson Brown, this book has been a chance to commune with her in memory, in reading through her library of languages and ethnographies of the central Sahel, in recalling my childhood in Senegal, holding her hand on the white beach and watching the long fishing boats roll on logs into the water. I find myself looking at the picture of her doing *sujud* with me as I imitated prayer. How many people can know with certainty that their mother only ever loved them and never did or said anything to hurt them? She did not fail in shaping me. And she would have loved this book.

# Date and Spelling Conventions

In this book I have hewed to a fairly academic standard in transliteration, mainly because much of the writing I have seen on 'Islam & Africa' does not follow the conventions used in Islamic intellectual history, and I have been frustrated at not knowing how particular words or names should be pronounced or rendered.

One exception to the conventions followed in this book is proper names that have become commonly transliterated in European languages, such as Senegalese names or many names and proper nouns in South Asia. Particularly in the case of West Africa, I have transliterated first names but retained conventional spellings for last names (so Aḥmad Bamba instead of Amadou Bamba; Ibrāhīm Niasse as opposed to Ibrāhīm Anyās).

Transliteration generally follows the Library of Congress Arabic transliteration conventions. The long vowels in Arabic and Persian are represented by ā, ī, and ū. The ' character in the middle or end of words represents a simple glottal stop, like the initial sounds of both syllables in 'uh oh.' The ʿ symbol indicates the Arabic letter ʿ*ayn*, a sound that resembles the beginning of the 'Aaah' noise a person makes when getting their throat checked. In Arabic and Persian words, q represents a voiceless uvular sound produced at the back of the throat and is non-existent in English. One could most closely approximate this sound with the 'c' sound at the beginning of the crow noise 'caw! caw!' Gh indicates a sound similar to the French 'r', and kh represents a velar fricative like the sound of clearing one's throat. Dh indicates the 'th' sound in words like 'that' or 'bother.' Th represents the 'th' sound in words like 'bath.' The ḥ represents a hard 'h', the ṣ an emphatic 's', the ḍ an emphatic 'd' (Arabic *ḍād*), the ṭ an emphatic 't', and the ẓ an emphatic interdental (like an exaggerated 'th' in 'bother').

In the main text, I have used bin and bint for the Arabic 'son/daughter of' naming convention, but in the footnotes and bibliography, I have used the Library of Congress b. / bt. abbreviations. The (s) indicates the honorific Arabic phrase 'May the peace and blessings of God be upon him (*ṣallā Allāhu ʿalayhi wa sallam*),' which is commonly said and written after Muhammad's name.

The only unusual citation conventions in this book are those for citing mainstay Sunni Hadith collections. I have followed the standard Wensinck system of citing to the chapter, subchapter of every book (e.g., *Ṣaḥīḥ al-Bukhārī: kitāb al-buyūʿ*, *bāb dhikr al-khayyāṭ*) except the *Musnad* of Ibn Ḥanbal, which is cited to the common Maymaniyya print.

For dates, I have used a Common Era/Hijri date format with the exception of names or events that are commonly only discussed in the Common Era context.

All translations are my own unless otherwise indicated.

# 1

## Introduction: Reading and Misreading

> The son of ʿImrān's dark skin was of no matter,
> since the Most Worthy of Worship chose him to speak to.[1]
>
> Ibrāhīm bin Muḥammad al-Kānimī (d. 608–9/1212–3),
> a scholar from near Lake Chad who moved
> to Marrakesh, on the blackness of Moses

Mālik bin Dīnār (d. circa 127/745) was a pious scholar of Basra. The son of a Persian slave, he lived off pennies made copying the Quran.[2] Yet Basra's wealthiest man, whose daughter had been courted by elite Arabs, offered the scholar her hand in marriage (it was her idea). Mālik bin Dīnār refused, saying that he had long ago divorced the world. He had little concern for the conventions around him if they led him away from God. On another occasion, when Mālik bin Dīnār realized that a black slave in Basra was actually the truest 'friend of God' in the city, he bought the slave and freed him so that he – Basra's most esteemed worshipper – could serve him as a student.[3]

What Mālik bin Dīnār and the wealthy Basran family both knew was what all those who have ever sought knowledge (*ʿilm*) or blessing (*baraka*) quickly discover: that once one gains a taste for either, one pays little heed to the shape or color of the vessel that bears it; that, as the Quran says, "the noblest among you before God is the most pious" (49:13). They knew what one of the Prophet Muhammad's senior disciples explained in an early book on Islamic piety: that there is no person, free or slave, black or white, "whose skin I wouldn't rather be in if they were more conscious of God than I."[4]

Yet prejudices and chauvinism die hard, even in the early Muslim community that formed with undeniable sincerity and devotion around the Prophet in his city of Medina. At moments of stress, his followers could lapse into the tribalism that had long riven Arabia. When they belittled each other's clans, the Prophet decried their divisive bigotry as "putrid" (*muntina*).[5] A devout Muslim might aspire to be in the skin of those more pious, but skin color has never stopped mattering. The story of Mālik bin Dīnār and the black saint has a disturbing ending. When the saint dies while prostrating in prayer, Mālik turns him over to lay him on his back. He sees that "the blackness had vanished from his face, which had become like the moon."

For me, this story was the starting point of this book. Mālik bin Dīnār could perceive with a clarity unimaginable to me. He looked through the social and economic strictures of his day. He did not care who would see him following and serving a black, former slave. He saw only a guide to the countenance of God. Yet even with all that understanding, a story clearly meant to inspire and challenge our priorities ends by saying black skin is something to be wished away.

How can we reconcile piety wise to the superficiality of race with a sense that blackness is worth less? It is a question prompted repeatedly by Muslim writings and Muslim lives in the centuries since Mālik bin Dīnār's day. And it is very much alive in our time. From the streets of Dakar to 'Little Senegal' in Manhattan and the African suburbs of Paris, no visage is more recognized than that of Shaykh Aḥmad Bamba (d. 1346/1927, see Figures 1–3). A black Sufi master from the Wolof of Senegal, he knew that he was looked down on by many Arabs and Berbers to the north. In the opening of his famous work *Pathways to Paradise* (*Masālik al-jinān*), Bamba wrote, "Do not turn down [this book's] benefits because I am from among the blacks. The most honored servant with God is, without a doubt, the most reverent. And blackness of body signals neither weakness of mind nor lack of understanding." Bamba's awareness and preemption of prejudice was echoed by a younger contemporary and another of Senegal's most revered saints, the Sufi scholar Ibrāhīm Niasse (d. 1395/1975, see Figures 4–5).[6]

If this book begins with Mālik bin Dīnār and the unnamed black saint, it ends with the 'white' Mauritanian clerics who met and surpassed Bamba's and Niasse's challenge. One of the first prominent figures to aver Niasse's sainthood was the 'white' Mauritanian ʿAbdallāh bin al-Ḥājj (d. 1345/1927). After meeting a young Niasse, he told his community, proud Arabs descended from the Prophet, that they would be humbled by "the flood [of divine grace that] will come to a black man. And you will be forced to take knowledge from him."[7] His clan soon came to embrace Niasse as a guide.[8] Another Mauritanian peer was the Sufi master Shaykh Saad Bouh (d. 1335/1917), whose center of instruction lay just north of the river that would divide Senegal and Mauritania. Shaykh Saad Bouh was of noble Arab and Berber stock, and he too traced his ancestry back to the Prophet. Yet he instructed some of his close relatives to settle among the 'blacks' south of the river. "Your blood (*nasab*) will mix with theirs," he told them. Their descendants carry on Shaykh Saad Bouh's teachings in Dakar today, in Wolof, not in Arabic.[9]

In one sense, this book is a study of the space between the ideal of transcending what the Prophet called "the arrogance of the age of ignorance and its pride in descent" and the historical reality that prejudice taints even pious hearts.[10] But the stories of Mālik bin Dīnār and Senegal's scholars show that the terrain of what blackness has signified socially and metaphorically is far too complex to be reduced simply to ideals and their betrayal. It is a terrain of tensions and layered meanings that this book seeks to explore.

## THE ARGUMENT OF THIS BOOK

Though a contested concept, antiblackness is most succinctly understood as racism directed against people of sub-Saharan African descent. Stereotypes about real or imagined Black Africans are nearly as old as historical records. From ancient Rome to medieval China, however, these stereotypes rarely stood out markedly in societies that were often cosmopolitan and where skin color played a less important role than other markers of identity. The notion that the rights and standing of people racialized as Black African were determined by that racialization became pervasive only in the early modern period, with the rise of the Atlantic slave trade and Europe's powerful colonial states. The understandings of race and blackness that formed in the West, particularly in the United States, have profoundly shaped global discourse. They have forced a dualistic template of black and white onto social terrains from Mali to Karachi which are often too dissimilar or complex for such a binary. They have bound Black Africanness and slavery in an essential relationship when the link between the two has often been incidental. And they continue to insist that 'black' as a mundane color descriptor cannot be separated from 'black' as a negative metaphor when no such essential relationship exists. Not everyone, everywhere, and particularly not speakers of African languages south of the Sahara, has collapsed blackness as skin tone and blackness as metaphor. Neither has aesthetic preference always entailed judgments of human worth. Not all description of color is prescription of value.

In the West, Islam and Muslims have been particularly singled out as antiblack, an accusation emanating from a centuries-old Western stereotype of Muslims as slavers as well as from contemporary American conservative cultural and political agendas. Antiblackness is rampant in much of the Muslim world, from North Africa to South Asia. It causes real pain that goes unrecognized.[11] But it does not originate in Islam's scripture or its system of law and ethics. Islamic civilization inherited stereotypes about Black Africans from the Greco-Roman conviction that climate shaped both body and personality and from Judeo-Christian lore about Africans being cursed with blackness and enslavement. Though prominent Muslim scholars opposed these ideas as antithetical to the Quran, the bulk of Islamic tradition indulged and added to this body of material. While antiblackness did not define the lives and destinies of people with darker skin tones, from Morocco to India 'Black African' came to stand in for 'slave' and correlate with inferior social status. The Sufi tradition, however, inverted this image, using it to represent the saint's journey from earthly subjugation to liberation through union with the divine. And it portrayed the Black

African as the pious and devout 'slave of God' who taught and inspired his or her social betters. In Islamic law, particularly norms around marriage, when the correlation of blackness with low status and undesirability was recognized, it was as a social reality that law had to manage, not as a norm for it to protect.

Whether in Islamic law or in how Black Africans have been perceived in other genres of Islamic scholarship, antiblackness has been incidental, not essential. In law, Muslim jurists recognized that what blackness meant, whether it was attractive or unappealing, depended on where, when, and who was perceiving it. Negative stereotypes about Black Africans in Muslim writings on geography and ethnology were often mirrored by stereotypes about Slavs and Turks. And the association of blackness with slavery and primitiveness, including in the writings of many Black Muslims from the Sahel, ultimately turned not on phenotype but on their locating blackness beyond the southern boundaries of the Abode of Islam.

Whether antiblackness was incidental or accepted as social custom, however, leading voices of Muslim scholarship from medieval to modern times have rejected it and advocated vigorously for the Prophet's teaching that no race or tribe has any inherent value over another. As judges, jurists and moral guides, Muslim scholars have had to balance a realistic accommodation of custom with their duty to enjoin right as 'heirs of the prophets.' In light of the severity of the blight of antiblackness today, it is clear that their duty as moral guides must be to promote the erasure of the color line.

## THE VIRTUES OF BLACK AFRICANS . . . *SŪDĀN, ḤABASH, ZANJ*?

Though I had puzzled over the story of the Basran saint's vanishing blackness for some time, this book came about by accident. In the summer of 2020, a debate broke out on an academic listserv devoted to African history. The matter of dispute was whether Islam was inherently antiblack. As we discuss in Chapter 4, this was not a new debate. Several participants contacted me with questions relating to topics I had published on in the past, such as reports attributed to the Prophet Muhammad (Hadiths) and slavery in the Shariah (Islamic law). As I tried to answer those queries, I found that every step I took in what was supposed to be a quick research foray required finding the answer to broader and more profound questions. Before I knew it, I was writing a book.

This is not the first book on the subject of Islam and blackness. It stands on the shoulders of impressive tomes produced by Black Muslim scholars in the recent past. Su'ad Abdul-Khabeer's *Muslim Cool: Race, Religion and Hip-Hop in the United States* focuses on the modern intersection of Islam and Blackness in the context of American society and its entrenched racism. Other books address the historical questions on which this present work focuses. They include *Islam and the Blackamerican* by perhaps the most influential figure in Islamic scholarship in North America, Professor Sherman Jackson. Other works include Abdullah Hamid Ali's *The 'Negro' in Arab-Muslim Consciousness*, Ahmad Mubarak and Dawud Walid in their *Centering Black Narrative*, Dawud Walid on his own in *Blackness and Islam*, AbdulHaq al-Ashanti in his *Defining Legends: An Analysis of Afrocentric Writings Against Islam*, Habeeb Akande in his *Illuminating the Darkness*, Shaikh Mustafa Briggs' recent *Beyond Bilal*, Imam Zaid Shakir in an essay on "Islam, the Prophet Muhammad (s) and Blackness," Rasul Miller in "Is Islam an Anti-Black Religion," and Iskander Abbasi in his essay "Anti-Blackness in the Muslim World."[12] Here I hope to update and expand on these efforts, particularly in light of recent debates and specific accusations of antiblackness in Islamic law and scripture.

These books, in turn, build on a long tradition of documenting the accomplishments of Black African Muslims and their contributions to Islamic civilization. Pushing back against antiblack prejudice in the Muslim world has formed a veritable genre of scholarly writing, beginning in the early Islamic period. Though they fall short of what is called for by modern antiracist activism, these books took on the question of antiblackness in Islam before it was ever phrased in its modern form. These works include:[13]

- *The Pride of Blacks over Whites* (*Fakhr al-sūdān ʿalā al-bīḍān*), an epistle by the famous Basran intellectual and overall man-about-town, al-Jāḥiẓ (d. 255/869);
- *Treatise on the Virtue of Blacks over Whites* (*Risāla fī tafḍīl al-sūd ʿalā al-bīḍ*) by the Baghdad intellectual Ibn Shirshīr al-Nāshī (d. 293/906);
- *On Blacks and their Virtue over Whites* (*Kitāb al-Sūdān wa faḍlihim ʿalā al-bīḍān*) by the Baghdad litterateur Ibn al-Marzubān (d. 309/919);
- *On the Asceticism of Blacks* (*Kitāb Zuhd al-sūdān*) by Jaʿfar bin Aḥmad al-Muqrī (d. 500/1107);
- *Illuminating the Darkness concerning the Virtue of Blacks and Ethiopians* (*Tanwīr al-ghabash fī faḍl al-sūdān wa'l-ḥabash*), an encyclopedic work by the famous Baghdad polymath Ibn al-Jawzī (d. 597/1200);
- no less than three treatises by the great Egyptian scholar al-Suyūṭī (d. 911/1505): *Raising the Standing of Ethiopians* (*Rafʿ sha'n al-ḥubshān*); *The Trellised Flowers on Reports of Ethiopians* (*Azhār al-ʿurūsh fī akhbār al-ḥubūsh*); and *Life's Promenade in Choosing Preference between the White, Black and Brown* (*Nuzhat al-ʿumr fī al-tafḍīl bayn al-bīḍ wa'l-sūd wa'l-sumr*);
- *The Embroidered Brocade on the Virtues of Ethiopians* (*al-Ṭirāz al-manqūsh fī faḍā'il al-ḥubūsh*) by the Meccan scholar Ibn ʿAbd al-Bāqī (d. *circa* 993/1585);
- *The Splendor of the Beautiful on the Virtues of Ethiopians* (*Kitāb Rawnaq al-ḥisān fī faḍā'il al-ḥubshān*) by the Meccan scholar Khalīfa al-Zamzamī (d. 1062/1652);
- *Alerting the Oppressors to the Freedom of Blacks* (*Tanbīh ahl al-ṭughyān ʿalā ḥurriyyat al-sūdān*), a treatise rebutting those in Morocco who believed Black Africans should be perpetual slaves, stressing the long presence of Islam and Islamic scholarship south of the Sahara, by Muḥammad al-Sanūsī al-Jārimī (writing 1320/1900, NB: some have identified this author as al-Ghānī al-Sūdānī, suggesting he was from a sub-Saharan region. But it seems clear in the text that he does not identify as one of the *sūdān*);[14]

- a book on freed black slaves who had attained excellence by the Moroccan Muḥammad al-Adūzī (d. 1323/1905);
- *A Boast-Off between a White, Brown and Black Woman* (*Mufākhara bayn al-bayḍā' wa'l-samrā' wa'l-sawdā'*) by the Damascene Muḥammad Bahā' al-Dīn al-Bayṭār (d. 1328/1910);
- *Jewels of the Gorgeous from the History of Ethiopians* (*Kitāb Jawāhir al-ḥisān fī tārīkh al-ḥubshān*) by the Egyptian Azharī Aḥmad al-Ḥanafī al-Qinā'ī, published 1903;
- *Blacks and Arabic Civilization* (*al-Sūd wa'l-ḥaḍāra al-ʿarabiyya*) by ʿAbduh Badawī (d. 2005);
- and *The Legacy of Blacks in Islamic Civilization* (*Athar al-sūd fī al-ḥaḍāra al-islāmiyya*) by Rashīd Khayyūn, published 2020.

[Some of these important works have been translated: selections from al-Suyūṭī's *Rafʿ sha'n al-ḥubshān* as *The Spirit of Black Folk*, trans. Adeyinka Muhammad Mendes and Talut Dawood; al-Jāḥiẓ's *Fakhr al-sūdān ʿalā al-bīḍān* as *The Glory of the Black Race*, trans. Vincent Cornell (rare); and Ibn al-Jawzī's *Tanwīr al-ghabash* as *Illuminating the Darkness: The Virtues of Blacks and Abyssinians*, trans. Adnan Karim.]

These book titles invoke a number of ethnonyms (names for ethnic groups), phenonyms (names for a certain 'look') and toponyms (names based on geographical location). The terms that Muslim authors, including ones from Africa south of the Sahara, have used to denote Black African people have often overlapped and at other times been complementary. Further confusion results from several of them being used for places as well as peoples. Exactly how these terms have been used across the centuries would require another book-length study, but generally the terms are as follows.

As we will see, ***aswad*** (black, fem. *sawdā'*) means either very dark skinned or having a 'classical' sub-Saharan, Black-African phenotype. The plural, ***sūdān*** (blacks, with the term *sūd* replacing this in twentieth-century formal Arabic) means people with the generally dominant phenotype from Africa south of the Sahara. The *bilād al-sūdān* (lands of the blacks) is the term that Muslim authors, including those living in that region, have used to refer to the Sahel and south into Africa's forest zone. ***Zanj*** (a toponym as well as an ethnonym, with *zanjī* as a singular and *zunūj* as an occasional plural) refers to East Africa and the people coming roughly from the area between Mozambique and the southern Horn of Africa and extending inland and up into the Nile.[15] *Zanj* can also be used more generally as a synonym for *sūdān*.[16] ***Ḥabash*** are the people from the Horn of Africa (an area called *Ḥabasha*). From the ninth through the sixteenth centuries CE, this was often used only for the region of modern-day Ethiopia and Eritrea, but it has also included people from Somalia and even northern coastal Kenya. *Ḥabashī* (the adjective) is first and foremost defined by a certain 'look' well known among Ethiopians and Somalis, including an aquiline nose.[17] Although *Sūdān*, *Zanjī* and *Ḥabashī* have often been used interchangeably, they have also been used with their specific meanings. Writing in the Hejaz in the 1500s, for example, Ibn ʿAbd al-Bāqī clearly distinguished East Africans (*zanj*) from people from the Horn of Africa (*ḥabash*).

Other specialist terms used in this book will be familiar to those with a background in Islamic thought. The Shariah (Islamic law) is the sacred law deposited in the world in the form of the Quran and the Prophet Muhammad's authoritative precedent (***sunna***). It has been interpretively unpacked over the centuries, debated and applied to novel questions of ritual and daily life by Muslim scholars (***ʿulamāʾ***). The Quran was set down in permanent, written form within two decades of the Prophet's death. His precedent and teachings, however, which explain and build on the Quran, have been preserved in much more contested forms. **Hadiths**, which are reports about the sayings, practice and judgments of the Prophet, were transmitted in mostly oral form for several decades before being written down in progressively more systematic ways. The forgery of Hadiths proved rampant as different groups sought to promote their agendas. Because of this, and also because of the inevitable errors that seep into even well-intentioned transmission, Hadith authenticity emerged as a major source of disagreement among Muslim scholars, who worked to sort out reliable attributions to the Prophet from forgeries. In the 800s CE, a number of Hadith collections were compiled which came to be seen as mainstay, if imperfect and incomplete, representations of the Prophet's sunna.

Besides Hadiths, the Prophet's teachings were passed on by two other means. The Prophet's Companions (the first generation of Muslims) embodied his practice and conduct in the form of communal practice and through the methods of understanding and applying the Quran that they learned from him. Because the first three generations of the Muslim community were so integral to the preservation and transmission of Islam's two scriptures, the Quran and sunna, the thinking of Muslim scholars from that period effectively forms a third pillar of the Shariah's foundations.

By the 900s CE, the efforts of Muslim scholars to understand, authenticate and apply the sources of the Shariah had coalesced into several interpretive approaches centered around the work of seminal personalities. These included Abū Ḥanīfa (d. 150/767) in Kufa, Mālik bin Anas (d. 179/796) in Medina, al-Shāfiʿī (d. 204/820) in Iraq and Egypt, and Ibn Ḥanbal (d. 241/855) in Baghdad, among others. Their opinions on matters of law and theology, as well as those of other leading contemporaries, matured into four major Sunni **schools of law** (the Ḥanafī, Mālikī, Shāfiʿī, and Ḥanbalī), two Shiite schools of law and several schools of theology. Specific schools of law in particular came to predominate in different regions. For the subject of this book, the Mālikī school of law, with its near monopoly in Africa, and the Ḥanafī school's predominance in India will be most relevant.

## Blackness OR blackness? THE QUESTION OF CAPITALIZATION

Black is a color or, more properly speaking, the absence of color. As we will see in Chapter 3, people from the Mediterranean and the Middle East were describing people from south of Egypt as 'black' over three thousand years ago and even depicting them with black paint. But few humans actually have black skin (at least that I've seen). When talking about skin tone and phenotype, black is a word used to racialize – in other words, to construct a category of bodily distinction. In short, as we will discuss later, 'black' is either a racial or proto-racial label, depending on how race and racism are defined and when they are thought to have originated. In any case, describing someone as 'black' is really to say that they have been racialized as black.

One way to acknowledge that phrases like 'black people' are not neutral but rather the product of racialization would be to replace a phrase like 'black people' with 'people racialized as black.' This is clear but awkward in prose. One could capitalize Black to distinguish this racialized adjective, but aspects of ambiguity would remain. First, capitalized Black has come to denote ethnic and cultural identities formed among African diaspora communities, such as in the United States. Second, the details and histories of racialization in particular locales have not been uniform. From ancient Egypt and Greece to Sung China and, of course, early modern Europe, 'black' has meant racialized as possessing the features and skin tone associated with what people outside Africa south of the Sahara perceive to be the recognizable sub-Saharan African phenotype. But, as we will see, the definitions of 'black' in places like South Africa, Brazil and the U.S. have marked very different boundaries. Moreover, in some times and places, 'black' has indicated only dark skin tones, whether African, Arabian, or Indian, without connoting any of the other somatic features associated with Africa. Crucially, this was the case in the formative period of the Islamic tradition at the center of this book.

An additional challenge in how we translate or render 'black' is that speakers and writers could be intentionally exploiting or unintentionally reproducing the multivalence of the word. Capitalizing or qualifying their use of 'black' might impose a set meaning on the word when ambiguity, such as that between literal and metaphorical, was intended by the speaker or demanded by the context. Choosing to capitalize 'black' would be making a decision that should perhaps be left to the reader.

White and whiteness present a similar problem. In the early Islamic period, Arabs used 'white' to refer to a light-olive skin tone. Later Muslim writers in medieval North Africa and south into the Sahel referred to people with Arab or Berber ancestry as 'white' regardless of their actual appearance (Shaykh Saad Bouh was thus 'white' but would likely be considered 'black' in France and the U.S.). There have been justified objections to capitalizing white when speaking about White Americans as counterparts to Black Americans, since this is seen as validating an inherently problematic 'White' culture. But capitalized White, along with Caucasian, is still used to denote the phenotype common to northwest Europe.

No convention for these labels can pay just heed to all the historical and communal concerns around race while still allowing the effective translation of the terms used in Islamic civilization. With apologies for their shortcomings, in this book I will thus use the following conventions:[18]

- **black/blackness**: for default usages, particularly if it is unclear what the speaker means in terms of metaphor, literalness, racialization, etc.
- **Black African/Africanness**: when what is intended is clearly the somatic features common in Africa south of the Sahara or the people racialized as possessing what is imagined as the 'classical' sub-Saharan African phenotype.
- **'black'/'blackness'**: when it is precisely the word and its meaning that is being contested.
- **Black American/Black British, etc.**: for communities in those societies in which racialization as black, a synthesis of African and other descents and cultures, a diaspora experience, exploitation and discrimination have created distinct cultures.
- **White/Whiteness**: for the phenotype associated with Europe as well as the globalized power structure and system of norms and standards of beauty that emerged in the early modern and modern periods with and through European colonialism and global consumer capitalism. Capitalization distinguishes this from uses of white in Islamic civilization for other phenotypes or racial categorizations.

## BLACKNESS IN THE MODERN MUSLIM WORLD

Writing in the early 2000s, the late historian of Islamic West Africa John Hunwick (d. 2015) pondered why no real sense of 'black consciousness' had arisen in countries like Algeria as it had in places ranging from Zanzibar to Brazil. Perhaps, he suggested, this was due to the descendants of enslaved Black Africans having been integrated into their societies, to the point that there were "a relatively small number of clearly identifiable descendants of slaves." Perhaps, Hunwick added, the explanation lies in the low social status and marginalization of those who are or who are seen as descendants of slaves.[19]

The question 'Where are the black people in the Muslim world?' might appear simple, but it involves manifold complexities. As we will discuss in Chapter 3, what blackness means and who defines it have long been contested, and that contestation has only grown more intense in recent decades. Locating a 'black' community means choosing whether the answer will come from people's self-identification or from outside ascription, both of which could hinge on very particular ideas of what blackness means. In the twentieth and twenty-first centuries, identification as black has often taken place amid competing local and transnational identities as well as in the climate of global activisms like decolonialism, Pan-Africanism, and Black Consciousness, some of which originated in the West.

In the last decade, there has been increased interest in identifying 'black' communities and also in identifying as 'black' in the Muslim world. Afifa Ltifi has done preliminary research on Tunisians of Black African descent.[20] Chouki El Hamel has studied a sizable and identifiable Black African population in Morocco, with its own cultural presence in the musical style of Gnawa. Numbering around half a million at the beginning of the twentieth century, this Moroccan Black diaspora is most concentrated in the country's historical capitals of Marrakesh, Meknes, and Fez, where large numbers of freed slaves settled over the centuries.[21] Recent years have seen journalism and preliminary academic research on other 'Afro-Arabs,' such as Afro-Palestinians and Afro-Iraqis.[22] There have also been initial studies on a community of hundreds of thousands of South Asians of African descent, known as Sheedis, concentrated in the Sind and Baluchistan regions of Pakistan.[23] As Hunwick alluded, one basic problem is how one could locate or identify who belongs to these communities. How would one establish whether such a group even exists in any number as opposed to being an expression of a relatively small network of people who have begun identifying as such?[24]

Less logistically difficult but much more politically inflammatory is the inevitable question of whether a Black/Afro-__ identity is 'authentic' or a reflection of an Atlantic Black diaspora identity inspiring imitation elsewhere. This question has been contested both by outside scholars and those within the societies in which such communities are situated. The issues of whether or not slavery, blackness, and race in Muslim or other non-Western societies are comparable to slavery, blackness, and race in the West have been debated in the West since as early as the 1500s.[25] These discussions are paralleled in many non-Western societies (and in the Muslim world in particular). They remain riven by the same colonial and post-colonial tensions that have characterized so many claims of comparison and solidarity across civilizational boundaries, from Marxist claims about downtrodden proletariats to feminist claims about the oppression of women in the 'Third World.' When someone claims that a phenomenon associated with a once-or-present colonizer also exists in a society it colonized, is that claim an accurate identification of some shared phenomenon? Or is it simply an ongoing act of colonization by which people in the colonized society have begun seeing themselves through the eyes of their colonizers? Are non-elite people working in a factory in Iran part of an international proletariat or part of a system of society and labor specific to their region and its particular history? Does a man who engages in sex with another man in Java fall under the identity and activist jurisdiction of an American LGBTQ group, or is his sexuality part of a local tradition incommensurable with gay identity in the West?[26]

Such tensions seem impossible to resolve because, even in a clear case of ongoing colonial imposition, once a perspective has been assimilated by members in the colonized or post-colonial society, it is as 'real' and sincere a part of their culture as any other. The case of the Shirazi community in Zanzibar offers a useful example. This group claims patrilineal descent from Persian merchants who settled in Zanzibar centuries ago. In the last century, Africa passed from colonialism to independence within a swirl of competing identities, some old, some new, some locally generated and some international. In the mid twentieth century, members of the Shirazi community embraced several competing notions of race and identity. Some claimed they were not African but Persian, gaining Islamic social cache in majority-Muslim Zanzibar by associating with their roots in the Islamic 'heartland.' Some invoked their families' long presence in Zanzibar to argue they were the island's true 'natives,' asserting their place in the face of 'later' arrivals from the African mainland. Others claimed that, Persian or not, their black skin made them part of the great African nation long oppressed by Arabs and Europeans alike.[27] How would one assess which of these identities or associations were more authentic or real than others?

## ANTIBLACKNESS IN THE MODERN MUSLIM WORLD

Antiblackness is shockingly rampant in the Muslim world, namely those countries and regions in which Muslims are the majority. In Cairo, for example, Westerners (including Western Muslims) with skin tones and features prominently associated with Black Africa are frequently teased or taunted in the streets. In testimony that is far from rare, a Black British student studying in Egypt recalls losing count of how many times people have yelled out at him in Arabic, "Hey chocolate!" The irony is that he hails from the family of Ḥājj ʿUmar Tal (d. 1280/1864), an anti-colonial leader of Senegambia. Worse treatment is suffered by Cairo's sizable population of Sudanese migrants and refugees, who often have the 'blue' black skin tone and pronounced height common in their home region.[28]

Of course, statements about antiblackness in the Muslim world imply qualification. A substantial part of the Muslim world lives in the Sahel and south into Africa's forest zone and along the East

African coast. Unlike medieval Christendom or even the early-modern and modern West, there are thus vast swaths of territory in the premodern and modern Muslim world where effectively the entire population is Black African. Yet antiblackness is an undeniable blight in a geographic band running eastward from the Senegal River, through the Sahel and the Horn of Africa, down onto the Indian Ocean coasts of Africa, Arabia, and India, then up through Muslim Central Asia and westward back through the former Ottoman Middle East and North Africa (I have not found any comparable indication of this in Muslim Southeast Asia).

Of course, antiblackness is a global problem. Antiblackness is rife among Arabs in the U.S.[29] It is just as present among Arab Christians as Arab Muslims, among Muslim and Hindu Indians alike. Antiblack racism in Muslim communities must be addressed with all seriousness. In this book, however, I am not engaging the prejudices of individuals or even communities. I am addressing the accusation that Islam *as a religion*, either in its founding scriptures or its normative traditions of law, theology, and spirituality, is antiblack.

The high lettered tradition of Islamic scholarship, however, has never been sealed off from the Muslim masses and popular culture. In fact, aspects of antiblackness in Islamic scholarship and among lay Muslims have fed, influenced and complemented each other over the centuries. At the very least, a cursory exploration of antiblackness in parts of the modern Muslim world is essential to appreciate the extent of the affliction and glimpse the forms that premodern antiblackness has taken after germinating in modern soil.

One of the most egregious and well-known manifestations is that the principal word for Black African in many dialects of colloquial Arabic is the word for 'slave.' *ʿAbd* (pl. *ʿabīd*) predominates in the Levant, Iraq, and the Arabian Peninsula, though usages of *aswad* (black) and *zinjī* (Zanj) are also attested. In Morocco, the slave-related term *ḥarṭānī* (pl., *ḥarāṭīn*, freed slave) is the most common, though *kḥal* (kohl-colored) and *akhḍar* (green) also appear. The synonymity of slave and Black African in the social lexicon of Moroccan Arabic is evident in sayings and adages. One states, "If there were good in slaves, their faces would not be [black like] iron," another that "People say to the slave, 'The face that shows shame [in others] for you is black (*kḥāl*).'"[30] In Libya and Tunisia, *khādim* (servant, slave) is the main word for Black African, and in Algeria and Libya *wṣīf* (handmaid, slave) is common. The most populous Arab country, Egypt, whose dialect is the most culturally influential, is an exception. There 'black' (*aswad*, pl. *sūd*) is used.[31]

Even when slave and Black African are not synonymous in Arabic, blackness is often associated with undesirable status and ugliness. For example, both Palestinian and Egyptian dialects of Arabic have their own versions of the saying, 'You love who you love even if they are a black slave.'[32] These two Arabic dialects, as with others, are also replete with metaphors and similes that utilize the black = bad and white = good metaphor, such as whiteness of face meaning fortunate, beautiful or noble and blackness of face meaning the opposite. Many counterparts are found in modern Persian as well.[33] Some idioms mix somatic color and moral metaphor, such as the Palestinian saying, 'Abū Zayd is black [read: skin color] but his inside is white [read: nobility of character].'[34] This last case seems the most insidious, building a clear bridge between the physical and the moral. But as we will see in Chapter 3, this is misleading. The negative associations of Black African in modern Arabic are undeniable. But the parallel usage and intermingling of black/white as metaphor and black/white as color descriptors is common in languages, including languages whose speakers consider themselves black.

The lexical antiblackness in these Arabic dialects is not uniform. There are important elements of class and education involved in word usage. An erudite and upper-class family in Jerusalem or Damascus is much less likely to use 'slave' (*ʿabd*) for a Black African than a poorer and less educated one. And there are important exceptions to general usage as well. In Saudi Arabia and the Persian Gulf countries, for example, *kḥāl* or *kaḥlānī* (kohl-colored) are commonly used in the colloquial speech among male youth.[35]

Most fascinatingly, in parts of Mauritania as well as in Kuwait, Qatar and the U.A.E. the most common term for black person is *khāl* (pl. *akhwāl*; note: not *kḥāl*), which literally means maternal uncle.[36] This merits repetition. In these speech communities, the phrase for 'black people' literally translates as 'maternal uncles.' This draws attention to one of the significant differences between the knot of race and slavery in the Muslim world and its counterparts in places like the United States and South Africa. Since the earliest decades of Islam, it has been established in the Shariah that children born of a slave concubine and her owner were free, legitimate and of the same social standing as a child born of a free wife.[37] In the case of communities in which *akhwāl* denotes black people, it is highly probable that this usage originated from the salience of Black African slave concubines among mothers.[38] Such acknowledgment of a more intimate connection to Black Africans may be linked to Gulf societies like Kuwait and Qatar having much better integrated populations (including citizens) of African descent than many other places. Africans, mainly slaves, made up between 11 and 22% of these two communities *circa* 1900. More important than population size, the formative experience of these societies in the modern period, namely the total economic collapse that followed the end of commercial pearling and date farming in the 1920s and '30s, bound former slaves and former owners together with relatively strong social cohesion.[39]

## ROOTS AND BRANCHES OF ANTIBLACKNESS

Antiblack racism in the modern Muslim world falls into two broad categories: enduring civilizational bias, and the stigma of perceived or actual descent from slaves. Like European writers and explorers, premodern Muslim scholars viewed the interior of Africa as a 'dark continent.' Beyond the frontiers of the Abode of Islam lay savage people who went naked, engaged in cannibalism and had neither achieved any form of civilization nor received any revealed books. Of course, as noted above, these were not characterizations of Black Africans per se but rather of Black African *pagans*. By the 1300s CE, a significant population in Africa south of the Sahara had embraced Islam, and the lands in which they lived had become part of the Abode of Islam.

This perspective on the 'dark' African interior thrived into modernity. In the nineteenth century, as Muslims in the Ottoman Empire struggled to negotiate their place in a world dominated politically, economically and militarily by the European great powers, Ottoman public views on Black Africa dovetailed with those of Conrad. Rifaʿat al-Ṭahṭāwī (d. 1290/1873), an Egyptian religious scholar sent to France as part of a delegation charged with learning what was needed to model European reforms, wrote about the distinction in types of human societies. Those who had achieved civilization and urbanity, such as Europe and the Muslim world, stood in stark contrast to "those wild and neglected peoples" exemplified by the inhabitants of the "lands of the blacks, who are forever like untamed animals, not knowing right and wrong (*ḥalāl wa ḥarām*) and unable to read or write . . ." Al-Ṭahṭāwī was hardly alone in this view. It is as easy to find in the writings of the intellectual elite of the late Ottoman world as it is in the works of Kipling.[40]

We see the same attitude even decades later with a figure who, ironically, devoted his life to pan-Islamic solidarity against European domination before and after World War I. Shaqib Arslan (d. 1366/1946) of Lebanon was livid at the League of Nations' decision to place the post-Ottoman Middle East under French and British tutelage. But part of his anger was expressed in his rejection of Arabs being lumped in with the rest of the colonized world. The cradle of civilization was Arab, he insisted. Arabs were part of the "the white race" and would not accept being made "the equal of the blacks of Cameroon and Togo."[41] Another Arab leader with avowedly anticolonial intentions exhibited similar condescension. In 1955, Egypt's dynamic president Gamal Abd al-Nasser (d. 1970) publicly underscored his country's commitment to its African heritage and its destiny as part of Africa. Egypt would never waver in its support, he vowed, for "the spread of enlightenment and civilization to the remotest depths of the jungle."[42]

A more pervasive vector of antiblackness, particularly in the Arab world, has been social contempt due to perceived patrilineal descent from slaves. A persistent and denigrated status resulting from slave descent is an undeniable social reality in Mauritania, Oman, and Yemen as well as parts of Mali and Niger.[43] In some instances, such as in Yemen, this extends to taboos about ritual filthiness that verge on caste anxiety. Such attitudes stand out in Islamic civilization, since the norm historically has been that descent from slaves is not a social liability.[44] As we will see, a sizable plurality of the most influential early Muslims were either freed slaves or their immediate offspring. Though this is only speculation, in some cases, such as Oman and Tuareg areas of West Africa, this slave stigma may have resulted from slavery ending by governmental decree as opposed to by a more gradual and economically organic process. Families emancipated in such a way may have been frozen in a sort of social stasis, unable to find complete acceptance in their new status.

The case of the Sahelian countries that emerged from French colonial domination is one in which antiblack racism is tied to former slave status and to the perception on the part of Berber and Arab communities that they were losing power to the Black Africans they had long looked down on. During the mid twentieth century, tensions crystalized in French West Africa between the Tuareg and Arab 'whites' and the 'black' Africans, both those who were the hereditary slaves of the 'whites' and the other non-Muslim ethnic groups to the south of the Niger River. Fears arose among the Tuareg of losing social control and property to their former slaves as well as to the large non-Muslim, Black African populations that they worried would dominate the states that seemed likely to emerge as colonialism ended. As independence loomed in the 1950s, France promoted the idea of a unified north Sahelian region. Though it never materialized, it was thought that such a state would allow France to isolate and control new oil discoveries in Algeria and assuage Arab and Tuareg fears of being swamped by non-Muslims. The 'whites' sometimes phrased the need for separation as due to differences in heritage and interest between two distinct communities. But they also expressed it through their contempt for Black Africans, whom they associated with enslavement.[45]

Two egregious cases of antiblack racism are also the best known internationally due to the attention they have received from human rights organizations: the plights of the Haratin in Mauritania and the Akhdam in Yemen. The Arabic word *ḥarāṭīn* (probably derived from a Berber word for mixed bloodlines) is used to refer to descendants of slaves racialized as black in both Mauritania and Morocco, which share the common thread of the antiblack racialization of slavery and the stigma of slave descent.[46] As Chouki El Hamel has detailed, going back at least to the 1500s CE, there existed a strain of thinking among Muslim rulers and an extreme minority of Muslim jurists that conquered populations could be drawn on perpetually as a source of slaves. Though this had been roundly condemned by prominent Muslim jurists in the region, in 1698 the powerful Moroccan sultan Mawlāy Ismāʿīl (d. 1139/1727) ordered the enslavement of the free black Muslims in his realm to serve in his army. This violated undisputed boundaries of the Shariah, including the red lines that Muslims could not be enslaved and that, once manumitted, former slaves could not be re-enslaved. The Muslim scholars of Fez and Meknes objected vociferously to the order, many paying with their welfare, freedom and one even with his life. But the sultan justified his decision on the flimsy argument that Black African slaves captured during the Moroccan conquest of Timbuktu a century earlier had not been freed officially. They and their descendants were thus still government property. Within a few years, some 221,000 Black Africans had been rounded up from the cities and countryside.[47]

The enduring slave or semi-slave status of the descendants of enslaved Africans has survived in to the present day in Mauritania with the Haratin, the descendants of former slaves. This is compounded by the persistence of actual slavery in the country. Though the Mauritanian government formally ended slavery in 1980–1 (for the third time), and owning slaves was criminalized in 2007, the practice continues informally.[48] The best estimates are that about two thirds of Mauritania's population consists of *Bīẓān* (whites) and their *Sūdān* (blacks) clients. Within these two thirds, 51% is made up of the two high status, Arabic-speaking groups making up the *Bīẓān*. Around 13% are their Black African slaves and another 29% Haratin, which together form – and self-identify as – *Sūdān* (Blacks).[49] Though the Haratin live among the *Bīẓān*, share in their Arabic language and culture and are legally free, the *Bīẓān* do not consider Haratin status equal to their own. The taint of slavery means that Haratin freedom is never complete. They remain second-class citizens in Mauritania, unable to attain anything beyond the lowest jobs and shunted towards work like waste disposal. Since the 1970s, Haratin organizations and activists have lobbied for better treatment and equal rights, some within the limited purview of Mauritania's unique racial-social make-up and some through solidarity with other Black African groups.[50]

Though their origin is impossible to prove conclusively, the Akhdam (Ar. *akhdām*, literally 'servants,' sing. *khādim*) of Yemen may be descendants of an Ethiopian tribe that established control on Yemen's Red Sea coastal plain in the eleventh century. But in Yemen they are uniformly believed to be the descendants of Ethiopian invaders who were defeated in the years just before Islam and subjugated to serve the Yemenis.[51] The Akhdam, an ascribed term which is rarely if ever used by members of this group to refer to themselves, form a hereditary underclass in Yemen, severely limited in terms of employment, intermarriage, and even socialization with the rest of society. In cities and many towns, they live in marginal slum areas, though in the villages of some regions they are much more integrated. Particularly in cities, they have long been associated with demeaning and disgusting work like emptying latrines and cleaning sewers. In recent decades, they have been employed by municipalities as sweepers and cleaners, to the point that the word Akhdam is synonymous with those jobs.[52] Akhdam are generally looked down upon and considered base, stupid, and even ritually filthy. One Yemeni saying holds, 'If a dog licks a plate, wash it seven times [in reference to a Prophetic Hadith ordering this], if one of the Akhdam, break it.' Another says, 'Do not let the beauty of any of the Akhdam delude you, filth is in their bones.'[53] Though in reality the relationships and interactions between Akhdam and other parts of Yemeni society vary from locale to locale and can often be quite normal, the Akhdam are always subordinated.[54]

Both the Haratin and Akhdam are unequivocally racialized as Black African by the societies in which they are embedded. In the case of the Haratin, they actually prefer self-identifying as black (*sūdān*) over the term Haratin. But in neither Yemen nor Mauritania, both countries with wide phenotypical diversity, are skin tone or physical features reliable indicators of who is Haratin or Akhdam.[55] This fact points to what often appears as a major stumbling block in how issues of race and racism in the non-Western world are approached in Western discourse: **in many settings, physical appearance does not reliably indicate race even when race is phrased in the language of physical appearance.**

Furthermore, in neither Yemen nor Mauritania can a binary, black-and-white framework of race be applied with any accuracy. Indeed, one cannot even apply a coherent and unified conception of antiblackness. Both the Haratin and the Akhdam are parts of societies in which racial constituencies and identifications are much more complex. In Yemen, the Akhdam are one of several marginalized and subordinated groups. Another is the *khaddāma* (servants, sing. *khaddām*, from the same Arabic root as Akhdam), who are people whose families have been expelled from their tribes for some perceived or actual trespass and have had to resort to menial and low-prestige work. Unlike the Akhdam, however, they are not racialized as black and are not generationally casted. They are often able to recover some degree of dignity and advance themselves.[56] Yemeni society also includes a category of freed slaves, who are often much more clearly phenotypically Black African than the Akhdam but who also are much more integrated into tribal structures due to their relationships with their former owners.[57]

Most importantly for our purposes, the status of Akhdam is not seen as due to their blackness. For example, Dolores Walters' fieldwork in ʿAbs in the northern Tihama plain of Yemen in the 1980s showed that *everyone* in that area identified as being of mixed Arab and Ethiopian stock, tracing their ancestry back to the famous black Arab poet ʿAntara bin Shaddād (see Chapter 5). Moreover, in some areas of mountainous north Yemen, it is common to refer to *all* the people on the Tihama coastal plain as black, not just the Akhdam.[58] In Mauritania, the Haratin are subordinated as a class to the *Bīẓān*. Though some Haratin-rights activists stress the class' origins in the Black African ethnic groups to the south in Mali and Senegal, the Haratin generally do not identify with those ethnicities. Rather, they identify with the Arabic-speaking, Muslim society of the *Bīẓān*.[59]

Moreover, the Haratin are not the lowest or most vulnerable part of Mauritanian society. The most serious concerns voiced by human-rights NGOs do not even involve them. They address the treatment of the country's sizable 'ethnic African' communities, which constitute about one third of the country's population and consist of groups like the Fulani (called Halpulaar) and Wolof. They have been racialized as Black African by the *Bīẓān* and Haratin alike, not with the label *sūdān* but as *kwār*, a word that means black but may also originate from a North African Arabic dialect word for unbeliever (see Appendix III). Beginning in 1989, the Mauritanian government exploited tensions between *Bīẓān* and ethnic Black Africans settled on both banks of the Senegal River to expel tens of thousands of mainly Halpulaar, many of them Mauritanian citizens. Months of rioting and attacks on ethnic Black African individuals and businesses in Mauritanian urban centers followed. Hundreds were killed and arrested, and the Mauritanian military engaged in a vicious purge and victimization of Halpulaar soldiers and officers in its ranks.[60] Most tellingly for our purposes, during protests in 1966 by Mauritanian ethnic African students over Arabization policies and again during the purges and expulsions of the 1990s, it was mobs of Haratin who were encouraged by the Mauritanian government to attack and disperse ethnic African crowds.[61]

Finally, there is another social group in Mauritania that is considered to be even lower status than the Haratin. These are the Znaga, descendants of defeated Berber clans who, like the Akhdam in Yemen, are viewed as ancestrally bound to serve the *Bīẓān*. Far from being racialized as black, however, the Znaga are actually light-skinned Berbers.[62] Such commonalities suggest that, with the Akhdam and the Znaga, their hereditarily demeaned status originates not in a racialization as black but in the understanding that they were tribes defeated by the majority in the society and condemned to perpetual service.

## THE COLOR LINE IN OTHER TIMES AND PLACES

A reoccurring theme in this book is that how race in general and blackness in particular are understood in the modern West differs greatly from how they are and have been understood in Islamic civilization. Of course, how race and blackness have been understood in the vast ocean of Muslim diversity that stretches from Dakar to Java has varied internally over expanses of space and culture and across the centuries. But one important generalization is that the status and identity of one's father is much more important than somatic characteristics, such as one's skin tone. This holds true even in the rare cases of Muslim societies that are to some degree matrilineal, like the Tuareg.[63]

What often proves confusing in studying blackness in Islamic civilization, whether in the premodern or modern periods, is that phenotype is neither irrelevant, as is sometimes claimed, nor definitive, as it has been in places like the U.S. Somatic features are not of paramount importance, but they have often been significant. This significance depends a great deal on the salience of other aspects of a person's identity, such as social position, wealth, religious credentials, and reputation.

Mawlāy Ismāʿīl is a case in point. This powerful and longevous Moroccan sultan inspired awe and fear within his realm and beyond it. We have already seen that he carried out a policy of re-enslavement that was and remains unparalleled in Islamic history.[64] Yet Mawlāy Ismāʿīl himself was the son of a Black African concubine. This was of no significance for Muslim biographers, but contemporaneous British writers agonizing over capture by Barbary raiders attributed his allegedly unnatural cruelty to his being "begotten of a Negro Woman by a white Man" (see Chapter 4).[65]

The Egyptian president Anwar Sadat (d. 1981) is a similar case. Sadat would almost certainly have been considered black in the U.S. His biographer, a famous Egyptian journalist who knew him well, reported that the president inherited his dark complexion from his mother, who was the daughter of an African slave brought to Sudan. Yet Sadat was a prominent figure in Egyptian politics for four decades and rose to the apex of political power. It would be tempting to conclude that skin color did not matter in Egypt. It certainly meant much less than it did in the West. But sources who knew the president well recall that his color was always a source of anxiety for him and that skin color in general was his "obsession."[66]

An interesting parallel in the realm of culture and politics is the Saudi intellectual, businessman, philanthropist, and politician Muḥammad Surūr al-Ṣabbān (d. 1391/1972). A major figure in the establishment of literary scholarship in the Hejaz, al-Ṣabbān rose through local politics in Jeddah and Mecca to eventually become the Saudi Finance Minister. Though an apocryphal story, I once heard in Jeddah that al-Ṣabbān had been denied entrance to a hotel in the U.S. because of his features; he responded by buying the hotel. This story was clearly meant to juxtapose what was possible for a 'black' man in 1960s America as compared to Arabia (as well as invoking the karmic role of oil wealth). Malcolm X, who worked with al-Ṣabbān, was so impressed with him that he gave his daughters Sabban as a middle name. He recounted how his mentor had been born a slave yet had risen to high office.[67] For Malcolm, this no doubt showed how neither slavery nor race stood in the way of merit in Islam. Ironically, anti-blackness loomed closer than the famous martyr realized. In fact, al-Ṣabbān had never been a slave; his family was free and hailed from Yemen.[68] Al-Ṣabbān certainly could never have attained the success he did had he been in the U.S., but it was the association of blackness and slavery in Arabia that made rumors of a slave background plausible.

The thirteenth-century poet whose words open this book, the black-skinned al-Kānimī, demonstrates the significance of the color line even if it was not paramount. A Muslim scholar from near Lake Chad, he voyaged to Marrakesh, where he married a local Arab woman and earned esteem in scholarly and literary circles for his impressive Arabic poetry. That the common valuation of Islamic learning and a literary mastery of Arabic could carve out a niche in North Africa for a Black African foreigner lends credence to the truism that Islamic high culture did not see skin color. Yet al-Kānimī's skin color is at the center of much of his surviving poetry, which suggests either his own insecurity or that in Marrakesh he was at best a curiosity and at worst mocked for his appearance. Asked why he did not engage in poetic invective in return, he replied:

> It is the noble who dislike insults, and the meanness of base people
> is not my path.[69]

Nine centuries later, the son of parents taken as slaves in the Sudan and later freed in Cairo found himself in a similar position. Muḥammad Imām al-ʿAbd (d. 1329/1911) gained renown as the captain of the Egyptian soccer team, but his true fame came as a popular poet. His poems ranged widely, but playful satire about the contradictions and absurdities of daily life was a common theme. He often portrayed himself as the comic fool, whether a hapless observer or victim. But his blackness, which his biographer called "ebony," features frequently and is tied to his inability to find love. He references his appearance as a humorous shortcoming, as it is here when tacked on to his skewering the costs of marriage:

> O my friend, such a good friend, don't blame a monk without
> evidence.
> I'm the night and all beautiful ladies the day. My conjoining with
> them is impossible.[70]

In another poem he courts a fair-skinned woman (*shaqrāʾ*), who tells him:

> You're a slave, and love has told me that a love union with a slave
> is forbidden.
> I replied: Yes, I am a slave, a slave of love. And love rules among
> humankind.
> And while I am a black slave, know that I'm also a man whose
> speech is free.

And he draws attention to how his blackness was a target of teasing among his literary companions, including prominent poets like Aḥmad Shawqī (d. 1351/1932):

They associate me with slaves figuratively, despite my virtue,
citing my blackness as their evidence.
My destiny wasted, I bemoan my bad fortune. So my blackness
wears mourning garb.[71]

Al-ʿAbd's lengthy ode to a black woman (*zanjiyya*) doubles as a response to his friends' teasing. Some lines betray a connection he feels to her. She is:

Black but Arab. Her cheek resembles mine.[72]

Because there was no clear 'color line' in Egypt, it is hard to know how much of al-ʿAbd's poetic play on his blackness was his own choice and how much was forced on him by the role society set for him. One gets the sense that he was in a position similar to Black American artists of the mid twentieth century, like Sammy Davis, Jr. They were able to succeed in the wider public square only if their blackness was part of the entertainment.[73]

## MISREADING FOR RACE AND THE BURDENS OF THE PRESENT

When Francis Moore (d. 1756), a British geographer, visited West Africa around 1730, he noted descendants of Portuguese traders living on the Gambian coast. Though they had intermarried with the local population, "they reckon themselves still as well as if they were actually White." Nothing angered these people more, noted Moore, than calling them "Negroes," since this was what they called their slaves. They had forgotten, Moore concludes, "the true Meaning of the Word."[74] When the prominent Black American professor Henry Louis Gates, Jr. traveled to Zanzibar to interview members of the island's Shirazi community, he had a similar reaction. Like Arabs in Mauritania (and, indeed, most Muslims historically), Shirazis identify patrilineally. Their paternal ancestors, Persian merchants, had settled in Zanzibar centuries earlier and had intermarried and taken slave concubines from the local population. When Gates asks the Shirazis he is speaking to if they are African or Persian, they reply, "Persian." Gates remarks off-camera, "To me the people here look about as Persian as Mike Tyson."[75]

Race, color and identity function differently in different societies. As Moore's observation shows, this obstacle is not a new one. But it seems a particular challenge for people accustomed to modern American discourse on race and blackness. As Gates demonstrates, the tendency to impose American racial categories can distort discussions about race and blackness.[76] And this is particularly true when these issues intersect with Islam.

We must be very careful not to read sources from the Islamic past with too relentless a demand that they tell us what 'we' want to know about race, for example, if a certain historical personage was 'black' or not. When I conducted an informal poll on social media about well-known black Muslim scholars, many educated and well-intentioned responses mentioned the famous Muslim jurist Aḥmad Bābā (d. 1036/1627). This prolific scholar hailed from the storied African city of Timbuktu, and the students that he taught during his years living on the other side of the Sahara in Marrakesh often elegized him as Aḥmad Bābā al-Sūdānī, which could be translated as 'the Black' or 'of Black Africa.' But Aḥmad Bābā was a Sanhaja Berber and referred to himself as such. He saw himself and was seen by others in Timbuktu as one of the 'whites' (*bīḍān*) in that predominately 'black' (*sūdān*) city. Indeed, Bābā's Moroccan student Aḥmad bin ʿAlī al-Sūsī explicitly states that his teacher was "not one of the blacks" (*al-sūdān*) but rather a Sanhaja Berber. Yet none of this has anything to do with how Aḥmad Bābā looked. His North African students probably called him al-Sūdānī because he came from what was unanimously known as the Land of the Blacks (*bilād al-sūdān*). On the other hand, neither this observation nor Bābā's own self-identification as Berber preclude that he would be considered 'black' if he visited the U.S. today. He may well have been very dark skinned, since lineages in the region and labels like Sanhaja, 'white,' and 'black' were defined by one's patrilineal ancestors and ethnic identity, not by one's appearance (al-Jārimī includes him as evidence that there were great scholars among Black Africans).[77] The truth is we have no idea what Aḥmad Bābā looked like.[78]

Neither should we jump to call out antiblack racism when other dimensions of discrimination and difference may really be at play. Aḥmad Bābā's great-great-grandfather had left the Masina region of Mali for Timbuktu because he disliked the Fulani who lived near him and was worried his children might intermarry with them. This certainly was an instance of a Berber scholar espousing a discriminatory view towards another group with which he did not want his family to intermingle. But it is a mistake to read it along white/black lines in which the lighter-skinned and 'nobler' group seeks to avoid miscegenation with the darker and 'less noble.'[79] In fact, it was likely more a matter of aversion to cultures mixing. When this scholar's grandson, Maḥmūd bin ʿUmar Aqīt (d. 955/1548), also a respected scholar in Timbuktu, was approached by his esteemed Arab student, al-Muṣallī (d. 995/1586–7), for his daughter's hand, Maḥmūd preempted him. "Birds of a feather flock together," he explained. Just as this Sanhaja Berber family was unwilling to intermarry with the 'darker' and less-Islamically rooted Fulani, they were equally unwilling to accept a 'white' Arab scholar despite his ancestry having an allegedly higher Islamic pedigree.[80] Maḥmūd bin ʿUmar was not antiblack in his preferences for marriage. He was anti-non-Sanhaja Berber.

What this means is that, despite the subjects we encounter in the past actually deploying terms like black and white, and despite them voicing what seem like clear racial preferences, we must not assume that any of the lines or views they mention match our understandings of those concepts. Again, Timbuktu provides an excellent example. By the 1300s, the city was flourishing at the junction of the rich, alluvial plain of the middle Niger River and the trade routes across the Sahara. Timbuktu was the meeting point of 'white' Berbers and Arabs, who were associated with trade and herding, and the 'black' Songhay, Soninke, Wangara and others, all associated with agricultural backgrounds. In Timbuktu these groups mixed, mingled and jockeyed for position and wealth, adopting common languages and even intermarrying. Walking the city's streets in the 1400s, one would have heard spoken Songhay, Arabic, and the Berber Tamasheq. One feature that was *not* a reliable indicator of who was who was 'the color line.' Factors like the predominance of patrilineality in identity along with the prevalence of slave concubines, who were often from Black African populations, meant that, throughout West Africa, skin color was a highly inaccurate guide to who belonged to the 'white' or 'black' communities.[81] Moreover, though Timbuktu's division into 'white' and 'black' communities was certainly important, it was not at all definitive. At the prompting of the city's ruler, who belonged to the 'black' Songhay ethnicity, the same Maḥmūd whose marriage selectiveness we have already encountered married a 'black' Songhay woman. Their son Muḥammad (d. 973/1565) eventually took up the chief judgeship of the city.[82]

Our caution must go further. Even in historical contexts in which antiblackness had become undeniably common, this does not mean that we should read everything through that lens. Not everything *we* read as racially inflected was intended or perceived that way. An example comes from one of history's most famous poets, a superlatively skilled and incredibly arrogant Arab called al-Mutanabbī (d. 354/965). This poet also features reliably among the examples given of premodern antiblackness in Islamic civilization, and not without reason. His satirical attacks on his one-time patron, the Nubian slave ruler of Egypt, have moved from legendary to infamous. Al-Mutanabbī had originally sought out this ruler, Kāfūr al-Ikhshīdī (d. 357/968), for patronage but was greatly disappointed when the ruler did not grant him the rewards he felt he deserved. He wrote in one of his savage salvos against his former employer:

> And if doubt should come over you about his condition, then
> look at his type (*jins*).
> Rarely is one base when clothed (*thawb*) without also being base
> at birth (*ghirs*).

Today, al-Mutanabbī's invectives against Kāfūr are often read through the lens of antiblack racism. Some Western scholars have translated *jins* in the above lines as 'race' and *ghirs* as 'origins,' interpreting the verse as averring that race and descent determine a person's essence.[83] The doors of poetic interpretation are wide, and I would not impose my own interpretation over another's. Scholars who see these verses as antiblack, however, are not claiming that al-Mutanabbī was some racist ahead of his time. They see him as representative of antiblack views that no one (including myself) would deny were palpably present in high Islamic culture in his day. In this light, then, it is instructive that medieval Islam's most famous commentators on al-Mutanabbī's poems did *not* read such verses as satire targeting Kāfūr's Black Africanness. These medieval commentators, who, as we will see in Chapter 5, had no qualms about stereotyping nations or disparaging Black Africans, nonetheless read the word *jins* as referring to the category of slaves, not 'race.' They read the word *ghirs* as the caul membrane that sometimes covers newborn infants, not as 'origins.' These medieval Muslims understood al-Mutanabbī as juxtaposing the robes of an adult with this 'clothing' of a newborn, declaring that Kāfūr's bad qualities were present at birth.[84] This constant in his nature is not blackness, however, but slaveness. As described by a famous commentator, al-Wāḥidī of Nishapur (d. 468/1076), the centerpiece of al-Mutanabbī's many attacks on Kāfūr is how slaves lack honor and have base, appetitive and fickle characters.[85] This is true for all slaves, not just Black African ones.

Similarly, it is tempting to read the following verses that al-Mutanabbī launched at Kāfūr through a modern Western racial lexicon of black and white:

> Who ever taught the black castrate a noble deed? His noble (*bīḍ*) kin? His regal (*ṣīd*) forebears?
>
> . . .
>
> For if white stallions are incapable of magnanimity, how then gelded blacks?[86]

Certainly, the word translated above as noble (*bīḍ*) can mean 'white people' (in fact, *bīḍ* is the term used in modern Arabic for precisely that meaning). But premodern commentators like al-ʿUkbarī (d. 616/1219) glossed whiteness here as denoting nobility (*kirām*), not appearance.[87] Al-Mutanabbī certainly plays on Kāfūr's appearance as opposed to those of other rulers, but that is only one of several themes the poet draws on in his brutal invective. That Kāfūr was a eunuch is another. As Kevin Blankinship points out, in the genre of satire, poets exploited whatever social weakness they could. The single most dominant theme that al-Mutannabī draws on in his attacks on Kāfūr thus reveals the ruler's weakest point. For al-Mutanabbī, and presumably for his audience, it was that the character of slaves is inevitably low and vile, and that the world had become inverted and corrupted when the free Muslim polity had submitted to a slave's rule. In Kāfūr's Egypt, al-Mutanabbī wrote:

> . . . the free person is enslaved and the slave worshipped.[88]

At times, the heightened suspicion of racism with which the modern, Western reader approaches the Islamic past exceeds interpretive license and trespasses into blatant misrepresentation. One example comes from an otherwise excellent study on domestic slavery in medieval Egypt and Syria. The author's anticipation of antiblackness leads them to conclude that part of an influential manual on purchasing slaves by the Christian physician of Baghdad, Ibn Buṭlān (d. *circa* 458/1066), was nothing short of "racist." The author renders part of Ibn Buṭlān's text as, "If the offspring of an East African woman (*zanjiyya*) is purified (*takarrara*) with whites over three generations, black becomes white, a flat nose becomes curved, limbs become tender, and the character changes accordingly . . ." (quoting the author verbatim).

The distinctly judgmental wording of purification in this passage, however, appears nowhere in the Arabic original, neither literally nor conceptually. The Arabic *takarrara* simply means 'repeated.' The author's conclusion that Ibn Buṭlān is explaining how, as they put it, "the negative character traits of dark-skinned people could be removed by breeding them with light-skinned people to produce offspring whose lighter appearance would attest to their superior character" is plainly imposed on the text.[89] Ibn Buṭlān actually leaves no doubt about his intention in this section, and criticism of blackness is not involved. He explicitly states that he will explain the meanings of phrases used by slave merchants to indicate a slave's origin. Right before the sentence translated above on interbreeding black and white, Ibn Buṭlān explains, "If you hear me say, 'Persian female,' know that [this means] she was born of a Persian." He then adds the above sentence to demonstrate that such descriptions lose meaning with intermarriage. Black and white is merely used as an example, with Ibn Buṭlān adding, "And know that this applies to all races (*ajnās*)."[90]

It is perhaps more understandable for scholars today to accuse figures in the modern period of antiblack racism, since less space for anachronism separates scholar from subject. But misreading can nonetheless prove egregious. One recent scholarly monograph, for example, accuses the famous Muslim scholar Muḥammad Amīn al-Shinqīṭī (d. 1393/1973) of antiblackness.[91] A 'white' Mauritanian Arab who emigrated to the Saudi Hejaz in 1948, al-Shinqīṭī wrote a memoir of his voyage by car from Mauritania, southeast to Bamako and then eastward through the Sudan to the Red Sea. His alleged antiblackness rears its head when al-Shinqīṭī passes by Mopti and sees people who were "black in color," wore almost no clothing and, he "was told reliably," worshipped trees and may have engaged in cannibalism. A second instance occurs when the scholar is making his way by road from N'Djamena towards Darfur. He recounts how all the cars around him were "loaded with blacks (*sawādīn*) who did not understand our language, and we did not understand them, and most of them were like cattle (*bahā'im*)."[92]

This accusation of antiblackness collapses precisely because it reads al-Shinqīṭī as modern and not as a Muslim scholar whose cognitive universe was shaped by over a millennium of Islam's magisterial heritage. The two situations mentioned above are not marked out by al-Shinqīṭī encountering blackness. His entire trip from Bamako to the Red Sea coast proceeded through the 'land of the blacks' and among peoples whom everyone in the world, including al-Shinqīṭī and those people themselves, would consider black. Throughout his journey, al-Shinqīṭī lavishes praise on many of the African Muslims he meets and who host him, including some in the same areas where he had made his above criticisms. What prompted al-Shinqīṭī's remarks on those two occasions was not the phenotype of the people around him but his feeling first of encountering the pagan, unbelieving 'black savages' that Muslim geographies had long placed in the south, beyond the frontiers of the Abode of Islam (see Chapter 5) and second of being totally isolated from Muslims.[93] Al-Shinqīṭī's remarks are not antiblack. Considering how reminiscent his comments about nude natives and cannibalism are of medieval Muslim writers describing pagan Africans, they are, if anything, anti-pagan.

## GUIDANCE AFTER WAYWARDNESS

Writing his book on the virtues of Ethiopians in the latter years of the 1500s CE, the Meccan scholar Ibn ʿAbd al-Bāqī offers a concise view of antiblackness in the Islamic heritage, with its paradoxes, internal tensions, and its conception of blackness that is so often incommensurate with modern ideas of race. Ibn ʿAbd al-Bāqī left his reader in no doubt about two matters. The first was his total enamorment with women from the Horn of Africa. As we will see, he was far from alone in this. The second was his utter distaste for women from further south along the East African coast and its interior. His book includes a warning against having children with these *zanjī* women, parroting the worst stereotypes about Black Africans circulating at his time throughout the Eurasian world, inside and outside the Abode of Islam: they are lazy, base, and submissive, but also volatile and unreasonable. He cites unironically Hadiths (forgeries, as it happens) calling East Africans disfigured and saying they steal when hungry and fornicate when full.

But Ibn ʿAbd al-Bāqī then strikes a totally different note. Turning away from such stereotypes, he tells his reader, "Such talk is the convention of some sophisticated folk (*akyās*). But what is the truth (*ḥaqīqa*) and what is held by those on the path (*ṭarīqa*) [of guidance] is that 'The noblest among you before God is the most pious' (Quran 49:13)." He then runs through a list of numerous sound Hadiths in which the Prophet praises Black Africans and enumerates pious exemplars among them.[94]

These few lines from this sixteenth-century book offer a concise answer to the question 'Is Islam antiblack?' Ibn ʿAbd al-Bāqī was an educated Muslim scholar, esteemed enough to have been selected to deliver the Friday sermon in the Prophet's Mosque in Medina. And yet he had no problem repeating awful expressions of antiblackness framed in and apparently justified by the Prophet and his successors among the ulama. But Muslim scholars far more respected and influential than Ibn ʿAbd al-Bāqī had long before him exposed as forged those Hadiths he cited as evidence for demeaning Africans and had thoroughly rejected the ideas they supported. And even as his pen moved across the page, Ibn ʿAbd al-Bāqī turned away from his antiblackness and towards the clear guidance of God and His Prophet. Those wondering if Islam is antiblack need look no further than how this scholar was rescued from the racism endemic in his society by the revelation of Islam itself.

# 2

## The Background of Race and Racism

I think there is such a thing as *reverse racism* . . . all I would need would be a, uh, time machine, right? And, uh, what I'd do is I'd get in my time machine, I'd go back in time to before Europe colonized the world, right? And uh, I'd convince the leaders of Africa, Asia, the Middle East, Central and South America to uh, invade and colonize Europe, right? Just occupy them, steal their land, resources; set up some kind of like, I don't know, trans-Asian slave trade where we exported white people to work on giant rice plantations in China – just ruin Europe over the course of a couple centuries, so all their descendants would want to migrate and live in places where black and brown people come from . . . I'd make sure I set up systems that privilege black and brown people at every conceivable social, political and economic opportunity, and white people would never have any hope of real self-determination. Just every couple of decades make up some fake war as an excuse to go and bomb them back to the Stone Age and say it's for their own good because their culture's inferior. And then just for kicks, subject white people to colored standards of beauty so they end up hating the color of their own skin, eyes and hair.

And if, after hundreds and hundreds and hundreds of years of that, I got up on stage and said, "Hey, what's the deal with white people? *Why can't they dance*?" That would be *reverse racism.*

Aamer Rahman, "Fear of a Brown Planet"[1]

One cannot respond to questions about antiblackness without first talking about race and racism, two immensely complex topics with their own contested histories.[2] Race and racism are closely related but must be treated distinctly, in part because each has generated its own polarizing debates among scholars and the general public alike. They are among the few issues on which the contents of academic journals and news headlines converge. Are race and racism products of the modern world or of ancient pedigree? How does race differ from earlier concepts like the Greek *ethnos*, the Latin *gens*, or the Arabic *sha'b*, peoples or nations who share a common culture, language, polity, or heritage? How real is race, and does that mean that it must be a feature of our bodies and genes? Or can race be a reality constructed by society? How is race marked and how have races been distinguished? What is racism and how does it differ from other forms of prejudice? Does being racist require holding racist beliefs? If so, what would define them? Does it require actions as well? Finally, can race exist without racism?

## RACE AND REALITY

One succinct understanding of race is that it is a system of categorizing people based on some common characteristic, often assumed to be an aspect of descent or physical appearance. But this simplistic understanding obscures hotly debated questions, such as when and where the concept of race emerged. The classical and – until recently – dominant understanding of race has been **biological**, that race is linked to the body. This general view has had many shapes and forms, but it basically holds that humans can be divided into a number of groups defined by shared hereditable features. These originate in geography, genealogy, climatic conditions, or divine will, depending on whom one asks, and are associated with certain phenotypes, physical qualities, character traits, and even moral worth. The biological conception of race used to enjoy broad support, but in the last seventy years it has been discredited at a popular level by the abuses committed in its name in the last century and academically by studies in genetics.

Recent decades have seen the triumph of a **social** understanding of race. Since the science of genetics has disproven any biological reality to discrete races – there is often more in common genetically between a random White American and a random Black American than between two members of the same race – these groups must have been *socially* constructed.[3] Blackness in America, for example, was constructed through laws around slavery, miscegenation, citizenship, segregation, etc., and it was the foil against which American Whiteness was formed.[4]

Debates over the merits of the biological versus the social nature of race, however, continue in popular discourse, where misunderstandings and inexact definitions have sown much confusion. Choosing the biological versus social conceptions of race is often read as pronouncing on whether race is 'real' or not. The answer is erroneously seen as a proxy for whether steps to address racism are merited. This misconstrual stems from reasoning that what is 'real' in our identities must be physical, set by biology, or genetics. If, common reasoning goes, there is no biological reality to race, then race is not 'real.' It is made up and should have no importance. Anxieties over race and hence racism should thus cease. This thinking overlooks how social constructions are just as real in people's lives as genetics. Although social constructions are constructed, the role of the construct of race in shaping society is among the most impactful forces in many people's lives. As a result, many scholars and activists who accept the social construction of race nonetheless argue that it is incredibly 'real' in the sense of being omnipresent and massively consequential. As a result, we must continue to speak about racial categories in order to rectify historical inequities brought about by racism.[5]

A major reason that the biological conception of race persists in scholarly and popular discourse is that even non-experts see it staring them in the face. How can race be socially constructed when there are obvious bodily differences between a random person from Norway and a random person from Senegal? On the one hand, there is an understandable urge to reject the biological understanding of race, with its historical baggage of master and inferior races. But, on the other, looking at these two random individuals, one cannot miss the physical reality of the differences in their appearances.

This conundrum results from the mistaken assumption that the biological and social conceptions of race are mutually exclusive.

Accepting the social construction of race does not necessitate ignoring *some* undeniable biological realities. It just means denying that this reality has any importance *in and of itself*. The differences in appearance between our random Norwegian and our random Senegalese person are obvious to our eyes, but the outward difference in phenotype has negligible significance for the overall genetic make-up of those two people. This visible biological difference is what Michael Hardimon has termed **minimalist race** – the obvious differences in skin color, hair texture, and common facial features that correspond to ancestry and geographical origin. It exists not just as a social but as a biological reality. There may even be *some* biologically significant differences between racial groups, such as susceptibility to some diseases (though our categories of race are poor proxies for this; identifying someone's actual ancestry regardless of how they look is much more accurate).[6] But what is and is not important about people's physical appearances, about minimalist race, is not determined by nature. It is chosen by societies. What differences matter to us, the ones that mark the categories in which we place people – skin color and hair texture as opposed to earlobe shape, for example – is a socially constructed distinction. In fact, what genetic characteristics of race there are, such as those that might result from two groups living in natural or artificial genetic isolation from one another, can actually be the result of social construction, like policies against miscegenation.[7]

As Hardimon explains, acknowledging the biological reality of minimalist race is not to deny that race overall is socially constructed, let alone to validate the discredited ideas of biological race.[8] It is simply acknowledging an undeniable reality there for all to see. We certainly reject the claim that a certain race has specific moral qualities, for example, but we still talk about 'black people,' associate this category with certain physical features passed on genetically, and associate that group and those features with Africa. Indeed, working with this reality is necessary to rectify the social ills of racism.

That biological difference only matters to the extent that it is recognized as socially significant is not only true for race. What biological differences matter is *always* a social decision. Just as there is no discrete genetic division between a black person and a white person, as we might imagine the division between black and white squares on a chess board, there is also no discrete, singular genetic line dividing human beings (*homo sapiens sapiens*) from Neanderthals (*homo sapiens neanderthalensis*). They very likely interbred.[9] Nor, indeed, is there a discrete, singular genetic line dividing humans from chimpanzees. Yet few would deny the manifest 'reality' of the distinction between those two groups. One might object that the difference between humans and chimpanzees is hardly only social. The two types cannot, for example, reproduce with one another. But nature has not been sufficient for enforcing the division between humans and the domesticated animals that have surrounded them for millennia. Though many have perceived this division as 'natural,' it has had to be policed and maintained *socially* as far back as records go, as we see with laws and taboos against bestiality from ancient to modern times.[10]

## RACE AND RACISM: ORIGINS AND MODERN DEVELOPMENTS

Whether or not race must be tied to the body, biology, or descent has directly affected conclusions about whether race and racism are ancient or relatively recent in origin. Much of this debate centers on to what extent race and racism must be defined by ideas of blood and descent as opposed to other categories like religious identification, geography, and culture. Humans have always engaged in forms of **othering**, whether tribal, religious, ethnic, linguistic, etc. Xenophobia, tribal chauvinism, ethnocentrism, and associating certain cultural, moral, and physical characteristics with particular 'nations,' whether due to geography or descent, are as old as recorded history. Scholars like Geraldine Heng and Thomas Gossett have argued that race and racism are best understood as recent manifestations of these ageless conventions, with medieval Christian representations of Jews, Muslims, Mongols, and Ethiopians often strikingly familiar to us. Scholars like Ivan Hannaford and Nell Irvin Painter, by contrast, have argued that race and racism are particularly modern ideas, with no real concept of race or racism as we understand them predating the seventeenth century.[11] Much attention has been paid to Iberia in the fourteenth and fifteenth centuries as the genesis of what would become modern notions of race. Numerous scholars have concurred that prototypical forms of race and racism emerged as the Christian Spanish began conceptualizing their own identities in contrast to Jews and Muslims in Iberia, subsuming ethnic and religious difference into distinctions of pure and impure blood.[12]

There does seem to be a fairly clear consensus, however, that something new and drastically important about race and racism came into being in late-eighteenth- and nineteenth century European and American discourse with the advent of 1) modern science and 2) the modern, industrializing, technologically capable, and societally expansive state. Such states also happened to be, in most cases, nation states, or states founded on and around an identity that often involved race. This was the nineteenth- and early-twentieth-century heyday of scientific racism, the European colonization of Africa and Asia, and articulating theories of race to justify imperial attitudes. This was also the era of contests over the global African slave trade, segregation, and eugenics. Ethnicity, national identity, and phenotype had all meant *something* to some degree or another in the premodern era. What changed with early modern and modern notions of race and the phenomenon of racism, particularly in the West, was that phenotypical race came to mean *everything*, increasingly because it was seen as indicating the scientifically established parameters of one's value and being.

Though scientific racism largely lapsed into infamy and discredit after World War II, premodern notions of cultural essentialism or group solidarity have returned with vigor to accomplish the same task. In the 1980s, scholars noted a phenomenon they labeled **new racism** or **cultural racism** among White communities in the U.K. and Western Europe. These scholars observed that such communities were concerned with preserving their own coherence and saw outsiders, particularly immigrants from former colonies, as threats to their culture and identity.[13] Attitudes towards such minorities proved complex and layered, with the dominant majority granting levels of acceptance to some groups in certain contexts while withholding it from others and at other times.[14] New/cultural racism differs from conventional racism in that voices in these majority communities expressed their negative views about minorities or perceived interlopers not through the language of body or descent but through the language of culture, values, and lifestyle. It is perhaps best understood in expressions like, 'I don't have anything against black people, I just don't like hip-hop culture' or 'I have nothing against immigrants, I just don't like Mexican values.'

But is it correct to classify such sentiments as racist, since they are evaluations of a culture or lifestyle and not someone's race – i.e., not something about social constructions based in people's biology or descent? Moreover, isn't it normal and perhaps excusable for people to want to 'live with their own kind'?

Answering these questions requires understanding that race and racism are less about the body and more about the power to decide what defines people and their station relative to one another. It is true that many scholars still insist that, in order to distinguish race from other categories of identity and racism from other forms of prejudice, race must be tied to the body, biology, or descent (though with an acknowledgment that what about these is granted significance and by whom is a social and political process).[15] Other scholars have convincingly argued that race is less about the body and more about essentialness and inalterability. It is not that a person's skin is black. It is that they cannot change that. It is their black skin that defines them in the eyes of those who matter, and they cannot do anything about it.[16]

Culturally racist sentiments are thus fundamentally racist because, though they appear as generalized assessments of cultural norms ('I don't like hip-hop culture,' 'I don't like how violent Islam is'), they actually assign people to categories of judgment regardless of their individual qualities and deny them the practical possibility of changing how they are viewed. This predominant understanding of race is thus about defining a group according to a common characteristic that is ascribed as essential to a person or a group and considered unalterable. This essentiality and inalterability are what distinguish racism from other types of prejudice or discrimination, such as religious bigotry. If a religiously discriminatory Christian community did not accept Muslims, they should, in theory, welcome former Muslims who had embraced Christianity. If there was still something about those former-Muslims-now-Christians that left them excluded or discriminated against nonetheless, as was the case in late-medieval Christian Iberia, then racism has reared its head. As Fredrickson says, mere dislike, bigotry, or intolerance becomes racism when "differences that might otherwise be considered ethnocultural are regarded as innate, indelible and unchangeable . . ."[17]

Who defines that characteristic and endows it with importance is, of course, the heart of the matter, and it points to an intrinsic element of race and racism as lived concepts: race and racism are frameworks created and maintained by the powerful and applied to those over whom they exercise power.[18] This is a crucial reason that race and racism are fundamentally modern phenomena. Only in the modern period has the mechanism of state power become both unmatchable and put at the service of racial hierarchies that serve as the primary templates for distributing power and privilege.

Here Kwame Anthony Appiah's distinction between racialism and racism is instructive. **Racialism** is the assertion that races exist: humans can be divided into groups, each defined by heritable traits and tendencies. **Racism** presumes racialism, but it adds that these races are morally significant either because they correlate with morally relevant characteristics (he calls this "extrinsic racism," e.g., 'Jews are stingy') or because they are intrinsically morally significant (he calls this "intrinsic racism," e.g., 'We need to make sure our tribe ends up on top'). Racism creates a hierarchy. Intrinsic racism, he notes, might be more akin to family, tribal, or national solidarity, and it is not necessarily morally noxious. What makes racism morally repugnant is when it is used to cause harm.[19]

Skepticism about the prevalence of racism, commonly associated with conservative outlooks in the West, generally hinges on ignoring this vital element of power disparity, both in reoccurring complaints about 'reverse racism' (e.g., 'If a White person said that, they'd be fired!') and in the claim that what is being condemned as racism is actually just a normal desire to be 'with one's own kind.' Reverse racism is not possible because the marginal or subaltern have no power over those above them. Even if they despised the more powerful for some inalterable characteristic, this would have little impact. Certainly, we can imagine two races of equal size and equal power living in a country. If each decided they wanted to 'live with their own kind' and disliked each other's culture and manners, this would not be racist. Where this differs from cultural racism, however, is that cultural racism is the sentiment of an established, powerful and (most often) majority group towards a marginal, less powerful group whom it is trying to deny opportunities and resources that the powerful control.

Are all forms of 'wanting to be with one's own kind' racist, however? George MacDonald Fraser (d. 2008), a Scottish journalist, author of the Flashman novels, and World War II veteran who would today probably be a conservative in the mold of Nigel Farage, deemed it an undeniable universal that people prefer to be with those whose culture and experiences they share, whether on the train or in a neighborhood. Race "is simply an extension of the family." The people we save first are our own, whatever their skin color, Fraser avers. In many ways, Fraser's 'own' were those who had fought and bled for Britain, whatever their color. He was outraged by the U.K.'s immigration and refugee policy not because it meant the arrival of foreigners but because he considered those foreigners unworthy. Many had never demonstrated any allegiance to Britain. The Gurkhas, Sikhs, and Pathans he served with in the war and who had served Britain, however, he would happily welcome.[20] Is Fraser's view a form of cultural racism, or is it more similar to a religious community that grants full membership to those who embrace its creed? If a person can prove they belong, is their status unalterable?

## RACIALIZATION, RELIGION, AND COLOR

Thinking about race and racism as ideas that can be elaborated along all sorts of lines, from ancestry (Arabian tribal notions of *nasab* [lineage] and *ʿirq* [bloodline]), to ethnicity (Irish), reveals much about how cultural racism operates and disguises itself today. Even religion can be racialized, as with the Russian Empire's categorization of its Muslim subjects as the race/nation of Tatars or the early modern European labeling of Muslims as Moors or Turks. Indeed, 'Muslim' has become a racialized identity in the West. 'Muslims' are assigned to that category, their acts and words are interpreted through the ways that Western society has defined it (e.g., terror, extremism, honor killing, etc.), and they are dealt with as such by the power structures of their societies. This kind of racialization erases what any one Muslim actually believes or thinks. Their Muslimness already defines them.[21] Serb nationalists carried out genocide against Bosnian Muslims who looked and spoke just like their Serbian and Croatian neighbors but were demonized as 'Turks.'[22]

Of course, **phenotype** – how one presents physically with hair, skin color, bone structure, etc. – is a convenient vector for defining race because it is immediately visible to everyone. Everyone can know your category.[23] Color prejudice and other types of phenotypical prejudice have thus been widespread in history. The way we look, our minimalist race – the somatic realities of our bodies – may be part of nature. But where our 'color' starts and stops and what it means are still social constructs, often within the overarching construct of race.

Linguists debate whether humans share a universal template for labeling colors at the basic level of language. In other words, do all societies see the same basic colors in the world, and how do they classify them?[24] But there is no debate that societies differ in how they deploy colors to describe people's appearance and, more importantly, to place them in social categories and hierarchies. In the next chapter, we will explore how conceptions of blackness as a phenotype and identity have developed and interacted with race and racism in history, but here we can look briefly at the contrast presented by how color and race function differently in the United States and Brazil. Both are polities that have been deeply invested in exploiting and controlling enslaved people from Africa. In Brazil, however, slavery was a strictly legal status not defined by race, while in the U.S. slavery was intimately tied to, defining and defined by race. Mid-nineteenth-century American defenses of slavery justified it on the basis of Africans' 'natural inferiority.' If people could be enslaved because they were black, then all slaves had to be black regardless of how much non-African parentage they had. The sizable mixed-race slave population in the U.S. was thus black by the necessity of definition, a definition of blackness that applied to free mixed-race people too.[25] This 'One Drop' rule, technically known as hypodescent, had its legal origins in a 1656 Virginia court case. Its true cradle, however, was not in the law but in colonial American society.[26] From the late 1600s to the early 1900s, the One Drop Rule would move from the dominant *social* definition of blackness to a legal one as well, particularly during the late-nineteenth- and early-twentieth-century establishment of Jim Crow segregation and the migration of Black Americans to the north.[27]

In Brazil, slavery had been conceived much more distinctly as a legal category apart from phenotypical race. One result of this profound difference in the relationship between race and slavery is that Brazilian society has construed color and race very differently, with many more color- and ethnic-based racial categories than in the U.S. In the early 2000s, Brazilian governments and institutions imposed a new system on top of these social categories. It asked Brazilians to identify with official racial groups: *branco* (white), *pardo* (brown), *preto* (black), and *amerelo* (yellow). Unlike the U.S., Brazil's long-standing social system of identification and the new government categories both give much more weight to how people identify themselves as opposed to how authorities would categorize them. In fact, Brazilians can even choose to switch racial identifications. In addition to the social and new government systems of race/color categorization, Black consciousness activists in Brazil have argued for merging *preto* and *pardo* into one category of self-identification, *negro*, so as to more accurately reflect the true population of Brazilians of visible African descent. These activists encourage a view of race similar to that of the U.S.

It is left to Brazilians to choose what race they are. The answer is not always clear to them. Brazilians of African or mixed African descent, for example, tend to use *moreno* ('tanned, dark-haired') to identify themselves far more commonly than they use the official term *preto* or the activist term *negro*. Because these racial categories are used in quotas for higher education, there has emerged a tension between the historical self-determination of someone's identity and the need of institutions to police who is claiming access to resources reserved for underprivileged groups. In 2004, for example, the University of Brasília established a tribunal charged with the uncomfortable task of assessing whether applicants who claimed to be *negro* actually were.[28]

As is evident in Brazil, color can function on a spectrum in the economy of preference and privilege that is an essential part of racism. **Colorism** is a concept that has gained salience in recent decades as scholars have recognized the prevalence of social norms that value lighter skin and devalue darker skin, both within regimes of race with discrete categories like black and white and in societies with no such clear regime. One factor commonly identified as shaping the economy of color and the desirability of a lighter skin tone has been the class association of lighter skin with not having had to labor in the sun. This has been historically prominent in Europe and Asia, particularly in considering a woman's marriageability. In this wide area, light skin suggested higher relative social status. As a result, for millennia in regions from Rome to medieval Japan, lighter skin has been seen as a premium for women.[29]

South Asia has been the focus for the investigation of colorism.[30] Mirroring debates around race and racism, scholars of colorism continue to debate whether it is a premodern phenomenon or a product of European colonialism and the spread of global Western standards of beauty. Those who favor the premodern origins of colorism point to the *Rigveda*'s (*circa* 1500 BCE) account of lighter skinned Aryans from the north subduing the indigenous Dasyus and occasionally associating these natives with black skin.[31] There is also a common assumption that upper-caste South Asians are generally lighter skinned than those from lower castes, such that in some Indian languages the phrase 'a dark Brahmin' is invoked as an idiom for an oxymoron.[32]

Advocates of the modern or early modern origins of colorism reply that the *Rigveda* mentions heroes and heroines of dark as well as light complexion.[33] They also undermine the claim of a correlation between caste and color by pointing out that, though there has long been an association of darker skin with manual labor in the sun as well as with lower castes, skin color in India correlates much more closely with region. People from southern India – high and low caste – are generally darker and shorter than those from northern India, where low caste and high caste Indians alike are generally lighter skinned. These scholars add that it was only during the period of British rule that lighter complexions became prized, both because the British administration and military favored lighter-skinned Indians for employment and because they created an infrastructure and regime that discriminated between the White colonials and the colonized locals.[34] As with the valuation of lighter skin tone among Black Americans in the U.S., this formed an economy in which the closer one's skin tone was to the European norm, the better. Already in the 1930s and '40s the Anglo-Indian starlet Merle Oberon (d. 1979) was using skin bleaching treatments that ended up destroying her career, and in recent decades the industry of skin whitening creams has burgeoned in South Asia.[35] The globalization of colorism has been well documented, even when it is not a specifically White standard of beauty that is held up as the ideal. A particularly outrageous example suffices here. In 2016 a Chinese detergent ad featured a Han Chinese protagonist stuffing a young black man eager to flirt with her into the washing machine. He emerges a handsome Han Chinese like her.[36]

## WHEN IS SOMETHING OR SOMEONE RACIST?

As evident in recurring debates over whether something that some celebrity or politician said or did was racist or not, and whether or not that person is therefore racist, there have been intense debates over what constitutes racism in the present day. Does racism require no more than holding certain beliefs or prejudices about some racial group, or does it require acting on those beliefs? Are certain actions racist even if the person who does them has no racist beliefs, or if they are unaware that their beliefs are racist? In other words, is intent or malice required? Does one racist statement or action (or non-action) alone make someone a racist?[37]

These questions have been extensively debated by scholars since the 1930s, when the term racism was coined to describe Nazi views. More restrictive theorizations of racism have proposed definitions that require some underlying prejudicial belief (Painter's concise, "the belief that races exist and that some are better than others") and limit racism to the intentional, malicious, or severe, often with a requirement that the distinction in question be related to biology or the body.[38] This narrow definition stems from a concern that, if racism is defined as patterns of conduct that result in discrimination without originating in some prejudice, or if racism can be detached from some reference to the body, then the term racism will be "inflated," as Miles and Brown (1989) put it, beyond any utility. It would expand to absorb what would otherwise be sexism, religious bigotry, or other modes of discrimination. Miles and Brown insist that racism must rest on an ideology that defines some groups as better than others based on some racialized aspect of their biology.[39] Lawrence Blum (2002) worries that an overly expansive definition of racism leaves us with moral labels too clumsy to address the subtleties of social reality; people, statements, or actions are either racist or acceptable, with no category in between. Blum thus limits racism to believing other racial groups are inferior or viewing them with antipathy (which ranges from conscious or unconscious prejudice, i.e., a general antipathy towards a racial group, to hatred). For Blum, racism should not be conflated with less severe phenomena like racial insensitivity, and he distinguishes between three elements: racism as a motivation, acts perceived as being done for those motives, and finally the people who do them, who may or may not be so motivated. For Blum, to be a racist one must display "an ingrained pattern" of such acts and motivations.[40]

Where scholars like Blum worry about racism losing its meaning at a pragmatic, social level, Jorge L.A. Garcia worries about the term becoming theoretically detached from the moral judgment he feels is essential to how the term racism is used. In an influential but controversial 1996 article, Garcia proposed that both one's beliefs and the results of one's actions are incidental to racism. Beliefs have no moral manifestation if they do not direct our will. The results of actions can be good or bad regardless of how we intend them. Racism is to deny some group or individuals the rights or degree of care that their humanity and our morality should secure for them. But, for Garcia, this is not racism's moral heart. When people talk about racism, they really understand it as involving a degree of "hatred, ill-will, directed against a person or persons on account of their assigned race." Actions or institutions can be racist only in that they are characteristic of racist motivations, since, for Garcia, racism must always originate in individuals and their morally reprehensible intent. If we use the term racist without this moral dimension present, we lose the core of what the word means to us.[41]

In contrast to conceptions of racism that turn on ill will, dislike, or express beliefs about a group's inferiority, recent years have seen the wide acceptance of what we might term the 'substantial' understanding of racism. This focuses not on the nature of beliefs, intent, or malice but on the discriminatory circumstances and conditions that result from actions, non-action, and expression. As J. Angelo Corlett's (2003) definition of racism shows, such an approach sees racism as essentially ubiquitous. This results from, first, shifting the focus of racism from intent and belief to the pervasiveness and influence of ethnic and racial stereotypes in society. Second, it results from the recognition that racism can be about more than the body or descent, since racialization is about assigning essentiality and need not involve a bodily characteristic. Cut loose from intent, racism is pervasive because ethnic and racial stereotypes so often guide our actions even without us being aware of them. People are so often unaware that their beliefs are prejudicial (for example, 'Jews are intelligent'). People are so often unaware of how those beliefs subtly shape their actions or words (for example, praising the Williams sisters for 'athleticism' but a White tennis player for a 'brilliant' performance). Finally, since racism does not require malicious intent, it manifests even when people think their actions are beneficial ('benevolent racism') or are nothing more than private, practical conduct (crossing the street when Black youths are coming). For the substantial understanding of racism, the issue, as Corlett puts it, is "not whether or not one is a racist, but the degree of racism we exhibit, the frequency in which we are racists, and the kinds of racism in which we are engaged."[42]

The divergence over intent lies at the crux of contemporary controversies over assessing what is and isn't racist. Blum's concern that 'everything is racist now' has only become more apt in the nearly two decades since his book appeared. In the U.S. and Western Europe, anxiety over the spread of Critical Race Theory and the sense that all White people are racist by dint of their race has become so inflammatory that it has emerged as a potent political rallying cry. While much of this anxious energy is yet another expression of nativism or White nationalism, there is also the sincere outrage of people who feel they are being called racist despite their deeply held conviction that race does not define a person's worth – that they do not hold negative views of other races or intend discrimination.[43] This sense of injury, however, misses the disjunct between the traditional understanding of racism as a reflection of someone's prejudiced beliefs or malign intentions – the image of the villainous, racist Southerner or Afrikaner – and the substantial approach to racism, which recognizes that a person can be racist without articulating any belief about racial superiority or harboring any bad intentions. They are racist because they abet in the production of a discriminatory reality.

This miscommunication is clear in reactions to Professor Ibram X. Kendi's best-selling book on systematic racism and antiracism, *How to Be Antiracist* (2019), which emerged as highly influential and controversial in the wake of the 2020 killing of George Floyd. Critics from the right and left, including Black American critics, have mocked Kendi's definition of racism as absurdly tautological: Kendi defines racism as "a collection of racist policies that lead to racial inequities that are substantiated by racist ideas."[44] Kendi advocates what I've described here as a substantial understanding of racism. In this case, racist ideas (for Kendi, ones that hold that one racial group is superior or inferior to another) lead to and justify policies that result in racial inequity (for Kendi, when racial groups are not on equal footing). The result is racism, and the result could remain intact even if the racist ideas that sparked it are no longer widely believed. In effect, America is racist because the racial inequities in property ownership, incarceration, education, income, and a number of other areas are beyond dispute. America is a racist society in which people are racist because the U.S. is a society in which racial inequities along a White/Black divide are omnipresent. Whatever policies and cultures have resulted in this racist situation are therefore racist, as are all the individuals involved, knowingly or unknowingly, in this system.

Kendi defines racism tautologically not because, as some of his critics aver, he is a fraud or uneducated. He does so because, for him and for adherents of the substantial approach to racism in general, it is the racially inflected hierarchy of power and inequity that matter and must be combatted, not individuals' intentions or abstract -isms that people may or may not be aware they even believe. From this perspective, a person can be at fault for being racist not for the severe infractions of having malign intentions or a belief in racial superiority but rather for not realizing that they are a participant in a racist system that all have the moral duty to undo.

The intentionalist-versus-substantialist distinction has also shaped a relevant subset of discourse around racism, namely current uses of the term antiblack. One recent example is a debate on social media over a Turkish artist who shared a painting he had made of nine minarets he had found particularly beautiful. Several respected Muslim academics who work in the fields of racism and antiblackness labeled this antiblack because none of the minarets were from Africa south of the Sahara.[45] Many others, academic and non, objected to what they saw as an unfair accusation leveled at an artist who had never claimed to be offering a comprehensive survey of minarets. From the substantialist perspective, however, the accusation of antiblackness made sense. Whatever the artist's intention, his painting was a representative product of a global Muslim discourse of memory and appreciation that has consistently omitted or patronized Black African Islam. It was this ongoing phenomenon that should be highlighted, not the author's intent or personal merit.

## WAS ISLAMIC CIVILIZATION RACIST?

In many ways, mapping the background of race and racism only reveals how inapplicable much of the scholarship on these topics is to the core of this book. At present, the bulk of scholarship views race and racism as modern or early modern phenomena. The heart of this book, by contrast, is the Islamic scriptural and normative tradition, the formative and most productive periods of which all took place long before the early modern period. In the Islamic tradition, what we encounter are premodern notions of national groups or phenotypical characteristics, along with accompanying assessments and prejudices. Whether scholars today would label such ethnotypes or beliefs as 'racist,' insist they were merely 'proto-racist' or object to both pronouncements is the subject of vigorous debates still ongoing among historians and social scientists.[46] Preoccupation with labeling the past with present concerns detracts from studying it on its own terms.

Questions about race and racism, however, do prompt us to consider useful generalizations about Islamic civilization. In the premodern heritage of Islamic law, theology, and ethics we certainly find examples of **othering**, Appiah's **racialism** and perhaps what he terms **intrinsic racism**. As we will see in the coming chapters, the Islamic tradition was replete with geographies and ethnologies, descriptions of phenotypes and common discourses around the various characteristics associated with each people and nation. These ethnotypes were not tied strictly to the body or common descent (i.e., race). Rather, they were based on a conflation of geography, environment, common descent, physical characteristics, and cultural and personal characteristics. In this regard, premodern Muslims were no different from their Greek, Roman, Persian, or Indian predecessors.[47] Phenotype had significance, but it was not definitive of one's status or even markedly correlatory to it. Furthermore, a massive swath of the Muslim world was phenotypically black, nobles and tillers alike.

Premodern Islamic civilization, like many premodern societies, did not reify aspects of the body or descent into inalterable lines along which power and resources were primarily distributed. Categories of identity such as religious confession were more important and shaped the most salient hierarchies, but they were also open and fluid. Anyone could convert to Islam. Some aspects of identification were more fixed, like tribe or lineage. But, ironically, even these 'bodily realities' were frequently constructed and reconstructed as individuals, families and tribes moved and created new associations. Berber tribes and Fulani communities in West Africa, for example, reconsidered and re-remembered their geographical origins and lineages as they made their homes in new regions and shifted their directions of identification according to religion, commerce, or demographics.[48] At any rate, such classifications of the body were either secondary to the category of religion, or the structure of power in society was too feeble to empower them in the way that race has been empowered since the early modern period.

Finally, premodern Muslim states, like premodern states in general, did not wield the capacities of control and resource monopolization needed to overwhelmingly disadvantage particular groups. The component parts of racism as the term is used today – hegemonic views of race and structures of power that could utilize those views to deprive and privilege according to a racial hierarchy – were not present. Moreover, we can actually pinpoint crucial moments when the situation changed. They are contemporaneous with the emergence of race and racism as governing ideas in Western Europe.

For example, the Moroccan sultan Mawlāy Ismāʿīl's (d. 1727 CE) shocking decision to enslave all 'blacks' in his realm for military service regardless of their being either freeborn Muslims or former slaves who had been freed was a definite turning point in the relationship between race and power. As Chouki El Hamel has noted, at that moment slavery in Morocco took a "racist turn."[49]

In the normative areas of premodern Islamic thought, we do encounter elements reminiscent of cultural racism, such as the frequency and confidence with which Muslim jurists spoke about how the customs (*ʿāda, ʿurf*) of particular cities, tribes, or communities dictated people's conduct and expectations. And these scholars could be judgmental in their descriptions of minorities or far-off peoples. But, in their recourse to custom and national characteristics, Muslim *jurists* (as opposed to scholars writing ethnology or geography) were almost always concerned not with demeaning or depriving minorities they governed but rather with managing the daily disputes and expectations among the majority to which they belonged.[50] Muslim jurists did frequently act as if their stereotypes about custom applied uniformly to all individuals in a group. They acknowledged individual or anomalous exceptions, but these could not threaten the rule. They were dismissed with axioms like "The rare case has no legal weight (*al-nādir lā ḥukm lahu*)."

This was not racialization of minorities along cultural lines, however. This was the generalization necessary for preserving legal and communal order, similar to how the common law holds individuals to a generalized 'reasonable person' standard regardless of their intelligence or psychological impediments. And it was class and gender, not race, national origin, or sub-culture, that the Shariah was most sensitive to. The law was deeply aware of class difference, in the sense that it viewed the social classes as functioning according to their own customs and general conventions. A slave might need to be punished by lashing, while a free person of high standing might be equally cowed by a public rebuke.[51]

When they were admitted into discussion by Muslim scholars elaborating or applying norms, stereotypes about ethnic or racial groups were similarly seen as nuggets of common sense useful for the pursuit of justice, not as devices for subordination. A (likely forged, see Appendix I) story of the influential jurist al-Shāfiʿī (d. 204/820) deducing that a missing Black African slave was in jail because, as it was 'well known,' "Black Africans, when they are hungry, they steal; when they are sated, they fornicate," was certainly demeaning to those racialized as black. In the culture of Islamic civilization, however, al-Shāfiʿī's deployment of 'common sense' was seen as nothing more than a cunning way to solve a mundane problem. The stereotype in no way governed how al-Shāfiʿī or other jurists treated students, colleagues or litigants racialized as black. In fact, one of al-Shāfiʿī's main teachers had been dubbed 'The Black African' (al-Zanjī), either because of his phenotype or because his love of dates corresponded to another stereotype, namely that Black Africans loved dates.[52]

# 3

## Blackness Contested

OLSON JOHNSON: All right. We'll give some land to the n—gers and ch-nks, but we don't want the Irish.
SHERIFF BART [who is Black American]: No deal.

*Blazing Saddles* (1974)

JIMMY RABBITTE: Do ya not get it, lads? The Irish are the blacks of Europe. And Dubliners are the blacks of Ireland. And the Northside Dubliners are the blacks of Dublin. So say it once, say it loud: I'm black an' I'm proud!

*The Commitments* (1991)

I no longer recognize white men, my brothers. Like this evening at the cinema, lost as they were past the void made around my skin.

Léopold Sédar Senghor (d. 2001),
"Lettre à un prisonnier" (Paris, 1942)[1]

A century and a half before a fictional Irish James Brown enthusiast pitched the idea of a White soul band in Ireland, broadsheets in the U.S. had talked about Irish immigrants as "n—s turned inside out." Indeed, at times there had been significant intermarriage between Irish immigrants and Americans of African descent. But, ironically, this tabloid epithet only underscored the reality that, even if the Irish were the 'blacks' of somewhere, they were not actually recognizable descendants of enslaved Africans. And when, in 1842, Irish Americans were called to join the campaign to end slavery in the U.S., a representative reply was that they would in no way consider Black Americans their "brethren."[2]

Yet in 2008, when another – apparently – son of Ireland, Barack Obama, became the first Black president of the United States, Ireland rejoiced.[3] Back in the U.S., meanwhile, respected Black American voices like Dr. Cornel West questioned whether Obama, the son not of centuries of enslavement and discrimination but of a highly educated Kenyan father and a White American mother, was really 'black' enough or not 'black' at all.[4] Indeed, recent immigrants to the U.S. from African countries like Nigeria have tended to avoid settling in Black American neighborhoods.[5] Some even use their mother tongue's word for black to refer to themselves in distinction to Black Americans.[6]

Before Obama emerged on the national stage but after I'd seen *The Commitments*, in a college course I took on Black Liberation Theology, a Cameroonian student told the class that the whole concept of blackness made little sense to him. He was Bantu. Yet, as he likely discovered living in the U.S., and as Obama retorted to his critics, when trying to hail a taxi, an African immigrant and a native-born Black American find themselves in the same predicament. On another occasion in university, as I walked with a Gulf Arab friend across campus, he told the students manning the Black Student Alliance table that he was black. They were nonplussed. "See, look at my lips," he added, pointing to his admittedly full lips. The students could barely marshal a reply. I considered the feasibility of denying I knew him. But sometime later, when I met my friend's family, his grandmother was visibly Black African, as were several of his siblings.

Is blackness about having a phenotype that certain people identify with Africa? If so, then who and what defines that look? Is it skin color only or other features as well, like hair texture and the shape of one's nose and lips? If blackness is about such phenotypical features, why did the Black American college students (and I) react with such discomfort to a person pointing out how his full lips revealed his actual African ancestry?[7] Was it that my friend, whom none of our friendship group had ever thought of as black, was performing out loud, in that charged space between my Whiteness and the students' Blackness, that shameful test we Americans run on one another daily, a test for something not locatable by instruments but made an inescapable reality by our own actions in history? Our laws betray how uneasy and ineffable this test is. Sundry definitions of 'black' in contemporary American legal codes and documents only state that it denotes a person who has "African ancestry."[8]

Or was it that the Black students were insulted that a wealthy Gulf Arab thought that the physical features he pointed out allowed him to identify with a people whose experience for the past four hundred years has been one of oppression and discrimination? Indeed, the Cameroonian student seemed eager to stress that a Black African phenotype did not entail a shared identity. The recent Movement for Black Lives Glossary would agree, defining a Black person as someone "who identifies as Black AND has African indigenous ancestry that predates colonization . . ."[9]

Can identifying as black be done separated from color and the body? What Jimmy Rabbitte and Obama's critics were both arguing, albeit from different directions, is that blackness is a condition of oppression, uprootedness, and marginalization. But, unlike Obama, Jimmy Rabbitte would not have any trouble finding a taxi in the U.S. or anywhere in the world for that matter. If blackness is a political condition and not the shape and color of one's body, political conditions can change. Bodies cannot. This is what happened when Irish Americans generally washed their hands of the struggle against slavery in the U.S. Maybe blackness is about that group always left behind and even stepped on by others seeking to rise, since few people offer the solidarity shown by Sheriff Bart and his motley band of railway workers in *Blazing Saddles*, who demanded they all be taken or none.

One can speak of blackness in many ways, and many definitions have been proffered.[10] As Michelle Wright observed, "Blackness remains undefined and suffering under the weight of many definitions."[11] I am not qualified to offer another or attempt anything approaching a comprehensive coverage. Nor would it serve the purposes of this book. In this chapter, we will only outline four important ways in which the concept of blackness (and antiblackness) intersects with the Islamic tradition. The first is simply through the notion of a phenotype, skin tone and physical features, that has long and widely been associated with the geography of Africa south of the Sahara and descent from its inhabitants. The second is both blackness as metaphor in language and what happens when that metaphor starts to blend with the somatic reality of black bodies, when, as Lewis Gordon alludes, the concrete and the metaphorical begin "bleeding into each other."[12] The third is the idea of blackness as the political condition of oppression, exploitation, and disenfranchisement. Finally, we will ponder blackness as a state of non-being and antiblackness as dehumanization distinct from any other type of racism. This is blackness as subjugation below the realm of the human and outside the sphere of political contestation and social life. It is, as Senghor described, to be apart from all else and to sit as the dominant White gaze merges the darkness of the cinema and the darkness of one's skin into the void of the unseen.

## BLACKNESS AS PHENOTYPE, WHITE AS THE NORM

The archetype of what we could term the 'classical' Black African phenotype has been remarkably stable from an early date. Full lips, a broad nose, tightly coiled black hair and dark brown or 'black' skin appear again and again in depictions and descriptions of Black Africans in distant times and places. With the exception of 'black' skin, we see these features in premodern artistic expressions by sub-Saharan Africans themselves. The Benin Bronzes depict figures whose features, though stylized, are easily recognizable to a Western viewer. An ivory pendant mask believed to have been produced for a king of Benin in the early sixteenth century is an almost realistic portrayal of a royal visage, with the novel contrast of a ring of what seem to be small, stylized busts of bearded Portuguese mariners around its edges.[13]

In the ancient Mediterranean world, the identification of a Black African phenotype that, though showing some variation, was generally stable can be traced back to at least the third millennium BCE in Egypt and the seventh century BCE in Greece.[14] Paintings from the tomb of the Egyptian governor of Nubia (the land south of Upper Egypt, between the first and sixth cataracts of the Nile) around 1330

BCE depict Nubians as having dark skin, represented using black and dark red paint. They stand in contrast with how the Egyptians depicted themselves in wall art, painted in a color Egyptians called red but which appears to us to be cedar, brownish ochre, or what Renaissance artists would call burnt sienna.[15] A statue of a Nubian captive depicts full lips and ritual scarring on the forehead. Old and Middle-Kingdom (*circa* 2700–2200 BCE and *circa* 2040–1782 BCE) carvings and paintings depicting Nubian wrestlers competing with Egyptians show a variety of black phenotypes with pronounced, thick lips, and coiled hair. Captions even show the Egyptian contestants taunting their foes as "black" and "kinky haired" as they force submission.[16] Scattered Assyrian epigraphy includes similar depictions.[17] A text from the seventh century BCE describes the Assyrian king's amazement at the "pitch-black" skin of Egypt's then Nubian Pharaoh.[18]

Another artifact of the ancient Near East, the Old Testament, refers to the Black African phenotype in a proverbial expression of inalterability: "Is a Cushite able to change his skin?" (Jeremiah 13:23), referring to the land of Cush, often identified as Ethiopia but generally referring to Black African peoples south of Egypt. This phrase echoes a similar Egyptian saying from as early as the sixth century BCE.[19] Here as well as in Numbers 12:1, which tells of some Israelites' anger with Moses for having married a Cushite woman, the Old Testament refers to Black Africans as the archetypal symbol of otherness and difference. Crucially, this image of difference was not necessarily pejorative.[20]

Ethiopia, which in the Hellenistic Biblical and Greco-Roman traditions more widely denoted the lands south of Egypt, played a similar role in the ancient Greek cultural lexicon. It was one extreme of the inhabited globe, "at the edge of the world," as it is described in the *Odyssey*. Some ancient Greek depictions of the Homeric hero Memnon, prince of Ethiopia, on pottery from as early as the sixth century BCE are recognizably (to me) Black African. In some depictions, however, he looks no different from the Greek characters, showing the way that classical Greek imaginings of Ethiopians ranged from mythical, distant folk to real Black Africans (Homer does not mention Memnon's skin color; Virgil describes him as black, *niger*).[21]

For Greco-Roman authors, the salient feature of the Black African phenotype was dark skin, with the Greek and Latin words for black used most frequently to represent this. The toponym most often used by Greco-Roman authors for where such folk dwelled was Ethiopia (literally, 'burnt face' in Greek), which indicated Africa south of Egypt and often all of Saharan and sub-Saharan Africa. The inhabitants of North Africa were also sometimes referred to as *Afer* (African) or *Maurus,* which may have been the name of a people there but which Isidore of Seville (d. 636 CE) claimed was derived from the Greek *mauros,* for black.[22] There was some slippage in the minds of Greco-Roman authors (as there still is in the West today)[23] between how they envisioned the inhabitants of North Africa, the majority of whom were Mediterranean in phenotype, and how they saw other 'Africans' further to the south. Greco-Roman geographies noted various shades of skin tones among those living south of the Mediterranean zone and Egypt, including some they described as 'swarthy' (*fuscus*) and even 'White Ethiopians,' as well as some Berbers who were 'black' in color but without the other Black African phenotypical features.[24]

Yet blackness was not coterminous with Africa for Greco-Roman authors. Latin writers might also describe people with 'black' skin as *Indus,* as they would sometimes use black to describe the skin color of the inhabitants of southern India.[25] But there was equally an awareness of a difference between Indian and Black African appearances, which demonstrates a more detailed Greco-Roman image of the Black African phenotype: a flat nose, thick lips, "woolly" hair, and bowlegs.[26] As with the Old Testament, such descriptions were not necessarily (or even not mainly) negative.[27] Herodotus (d. *circa* 425 BCE), for example, calls the Ethiopians (i.e., generically all Black Africans) the "handsomest" of people.[28]

Greco-Roman scholars elaborated various theories to explain different human phenotypes. Most were climatic, explaining different physical features and temperaments by proximity to the sun, heat, humidity, and water. Such theories can be found in the works of Strabo (d. 24 CE), Pliny the Elder (d. 79 CE), and Galen (d. *circa* 216 CE), among others.[29] Even Ovid (d. 17–18 CE) tells of how some believed that, because of the hot sun, "the creatures of Ethiopia turned black, their thick blood drawn to the surface of their skin."[30] Other theories posited a relationship between the four humors and climate.[31]

By the Antonine age, a robust physiognomy literature had accrued in Greek and Latin, with works by Galen on the subject and another influential treatise attributed (incorrectly) to Aristotle. These theorized an association of character traits with the climatic origins of varied somatic features. According to these views, the Mediterranean sphere of the Greeks and Romans produced moderation and excellence in body and character. When describing their own idealized appearances, classical Greek authors had tended to stress the bronzed and ruddy color of a healthy man out in nature and the pale color of women who had been shielded from outdoor labor. Hence Homer's extolling "white-armed Nausicaa" (*leukṓlenos*) in the *Odyssey*. This was further cemented in Republican Rome, where what Harmannus Hoetink called the 'somatic norm' (that collections of physical characteristics which a group sees as its norm) for Roman men was a 'white' (*albus*) color, understood as a light olive complexion. A slightly paler color was considered ideal for women.[32] This Roman convention would be momentous because, it would seem, this is the origin of designating the 'average' southern European phenotype as 'white.' This would be the base from which later conceptions of European whiteness took off (though ancient Egypt may also be a source: a wall painting from 1400 BCE depicts Canaanites as much lighter than the reddish-brown Egyptians. In the famous painting from the tomb of Seti I, the Egyptian artist depicted a Cushite with black paint and an Asiatic, probably someone from the greater Syria region, as well as a group of Libyans, with an ivory white).[33]

To the far north and south of this virtuous median were the climes of extremes and intemperance, both positive and negative. People in the cold north were pallid or pale in color (*pallidus*, *candidus*) and cold in disposition, along with the associated physical features of tallness, blondish hair, and snub noses. People in the hot south were characterized by the typical African phenotype and a heated temperament. In terms of the clearly negative, the hot southerners (i.e.,

Black Africans and perhaps southern Indians) were characterized by fickleness, frivolity, untrustworthiness, cowardice, thievishness, and, most of all, hypersexuality (including a large penis for men). This last feature became a trope that redounded in many a bawdy Roman tale of Roman women tempted by African slaves. But, on the positive side, their hot climate also cultivated in Africans quick minds and sagacity.

It is tempting to see in the Greco-Roman physiognomy an obvious antiblackness. But the inhabitants of the moderate, civilized world of the Mediterranean looked on the blue eyes, pale skin and blondish hair of the northern Europeans with distaste similar to what they felt towards Black African features. Indeed, Black Africans escaped relatively unimpugned compared to the disapproval directed at those who dwelled far to the north. Northerners (such as Germans and Slavs) might be courageous, but they were more characterized by rashness, simplemindedness, obtuseness, stupidity, an incapacity to reason, laziness, and drunkenness.[34]

As we saw in the previous chapter, the debate about whether race and racism are modern phenomena or of ancient date has exercised scholars for decades. Classicists are no exception. Were the Greeks and Romans racist, or did their ideas and remarks about various peoples and climes carry little in the way of prejudice or discrimination? The landmark work of Frank Snowden (d. 2007) argued that Greco-Roman sensibilities did not constitute modern color antipathy, color prejudice, or biological racism. He argued that they "attached no stigma to color," since it was widely understood that phenotype was the result of the accidents of climate and geography. Any positive or negative assessment of color or phenotype was a matter of personal preference, since the net assessments of the values or qualities associated with people from very northern climes did not differ much from those from the south. The "expressed preference," Snowden concluded, for white or black, dark or light, in Classical literature "is approximately equal."[35] Taking an example from the famous *Satyricon* of Petronius (d. 66 CE), we find comic characters mooting the idea of disguising themselves as Ethiopian slaves to escape being discovered by rivals. But they realize that, even if they dye their skin black, "can we make our lips swell to a hideous thickness? Or transform our hair with curling-tongs? Or plough up our foreheads with scars? Or walk bow-legged?"

Here Petronius is repeating well established physiological stereotypes associated with Black Africans in Classical culture. But to read the *Satyricon* as antiblack we must ignore the characters in this episode poking fun at the physical characteristics of several nations. Should they circumcise themselves like Jews, they ask themselves, pierce their ears like Arabs, or chalk their faces like Gauls?[36] It is a parade of stereotypes of non-Roman 'others.' While Jews and Arabs – other Mediterranean types – were marked by piercings, etc., the northern Europeans and Black Africans were equally alien in their skin color. One required white face, the other black. As Lloyd Thompson observed, such attitudes towards ethnic and national 'others' was not so much racist as it was an elite contempt doled out to all those seen as other than proper Romans – or at least all those other than whatever elite author was writing.[37]

Snowden's position has been seconded by many scholars, but it has also been criticized in the last three decades. Critics observe that Snowden was too focused on the description of physical traits and insufficiently attentive to how Greco-Roman culture constructed social understandings of race. What Snowden saw as value-free description or personal preferences Lloyd Thompson views as undeniable prejudice. Body and disposition might be shaped by climate, but these stereotypes were certainly prejudicial. Thompson argues that, taken as a whole, these views entailed widespread bias on the basis of color, phenotype and their national associations.[38] Benjamin Isaac added to this point, arguing that climatically governed physiology and ethnology were "proto-racist," since they fixed specific characteristics to certain groups. Moreover, such visions of Barbarian others had consequences. They figured into Greco-Roman justifications for imperial expansion.[39] But, even if we concede that Greco-Roman understandings of phenotypes, character, and nations were contemptuous or proto-racist, they were surprisingly contemptuous and proto-racist toward northern Europeans as well as Black Africans. In fact, considering that their physiognomy assessed northern Europeans as stupid and Black Africans as quick minded, and considering Greco-Roman literature featured a trope going back to Homeric epic of Ethiopia as a semi-mythic font of wisdom, it is not clear which group was seen in a worse light (though Thompson points out a late Republic trend of elite Roman women mimicking a more northern European appearance by using whitening cosmetics and blond wigs).[40]

The descriptions of the Black African phenotype established in the ancient Mediterranean and Near East are also found later on in China, during the Tang and Sung periods (together, 690–1279 CE). When a delegation of Muslims from Iran visited the Sung court in 977 CE, it was observed that their servants had deep-set eyes and black skin.[41] Though it is not clear if Chinese authors derived this from Muslim sources, they also seem to have shared the general, Near-Eastern impression of the character traits embodied in 'hot' southerners from Africa and other southern locales. Interestingly, however, the earliest descriptions that Chinese authors received about Africa, from the ninth century CE, note what trade goods were available, some customs and even that the inhabitants were raided by the Arabs. But they do not note the inhabitants' phenotypes. A twelfth-century text, however, does describe a part of Africa where the people are 'black' and regularly taken as slaves by Arabs.

Some of these slaves were transported to China, often identified with a Chinese transliteration of Zanjī (*Seng-chih*, from *Ts'eng-ch-'i*). They were evidently common in Guangzhou, where a twelfth-century source says many wealthy families owned them, referring to them as "devil-slaves," "wild men," or "black servants."[42] They were described as having "lacquer-black" or ink-black skin, red lips, white teeth, and frizzy, yellow hair. This last feature, which Kristina Richardson points out is almost certainly a description of 'blond' Melanesians from Oceania (whose phenotype resembles the image of Black Africans but with blond hair), shows the composite that made up the Chinese view of blackness. Slaves from Africa were sometimes lumped in with all the other slaves brought to China from India and the archipelagos of southeast Asia during the Tang and Sung periods.[43] These peoples were collectively described in ways similarly to Greco-Roman descriptions of Black Africans in terms of their phenotype, customs, and character.[44] Subsuming everyone perceived as coming from the south and Indian Ocean world under the color descriptor of black seems to have been a trend; a Tang court history produced in 945 CE also describes Arab men as "black and bearded."[45]

These remarkably consistent conceptions of what Black Africans looked like raise a basic question. Why were African people described as black and not brown?[46] Why did ancient Egyptians and Romans depict their skin using black paint, why did the Babylonians describe Nubians as "black as pitch," and why did the Chinese call them lacquer- or ink-black (a Japanese envoy to the U.S. in 1860 described Black Americans as having ink-black skin as well)?[47] There are not many people who actually have black skin, just as there are few who actually have white skin.[48] In modern studies and anecdotal accounts, children with Black African features who are asked to pick colors that match their skin tone choose shades of brown, not black.[49] Why didn't ancient Egyptians, Greeks, or Chinese describe or paint Africans in browns as well?

One reason may be that languages develop specific descriptors for brown relatively late in their maturation. In 1969, linguists Brent Berlin and Paul Kay advanced the influential theory that languages evolve in their vocabulary for color naming. Descriptors for black and white (or, according to later revisions, dark-cool/light-warm) exist at the earliest stage of a language. More color terms and distinctions are added in a total of seven stages. Brown usually appears in the second to last.[50]

In the cases of ancient Egyptian, Sumerian, and Akkadian, the earliest evidence shows that the languages had only four basic color terms: white, black, red, and blue/green. The Berlin and Kay theory does not suggest that Egyptians could not see any colors other than white, black, red, or blue/green. It does not mean that they could not describe or name other colors. It only means that the names for other colors were either derived from those basic color names (e.g., in theory, 'pink' might be called 'light red'), indicated by referring to some object (like 'tea colored' for 'brown' in Chinese) or were developed later on as vocabulary matured.[51] As Egyptian painting and painted sculpture developed, Egyptian men were depicted in shades of what Egyptians called 'red' (verging on what we would see as brown) and Egyptian women in 'yellow,' mirroring the Greek and Roman ideal of lighter skin tone for desirable women shielded from work in the sun. There is some indication that darker reds could be used for manual laborers and yellow occasionally used for a man who was portrayed as sedentary or bureaucratic, a youth or very old.[52] It may be the case that, at the very early point at which communities in the ancient Near East and Mediterranean first selected color names to describe Black Africans, their languages had not yet developed robust labels for browns, and hence they chose black. This may be the case among Africans south of the Sahara as well. As we will see later (see Appendix II), sub-Saharan languages generally use 'black' to describe the average skin tone of their speakers, with 'red' for lighter skin tones in their communities. In Mbay, a language spoken mainly in Chad, a warm brown is referred to as 'red' and a dark brown is referred to as 'black.'[53] Black and white descriptors of skin tone can also be more clearly figurative, with no evident mimetic function. In medieval Japanese, for example, lighter-toned skin was called 'white,' while very tanned Japanese skin was called 'black.' Anything in between was labeled in relation to one of these, like 'light black.'[54]

## BLACKNESS AS SIN, BARBARISM, AND FILTH

Whether they had been preference or prejudice before, during Late Antiquity (roughly 250 CE to the rise of Islam) Greco-Roman physiognomic and social stereotypes regarding Black Africans acquired an unmistakably negative valence. This was at least in part due to a blending of somatic description with the metaphorical association of blackness with sin in Christian discourse. The blackness of Africans was linked to sin and whiteness to baptism and grace. Here we should recall that words for white (e.g., *albus*) in Latin were used to describe the 'normal' phenotype in the Roman world. As Christianity became the norm in the Late Antique Mediterranean and Near East, whiteness became the color of 'normal' faith.

It is not surprising that humans portray error as darkness and guidance as light (Isaiah 9:2, Ephesians 5:8), but this metaphor seems to have taken on a more corporeal form in early Christian expression. Even in the late first century CE the Devil was labelled "The Black One" (*ho melas*), using the same adjective for black as was often used for black skin.[55] Inspired by the story of the apostle Philip baptizing an Ethiopian (Acts 8:26–39), the Cappadocian bishop Gregory of Nyssa (d. 395 CE) proclaimed that Christ had come into the world to make Black Africans (lit., Ethiopians) luminous and splendid, as they would be in the Kingdom of Heaven. In a false attribution to Dio Chrysostom (d. *circa* 120 CE), the famous orator purportedly celebrated how "baptism whitens Ethiopians."[56]

For many Church fathers, the blackness of the Ethiopian was the blackness of distance from God awaiting the salvational whitening of the Church.[57] In the writings of Augustine (d. 430 CE), we see a blending of Greco-Roman climatic physiognomy with the Biblical notion that the descendants of Noah's son Ham had been cursed with slavery and thereafter had populated Africa (Genesis 9:21–29). Augustine argues that the very name Ham comes etymologically from heat. Hence the descendants of Ham would be apart, hot and blazing with impatience and heresy, unlike the Semitic and Greco-Roman descendants of Noah's more favored sons in more moderate climes. His description of Ham's descendants resonates with contemporaneous depictions of slaves, in particular what de Wet calls "an unmanly and servile loss of control and mastery over the self, practically a return to animality." Though de Wet does not perceive any explicitly ethnic or racial element in Augustine's imagery, I think the continuity with the appetitiveness and carnality of the 'hot,' southern, African is evident.[58]

The devaluing of blackness/darkness crept into Biblical exegesis and even translation. We see in Origen's (d. *circa* 253 CE) commentary on *The Song of Songs* that the Bride (i.e., the Church) is transformed from black into white through God's grace. Jerome's (d. 420 CE) authoritative Vulgate translation of the Bible from Hebrew and Greek into Latin renders the Bride's words "I am black and beautiful" as "black *but* beautiful" (Song of Songs 1:5, emphasis mine).[59] In the

Late Antique period the stories making up the knot of the infamous Curse of Ham expanded beyond the curse of slavery to include the curse of blackness as well (see Chapter 4).

In the medieval Latin West, meanwhile, the somatic norm of the 'white' Roman Christian morphed smoothly into that of the Anglo-Germanic Christian.[60] Against this Christian image medieval Western European art and literature drew on a language of blackness in their depictions of two foes, the imagined demon and the very real Saracen (i.e., Arab Muslims). The overlap in artistic depictions of Ethiopians and devilish demons was noticeable. Medieval Christian art and literature like the *chansons de geste* regularly depicted Saracens as Black Africans or simply with very dark skin. In the *Song of Roland*, the evil Saracens are "black as ink" and "black as melted pitch to see."[61] This was primarily because of their association with sin, evil, and heresy, but their blackness also resulted from a geographical and somatic collapsing of the Arab with the Ethiopian. In an early-fourteenth-century English depiction of Richard the Lionheart impaling Saladin (the two probably never met), Saladin's face is a demonic blue, while his shield bears a much more realistic dark-brown-skinned, curly-black-haired image of what we assume is Muhammad.[62] Evil and Black Africa are combined. Meanwhile, the English epic (*circa* 1400) *The King of Tars* features an imaginary black Muslim sultan becoming physically white when he embraces Christianity.[63]

In sixteenth- and seventeenth-century Western Europe, the normativity of European Whiteness and its contrast with disdained African blackness gained wider purchase in cultural expression. This was in large part the result of increased European trade and exploration, which brought Europeans into contact with people who looked dramatically different from them. A host of such 'others,' from Native Americans to Pacific Islanders, served as the foil against which national and cultural identities formed and Europeans defined themselves. But the image of the Black African eclipsed all others, offering a physical reality for the Christian metaphor of black sin and white purity in which valuations were clear.

This conceptualization of the Black African as the other to the English, the French, or the Christian, White European burgeoned in the Renaissance and early modern periods. The Greco-Roman saying 'washing an Ethiopian' and the Biblical reference to an Ethiopian changing their color began being phrased more consistently as 'whitening an Ethiopian.'[64] A seventeenth-century French engraving of the baptism of an Ethiopian portrays him emerging not as a Semitic inhabitant of Palestine but as a cherubic, European youth. A European phenotype was thus not only normal but righteous, a sentiment that only increased during the Age of Discovery and the period of European colonialism.[65] European Whiteness was not only normal and righteous but *natural* as well. The French naturalist Buffon (d. 1788) was convinced that humanity was one species, but Whiteness was clearly "the true natural color of man."[66] The Greco-Roman physiognomic stereotypes remained alive and well. The Englishman Thomas Nabbes' (d. *circa* 1641) play *Hannibal and Scipio* portrays the African Carthaginians as black, sexually uncontrollable, driven by appetites and undisciplined. The Romans, progenitors of the Christian Europeans, are their opposites.[67]

Kim Hall has argued that, in the Elizabethan period, imagery of blackness and whiteness proved key to how the English were formulating notions of self and other, arising at a time of novel contact and trade with Africa.[68] The otherness of the Black African was incorporated into a white/black binary construction of English/non-English identity. English literature and letters swam with monikers encompassing blackness, such as Ethiop, Moor, Blackamoor, and Indian. These could be interchangeable, and the lines between them were not yet clearly drawn. But, by the 1600s in England as well as in France, recognizable representations of an African phenotype were clear and common.[69] So were its caricatured elements. Shakespeare has a character slur Othello as "Thick-lips." This image of the Moor, the African, and the Ethiop was ubiquitous in seventeenth-century English drama and literature, in the new American colonies as well as in Britain.[70] Black was barbaric, dirty, infidel and other, everything England and English was not.

Oddly, as Nabil Matar has shown, in England, cultural imagination and reality forked in this period. Even as interaction and familiarity with North and West Africa increased, depictions of Africa became more homogeneous and caricatured.[71] In English in particular, in the late 1600s the word 'Negro' and slave were becoming increasingly synonymous.[72] Cedric Robinson (d. 2016) observed that, as the Trans-Atlantic slave trade grew in scale, the previous ciphers for the African other, such as Moor, Ethiopian, etc., were all subsumed under the new racial category of 'black/negro.' Whereas, as we will see in the next chapter, the African Muslim Moor was in reality often a partner of Europeans and in the European imagination a fearsome foe, the 'black/negro' was a uniform and contextless color, their varied African histories and long interactions with Europe erased. 'The Negro' would be nothing more than a non-human, exploitable source of labor.[73]

The European Age of Exploration and the Enlightenment brought unprecedented exposure to other peoples, often observed empirically, as well as new, scientific justifications for dismissing their claims to humanity. The era brought a novel and expansive championing of human liberty but also scientific and legal reasoning for why Black Africans could be denied it.

Though some scholars have argued his comments were ironic or not representative of his views, Montesquieu (d. 1755) offers horribly disparaging descriptions of Black Africans. He even wonders how a wise God could deposit souls in such bodies. Montesquieu was a seminal critic of slavery who terminated its dominant, two-millennium-old Roman and natural-law justifications. Yet he also suggests that, if slavery were to be countenanced anywhere, it would be in those tropical lands where the climate makes people languid, lazy, and happy to surrender their political freedom.[74]

What Montesquieu could look past due to his climatic understanding of culture, John Locke (d. 1704) was able to look past with his novel legal conception of the right to liberty. It was acceptable (and profitable) to enslave Africans, Locke acknowledged, because they existed in a primitive state in which they raided one another and transgressed each other's rights to property and inviolability. Anyone who disregards others' rights to that extent, proposed Locke, forfeits their own right to liberty.[75]

Thomas Jefferson's (d. 1826) views about blackness, though they seem to have fluctuated during his long life, echoed the budding scientific racism of the era. He is unsure whether Black Africans and European Whites had always been distinct races or whether they grew apart. But, whatever the link between skin color and faculties, Jefferson wrote, the differences between the two races were essential and indelible. Though he acknowledged that Black Africans were better endowed with basic musical skill than Whites, he doubted whether they would ever produce a great composition. They were simply too inferior in reason and intellect, in oratory and expression. Jefferson's outlook is self-consciously that of the empirical and observational scientist. Black Africans themselves, he had observed, preferred Whites aesthetically and in terms of character, "as uniformly as is the preference of the Oranootan for the black woman over those of his own species."[76]

Like some other Enlightenment champions of liberty, it was the scientific mode of Jefferson's thought that allowed him to both condemn slavery morally and accept the enslavement of Black Africans. Though he does not seem to have gone to the extreme of contemporaneous thinkers like the Scottish James Burnett (Lord Monboddo, d. 1799) or Carl Linnaeus (d. 1778), who both speculated about blacks having interbred with apes, Jefferson's language is not far off.[77] The biological distinction between Black Africans and Whites is large enough to have created enormously divergent capacities and possibly different rights.

Of course, the Enlightenment period also saw arguments for abolition based on an insistence of unmitigated common humanity. The trend of scientific racial distinction at the biological level stands in stark contrast with Josiah Wedgewood's (d. 1795) famous porcelain medallion of a kneeling Black African man raising his eyes and manacled hands upward to the assumed viewer along with the plea, "Am I not a man and a brother?" And we see a similar plea in the form of philosophical argument in the spirited condemnation of slavery and its racial basis penned by Condorcet (d. 1794). The French nobleman's two treatises on slavery mock how Europeans had made feeble arguments for the inferiority of Black Africans and their lack of reason, then used those arguments to justify depriving their fellow human beings of their natural liberty.[78]

By the twentieth century, Whiteness had become the undisputed standard of civilization and beauty alike. And blackness was its opposite. Studies on how people racialized as non-White exhibit preference for skin tones and features closer to the standard of Whiteness are legion.[79] In a modern, secular descendant of the baptized Ethiopian, early-twentieth-century French detergent ads depicted a caricatured Black African man removing his hand from soapy water and revealing it Whitened.[80]

## BLACK AS METAPHOR; METAPHOR SHAPING REALITY

We have already seen how the metaphor of darkness and light came to inform early Christian thinking on Africa. Blackness as metaphor, however, has a much more expansive history. Race and how the language of color is used to make it may be social constructs, but humans are still part of nature. This seems to have influenced in nearly universal ways how humans relate to metaphors of color and value, from Britain to China.

Humans are a species that sees light and dark, the relative safety and comfort of the day and the dangers and mystery of the night.[81] Moreover, for many human populations, skin darkened by the sun is a trait of those who have been forced to labor outdoors, while lighter skin is the luxury of those who can afford to stay in the shade ('having a nice tan' today is the exception that proves the rule – only wealthy northerners can enjoy the sun or artificially tan all year round). It is certainly true that in associating lighter skin tone with higher socio-economic status we are centering the global north; the impact of exposure to sun is much less visible among darker-skinned populations. But even in Africa south of the Sahara, we find evidence of darkness acting as the metaphoric indicator of the lowest rungs of society. In such cases, the darkness associated with low status is the blackness of dirt and uncleanliness, not of more sun or melanin.[82]

It is not surprising that languages seem to have a near universal association of black/dark with bad and often also of white/light with good. This is true even in Africa south of the Sahara.[83] Language-specific studies have found associations of brightness or white with moral or a positive valence, while darkness and black are associated with immoral or negative meaning.[84]

Crucially, however, this metaphoric association does not necessarily govern how a society thinks about phenotype and value, let alone about race. Color descriptors like black or white *can and often do* work as part of the social construct of race to include and exclude, to empower and disempower. But in some societies color descriptors also simply work to describe someone's features with no relation on their status. We must note a crucial point here: in some societies, the language of color can do both jobs depending on context. While color is central to some systems of race (like that in the U.S.), it is less important in others (like that in the Arabian Gulf), which define the racial hierarchy of power, insider/outsider by means other than phenotype, such as descent, lineage, and/or citizenship. But color can still play a role. **Even in societies in which race is not primarily indicated by color, color can still sometimes be used as a proxy for racial status. But, in this case, color is indeterminate and secondary.** In other words, though color may be invoked, some other factor, like lineage or citizenship, is primary and all-important.

Moreover, **the metaphoric meanings of 'black/dark = bad' and 'white/light = good' are often used in ways that are totally unrelated to people's actual appearances.** The metaphor of 'black = bad' may appear nearly ubiquitously in world languages, but it often does not apply consistently *within* a language. Describing someone's appearance as 'black' often has no negative connotation. In many languages from Africa south of the Sahara – spoken by populations in which the Black African phenotype predominates – the word 'black' (the same used to describe the color of a piano, for example) is also used to describe the skin tone of the vast majority of the population. It carries no negative connotation. Yet that same word in those same languages is also used to register malice or negativity in phrases like 'black hearted.' But this negativity associated with blackness as metaphor does not transfer over into the literal descriptions of the skin tone of the populations speaking those languages (see Appendix II).

This equanimity around 'black' as a descriptor breaks down noticeably in the Sahel (see Appendix III) and the Horn of Africa (see Appendix IV), where darkness and blackness, either real or perceived, are bound up in racial categories of power and acquire a status denotation.

So, in the case of many African languages, what we might deem metaphorical antiblackness exists alongside a neutral view of blackness as a physical descriptor without one influencing the other. But in some cases in world history, metaphorical antiblackness can actually shape how physical features are described. It can bend the way language is used to talk about physical description even when all the people in question look the same. In other words, even when the metaphor of 'black = bad' is explicitly transformed into a literal description of someone's physical color, *it can still have nothing to do with their actual appearance.*

Literary evidence from medieval Scandinavia often depicts slaves (sing., *thrall*) as 'black' or dark in complexion. The *Rigsthula* poem, which has been dated to between the ninth and thirteenth centuries, tells of the mythic origin of Scandinavia's social classes. The first nobles were fair-haired and bright-colored. The first farmers were ruddy. But the first slaves were black (*svartan*)-haired or black-skinned (depending on the reading). But, in reality, these slaves were *not* literally 'black.' They were not even darker skinned than their owners. Slaves in medieval Scandinavia were either from the indigenous population, or they were Celtic (from Scotland or Ireland), Saxon, Germanic, or Slavic. None of these groups could be described as darker than the average Dane, let alone as black. Indeed, Scandinavian literary evidence just as often makes the point that one cannot tell a slave by their looks.[85] We also see this in medieval English literary depictions of the Welsh as the near other, subject to enslavement. We find, for example, in a late-tenth-century book of Anglo-Saxon riddles references to the "dark haired" (*wonfeax*) Welsh slave and the "swarthy" (*swearte*) Welsh, in contrast to the light-haired or blond English.[86]

How can we make sense of describing slaves who were the same color as their owners, and all of them among the palest humans around, as 'black'? First, we must recall the widespread link between the desirability of 'light' and basic economics. The description of the archetypal slave in the *Rigsthula* centers not on blackness of skin or hair but on dirtiness and an ugliness stemming from a life of manual toil, on "rough hands" and "sunburned arms." Slaves are dark because they are constantly in the sun and dirt and do not have the luxury of cleanliness. Second, race is a construct that takes something people make up – different social categories for humans – and endows it with the legitimating veneer of biological reality. Ruth Karras notes that the Scandinavian slave's ugliness and unhealthiness was not literal even though it claimed to be a physical description. It was a foil to contrast the subhumanity of the slave with the human normality of the ruddy and healthy free folk. The physical description of the slave as black and ugly, as foreign, "was part of the social construction that made the slave an other."[87] It was the otherness, not the color, that was important.

## BLACKNESS AS A POLITICAL CONDITION

It seems unlikely that Jimmy Rabbitte was identifying as black because he recalled some ancestral enslavement to the Danes. The notion that the Irish (or at least some Irish) might identify with blackness assumes that blackness can mean something other than skin color. It is the same metaphor of blackness that has led, with the recent internationalization of the Black Lives Matter movement, to Palestinians under siege in Gaza painting murals expressing shared suffering in solidarity with the family of George Floyd. This political metaphor of blackness takes the suffering of Black Africans in the Middle Passage and then plantation slavery in the Americas, the segregation of Black Africans from South Carolina to South Africa and the Western colonial exploitation of Black Africa, and renders blackness the very color and idiom of systemic oppression and the infliction of injustice. This blackness stands in opposition to Whiteness as the transnational system of exploitation, what in language is the 'Babylon system' in Jamaican Iyaric and 'the Man' in African American English, what in geography is the northern colonial exploitation of the global south. The black worker in the U.S., laborers in India, China, Africa, etc., who make up what Du Bois (d. 1963) called that "dark and vast sea of human labor," have all shared the common experience of immense exploitation to enrich the wealthy of New York, London, and Rio. They are "the dark proletariat."[88]

Responses to disenfranchisement, oppression, and exploitation under colonial rule have taken the form of local, community-specific resistance. They have also manifested as efforts to phrase and inspire resistance by linking it to broader frames such as Marxism in order to help build solidarity with others and draw on their moral and material resources. Blackness has appealed at various times and places as the idiom for such movements. The first seeds of what we can call political blackness likely lie in the thought of the Moorish Science Temple in 1920s America. This Black Nationalist movement developed the idea of the common Asiatic roots of non-Europeans. The Nation of Islam soon further elaborated this concept, both ethnological and political, transforming it into the 'Asiatic Black Man.' The Nation's most charismatic spokesman, Malcolm X (d. 1965), popularized this idea, insisting that blackness was an international, historically-deep political condition imposed by White, Euro-American persecution. "When I say Black," he explained in a 1964 speech, "I mean non-white – black, brown, red, or yellow."[89] For the Black radicals of the 1960s and '70s, blackness was a transnational political condition of oppression and cultural and physical occupation as present in Palestine as in the American South.

A major theoretical pillar for this perspective was the writing of Frantz Fanon (d. 1961), a Francophone Martinican racialized as black. His *Peau noire, masques blancs* (1952, translated as *Black Skin, White Masks*) and his famous *Les Damnés de la terre* (1961, translated as *The Wretched of the Earth*) provided a crucial theoretical foundation for moving from the experience of blackness in Europe and the Americas to the shared condition of the colonized.

One of the most influential articulations of blackness as a political condition came from Apartheid South Africa, in particular from the Black Consciousness movement and the South African Student

Association (SOSA) founded in 1969 by Steve Biko (d. 1977). The Black Consciousness movement focused extensively on forming Black Africans into agents of change and throwing off value systems and aesthetics that had long held Whiteness as the point of reference (with slogans like "Black is beautiful"). Although in early articulations of its mission SOSA's founders had gravitated towards the phrase "non-Whiteness" as their anchor of solidarity, there was concern that this left Whiteness the reference point.[90] So blackness was adopted as the ideological touchstone, and in 1971 SOSA defined Blacks as "those who are, by law or tradition politically, economically and socially discriminated against as a group in the South African society and identifying themselves as a unit in the struggle towards the realization of their aspirations." Many South African students of Indian descent began referring to themselves as black and felt represented by SOSA and the Black Consciousness movement.[91]

A movement of Political Blackness, actually referred to by this proper noun by its proponents, also formed in the U.K. in the 1970s. Political Blackness was developed by leaders in the country's South Asian, Black African, Afro-Caribbean, and Indo-Caribbean communities, who recognized they shared similar experiences of ghettoization, marginalization, and victimization by law enforcement. Not only was the power elite and state establishment of the U.K. almost exclusively White, but these minority groups had often all been referred to by spokespeople or representatives of that establishment as black, whether they had African ancestry or not.[92] In this sense, Political Blackness grew in ground conditioned by British colonial literature and governance. Madras, for example, had been founded by the East India Company with an exclusively European "White Town" and a "Black Town" for local Indians. The Scottish explorer Mungo Park (d. 1806) spoke of "a black merchant of Hindostan," the British troops fighting against the 1857 Indian uprising referred to their foes as "n—rs" and "black creatures," and Kipling's (d. 1936) narrator in *Gunga Din* referred even to loyal Indian Sepoys as "all them blackfaced crew."[93]

Blackness as a political condition has not simply been the purview of activists. It has also been theorized with sophistication by scholars who see it as a way of understanding the pervasiveness of White supremacy and how the expropriation of land and resources in recent centuries has weaponized antiblackness. For example, anthropologist Sarah Ihmoud argues that blackness is a condition experienced by Palestinians under Israeli settler colonial rule, not simply due to the crude analogy of oppression but because the Israeli dispossession and erasure of Palestinians is a White supremacist project that follows "an antiblack logic" governed by anxiety over racial purity and threats to it.[94]

There has been great tension, however, around the extent to which blackness as a political condition is isomorphic with other prominent frameworks for comprehending oppression and exploitation. Are the international proletariat, the colonized world, and, more recently, those exploited by the post 1990s neo-liberal global economy all truly categories fungible with those racialized as living in black bodies? Black activists and intellectuals who have understood themselves to be part of or associated with struggles against capitalism, colonialism, and Apartheid have faced the question of whether they should sublimate the idiom of blackness into, for example, a Marxist framework of class struggle or maintain the idiom of blackness intact but in solidarity with such a framework.

One question has persistently loomed. Whether one proposes solidarity with fellow workers or with other colonized peoples, do these lenses for explaining and addressing suffering in human history really take into account non-Western people and their experiences? More importantly, does the progress promised by these models for identifying and rectifying modes of oppression come at the expense of some who are left behind?

As we will see, Afropessimists see Marxism and political blackness as mirages that allow those without black skin to contest power politically, ultimately at the expense of those racialized as black. Yet many others have been clear that racial distinction is a distraction. Huey Newton (d. 1989) and Malcolm X did not have any illusions about the horrors faced by enslaved Africans and their descendants in the U.S. But in realizing that they were "a colonized people" and that their cause was part of a larger, global anti-imperial and anti-colonial struggle, as Newton put it, "we're latecomers." What made the U.S. exceptional was not the particularity of the American enslavement and oppression of Black Africans but its centrality to a racist and exploitative world order that remained regnant.[95]

Similarly, many Leftist activists have long argued that racial distinction is a distraction from the true structures of oppression: class and capitalism. Even the most prominent critic of Marxism from the perspective of race, Cedric Robinson, still saw Africanness as essentially incidental to racial capitalism. In modern times, Robinson argued, European racism had certainly metastasized into a global structure to exploit African labor and keep White workers in line. What Marxism and other Eurocentric lenses of revolution had missed, however, was that racism was not an epiphenomenon of capitalism or modernity. It had been a crucial component of how power was structured within Europe long before the rise of industrialization and exploration. What Robinson held out as the solution, the Black Radical Tradition, made up of those tools of resistance drawn from the African past and experience of slavery, from gospel and Black Christianity to sabotage and open rebellion, was the means for *all* to bridge the economic and social crises gripping the Western world today.[96]

The main movements of political blackness, however, stumbled over race. For Political Blackness in the U.K., Black Consciousness in South Africa and the Black radicals in the U.S., the forces of internal fission and the divide-and-conquer policies of the state proved either daunting or overwhelming. In the U.S., U.K., and elsewhere government compartmentalization of minorities into discrete ethnic or racial communities undermined intra-national and international solidarity by, as Annie Olaloku-Teriba explains, "determining the language through which communities could seek funding and redress for harms from the state." "Anti-racism," she concludes, "was largely shorn of its internationalism as political horizons retreated into 'community organizing.'"[97] In the 1980s, Black radicalism in the U.S. gave way to the struggle to liberate African Americans, with figures like Jesse Jackson significantly attenuating their support for international issues like Palestinian rights as he sought to navigate the strongly pro-Israel mainstream of American politics.[98] In recent years, some Black American activists, such as many advocating for reparations for American slavery, have deemed terms like Black and People of Color to be too expansive. As with critics who saw Barack Obama as a product of comfortable Whiteness and aspirational African immigration, they view Black African immigrants to the U.S. as inappropriate partners in solidarity, since they do not carry the legacy of American enslavement and discrimination. Some such activists have adopted the narrower concept of ADOS (American Descendants Of Slaves) instead of blackness or color.[99]

In the U.K., internal differences and the state's carrot-and-stick strategies of hiving off groups doomed the Political Blackness movement.[100] In South Africa, the hesitancy of some Indians to either identify as Black or sacrifice their marginal advantages over Black Africans in the Apartheid system hampered solidarity. In the U.S., as Hisham Aïdi has noted, there had long been suspicion that Islamically inflected Black Nationalist movements offered conversion to Islam or the adoption of a Moorish identity as forms of passing.[101] The Moorish Science Temple's leaders had claimed that American Blacks were originally "olive-skinned" and from Morocco, and Elijah Muhammad (d. 1975) romanticized Arab North Africa and the Arabian Peninsula, seemingly in preference to sub-Saharan Africa.[102]

That political blackness failed has become a truism among many intellectuals, with scholars like Kwame Anthony Appiah offering post-mortem analyses of the movement. Maya Bhardwaj observes a trend among those calling for social and political justice to move beyond blackness as the select idiom of solidarity, since it has proven both too broad (and thus subject to internal fragmentation) and too narrow (with national and even sub-national strains like ADOS activism claiming the true mantle of blackness).[103] One approach taken by contemporary social justice activists aims to create the large tent imagined by political blackness but to do so along non-racialized lines. It draws on critical and queer theory to argue for a broad alliance of historically marginalized and oppressed segments of society, with concepts like BIPOC (Black, Indigenous, People of Color) and other groups (women, LGBTQ, etc.) identifying racial capitalism and heteropatriarchy as, in Bhardwaj's words, "the root causes of our ills."[104]

Yet many still insist that blackness is either *the* political condition of oppression or that the social and political activist energy devoted to fighting racialized antiblackness is better directed at racial capitalism, imperialism, or a mixture of both. Leftists of various stripes and adherents of the de-colonial school of thought are the most vocal. As we saw with the taming and nationalizing of Black radicalism in the U.S. and as we will see with Afropessimism, the question of Palestine continues to be both divisive and a litmus test. As Olaloku-Teriba explains, the Palestinian cause reveals how one understands blackness and black liberation.[105] If blackness is a political condition, either equal to or part of the oppression wrought by capitalism, imperialism, etc., then black liberation and Palestinian liberation are bound together. But in countries whose governments are habitually pro-Israel, like the U.S. and U.K., then solidarity with Palestine carries a cost. As we will see now, however, an influential strand of thinking about blackness voices open suspicion about whether *any group* not racialized as Black in body can stand in solidarity with Blacks. And Palestinian Arabs are the most prominent example.

## BLACKNESS AS NON-BEING: AFROPESSIMISM

The Civil Rights movement in the U.S. and the broader movement for Black liberation has long held out the eventual hope of freedom, even if it lies beyond a distant horizon. Whatever reforms might be achieved in the present, it is a present still far from free. But someday discrimination will end.[106]

But what if there is no hope? What if there is no overcoming for some people because those people's abject subjugation is the floor upon which humans stand to be human, on which society is built so that it can be the space where disputes about oppression and racism play themselves out with all their rancor? This is the view of Afropessimism, a theory articulated and advocated by American academics such as Professors Jared Sexton and Frank Wilderson III.

Afropessimism might enjoy no more than the niche appeal that academia offers any subfield, except that it has increasingly influenced the activism against antiblack racism that has become prominent in recent years.

Like so much thought on race and oppression, Afropessimism builds on the writings of W.E.B. Du Bois and Fanon.[107] But it also draws on the sociologist Orlando Patterson's efforts to define slavery in world history. Patterson introduced the idea of social death to discussions of slavery, which he argued is in part defined as a condition in which individuals are, in effect, dead to their descendants and ascendants, unable to benefit from what their families could have passed on to them and unable to benefit their own children.[108] Afropessimists add to this the literary scholar Saidiya Hartman's notion of "the afterlife of slavery," that, even after abolition, the condition of slavery continues to define the existence of communities who had suffered through it.[109] As slavery came to define blackness and blackness became the same as slaveness, blackness became the ontological state of social death, of non-being. Since identities and meaning are defined in opposition to something other, blackness is the other against which the socially alive and human is defined.

If one posits blackness as a political category defined as the excluded, oppressed, or exploited that allows the powerful, enfranchised, etc. to constitute themselves, then Afropessimism *could* coexist or overlap with the theory of blackness as a political condition. But the most prominent articulators of Afropessimism seem, at least implicitly, to define blackness as the condition of those people who have been racialized as black bodies. Black people are those whose destinies were shaped and defined by enslavement and its afterlife. They are unmistakably of African descent.[110]

Discussions of social death and ontology are abstruse even for academics, and Afropessimism might not have achieved any relevance beyond academia had the theory not entailed profound consequences for broader antiracism activism around the world. Put simply, for Afropessimists, antiblackness is not a form of racism. Racism is a phenomenon that occurs *within* society, and groups that suffer from it or from other forms of discrimination can organize and contest them. Blackness, by contrast, exists outside society, and so other forms of oppression are simply incommensurate to antiblackness.[111] What this means is that calls for solidarity between those racialized as Black and victims of racism such as Latinos, not to mention those who suffer from sexism or economic exploitation, are misplaced. As Wilderson, a compelling writer to be sure, has put it, "The antagonist of the woman is the man; the antagonist of the worker is the boss; the antagonist of the queer is the straight – but the antagonist of the Black is the Human." Workers, women, and LGBTQ folk struggle for a better and more just future, but "the future is what happens when one is not Black."[112]

Not only is the injustice suffered by other groups not analogous to that suffered by those racialized as black, black solidarity with those other groups is inevitably rewarded with betrayal. As Wilderson describes, however much an oppressed group might feel in common cause with blacks, the moment they overcome whatever oppression they face, they will be – as they always were – human beings standing in opposition to black non-being.[113]

The pessimism of Afropessimism may not be as inscribed as authors like Wilderson would have it. For him, Afropessimism differs from well-known revolutionary perspectives like Marxism because it offers no prescription for salvation.[114] For other scholars of race who subscribe to Afropessimism, however, it does hold promise. It alerts us that any real solution to antiblackness would require "radically alternative conceptions of what it is to be human and live in society," as Moon-Kie Jung and João H. Costa Vargas have concluded.[115]

Whether or not Afropessimism denies the possibility of resolution may not be its most important facet. As Professor Jesse McCarthy observes, Afropessimism's significance lies as much in how it steers our conversations and marks a certain mood in intellectual culture and activism at a moment in which the deepness and pervasiveness of antiblack racism has become widely recognized. It questions whether, as Martin Luther King described it, the long arc of history really does bend towards justice.[116]

More practically and arguably more consequentially, Afropessimism also casts a spanner in the works of efforts at solidarity among non-black people of color and other marginalized populations. In many Western countries like the U.S., where the Cold War placed Leftism either at the margins of discourse or under extreme suspicion, the Civil Rights tradition – synonymous with the cause of Black American liberation – is one of the few mainstream avenues for contesting racism and exploitation. But Afropessimism not only delegitimizes non-black adoption of this tradition, it also seems to have resulted in accusations that non-blacks are perpetuating antiblackness by daring to analogize their experiences with blackness or trying to trade on black suffering.

It is thus no surprise that the main critics of Afropessimism are those who advocate for solidarity among workers, the colonized, victims of racism and sexism more broadly, etc. For them, Afropessimism entails nothing less than a betrayal of the intercommunal solidarity championed by Black radicals like Huey Newton and Malcolm X.[117] This critique is voiced loudly in activist circles, but it is equally present at the theoretical level in the academy. In addition, the Afropessimist claim to an exceptional experience of violence and dehumanization has also been challenged by scholars of indigenous studies, who have worked to uncover the histories of dispossessed and liquidated native populations from Australia to Palestine. Scholars like Justin Leroy have pointed out that black and indigenous claims need not be in competition, since the logics of antiblackness and settler colonialism have fed off and strengthened one another.[118]

How fair are these criticisms of Afropessimism? On the one hand, pessimism about solidarity with those racialized as black is born of experience. Considering episodes like the Irish American refusal to commit to abolitionism and the fragmentation of political blackness in the U.K. and South Africa, it is understandable that those familiar with the history of activism would expect that black people will eventually be thrown under the bus. One also wonders to what extent this pessimism is really a matter of principle. It may be closer to well-deserved skepticism. Referring to an incident in which a Palestinian friend betrayed what Wilderson had thought was their solidarity and shared commitment to each other's causes, Wilderson shows himself not so much unwilling to support Palestinian liberation as committed to holding Palestinians accountable for their past and future antiblackness.[119]

On the other hand, one wonders whether Wilderson's dismissal of his Palestinian friend was too hasty. As we will see in the next chapter, the accusation that 'Arabs' writ large use the word 'slaves' (*'abīd*) to refer to Black Africans has become a trope not just in Afropessimist discourse but also in other contemporary instances of Black/Muslim encounter, including Black Muslims in the U.S. voicing frustration with immigrant Muslims from the Arab world and South Asia.[120] In fact, this usage is only found in some dialects of spoken Arabic and, even then, often only in less refined registers of the language.[121] Moreover, in the lengthy and carefully considered account that Wilderson gives of his Palestinian friend's moment of betrayal – when he confided to Wilderson that the most humiliating instance of being searched at an Israeli checkpoint was when the soldier doing so was an Ethiopian Jew – Wilderson omits any attempt he might have made to ask his Palestinian friend what he meant. Wilderson seems to have immediately understood this comment as meaning, definitively, that the "collective consciousness of Palestinian insurgents has more in common with Israeli state and civil society than it does with Black people."[122] But is that really a fair induction from what the friend said? Could he not have meant that it was uniquely humiliating because Ethiopian Jews are so looked down on by other Israelis, so this experience was an even clearer reminder that Palestinians are the non-human other in Israel?

In any case, the criticism that Afropessimism undermines solidarity is an argument from consequence, not a critique of Afropessimist arguments themselves. A major fallacy identified within Afropessimism, by contrast, is its assumption of a transhistoric, global concept of blackness and a transhistoric, global concept of slavery that is racialized as black. Afropessimists like Wilderson might reply that they are addressing blackness only as it has existed since trans-Atlantic slavery, at which point slaveness "consumed Blackness and Africanness, making it impossible to divide slavery from Blackness."[123] But this still leaves Afropessimism forcing its understanding of blackness – a markedly U.S.-centric view of blackness as synonymous with slavery and its afterlife – on all those who are seen as or see themselves as black around the world. What about the one billion Black Africans who live in Africa south of the Sahara but whose identity and past are not necessarily defined by slavery?[124] Finally, as Kevin Ochieng Okoth has objected, one cannot conceive of blackness and antiblackness as morally prior to and independent of colonialism and capitalism when it was colonialism and capitalism that created the modern world in which blackness and slaveness have become one and the same.[125]

The conflation of slaveness and blackness in Afropessimism seems to be the theory's Achilles heel. In reality, it is not so much that it is "impossible to divide slavery from Blackness," as Wilderson claims, but rather that the two have become closely associated because of particular historical contingencies. One such contingency is the assumed synonymity of blackness and Africanness. 'Slave,' 'black,' and Africa might be synonymous in many contexts, whether in the modern Americas or the modern Arab world. But this process of association was one that could extend itself beyond the Black African, such that there is no necessary link between 'slave' and the Black African body. Seventeenth-century Dutch East India Company merchants in Southeast Asia racialized their slaves and even sometimes their servants as black even though Africa was an insignificant source of slaves compared to peripheral Southeast Asian communities and the coasts of India and Burma.[126] Here 'slave' and 'black' were coterminous, but the Black African was absent.

An Afropessimist might object that the association between 'slave' and 'black' could only have been made in the wake of the synonymity of slavery and Black Africanness. But, first of all, the seventeenth-century Dutch seem to have conceived of the blackness of slavery as the blackness of the Moor, the label that Dutch slaveholders in the Netherlands gave to Black African domestic servants.[127] And Moors were competitors, not subhumans or natural slaves.[128] Second, if Afropessimists accept that slaveness and blackness can be synonymous even though the body in question is not Black African, then how is this any different from thinking of blackness as a political condition? The Burmese slaves of the Dutch East India Company in Java met every condition for blackness demanded by Afropessimism. Perhaps, in some time and place, some Irish did too.

## SO WHAT ABOUT ANTIBLACKNESS AND ISLAM?

A common definition of antiblackness is that it is antiblack racism, namely racism directed against people racialized as black.[129] Though they have not always deployed labels based in color, we have seen that people outside of Africa south of the Sahara have long shared a fairly stable mimetic vision of the Black African phenotype. Antiblackness could thus simply be racism directed at those seen as recognizably of Black African origin. This seems clear enough provided one can agree on what racialization as black means.

Though the U.S. is not the starting point for this question, U.S. discourse on race has greatly complicated it. In many ways, how blackness and antiblackness are conceived in the U.S. stands out in the world. On the one hand, blackness in the U.S. is both more inclusive as a phenotype while also being – according to some – more exclusive as an identity. The 'One-Drop' rule of hypodescent and the exclusivity of slavery and later Jim Crow discrimination to people racialized as black according to this rule meant that the phenotypical markers of blackness in the U.S. took in a greater swath of the population than the Black African phenotype as imagined from ancient Greece to Elizabethan England would have.[130] Yet the experience of slavery and systematic discrimination has led to an insistence among some Black Americans that recognizably Black African features or African descent are not enough to be Black in America.

On the other hand, Afropessimism has taken the U.S. (and arguably the broader American) experience of blackness as the black-body-made-slave and generalized it globally and transhistorically. From the point of view of Afropessimism, antiblackness is expansive. It is antiblack simply for those not racialized as black by U.S. standards to analogize their suffering to that of Black Americans. But the generalization of a U.S.-centric conception of blackness and a capacious definition of antiblackness are truly narrowing in that they close the door on blackness as a metaphor of political oppression.[131]

If Afropessimism is U.S.-centric, however, then in an important way it charts a continuity in the role blackness has played in the formation of a Western identity. What was one of many, sometimes exotic ethnotypes in the cosmopolitan world of Rome became the non-Christian or not-yet-Christian other of the early Church, then the dark barbarian other to the White and civilized English or French. This foil of blackness allowed Enlightenment Europe to guarantee liberty and rights to the fully human while exploiting the labor of the not fully human. And blackness has helped keep those racialized as White in line in a capitalist system that has also allowed other colonized or subordinated groups to negotiate belonging against the floor of blackness.[132] Yet blackness has been embraced by many among the downtrodden or non-Western, providing an important idiom of resistance against colonialism and racial capitalism.

One variation in the strikingly stable conception of black as a somatic description is relevant to blackness in the Islamic tradition. Like the Greco-Roman tradition, Islamic sources (particularly early ones) can use black to describe both the standard Black African phenotype as well as someone who has very dark skin but no African descent. Otherwise, as with the question of racism, much of the discourse and debate around blackness and antiblackness seems set too late in time to influence how we answer the question 'Is Islam antiblack?' If antiblackness is racism against those perceived as descending from Black African origins, then the question is straightforward (though its answer would still hinge on how one defines racism). Some scholars have suggested an association of blackness and slaveness in medieval Islamic civilization even prior to the early-modern coalescing of racism proper. This we will address in the next chapter. But Afropessimism's most compelling argument is for the conflation of blackness and slaveness *after* the intensification of the Atlantic slave trade. As with the most widely held view on the emergence of racism, this would be long after the maturation of the Islamic normative tradition.

By connecting slavery and social death to the ontological contrast between being and non-being, human and non-human, however, Afropessimism poses a relevant question to the Islamic tradition. Islamic law only allowed the enslavement of non-Muslims outside the borders of the Abode of Islam (*Dār al-Islām*), the land where God's law ruled. Islamic law built on and took for granted many crucial aspects of slavery in the pre-Islamic Near East, including theorizing the legality of enslavement on the basis that captives taken in war had been spared death. As in the Roman law etiology of enslavement, the death spared captives was fungible with their enslavement (Islamic law also allowed ransoming or simply freeing them). So can we think of the populations from which Muslims could draw slaves as subjected to the ontological state of non-being? Does blackness as non-being lie outside the borders of the Muslim abode of humanity?

There are serious limits to this analogy. For example, leading Muslim scholars extended to non-Muslims living outside the Abode of Islam the right not to be enslaved or sold off by their own kin. This was because these jurists considered it a violation of human rights to own a close relative – a prerequisite for selling them.[133] And Muslims could conclude treaties with such peoples, as in the case of the Abbasid caliphs' treaty and gold-sharing production deal with the non-Muslim, Black-African Bujja south of Egypt.[134] As we will see, Muslim scholars writing their geographies and ethnologies sometimes spoke of the Black Africans (*sūdān*) who lived outside the borders of the Abode of Islam as savages closer to beasts than men. If blackness in the ontological sense is the non-being and non-human beyond the borders, however, in this case it cannot be the same as being racialized as Black African. We will see that, as the borders of the Abode of Islam spread to the south and more Black Africans embraced the faith, the boundary line of the human and unenslavable moved as well. Swaths of Muslims racialized as black lived within it. Those Black Africans who had become Muslim were identified by tribe and nation and affirmed as fully-human recipients of God's revealed law.

# 4

## The Western Narrative of Islam, Slavery, and Antiblackness

The Muslim slave trade was 200 times greater than the American slave trade. Moreover, while Westerners had fought to end slavery globally, Muslims continued to buy and sell human beings. White guilt, it would seem, was uncalled for. So tweeted the Canadian far-right identitarian Stefan Molyneux in 2018, not long before he was banned from the platform.[1] Two years later, in the wake of the 2020 killing of George Floyd, a conservative Israeli news outfit responded to efforts to promote Palestinian–Black solidarity in the U.S. by pointing out how a young Palestinian American activist had referred to Black people as *ʿabīd* (slaves). This was due, the journalists claimed, to a strain of racism endemic among Muslims and Arabs. It was on display in Saudi Arabia, they alleged, where citizens of African descent "are treated like slaves."[2] In early 2021, a Clubhouse room hosted by Black Hebrew Israelites was convened to expose Islam as an antiblack, slaver religion, complete with an exhaustive reading from the Quran and Hadiths.[3] Around the same time, the Vanderbilt University historian Moses Ochonu published an article on how, at its very scriptural foundations, Islam had a mandate for "divinely ordained racial slavery." The historical role of Arabs and Muslims in Africa should be criticized, he argued, just as European colonization of the continent has been.[4]

Though they came from very different angles, these four voices were all entering into the same long-standing debate: is there such a thing as 'Arab-Islamic slavery' (AIS)? What does that mean about Islam's place in Africa? And is Islam antiblack? Though it may seem obscure, this debate has been vigorous and regularly surfaces in pockets of Western public life beyond the academy. In part this is because it serves as a proxy for a set of accusations that, while deserving scholarly attention, also advance three very different ideologies thriving in segments of society outside university classrooms.

The first ideology, what one could term **Western supremacism**, is the broad belief that, whatever its flaws, 'the West' has forged a path for mankind into a better future. The second, **Afrocentrism**, holds that Africa once housed a Black civilization that laid the foundation of mankind's cultural and philosophical heritage before succumbing to invasion and centuries of exploitation by outside forces. The third, **pro-Israel public diplomacy (Hebrew, *Hasbara*)**,[5] has functioned to insulate Israel's displacement of Palestinians and its apartheid policies from international criticism. Western supremacism is a major force in the consuming contest over identity and history in countries from the U.S. to Australia. Afrocentrism has inspired cultural phenomena from Michael Jackson's 1991 video "Remember the Time," in which Eddie Murphy and Iman play a Black pharaoh and his queen, to the 2018 blockbuster film *Black Panther*. Hasbara – the term used by those involved in pro-Israeli public diplomacy themselves – is a remarkably enduring political strategy that is fueled and promoted by an ideological alliance between Western security hawks, Jewish (religious) Zionists, and American Christian Zionists.

The claim of 'Arab-Islamic slavery' has proven useful to Western supremacism, Afrocentrism and pro-Israel public diplomacy alike because it helps advance the following accusations: 1) that Islam/Arabs/Muslims have some inherent tendency to enslave; 2) that Islam/Arabs/Muslims are a colonizing force in Africa as opposed to being an indigenous part of African history; and 3) that Islam/Arabs/Muslims harbor inherently antiblack sentiments. All three points resonate with Afrocentrists like Kwame Zulu Shabazz, who see Islam as both foreign to Africa and predatory.[6] For American conservatives like Rod Dreher, 'Arab-Islamic slavery' shifts denunciatory attention away from American history to the 'Arab slave trade.' Americans can thus proclaim that slavery was not only "*our* original sin" (italics mine). Others are guiltier, so Americans can bask in the moral contrast between the West's realization that slavery is evil and the alleged unrepentance of the Arab world.[7] For pro-Israel public diplomacy, 'Arab-Islamic slavery' has worked to fracture 'Third World' or anti-colonial solidarity between Arabs and Africans and redirect attention from Israeli apartheid to Arab/Muslim discrimination against people racialized as black.

For all these agendas, 'Arab-Islamic slavery' portrays the Arab/Muslim as the historical villain and enemy of enlightened progress. It is the Arab/Muslim who was truly culpable for the rape of Africa – an act for which, unlike White Westerners, he feels no remorse. Indeed, the Arab/Muslim may still be enslaving today. And, at the very least, it is he whose racial discrimination should be the center of global attention, not the Israeli treatment of Palestinians.

## THE ROOTS AND BRANCHES OF AFROCENTRISM

Afrocentrism has its roots in Black Nationalism, which arose in the U.S. among the new concentrations of Black Americans who settled to work in the industrial cities of the north during and after World War I. It was also inspired by trans-Atlantic Black intellectuals like Edward Blyden (d. 1912), who promoted a unified Black (diaspora and African) destiny. Black Nationalism birthed movements like Garveyism, the back-to-Abyssinia movement and the Nation of Islam in the early and mid twentieth century. Black Nationalism sought a historical anchor for Black American identity in one of several brilliant African civilizations (imagined or real), creating a sense of solidarity with some aspect of Africa of the present – real or imagined – and simultaneously claiming for Black Americans a sense of future meaning, purpose and hope. Movements like the Moorish Science Temple and the Nation of Islam based their worldview on identifying with Islam (an idea explored by Blyden). The Black heritage they conceptualized was an Islamic one, spanning Africa and Arabia. They identified closely with the Arabic-inflected north of Africa at the expense of Africa south of the Sahara. Afrocentrism took the opposite approach. Some of its leading ideologues have defined Africa as excluding the region north of the Sahara – indeed all Muslim parts of

Africa. For them, Islam is altogether foreign to Africa's essential religious and cultural body.[8]

The scholarly flourishing of Afrocentrism, however, occurred not in America but in Senegal, in the writings of the French-educated historian, philosopher, and scientist Cheikh Anta Diop (d. 1986). Though his writings had been published in French in the 1950s and '60s, Diop's thesis landed like an obelisk in the Anglophone academy when his *The African Origin of Civilization: Myth or Reality* appeared in 1974. Diop argued that the Western version of African history had turned reality on its head. Black Africa had never been beyond the margins of the great civilizations, and ancient Egypt was not Semitic and European property. Rather, Egypt had been a Black civilization, and the history of Africa had to be understood as the story of that genius's intimate connection to the rest of the continent.

Diop provided the scholarly momentum for Afrocentrism, but fellow travelers across the Atlantic took it in a different direction. Diop was a Muslim who dismissed the idea that Arabs had violated Black Africa or forced their religion on it. He held up the madrasas of Timbuktu as paragons of Africa's scholarly heritage. American articulations of Afrocentrism took the opposite view of Arabs and Islam.[9] Their landmark work was *The Destruction of Black Civilization* (1971) by the Howard University historian Chancellor Williams (d. 1992) (see Figure 6). In this book, Williams argued that Black African civilization was the world's oldest and most brilliant, possessed of immense wisdom and accomplishment. Black people had ruled in ancient Egypt, built the pyramids and birthed monotheism. Europe and Christianity were foreign subjugators. But, in Williams' view, Africa had suffered white colonization just as intensively at the hands of Islam and Arabs. Their descendants in North and East Africa remain as foreign to Africa as Dutch Afrikaners. Indeed, for Williams, Islam and Arabs were "even more devasting for the African people" than European colonialism or the Atlantic slave trade. Turning to Black Americans, Williams argued that those who embraced Islam merely exchanged one oppressor for another. Giving up their Christian 'slave names' for Muslim ones meant nothing more than adopting the names of their Arab slave masters.[10]

Professor John Henrik Clarke (d. 1998) built on Williams' theories but took a harsher line on all that was extra-African, particularly Islam. Just as Christianity was originally African but was taken over and dominated by Whites for their political purposes, Clarke argued, Islam's original form was also African – found in the faith of the Muslims who sought refuge in Ethiopia early in the Prophet's mission (see Figure 8). But that Islam was almost immediately taken over by Arab "foreigners," who warped it into a vehicle for their political domination. Islam quickly became mere "Arabism" in Clarke's view. Even worse, those Arabs soon cooperated with Europeans in the slave trade.[11]

Williams' and Clarke's intellectual descendants have further elaborated Afrocentrism, sometimes with more or less flare. Kemet Afrocentrism, most famously articulated by Professor Molefi Asante, further developed the idea that Egypt had been the wellspring of Black civilization and global wisdom (the Ancient Egyptian word *k-m-t*, possibly meaning 'black land,' was a main endonym for ancient Egypt). Although Arabs/Muslims destroyed the Egyptian heartland of Black civilization, its heritage had been preserved among African peoples like the Wolof, Yoruba, and Ashanti.[12]

An offshoot from Asante's relatively moderate views is a more strident and xenophobic strain. One of its main themes is that nothing extrinsic to their conception of Afrika [sic] can be of any significant value, and that the Black Holocaust of slavery was perpetrated by Europeans and Arabs alike. Arabs *cannot* be autochthonously Afrikan, according to this view. Some adherents to this strain of Kemet Afrocentrism actually identify as Muslim, placing the blame for the enslavement of Africans not on Islam but on Arabs. As one such writer puts it, "Despite the fact some Arabs believed in the religion of Al-Islam, they were still involved in slavery."[13] But others, like the Black American preacher Olatunji Mwamba, are more stridently anti-Islamic. They represent what Nathaniel Mathews describes as a more "amateur populist approach" to Kemet Afrocentrism, leaning towards default American cultural conservatism and highly suspicious of LGBTQ activism and Black feminism as conspiracies against Black manhood.[14] They argue that Islam is nothing more than a jumbled patchwork of Near Eastern religious ideas along with some African ones (Arabia – and Greece – having originally been populated by Blacks, according to Mwamba).[15]

A more sensationalist and caustic dispensation of Black Nationalism and Afrocentrism is that of the Black Hebrew Israelites (who refer to themselves either as Hebrew Israelites or simply as Israelites). This is a subset of the phenomenon of Black Judaism, a diverse African American religious movement that identifies literally, not metaphorically, with the tribe of Israel and what it understands as Israel's journey of redemptive suffering. Black Hebrew Israelites hold diverse views and have fragmented into a number of organizations, many of them mutually antagonistic. But they generally believe that the original Israelites were black and that the African diaspora are their true descendants. Some aggressively pursue anti-Islam polemics at places like Speaker's Corner in London and online.[16] Many are virulently antisemitic as well, particularly what Andre Key identifies as the Messianic trend among Black Hebrew Israelites, such as the Israelite School of Universal Practical Knowledge.[17]

## THE PROBLEMS WITH AFROCENTRISM AND 'ARAB-ISLAMIC SLAVERY'

There have been numerous, solidly grounded replies to Afrocentric polemics against Islam and Arabs. Two decades ago, the late Ali Mazrui (d. 2014) launched a searing critique of Afrocentrism when he identified it as a manifestation of what he termed 'Black Orientalism': African American conceptualizations of Africa that grant diaspora Africans roots in select moments of African civilizational greatness while simultaneously condescending the reality of the African present, selectively ignoring African voices and minimizing the role of Euro-America in the slave trade.[18]

What of the claim made by Williams, and picked up by others like Molyneux for their own purposes, that the 'Arab' slave trade exceeded or even dwarfed the Atlantic one? If we limit the European extraction of enslaved people from Africa to the Atlantic slave trade, omitting the much earlier transportation of African slaves to Roman Italy or Gaul (though this seems arbitrary, since Europeans gladly claim Rome's accomplishments), then the 'Arab' slave trade was certainly longer than the European one.[19] But it was not much larger in volume. And it was certainly much less intense. According to the Trans-Atlantic Slave Trade Database, between **10.7 and 12 million people** were removed from Africa by European slave traders bound for the Americas in the merely three and a half centuries between 1514 and 1866, an average of 3–3.4 million people per century.[20] Combining and extrapolating scholarly estimates for the 'Arab' slave trade out of sub-Saharan Africa (via the Trans-Saharan, Indian Ocean, and Red Sea routes), it would seem that, over twelve centuries, between **12.2 and 15.6 million** people were enslaved and transported. With an average of 1–1.3 million people per century, this 'Arab' slave trade was around a third less intensive than its European counterpart.[21] As Cedric Robinson observed, the Arab/Islamic slave trade out of Africa came nowhere close to the impact of the Atlantic one, which was created and justified by a "racial cacophony" that yielded not only the vision of superior White and inferior black races but also the incredible violence of the European colonization of Africa.[22]

The very concept of an Arab-Islamic slavery (AIS) itself has come under withering criticism by historians of Africa and the Islamic world. Professor Dahlia Gubara has neatly pointed out that AIS depends on a parade of ahistorical, artificially sealed essentializations: 'Arab,' 'Islam,' 'Slavery,' and 'Africa.' Each of these is so historically rich, internally diverse, and blurry at whatever edges it might have that casually referring to AIS reveals more about the selective perspective of the person deploying it than about any discrete, historical phenomenon. Are Black Africans who speak Arabic Arabs or Africans? Is a slave taken from Lake Chad to Marrakesh leaving Africa? Why is slavery always understood as removing people out of Africa, when Africa had centuries-old internal networks of enslavement and slave trade that continued into the twentieth century? If a person in one of those networks becomes nominally Muslim, altering little in their lifestyle or livelihood, is that suddenly 'Arab-Islamic slavery'? There had been a trade in slaves from areas like Nubia and Ethiopia up the Nile to Egypt since at least 1200 BCE, continuing through Roman times.[23] Did this become 'Arab-Islamic slavery' simply because Coptic-speaking Egyptians embraced Islam and started speaking Arabic?

Gubara also draws attention to the performative, self-congratulatory aspect of the discourse around AIS. Like the narrative of Barbary captivity we discuss below, AIS is a conversation in which the civilized West laments the evils of the barbarian other. Gubara traces how AIS discourse is woven by the once-and-always enlightened Westerner between the timeless and thus backward Arab/Muslim and the essentialized Black African.[24]

Nathaniel Mathews builds on Gubara's work to provide the most comprehensive rebuttal of the idea of AIS. While all other slave trades are identified by their geography (e.g., the Atlantic slave trade) or the populations suffering enslavement (e.g., the Circassian slave trade), Mathews notes that AIS is defined by those carrying it out. Yet the Arab/Muslim voice is only counted to Islam's detriment. When Muslims cite religious motivations or justifications for their involvement in enslavement (e.g., 'We are bringing civilization to them'), Western audiences take them at their word. Yet Muslim criticism of the slave trade or calls for its abolition are dismissed as affected or derivative of European morality.

These are not the main failings of AIS discourse, however, three of which are summarized by Mathews. First, AIS confuses religion and ethnicity. This results in a matrix in which "Arabs are non-African, North Africans are non-black, [and] sub-Saharan Africans are non-Muslims." Each of these assertions is *prima facie* nonsense. Millions of native Arabic speakers who identify as Arab live in Africa. Many North Africans are 'black' according to their own society's definitions as well as Western ones. And Africa south of the Sahara is home to hundreds of millions of Muslims who are among the world's most devout in terms of professed belief and practice.[25] Second, AIS discourse is ahistorical, ignoring context such as diverse trade systems and historical continuities. An eighteenth-century king on the Senegal River selling Africans captured inland (including many Muslims) to Europeans for use on Brazilian plantations in return for guns and alcohol, and an Omani slave merchant selling east Africans for use as military slaves in India in return for textiles are thus summarily lumped together as one 'trade' because someone involved happens to be Muslim. Finally, AIS discourse is Islamophobic and Orientalist, premised on the ideas that Islam is a pernicious force in history and that its adherents are homogeneous, monochromatic, and incapable of authentic change.[26]

As for the accusation that Islam is not indigenously African, Sherman Jackson has pointed out that this assumes the existence of some quintessential 'Africa' throughout time.[27] The majority of Afrocentric definitions of Africa, however, are either arbitrary, artificial or hopelessly Eurocentric. The Nigerian writer Wole Soyinka stresses that Islam cannot be African because it is intolerant of apostasy, which he claims, *petitio principii*, is "anathema" to the real Africa.[28] But why is Soyinka's definition of what is truly African any more meaningful than the opinion of Souleymane Bachir Diagne, a Senegalese philosopher? Diagne has pointed out the absurdity of trying to subdivide the continent into the real and not real Africa, of making the perennially fluid and traversed Sahara "into the wall that it has never been."[29] Why is Soyinka's definition of Africa any more authoritative than that of Professor Ousmane Kane, a Senegalese historian? Kane reminds us that Islam, Muslims, and Arabic were present in 'Africa' from the religion's earliest years, when Muslims sought refuge in Ethiopia (see Figure 8), even before Islam reached the greater Middle East, where it is uncontroversially considered at home.[30]

Finally, as Mazrui notes, it was early-modern European cartographers who defined Africa by its current continental boundaries. Why, he wonders, is Ethiopia part of Africa anyway? Why not group Ethiopia with Arabia, since it is a Semitic-language-speaking, ancient Christian (and Muslim) land that once ruled Yemen and may well have been ruled *by* Yemen at one time?[31] Afrocentrists might reject the current continental definition of Africa by excluding the continent's north. But this only embraces another European definition of

Africa. While scholars like Walter Rodney (d. 1980), Diop, and Mazrui understood Islam as an integral part of Africa's heritage, it was the German philosopher Hegel (d. 1831) who asserted that North Africa and Egypt were not part of what he called "Africa proper," namely Africa south of the Sahara.[32] Certainly, where Hegel saw "Africa proper" as a civilizational void, Afrocentrists see it as a teeming civilizational treasure. And where Islamophilic Afrocentrists like Diop viewed ancient Egypt and Timbuktu as African accomplishments, Islamophobic Afrocentrists view the first as lost to un-African, Arab/Islamic invasions and the second as damage wrought by them. But, though they might have changed the contents, Islamophobic Afrocentrists nonetheless adopt the Hegelian structure of what Africa is.

As for some innate 'slavery gene' in Islam, or what Ochonu calls Islam's "divinely ordained racial slavery," this is patently false.[33] As I dealt with at length in *Slavery & Islam*, something we could label slavery was an uncontroversial feature of all premodern civilizations. The Quran and Sunna of the Prophet, however, stand out for their unparalleled obsession with emancipation.[34] There is no denying that antiblack sentiment is rampant among many Muslims. This is indefensible. But if this were a problem with Islam then it would be uniquely pronounced in Muslim communities. And it is manifestly not.

"The bedrock of Arab anti-Blackness," argues Ochonu, was enslavement across the Sahara and Indian Ocean. It is true that, even in Arabia before Islam, slaves had been brought across the Red Sea from Ethiopia. But only a minority of slaves in Islam's founding Arabian community were African. As we will see later, the largest group of slaves in Mecca and Medina were other Arabs, not Africans, and Persians were not far behind (see Chapter 5). Moreover, later on during the classical Abbasid period, the number of Slavic and Turkic slaves imported into Islamic civilization surpassed the number of Africans. If, as Ochonu presumes, enslavement of a group leads to racial contempt for them, why do we not speak of Arab anti-Slavicness or anti-Turkicness?

Ochonu rightly notes the Curse of Ham as a crucial cause of antiblackness. This was the infamous tradition the core of which is found in the Old Testament book of Genesis. After Noah falls asleep naked while intoxicated, his son Ham does not cover his father up, while his two brothers, Shem and Japheth, do. When Noah awakens, he declares:

> "Cursed be Canaan [one of Ham's sons]; lowest of slaves [Hebrew *'bd*, Latin Vulgate, *servus*] shall he be to his brothers." He also said, "Blessed by the Lord my God be Shem; and let Canaan be his slave. May God make space for Japheth, and let him live in the tents of Shem; and let Canaan be his slave." (Genesis 9:25–27, NRSV)

Of course, it is not actually Ham who is cursed but his son, Canaan. And Canaan was not the son of Ham who was believed to have populated Africa. But the vagaries of text and interpretation through which the Curse of Ham became cursing Africans to dark skin and slavery are not our concern here. Suffice it to say that, by the Late Antique period, it had been established in strains of Near Eastern Jewish and Christian tradition that it was Ham and his descendants who had been cursed with slavery, that they were dark skinned and that they inhabited great parts of Africa.[35]

But Ochonu somehow turns the Curse from a Judeo-Christian product long predating Islam into something Muslims are responsible for. He compounds his indictment by accusing Muslims of passing on the Curse of Ham myth to Europeans, thus assigning to Islam the blame for European antiblackness as well.[36] But centuries before Islam appeared, Augustine had already affirmed that Ham's African descendants had been cursed to slavery, burning in the heat of heresy and apart. Some Church Fathers of the time portrayed slaves as sexually appetitive and gluttonous, while others like Gregor of Nyssa (d. 395 CE) equated blackness with sin.[37] Surely, if we are to seek a religious grounding for antiblack sentiment in Western civilization, we should look to figures like Augustine before Muslim scholars.

## ENDURING TEMPLATES: MOORISH BONDAGE AND THE ARAB SLAVE TRADE

In the 1921 silent film *Adventures of Tarzan*, the feral hero saves Jane from Arab slavers in Africa. That same year, Rudolph Valentino earned immortal fame as *The Sheik*, abducting and soon proving irresistible to a British lady in Algeria. The era of silent film seems like the distant past, but when these films were made the literary trope of enslavement at Arab/Muslim hands had already existed for three centuries.

'Arab-Islamic slavery' may seem a product of recent political phenomena like Donald Trump's prized 'radical Islamic terrorism' and ISIS, but it is actually a motif that has wound its way through Western cultural expression as far back as Elizabethan England (in fact, Eastern Christian moral disgust and fretfulness over perceived Muslim indulgence in the sexual license of slave concubinage and pederasty can be traced back to the 700s CE).[38] This salience in the Western cultural imagination has two roots. The first is anxiety and fascination with the enslavement of Europeans and Americans by the 'Turks' and 'Moors' of North Africa from the sixteenth to the nineteenth centuries. The second is moral outrage at the Arab/Muslim enslavement of Black Africans from the nineteenth century to the present. These two roots have grown together, however, in depictions like *Tarzan*, of Arabs and Muslims preying on White women and Africans alike.

As Nabil Matar and others have shown, the narrative of Barbary captivity became an established trope in Western Europe and North America as early as the 1600s. Accounts and memoirs of French, British, Irish, and American seafarers being captured and enslaved at sea by Moors – Muslims from North Africa – flew off the presses regularly in Britain from 1577 through the 1700s. Some became runaway bestsellers in America. Narratives by French captives appeared in France from the late 1600s through the early 1800s.[39]

The trope of Barbary captivity lived on and thrived long after its reality had faded and, in fact, inverted. The specter of White slavery grew precisely as the actual threat receded, inflating its impact in retrospect. After 1690 there was a precipitous drop in the number of Christians taken captive off the Barbary coast.[40] In fact, by the early 1700s, the power of the British Royal Navy and the rise of European states meant that many more Muslims were actually being taken captive by 'Christians' than vice versa.[41] Such was the allure of this genre, however, that in the nineteenth century several popular accounts of Barbary captivity, including two allegedly by English and American women, turned out to be fictional.[42]

The fear and fascination intertwined with captivity at the hands of Barbary Moors continues to entrance historians and pseudo-historians alike. Modern estimations of how many Western Europeans were captured by the Barbary corsairs have proven gross exaggerations. One estimate from 1979 posits half a million to one million people. One from 2003 put the number taken captive/enslaved between 1530 and 1780 at some 1–1.25 million.[43] These estimates, however, have been shown to be based on inaccurate and, indeed, physically impossible assumptions. Such numbers could not have actually fit into the cities that allegedly housed them. A more grounded estimate puts the number of people from the British Isles taken captive between 1600 and 1750 at only around 20,000 (including many prisoners of war).[44] Looking back at estimates by French diplomats, former captives, and writers at the time, the number of 'Christians' *overall* in captivity (but not necessarily taken captive that year) in Algiers, Morocco, and Tunis was an average of around 26,000 in any given year between 1530 and 1690, then around 6,000 in any given year between 1690 and 1820.[45]

This narrative of Barbary captivity was always and has remained greater than its reality because it titillates, terrifies, and exonerates in equal parts. It emerged at precisely the point in time when a sense of English identity, for example, was being constituted against the foil of a dark, infidel, barbarian, and African other.[46] The famous Boston minister Cotton Mather (d. 1728) sermonized against the horrors of enslavement to the "hellish" Moors and "barbarous Negroes," and his "Monsters of Africa" soon emerged as the image of the barbarous, dark other (i.e., Muslim) to the White, good, civilized, and Christian American victim.[47] Accounts regularly emphasized the role of the

Black African slaves that the Moors put in charge of the Christian captives, a trope that blossomed during the same period that European colonists in North America were constructing their systems of slavery and race. The image of the White Christian slave being abused and humiliated by the Black Muslim master allowed slave-holding American society to portray itself as the victim and simultaneously express its paranoia over the vengeful Blacks it perceived in the Haitian Revolution and Nat Turner's rebellion.[48]

Reality was, of course, not so simple. The stark distinction in European and American depictions of dark-skinned Muslim pirate slavers and the White Christian victims belies the fact that Barbary states like Algiers were incredibly cosmopolitan and multilingual places. Many corsair crews were made up of as many Europeans as Muslims, the former having taken to the sea to make their fortune, sometimes converting to Islam in the process.[49] The corsair raid on Iceland in 1627 and the epic raid on the Irish coast in 1631 were both led by a European convert to Islam, probably the same Dutchman.[50] Nor did pirates and raiders make sail only from the southern, Muslim coast of the Mediterranean. 'Christian' ports also had careers as pirate and slaver coves. As Fernand Braudel noted, "Malta and Leghorn [Livorno] were Christendom's Algiers."[51]

White slavery at Moorish hands, particularly the capture of White women by the swarthy 'Turks,' took lasting hold on popular literary imaginations. The figure of the Moor as both sexually alluring and sexually (and otherwise) dangerous, already seen in Jacobean English characters like Othello, would remain a fixture in the Western cultural vocabulary. It was in the late eighteenth century that the lurid fascination with what Lila Abu-Lughod has termed "the pornography of Muslim bondage" began to flower, with salacious works appearing like *The Lustful Turk* (1828).[52] This novella, framed as the letters of European women enslaved in the harem of the ruler of Algiers, has to be read to be believed. Its pioneering pornographic content could be described as *The Abduction from the Seraglio* (1782) if *The Abduction* had been written for Penthouse Forum with rape fantasies instead of *arias* and with the protagonist departing with her rapist/lover's penis in a jar. *The Lustful Turk* features a motif common in Barbary captivity narratives, one that highlights their psycho-cultural significance: an intense fear of and obsession with being sodomized by Moors.[53]

The trope of the American battling the immoral, salacious Barbary Turk/Moor thrived into the twentieth century. It spawned a children's board game (1930) and pulp novels through the 1950s.[54] Books became motion pictures starting in the first decade of feature films with *Robinson Crusoe* (1916). At least twelve Barbary captivity feature films have followed since, in English, Italian, and other languages (see Appendix V).

It was the more specific motif of White women being captured, enslaved, bought, sold, seduced, and/or violated by Muslims/Arabs, however, that truly flourished on the silver screen. From 1914 to the present, no fewer than fifty-eight feature-length films have incorporated this theme into their plots.[55] An entire genre of film – the Oriental romance, or sheik, genre – followed Rudolph Valentino's blockbuster silent role in *The Sheik* (1921) (movie posters read, "When an Arab sees a woman that he wants, he takes her."). So established was this theme that films were parodying it as early as the 1920s. The threat of a White maiden being violated by an Arab slaver proved so enduringly titillating that it was invoked decades later in *Paradise* (1982) in an effort to outbid the hit *Blue Lagoon* (1980). Whereas *Blue Lagoon* featured two gorgeous but innocent teens (one of them Brooke Shields) exploring their sexuality and showering/swimming nude against the backdrop of a tropical island, *Paradise* had two gorgeous but innocent teens (one of them Phoebe Cates) exploring their sexuality with even more showering/swimming nude against the backdrop of desert oases and being pursued by lascivious Arab slavers. Arabs/Muslims enslaving and sexually threatening White females continues to exert its voyeuristic pull of excitement and anxiety in films like *Taken* (2008), with occasional semi-sympathetic portrayals like the late Sean Connery as "the last of the Barbary pirates," acting opposite Candice Bergen's feisty captive American beauty in *The Wind and the Lion* (1975).

As the Barbary captivity genre was entering its baroque period in the nineteenth century, American and British attention turned to moral outrage at 'the Mohammedan slave trade.' Anglophone abolitionists were fairly unaware of the slave trade within Africa until the 1820s, when British abolitionists in particular began investigating slavery in Africa and the slave trade to the Ottoman and Persian realms.[56] Popular interest was drawn by Thomas Buxton's (d. 1845) *The African Slave Trade* (1839). This serious tome was popularized in an abridged, Evangelical form issued by the Society for the Extinction of the Slave Trade, founded in 1839 with Buxton as a principal member. The abridgment baldly identified the "Mahommedan slave trade" as the sole counterpart to what it was at pains to admit was still a much larger Christian ("as it is called falsely") trade.[57]

Here we see the unmistakable shaping of a narrative binding modern slavery and Islam. Not only did the Society for the Extinction of the Slave Trade (today known as Anti-Slavery International) define one of the two slave trades it claimed plagued Africa as Islamic while denying the Christian association of the Atlantic trade. It also made Muslims and Islam the sole culprits for all non-European/American-run trade in slaves within and out of Africa.

This was indisputably fallacious. For example, after the end of the British and U.S. slave trade in 1807, the internal, non-Muslim slave trade in the coastal region of Ghana burgeoned. Even after the Atlantic demand for slaves had dropped, slaves brought from continuing wars inland in Asante areas were purchased by the local Fante people in unprecedented numbers. The increase in internal enslavement within West Africa that resulted from the nineteenth-century jihad movements is well known. But a significant number of these slaves were purchased by the "virtually limitless" labor market in the non-Muslim areas of Ghana's south.[58] Far from being unaware of this non-Muslim, internal African slave trade, the British colonial authorities pursued a policy of studied non-interference.[59] Similarly, in the non-Muslim Biafra region of what would become Nigeria, domestic slavery intensified after the end of the Atlantic slave trade, with British colonial authorities allowing the necessary loopholes for slavery to continue through the 1920s and '30s. Indeed, the social stigma of descent from such African slaves enslaved by Africans (and perhaps the enslavement itself) continues to this day in Igbo communities in

Nigeria.[60] Across the continent in Ethiopia, the late nineteenth and early twentieth centuries saw a booming internal slave trade within that Christian kingdom, which even spilled over its borders, all facilitated by the conquests and domination of the Christian Emperor Menelik II (d. 1913).[61]

This is not to say that Arabs/Muslims were not involved in the African slave trade in the nineteenth century. They certainly were, the most infamous agent being the British ally in East Africa, Ḥamīd bin Muḥammad, a.k.a., Tippu Tip (d. 1905). But matters cannot be neatly bisected into Arab/Black, Arab/African, or Muslim/non-Muslim. The caravans that went inland from the coast off Zanzibar were led by Arabs *and* local Africans. Inland, they bartered with other leaders for slaves those leaders had captured in raids in exchange for American-made textiles, guns, and gunpowder. Tip was indeed of noble Arab ancestry. But those ancestors had taken African wives in Zanzibar and, despite being Arab, Tip was "perfectly black," according to one British observer. Nor were the Arabs, Persians, and other Muslim inhabitants of Zanzibar part of some unified, predatory Islamic front. In the nineteenth century, the Arab sultans of Zanzibar objected strenuously to the Arab raiders and slave traders who would come from the Arabian Gulf and terrorize the island in the summers, wandering around kidnapping local Muslims (especially children) to take as slaves.[62]

None of this is to say that Western abolitionists or advocates for the rights of women or children in the European colonies in Africa were unaware that there was domestic slavery in Africa that did not involve Muslims. They were aware. But their activism, like that which started up in Biafra in the early 1900s, long postdated the solidification of the association of slavery in Africa with 'Mahommedanism' and did nothing to correct this stereotype.

The association of Islam and slavery in Africa quickly permeated Western cultural production, attaining undeniable prominence in cinema. The image of Arabs raiding and enslaving Black Africans has appeared in at least twenty-three feature films in multiple languages, often at the core of the story. In *Tarzan of the Apes* (1918), intertitles tell us that the reason that Tarzan's family had voyaged to Africa in

1886 was to "suppress Arab slave trading in British Africa." The German-produced *Slavers* (1978) portrays White slavers (American, English, Portuguese) working alongside an Arab slaver, who proves so brutally evil that the American repents his ways and struggles to free the enslaved Africans. Even *A Daughter of the Congo* (1930), a rare film made by an African American studio, casts Arab slavers as the villains. It differs from mainstream productions only in that its African princess is saved from the Arabs' evil clutches not by White heroes but by African American cavalry officers.[63] Films like *East of Sudan* (1964) mixed themes, with White saviors trying to save themselves and Black African tribes from Arab/Muslim slavers. One of the film's advertising taglines was "The Arab slaver is only one day away!"[64]

Arabs/Islam and slavery have been closely associated in ongoing abolitionist work in the last century. The Society for the Extinction of the Slave Trade (after several name changes, now Anti-Slavery International) has been active in combatting the slave trade globally since 1839, joined more recently by other groups like Free the Slaves (2000) and the Walk Free Foundation (2011). A significant portion of these groups' work has taken place in Africa and in or adjacent to Muslim-majority areas. Anti-Slavery International, for example, has been involved in reporting on and combatting first legal slavery and, more recently, modern-day slavery in Sudan since British colonial rule began there in the late nineteenth century.[65]

To be sure, slavery was indeed legal in many Muslim countries into the 1950s and '60s. And there is no doubt that *de facto* slavery continued in some Muslim-dominated regions like Sudan, particularly amid the civil conflicts that fragmented that country from the 1980s through the 2000s. Indeed, groups and states identifying as Arab and Muslim in what became northern Sudan had been carrying out slave raids on non-Muslims to the south since the sixteenth century.[66] But raiding and captive-taking had been longstanding on both sides in conflicts between Arabs and non-Arabic speaking, non-Muslim communities in Sudan.[67] And, *de facto*, slavery and the associated trafficking of women and children remains a serious problem in Nigeria, in Muslim areas and the non-Muslim south alike.[68] Yet only the narrative of 'Arab-Islamic slavery,' particularly of Black Africans, grabs global headlines.

So powerful is the narrative of the Arab/Muslim enslaving Black African victims in the eyes of the Western viewer that it has helped shape political reality. In the 1990s, the spike in capture and enslavement in Sudan caused by the civil war between the Arab-dominated government and the Sudan People's Liberation Army (SPLA) in the south became a cause célèbre in the U.S. Though it convinced few in Sudan, internationally the SPLA portrayed themselves as African victims of an oppressive Arab regime that enslaved its people.[69] Huge charitable donations from Western donors flooded into organizations like the American Christian Solidarity International (CSI) to 'redeem' and free slaves taken into the Arab north. Yet CSI's claims about the number of southern slaves held in northern Sudan were orders of magnitude greater than the number estimated by other NGOs and UNICEF. Numerous witnesses and participants testified that many slave 'redemptions' were actually scams run by rebels or local leaders, who had their own people pose as slaves and then pocketed the money used to 'free' them.[70]

My point here is not to deny enslavement or suffering in Sudan. Neither is it to minimize Muslim participation historically in the slave trade or dismiss the work of anti-slavery campaigners. It is to note how the nineteenth century saw the tailoring of a template for 'Arab/Muslim slaver and Black African slave' that was selective and essentializing. Exploitation that fits this narrative seems often to be the only type that Western eyes see.[71] This is not surprising, considering the prominence of this motif in Western cultural production in literature and film. And it explains how quickly and unreservedly the conflict in Sudan in the 1990s and 2000s, with its oversimplified narrative of Arab/Muslim slavers and Black African victims, caught on among Western populations, for whom it fit the enduring template of the 'Mahommedan slave trade.'

## GATHERING THE THREADS: ARAB-ISLAMIC SLAVERY AND THE ISRAEL–PALESTINE CONFLICT

The tropes of sexualized Barbary captivity and Arab-slaver/African-slave came together and crystalized most completely in *Ashanti* (1979, see Figure 7), a film based loosely on the Spanish novel *Ebano* by Alberto Vázquez-Figueroa. The spectacular cast (Michael Caine, Peter Ustinov, William Holden, Kebir Bedi, Rex Harrison, Omar Sharif, and Beverly Johnson) contrasts with *Ashanti*'s poor quality. The film was beset with production problems, and Warner Brothers distanced itself from the finished product. Caine admitted he only made the movie for the money, "loathed every second on it" and "hopes you never see it."[72]

The film's heroine and chief victim, Anansa, is played by Beverly Johnson, the stunning African American fashion model who had only a few years earlier been the first woman of color to grace the cover of *Vogue*. Her character embodies both the Western and African victim of the Arab slaver. She meets White standards of beauty (even appearing nude), and her character is an accomplished U.N. doctor married to a strapping fellow aid physician (Caine). But Anansa is also a native of the African country she is visiting. While the African villagers dance and frolic as her British husband administers vaccines, Anansa bathes in the river and is abducted by Muslim slavers. The henchmen are black Muslims (the 'Negro' of the Barbary narrative), but they are led by the Arab Suleiman (Ustinov), whose cruelty seems born of his amusingly cynical greed. Caine's hero pursues Anansa bravely, with the help of a Bedouin warrior named Malik (Bedi), whose Muslimness is totally unrecognized in the film. They are able to rescue Anansa just before she is secreted away on the yacht of Omar Sharif's Arab shaykh, who, though urbane and sympathetic, is still Arab/Muslim and thus, we learn, compelled to populate his harem with gorgeous slave women. *Ashanti* even pays homage to the obsessive sodomy motif of the Barbary narrative, as an enslaved African boy is lusted desperately over by one of the Muslim slavers. After Suleiman relents, the boy is led away to an off-camera rape scene marked only by his pitiful squeal. Later, however, Black Africa takes revenge on Arab Islam. The boy uses a voodoo doll he has constructed of his rapist to make his organs explode inside him.

*Ashanti* was filmed primarily in Israel, which doubled for 'Africa.'[73] This is not surprising for a film featuring the 'Arab-Islamic slavery' motif, at least four of which have been Israeli productions. Pointing to pro-Israel public diplomacy when discussing a 1979 film on slavery in Africa might rightly raise an alarm of conspiracy mongering along the lines of the *Protocols of the Elders of Zion*. It may be best thus to work backwards, tracing the trend of Hasbara's widely studied, recent role in shaping and fueling American Islamophobia (anti-Muslim prejudice) back to its contribution to the global narrative on 'Arab-Islamic slavery.'

The role of Christian Zionist, Jewish Zionist, and American conservative institutions and individuals in arguing, funding and promoting the vilification of Islam and Muslims – what Nathan Lean has termed the 'Islamophobia Industry' – has by now been well documented. During the past two decades, prominent activist and philanthropic organizations like the Anti-Defamation League, the American Jewish Committee, and the Newton D. & Rochelle F. Becker Foundation have worked to move previously marginal, small anti-Muslim thinktanks like the Center for Security Policy into the U.S. conservative mainstream and amplified their message that Islam and Muslims are dangerous, barbaric, and incompatible with life in the West.[74]

Long before 9/11, making Islam and terrorism synonymous was a specific Hasbara objective. This aim extended back to conferences convened in 1979 and 1984 by the right-wing Israeli think-tank The Jonathan Institute. As explained by the lead convener, the Israeli historian Benzion Netanyahu (d. 2012) (father of Benjamin Netanyahu), these conferences aimed at and were instrumental in focusing global attention on the threat of international terrorism, a threat that the conveners argued at the time was primarily funded and carried out by the Soviet bloc and Palestinian resistance organizations. This effort aimed at presenting Israel's war on 'Palestinian terror' as part of a larger, global battle against Soviet, state-sponsored terrorism.[75] With the fall of the Soviet Union, this global threat of terrorism was no longer Soviet. It was Islamic. This threat became a terrible reality after 9/11, an event that Benjamin Netanyahu assessed as "very good," since the attacks would rally American sympathy for Israel as a fellow victim of terror.[76]

Vilifying Arabs and Muslims did not only serve to make Americans see them as enemies abroad. It also helped nip in the bud any efforts on the part of Arabs or Muslims in the U.S. to create a domestic lobby that could compete with what Stephen Walt and John Mearsheimer have exhaustively detailed as the pro-Israel lobby. Arabs, Muslims, and Islam could not be embraced as indigenously American. As one career pro-Israel think-tanker wrote in a 2011 JINSA (Jewish Institute for National Security of America) report, Western support for Israel will follow from Western fear of Islamic terrorism, "[f]ear of large Muslim minorities – unassimilated and unassimilable . . ."[77]

Anti-Muslim and pro-Israel sentiments have dovetailed easily in the eyes of a public inured to the imagery of Arabs/Muslims as barbaric slavers. In a 1977 review of the landmark TV series *Roots*, James Michener (d. 1997), the American novelist who had openly expressed contempt for what he viewed as Arab savagery in the face of the civilizationally superior Israelis, objected to the depiction of the enslaved Kunta Kinte as a Muslim "praying to Allah while chained in the bottom of a Christian slave ship." Yes, Europeans were involved in the trans-Atlantic slave, Michener admitted. Yes, Africans were involved, though they were merely "corrupt or ignorant or deceived." But "the most relentless collectors [of slaves] were always the Arabs," ended Michener.[78]

The unquestioned elder statesman of Islamophobia in the U.S., who has devoted his career to vilifying Muslims and relentlessly depicting them as barbaric and incompatible with Western life and values, is Daniel Pipes.[79] In 1993, this Middle East historian and founder of the Islamophobic platform Middle East Forum presented a lengthy excursus on how Muslims in the U.S. were unhygienic, misogynist extremists bent on creating a parallel religious society in America. They were, according to Pipes, both angling dangerously to take over the West yet also helplessly dysfunctional. The fatal impediments to Muslim cohesion in the U.S. and advancement in Europe, according to Pipes, were the perennial faults of Arab-Islamic slavery and Muslim antiblackness. The relationship crucial to potential Muslim unity in the U.S., that between Muslim immigrants and native-born African American Muslims, Pipes concludes, could never cohere due to the undeniable reality that Muslims from the Middle East, "whatever theory holds, are endemically racist." He alleged that Muslim immigrants to Western Europe in the 1960s and '70s "tended to specialize in one or another type of criminal activity." One was to traffic European women to the Middle East, "the so-called white slave trade."[80] In the almost three decades since Pipes wrote this, American pundits functioning as cogs in the Islamophobia Industry have returned again and again to the task of highlighting the 'Arab slave trade' and equating Islam and antiblack oppression.[81]

Proponents of pro-Israel public diplomacy have not just played a substantial role in cementing the narrative of Arabs/Muslims as antiblack slavers. They have actually helped shape modern abolitionist discourse and policy. In 1994 the American management consultant Charles Jacobs founded the American Anti-Slavery Group to combat slavery in Mauretania and Sudan. The organization proudly displays photos of Jacobs participating in trips to Sudan to 'redeem' slaves and posing with grateful locals. Jacobs' other career, however, has been that of a predacious opponent of public critics of Israel in the U.S. In 1982 he founded CAMERA (Committee for Accuracy in Middle East Reporting and Analysis), a vehemently pro-Israel media watchdog dedicated to combating criticism of Israeli policies in the media. It remains active to this day. Jacobs was also a founder of the David Project, a pro-Israel organization that in 2004 funded an attempt to oust the pro-Palestinian professor Joseph Massad from his position at Columbia University.[82]

I do not question the sincerity of Jacobs' abolitionism. But it is clear that his zeal has only ever been directed at Muslims. In a lengthy public conversation with the Institute for Black Solidarity with Israel (7 July 2021), we see Jacobs sounding the standard motifs. For example, the Arab slave trade was as large in volume and more savage in quality than the Atlantic slave trade and American slavery. More shocking is Jacobs' insistence that Islam alone is responsible for modern-day slavery, that Islam and Arabs are synonymous with slaving and Black Africans with its victims. Americans have "freed our souls" from the sin of slavery, Jacobs opines, "whereas the Islamic world has not." Jacobs claims that, today, there are five countries (Nigeria, Mauretania, Sudan, Libya, Algeria) where slavery still exists, and "all the slavers are Arab and/or Muslims, and all the slaves are black." This is a striking break with the U.N.'s International Labor Organization (ILO) and the other major New Abolitionist NGOs, which have established that by far the largest number of modern-day slaves are in Asia and the Pacific – 62% of slaves in the world today, compared to 23% in Africa. Even measured *per capita*, modern-day slavery in Asia & the Pacific (6.1 people out of 1,000) is not far behind that in Africa (7.6/1,000).[83] The Thai seafood industry is a particularly egregious culprit.[84] For Jacobs, however, slavery is equated with Islam, an obsession that leaves no doubt as to his political agenda.

Jacobs' career culminated in the clearest intersection of Hasbara, the trope of 'Arab-Islamic slavery,' and Black Orientalism, namely the cause of South Sudan. The founding of the sovereign state of South Sudan in 2011 consummated an independence movement set in motion in the 1950s, when the newly independent country of Sudan instituted a policy of promoting Arabic language and identity across a country whose south was linguistically and ethnically diverse. Early on in the worsening conflict between parties in the south and the Sudanese government in Khartoum, Israeli foreign policy identified aiding south Sudanese separatists as a priority. As Yotam Gidron notes, "the war in Sudan represented a golden opportunity for fueling the tensions between Africans and Arabs, something that could only strengthen Israel in the international sphere."[85] And, since 1968, Israel has provided three generations of southern rebels with arms and extensive training.[86]

During the 1990s and 2000s, the Sudanese government regularly dismissed accusations of northern enslavement of south Sudanese as political slander instigated by Zionists in the U.S. and Israel. The Khartoum government's denial certainly rings hollow. But, as with many a conspiracy theory, it sells because it also strikes a clear note of truth. On the scholarly plane (though not on the humanitarian one), disavowing the role of pro-Israel public diplomacy in the Sudan slavery issue is as intellectually dishonest as denying northern slaving. Jok Madut Jok, a Dinka academic and activist who advocated extensively for international intervention against northern Sudanese slaving and has since served in the government of South Sudan, dismisses the accusation by responding that Jacobs only "happened to be Jewish."[87] This not only brushes aside the pro-Israel element in Sudan activism but implies that affirming it is nothing less than Arab/Muslim antisemitism.

But whether or not Jacobs is Jewish is irrelevant. What is relevant and also quite undeniable is that the single most consistent and salient thread in his career has been aggressively attacking sound critics of Israeli policy, demeaning Islam as a religion and Muslims as a faith community, and founding institutions to accomplish these tasks. Throughout Jacobs' involvement in anti-slavery work in Sudan and promoting the cause of southern Sudanese independence more broadly, he and his southern Sudanese associate, Simon Deng, have "railed against Islam while treating the Sudan conflict as part of a larger war in which Israel was a key protagonist," as Melani McAlister notes.[88] Jacobs clearly sees his role in the partition of Sudan as substantial, explicitly claiming credit for persuading U.S. President George W. Bush to push for a referendum in Sudan to begin the process of secession.[89] Along with the support of American Evangelical Christians, who followed on the heels of British missionaries in southern Sudan, these efforts eventually resulted in the creation of the new state of South Sudan.[90] As *The Daily Standard*, a conservative American journal, wrote, South Sudan's new capital was the only one in the region "where American and Israeli flags hang proudly from taxi drivers' windshields."[91]

South Sudan is a sovereign landmark to saving 'Black Africa' from 'slaving Arabs,' a narrative that activists and intellectuals from the south like Dunstan Wai (d. 2005) had been promoting since the 1970s. As Wai wrote, the Sudan conflict was one of warring essences, Arabs in the north and southern Sudanese "who feel themselves to be authentically Negroid Africans in every way." Northern Sudan was part of the Middle East, while the south "is culturally a part of tropical sub-Saharan Africa."[92] Being a victim of Arab/Muslim slavery was an essential part of this southern identity claim. As a South Sudanese intellectual later wrote, "Arab-led slavery of Africans represents the largest and, in time, the longest involuntary removal of any indigenous people in the history of humanity."[93]

Highlighting 'Arab-Islamic slavery' and Arab/Muslim antiblackness has only grown in importance for pro-Israel advocates with the rise of social justice activism in the U.S. in the 2010s. Support for Palestine among Left-Progressive activists has recently portended a return to the Black–Palestinian solidarity of the 1960s and '70s at precisely the moment when Black Lives Matter and related movements for racial justice have earned unprecedented acceptance in the American public square. This is best demonstrated by the 2018 election – and 2020 reelection – of Ilhan Omar, an avowedly pro-Palestinian, visibly Muslim Somali American, and Rashida Tlaib, a vocally Palestinian Muslim from an overwhelmingly Black district, to the U.S. House of Representatives.

Hasbara efforts to drive a wedge between Black activism and the Palestinian cause have correspondingly intensified. In 2016 the *Forward*'s Sam Kestenbaum trumpeted how the "prominent African-American Zionist" Chloé Simone Valdary had objected to Palestinian American organizations claiming solidarity with African Americans since, she claimed, "Today Arabs are still engaged in the African slave trade."[94] A more extensive polemic appeared in the *Jerusalem Post* and the *Times of Israel* in 2017 in response to the Black American scholar and activist Marc Lamont Hill's support for Palestinians facing Israeli discrimination. The American lawyer and self-described public pro-Israel advocate Clyde Zamir sought to rebut Hill by pointing out how "he completely ignores the struggles faced by Africans in the Arab World, which exist in the form of institutional racism and even slavery." Drawing on the Islamophobic writings of the Ghanaian Evangelical pastor John Azumah, he touches on mainstay points of the Arab-Islamic Slavery narrative: the Arab/Muslim slave trade was more enduring and savage than the Atlantic slave trade, it is still ongoing in Mauretania and Sudan, and antiblack racism is endemic in the Arab world.[95] In 2020 Pipes' Middle East Forum published an article on "Islam's Hidden Role in the Atlantic Slave Trade."[96]

## ISIS, BOKO HARAM, AND THE NARRATIVE OF BARBARY CAPTIVITY

Over a decade ago, Paul Baepler wondered if the jihadi terrorists of the post 9/11 world were the modern Barbary pirates, functioning outside or alongside the nation state and provoking a fear that would become as much a reality in the public mind as the actual dangers presented by the groups themselves.[97] In one sense, the parallels seem only to have grown stronger in the years since the question was asked. There are few names that jump more quickly to mind upon mention of slavery and capturing women than Boko Haram and ISIS. In April 2014, Boko Haram shocked the world by kidnapping 276 schoolgirls from the northern Nigerian town of Chibok. Some of these girls were married off to Boko Haram commanders. Others were sold as slaves. Some were eventually returned to their families. Several months later, ISIS followed with its stunning takeover of much of Iraq and Syria and its enslavement of thousands of Yazidi men, women, and children. As with Boko Haram, some Yazidi women and girls were taken as sex slaves by ISIS fighters. It is disturbing to think that the Barbary captivity trope may have been right and that there may be something about 'Islamic' militant groups that makes them indulge in slavery. It is tempting to think that these groups were aware of how large Arab/Muslim slavery loomed in the repertoire of the Western cultural imagination and that they knowingly played to this fear.

In some ways, however, all this seem to be no more than a tragic coincidence. If Islamic commitment leads to enslavement and sex slavery, why have these actions been so rare among Islamic militant groups? As Professor Aisha Ahmad has noted, whatever the faults of many Islamic militant groups in their treatment of women, their commitment to the Shariah has often kept them from inflicting sexual violence on civilian women, let alone enslaving them.[98] Where conviction might lack, pragmatism may govern. The Muslim scholar and ideologue of the Islamic resistance to the Soviet Union in Afghanistan, ʿAbdallāh ʿAzzām (d. 1990), forbade the Mujahidin fighters from taking 'Communist' women as slaves out of tactical concern that the enemy would do the same to Muslim women.[99]

It is still not clear why enslavement, especially sex slavery, has emerged as a particular tactic of Boko Haram and ISIS. In the case of Boko Haram, Aisha Ahmad has argued that it was the Nigerian government's 2012 capture and detention of the wives of several Boko Haram commanders, including its leader, and then the government's refusal to exchange these women for other captives that prompted an outraged Boko Haram to the drastic action of kidnapping the schoolgirls. Ahmad argues that the Islamic religious justification for enslaving the girls offered by the group's late leader, Abu Bakr Shekau, was merely *post hoc.*[100] That kidnapping groups of school children for ransom has emerged as a terrible new criminal enterprise in Nigeria without regard to confessional lines, often with no international attention because these acts do not fit the standard "media narrative," further suggests that there is much more at work in Nigeria than 'Islamic slavery.'[101] In the case of ISIS, Will McCants has argued that Islamic religious motivation was front and center. ISIS leaders inquired from their scholars if they could take captives as slaves according to the laws of jihad. The answer was yes, but this tactic also fulfilled the group's grandiose ideological claims. Not only was restoring the practice of enslaving captives an example of how fully ISIS was reviving the Shariah, it also heralded the looming end of days.[102]

There remains the possibility, however, that, in the case of ISIS, the return of 'the Muslim slaver' is more than just coincidence. Some scholars studying ISIS have argued that the group consciously pursued a tactic of psychologically crushing its opponents with sheer savagery and that the group's leaders were keen to make a name for ISIS in the minds of a global audience.[103] In much, perhaps most, of the distant past, enslaving captives and taking their women as concubines would have been unremarkable. But today there are few things more shockingly savage. Any glimpse at a now globalized Western culture would tell you that.

# 5

## The Prophet, Arabia, and the Rise of Antiblackness

MELKITE BISHOP OF EGYPT: How can you accept this black man being the best among you? He should be below you in standing.
MUSLIM DELEGATION: Not at all! Though he is black, as you see, he is the among the best of us in station, among the first of us to embrace Islam, and among the best in reason and judgment. And blackness (*sawād*) is not something disparaged among us.

A report about ʿUbāda bin Ṣāmit leading a Muslim delegation during the conquest of Egypt, 639–42 CE[1]

### THE EASY ANSWER

For many Muslims, the answer to the question 'Is Islam antiblack' is simple. God tells humans that "among His signs . . . is the diversity of your colors and languages" (Quran 30:22), and His revelation clearly rejects ethnic and tribal chauvinism. God has created mankind "in peoples and nations so that you may come to know one another. And the noblest among you before God is the most pious" (Quran 49:13). Indeed, this verse was revealed to the Prophet in order to rebuke some recalcitrant Meccans who had mocked the Muslims for "having no one better" than Bilāl (d. *circa* 20/640), "this crow," as they called him, to perform the call to prayer. This led the Prophet to address the people of Mecca and tell them that God had driven from them the arrogance and pride in ancestry that were rampant in the Jahiliyya, the age of ignorance and arrogance before Islam. All people were the children of Adam, the Prophet announced, and "God created Adam from dust."[2] As the Prophet further explained, it was the varied colors of that dust that gave humans their different skin tones.[3]

The rejection of racism and denying the significance of descent are even more explicit elsewhere in the Prophet's teachings. On the Day of Judgment, "Those whose deeds have slowed them down, their lineage will not speed them up," he explained.[4] The Companion Abū Hurayra (d. 58/678) recounted that there was a black person who used to clean the mosque in Medina. When they died, no one told the Prophet. When he asked how the person was and was informed that they had died, the Prophet replied with sadness, "Would that you all had told me." Abū Hurayra explains that some Companions "had viewed the person with contempt," but the Prophet asked to be taken to their grave so he could pray over them.[5] When an Arab family would not accept Bilāl's proposal to marry their sister (their specific objection is not mentioned), the Prophet rebuked them and made them agree.[6] The Prophet told his followers, "By Him who sent down the book upon Muhammad, no one has any virtue over anyone else except by deeds."[7] And he reiterated this point during his farewell sermon, when he reaffirmed that all mankind descends from one ancestor and is beholden to one God, so no race or nation could be better than any other except through piety (*taqwā*).[8]

Tajul Islam, a Muslim intellectual from the U.K., offers a profound insight about how the Quran and the Prophet's teachings address the disease of racism. He notes how people often remark that there was no premodern word in Arabic for racism (the word racism itself is novel in European languages too, appearing in the 1930s). But Tajul points to a famous Hadith that the Companion Abū Dharr (d. 32/652–3) recounted years after the Prophet had died. When some Muslims found Abū Dharr sitting in his desert homestead beside his slave, both of them wearing the same simple clothes, they asked him why he didn't take part of the slave's clothing to make himself a more dignified outfit. Abū Dharr replied by telling them how he had once insulted a slave by bringing up how his mother was non-Arab. When the Prophet was told about this, he confronted Abū Dharr and told him, "You are a person with Jahiliyya in you." He then instructed the Muslims that slaves "are your brothers. God put them in your charge.

So whomever God has put in charge of his brother, let him feed him from what he eats, clothe him from what he wears, and let him not give him more work than he can bear. And if he gives them work that overwhelms him, then let him help him."[9] Tajul explains that there *was* a word for racism in classical Arabic. There *was* a word for assigning certain people to a group because of something those in power had declared unchangeable about their body or being in order to subordinate or belittle them. That word was Jahiliyya.[10]

## BLACK CROWS: WHY WAS BLACKNESS BAD IN ARABIA?

There seems to be a contradiction, however, in what we have seen so far. The Muslims who responded to the Christian bishop in Egypt told him that "Blackness is not something disparaged among us." But then why was the black servant at the mosque viewed with contempt? Why did the Quraysh call Bilāl a crow, a clear reference to his color? The Quran and the Prophet's teachings might have clearly condemned discrimination on the basis of tribe or nation and rebuked the disparagement of those seen as black, but this would presume that blackness was viewed as something negative in Arabia on the eve of Islam. Were the Arabs of the Hejaz in the seventh century antiblack or not?

Here we must take care not to fall into the trap of reading all negative references to blackness or black skin as expressions of antiblack sentiment and assuming that everyone in history has understood race, color, and value like modern Americans do.[11] In our sources on early Islamic (and some pre-Islamic) history, we do find instances of someone's blackness being referred to pejoratively. But we also find it referred to in a matter-of-fact way with no negative connotation at all. Authors of some of the earliest works in the Islamic tradition, like Ibn al-Kalbī (d. 204–6/819–20) and his student Ibn Saʿd (d. 230/845), often mentioned that an Arab of respected lineage was black or that their mother was black without any hint at negative signification.[12]

Often a report notes a person was black while recounting some unrelated matter.[13] The *Muwaṭṭa'* of Mālik (d. 179/796) contains a report of a man who brings "a black slave girl" to the Prophet to see if she was Muslim because he needed to free a Muslim slave to expiate (*kaffāra*) a sin he had committed.[14] Her blackness was irrelevant. Before the Battle of Qadisiyya (636 CE), as the caliph ʿUmar bin al-Khaṭṭāb reviewed the troops, a clan known as the Sukūn passed before him. The narrator tells that "There were among them very black young men with straight hair (*dulm sibāṭ*), and ʿUmar kept turning away from them." When the caliph was asked why he reacted so, he replied, "I am hesitant about them. No group among the Arabs has passed by me more disliked to me than them." But ʿUmar's reaction to this group has nothing to do with their appearance. The narrator explains that some of those who would later assassinate the caliphs ʿUthmān and ʿAli were among the Sukūn.[15] The aim of this report seems to be showing that ʿUmar could foresee the evil that some Sukūnīs would do. Their appearance was incidental, particularly since they were not all bad. The narrator adds that one of the men who avenged ʿUthmān's murder was also from the Sukūn (also, ʿUmar's mother and paternal grandmother were black).[16] Sometimes someone's color is mentioned to stress that two people are biologically unrelated, for example, juxtaposing a black person with someone with a Mediterranean skin tone. In one more scandalous case, a black freeman is confronted with his wife giving birth to a child "[white] as someone with vitiligo" nine months after she had been romanced by a "Greek" (*rūmī*) slave.[17]

Of course, blackness is certainly invoked negatively in our sources on the dawn of Islam. In order to understand why this is, we must remember that tribe was everything in western Arabia, where the Prophet lived and delivered his message. There was no government or formal mechanisms of law as we would recognize them. There was only the family and tribe to offer security and only custom and the ways of the ancestors to distinguish right from wrong. To be part of a powerful or large family and, on a larger scale, tribe, was to be safe. Those who lacked such support lived precariously. Outsiders, whether people with no tribe or people from a distant place whose family was far away, were the most vulnerable and the least respected. And there was no greater outsider than the slave. In fact, some leading scholars of slavery in world history have argued that it is marginality in society that defines slavery.[18]

Arabia at the time of the Prophet was not a society in which slaves played a crucial economic role, like the Roman Empire or the American South. Slaves were found throughout Arabia but not in huge numbers. Some were bought at markets like those near Mecca, and some were people captured on raids and then either kept as slaves or sold. A study of Medina at the time of the Prophet shows that many slaves were from Ethiopia and some from the Byzantine world of Syria. But the largest group were captives from other Arab tribes.[19] Of the twenty-two slaves the Prophet owned at some point in his life (he freed all of them), including captives he married (Ṣafiyya and Juwayriyya) or took as concubines (Māriya and perhaps also Rayḥāna), only four – or perhaps six – were either described as black (*aswad*) or being from lands associated with that (Ethiopia, Nubia). Almost as many – three, or perhaps five – were Persian. Many, perhaps all, of the rest were Arabs.[20]

Slaves in Arabia on the eve of Islam were all marginal outsiders, regardless of their skin color or place of origin. When a delegation of noble Arabs came to see the Prophet in Medina, they found him seated with Bilāl, Ṣuhayb, Khabbāb, and ʿAmmār, among "the weak of the believers." These Arabs complained to the Prophet because they did not want other Arabs to see them "with these slaves."[21] The four Muslims named in the group were among the earliest and most committed converts to Islam. What joined them was not their skin color. Bilāl looked African and ʿAmmār's mother may have been Ethiopian. But Ṣuhayb was "extremely ruddy," hailing from northern Syria, and Khabbāb was an Arab from the Tamīm tribe who had been captured and taken as a slave to Mecca.[22] What united them in the eyes of the Arab delegation was their marginality in Arab society, their "weakness." Hence the Arab delegation erroneously calling them all slaves, the ultimate outsiders (most in the group had, in fact, been slaves who had converted to Islam and were then bought and freed by other Muslims). In this and other instances in which the Prophet affirmed that what God esteems is not wealth, family, or status but rather faith and good deeds, we see that what was in common among those Muslims he embraced was not color or slave status but marginality, their status as outsiders in a tribal society.

Blackness or Africanness was not negative in and of itself in Arabia of the Prophet's time. Blackness could provoke contempt or prejudice because it was a strong marker of being an outsider. We see over and over again in the life of the Prophet that it is outsider status that is denigrated, not blackness, even if blackness is invoked. Bilāl, the "crow," had trouble finding a wife. But there are even more stories of the Persian Companion Salmān (d. 35/656) being rebuffed for marriage.[23] Salmān was not black like Bilāl. But he had been a slave like Bilāl, and like Bilāl he was totally out of place in Arab tribal society. While Bilāl was demeaned as black, Salmān was peppered with requests to state his ancestry. These taunts served the same purpose in both cases: a cruel reminder of the two men's outsider status. When challenged about his ancestry, Salmān would respond that he was Salmān, the son of Islam.[24]

In Arabia at the dawn of Islam, the worst situation to be in was that of an outsider, to be marginal, whether one was a captive taken near Antioch or from Ethiopia. Blackness was seen as one of its potential markers. But we should not confuse a possible indication of a cause with the cause itself. The famous pre-Islamic poet-warrior ʿAntara bin Shaddād referred to his own blackness – he was the son of a noble Arab of the ʿAbs tribe and his African slave woman – and the contempt with which he had been treated until he won the respect of his father and tribe through his deeds in battle. But ʿAntara was not treated with contempt because he was black. He was treated with contempt because he was the son of a slave woman (and thus a slave himself) whose father had long refused to acknowledge him as his son.[25] He was thus a marginal outsider.

In fact, blackness was insignificant when it did not indicate outsider status, as we see in the cases of individuals ensconced within Arabia's patrilineal tribal system. Noting that a noble Arab's mother was black meant nothing, since their belongingness and even their nobility was assured by their father's standing. Noble Arabs of the Quraysh tribe like Ṣafwān bin Umayya, ʿAmr bin al-ʿĀṣ, and ʿUmar bin al-Khaṭṭāb (contested) were either described as black or of

African descent. Ṣafwān's mother was Ethiopian, while ʿAmr's and ʿUmar's mothers were Arab but black (*sawdāʾ*). ʿAmr was even described as "short and tinted with blackness (*sawād*)," and ʿUmar's paternal grandmother was from Ethiopia as well.[26]

Blackness ceased to have meaning when a person's standing in the tribal system was affirmed. Compare ʿAntara's precarious situation with that of ʿArār, the son of another Arab poet, ʿAmr bin Sha's, from his black slave woman. ʿAmr's wife belittled the son her competitor bore him, so ʿAmr replied:

> She sought to punish ʿArār, and those who seek
> His punishment, by my life, they've wronged [him].
> For if ʿArār is not fair (*wāḍiḥ*),
> I do love blackness (*jawn*) in one full in form (*dhā al-mankib al-ʿamam*).
> And if ʿArār doesn't bridle himself,
> I've taken this from him; I cannot conceal.
> So, if you are with me or wish my company,
> Be to him likc butter, readied in its bowl.
> Otherwise, depart! Like the rider
> Rushing their thirsty mount [to water], on the road without ease.[27]

Another telling example of this appears in a set of questionable Hadiths, which reveal much about the dynamics of early Arab-Islamic society even if they are not historically reliable. One Hadith describes how the Prophet supposedly delayed the departure of all the pilgrims from the plain of ʿArafa during Hajj so that his Companion Usāma bin Zayd could return from an errand. When he returned, the people there from Yemen saw that Usāma was "flat-nosed and black." They complained to the Prophet, "This is the reason you detained us from departing today?" The narrator of this report, Yazīd bin Hārūn (d. 206/821–2), adds that the people of Yemen rebelled against Islam in the Ridda Wars (632–4 CE) because "they had contempt for the Prophet's (s) command," meaning, we are meant to understand, his command regarding Usāma bin Zayd.[28]

This is an isolated report transmitted via only one chain of narrators for three generations, so it is not particularly historically reliable. Yet it was nevertheless circulated by at least some Muslims during the early Islamic period and seems to express real antiblack sentiment. But to stop at this conclusion is to miss the real cause of tension and controversy that shaped this report. Once again, blackness here is merely a proxy for being an outsider. Usāma's father, Zayd bin Ḥāritha, was one of the first converts to Islam and one of the few individuals mentioned by name in the Quran. He was raised by the Prophet and was beloved to him, as was Zayd's son. When Zayd grew to adulthood, the Prophet saw him as a capable leader and put him in charge of important campaigns. There was even some notion in the years after the Prophet's death that, had Zayd outlived him, the Prophet would have made him his successor.[29] The Prophet's affection and esteem for Usāma matched that for his father. Usāma was raised like a grandson of the Prophet, who doted on him as a child and who saw him as a capable commander and leader as an adult.[30] The "command of the Prophet (s)" that Yazīd bin Hārūn mentioned regarding Usāma, which angered some Muslims, was not him delaying leaving ʿArafat. It was that the Prophet, immediately after Hajj, put Usāma in charge of a mission even when more senior Companions were present, something that the Prophet had already done several times before. After the Prophet's death, his successors continued to hold Usāma in high esteem. During the Ridda Wars, the caliph Abū Bakr left him in charge of Medina.

Zayd and Usāma had high standing in Islam, but they were very much outsiders in the tribal society of the Hejaz that still dominated the early Muslim community. Not only was Zayd not from the Quraysh or from any major tribe, he had come to Mecca through its slave market. He had been enslaved in Yemen as a child and sold near Mecca, where he was purchased by the Prophet's wife and soon freed. Authentic Hadiths reveal how controversial it was for the Prophet to put such an outsider in command over noble Arabs of Mecca and Medina, and the Prophet had to face this outrage again when he granted Usāma bin Zayd the prominence he felt Usāma merited.[31]

We are not sure how Zayd looked, in part because it seems clear that claims about his appearance functioned to emphasize his outsider status. All available reports are that both Zayd's parents were Arabs from Yemen, but there is an early report that he was short, extremely dark (*shadīd al-udma*), and had a flat nose. In contrast, Ibn Saʿd notes that it was also reported that Zayd was light skinned (*abyaḍ*), and scholars like al-Dhahabī (d. 748/1348) consider this to be the most reliable position.[32] On the other hand, scholars agreed that Usāma was dark skinned (*aswad*), like his Ethiopian mother. But while this was unremarkable in the case of noble Arabs like Ṣafwān bin Umayya, ʿAmr bin al-ʿĀṣ, and ʿUmar bin al-Khaṭṭāb, reports circulated in the early Islamic period that referenced Usāma's color functioned to denigrate him.[33] In this tension around Zayd and Usāma, blackness stands in as a proxy for the resentment over the Prophet's estimation for someone's merit as opposed to their station in tribal society.

Blackness was not the only concept that served as a proxy for outsider. Nor did 'outside' remain limited to the Arabian tribal arena. As the Muslim community expanded geographically and in population and fell into the first of many internecine disputes, any number of heresies or misguided political causes were perceived as coming from 'outside' of Islam. This is clearest in the way that Muslims viewed the figure of ʿAbdallāh bin Saba' (d. *circa* 40/660), who was blamed for introducing heretical ideas about the deification of ʿAlī. Al-Ṭabarī (d. 310/923) reports that he was "a Jew from Sanaa whose mother was black."[34] It is interesting that almost all the personas discussed here (Usāma and Zayd) as well as the early Shiite figure Muḥammad bin al-Ḥanafiyya (d. 81/701) and the rebel against the Abbasids Muḥammad the Pure Soul (d. 145/762) were all viewed as sites of contesting Islamic authority and described or demeaned as black.

## BLACKNESS IN BODY AND METAPHOR IN ARABIA

In the ruins of Qaryat al-Fāw, an ancient town southeast of Mecca whose people had spoken a version of pre-Islamic Arabic, archaeologists unearthed a stunning wall painting. Its surviving section depicts the head of a nobleman, with two women in the background offering him grapes. His large eyes, wavy hair, stubble, and fine mustache are black. Their faces are all rounded, contoured with light and shadow, and their noses straight. Their skin is an ochre red color like burnt sienna, probably painted with pigment made from red iron ore. Most likely produced in the first century CE, it is a rare insight into how Arabs in the region saw themselves.[35] Their faces and clothes do not differ dramatically from contemporaneous paintings and mosaics in the Mediterranean world.

Debates continue about the extent to which our earliest Islamic historical and legal texts, dating from the mid eighth century CE, preserve eye-witness accounts from the life of the Prophet and the early Muslim community, not to mention the pre-Islamic period. Yet one source stands out. The Quran remains essentially unchanged from the mid seventh century CE. That means that its text preserves not only Islam's foundational teachings but also offers the best record we have for the language and culture of the Hejaz at that time.[36] The Quran does not describe the phenotypes of the characters it mentions, but it does on several instances describe faces "blackened" and "whitened" in this world and the next. The holy book upbraids the Meccans for their disappointment at having female children: if they are told of a female child "their face becomes black" (16:58). And the Quran distinguishes between the fates of those who believed during their earthly life and those who disbelieved "on the Day when faces will be whitened and faces will be blackened" (3:106, see Chapter 6).

We are thus presented with a challenge in interpreting black and white as descriptors in Arabic of the Prophet's era. Black (*aswad*) appears commonly both as a literal descriptor of skin tone and a metaphor for loss or debasement. It is not so much that we see blackness 'bleeding' between metaphorical and physical as much as the Quran's audience felt no anxiety about deploying both in their ordinary use of language.[37] White (*abyaḍ*), by contrast, was not primarily used to describe phenotype. As Abdullah Hamid Ali has shown, when used to describe people, white was employed mainly as a metaphor for nobility, joy, and purity.[38] As with the Quran's use of the image of blackened and whitened faces, whiteness often functioned alongside blackness in a metaphoric binary pair for good/bad.

There seems to have been little bleeding between the paired metaphor of black/white and descriptions of actual phenotype in early Arabia. Black/white was not a common template for phenotypical taxonomy or the juxtaposition of skin tone. In fact, white was not even the term Arabs used to describe those with the lightest skin in early Islamic Arabia or the phenotypes closest to White people today. Contrary to its metaphoric import of honor or purity, when white was used in regards to skin color, it was not necessarily positive. It was often used to describe the loss of pigmentation caused by vitiligo or some sort of mild leprosy (*baraṣ*).[39] Otherwise, as the famous Damascene scholar al-Dhahabī explains, when early Arabs described someone's skin as white (*abyaḍ*), they meant "wheat colored (*al-ḥinṭī al-lawn*) with a darkish hue (*bi-ḥilya sawdāʾ*)." This appears to be exactly what Romans had meant by 'white' (*albus*) skin, namely a sort of olive tone in our terms. Arab-Islamic authors described the fairer and ruddier complexions seen in Syria and Anatolia as red (*aḥmar*) or fair and ruddy (*ashqar*).[40] When trying to stress how light-toned one man was, an Iraqi scholar of the late ninth century described him as "fair and ruddy like an onion (*ashqar mithla al-baṣala*)."[41]

It is very important to note that when black (*aswad*) was used to describe the color of a person, it could mean either the range of dark browns associated with a Black African phenotype as well as such a color for **someone who had no link to Africa**. Furthermore, black described skin color first and often exclusively. In this regard, Arabs at the dawn of Islam were similar to Herodotus in his usage of black. The color descriptor did not automatically connote other features stereotyped as part of Black Africanness, such as tightly coiled hair, a wide nose, or thick lips.[42]

In the Hadith corpus, the chief color categories for describing humans were not white and black but either the bipartite 'red and black' or the tripartite 'red, white, and black.' When the Prophet came out of his quarters and found his Companions reciting the Quran, he said, "Praise be to God! The Book of God is one, and among you there are red (*aḥmar*), white (*abyaḍ*) and black (*aswad*) . . ."[43] In the case of the 'red and black' division, evidence suggests that the early Arabs considered themselves part of the 'black' group.[44] And if among the Companions the Prophet saw red, white, and black, and if the lightest skinned were Syrians or Greeks and the darkest had skin tone resembling Africans, then the middle group, the 'white,' were average Arabs of the day. This supports what al-Dhahabī stated, that white skin color in the context of early Islamic history was what we would today call an olive or wheatish tone.

When confronted by what we call a White phenotype today, namely that of Europeans, scholars and travelers of the early Arab-Islamic world were at the edge of their descriptive envelope. They had to categorize them either as fair and ruddy (*shuqr ḥumr*), as Ibn Faḍlān did when he encountered Rus (Scandinavians or Slavs) on the Volga River in 921–2 CE, or they went so far as to describe them as verging on blue, as al-Masʿūdī (d. 345/956) described Slavs and Germanic peoples.[45] One ninth-century Muslim scholar disparaged the complexions of Slavs and their ilk as "between light-skinned, ruddy, albino and ugly white (*mughrab*)."[46] Ibn Faḍlān was more impressed, noting how the Rus were massively built. Sometime later (though it is not clear exactly when), a traveler named Ḥasan al-Rūmī said of the peoples living in the distant lands of the northeast that "there is no type of slave with finer bodies or more beautiful than their whiteness (*aḥsan min bayāḍihim*). They are of full form, in their beauty, whiteness, wonderous softness, and blue eyes."[47]

The difficulty of fixing exactly how early Muslims used color to describe phenotype is clear in descriptions of how the Prophet looked, a case in which we see the oscillation of color as metaphor and color as physical description. Descriptions of the Prophet's skin color in Hadiths seem perplexing, since they range from "white with a reddish hue" to brown. This is clarified, however, when we remember that white as a skin color meant a light brown or olive tone and that descriptions of the Prophet's face stressed not its color but its luminosity.[48] A Hadith in the famous *Ṣaḥīḥ Muslim* collection features the Companion Abū al-Ṭufayl describing the Prophet's face as "white and lovely" (*abyaḍ malīḥ al-wajh*).[49] In another, less reliable Hadith that would become famous in praise poems about the Prophet, ʿAlī describes his face as "white with a reddish hue" (*abyaḍ mushrab*), while another solitary narration from his servant Anas bin Mālik describes him as "brownish" (*asmar al-lawn*).[50] Very widely transmitted and authentic reports have Anas describing the Prophet as "not unhealthily white and not very dark (*ādam*)," with the most accepted explanation of that not-unhealthy whiteness being that it was not the whiteness associated with vitiligo or albinism.[51] Anas' description of the Prophet would be celebrated in the gorgeous tradition of the Ottoman *hilye*, an ornately illuminated calligraphy of the Prophet's description.[52] The most famous descriptions of the Prophet's face, however, simply describe it "luminous" (*azhar*), and al-Nawawī (d. 676/1277) stresses that the Prophet's whiteness was "a luminous white."[53] It seems that, though he was lighter skinned than many Arabs of his time, the Prophet did not have the complexion they associated with Greeks or Persians (*aḥmar*). And he was certainly nothing like what is considered White today.[54]

## THE RISE OF ANTIBLACKNESS, PART ONE: BLACK AS SLAVE

The 700s and 800s CE saw an unusual phenomenon in Arabic literature: interest in a group of pre-Islamic and early Islamic Arabic poets who were dubbed 'The Crows of the Arabs.' These were three poets, ʿAntara bin Shaddād, Khaffāf bin Nadba, and Sulayk bin ʿUmayr (along with a few others sometimes), whose fathers were Arab but whose mothers were Black African slave women or very dark-skinned Arabs and whose appearance was black. A theme that appeared in much of their poetry was contrasting what they seemed to admit as the ugliness and lowliness of their appearance and sometime slave status with the nobility of their character.

Though he has been criticized for many things, the Orientalist Bernard Lewis (d. 2018) was quite right when he observed that the 'Crows of the Arabs' theme was a momentary fad in Arabic poetry. And he was even more correct when he explained that much of their poetry and the stories around them betray traces of later invention as opposed to being authentic expressions of pre-Islamic and early Islamic Arab culture.[55] As we have already reiterated, for Arabs of the time of the Prophet, skin color or appearance were not important in and of themselves. And the Quran and the Prophet had made clear that invoking someone's lineage or color to draw attention to their status was unacceptable. When Meccans had mocked their former slave Bilāl as a 'crow,' the Prophet and the Quran had rebuked them. In the 800s CE, however, noted Muslim scholars wrote books on poetry that fetishized the 'Crows of the Arabs.'[56] As al-Jāḥiẓ imagined, those of African descent in the salons of Basra were now wondering, "You [Arabs] saw us as matches for your women during the Age of Ignorance (*jāhiliyya*). But, now, when the justice of Islam has come, you decide that was wrong?"[57] What had changed?

Lewis offers a compelling and sound explanation. In Arabia of the Prophet's time, Ethiopia was not seen as some backward land of primitive people. It was a respected neighbor and refuge where the Muslims had sought safety and lived for years.[58] The Old Ethiopian language and culture was familiar to Arabs in the Hejaz, who regularly referenced its vocabulary and customs.[59] Many of the Ethiopians that Arabs in the Hejaz would have seen would have been slaves, captured in raids or bought in the market. But Ethiopians were present in places like Medina for other reasons as well, as visitors or delegations.[60] Even during the civil war between Ibn al-Zubayr and the Umayyads (680–92 CE), an Ethiopian unit fought in support of Ibn al-Zubayr in Mecca. They were not slaves. Rather, they were soldiers sent by the allied ruler in Ethiopia (meanwhile, the Umayyad opponents of Ibn al-Zubayr had units in their armies made up of Berber and Bukharan slaves sent as tribute, as well as a unit of Slavic freed slaves from around Antioch).[61]

Whatever their origin (the largest group seems to have been Arabs), slaves were present throughout Arabia of the Prophet's time, though not in great numbers. They were the result of raids and small-scale trade in labor. When the Muslims conquered the greater Near East, however, they found themselves right in the middle and in charge of a region in which slave labor had been a significant part of the economy and society for centuries and in which the international slave trade was a major commerce. There had been a trade in slaves from areas like Nubia and Ethiopia to Egypt since at least 1200 BCE.[62] But most of the slaves in the Roman Mediterranean and Near East were not Black Africans. They were Berbers, Persians, Turkic peoples, Germanic folk, Slavs, etc. As Lloyd Thompson put it, "The overwhelming majority of slaves in Roman society was always white."[63]

Crucially, however, most of the Black Africans present in the greater Near East *were* slaves. A rabbinic exegetical story (*midrash*) from the fifth century CE reveals the assumption that, presented with a dark-skinned African (*kushi*) and a random inhabitant of the Mediterranean world, it would be assumed that the Black African was the slave of the lighter-skinned person, not the other way around.[64] This was the socio-economic reality that the Arab-Muslim conquerors of the Near East found themselves ruling. When they began encountering Black Africans from far away regions like the East African coast and the upper Nile Valley, they encountered them mainly as slaves, often as tribute paid.[65]

Yet, as the new political and religious order of the caliphate gelled under the Umayyad and Abbasid dynasties, most of the slaves brought into the central Islamic lands were Slavic, Turkic, Greek, or others from Europe or even India.[66] In a historical report circulating in the mid 800s and probably reflecting eighth-century sensibilities, the rebel Mukhtār bin Abī ʿUbayd (d. 67/687) and his accomplice kill two people, one very black and one "very red, like the redness of a Greek (*rūmī*)." Mukhtār assumes both are slaves.[67] In histories composed in Iraq in the tenth and eleventh centuries, the mention of slaves, male or female, presumes they are Greek, Slavic, Persian, or Turkish (see Figure 9). The default slave is not Black African, since this descriptor is added when authors choose.[68] In al-Ṭabarī's *History*, finished in 915 CE, the caliph's slaves (*ghilmān*, *khadam*) are generally mentioned without any specification about their color or origins. Presumably these are Slavic or European. When black slaves are mentioned, they are described as such specifically. ʿArīb bin Saʿd's (d. *circa* 370/980) history describes the Abbasid caliph summoning "around one hundred of his slaves (*ghilmān*), young and old, and four hundred black slaves . . ."[69] We find a similar case in al-Khaṭīb al-Baghdādī's (d. 463/1071) *History of Baghdad*, which focuses more on the lives of scholars than the political and military elite of the Abbasid capital: slaves who are black are specified as such. In the *History of Baghdad*, occurrences of the word 'slave woman' (*jāriya*) most commonly refer to women who are either objects of infatuation, expensive courtesans, and/or highly cultured, or they are or essentially anonymous servants, though some are highly skilled at proofreading or dictation. Their race or color is hardly ever mentioned. Al-Khaṭīb only includes two reports mentioning black slave women. The first reports a black slave woman providing companionship for the successor Qays bin Abī Ḥāzim (d. *circa* 97/715) during his senility, and the second is a woman mentioned as part of the household of the Kufan scholar Wakī' bin al-Jarrāḥ (d. 197/812). He would have everyone in his house offer extra prayers late at night (*tahajjud*), "even a black slave woman of ours."[70]

Despite the default ethnicity of slaves not being Black African, however, in the central Islamic circuit of Baghdad to Khurasan in the crucial period of the 800s–1000s CE the association of blackness and slavery simply grew stronger and stronger. The prominent early Egyptian jurist Ibn al-Qāsim (d. 191/806) reported that the famous Medinan jurist Mālik bin Anas held that it was not slanderous to say to someone of a darker complexion (*aṣfar*) "Get out of my way, slave!" provided that his mother was black or Indian (*sindiyya*) and that the comment was a reference to the man's dark color and not a suggestion that his mother had committed adultery with a slave.[71] In the tenth century, a black Sufi saint from Kufa set out for Hajj but was confronted just outside Kufa's gates by a man who mistook his identity and claimed he was his slave.[72] In the mid 800s, a pious scholar on the way to Hajj from Baghdad met a black man praying on the road near Mecca and assumed – correctly – that he was a slave (he bought and freed him).[73] These may be actual incidents or literary tropes, but the import is the same: a random Black African, presumably dressed in modest attire, could be (mis)taken for a slave.

Examples of the conflation of blackness and slaveness in the Abbasid period can even be seen in the transmission of a single

Hadith in Basra in the 700s CE. The best preserved and most reliable narrations of this Hadith (in *Ṣaḥīḥ al-Bukhārī*, compiled *circa* 860 CE), in which the Prophet tells a story from the Children of Israel, mention one character described only as a pious "slave woman" (*ama*). A narration found in the *Musnad* of al-Bukhārī's teacher, Ibn Ḥanbal, had been passed on by at least one less fastidious transmitter, who seemed unconcerned with preserving the story's original form from the push and pull of cultural change. It refers to the slave woman as simply "an Ethiopian or Zanjī woman."[74] With this Hadith, we see how 'slave' morphed into 'Black African' in Basra as the terms began to overlap in the minds of Muslim scholars and their audiences in that city.

In a crucial development that would feature in the lettered culture of Islamic civilization from Morocco to India from the late Abbasid period onward, 'black' (*aswad*, fem. *sawdā'*, pl. *sūdān*) became a broadened metonym for slave.[75] In one sense, this was the obverse of what we might call a weak racialization of slavery. It is well established that slavery in Islamic civilization writ large was not tied to or defined by a particular race, and the majority of slaves in the Mediterranean and Persianate regions in the Islamic middle period were not black. Yet, as with American films casting dark-skinned actors as criminals despite Black Americans making up a minority of arrests, stereotyping linked slavery and blackness.[76] We see this illustrated in a volume of popular sayings in Andalusian Arabic collected in the late 1200s CE, by which time Black Africans seem to have replaced the region's earlier reliance on Berber and European slaves. It features expressions like "As blacks have served you, you'll serve whites," and "As long as you find a black, don't put a white to work."[77] There seems to be little alternative to reading black and white in such texts as standing in for slave and free. The broadened metonymy of black-for-slave in the literature of Mediterranean, Middle Eastern, and even South Asian Islamic civilization is the counterpart of 'slave' (*'abd*) coming to be a main word for Black African in spoken Arabic in the Levant, Syria, and Iraq.[78]

Why associate slavery with Black Africans? Why didn't Muslims in the eighth to the tenth centuries CE start associating Turks,

Indians, or Slavs – all groups from whom slaves were drawn in massive numbers – with slavery? It is possible that, because the Abbasid Empire abutted Turkic regions and had commercial links with India that Muslim interactions with these groups were too complex for such a stereotype to form. But that does not explain why the more distant Slavs were not associated with slavery (as they would be in medieval Europe).

Perhaps the phenotypes of Africans brought from south of the Sahara or the interior of the East African coast simply stood out much more strongly than any of these other groups. This has been observed in the depictions of Black Africans as slaves in Roman art. As Lloyd Thompson has put it, it may be that the 'somatic distance' (borrowing this concept from H. Hoetink) between the phenotypes common from Baghdad to Khurasan and Black Africans was much more striking than in the case of a Turkic or Slavic person.[79] It does not seem like many Black Africans *not* brought as slaves were present in cities like Baghdad or Nishapur in this period. Persians and Turks converted to Islam in massive numbers, and even by the 1100s CE Muslim scholars and merchants from Baghdad, Iran, and Egypt were familiar with India as a station on commercial and even scholarly circuits. This would not be the case for Africa south of the Sahara for some time. *Circa* 1200 CE, in Baghdad there was a hostel for Ethiopians (*ribāṭ al-ḥabashiyya*).[80] In the 1240s CE a wealthy pilgrim from Kanem-Bornu who had stopped in Cairo on his way to Hajj endowed a madrasa there for students from his home region to come and study Mālikī law.[81] But it is not until the 1300s that people from places like Zayla and later Timbuktu were noticed as visitors in the Nile-Oxus region.[82] By the early 1400s, in fact, migrants from the northern Horn of Africa had become a familiar presence in Cairo.[83]

This theory of somatic distance makes significant assumptions about what 'average' Muslims in a city like Baghdad were used to seeing. We already know that dark-skinned Arabs were not at all unknown. There is significant distance, however, between being unknown and being familiar enough not to be stereotyped. Dark skin may well have been visible in cities like Baghdad and even Khurasan, but the Black African slave had nonetheless become a symbol of foreignness. By the early Abbasid caliphate, an African slave was no longer an Ethiopian laborer, speaking a Semitic language close to Arabic, owned by an Arab family that was scratching out a living on the desolate fringes of the desert. They were exotic trade items brought from far off lands into the wealthy circles of the new conquerors. A scholar in Nishapur in the eleventh century notes a saying, 'She's been drawn to blacks, though there are whites aplenty (*ghariyat bi'l-sūd wa fī al-bīḍ al-kuthr*),' to refer to someone who sticks with a preference regardless of other, easier options.[84] Some early Muslim scholars, like the Basran Ibn Ṭāwūs (d. 132/750), would not eat meat prepared by an East African (*zanjī*) because they assumed that this person was neither Muslim nor from the People of the Book.[85] The African slave was assumed to be linguistically and culturally incommunicado. Although we cannot be sure when this report entered circulation, since it appears first in the writings of the Damascene polymath Ibn Taymiyya (d. 728/1328), we see the Black African as the personification of isolation from the undulating waves of Islamic culture. Though Ibn Taymiyya denounces it as a forgery, he recounts a report of ʿUmar allegedly saying, "The Prophet (s) and Abū Bakr would talk with each other, and I was like a Zanjī between them." In other words, the Zanjī was completely unable to understand anything being said by Muslims around them.[86]

Somatic distance may well have played a role in the association of Black Africans and slavery, but there is little doubt that a major contributor was a noxious element inherited from the Near Eastern heritage: the tradition of the Curse of Ham. As we saw earlier, by the rise of Islam it had been established in strains of Near Eastern Jewish and Christian tradition that it was Ham and his descendants who had been cursed with slavery and/or blackness, that they were dark skinned, and that they inhabited great parts of Africa.[87] Early Muslim historians and exegetes of the Quran absorbed this material, sometimes explicitly quoting 'The Torah' (by which they meant Jewish lore in general), sometimes citing early Muslim scholars who specialized in collecting exegetical material from the Jewish and Christian traditions, and sometimes not citing their sources at all (see Appendix VI).[88] Although Muslim scholars like Ibn al-Jawzī (d. 597/1200),

Shams al-Dīn al-Dimashqī (d. 727/1327), Ibn Khaldūn (d. 808/1406), al-Suyūṭī (d. 911/1505), and others rejected the various Curse of Ham versions as either unfounded and contradictory to the established teachings of the Prophet or as clashing with climatic explanations of phenotype, it is clear that even in the 700s CE Muslims were being strongly influenced by the belief that Noah cursed Africans with blackness and slavery.[89]

The general characteristics of slavery in Islamic civilization, in particular the ubiquitous phenomenon of elite slavery, means that we must be careful in how we read for antiblackness in the association of blackness and slavery. The image of the Black African slave as an administrative face of the state goes back to at least the 800s CE. In 284/897 CE, the Abbasid caliph was outraged to hear that a random rabble in Baghdad were heckling his black slaves as they made their way through the streets on official errands. Were these rude Baghdadis indulging themselves in antiblack mockery? Or, more likely, were they taunting elites, namely people who were clearly the caliph's personal Black African eunuchs?[90]

It is noteworthy that the association of blackness and slaveness in Islamic thought did not metastasize into a widespread theory of Black Africans as particularly or exclusively suited to slavery by nature (though this did obtain in early-modern, northwest Africa). Modern critics often point to the well-traveled Christian physician Ibn Buṭlān (d. *circa* 458/1066), who wrote an influential guide to buying slaves, as expressing this idea. He does indeed describe Nubian women as submissive and obedient, "as if they were created for slavery." Such a reading is unduly selective, however. Ibn Buṭlān's claim comes as part of a lengthy taxonomy of slave women from various ethnicities, each one listed with its strengths and weaknesses. It is not blackness that Ibn Buṭlān associates with slavery. It is Nubianness. In the case of three other groups that both modern Americans and the Arab-Islamic tradition would categorize as Black Africans, they are not described as naturally slave-like by Ibn Buṭlān.[91] His contemporary, the humanist scholar Miskawayh (d. 421/1030), does indeed observe that the virtue of loyalty in slaves is prominent in Ethiopians and Nubians. But it is equally present in Greeks.[92] An even more illustrious contemporary, the Bukharan philosopher and physician Ibn Sīnā (d. 428/1037), repeats Aristotle's theory that some people are natural slaves. While Aristotle never linked this to specific nations or regions, Ibn Sīnā does . . . to both the Turks and Black Africans (*zanj*).[93]

## THE RISE OF ANTIBLACKNESS, PART TWO: BLACK AS HYPERSEXUAL, BLACK AS STUPID, BLACK AS ANIMAL

Beyond the Curse of Ham, the pre-Islamic heritage of the greater Near East contributed another prominent element of antiblackness to the Islamic intellectual tradition. Muslim scholars of the Abbasid period and beyond received and built on the fields of ethnology and physiognomy traced back to Galen (d. *circa* 216 CE) and the geographical oeuvre associated with Posidonius (d. *circa* 50 BCE) and Ptolemy (d. *circa* 170 CE), with its division of the world into different climatic zones and the theory that climate shaped bodies and temperament.[94] The offensive stereotypes of Africans as unconstrained in their appetites and hypersexual, which abounded in Islamic civilization, were direct inheritances from this Near Eastern corpus.

As with their Greco-Roman predecessors, it was common for medieval Muslim authors to claim that the middle zones containing the modern Middle East were the most temperate and thus produced people with the most balanced minds and bodies.[95] While negative stereotypes of Black Africans were much more culturally salient, as before, this climatic ethnology meant that the negative assessments of those Africans in the south found negative counterparts in those in the extreme north, such as Slavs and Turks. The people who inhabited the extreme north (Slavs, Turks and others) and the extreme south (Black Africans) were both characterized by stupidity and an inability to reason, though Slavs were of a cold disposition, while Black Africans were 'hot' and savage.[96] Ṣā'id al-Andalusī (d. 462/1070) describes how the climate in the hot south had turned Africans foolish and ignorant. But the people of the far north, such as Slavs, became rude, ignorant, and stupid as a result of the cold.[97] Shams al-Dīn al-Dimashqī, whose geographical compendium cites Galen directly for its explanation of phenotype and character and whose description of Black Africans is among the most negative, notes how the most distant Ethiopians share some customs with the Slavs.[98] Ibn Khaldūn's Greco-Roman scientific description of why the Africans living in the extreme south are primitive of mind and never received revelation applies equally to Slavs, he notes.[99] Ibn Mājid (fl. mid 1400s) in his navigational guide says that south of Kanem lived whites whose appearance was caused by their great distance from the sun, just like the Turks.[100] A thick slave-purchasing manual from mid-thirteenth-century Cairo lists very unfavorable views of Circassian and Frankish (Western European) slaves. They might be skilled or good fighters, but they were stupid and arrogant.[101]

Unfortunately, these Muslim scholars adopted the negative assessment of the notional Black African temperament without the positive counterparts that Greco-Roman authors had posited, such as sagacity and quick mindedness (though the Cairean slave-purchasing manual affirms this for Ethiopians).[102] Yet many Muslim scholars writing on geography and ethnology do praise Africans of the Sahel for the justice of their rulers and regularly note the immense wealth of their kingdoms. A compilation of popular sayings from medieval Andalusia includes one that, "The blacker he is, the more magnanimous (*aswad huwa ajwad huwa*)" (meanwhile, another saying associates the European world to the north with catamites).[103]

It is also important to note that, in the case of writers with direct experience in the Sahel or whose sources had visited the region, the most negative assessments are reserved for the populations who live south of Sahelian kingdoms like Ghana and Borno. These distant Black Africans are frequently described as going naked, as cannibals, as never having received revelation, of being incapable of reason, and as being "closer to wild animals than humans."[104] Incidentally, it is from these very distant African lands that geographers like al-Iṣṭakhrī (d. mid 900s CE) note the bulk of African slaves are drawn.[105] The savagery and stupidity seen as caused by living in that extreme clime is thus really manifested in the African populations to the south of the Sahel areas, beyond the areas into which scholars like Ibn Khaldūn note Islam and Christianity had already spread.[106] The Grenadine scholar Ibn Saʿīd (d. 640/1243) describes the people of Kawwār, north of Lake Chad, as "Muslim blacks" who have "taken on the customs and conduct of whites" in their dress and manners.[107] Another Andalusian traveler, Abū Ḥāmid al-Gharnāṭī (d. 565/1169–70), dismisses those Africans who live beyond the southern borders of the Abode of Islam as bereft of reason and revelation as well as being physically unappealing. But the Black African people of Ghana he praises not only as the best looking of the *sūdān* but also the best in lifestyle, possessed of reason and understanding. They, after all, were Muslim.[108]

Of course, this frontier between the Abode of Islam (*dār al-islām*) and the realm of unbelief and, metaphorically, the savage and perhaps even the unhuman, was not fixed. It could move both in perception and through further conversion. The case of the people in the Aïr region of Agadez in modern Niger provides an instructive example of the region's liminality. In a letter sent to al-Suyūṭī in Cairo *circa* 1500 CE inquiring about some minutiae of Islamic law, the scholars of Agadez explicitly state that theirs is a "land of Islam" inhabited only by Muslims. But a Berber Sufi master resident there, Sīdī Maḥmūd (d. *circa* 1640 CE), seems to have disagreed. He instructed his students, who had asked if they were in the Abode of Islam, that they lived in a land that had once been "the land of the blacks." It was not "the land of Islam." Rather, it was "the land of fire." Yet some of Sīdī Maḥmūd's followers were *sūdān* from the Hausa and Fulani peoples, and other Sufi masters in the region had won converts among the Toubou as well.[109] Writing in the early 1800s, the Sokoto caliph Muḥammad Bello's (d. 1253/1837) history of West Africa describes the vantage point of his Fulani Muslim polity as teetering on the edge of a land of unbelief and ignorance. To the south are the blacks (*sūdān*, *sūdāniyyūn*), often referred to as the "black rabble" (*ajlāf al-sūdāniyyīn*), in their undifferentiated tribes. They are unbelievers who overwhelm the Muslims in their midst. If they are guided to Islam by righteous leaders, they are nonetheless prone to backslide into unbelief, into their "madness and brazenness." Some are the historical slaves of the Fulani, stubborn and rebellious.[110] But the boundaries of the Abode of Islam and the realm of the human could extend even in this one individual's view. Just a few years later Bello affirmed that his Fulani people were actually not descended from Arabs, as he had previously claimed, but from "the Bambara, from among the peoples of the *sūdān*," in what the historian Paul Naylor feels was an expression of Bello's identifying more with the Sahel region and its diverse populace.[111]

Interestingly, Black African (*sūdān*) seems to have been almost exclusively an exonym or ascribed label when it came to people (as opposed to geography), at least until the early modern period. It is rare to find a person identifying as 'one of the *sūdān*' (see Appendix III). Muslim writers in the western Sahel and trans-Saharan regions referred to the unbelievers south of the Abode of Islam's borders as Black Africans (*sūdān*), often in an undifferentiated mass. This despite, as we have seen, the fact that, by the 1300s, the actual boundaries of where Islam had been embraced had already long subsumed sizable Black African communities. But, once they embraced Islam, Black African ethnic groups and communities become known by their endonymic names.

Perceptions of where the borders of Islam should be traced and who fell within them differed abundantly. In influential instances, the governing factor was more the theological or political idiosyncrasies of those making the judgments than the confessional identity professed by those being judged. Al-Maghīlī (d. *circa* 910/1505), a doctrinaire Moroccan scholar who visited the Niger bend region, brought the severe opinion that even a population who claimed to be Muslim was actually not if they continued to engage in even innocuous pagan rituals and customs.[112] This perspective was adopted by the leaders of the Sokoto Caliphate in their justification for their jihad against neighboring states, whose inhabitants often pleaded strenuously that they were Muslim. Aḥmad Bābā of Timbuktu was both more charitable than al-Maghīlī and more representative of Islamic scholarship, ruling that people from Kano, Gobir, and other major communities in the Sahel were all Muslims, including those whose

"Islam is shallow."[113] Other Timbuktu scholars like al-Sharīf Ḥamā Allāh (d. 1169/1755) show how difficult such questions could be. When asked if a Black African who claimed to be a Muslim but did not believe in resurrection was actually a Muslim, the scholar had no choice but to answer that one could not be Muslim if one denied this core tenet of faith.[114]

Muslims from phenotypically Black African communities in the Sahel and south were eager to register their belonging to the realm of Islam. Van Dalen has shed light on the anxiety motivating local scholars to distinguish their Muslim communities from 'pagan' African neighbors in seventeenth-century Bagirmi.[115] A note from the British consul in the North African principality of Tripoli in 1789 records that, when the 'prince' of Borno passed through, his conversation with the consul touched on how the barbaric customs of human sacrifice and selling one's people into slavery were not found in Borno but only among the unbelievers beyond its southern borders.[116]

# 6

## Antiblackness in the Quran and Sunna?

> The people who walked in darkness have seen a great light; those who lived in a land of deep darkness – on them light has shined.
>
> Isaiah 9:2

> Then in a pack they charge off, jaws all dripping blood,
> to lap black surface water with their slender tongues
> in some dark spring, vomiting up clots of blood
> from their crammed bellies, while in their chests their hearts
> are resolute. That's how the leaders and commanders
> of the Myrmidons rushed around brave Patroclus . . .
>
> *Iliad* XVI:156–64

### TYRANNY OF THE PRESENT

Discussions of Islam and antiblackness frequently raise the question of how blackness and Black Africans are referenced in the Quran and Hadiths of the Prophet Muhammad. The vast majority of the Hadiths that critics bring up have either long been deemed inauthentic by Muslim Hadith scholars or are demonstrably unreliable according to those scholars' criteria. In the case of the Quran and several well authenticated Hadiths, the often anxious and spirited discussions they spark labor under what has often been called the tyranny of the present.

Whereas nearly a century ago Walter Benjamin (d. 1940) described how a moment in the past could be "blasted out of the continuum of history" to overwhelm the present, ours is a present that turns back on the past and consumes it.[1] In its moral urgency, it dissolves the past's complexities. This may only worry historians, but our present also consumes and dissolves the past's perspectives and, more dangerously, its sincerities. This is not to say that the convictions of long-gone generations were always or even often right. But they nonetheless *were* sincerely held. That they were held by people as capable and as human as us demands that we at least take them seriously in evaluating them. To refuse to even try to understand is to stake feeble and fallaciously narrow claims around what we think it means to be human and to triumph falsely in our present certainties. The tyranny of the present cuts us off from the experience of our species. It costs us whatever in our past is alien to us now because these now foreign views must give way to a present that need be all familiar. And it costs us our connection to the continuities of that past, because it is only the continuities projected backward from the present that matter.

The phrase 'the tyranny of the present' is often (inaccurately, I think) attributed to Cicero (d. 43 BCE). For the cultural critic Neil Postman (d. 2003) it nonetheless provided a productive foil. "Cicero remarked that the purpose of education is to free the student from the tyranny of the present," he wrote. But this involves painful irony. For young people, Postman explained, it is precisely to the present that they are desperately trying to accommodate themselves.[2] I have seen many young Muslims embrace the admirable fight against antiblack racism, feeling empowered by their new cause. Even more, they finally feel at home. But I have also seen how their zeal can lead them to voice outrage at how the Quran speaks of unbelievers as having "blackened faces" on the Day of Judgment. Some all but explicitly call the Prophet antiblack for freeing one slave of unknown background by exchanging two black slaves for him. To dismiss so hastily what for Muslims is revelation and prophetic guidance, and what for non-Muslims should at the very least be great literature and a man of immense historic importance, is too high a price to pay without at least trying to break free of the constraints of the present.

Whether in their figurative language or the episodes they recount, texts from the distant past can be movingly familiar to us as well as jarringly alien. Isaiah's image of great light illuminating the path of a people who had long walked in darkness is immediately comprehensible to us even thousands of years after it was written because it draws on the nearly universal imagery of darkness and light. To reflexively label such use of language as antiblack is to overlook how this same imagery is used in languages from Africa south of the Sahara whose speakers also refer to their own skin tone as black (see Appendices II, III, and IV).[3] The *Iliad*'s perplexing simile of the bloody beasts vomiting up chunks of flesh as they lap the black waters of a dark spring is as bizarrely foreign as Isaiah's is familiar. Were we to read the mentions of blackness in this imagery through the meaning of blackness in our racially charged present without even trying to understand what the image meant to those for whom it *was* familiar would be to ignore the past's plea to inquire into why these words were strung together for those ancient ears. Livy (d. 17 CE) described the study of history as the best medicine for a sick mind. Curiosity about imagery and reasoning in the past, in its familiar and foreign parts, can temper the present's arrogance.

## BLACKENED AND WHITENED FACES IN THE QURAN

We have already seen how, in Arabia of the Prophet's time, the black/white binary was employed more as a metaphor for bad/good, ignoble/noble than to describe actual phenotypes. The Quran reprimands pre-Islamic Arabs for the gloom they felt at the birth of daughters, which caused their faces to "become black" (16:58). The holy book describes how the Day of Judgment will reveal the contrasting fates of those who denied God as opposed to those who believed and did good deeds. It will be "the Day when faces will be whitened and faces will be blackened" (3:106 and 39:60).

We can thank Christian Lange for an excellent study on the imagery of the face, as well as its blackening and whitening, in the classical Islamic tradition. But his assertion that, "All in all, there seems to have been little disagreement that on the Day of Judgment the faces of sinners would literally be black" can be misleading, as is his conclusion that the famous Central Asian theologian and exegete Fakhr al-Dīn al-Rāzī (d. 606/1209) argued for this literal position.[4] Al-Rāzī merely restates the figurative (*majāz*) and literal (*ḥaqīqī*) positions, along with the arguments supporting each. He picks no favorite at that point in his commentary. He does describe the blackening of faces in unmistakably metaphoric terms, however, when discussing a verse on how one will see "those who had lied against God with blackened faces" (Quran 39:60) as well as in his commentary on faces blackened at the birth of a daughter.[5] But Lange is correct that al-Rāzī does refer numerous times to what is presumably a literal "blackness of faces" on the Day of Judgment in verses that mention how unbelievers will be recognizable on the Day of Judgment (e.g., Quran 55:41–42, though some scholars like Ibrāhīm Rufayda have argued that this part of the book was not actually written by al-Rāzī).[6]

Yet with al-Rāzī and Sunni exegetical literature overall, even if the blackening/whitening of faces on the Day of Judgment were understood literally, there was no notion that this was connected to a Black African phenotype. Al-Rāzī describes any literal blackness on the Day of Judgment as the darkness of the heart that results from ignorance and then manifests in the face. It has an unearthly quality and is totally other, "a blackness different from all other types of blackness (*sawād mukhālif li-sā'ir anwāʿ al-sawād*)."[7] Similarly, al-Qurṭubī (d. 671/1272) and al-Thaʿlabī (d. 427/1035) provide a report that those whitened will have faces "white as ice," not white in the sense of some conventional Mediterranean or European phenotype.[8] We see this coloring of faces not along ordinary phenotypical lines but in much more dramatic, unnatural ways in a story about how the Arabian people of Thamūd were punished for slaughtering a camel God had ordered them to leave unmolested (Quran 91:13–15). This story, which was circulating as early as 700 CE, tells that, when the people hamstrung God's camel, their impending doom was presaged by their faces first turning yellow as if painted, then red as if covered with blood, then black (*muswadda*) as if covered with pitch.[9]

Interestingly, al-Rāzī resorts to his own earthly analogy of a Black African phenotype for the verses describing how "faces that Day shall be shining, radiant, laughing, joyous. And faces that Day shall be covered with dust, overspread with darkness" (Quran 80:38–41). He explains that this language conjures the image of dust on Black African skin. "You will not see anything uglier (*awḥash*) than the mixture of dust and blackness on a face, like when you see the faces of Black Africans (*zunūj*) covered with dust." In explaining this analogy in such terms, however, al-Rāzī is using a simile to communicate the Quran's imagery, not claiming that this will literally be the case on the Day of Judgment.[10]

Al-Rāzī was a titan of Sunni scholarship, but he was not always representative of it. In this case, however, the metaphoric understanding of whitening/blackening of faces on the Day of Judgment seems to be the leading opinion. It is clearly favored by Rāghib al-Iṣfahānī (d. 502/1108) and al-Samʿānī (d. 489/1096).[11] For the Sokoto Caliph Muḥammad Bello and the modern Senegalese Tijānī master Ibrāhīm Niasse it is obvious that it is the metaphoric whiteness of their belief that whitens their faces and the metaphoric blackness of disbelief that blackens the faces of others.[12] The metaphoric reading seems to be favored (or presented as the only reading for Quran 3:106) by al-Qurṭubī, al-Qushayrī (d. 465/1072), al-Baghawī (d. 516/1122), al-Thaʿlabī (who also includes a report about the ice color of the whitened faces), al-Māwardī (d. 450/1058), al-Bayḍāwī (d. 719/1319), and al-Thaʿālabī (d. 875/1470).[13] Scholars also emphasized the disconnect between blackening on the Day of Judgment and the earthly body. Maybūdī (d. *circa* 540/1145), a Sunni scholar from Yazd who penned a monumental Quranic commentary, reminds the reader that God does not refer to "black faces" (*sūd*) or "white faces" but to faces *being* blackened (*taswaddu*) or whitened precisely because this was something that happened to people on the Day of Judgment, not how people were born in the world.[14] Of course, some scholars have disagreed. Al-Ālūsī (d. 1270/1854) suggests that it is literal and applies to the whole body, not just the face.[15] The Iraqi jurist al-Māwardī understands the blackening of faces at the birth of a daughter to be literally that one's face "turns black in color," claiming that this is the "opinion of the majority (*jumhūr*)."

Al-Māwardī's claim is anomalous, however, and not borne out by even a cursory reading of other Quranic commentaries.[16]

In fact, even when the Quran uses language that suggests the literal covering of the face by dust or darkness on the Day of Judgment, leading exegetes have still read this as figurative. In the verse "neither dust nor abasement will cover their faces [on the Day of Judgment] (*wa lā yarhaqu wujūhahum qatar wa lā dhilla*)" (Quran 10:26), the word translated here as dust (*qatar*) is just as often translated or directly glossed as darkness or blackness (*sawād*). While many commentators interpret this as the dust of trial or even the smoke belching from the fires of Hell, al-Ṭabarī (d. 310/923) understands it as immense sorrow (*ka'āba*).[17]

## THE FORGERY OF ANTIBLACK HADITHS

The Prophet's proclamation that no nation, tribe, or people has any claim to standing over another except through piety seems categorical. Indeed, if matters were as simple as the Prophet's teachings in his farewell sermon, there would be little debate over antiblackness in the Hadith corpus. But there are some Hadiths attributed to the Prophet that do denigrate Black Africans (often referred to as *zanj*), stating that they are lazy, stupid, beholden to their base appetites, and even disfigured. These include alleged Hadiths like "Don't mention Black Africans to me, for the Black African is beholden only to his stomach and genitals (*daʿūnī min al-sūdān . . .*)," "The Zanjī, when he is hungry, he steals and when he is sated, he fornicates," "The Zanjī is an ass," or, in marriage, "Beware of the Zanjī, for they are a deformed creation (*khalq mushawwah*)."[18]

These supposed sayings of the Prophet, however, do not appear in mainstay Hadith collections, such as the Sunni Six Book Hadith canon. More importantly, leading Muslim Hadith critics have insisted they are forgeries. Since at least the 1300s CE it has been an uncontroversial point in manuals of Hadith criticism that any Hadith belittling a race or ethnicity cannot come from the Prophet and must be forged or an error.[19] Though Ibn al-Jawzī (d. 597/1200) and Ibn

Qayyim al-Jawziyya (d. 751/1350) were the first to articulate this as a rule, its application can be seen even among earlier critics like Muḥammad bin Ṭāhir al-Maqdisī (d. 507/1113) and Abū Dāwūd (d. 275/889), the compiler of one of the most respected Sunni Hadith collections.[20] When Abū Dāwūd was asked about a narrator who had quoted Aisha, the Prophet's wife, as saying, "Beware of Zanj, for they were created disfigured," he replied, "Whoever narrates this, accuse them [of unreliability]."[21]

We do find such alleged Hadiths in uncritical Hadith collections and histories, such as the *Muʿjams* of al-Ṭabarānī (d. 360/971) or the works of Abū Nuʿaym al-Iṣbahānī (d. 430/1038), both prominent Hadith scholars of Isfahan. But such authors made no pretense that they considered the material in their Hadith books to be reliable. Indeed, they were criticized by noted Muslim scholars such as Ibn al-Jawzī and al-Dhahabī for misleading people by including such dubious content.[22] Aḥmad al-Ghumārī (d. 1380/1960), a remarkable Moroccan Hadith scholar who embodied the oceanic rigor of that science in the modern era, slammed a famous scholar for including these racist Hadiths in one of his collections. The best of God's creation, His noble prophet, al-Ghumārī explained, would never speak in such a way that "injures people's feelings, especially as we see among blacks those who are more noble than whites!"[23]

Some Muslim scholars pushed back against the criticism of specific Hadiths belittling Black Africans, but it is a mistake to read this as them approving of such Hadiths or defending their contents. They simply disagreed with the methodologies used by some earlier critics to prove the falsity of such Hadiths. Ibn al-Qayyim and scholars in the Sunni Hadith tradition who came after him stated *as a principle* that no Hadith belittling a nation or race could really have been something the Prophet said. By contrast, the earliest works listing forged Hadiths did not cite unacceptable meanings as proof of forgery. They demonstrated the forgery of each report by pointing to the transmitter who had erred or intentionally forged it or by identifying some break in the chain of transmission. Al-Suyūṭī (d. 911/1505) objects that this was sometimes not sufficient for invalidating *all* the Hadiths with some specific, abhorrent meaning, since this method did not account for other chains free of those problematic transmitters.[24] In his critique, however, al-Suyūṭī was not committed to defending the authenticity of Hadiths denigrating Black Africans, much less their meaning. Al-Suyūṭī himself criticizes many of these in his *three* books on the virtues of Black Africans.[25]

Other Hadiths do not explicitly demean people racialized as black, but they do cast phenotypic blackness in a negative light. These Hadiths, however, are either plainly unreliable or highly suspect and unworthy of any confidence. In two of the *Muʿjam*s of al-Ṭabarānī we find the Prophet telling a pious Ethiopian man that, in the Afterlife, "the whiteness of a black man will be seen across the distance of a thousand years in the Garden (*la-yurā bayāḍ al-aswad fī al-janna ʿalā masīrat alf ʿāmm*)." This Hadith, however, was roundly criticized by scholars as an uncorroborated addition to an already flawed narration. It is quite simply unreliable.[26]

In another Hadith attributed to the Prophet, a black man comes and asks, "O Messenger of God, I am a black man, putrid smelling (*muntin al-rīḥ*), with an ugly face and no money. If I were to fight against those [unbelieving] folks until I were killed, where would I end up?" The Prophet replies, "In the Garden." The man then fights in the path of God until he is slain. The Prophet approaches his body and says, "God has whitened (*bayyaḍa*) your face, sweetened your smell and given you great wealth." He then adds to those present, "I have seen his wife among the black-eyed beauties [of Paradise], pulling aside his woolen cloak and sliding in next to his body."[27] Although this Hadith is judged to be sound (*ṣaḥīḥ*) by the famous collector al-Ḥākim al-Naysābūrī (d. 405/1014), it appears only in his Hadith collection, which came along very late in the process of collecting and authenticating Hadiths. Not only have Sunni Hadith scholars long been wary of al-Ḥākim's seal of approval (see Appendix I), material attributed to the Prophet that appears first and only in the 1000s CE is highly suspect. Why was it not recorded in the mainstay Sunni Hadith collections of the 800s CE or the massive and totally uncritical collections of scholars like al-Ṭabarānī in the 900s? It is too likely that it simply was not there.

Al-Ṭabarānī never claimed the contents of his collections were reliable. But al-Ḥākim did. Why would either of these scholars include in their works reports that were demeaning to blackness as a somatic trait? As we will see in Chapter 7, this is partially because of how blackness and whiteness as a paired spiritual metaphor mixed with somatic blackness and whiteness in the Sufi tradition. But the question can be asked even more forcefully. Despite their frequently impugning alleged Hadiths dismissing Black Africans as appetitive and hypersexual, many leading Muslim scholars from the 1000s CE onwards treated these Hadiths as unproblematic. For example, Imam al-Shāfiʿī (d. 204/820) is described as using the alleged Hadith describing Black Africans as prone to theft and fornication to predict that a Black African slave had been up to no good. I think it is clear that such attributions to al-Shāfiʿī are as unreliable as the alleged Hadith itself (see Appendix I). But several prominent biographers of that seminal jurist include this vignette as evidence of al-Shāfiʿī's perspicacity. It is troubling that the scholars who made such attributions or repeated them found nothing objectionable about the ideas they were reporting. Sadly, as we saw with the rise of antiblackness in Islamic thought, antiblack sentiment affected even respected Muslim scholars.

## RAISIN-HEADED: THE QUESTION OF ANTIBLACK RACISM IN THE SUNNA, PART ONE

In 30/650 CE, a slave placed in charge of wealth collected in charity visited the famous ascetic Companion Abū Dharr (d. 32/652–3) at his home in Rabadha, a remote station on the road from Mecca to Iraq. When prayer time came, the slave, an Ethiopian named Mujāshiʿ, said, "Go ahead [and lead the prayer], O Abū Dharr." The elderly Companion replied, "No, you go ahead, for the Messenger of God (s) said to me, 'Listen and obey, even if the one placed in charge over you is a mutilated slave (*ʿabd mujaddaʿ*).' You are a slave, though not mutilated." In another, probably more accurate report of the encounter, Abū Dharr replies by citing a version of the Hadith with the wording "even if the one placed in charge of you is an Ethiopian slave," then adding, "And you are an Ethiopian slave."[28]

Another version of the Hadith cited by Abū Dharr has the Prophet command, "Listen to and obey [your commander], even if the one put in charge of you is an Ethiopian slave whose head is a like a raisin."[29] Unlike the antiblack Hadiths discussed so far, both this Hadith overall and the specific narration with the raisin simile have been authenticated by Islam's leading scholars of Hadith criticism. The version with the raisin simile appears in the most esteemed collection of Hadith in Sunni Islam, the *Ṣaḥīḥ* of al-Bukhārī (d. 256/870). It is noteworthy that the most common – and likely the most reliable – narrations of this Hadith, including those based on Abū Dharr's own recollection, do not contain the raisin simile.[30] But, in any case, no scholar in the premodern period identified anything unacceptable about the Hadith overall or the raisin simile in particular, and I know of no respected Muslim scholar of Hadith who has done so in the modern period either.

The plain meaning of this Hadith is clear and uncontested. By conjuring the hyperbolic image of the person at the bottom of Arabian social hierarchy, the Prophet makes it clear that one must obey the commander placed in charge even if they are the lowest of the low. Another early report also uses this hyperbole. When the early Basran scholar Ibn Sīrīn (d. 110/728) was asked by apparently frustrated students about a person he was narrating Hadiths to, he replied that, "even if he were a man from the Zanj, he would be equal to [my own son] ʿAbdallāh in this matter."[31]

The 'Hadith of the Raisin' has been understood as conveying two lessons. At the moral level, as Ibn Taymiyya explains succinctly, it shows that a person's standing is determined by their piety and faith.[32] Its more frequently cited significance, however, is practical. The Hadith's immediate context suggests the specific duty to obey commanders when out on campaign, but the Hadith has been understood as applying to authorities in the civilian government as well. Of course, the Hadith of the Raisin must be understood in the context of other Hadiths in which the Prophet makes clear that obedience is only owed "in that which is right" and that a Muslim cannot obey a person ordering them to disobey the Creator. One narration of the Raisin Hadith includes the added condition ". . . as long as he establishes among you the Book of God."[33]

What concerns us here, however, is this Hadith's depiction of blackness, in particular the use of a raisin as a simile for the Ethiopian's head. Muslim scholars' interpretation of this aspect of the Hadith seems to have gone through two stages. Until the mid 1200s CE, the raisin simile was read as a straightforward imagery of how an Ethiopian looked (at least in the eyes of scholars from Andalusia to Central Asia). After the mid 1200s CE, commentaries on the raisin simile took on a much more contemptuous tone.

Early commentaries by the Persian al-Khaṭṭābī (d. 386/996) and the Andalusian Ibn Baṭṭāl (d.449/1057) do not pay much attention to the raisin simile, treating it as self-evident. Another Andalusian, the famous Qāḍī ʿIyāḍ (d. 544/1149), explains it as describing the slave's blackness, like the dark color of a raisin, and the texture of his coiled hair, which is like the wrinkled texture of the raisin. Qāḍī ʿIyāḍ describes this texture as "peppercorny" (*tafalful*), wording that would be repeated often by later scholars. If one pictures peppercorns packed next to one another on a flat surface, the image is similar to tightly coiled hair (the French ethnographer Dominique Champault similarly described the hair of black inhabitants of a Saharan oasis as "like peppercorn").[34] The Baghdad scholar and vizier Ibn Hubayra (d. 560/1165) holds that the simile is based on the blackness of the Ethiopian's head and its "diminutiveness" (*qamā'atihi*).[35] Another Baghdad Ḥanbalī, Ibn al-Jawzī, simply explains it as a reference to how Ethiopians are known to have small heads.[36] Ibn al-Munayyir (d. 683/1284), a judge and preacher in Alexandria, explains that the Prophet chose this image because the Ethiopian slave was "the least likely of people to be obeyed." This required summoning the image "of a non-Arab, new convert to Islam," he explained, who would have had very little knowledge of the religion.[37]

With the influential Damascene scholar al-Nawawī (d. 676/1277) and later the Iraqi scholar al-Ṭībī (d. 743/1342), we see the readings of the raisin simile become explicitly pejorative. In addition to the image of smallness, black color, and tightly coiled hair, the comparison with a raisin serves to "demean the standing of the slave" (*taḥqīran li-sha'nihi*).[38] The wording of the Baghdad scholar al-Kirmānī (d. 786/1384) in his commentary on *Ṣaḥīḥ al-Bukhārī* would prove influential and would later be reaffirmed by the Cairene Ibn Ḥajar (d. 852/1449) in his definitive commentary on the *Ṣaḥīḥ*.[39] Ibn Ḥajar, however, includes two discussions of the Hadith with two very different tones. In his commentary on the Hadith in the chapter on leading prayer, he focuses on physical description without mentioning any pejorative element. It is a simile based on "the smallness of his head, and that is known regarding Ethiopians. And it is said: due to his blackness, or the shortness of his hair and its likeness to peppercorns." In the chapter on leadership in the *Ṣaḥīḥ*, Ibn Ḥajar focuses much more on the pejorative dimension. There he discusses that the Prophet may have chosen this simile due to the raisin's wrinkliness and because Ethiopian hair is black. But more it is "a representation (*tamthīl*) of [the Ethiopian slave's] demeaned standing (*ḥaqāra*), ugliness (*bashāʿat al-ṣūra*), and unimportance (*ʿadam al-iʿtidād bihā*)."[40] Interestingly, it is this second, loaded discussion that would set the course for commentary on this Hadith in subsequent centuries.[41] Later on, the Indian-born scholar of the Hejaz, Abū al-Ḥasan al-Sindī (d. 1138/1726), would add another level of contempt: the raisin simile is a sign of this hypothetical slave's "low intelligence and great stupidity."[42]

Though I cannot offer a definitive answer, the question of whether or how this Hadith, particularly its raisin simile, is antiblack can be approached via the three general readings offered by Muslim commentators. In the first reading, which uses the raisin simile simply to describe skin color and hair texture, the question of antiblackness is one of description versus objectification. Is it appropriate to invoke any sort of imagery, particularly mundane imagery, to describe a Black African phenotype? Or is such description itself an act of objectification? This is redolent of the controversy around the work of the award-winning British author Kate Clanchy, whose 2019 memoir caused an uproar because it described a student as having "chocolate-coloured skin."[43]

The second reading involves the use of imagery that seems diminishing or demeaning. If one is going to compare a person's head to something, a raisin does not seem like a complimentary choice. The African-American Muslim scholar Dawud Walid has rejected this impression as privileging modern Western sensibilities. He argues that raisins were not objects of particular contempt for Arabs of the Prophet's time, nor should we interpret them as such.[44] While some Muslim scholars have understood the raisin simile as conveying the image of color and texture only, for others it implies size as well. In this case, reading the raisin simile as inoffensive would require accepting that one could inoffensively describe a particular people or phenotype as having noticeably small heads. This is certainly how many Muslim scholars, even before the post-1200s turn to pejoratives, understood the simile. Books of physiognomy that Muslims wrote along the same lines as their Greco-Roman predecessors suggest that a small head could have been interpreted in a number of ways, positive and negative. Although a large head generally connoted intelligence and a small head the opposite, the actual meaning of head size depended on its size relative to other body parts. A small head with a large chest and neck, for example, indicated courage and strength, while a large head with a small chest suggested clumsiness.[45]

That there are variations in somatic features, such as average height, between regions is uncontroversial.[46] Inquiring into possible differences in skull size between various regions or populations, however, is *very* controversial. In the West, the association of measuring skull sizes (craniometry) with scientific racism, racist claims about superior and inferior intelligence, and discredited 'sciences' like phrenology has rendered this issue too toxic for any useful investigation.[47] But there is no reason to extend this understandable, contemporary suspicion anachronistically to readers and speakers in the distant past, particularly to the Prophet and his immediate context. With the exception of al-Sindī, Muslim scholars do not seem to have read the raisin simile as an allusion to stupidity. The pre-1200s readings by Muslim scholars simply understood it as a feature of a certain somatic type. It could well have been held as an uncontroversial fact by Arabs in the seventh century that Ethiopians had smaller, darker, and curlier-haired heads than Arabs.

The third reading, however, is that this Hadith intended to create an unambiguously negative image. Post 1200s CE, Hadith commentaries have understood the raisin simile as communicating a Black African's lowliness and ugliness and have read the simile as part of a larger image of the demeaned status of the slave, a status that this reading conflated with phenotypical blackness. This reading need not assume malicious intent on the part of the Prophet (in fact, any Muslim scholar would almost certainly revolt in horror at that idea). In uttering these words, the Prophet may only have intended to refer to tropes well known in his context, namely that a Black African slave (particularly a mutilated one) stood on the lowest rung of the social ladder. The image was invoked not to demean a segment of society but in order to make the point clearly about obedience to commanders. But doesn't such a reference reinforce this social hierarchy? The post-1200s commentaries on this Hadith were merely explaining its hyperbolic social image in clearer terms. But in referring to and explaining that brutal social reality, weren't they legitimizing it?

The Hadith of the Raisin in general and this third reading in particular raise important questions about the function and purpose of scripture and its interpretation. Much like the differing schools of thought on defining racism today, allegations of antiblackness in this Hadith seem to turn on how one weighs the importance of three elements: the speaker's intention, their cultural context, and the substantive effect of their words. Mirroring the predominance of what I described as the substantive definition of racism (i.e., racism is whatever contributes to racial inequity), many today would likely judge even the first, most innocuous reading of the raisin simile to be the objectification of a person racialized as black by someone not racialized as black and in a position of power. As one critic of Clanchy's above-mentioned book put it, "no one likes being described as 'chocolate-coloured' . . .," particularly by a person from the racial class that has long objectified non-White bodies for its own empowerment.[48]

From the perspective of the Islamic hermeneutical tradition, however, intent is key in determining the meaning of a text, particularly a normative one. Because the intent of the Lawgiver (God and, by His willed extension, the Prophet) can only be demonstrably known through the texts of revelation, Muslim scholars have long ruminated on how to mine scripture for its intended meaning. The revelation of the Quran and the Prophet's inspired instruction in Hadiths take the form of human language, specifically the Arabic of the Hejaz in the seventh century. As such, Muslim exegetes concluded that, though it in no way exhausts the richness potential in the Quran and the Prophetic teachings, the first step in determining their intended meaning is to read them through the conventions of language and rhetoric prevalent in their immediate contexts. As the contemporary Muslim theologian Saʿīd Fūda phrases it, "The presumption is that we interpret language according to the meanings predominant among its audience (*al-aṣl an naḥmila al-alfāẓ ʿalā al-maʿānī al-shāʾiʿa bayn al-mukhāṭabīn*)."[49]

How was the Hadith of the Raisin received by those who first heard it? The setting of Abū Dharr's homestead at Rabadha affords a glimpse. It was there that this early convert to Islam and prominent Companion had been seen sitting next to his slave, both of them wearing the same clothing. It was then that he had explained to his visitors that the Prophet had once upbraided him for mocking a slave for his descent and instructed him on the ethical treatment of slaves as one's brothers. In accounts of Abū Dharr at Rabadha, he is doing errands with his slaves. He tells his visitors that his property consists of his sheep and camels, one herd tended by his female slave, the other by his male slave. The male slave will be set free when the new year comes. The caliph has assigned an Ethiopian slave, Mujāshiʿ, to oversee the massive herds of camels collected in charity and pastured at Rabadha, and Abū Dharr praises Mujāshiʿ for his generosity.[50] When prayer time comes and Mujāshiʿ is present, he asks the elderly Abū Dharr to lead them all in prayer. Abū Dharr replies that it is the government representative's place to lead, not his. This is what the Prophet had taught, even if the person was a mutilated or Ethiopian slave. "You are a slave, though not mutilated," adds Abū Dharr in one account. Was he making a joke about how the Hadith, which applied bizarrely well to their situation, did not *quite* apply completely? "You are an Ethiopian slave," he says in another. Was there something special in a moment of living out a hypothetical hyperbole spoken by the figure that the two men, one a venerable early Muslim, free but civilian, the other a representative of the powerful new Muslim empire but a slave, both revered as God's last messenger?

How did Mujāshiʿ feel when he heard this Hadith? We have no way of knowing. In the centuries since, how have scholars who likely shared a Black African phenotype understood this Hadith and its raisin simile? The scholars whose commentaries we have reviewed so far have hailed from the Mediterranean and Persianate realms. None, that I am aware, would have been racialized as black by their own or modern standards. Al-Suyūṭī may offer a useful perspective. Though he hailed from upper Egypt and had a Circassian mother, he doted on his Ethiopian concubine, who bore him a son. In his commentary on *Ṣaḥīḥ al-Bukhārī*, al-Suyūṭī replicates Ibn Ḥajar's first, relatively neutral gloss about head size, color, and hair texture, and he does not mention the pejorative elements.[51] Unfortunately, finding discussions from Black African scholars on this Hadith has been challenging. Despite their extensive study of major Hadith collections, scholars from the otherwise intellectually dynamic world of West African Islam do not seem to have composed commentaries on them.[52]

But prominent African scholars have *deployed* the Hadith of the Raisin in their writings. And they betray no sense of discomfort with its imagery. ʿUthmān bin Fūdī (Usman dan Fodio, d. 1232/1817), the Fulani founder of the Sokoto Caliphate, cited versions of this Hadith on two occasions when dealing with the question of heeding commanders or allegiance to unjust rulers. One version contains the wording "black" and the other "Ethiopian," but in neither case does the caliph give comment or evince any concern.[53] His son and successor, Shaykh Muḥammad Bello (d. 1253/1837) cited this Hadith as well, including its raisin simile, in a letter he wrote to the commanders of his forces. He felt no need to explain or qualify it.[54]

One could theorize, perhaps, that the Sokoto leaders found nothing askance in the raisin simile because they were Fulani, an ethnic group that has sometimes considered itself (and been seen by some European explorers as) non-*sūdān* (see Appendix III). But we find exactly the same non-response in the work of a scholar who was actually Ethiopian and identified as such: the late Ethiopian Hadith scholar Shaykh Muḥammad Amīn al-Hararī (d. 1441/2019). In his massive commentary on *Ṣaḥīḥ Muslim*, al-Hararī simply copied al-Nawawī's explanation of the Hadith, saying all the images it invoked, from slavery to mutilation and blackness, serve to drive home the slave's "utmost lowness." "For a slave is low (*khasīs*) by custom (*fī al-ʿāda*)," al-Hararī explains. "And his blackness is another deficiency (*naqṣ*). His mutilation yet another, and in another Hadith [we read] that his head is like a raisin . . ." Elsewhere al-Hararī remarks that the adjective 'Ethiopian' was added "to increase his deficiency by his blackness."[55] Al-Hararī does add one unique insight to al-Nawawī's commentary. "The intended meaning is not that all Ethiopians were slaves, for [Ethiopia] was an ancient state from which Rome and Persia would learn statecraft," he explains, "to the point that Ethiopia gained control of Egypt and Yemen." He also says that, in the Prophet's day, Ethiopians would enslave children from other African communities and sell them to the Arabs.[56] Does this mean that the 'Ethiopian' slaves whose image the Hadith refers to were actually not Ethiopians at all but actually other East Africans? If this is a subtle effort on al-Hararī's part to rehabilitate Ethiopians' image, it is very subtle indeed. At every point at which he addresses the raisin image he does so without the slightest hint of discomfort or any adjustment to prior commentaries.

Uncomfortable as it might make some, the Quran and the Prophet's teachings draw on the lexicon of imagery and cultural tropes that permeated their Arabian world and, in fact, the premodern world more generally. This was not to endorse a resonant image but to use it to communicate. The Quran, for example, repeatedly invokes the disabilities of blindness and deafness in contrasting those who open themselves to guidance with those who stubbornly refuse it. "Say: Are the blind man and the one who can see equal? Will you all not then ponder?" (6:50), and "The parable of the two groups is like that of the blind and the deaf and then one who sees and one who hears. Are the two groups equal? Will you all not then take heed?" (11:24). Such images were not meant as indictments of the blind or deaf, nor did Muslim scholars receive them as such.

In an online discussion of the Hadith of the Raisin, a young British Muslim of West African descent, very active in opposing antiblack racism, plainly denied that the Prophet could have uttered the raisin simile. He may be right, as the raisin simile appears in an isolated and uncorroborated version of the Hadith. But our reactions reveal more about our sensitivities and worries about the demon of racism than about the meaning of the Prophet's words as he intended them and as they were heard for many centuries, from Central Asia to West Africa. If the raisin simile speaks to many today with what seems like at least some level of antiblack sentiment, this seems to have been wholly unremarkable to premodern Muslim scholars who were black themselves.

## TWO FOR ONE: THE QUESTION OF ANTIBLACK RACISM IN THE SUNNA, PART TWO

Accusations that Islam is inherently antiblack often mention a Hadith found in *Ṣaḥīḥ Muslim* and other collections that recounts a Muslim man coming to pledge allegiance to the Prophet and expressing his desire to emigrate to Medina. The Prophet did not know that the man was a slave. "Then his owner came seeking him," the Hadith continues, "and the Prophet (s) said to him, 'Sell him to me,' so he bought him with two black slaves. And the Prophet (s) did not take the pledge of allegiance from anyone after that without first asking if they were a slave."[57]

Like the Hadith of the Raisin, this Hadith has long been considered by Muslim scholars to be a sound and unproblematic attribution to the Prophet. It received a good deal of attention from jurists, but not for the reasons we might expect. It interested them first and foremost because it seems to indicate that one can exchange one item of a specific type of good (a slave in this case) for two of that specific good. This seemed to violate the legal principle that, when exchanging like for like, the items had to be of the same quantity (based on a famous Hadith).[58] One could not exchange one bushel of wheat for two, for example, or one gold coin for two (if one introduces a delay in payment, one can see how this could be a way of charging interest). Jurists saw the Hadith of the Prophet buying one slave with two slaves as a basis for analogizing to other living creatures being transacted. As a result, they agreed that animals were not subject to the like-for-like requirement; one could trade one (presumably great) horse for two (presumably not so great) horses.

The Hadith also attracted attention because it raised questions about the priority given to the religion of a slave compared to the property right of their owner as well as to the obligations that a Muslim polity has towards liberating Muslim slaves. What complicated all this was that the Hadith does not specify the religion of the slave's owner or the religions of the two slaves exchanged for him. There were several possibilities, each of which raised legal questions:

1. The slave owner was not Muslim but the two black slaves were. This would not be possible, jurists agreed, because Muslims could not be surrendered as slaves to non-Muslims.[59]
2. The slave owner was not Muslim and neither were the two black slaves. This would make sense, since jurists agreed that, if the slaves of the enemy fled their camp to join the Muslims, the Muslims should accept them and not return them. This is what the Prophet had done when his forces had besieged the town of Taif near Mecca. He had offered refuge to any slaves who abandoned the town and did not return them to their former owners after Taif surrendered.[60] And, in this Hadith, this seems to be what the Prophet was doing in refusing to return the Muslim slave.

   But several objections were raised to this possibility. First, in the case of Taif, the Prophet had not offered any compensation to the non-Muslim enemies from whose camp the slaves had fled. This suggests that the owner of the Muslim slave in the Hadith under discussion here had to be Muslim himself, since otherwise there would be no reason for the Prophet to compensate him for his loss. The great Indian scholar Anwar Shāh Kashmīrī (d. 1352/1933) raised another objection. A non-Muslim cannot legally own a Muslim according to the Shariah. If the slave owner were non-Muslim, then, by merely converting to Islam, the slave would have freed himself. And, if the slave were free because he had converted to Islam, then why did the Prophet buy him? It is possible, Kashmīrī suggests, that the non-Muslim owner was from a tribe that was allied with the Prophet even if the owner or maybe his whole tribe were not Muslim. In this case, the Prophet might have been trying to placate an ally for his loss.[61]

3. The slave owner was Muslim and the two black slaves were Muslim as well. In this case, one would assume that the Muslim owner lived outside Medina, since the Muslim slave had come to emigrate to Medina and live in the Prophet's community. The Prophet was trying to help the Muslim slave achieve his goal. Since his owner was Muslim, there were no communal lines that, if the slave crossed them, he would automatically gain his freedom as he would by embracing Islam. Thus, the Prophet paid his owner to release him. But in this case, if we assume the two black slaves were also Muslim, it hardly seems fair that the Prophet would send them to live outside of the City of the Messenger of God so that another Muslim could come live there.
4. The most likely case: the slave owner was Muslim and the two black slaves were <u>not</u> Muslim. This situation seems the most probable, since the Prophet would not be disadvantaging two unbelieving slaves by sending them away from Medina. It is not at all unlikely that the Prophet had non-Muslim slaves working for him or other Muslims in Medina, since one of his personal servants was a Jewish boy.[62]

Assuming that the two black slaves were non-Muslim helps us understand the dynamics at play in this Hadith. In Arabia at the time of the Prophet, and at least for the two or three generations after his death, Black African slaves seem to have generally had less market value than Arab slaves or slaves from areas to the north, such as Egypt, Persia, Iraq, etc. The vaunted Basran master of the Quran and Arabic, Abū ʿAmr bin al-ʿAlā' (d. *circa* 155/770), seems to make it clear that white (*abyaḍ*) slaves cost more than Black African ones. And the Medinan jurist Mālik (d. 179/796) also acknowledged that there were different price ranges for 'red' (*ḥamrān*) (i.e., Persian, Greek, Aramaic-speaking, etc.) and Black African (*sūdān*) slaves in Medina during the mid to late 700s CE.[63]

But, again, we should not assume that it was race or phenotype that was being valued here. Just as blackness was a proxy for outsider status in a tribal society, so geographic origin was often seen as overlapping with valued skills. Black African slaves were not seen as possessing the skills that the early Muslims needed. Mālik discusses how there was no problem with trading a slave who spoke Arabic and had commercial experience for several Ethiopian slaves "or several slaves of any other race who are not his equal in fluency, commercial expertise, judgment, and skill."[64] It is not the slaves' ethnic background that is being evaluated here. It is their skills and command of Arabic. But those features were associated with specific ethnic backgrounds.

Before the Muslim conquest of the Middle East, the largest ethnolinguistic group of slaves in Arabia was other Arabs captured in raids, followed by Ethiopians and Persians. After the early Islamic conquests, they were mostly Arabic-, Aramaic-, Greek-, and Persian-speaking captives from conquered Byzantine and Persian lands. In the period of the early Islamic conquests, Black African slaves came from a region that was not the commercial and political focus of Muslim life and society. The first Muslim 'emigration' (*hijra*) during the early years of the Prophet's mission had been to Ethiopia. After the early Islamic conquests, however, energy and attention shifted to the north. Within three decades of the Prophet's death, the capital of the Muslim state had moved from Medina to Kufa in Iraq, then to Damascus five years later. A century later it moved to the new city of Baghdad. 'Red' and 'white' slaves would be people from the new realms of Muslims' commercial and political future. They were either Arabs, perhaps from tribes in Syria, Berbers, and Aramaic- or

Persian-speaking captives. In the early years of the Muslim conquests after the Prophet's death, a man from an Arab tribe is described as "red, resembling the *mawālī* [i.e., new, non-Arab converts to Islam in Syria, Egypt, Iraq, and Iran]."[65]

We must also not be misled by the stereotype of slaves as silent and unskilled labor working in mines or fields. Especially in the Roman and Near Eastern world, slaves could be highly skilled and work as managers and commercial agents for their owners. This was clear even in the comparatively poor and marginal world of the Hejaz during the Prophet's time. The first *minbar* (pulpit) in Islam was crafted for the Prophet by a slave who was a skilled carpenter and whose female owner assigned him this task.[66] Slaves could be investments that yielded returns in other, more abusive ways as well. The Quran condemns the practice of prostituting out female slaves to enrich their owners, as the Medinan hypocrite ʿAbdallāh bin Ubayy had done.[67]

What is important for our purposes is not that some slaves were valued more than others because of their skills. It is that, at least in the Hejaz, the economy of slave labor in the early Islamic period assumed that Ethiopian slaves did not speak Arabic or have the commercial experience that buyers valued. Moreover, as al-Jāḥiẓ noted in the mid 800s CE, those slaves that Muslims has been acquiring via trade from India seemed to be relatively unskilled. They did not come from the segments of Indian society learned in the arts, sciences and crafts that Muslims knew flourished there.[68] Muslims had much more immediate access, on the other hand, to the cultural capital and skills of the Near Eastern populations they ruled directly and abutted immediately. The distant lands of Africa south of the Sahara are analogous to India in al-Jāḥiẓ's observation. Their inhabitants also had their skills and strengths. Al-Jāḥiẓ applauds Ethiopians for their eloquence, for example.[69] Yet the trope of the Zanjī slave as linguistically incapable suggests that, if al-Jāḥiẓ's praise was not simply a literary conceit imagined by Arabs musing about far-off places, the individuals brought as slaves from East Africa and south of the Sahara were not the best representatives of the skills and crafts of those lands.

The potential of enslaved Persian-, Greek-, and Aramaic-speaking people to help Arab Muslims integrate into the wider Mediterranean and Persian world is borne out when we realize that it was these slaves and their descendants who formed the backbone of early Islamic scholarship and administration. There were many early Muslim scholars who were Arab, including black Arabs of African descent like ʿAṭāʾ bin Abī Rabāḥ (d. 114/732) of Mecca, Saʿīd bin Jubayr (d. 95/713–4) of Kufa, and Yazīd bin Abī Ḥabīb (d. 128/745), whose father had been a Nubian slave acquired by the Muslim conquerors of Egypt.[70] But it was Persian, Aramaic-speaking, Berber, Turkic, and even Indian slaves and their offspring who would emerge as the foundation of early Islamic scholarship and statecraft. Their ranks are daunting. An easily accessible array includes leading scholars of the second generation of Muslims, such as al-Ḥasan al-Baṣrī (d. 110/728, Persian), Ibn Sīrīn (d. 110/728, Persian), Ṭāwūs (d. 106/724–5, Persian), Nāfiʿ (d. 117–20/735–8, Berber or Persian), and Makḥūl (d. 113/731, possibly Indian). We find also important early jurists and Hadith transmitters in the following generation, like Ibn Jurayj (d. 150/767, Egyptian or Syriac), al-Aʿmash (d. 148/764–5, Persian), Maʿmar bin Rāshid (d. 153/770, probably Persian), Ibn Isḥāq (d. 150/767, Persian), and Ibn al-Mubārak (d. 181/797, Byzantine and Persian).[71]

The association of certain skills or strengths with specific ethnic backgrounds would only grow more intricate as the centuries passed, becoming common knowledge in every area of Islamic civilization, among Muslims, Christians, Jews, and others alike. Sometimes these associations rested on sound experience, such as how young Turkic men made valuable soldiers. Many of them had, after all, grown up in a lifestyle in which a mastery of mounted archery gave them an edge in warfare. Other associations were more superficial, such as the association of Circassian women with beauty. And some were stereotypes, like Greek slaves being trustworthy and loyal.[72] Which linguistic or ethnic background was preferred for a specific job often changed based on time and place. Over the centuries, for example, Ḥanafī jurists commented on what kind of *waṣīf* (a slave woman who served as a personal handmaiden) a bride could ask for as part of her dowry (*mahr*). Living in Iraq in the mid 700s CE, Abū Ḥanīfa (d. 150/767) had said that the most in-demand maid was 'white' (*abyaḍ*), which likely meant anyone from Persia, Byzantium, or the Slavic or European lands beyond. For al-Sarakhsī (d. 490/1096), writing in the Ferghana Valley of Central Asia in the late 1000s CE, the most expensive *waṣīf* was Turkic. Al-Kāsānī (d. 587/1189), who hailed from Ferghana but settled in Aleppo, states that it was a woman from Byzantine lands (*rūmī*).[73]

# 7

## Antiblackness, Sufism, and Veneration of the Prophet

Before God, all souls are white.

Victor Hugo (d. 1885), in a letter to a Haitian correspondent

The first person to enter the Garden will be a black slave named ʿAbbūd.

Hadith of the Prophet, of dubious reliability.[1]

This quote from Victor Hugo appears in an otherwise stellar book on how blackness was perceived in ancient Rome. The author deploys it as a *coup de grace* to illustrate the effortless civilizational supremacy felt by Victorians, born of an utter surety that everything good was necessarily white, including human souls. The quote, however, is misleading. In his response to Monsieur Heurtelou, the Black Haitian editor of the country's *Le Progres* journal and a man for whom he expresses profound respect, Hugo does indeed write, "Before God, all souls are white." Yet the preceding line reads, "There are not on the earth whites or blacks. There are souls. You are one of them."[2] Hugo is not transposing onto the Hereafter his certainty about the earthly superiority of whites over blacks, comforting his correspondent with the good tidings that he will also be white one day. Quite the opposite, Hugo is denying the significance of black and white phenotypes in this world. All humans are souls. True, Hugo states all souls are white before God. But this cannot be the somatic whiteness that he has just denied exists. It is the whiteness of the empyrean realm, of purity and goodness.

It has been argued that Hugo, a vocal opponent of American slavery, had problematic views on race because his abolitionism centered the perspective of Eurocentric romanticism as opposed to that of Africans themselves. Of more concern to us here is what Timothy Raser argues is Hugo's unquestioned assumption about the positive valence and "aesthetic value" of whiteness.[3] If Hugo was wrong in assuming a positive metaphoric valence for whiteness, however, then his was an error shared by an enormous swath of world languages, including from Africa south of the Sahara.

We easily misread Hugo because antiblack racism has been so pervasive in the U.S., and to some extent in the global West more broadly, that many are justifiably suspicious of how blackness and whiteness are deployed even at the basic level of language. This has led some to argue, either in effect or explicitly, that one cannot disentangle blackness and whiteness as metaphor from blackness and whiteness as somatic or racial descriptors. In practice, the two bleed into one another, with the metaphoric subordination of blackness serving to reinforce a racial hierarchy. In 2020 numerous American tech companies suggested replacing industry terms like blacklist and whitelist (lists of who has or does not have access to programs under development) with allow/deny lists to avoid racial overtones.[4] Some women of color publicly called on dictionaries to rectify the colexification of black as a somatic descriptor with its well-known, negative figurative meanings.

Whatever is appropriate for issues of language and race today, however, collapsing the categories of metaphor and color descriptor or ignoring how they could interact in the Islamic tradition clumsily imposes a particular modern perspective on times and peoples with their own views of the world. In the case of Sufism, the Islamic mystical tradition, the metaphor of black and white as bad/good, sinful/righteous, damned/felicitous proceeds from the same starting point we found in the Quran: the metaphor is distinct from the somatic description of skin tone and phenotype. But in the Sufi tradition, the black-and-white metaphor and physical description *are* blended in imagery or narrative. When this occurs, the physical becomes symbolic. The Black African often appears as ʿAbbūd does in the above Hadith: a hyperbolic image of the saint as the ideal 'slave of God.' In other Sufi settings, somatic blackness works as a metonym symbolizing man's earthly state, while lunar whiteness represents transcendence and reaching towards the divine.

In later centuries in the Mediterranean and Persianate Islamic world, blackness and whiteness as metaphor and blackness and whiteness as somatic descriptors are noticeably blended in a way that merits our suspicion. This is particularly noticeable in texts used in the veneration of the Prophet. But this conflation is not representative of Islamic mystical expression or the profound veneration of the Prophet so characteristic of Sufism. The pious tradition among Muslims south of the Sahara, for example, veered away from what had become a precarious language of blackness in the Mediterranean Middle East in favor of emphasizing a language of luminosity.

Blackness also appears in the legal dimension of venerating the Prophet, with influential scholars asserting that describing the Prophet as black was a serious offense. Although this opinion clearly emerges from a context in which antiblackness had become endemic, prominent scholars reiterated that such prejudice and aesthetic preferences were mere matters of custom that would not apply in many regions.

## CASUAL ANTIBLACKNESS, OR BLACK AS HUMAN?

The famous Muslim mystic Jalal al-Din Rumi (d. 672/1273) is one of the best-selling poets in the English-speaking world (in liberal translation). For those who even know Rumi was Muslim at all, they certainly don't expect his famous *Masnavī* poem to include anything controversial. But we find in the long diwan the story of a caravan passing through the desert. A Black African slave accompanying it is sent out for water. When the Prophet miraculously appears before him, the slave attains true pious understanding, and his face then becomes "white like the full moon" when the Prophet touches his cheek.[5]

This story is not unique. The Egyptian Sufi Dhū al-Nūn (d. 246/861) met a Black African in the wilderness who possessed a true grasp of divine unity. Whenever he uttered a remembrance of God his blackness would vanish, and his face would become "like the halo of the moon."[6] In the story at the beginning of this book we encountered the famous early scholar Mālik bin Dīnār as he realized that a humble Black African slave was actually a saint who, alone among all the pious Muslims of Basra, was able to end a drought with his prayers. Mālik recounts how, when the saint died, "the blackness disappeared, and his face had become like the moon."[7] Such encounters were either not isolated occurrences or took on a life of their own as a trope in devotional writings. In one report, a famous early Muslim scholar, Muḥammad bin al-Munkadir (d. 130–1/747–9), encounters a Black African saint in Medina whose prayer (again) saves the city from drought. And a story of Ibn al-Mubārak (d. 181/797) meeting a Black African slave saint in Mecca closely resembles Mālik bin Dīnār's account, although neither of these latter two narrations include the saints' countenances whitening.[8]

To be sure, none of these scholars had any doubt that it was a person's piety that determined their station, not their race. Dhū al-Nūn's father was Nubian. Mālik bin Dīnār actually bought the slave saint from his owner in order to free him and act as *his* servant and be *his* disciple. Ibn al-Mubārak's father had been a slave, and he spoke to the slave saint whose freedom he had just purchased with the etiquette due a social better. Rumi turned his back on society to follow a penniless dervish whom he realized possessed the true keys to closeness to God. He saw all colors as clouds that obscured the primordial state of "without color (*bīrangī*), which is the moon."[9]

But why would a pious scholar like Rumi include such a story? Why would Ibn al-Jawzī, whose collection of Sufi biographies includes several such reports but who also wrote a thick tome defending the virtues of Black Africans? Aren't such stories transparently antiblack and objectionable? I think an honest and accurate answer to this question forces us into a very uncomfortable position, skating well over the line into what we would label in the present day as apologetics for antiblack racism. But I see this as inevitable if we are to take both the pious convictions of a sage like Rumi and his words themselves seriously. Mālik bin Dīnār was willing to become the disciple of a black slave. If we as individuals would not be willing to subordinate ourselves to whomever the basest person in our society is, we should perhaps extend charity to someone like Mālik bin Dīnār and assume he was neither careless nor trying to be insulting when he described the 'blackness' leaving the slave saint's face, which became like the moon. How then do we understand these episodes?

First, we should remember that the Black African slaves in these stories did not transform into White people, like the Semitic Jesus son of Mary becoming the blond-haired, blue-eyed Aryan of so many Western paintings, portrayed by the Swedish Max von Sydow in *The Greatest Story Ever Told* (1965). This is not the seventeenth-century French engraving of the Ethiopian literally emerging from the baptismal font looking like a cherubic White youth. These saints' color vanished and they became like the moon.

The Sufi path aims at spiritual transformation through discipline, worship, moral rectitude, and grasping the truth of God. It seeks to transcend the forms of this earthly world and rise upwards. In the vocabulary of the Islamic mystical tradition, the moon represented beauty visible in this immanent world but also reflecting the transcendent realm beyond. The moon represents the Prophet Muhammad. And in mystical cosmology it is the boundary of this lower world, beyond which lie the unchanging heavens and the transcendence of divine Reality.[10] If this was the end of the Sufi path, its metaphoric beginning was the black slave. This figure was not only the lowest rung of the earthly order of the medieval Near East, but the darkness of earth is the material origin of humanity. One explanation for the name *Ādam*, which as an adjective as opposed to a proper name generally means very dark colored, is the darkness (*udma*) of the earth from which humanity was formed (see Appendix VI).

In the stories of Rumi, Dhū al-Nūn, and Mālik bin Dīnār, the Black African slave represents the human as the slave of God, and his transformation into lunar brilliance is a metaphor of transcendence phrased as physical change. It charts the possibility of humans drawing closer to their Creator. This theme of somatic color in the transcendence of form appears in a Shiite account describing one of the disciples of Imam Muḥammad al-Bāqir (d. *circa* 114/732) meeting him for the first time. The disciple is struck by how slight and dark-skinned the imam is, but before he can complete his thought, the imam grows massive in size and cycles through all the colors of the rainbow before returning to his original state.[11] As Rumi intimated, colors are a distraction from truth.

From ancient Mesopotamia to Augustine, Near Eastern scripture had construed the relationship between God and humankind primarily as that between master and slave. This continued in Islam. The Sufi tradition is permeated with the image of the ascetic and mystic as the willing slave of God, liberated by their devotion and recognition of their utter dependence.[12] If the Sufi is the lowly slave of God, then it is no surprise that we find the black slave as an ideal image. We see this in the stories of black slave saints as well as in the trope of Sufis encountering anonymous black mystics dwelling as hermits in wastelands and possessed of profound mystical understanding.[13] This is arguably even present in the life of the famous Moroccan Sufi ʿAbd al-ʿAzīz al-Dabbāgh (d. 1132/1719), who describes his mystical apprenticeship at the hands of the enigmatic figure of the Bornu saint ʿAbdallāh al-Burnāwī.[14]

As we have seen, the somatic persona of the Black African (often *zanjī*) became a metonym for ugliness and undesirability in the Mediterranean and Middle Eastern lands of Islam from the Abbasid period onward. This crept into the Islamic scholarly tradition of the Persianate world of Iraq, Iran, and later the Ottoman and Mughal realms.[15] But in the Sufi tradition, the image of the Black African as ugly or debased was not indulged with crassness. It served to articulate either ideals of mystical transcendence or intensive servitude to God.

Yet we cannot dismiss the social environment in which these images were shaped. Muslim scholars knew well that the Quran's whitening and blackening of faces on the Day of Judgment was a metaphor for ennoblement and disgrace, felicity and despair. It very clearly had *nothing* to do with how people looked in their earthly life. But by the 1000s CE in the Mediterranean and Persian world the distinction began to break down between the metaphor of whitened/ blackened for ennobled/disgraced on the one hand and mundane descriptions of skin color and phenotype on the other. Al-Rāzī recounts how he had heard that, in Khurasan, a descendant of the Prophet notorious for his libertine lifestyle dwelled in the same town as a black former slave renowned for his knowledge and righteous conduct. This black scholar was sought out for his learning and his blessings. One day, the sinful, drunken man ran into the pious scholar and accosted him as he made his way to the mosque in the company of his students. "I am the son of the Messenger of God," the iniquitous man protested, "yet I am brought low and you magnified, I am scorned and you honored, I am insulted and you supported!" The black scholar replied, "O you of noble descent (*sharīf*), you have whitened my inner self (*bāṭinī*) and blackened yours. People see the whiteness of my heart before the blackness of my face, and so I have grown beautiful . . ."[16] Al-Ghazālī (d. 505/1111), who had taught al-Rāzī's father, recounts the story of a man who was told in a dream that his father had died and that "God had blackened his face." When he awoke, he uncovered his father's face and found him "dead, with his face black" (*aswad al-wajh*). Collapsing in grief, the son dreamt that the Prophet wiped over his father's face. When the son awoke, he found that his father's face was "white" (*abyaḍ*).[17] These stories are unproblematic when appreciated as spiritual metaphor, an element obvious in both of them. But they blend metaphor with phenotype, bringing metaphor unmistakably 'down to earth.' Why, in al-Rāzī's story, is the nobly born man's reprehensible conduct the counterweight of the pious scholar's skin color? What exactly does it mean that the father's face was 'black'? In death had his face taken on a Black African skin tone? Had he been 'white' before?

We see this gradual comingling of metaphor and physical descriptor in readings of the *Burda* poem of Imam al-Būṣīrī (d. *circa* 694/1294) in the Mediterranean and Persianate lands. One of the most famous and popular means of venerating the Prophet, at one point this poem mentions verses of the Quran that, if read, cool fires "as if they were the [Prophet's] Fount, which whitens the faces of the disobedient, who had come at first like coals." This is a reference to Hadiths telling of the Fount (*ḥawḍ*) by which the Prophet will meet the believers on the Day of Judgment as well as to the River of Life (*nahr al-ḥayāt*) that will cleanse believers of their sins. Mullā ʿAlī al-Qāri' (d. 1014/1606) of Mecca explains the poem as meaning that reciting and embodying these Quranic verses whitens the hearts (*bayāḍ qulūb*) of believers, and that the River of Life is where "blackness leaves them and whiteness shows."[18] In another work, Mullā ʿAlī refers to a novel (and bizarre) notion, which seems to have emerged in the 1500s (I have not found any evidence earlier), that the Quranic descriptions of the "whitening" of the believers on the Day of Judgment meant that black Muslims would enter the Garden actually "white."[19] In the Middle East, it seems commentaries on the *Burda* were increasingly stressing whiteness versus blackness as a theme and beginning to erode the distinction between moral metaphor and physical description.

The 'whitening' of faces at the Prophet's Font has its roots in sound Hadiths, but in these later interpretations one can trace a steady move away from sophisticated metaphors juxtaposing beauty, sin, and ruin with rebirth to a more simplistic and corporal metaphor of white and black. What are in al-Būṣīrī's and Mullā ʿAlī's language faces once black as coal now whitened have their roots in a Hadith in *Ṣaḥīḥ al-Bukhārī*. In it, the Prophet tells of a dream he had in which he was given a tour of Afterlife. One group he sees in the Garden are people whose bodies are "half as beautiful as you would ever see and half as ugly." Then those people immerse themselves in a river of "purest white" and come out with that "badness" (*sū'*) gone from them. The angels explain to the Prophet that those people were those who had mixed good deeds and bad, but God forgave them their bad deeds.[20] Blackness is absent here, unlike the *Burda*. Another narration of a Hadith in *Ṣaḥīḥ al-Bukhārī* does tell of people "blackened" by the Fire being thrown into the River of Life and emerging like new, yellow (*ṣafrā'*) shoots budding on the sides of a flood channel.[21] But the blackness in this narration is incidental. The core imagery is of being burnt, which all the other narrations of this Hadith explicitly describe with no mention of blackness. Their only color references are to the yellowness of young sprouts. What started as a metaphor of burnt land brought back to life in sound Hadiths becomes one of stark blackness and whiteness in the *Burda*.

The narrowing of metaphoric diversity and the channeling of imagery into a stark black/white language are visible in the Hadith corpus more generally. Similar to how 'slave woman' was conflated with 'Ethiopian or Zanji woman,' narrators in the eighth and ninth centuries sometimes allowed black and white imagery to seep into their transmissions. In one Hadith in the *Musnad* of Ibn Ḥanbal (d. 241/855) the Prophet is quoted as describing how, when God created Adam, He struck his right side, bringing out "progeny white as if they were red ants" (*dharr*). Then God struck Adam's left side, bringing out "progeny black as if they were coals." God declared that the first group were destined for the Garden, the second for the Fire.[22] This is a very isolated narration, however, of a well-known grouping of reports known as the Hadith of the Two Handfuls, which describes God's setting the fates of Adam's progeny in the Hereafter. Only this isolated narration includes the black/white element, however. Other narrations that were both transmitted more widely and have been regarded by Hadith critics as much sounder omit it.[23]

Other popular means of celebrating the Prophet in later centuries also highlighted his physical 'whiteness.' A very popular poem recited to praise the Prophet in the Arab world, the *Mawlid* of Imam al-Barzanjī (d. 1177/1764), draws on the physically descriptive language of some Hadiths when it sings of the Prophet as "white with a reddish hue (*abyaḍ mushrab*)."[24] A praise poem about the Prophet (one of many) by the conservative late Ottoman scholar Yūsuf al-Nabhānī (d. 1350/1932) draws on the classical Arabic language long associated with the Prophet's visage: his is "a face that effaces the darkness, its light burning; and his forehead, bright white, fair, radiant and joyous with beauty (*jabīnuhu al-waḍḍāḥ ablaju abhaju*)." Language straddling whiteness and radiance was not new in descriptions of the Prophet. But there is no doubt that the Prophet's physical skin tone was very present in al-Nabhānī's mind. Recounting his first dream vision of the Prophet in which he saw him in person, al-Nabhānī dwells at length on how his face was "radiant white" (*abyaḍ azhar*), which al-Nabhānī describes as "pure white" (*ṣāfī al-bayāḍ*), not even tinged with ruddiness.[25]

## THE PROPHET'S COLOR AND BLACK MUSLIMS

This trend toward blending metaphorical and physical whiteness was not universal, however. Much praise of the Prophet continued to hew closer to the metaphor of his luminosity. The *Guide to Goodness* (*Dalā'il al-khayrāt*) of the famous Moroccan scholar Imam al-Jazūlī (d. 869/1465), which was one of the most commonly owned books after the Quran in the Ottoman world, mentions the Prophet's glowing countenance, "more beautiful than the full moon."[26] It refers many times to his Fount on the Day of Judgment but never to blackness or whitening.[27] A nineteenth-century Swahili translation of the *Burda* by one Shaykh Muḥammad ʿUthmān Ḥājjī Alekuwako from Lamu renders the verse about the Prophet's Font as "It is like the pond Hawdh or the river Kawthar, the disobedient [souls] go there eagerly, it cleanses their faces which begin to shine, their sins disappear and they become good."[28] Again, blackness is absent.

Focusing on the luminosity of the Prophet instead of his somatic whiteness certainly seems to be a trend in Africa south of the Sahara. The famous *ʿIshrīniyyāt* (Twenties) poem praising the Prophet by al-Fāzāzī's (d. 627/1230) of Tlemcen, which in later centuries would be read out after every Friday prayer in Timbuktu, mentions the Prophet's face but not its color. It alludes to his appearance and invokes images and words used in classical descriptions of his features (ex. *ablaj*, bright, white; *azhar*, luminous; his Font, etc.) but often repurposed and always figuratively. They do not describe him physically. They convey his radiance of being, the communion of hearts, and the light of his message. "The lights of his footsteps glow radiantly (*tataballaju*)," drawing on the same root as *ablaj*. His forehead is like the bright morning sun, and hearts are purified through him on the Day of Resurrection. He is the sun and the moon, and his beauty is enchanting.[29] The Mauritanian Shādhilī Sufi master al-Yadalī's (d. 1166/1753) widely recited poem, *The Blessings of My Lord* (*Ṣalāt*

*Rabbī*), speaks only generally of the Prophet's "beautiful face" (*wajh jamīl*).[30] Nana Asma'u (d. 1280/1864), the learned daughter of Usman dan Fodio of Sokoto, penned several poems praising the Prophet and mentioning his Fount on the Day of Judgment. They all focus on his illumination. "The beauty of the full moon is nothing compared to the beauty of his face," she writes. Its light "exceeds the light of the full moon." Referring to sound Hadiths, Nana Asma'u writes of the river of Kawthar's water having a "whiteness [that] exceeds that of milk." But there is no mention of whitened faces or any contrast with blackess.[31] The Senegalese Sufi pillar Aḥmad Bamba's poetic recounting of the blessings of Paradise mention its rivers and hearts being washed of sin but with no element of color. A lengthy liturgy of prayer upon the Prophet includes his description of "not unhealthily white or very dark," but only as part of a full recounting of Anas bin Mālik's famous descripton of the Prophet's features.[32] Physicality is absent from the *Ramsa* praise poem of the Ethiopian Sufi shaykh Aḥmad Ādam (d. 1321/1903), in which the Prophet's light (*nūr*) is a major theme.[33] The Senegalese Sufi master Ibrāhīm Niasse's popular poem on the Prophet's appearance speaks of his "luminous color" (*azhar al-lawn*). Another of his poems (*Abā qalbu*, from his *Easing Attainment*) calls the Prophet "white" (*abyaḍ*), but it is a whiteness not of skin but one that illuminates "the dark night of ignorance."[34]

Dominant modern, Western racial understandings of black and white can certainly inform how Muslims invoke blackness and whiteness, particularly in the context of European colonial rule and post-colonialism. But this can take unexpected forms. In a cunningly subversive verse later in his *Easing Attainment* poem, Niasse pushes the black/white metaphor clearly into the realm not just of the somatic but also of modern racial language. He does so, however, in a way that inverts its power dynamic. Meditating on the power of the classical Islamic duo of love and hatred for the sake of God and the Prophet, he writes:

> And through loving [the Prophet] the blacks (*sūd*) are whitened (*tabyaḍḍu*); and through hating him depraved peoples among the whites (*al-bīḍ*) are blackened.

> And this, by God's praise, is the free disposal of our Lord; His is judgment and disposal through love and hate.[35]

Again, we see the Quranic metaphor of whitening-as-ennoblement and blackening-as-debasement but now deployed onto the modern racial divisions so well known globally. More so even than with the commentaries on the *Burda*, we are presented with the plural adjectives for racial phenotypes, *bīḍ* and *sūd*, literally white people and black people. These terms were not in common use in the Sahel in Niasse's day, however, even among Arabophone scholars. The alternate plurals *sūdān* and *bīḍān* are still used for Black Africans on the one hand and those of Arab and Berber descent on the other, with *Naṣārā* (lit. Christians) serving as a common word for European Whites.[36] Where *sūd* and *bīḍ* are usual terms for racial groupings, however, is in the Arab world, a world whose politics and language Niasse knew well. There these words mean blacks and whites in a manner familiar to the West today, though with Arabs clearly included within the fold of whiteness. It is possible that Niasse meant nothing other than a refrain of Quranic and Prophetic praise imagery, with a not unprecedented intermingling of metaphor and physical description. But his verses also seem to describe how venerating Islam has ennobled – metaphorically whitened – the Muslims of Africa, while contempt for the Prophet and his faith has humiliated – metaphorically blackened – the colonizing Europeans.

## ANTIBLACKNESS AND INSULTING THE PROPHET

An item often raised in discussions of Islam and antiblackness pertains to the legal dimension of venerating the Prophet. Several well-regarded Muslim scholars over the centuries have maintained that saying the Prophet was black constitutes an act of unbelief (*kufr*). Though rarely invoked, this position is repeated in standard books of law, often in sections on what takes a person outside the fold of Islam. The most famous is the influential *Book of Healing on the Rights of the*

*Chosen One* (*Kitāb al-Shifā bi-ta'rīf ḥuqūq al-muṣṭafā*) by the giant of medieval Andalusian scholarship, Qāḍī 'Iyāḍ (d. 544/1149), who traces this position to the early Mālikī scholar Aḥmad bin Abī Sulaymān (d. 291/904).[37] It results from the well-known tenet of Islamic law and theology that knowingly and intentionally insulting the Prophet is an act of unbelief. What concerns us here is the unspoken premise of this particular argument: that calling someone black is an insult.

As we have seen, the Prophet was not 'black,' neither by the descriptive standards of his own culture nor by global Western ones. So describing him as black is inaccurate, but no more inaccurate than calling him extremely light skinned. Why is calling him black singled out as an offense if there was not something particularly denigrating about it? Isn't this conclusive proof of virulent antiblackness among the Muslim scholars elaborating Islamic law and theology?

Not necessarily. Most discussions of this issue, including Qāḍī 'Iyāḍ's, center on making false statements about the Prophet. They list saying he was black among other assertions that were simply inaccurate, like saying he was not from the Quraysh tribe or that he died before reaching adulthood.[38] As another famous Mālikī jurist, Shihāb al-Dīn al-Qarāfī (d. 684/1285), wrote, if someone claims to have seen the Prophet in a vision but says that the person they saw was black (*aswad*), then the vision was not truthful. But blackness is but one of many physical features he lists as not attributable to the Prophet in reports about his appearances, along with having only one eye or no feet.[39]

Blackness had been singled out, however, by Aḥmad bin Abī Sulaymān, and no one needed to explain why. As we have already seen, an association of blackness with ugliness and lowness had become an undeniable cultural phenomenon in the central Islamic lands by the 800s CE. A profound treatment of this ruling comes from the famous Ḥanafī scholar Mullā 'Alī al-Qāri' (d. 1014/1606), who had moved from his native Herat to settle in Mecca. He explains that saying the Prophet was black is a sin only if it is meant as an insult. Interestingly, Ḥanafī scholars in the Persianate lands of Central

Asia and northern India had long been pondering whether cultural- and language-specific phrases in Persian would entail disbelief if directed at God, the Prophet, or some other revered early Muslim. The answer often turned on the intent of the speaker.[40] What a person means by describing someone as black, Mullā ʿAlī explains, "differs with the different customs (*ʿurf*) of mankind, as blackness is desired among Ethiopians and Indians just as whiteness is desired among Arabs, Persians and Greeks."[41]

Mullā ʿAlī's teacher, al-Haytamī (d. 974/1567), had implied something similar when discussing the Prophet's description. Although he felt the Prophet's phenotype was objectively the best, since he argued that a degree of ruddiness indicates healthy blood circulation, he acknowledged that what various cultures consider the 'best' color is based on custom (*ʿāda*).[42] Al-Haytamī's discussion of this point strongly suggests that what was at stake was less a substantial matter of belief than a minor credal point that had taken on a social life of its own. This Shāfiʿī scholar of Mecca, who had migrated there from his native Egypt and had become a star attraction for scholars as far away as India, explains that parents should make sure to teach their children the Prophet's skin tone "because of [scholars'] explicit statement that claiming he was black is unbelief." What he intends by this, explains al-Haytamī, is not that the Prophet's color is some core matter of faith. Rather, this should be taught "so that a person does not claim [the Prophet] was black and thus be declared an unbeliever."[43] Ironically, this explanation only confirms how prevalent antiblack sentiment had become in the Mediterranean Middle East. Al-Haytamī's discussion would be repeated in influential commentaries by Shāfiʿī scholars from Cairo and Mecca in the subsequent centuries.[44]

How was this ruling on calling the Prophet black received among Muslim scholars south of the Sahara? It is interesting that Qāḍī ʿIyāḍ's *Book of Healing* became a core text in the teaching of Islam in West Africa from the fifteenth century onward. Asked about the ruling it mentions for calling the Prophet black, contemporary scholars in Niasse's Tijānī tradition reply that "the Prophet (s) has no color." In fact, fortunate faithful around the world encounter him in dreams, where his manifestation appears truthfully in all the shades of human appearance.[45]

## BLACK AS BEAUTIFUL

Mullā ʿAlī al-Qāri' was not the first to understand that what people find attractive is based on custom. Eight centuries earlier al-Jāḥiẓ (d. 255/869) had explained that "desires [about color and features] are customs (*ʿādāt*), and most of them are just inherited traditions (*taqlīd*)."[46] We are not sure what al-Haytamī's and Mullā ʿAlī's own preferences were, but there is remarkable evidence from the 1500s CE that women from the region of Ethiopia and Somalia were considered beautiful and desirable by the elite of Mecca and Medina during their time. The Shāfiʿī preacher of the Prophet's Mosque in Medina, Ibn ʿAbd al-Bāqī (d. *circa* 993/1585), composed a book, *The Embroidered Robe on the Virtues of Ethiopians*, which is best described as a love letter to women from the Horn of Africa. It includes several poems from his teacher, a leading scholar in Mecca named ʿAbd al-ʿAzīz al-Zamzamī (d. 976/1569), praising their beauty and even apologizing to his wife for his obsession with them.[47] During a trip to Mecca in 1671–2, the Istanbulite Evliyā' Chelebī (d. *circa* 1095/1684) observed that Ethiopian singing girls were very popular there.[48] The Scottish explorer James Bruce (d. 1794), visiting the southern Hejaz in the 1770s, noted that Ethiopian concubines were preferred over local wives.[49] A Dutch Orientalist who visited Mecca in the late nineteenth century posing as a Muslim pilgrim observed that what men there found particularly attractive were dark-skinned African and Ethiopian women.[50] A British resident in Istanbul in the 1840s reported that female Ethiopian slaves were seen as attractive and valuable. Women from Sennar on the Sudanic Nile, however, fetched a low price, since they were considered stupid, lazy, stubborn, and untrustworthy. (This assiduous observer noted that it was rare for Turks to have children with African women, and that one rarely saw mixed-race children.)[51]

It is certainly true that Muslim writers in the Mediterranean and Persianate lands associated lighter skin with beauty and darker skin with unattractiveness, but exceptions were not rare. The Iberian litterateur al-Sharīshī (d. 619/1222) wrote, perhaps knowingly, perhaps fantastically, about the gorgeous slave girls brought from the region between the Senegal and Niger Rivers. They were beautiful, with gorgeous legs and "profusely black" (*tafattuq al-sawād*) skin.[52] Biographical data from sixteenth-century Cairo suggests that the majority of slave concubines there were Ethiopian.[53] A taste for diversity was shared by the Egyptian scholar Rifāʿat al-Ṭahṭāwī, who visited Paris in the 1820s. He felt pity for French men, whom he noticed found only white women attractive but not black ones. Arabs, he remarked, "have two directions in love."[54] His contemporary, the daughter of the Omani Sultan of Zanzibar, recalled how "at least eight to ten shades of color could be found in the faces" of her siblings and her father's wives and concubines, who were Arab, Persian, Ethiopian, Assyrian, and Circassian (though those with fairer skin seem to have been considered more beautiful).[55]

Ironically, finding darker skin tones or Black African features attractive was not uncommon among Arabs of the Prophet's time. A book praising the virtues of the Prophet's cousin Jaʿfar bin Abī Ṭālib includes a report that he preferred dark-skinned and dark-lipped women (*admāʾ laʿsāʾ*).[56] In his book on the virtues of Black Africans, the Persian scholar Ibn al-Marzubān (d. 310/919) includes a whole chapter on early Muslims who fell in love with Black African women or found them particularly gorgeous.[57] We should not assume such accounts are documentary evidence. There is clearly a literary flourish, which plays on how unconventional Abbasid-era high culture found the idea of Muslim elites being drawn to Black African women. Ibn al-Marzubān may include a report about the caliph Abū Bakr's son falling in love with a black slave girl and reciting poetry about how his love for her made him love all Black Africans. But this occurs against the background that such attraction and open devotion, while not necessarily blameworthy, was not normal.[58]

The final word on this matter should be the conclusion arrived at by al-Suyūṭī, who wrote two lengthy books on the virtues and noble qualities of Black Africans and mourned the death of his beloved

Eṭhiopian concubine Ghuṣūn, mother of his son. In a third book, focused on the virtues of 'brown,' 'black,' and 'white' complexions, al-Suyūṭī cites a poem from someone he felt had struck home:

> Listen to a word of truth,
> And be with your truth my aid.
> Beautiful is beautiful,
> Beloved in every shade.[59]

# 8

## Antiblackness in Mālikī Marriage Law

A woman is married for four things: for her wealth, for her merit (*ḥasab*), her beauty and for her religion. But favor religion, and may you prosper!

Hadith of the Prophet Muhammad[1]

Whoever says a dark-skinned man (*asmar*) is suitable, let them give him their daughter's hand.

ʿAbd al-ʿAzīz bin ʿAlī, a respected early-modern Moroccan scholar[2]

ʿAbd al-ʿAzīz bin ʿAlī, esteemed as a 'righteous jurist,' certainly spoke plainly. Today his words are shocking. They are also revealing. This Muslim judge was steeped in the pious ideals of God's law. But he was also intimately involved in the daily realities of domestic disputes in Morocco's verdant Sous valley. He knew well where ideals and reality met, and which tended to triumph. Those who wished to follow the Prophet's guidance and marry for piety first and foremost were welcome to. But would they accept their own daughter marrying a black man?

Or it may be that the scholar intended something else: that it was precisely the correct understanding of God's law to deem a dark-skinned groom unsuitable for a bride from a good family, and any scholar between Fez and Sous worth his salt knew it. In either case, ʿAbd al-ʿAzīz bin ʿAlī was heeding the wisdom of a fellow judge from the region: whenever possible, judges should defer to "what is customary in a land, regardless of where and when." The judge recalled how, in the hinterland of Casablanca, a local chief, wealthy, powerful, and with a sterling reputation, had married a woman from a good family. Because he or his family had once been slaves, however, the wife's clan suffered painful reproaches even years later.[3]

What was at issue in these cases was the question of whether, for purposes of marriage, the Shariah recognized hierarchies in lineage, wealth, or other measures of social standing, including skin color. ʿAbd al-ʿAzīz bin ʿAlī was debating fellow Mālikī scholars who believed it did not. For them, it contradicted the Quran's clear teaching that "the noblest among you before God is the most pious" (49:13) and the Prophet's undisputed edicts that no person or people enjoy standing above others except by faith and good deeds. ʿAbd al-ʿAzīz, by contrast, along with the majority of Mālikī scholars in North Africa, believed that such hierarchy was legitimate according to the Shariah. They were joined by the bulk of Muslim jurists from the other schools of law as well.

Though they differed in which they favored, this scholarly majority relied on three distinct arguments to prove that the Shariah recognized social hierarchy. First, some pointed to how God and the Prophet had empowered custom to define the details of the Shariah. Such custom could, in turn, involve rankings of class and value. The exact nature of custom was incidental, but it was acceptable provided it did not clearly transgress the Shariah's boundaries. Second, many scholars argued that, in addition to the empowerment of custom, there were Quranic verses and Hadiths that directly established aspects of hierarchy in lineage, legal status, and profession. Third, scholars contended the very nature of human society was inherently hierarchical, and that the law of God acknowledged this. The forms and intensity of this hierarchy might differ between societies, but it was always present, and the Shariah's affirmation of custom recognized this reality. Understanding how and why Mālikī scholars like ʿAbd al-ʿAzīz held antiblack positions as well as why other Muslim scholars opposed them requires understanding these different visions of the legitimacy or illegitimacy of hierarchy in Islamic law. This will be the task of this chapter and the next.

## THE CONUNDRUM OF CUSTOM

Chronicles and accounts of Islamic history regularly praise austere and devout ulama who smashed wine jugs and decried musical performances, who stood before rulers and refused to be silent about tenets of creed they found heretical. The great Hadith scholar ʿAbd al-Ghanī al-Maqdisī (d. 600/1203) did all three and feared neither seller nor sultan. And he was beloved. His student recalled that one could hardly walk the streets of Isfahan with him due to the crowds of people mobbing him for his blessings.[4]

But such individuals were pushing against the tide. A revivalist movement inspired by the likes of al-Maqdisī convulsed Istanbul in the mid 1600s, trying to force locals to abandon heretical innovations like tobacco and certain popular but non-canonical prayers. The Ottoman intellectual Kātib Chelebī (d. 1067/1657) did not approve of these reformist efforts, judging them futile and invoking a saying that it is foolish not to recognize the customs of one's time. The Shariah ordains a respect for custom, he explained, indulging it whenever possible. And all agreed that "there is a certain harm" in trying to stamp out even those habits that the Shariah frowned on. Chelebī could be sardonic; he quipped that the revivalists should try *encouraging* those practices so the masses would end up abandoning them the way they had their basic religious duties.[5] But his reticence was not born only of cynicism. It was not unusual for even senior Muslim clerics to avoid confronting social wrongs that seemed immovable. Al-Suyūṭī had experienced this when one of his teachers, a scholar of institutional repute named Shams al-Dīn al-Bānī (d. 885/1480 or 895/1490), ruled that a brothel operating next to a mosque in their Cairo neighborhood be left alone.[6]

In this chapter we will encounter more statements like that of ʿAbd al-ʿAzīz bin ʿAlī of Sous. Time and again ulama will invoke and discuss the role of custom (*ʿāda*, *ʿurf*) in contouring the contact surfaces of the Shariah to the mundanities of family and commerce. There are some matters on which the Quran and the Prophet's teachings empowered custom specifically, like what obligations husbands and wives owe one another in marriage and divorce.[7] Beyond these,

Muslim jurists drew on custom to build bridges between the principles and abstract rules set forth in scripture and the concrete questions arising from daily life. One of the legal maxims they articulated to express this process was 'Custom is dispositive' (*al-ʿāda muḥakkima*).[8] What conditions are allowed in contracts, what constitutes appropriate dress beyond the bare minimum of covering one's nudity (*ʿawra*), what kind of movements break one's prayers, and what is considered reasonable as opposed to transgressive conduct in everything from personal injuries to damage caused by animals – these are all examples of how many details of the Shariah are set by custom.[9]

What happens when the discretion given to custom begins to encroach on a principle or clear ruling from the Quran or the Prophet's teachings? At the opposing ends of the spectrum, the relationship between the established rules of the Shariah and custom was straightforward. Custom could never change, for example, the Quranic prohibition on eating pork and rulings that were agreed upon by all. When a Ḥanafī jurist in tenth-century Bukhara ruled that workers tying and retying their waist wraps could be exempted from the normal rules of modesty, namely that a man's nudity (*ʿawra*) begins at his navel, later Ḥanafī scholars looked back in stern disapproval. His stance had violated the definition of nudity agreed upon by all jurists.[10] Writing as a Mālikī jurist, Muḥammad Bello condemned scholars approving of practices in all areas of interactions and commerce that violated the clear dictates of Islamic law simply because they were customary (*ʿāda*). This amounted to "abrogation of the Shariah by custom." Yes, as those scholars insisted, "Custom is law" (*sharʿ*), but this was a qualified principle, not a categorical rule. Custom that is accepted "cannot infringe upon one of the bases (*qawāʿid*) of the Shariah."[11]

Conversely, Mālikī jurists in North Africa agreed to accommodate Berber customs by allowing fines as a punishment for drunkenness instead of lashes (some Berber tribes bridled at the use of corporal punishment). Although fines were not allowed in the Mālikī school of law, they were an acceptable form of punishment in other schools. Accommodating custom here did not break with any clear text of the

Quran or Prophetic teachings or transgress the outer limits of the Shariah.[12]

Matters became more complicated when custom came up against an ethical principle rather than a stark rule, or against a directive that may itself have been based in context and was less definitive than the prohibition on pork. The famous jurist of Cairo, Ibn ʿAbd al-Salām (d. 660/1262), was once asked if it was appropriate to stand up for people when they entered a room, as was custom, in light of the Prophet's warning that, "Whoever wishes for men to stand up for him, let him prepare his seat in the Fire." He replied that it might actually be required to stand up for people, since the Prophet had also instructed Muslims not to sow hatred or dissension among themselves, a likely effect of not standing up in Cairo in his day.[13] Was this a Muslim jurist acceptably changing a ruling as circumstances changed, balancing a realistic deference to custom with pursuing Shariah goals? Or was this the pressure of custom leading a Muslim jurist to indulge a display of arrogance that the Prophet had clearly discouraged?

Even if they did not have al-Maqdisī's zeal, Muslim scholars considered it a duty, at least in principle, to fulfill the Quranic charge of "commanding right and forbidding wrong." For scholars up to the task, this often meant confronting regnant customs. By the 1500s in India, for example, the ancient taboo against widows from high-caste families remarrying had become widely accepted among Muslims (see Appendix VII).[14] This was even the case among Indian ulama, who considered the 'choice' not to remarry on the part of a widow and her family to be a matter of discretion. But voices arose to challenge this. Sayyid Ḥusayn Bilgrāmī (d. *circa* 1000/1590), a senior scholar in Delhi and the Deccan, would visit widows and encourage them to remarry as soon as their Quranically ordained waiting period had ended. This was the teaching of the Prophet, he explained, who had himself married several widows. For this, Bilgrāmī was hounded and denounced by Indian Muslim men and women alike.[15] Two centuries later, the taboo was still strong. Even the revivalist scholar Shāh Ismāʿīl Shahīd (d. 1246/1831) would skip over Hadiths mentioning widows remarrying when they appeared in books he was teaching in Delhi's madrasas. It was not until one of his mentors convinced him that this was a Hindu custom that Shāh Ismāʿīl came out in opposition to the practice and even made sure his widowed sister remarried.[16] Major scholars in the Deoband movement, like Ashraf ʿAlī Thanawi (d. 1362/1943), continued this effort.[17]

Of course, the Shariah affected major social change wherever Islam spread. Archaeologists have long considered an absence of pig bones to be a telltale sign of conversion to Islam in a region, for example.[18] The unremarkable prevalence of Islamic ritual practice and Shariah norms is part of what defines 'the Muslim world.' But in particular places and times, the small-scale push and pull of Shariah norms and the customs that militated against them has often been dramatic. Respected scholars allowed the brothel near al-Suyūṭī's mosque to remain open. Serving a few sunny years as the judge in the Shariah court in the Maldives, Ibn Baṭṭūṭa (d. *circa* 774/1374) bemoaned how he "strove with all [his] might to establish the rule of law" and to get rid of "bad customs" like a divorced woman not being allowed to leave her ex-husband's house until she married again. But he could not manage to convince local women to cover their breasts in public, a mindboggling violation of basic Shariah norms. He could only oblige them to do so when in his court.[19] When Muslim scholars have decided that overturning established customs was worth the "certain harm" Chelebī had noted, conflicts have often ensued. The nineteenth-century reformist movements of Sokoto in West Africa and the Paderi movement in Sumatra aimed at, among other things, transforming pre-Islamic norms of dress, entertainment, marriage, and inheritance. For better or for worse, they involved violence and compulsion.[20]

How hard could Muslims be pushed to adopt completely the ethics, ritual, and praxis of the Shariah? There was always the dreadful possibility that the laity could take the course of a Berber clan that actually held a funeral for the Shariah and formally announced they would no longer have anything to do with it.[21] Or, less dramatically, they could do as 'enlightened' young, suit-sporting Cairenes did in the 1920s, when they so alarmed Egypt's Grand Mufti by arguing that laws and morality should be based solely on modern customs, not the ways of the Prophet.[22] Where does deeming black men unsuitable grooms for Arab or Berber women fit on this spectrum of balancing clear scriptural edicts and custom, ideals, and reality?

## DESIRABILITY AND BLACKNESS IN MĀLIKĪ LAW

A basic primer on Mālikī law written by Abū Zayd al-Waghlīsī (d. 786/1384–5), a Muslim scholar from Béjaïa in modern-day Algeria, takes up the question of what Muslims should and should not look at as they make their way through public spaces. The *Waghlīsiyya* textbook would end up on shelves in madrasas from Mali to Alexandria. And, on this point, it was typical of books of Islamic law: it is not permitted for a young man to look at the faces of unrelated women, "out of fear of temptation." But al-Waghlīsī adds a comment not typical in other schools of law. He makes an exception for looking at the face of a woman who is "old (*ʿajūz*), black (*sawdā'*), or the likes." By comparison, texts in the Shāfiʿī school sometimes mention old women in such discussions, but not black women.[23] Associating blackness with low status in suitability sometimes appears in Ḥanafī legal texts as early as the mid 900s CE. But this is rare and is not explicitly linked to undesirability.[24] (In what follows, we should understand the blackness referred to in Mālikī law books as either a Black African phenotype or simply as skin markedly darker than the average skin color in whatever society is under discussion.)[25]

Al-Waghlīsī's comment is even more shocking than the one that opened this chapter. Black Muslims, male and female, from the U.S. who have studied Mālikī law in Egypt testify to how painful it is to find that major scholars had deemed blackness to be a cause of undesirability in women and men.[26] The points of law in which this appeared could be relatively minor. But they have huge symbolic importance, since they suggest Islamic legal validation of antiblack discrimination.

The opinion of al-Waghlīsī and others like him, however, does not represent the Mālikī school as a whole. Nor would al-Waghlīsī have claimed it did. His assessment of desirability and undesirability was not intended or received as a timeless or universal declaration. Shocking to us, it reflected the society in which al-Waghlīsī lived, with its customs and practicalities. If the antiblack statements of jurists like al-Waghlīsī were matters of custom, jurists were the first to acknowledge that customs change. If they were practical responses to dealing with the social realities of class and identity, jurists knew well that the Shariah was supposed to shape society as much as it accommodated it. And, as we shall see, many Mālikī jurists felt, and continue to feel, that al-Waghlīsī had failed in that regard.

Beyond the question of who one should look at, blackness was taken into consideration as a significant factor in male or female desirability on three points of law in the Mālikī school. All were related to the issue of suitability (*kafā'a*) in marriage, those guidelines for choosing appropriate spouses, which Muslim scholars recommend or require brides, grooms, and their families take into consideration. For the majority of Muslim jurists, *kafā'a* is only a guideline, not binding, as long as the woman and her family agree on a groom.[27] Ironically, as we will see, Mālik himself took the most egalitarian stance among the founding figures of the Sunni schools of law on who was suitable to marry whom. But on these three points of law, Mālikī jurists in North Africa used the Shariah's deference to custom to excuse antiblack attitudes.

The first point of law was relatively obscure: a male relative's right to object to the marriage of a woman in his family. If the groom was unsuitable for the bride, a close male relative could prevent the marriage *if the bride was desirable*. He could *not* object to the marriage if she was 'undesirable' (*ghayr marghūb fīhā*). One of the features that rendered a woman 'undesirable' was blackness (an 'undesirable' woman was thus freer in her marriage choices than a desirable one).[28]

The second point was what defects (*'ayb*) constituted valid reasons for annulling a marriage. Mālik himself had explicitly stated that discovering one's spouse was black was not sufficient to annul the marriage. But an anomalous opinion from the early Mālikī jurist Ibn Ḥabīb (d. 238/852) held that a bride in particular could be rejected if it turned out she was black when the groom had had no reason to expect this (e.g., she came from a family in which no one else was dark skinned), or if her appearance had been made a specific condition in the marriage.[29] Particularly in Morocco in the seventeenth through the nineteenth centuries, many Mālikī judges, like Sayyid ʿArabī Burdula (d. 1133/1721) of Fez and Muḥammad ʿArabī al-Zarhūnī (d. 1260/1844) of Meknes, as well as ʿAbd al-ʿAzīz bin ʿAlī of Sous, treated this as their school's rule for grooms *and* brides on the basis of respecting custom.[30]

The third situation involved the suitability of a potential groom and when a woman's father or other male guardian could be prevented from marrying her off to him. In this case, it was not the physical unattractiveness of the groom but his social undesirability that was at issue. An early and influential Mālikī scholar of Kairouan, Saḥnūn (d. 240/855), gave the ruling that, if a woman's male guardian tried to marry her off against her will to an insane person or someone afflicted with mild leprosy (*abraṣ*), the state (*sulṭān*) could prevent it. This was also true, said Saḥnūn, if he tried to marry her to a black man (*aswad*), due to the disgrace (*maʿarra*) involved. This opinion was seconded by Abū al-Walīd (d. *circa* 606/1210), the main judge of the bustling city of Cordoba and author of a mainstay legal manual.[31]

When considering these legal rulings, we must keep three points in mind. First, at various points and times, discrimination on the basis of phenotype was a proxy for discrimination on the basis of class. In the case of North African grooms who were black or dark-skinned, what was at issue was the association of blackness with slave status or descent from slaves. What had caused so much reprobation to the family whose daughter had married the local chieftain near Casablanca was his slave origins, not specifically that he was black. While that might have been the case, his skin color was not specified by the scholar recounting the story. It did not have to be. We have already seen how medieval and early-modern Andalusian and Moroccan sayings treated 'black' as a broadened metonym standing in for 'slave.'[32] In much of North Africa, blackness had become a correlate of slave status or slave descent.

Of course, skin color and status were not *necessarily* linked. The relationship could be ignored depending on other social factors. Blackness and slavery were not synonymous or exact social equivalents. Ambiguity resulted from the common practice of upper-class men siring free children with their Black African slave concubines.[33] As a result, dark skin tone or a Black-African phenotype was *not* a liability if a man's standing was otherwise assured by his patrilineal descent. Yūsuf bin Tashufīn (d. 500/1106), the effective founder of the powerful Almoravid state in Morocco, was a Berber whose mother was probably a Black African slave concubine. He had a black complexion, but this was not held against him.[34] Mawlāy Ismāʿīl (d. 1139/1727), the Moroccan sultan who forcibly re-enslaved the free black men (*ḥarāṭīn*) in his realm, was born of a black concubine, as were two later sultans in his line.[35] And blackness could be socially imagined as an indicative trait even if it was not somatically obvious. *Ḥarāṭīn* were identified and even identified themselves as black despite there being no consistent or reliable distinction between their appearance and those of freeborn Muslims of high standing, for example.

North and Northwest Africa in the late medieval and early modern periods thus present an unfortunate irony. Despite the generally correct assertion that slavery in Islamic civilization cannot be understood along strictly racial lines, and despite the general trend in Islamic civilization that freed slaves or their descendants did not suffer discrimination, **in this particular context, blackness and an enduring stigma of slavery were social and semantic correlates**.[36]

The second point to keep in mind is that blackness was merely *one* of many features that the authors of the Mālikī legal texts in question, mostly Arabs or Berbers in Andalusia and North Africa, considered aesthetically or socially unappealing. Particularly in Morocco, having dark (*sumra*) or black skin or being a freed slave (*ḥarṭānī*) made potential grooms undesirable or unsuitable for a noble or light-skinned (*bayḍā'*) woman. Mālikī jurists listed several features deemed unappealing or characteristic of a lowly woman (*daniyya*). Along with blackness, others included the woman being a freed slave (in which case, she could as easily be Italian as African) and her being a non-Arab convert to Islam (*musalmāniyya*). Ironically, such non-Arab converts would almost certainly be much lighter in skin tone than Arabs and Africans alike, since they would probably be women from Persia, from north of the Black Sea or from Mediterranean Europe. So, according to these Mālikī scholars, something much more akin to a modern White phenotype could detract just as much as blackness from a woman's appeal.[37] An instance noted by the British consul in Tripoli in the 1780s provides some insight, although involving a husband, not a wife. The chief of the navy in this North African principality was actually a Neapolitan "of very low extraction." But he had somehow ended up in Tripoli, converted to Islam, and became so successful that he eventually married the governor's daughter. His wife, however, had the utmost contempt for her ill-bred husband and treated him with open disrespect.[38]

Third and finally, we must understand that including darkness or blackness among those qualities that detract from a woman's or man's appeal was not a prescriptive or universal claim being made by the authors of legal manuals like the *Waghlīsiyya*. It was highly contextual and based on the particular hierarchies and preferences of the authors' cultural surroundings. Exactly which qualities make a man or woman an appealing spouse are left to local custom to determine. Desirability is thus contextual and changes according to time, place, technology (e.g., cosmetics, gym availability, etc.), and culture.[39] The eighteenth- and nineteenth-century judges and muftis of Fez and Sous who held that blackness made a bride or groom unsuitable cited their main reason as the Shariah's deference to custom in such matters of personal and family preference, since "custom is like a legal condition."[40] Abū al-Walīd, the Cordoban judge who affirmed that it was disgraceful to be married off to a black man, was asked how Mālikī law could justifiably break with the egalitarianism demonstrated by the marriages of the Prophet and his Companions. He replied that what the Prophet had done had served to break the back of pre-Islamic Arab tribal chauvinism. It was appropriate for that time and place. But for the details of marriage law in later eras, Abū al-Walīd argued, "in every age one should look at what its people do (*mā ahluhu ʿalayhi*). With every land and locale, their people are held to what [is customary] there."[41]

Al-Waghlīsī's discussion of prohibited gazes influenced the commentaries that some Mālikī scholars penned on another influential epitome on worship in the Mālikī school. The *Mukhtaṣar* (Abridgement) of the Algerian al-Akhḍarī (d. 983/1575) states that a Muslim man should not look at an unrelated woman (*ajnabiyya*). A commentary on this text by a contemporary, another Algerian named ʿAbd al-Laṭīf al-Mirdāsī (d. 980/1572), adds the explanation that, while a man can look at the face and hands of an unrelated woman (since these are not part of her nudity, *ʿawra*), he should not look *at all* at a woman who is likely to cause him temptation. Old women and black women are exceptions to this, he adds, presumably because they do not excite attraction.[42]

Again, however, this scholar's opinion was not definitive for the Mālikī school nor reflective of how scholars in different environments thought. Even in North Africa, from Algiers to Egypt, where these specific legal texts thrived, respected jurists either qualified or ignored al-Waghlīsī's and al-Mirdāsī's opinions on blackness. Among the commentaries penned on al-Waghlīsī's epitome was one by the famous North African Sufi Aḥmad Zarrūq (d. 899/1493). He explains that the two exceptions to the prohibition on looking at unrelated women – old and black women – stood in for all types of lowly or ignoble women (*awkhāsh*) who are generally not heeded or paid attention. But Zarrūq insists that these exceptions are not absolute. "As for an older woman who is better (*khayr*) than some young ones and a black woman who is more desirable than free women, it is not permitted to look at them."[43] One such example seems to have been Ittifāq, a black female slave in fourteenth-century Cairo who so enchanted audiences with her singing and oud playing that she became the concubine of one sultan, married two more in turn and ended her long and jewel-bedecked life the wife of the grand vizier.[44]

Two major pivots of Mālikī law in Cairo, commenting on the characteristics that qualify a potential bride as undesirable, saw a more glaring problem with manuals that had given "a poor black woman" as an example of undesirability, along with the new convert. ʿAbd al-Bāqī al-Zurqānī (d. 1099/1688) and ʿAlī bin Aḥmad al-ʿAdawī (d. 1189/1775) objected that what the Mālikī tradition had originally referred to was not "every black woman" but rather the case of a specific tribe of dark-skinned, poor Egyptians who had migrated to

Medina in Mālik's time. Muḥammad Bannānī (d. 1194/1780), a leading Mālikī scholar of Fez, explained further. Lowly or undesirable status "does not apply to every black woman, just as it does not apply to every new convert . . . for each of these women could also be individuals of stature who would be desirable." Mālikī texts should not generalize these particular examples, stressed Bannānī. Rather, they should explain the general rule: lowly or undesirable women are those without any ties, standing, beauty, or wealth to speak of.[45] That what was really at issue was social status, not phenotype, is made even more evident in al-ʿAdawī's specification that the suitability or unsuitability of a slave as a groom depended on what kind of slave he was. 'White' slaves (by which he meant – literally – Caucasians), he explains, were actually in higher demand as husbands than free men, since they were a source of honor in Egypt at his time. In fact, they were the ruling class there. Black slaves, on the other hand, would be considered an insult to the bride.[46]

This could be understood as confirmation that it was blackness that was always the problem, not slaveness. This case in Egypt, however, actually confirms that local custom and conditions were ultimately determinative. The near synonymity of blackness and slaveness, and the stigma of slave descent were particular to northwest Africa. But, even there, blackness was not a problem if a person's standing was otherwise established, as with the case of the sultan Mawlāy Ismāʿīl. As the case of Egypt shows, even slaveness did not matter if the slave in question was high status.

Muḥammad Sālim al-Majlisī (d. 1302/1885), a light-skinned Arab scholar from Shinqīṭ in modern Mauritania, also broke with al-Mirdāsī's approach in his own commentary on al-Akhḍarī's work. He makes no mention of old or black women, choosing instead to note that the prohibition on ogling includes handsome young boys as well as women.[47] All mention of black women as unattractive is totally absent from a commentary on al-Akhḍarī's book written by a famous Black African Muslim scholar and educator from Segou in Mali, Saadou Oumar Toure (d. 1417/1997).[48]

Other Mālikī scholars have been more explicitly critical of how reference to custom had been misused and misconstrued on these issues of desirability. Their objections took two forms. First, custom had been overindulged and allowed to trespass onto the ethical principle that faith and deeds alone determine a person's value (whether this is really how the bulk of jurists understood this principle will be discussed later). Second, if it was legitimate and wise to defer to custom in many areas of law – and jurists all agreed it was – it was incumbent on scholars to recognize that customs change and that those in one region and time should not be assumed to apply in another.

It was a famous Andalusian exegete and immigrant to upper Egypt who pushed back hardest. Al-Qurṭubī (d. 671/1272) reminded his fellow Mālikīs of the egalitarian principle expounded by the founder of their school. The concept of lowliness as a distinction in marriage is not permissible, al-Qurṭubī pleaded, "because the Prophet (s) ruled that they [i.e., women] are equal in blood, saying, 'The blood of Muslims is equal (*al-muslimūn tatakāfa'u dimā'uhum*)' " (this Hadith is generally considered sound by Muslim scholars).[49] This egalitarian thread has been further developed by the modern Mauritanian scholar Aḥmad bin Aḥmad al-Shinqīṭī, who adds that lowliness (*danā'a*) is defined by sinfulness, not by blackness or by the other characteristics that Mālikī scholars had enumerated. The Prophet's nursemaid, Umm Ayman, was the best of women after the Prophet's wives, he reminds the reader, and she was a black former slave.[50]

Al-Qurṭubī and an earlier Mālikī scholar on whose work he often relied, Abū Bakr Ibn al-ʿArabī (d. 543/1148), leapt on other instances of what they saw as baseless prejudice. Ibn al-ʿArabī (not to be mistaken for another Andalusian, the famous mystic Ibn ʿArabī) served as a judge in Seville and Fez after years of travel and study in Baghdad. He came across a report that Ṭāwūs (d. 106/724–5), a leading early scholar of Persian descent who lived in Basra, would not attend weddings between mixed black (*aswad*) and white (*abyaḍ*) couples because he thought this fell under the Quranic condemnation of "changing God's creation" (4:119). Assuming Ṭāwūs actually thought this (the quote first appears four hundred years after his death), no one else shared his interpretation of the verse. Ibn al-ʿArabī made it clear that it was totally erroneous, pointing out that Ṭāwūs must have missed how the Prophet married his own white (*abyaḍ*) adopted son Zayd to an Ethiopian woman, Umm Ayman. A century later, al-Qurṭubī piled on, adding that the Prophet married off the child born from this marriage, the dark-skinned Usāma bin Zayd, to Fāṭima bint Qays. She was not only white (*bayḍā'*) but also a member of the noble Quraysh tribe.[51]

Other Mālikī scholars have objected to al-Waghlīsī's cultural milieu being immortalized in the text of a basic law epitome. Unlike al-Qurṭubī, the Sudanese scholar ʿUthmān bin Ḥusayn al-Barrī (d. 1380/1960) did not think that any egalitarian principle had been betrayed. He fully accepted that custom could create legitimate classes of suitability. But fixating on blackness ignored the diversity of customs. A woman's status and desirability depend on piety, wealth, looks, and livelihood. "And this is irrespective of if she is white or black," he explains, "especially in Black African (*sūdān*) lands, since blackness . . . is subjective and relative depending on various lands and the fancies of certain regions." To many in the world even some of the Prophet's own family would be considered black today, al-Barrī reminds his reader.[52] A similar and very forthright objection comes from Ḥasan al-Kattānī, a contemporary Moroccan jurist and Hadith scholar from one of Fez's grand scholarly houses. In a commentary on the *Waghlīsiyya*, al-Kattānī points out how many scholars had criticized al-Waghlīsī's statement about black women. As Zarrūq had intimated, there are beautiful black women just as there are beautiful women from every race. And, for people who live in Africa south of the Sahara, Black African women are the somatic norm. Al-Waghlīsī's words, stresses al-Kattānī, are rightfully criticized and "should never have been said" (*lā yanbaghī an yuqāl*).[53]

Not only does the context of custom and convention define the significance of phenotype and descent, changes in custom can also render its past legal meaning inscrutable. This is evident in the case of determining which statements are considered slanderous (*qadhf*), since the degree of insult borne by certain words or phrases depends on how they were understood in a particular environment. Sometimes a jurist like Mālik and his students provided explanation for why one phrase was insulting while another was not. Reporting the opinion of

Mālik, Saḥnūn explains that, if you address a white (*abyaḍ*) man of Arab descent as "O Ethiopian" (*yā ḥabashī*), then you merit the punishment for slander, since Ethiopians are a race (*jins*) distinct from Arabs. If you call a man who has no Black African ancestors "O son of a black man," then this is also slanderous, whether the man is Arab or not. Presumably this was understood as accusing his mother of committing adultery with a Black African. On the other hand, Mālik did not apply the punishment for slander to someone who called a Persian, Berber, Greek (*rūmī*), or Nabatean man any one of these labels incorrectly, since the above groups are all white (*bīḍ*).

Such rulings might have had their own logic, but they were often hard to make sense of just a generation or two later. Saḥnūn himself does not know what do with an opinion attributed to Mālik that it was not slanderous to call a Berber man Ethiopian (perhaps because there was often not much somatic distance between darker-skinned Berbers and Black Africans?).[54]

Although the notion of black women as unattractive became cemented in some Mālikī books of law because of al-Waghlīsī's unfortunate wording, the fact that other Mālikī jurists from Africa north and south of the Sahara did not replicate this strain of thinking and even explicitly opposed it demonstrates how much context shapes the details of Islamic law. Had specific mention of black women as unattractive not been fixed in the prose of a standard Mālikī textbook, it likely would not have elicited any comments outside the North African context in which that preference seems to have been endemic. It is noteworthy that, while the *Waghlīsiyya* textbook was certainly known in the western Sahel, it did not generate the scholarly engagement it did in North Africa. There are twenty-five copies in Timbuktu's manuscript libraries, two in Segou, and a copy of Zarrūq's commentary in Niamey in Niger.[55] Yet scholars in the regions of Senegambia to the Niger bend seem to have yielded no commentaries on the work.[56]

How would Muslims in an area like Segou, where a general Black African phenotype is the somatic norm, have perceived al-Waghlīsī's statement about the unattractiveness of Black African women or the reference to blackness as a factor in lackluster appeal? How could such language not be offensive? Abdullah Hamid Ali, a Black American Muslim scholar trained in Mālikī law at the Qayrawiyyīn University in Fez, points out that there is an almost unsurmountable incongruity in the accusation that the Mālikī school of law is anti-black. It has for centuries enjoyed near exclusive adherence and loyalty in Muslim Africa and among those Muslims who are overwhelmingly Black African in phenotype (Shāfiʿīsm on Africa's east coast is an exception to this). Ali argues that African adherents of the Mālikī school of law did not take offense at what legal commentaries written on the Mediterranean coast of North Africa listed regarding unappealing characteristics in women or men because they were irrelevant to their African context.[57] Indeed, in my own research on this issue, queries to West African ulama on these points of Mālikī law are almost always met with the polite befuddlement of someone being asked about a matter plucked from medieval obscurity.

A quick glimpse at the dominant custom of the global West shows how irrelevant other features Mālikī scholars deemed unattractive are today as well. Along with blackness, the non-Arab female convert to Islam (*musalmāniyya*) was also deemed lowly. Yet, if limited studies, the anecdotal testimony of the head of a global Muslim matchmaking service, and memes are any evidence, the White female convert to Islam is the most sought-after bride today.[58]

The famous Senegalese Sufi master of the Tijānī order, Shaykh Ibrāhīm Niasse, adroitly gathers together the threads of Prophetic egalitarianism and changing custom, putting Mālikī legal distinctions around race and color in their place. He cites the examples given by the scholars who had formulated these distinctions a millennium ago, subtly demonstrating how races like 'Nabatean' that might have made sense in the Middle East long ago are now archaic and meaningless in the greater Muslim world. Niasse acknowledges that "lineage is taken into account in customary usage and in Islamic law." "But lineage ceases to be of any consequence," he rejoins, "in the face of belief and true devotion (*taqwā*) . . . lineage in the face of *taqwā* is as the stars that disappear when the sun rises."[59]

FIGURE 3: Shaykh Aḥmad Bamba praying on the sea. His disciple Mūsā Ka composed a lengthy praise poem narrating Bamba's exile and return. In this famous scene, Bamba is taken by ship into exile. Aboard are a colonial official, a Catholic priest, and a Frenchwoman. When prayer time arrives, Bamba is told he cannot pray on the ship. The Frenchwoman also repeatedly touches the saint, thus breaking his ritual purity. To accomplish his prayer, Bamba casts his rug onto the water and prays there. (Painting on reverse glass, 1978, author's collection.)

FIGURE 4 (left): Sufi scholar Shaykh Ibrāhīm Niasse (d. 1395/1975). FIGURE 5 (right): Niasse with his daughter, the late Maryam bint Ibrāhīm Niasse (d. 1442/2020), who memorized the Quran as a teen and then devoted her life to teaching the holy book to anyone who wished to learn. She gained international renown for founding educational institutions for Quranic learning and childhood education. (Photo provided by her family.)

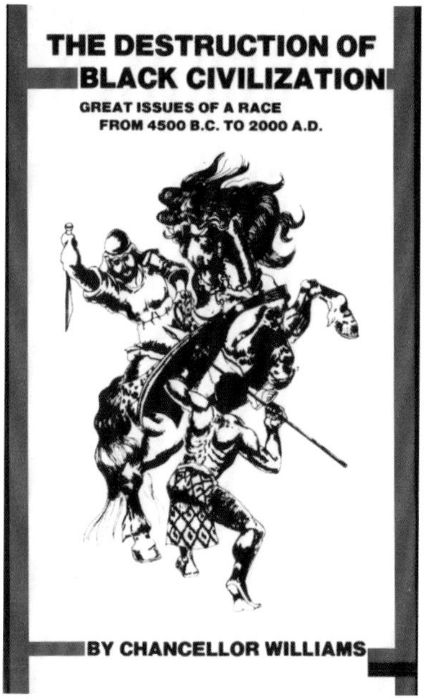


FIGURE 6: The cover of a revised edition of Chancellor Williams' *The Destruction of Black Civilization*. (From the book *The Destruction of Black Civilization* © 1987 by Chancellor Williams, reprinted by permission of Third World Press Foundation, Chicago, Illinois.)

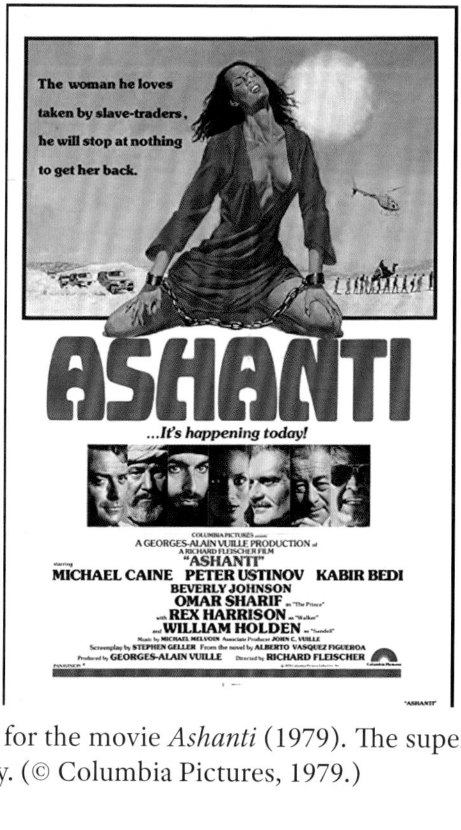


FIGURE 7: Poster for the movie *Ashanti* (1979). The superb cast belies the film's poor quality. (© Columbia Pictures, 1979.)

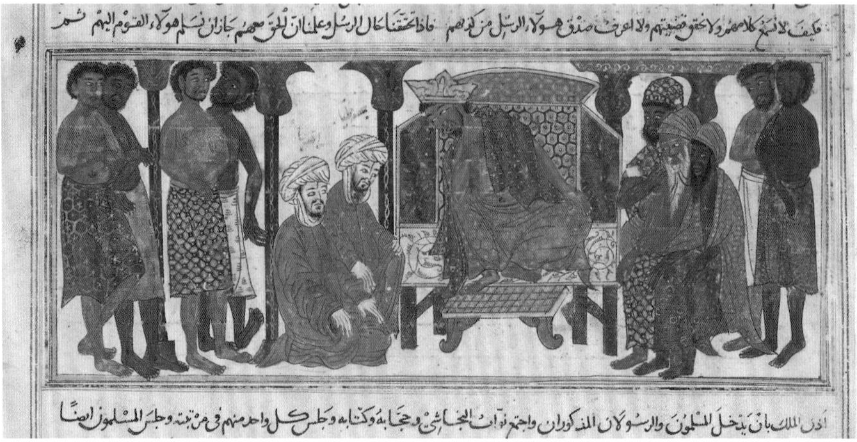

FIGURE 8: Fourteenth-century illustration showing two Muslim representatives, including the Prophet's cousin Jaʿfar bin Abī Ṭālib (right), in audience before the Ethiopian king, *circa* 615 CE. They are requesting refuge for the Muslims persecuted in Mecca. From the *Jāmi ʿal-tawārīkh*, a world history commissioned by Rashīd al-Dīn (d. 717/1318), vizier of the Ilkhanid court in Tabriz. (University of Edinburgh library collection, Or.MS.20, f.52r.)

FIGURE 9: An incidental depiction of how a female slave in an elite household was imagined in the 1300s in northern Iraq. An illustration, produced in 1315 CE, from al-Jazarī's *Kitāb fī maʿrifat al-ḥiyal al-handasiyya*. It shows a mechanical wine-pouring machine designed for the ruler of Diyar Bakr around 1200 CE. A papier-mâché slave woman (*jāriya*) emerges from a closet eight times an hour to serve wine. (© The al-Sabah Collection, Dar al-Athar al-Islamiyyah, Kuwait.)

older dispensations of the Cinderella tale end up buttressing class. In the 1697 French and 1812 Grimm Brothers urtexts of the story, Cinderella's father is wealthy. She is only made lowly by his second wife. In varied versions from farther afield, such as the Tang Chinese and twelfth-century Old French dispensations, 'Cinderella' is nobly born, but this status has been concealed.[2] Happily ever after is not breaking with social structure but rectifying it.

Aspects omitted in many (but not all) oral, written and film versions of the Cinderella tale are the difficulties and undesirable consequences faced by the couple after the story ends. Can individuals from two worlds really live happily ever after if those worlds differ in ways that their society, and perhaps even we, deem significant? Today even nods to the challenges of class and cultural difference are few and far between. In *Crazy Rich Asians* (2018), the low-born but successful heroine acknowledges that her wealthy beau forsaking his family to marry her would be too devastating for everyone involved. Fortunately, his mother relents. Kumail Nanjiani's *The Big Sick* (2017) is a rare exception. In this film, the young Pakistani Muslim protagonist finally tells his immigrant family that he cannot grant them the one thing they have asked of him – to marry a good, Pakistani Muslim girl – because he has fallen in love with a (non-Muslim) White American. In the confrontation scene, the father's grief over the son's disregard for his family is as moving as the son's profession of true love. The film ends with the son estranged from his broken-hearted mother, who is not without audience sympathy.

In North Africa, we saw how conceptions of blackness and anti-blackness were really proxies for value in a social hierarchy. They can be in the U.S. as well, even among communities all racialized as black. Though less dramatic than the king's reaction in *Coming to America*, what Ohimai Amaize has called the 'social distance' that African immigrants to the U.S. can feel toward Black Americans has been framed by some as antiblack.[3] In this case, antiblackness represents not racism expressed along lines of African descent but the social distance in culture and class felt towards those whom the *Crazy Rich Asians* matriarch would call "not our kind of people."

This suggests that one analytical approach to antiblackness can be as part of a broader question of how a society and legal system imagines hierarchy, egalitarianism, and appropriate relationships. It is no accident that antiblackness in Islamic law primarily surfaces under the rubric of marriage suitability (*kafā'a*).

At many points in this book, we have seen reference to Islam's egalitarian spirit, manifested in the faith's pure founts of the Quran and the Prophet's teachings. In this chapter, however, we will see how the Islamic normative traditions of law and political theory were markedly hierarchical, due to reasons both intrinsic and extrinsic. As with the Mālikī scholars who opposed their school's antiblackness, however, I argue that the Islamic legal tradition overall is nevertheless possessed of a relentlessly egalitarian ethos. It has risen to particular prominence with the drive to revive adherence to the Quran and Prophetic way in the last two centuries. The overlap of social hierarchy, law, and the body stands out in the question of caste and marriage in Muslim India. How and why Muslim scholars in South Asia affirmed, denied, or tolerated caste offers a useful analogy to antiblackness in Islamic law and raises the question of why, at the meeting of the Shariah and society, the guardians of Islamic law and ethics have not spoken with a more prophetic voice against discrimination. The answer lies partly in the competing responsibilities that Muslim scholars have borne as both the heirs of Muhammad's message and the agents charged with resolving everyday disputes in the social ocean around them. But it also lies in the priorities that Muslim scholars have identified for effecting change.

## JUSTIFYING HIERARCHY IN SUITABILITY (*kafā'a*)

This may seem ironic after a chapter on antiblackness in Mālikī marriage law, but at the foundations of its legal doctrine in the opinions of Mālik himself, his school is by far the least discriminatory in what regulations could be invoked to prevent couples from marrying. Mālik considered all free Muslims on equal footing, with the school of law built on his legacy differing as to whether slaves had a lower status (those who considered a slave groom unsuitable for a free wife pointed to sound Hadiths in which the Prophet gave a recently freed slave woman the choice of remaining with her still-enslaved husband).[4] This minimal position on suitability, upheld by Mālik himself and the egalitarian strain in his school, rests on two pillars. The first is the very famous statement of the Prophet that, "If a [man] comes to you whose religion and character please you, then marry [your daughter] to him." If one does not, the Prophet explains, there will be great strife.[5] The second was the overwhelming unreliability or ambiguity of the evidence for other criteria of suitability (*kafā'a*).

In contrast to Mālik, Sunni legal scholarship writ large elaborated an imposing list of characteristics that could potentially bar marriage. Scholars had the best intentions in doing this. They felt encouraging suitability in marriage was mandated by the Quran and Prophetic teachings. Furthermore, they considered it a general aim of these scriptures to promote felicity and harmony in Muslims' lives. Though the schools of law have differed in the extent to which they subscribe to all categories on the list, the characteristics that should be taken into consideration when selecting a spouse or approving of a marriage include: **confession** (*dīn*, e.g., a Muslim woman cannot marry a non-Muslim man), **lineage** (*nasab*), **slave/free status**, **piety and character** (called *ḥasab* or *dīn* by Ḥanafīs, *diyāna* by Ḥanbalīs), **financial status** (*māl*), absence or presence of **defects**, and **vocation** (*ṣan'a*).

There has been awesome variety in the rules for suitability elaborated by Muslim scholars over the centuries, with schools of law differing internally and changing their positions over time. In part this is due to the dearth of compelling scriptural evidence, which has left jurists to build up rulings according to custom and their own patterns of legal reasoning. Many Hadiths offer guidance on suitability, but most are weak, debated, or even forged. One Hadith that is widely considered authentic is the Prophet's saying "Choose well for procreation, and marry those who are suitable."[6] Though this affirms the importance of suitability in marriage, it does not specify what suitability means. To justify their more extensive criteria for suitability, non-Mālikīs have cited the following evidence:

**Sound Hadiths that explicitly give details on suitability**: A Hadith in which the Prophet advises a woman not to marry a man who had no money, and the Hadith of the newly freed slave woman being able to choose whether to remain married to her enslaved husband were considered reliable and generally applicable.[7] There are numerous other Hadiths, such as "Arabs are the equals of one another, and the *mawālī* (non-Arabs) are the equals of one another . . ." and "People are the equals of one another, except for weavers (*ḥā'ik*) and cuppers (*ḥajjām*)." These were of dubious reliability, however, as was admitted even by scholars whose schools held *kafā'a*-heavy positions, like the Shāfiʿī's al-Bayhaqī (d. 458/1066), and Ibn Ḥajar. Abū Ḥanīfa (d. 150/767) himself considered the Hadith about weavers to be anomalous and insufficient for evidence.[8] There are a massive number of Hadiths claiming the Prophet ordered Muslims to love and honor Arabs and that God had favored them by ennobling them with His final messenger. But, as al-Haytamī (d. 974/1567) shows in his digest of these Hadiths, the explicit ones are almost entirely unreliable.[9]

**Questionably broad readings of Quranic verses**, such as "God has granted favor to some of you over others in sustenance" (16:71).

**Hadiths deemed reliable but of questionable relevance**, like those praising the virtue of the Prophet's tribe and clan, the Prophet stating that "Merit (*ḥasab*) is wealth, and nobility (*karam*) is piety," and his command to "Look past the blunders of the virtuous, except in the Hudud" (i.e., even those of high status are subject to Hudud punishments, namely those offenses for which the Quran or Hadiths set punishments).[10]

**The rulings of early Muslims**, like the caliph ʿUmar's statement, "I prohibit the thighs of women of merit (*aḥsāb*) to any not their equals." (Scholars have debated this statement's reliability.)[11]

**General reasoning** based on custom and social norms, as we have seen more elitist Mālikīs employ for the suitability categories of phenotype and lineage.[12]

As we have already seen, for the pro-*kafāʾa* Mālikīs, the mandate to defer to custom did almost all the evidentiary work in justifying their position. Custom played a significant role in the other schools of law as well, in particular in justifying vocation as a category of suitability, as both Ḥanafī and Ḥanbalī scholars acknowledged.[13] In fact, leading Ḥanafī jurists even saw the Prophet's alleged diminishing of weavers and cuppers as contextual to his society, not a universal judgment. The Cairean Ibn al-Humām (d. 861/1457) explains that in Alexandria in his own day weavers would be on par with perfumiers, a generally esteemed profession, because weavers were held in good standing in that city.[14]

Custom was indeed so dominant in elaborating and justifying the legal recognition of social hierarchies that it did so far outside marriage law. On the question of who can offer testimony in court, many details depended on custom. The Quran had instructed Muslims who cannot find the ideal type and number of such witnesses to take the testimony "of those of whom you approve" (2:282).[15] Some Mālikī scholars did not accept the testimony of tanners, cuppers, or weavers, again on the basis that God and the Prophet had left Muslims to follow custom on this. Ḥanafīs have had no problem with the testimony of such occupations.[16] The important Shāfiʿī jurist Abū Isḥāq al-Shīrāzī (d. 476/1083) held that one cannot accept the testimony of someone with no honor (*muruwwa*), like a dancer or someone who does not cover their head in a place where custom (*ʿāda*) says one should. The school disagrees over whether this applies to those who perform lowly jobs (*ṣanāʾiʿ danīʾa*), such as sweepers, tanners, and garbagemen, if they are pious and goodly. Some concluded that this makes virtue impossible for them, while others, like al-Nawawī (d. 676/1277), returned to the Quranic rule about nobility emanating from piety.[17]

How did the pro-extensive-*kafāʾa* majority in the Sunni legal tradition address this Quranic pronouncement that nobility was defined by piety, or the very explicit and very reliable instruction from the Prophet that one marry one's daughter to any man whose piety and character were pleasing? In short, they read these proof texts as emphases on the importance of piety, not as proof of its exclusive role. The Shāfiʿī scholar al-Ṭībī (d. 743/1342) acknowledged that the Hadith of accepting the pious groom seems to favor Mālik's position that only piety matters, but he responds that it entails no more than a warning against looking *only* at a groom's wealth or status.[18] Earlier, leading Persian Shāfiʿī scholars of Hadith and law like al-Baghawī (d. 516/1122) had also treated this Hadith as meaning that religion was the *most important* aspect of suitability, not the only one.[19] The other schools of law have also commonly made the argument that egalitarian scripture like this Hadith and the Quran's statement that nobility comes from piety 1) were only warnings to Muslims not to insult or condescend people because of their lineage, and 2) were explanations that lineage, etc., does not bolster one's standing with God or in the Afterlife. But they did matter in this life.[20]

## ISLAMIC CIVILIZATION AND NATURAL HIERARCHY

For many, perhaps most, Muslim scholars, the agglomeration of Hadiths (even if unsound), intimations sensed in Quranic verses, the force of custom, and the compounded generations of legal reasoning clearly demonstrated that suitability in descent, wealth, and vocation were legitimate features of human society. Legal texts in every school of law but the Mālikī present statements like "a sweeper does not marry a noble woman (*sharīfa*)" as fixed points needing no justification. Moreover, such hierarchies were not just social realities that the Shariah accepted because they could not be expunged. They were seen as proper and beneficial. In this earthly life, the Egyptian Shāfiʿī scholar al-Damīrī (d. 808/1405) explains, "genealogies (*ansāb*) are taken into account for people's good."[21] The seminal Indian scholar Shāh Walī Allāh (d. 1176/1762), who knew Indian customs intimately but preferred hewing to Arabian tradition, saw suitability in wealth, nobility, and morality as reflections of something profoundly present in all societies. These facets were "among those things that people in their groups have been created with as part of their nature (*jubila ʿalayhi*) . . . and people are of various levels (*marātib*)."[22]

One might view the discussion over marriage suitability as an example of the tension between the egalitarian teachings of the Quran and a fractionating social tendency to hierarchy, between the impulse to locate merit in an individual's conduct and the aristocratic presumption that hereditary status, merit, and moral worth are all coterminous. Whether in the Arab system of tribal rankings, which soon began to reassert itself, or in the trenchant social stratification of Abbasid Persian culture, within decades of the Prophet's death Muslims found themselves engaged in what Louise Marlow has called "the taming of Islamic egalitarianism." The Near Eastern world into which Islam moved and whose culture it absorbed was one pervaded by hierarchy in theory and in reality, from Plato's three-part structure of the city to the Hermetic tradition and, most of all, the ancient Persian assumption that rigid class division was the single most essential feature of a just state and functioning society.[23] The Shariah notion that profession should be considered in marriage suitability had precedents in Greek and Persian understandings of the link between work and capacity and between capacity and social value. In the Greco-Persian Near East, it was a common notion that occupation reflected a person's ability to understand as well as their merit. The Islamic learned tradition adopted this view, as demonstrated by the great Islamic philosopher al-Fārābī (d. 339/950) in his commentary on Plato's *Laws*.[24]

Of course, the Muslim jurists elaborating rules of suitability did not think they were betraying any Quranic value. They firmly believed they were properly manifesting the message of God and His prophet. There were certainly those who, in some moments at least, stressed a purer and simpler egalitarian call. In his argument for Islam's virtues over other faiths and civilizations, al-ʿĀmirī (d. 381/992) attacked the pre-Islamic Persian structure of state and society that subordinated talent and initiative to social rank at birth. He compared this with Islam's teaching that "All people are from Adam, and Adam was from dust" along with its universal mandate for the acquisition of knowledge.[25] But the simple fact was that Islamic civilization came to be dominated by the same presumption that had reigned before the Prophet: that lineage and descent determined both nobility and ability, either because nobility of birth mattered more than merit or because it was inconceivable that the two could occur independently of one another. As with the just societies imagined in the works of Plato and the *Rig Veda*, Muslim intellectuals were able to, as Marlow describes, "rationalize inequality" by reasoning that people have innate dispositions that are complementary, if not equal, and hereditary. Communal success rests on people cooperating and each playing their role.[26]

Once inequality had been rationalized, scripture could be reread accordingly. If one believes that descent, lineage, or family culture plays a significant role in passing on excellence, then scriptural commandments to grant station by merit become mandates for hereditary hierarchy. When the Prophet says, "The best of you in the Jahiliyya are the best of you in Islam as long as they understand (*faquhū*) [the truth]," this makes devotion to God the essential component for social prominence.[27] But it could also be read as meaning that, once everyone is nominally Muslim and has "understood," pre-existing social hierarchies can legitimately reassert themselves.

Once social stratification has reasserted itself, statements like the Prophet saying "nobility is piety" or even the Quran's decree tying piety to nobility can have their polarity reversed. In a society in which noble birth is esteemed, including descent from the Prophet or a great Muslim saint, "nobility is piety" can be interpreted not as piety defining nobility but as nobility coinciding with piety – the highborn are also pious. The cosmopolitan litterateur of Abbasid Iraq and Iran, al-ʿAttābī (d. early 200s/800s), wrote of nobility as the root (*aṣl*) and piety as its branch.[28] Al-Rāzī pondered whether the Quranic verse "The noblest among you before God is the most pious" meant that being noble in God's eyes made one pious or being pious made one noble in God's eyes. In either case, however, al-Rāzī and his audience understood the nobility he was considering as ethical devotion to God, not lineage.[29] But a century and a half later, Ḍiyā' al-Dīn Baranī (d. *circa* 760/1360), a jurist and sometime advisor to the court of the Delhi sultans, read that verse in reverse. For him, "The impure (*palīd*) is born from the impure, base-born from base-born; they can never be 'the most pious.'" If one comes across piety in a merchant or someone else low-class, Baranī explains, one of their ancestors must have been of noble stock.[30] In effect, they are Cinderella recognized for her noble birth.

For the majority of Muslim scholars in Islamic history, the robust criteria of suitability in marriage were not a betrayal of some clear Quranic spirit of egalitarianism. They were the accurate understanding of God's revelation. The hierarchies traced back to the Quran and the Prophet were often not as dramatic or contemptuous as Baranī's. They could be quite virtuous in what they prized. One of the most compelling and widespread scripturally-grounded instances of an Islamic hierarchy was the standing of the 'People of the House,' as the descendants of the Prophet are called, in both Sunni and Shiite Islam. A famous seventeenth-century book on a clan of Yemeni scholars and saints from Hadramawt tells how it has always been the People of the House who have been consistently devoted to piety and good deeds and how the axis of sainthood is always among them. The book's author, al-Shillī (d. 1093/1682), concedes there are rotten apples. But he considers it beyond doubt that loving the Prophet's descendants is required for Muslims and that hating them is prohibited.

For al-Shillī and his readers, this is not chauvinism or tribal supremacism. It is simply, according to the majority trend in Sunni and Shiite Islam, a straightforward instruction from God and His prophet. Al-Shillī's heavy tome on the saints of Hadramawt features pages and pages of Hadiths (mostly unreliable, according to Muslim Hadith scholars) on the virtues of the Arabs, the Prophet's tribe, his clan, and his descendants. Yet this is followed by pages listing all the Hadiths warning against racism and tribal chauvinism, all buttressing the Quran's teaching that the "The noblest among you before God is the most pious." For al-Shillī, this is not a contradiction. God and the Prophet warn against arrogance and false pride in one's descent, declaring that an individual's standing before God is defined by their piety. But God nonetheless had granted some tribes, nations, and families more blessing and higher standing than others, bad apples excepted.[31]

Al-Shillī was no solitary voice on this. The same Bilgrāmī who had crusaded against the Hindu custom of widows not remarrying also raised eyebrows by declaring to any audience who would listen that the descendants of the Prophet were all guaranteed salvation in Paradise. When it was objected that these descendants were quite numerous in India and that such news would presumably not prove useful guidance for them, Bilgrāmī replied that this was the teaching of Islam and that he would announce it regardless. Indeed, the same position had been expressed by a towering figure of Islamic scholarship and administration in north India, Shihāb al-Dīn Dawlatābādī (d. 849/1445), as well as by the Meccan scholar al-Haytamī and the über-influential Sufi Ibn ʿArabī. (Though Ibn ʿArabī offers a useful reminder about the other-worldly nature of this advantage; it had no effect on earthly life, rights, or obligations. If a descendant of the Prophet committed a crime, they would be punished in this life like anyone else.)[32]

## A USEFUL ANALOGY: ISLAMIC LAW AND CASTE IN INDIA

Caste among Muslims in South Asia, a region in which the Ḥanafī school of law predominates, offers an interesting parallel to blackness in North African Mālikism. In both cases, we see the partnering of laws on *kafāʾa* with the presumption that human society was justly and naturally deeply hierarchical. In both cases, existing social hierarchies and Islamic norms intermingled in such a way that the resulting social and legal fabric earned the validation of many Muslim jurists. In both cases, however, prominent scholarly voices dissented. In examining how Muslim scholars have addressed caste in South Asia, we see in fine detail how a scholarly tradition has managed the tensions between egalitarian ideals and a hierarchy that, whether it accords with the Shariah or not, was socially daunting and even inescapable.

Baranī's elitist conviction that maintaining social hierarchy was essential for stability was not novel in Islamic civilization. But it likely owes its rare intensity to his Indian context. Indian converts to Islam would often preserve their caste sensibilities, and Muslims in South Asia were influenced by their cultural environment. Against this background, the Ḥanafī *kafāʾa* criteria of lineage and vocation – as well as the role that the Shariah granted custom in extending them – allowed Muslim scholars in India to effectively fashion a system of caste that at times paralleled the one surrounding them and at times formed an Islamicate counterpart within the space of the Muslim community (see Appendix VII). Muslims in South Asia have generally not matched their Hindu counterparts in the severity of their prohibitions on caste intermarriage, dining together, or the taboos of pollution by inter-caste contact. But South Asian Muslim society has been characterized by structures highly comparable to Hindu notions of caste based on lineage and vocation.

The majority of Muslim scholars in South Asia have defended *kafāʾa* and the structure of caste simultaneously. Whatever their motivations (it should be noted that all the scholars looked at here are high caste), South-Asian ulama have advocated the conservative Ḥanafī position on *kafāʾa* and applied it to the Indian caste distinctions of descent and vocation.[33] Ashraf ʿAlī Thanawi provides a representative voice. Though he advised parents first and foremost to consider the piety of potential spouses for their children, his opinions show a blending of Ḥanafī jurisprudence and South Asian caste consciousness. The Ḥanafī school has generally considered Arabs as one group, all suitable for one another, and *ʿajam* (non-Arabs) as a group suitable for one another. This fit Muslims in South Asia well, with their account of Arab, Persian, and Turkic Muslims entering India by land and sea and then locals embracing their faith. But further internal variegation was required beyond the standard Ḥanafī framework. Fortunately, the mandate to accommodate custom facilitated this. What emerged as the high Muslim castes (*ashrāf*) consisted of, at the top, those who traced their ancestry back to the early Arab Muslims, then those tracing descent to the Central Asian Mughal elite and, finally, those of Pathan and Afghan ancestry. According to Thanawi, among these high castes, those of Arab descent could intermarry and those of non-Arab descent could intermarry. Thanawi accepted the Hadith of the Prophet deeming weavers a lowly profession, which fortuitously accorded with the low-caste status weavers occupied in Indian tradition. And the Ḥanafī school's method of building on this Hadith by analogy and recourse to custom led Thanawi to import other South Asian caste sensibilities, ranking barbers and washers as lowly along with weavers.[34] That Thanawi's view was representative is indicated by the agreement of an arch rival in Indian Islamic thought, Aḥmad Riḍā Barelwi (d. 1340/1921). This influential Ḥanafī jurist similarly based his list of lowly (*danā'a*) vocational castes on what was considered ignoble by custom.[35]

## EGALITARIANISM RESURGENT: JAHILIYYA, CASTE, AND TRIBALISM

The belief that hierarchy on the basis of descent, wealth, vocation, etc. was not just recognized by Islam's scriptures and scholarship but also naturally embedded in human society came to dominate in Islamic civilization, at least in the areas between Morocco and India. If much of the Mālikī school of law seems to have had no qualms about abandoning Mālik's own egalitarian views on who was fit to marry whom, and if Muslim scholars in India effectively indigenized caste, is it really appropriate to speak of 'a tension' between egalitarianism and hierarchy in Islamic law? Or is the Islamic normative tradition simply, clearly, hierarchical?

In fact, is it even correct to speak of some Quranic or Prophetic egalitarianism to begin with? When Shāh Walī Allāh stated that "people are of various levels," he was expressing what Muslim scholars assumed to be a reality not just among humans as part of nature but also in the revelation God sent in parallel with nature. When God says in the Quran, "We have apportioned among [people] their livelihood in this worldly life, and We have raised some above others in degrees so that some may make use of others in labor" (43:32), the Quran is validating as natural, to one extent or another, hierarchy and distinctions in wealth and labor relations. When the Quran instructs Muslims to "obey those in authority among you" (4:59) and to "tend to the near of kin" (16:90), it is affirming as natural both political authority as well as, to some degree or another, the inclusivity and exclusivity of the family. When the Prophet's wife Aisha says that he "taught us to place people in their appropriate stations" (*nunazzila al-nās manāzilahum*), it is both as Muslims and as human beings with their varied capacities and talents that individuals are being placed.[36] People in society differ in their piety and devotion. They also differ in their family, talents, opportunities, and wealth. Money, family, and ability may be all tests from God – as the Quran says, "He has raised some of you over others in degrees to test you all with what He has granted you" (6:165). Lineage might be worthless if not accompanied by faith. But these distinctions and duties nonetheless form hierarchies. And, again, once it was assumed in a wide swath of Islamic civilization that those enjoying degree in status, wealth, and lineage do so *because* they are pious or inseparably *from* piety, then even profane social hierarchy accorded with God's revelation. Can we even speak of a Quranic egalitarianism Muslims can be accused of betraying?

I think we can. There was and has always been an egalitarian spirit, rooted in the Quran and sound attributions to the Prophet. Prominent and numerous scholarly voices throughout the centuries have consistently and passionately rejected the pull into discrimination on the basis of lineage, race, or wealth, whether such distinction rested on arguments based in Islamic scripture, its empowerment of custom, or assumptions about human society. Certainly, the Quran and the Prophet's teachings do affirm and endorse specific hierarchical relationships, as well as specific duties and rights that stem from inclusion and exclusion. These are balanced, however, by scriptural principles recognizing the equality of humans before God, the basic rights of all humans to physical inviolability, property, and due process before God's law, and that piety and good deeds define one's nobility.[37]

The pages of the Quran display a tension between hierarchy and egalitarianism not because the book is flawed but because that tension is inherent in the human condition. The French anthropologist Louis Dumont (d. 1998) observed that "to adopt a value is to introduce a hierarchy, and a certain consensus of values, a certain consensus of ideas."[38] For Dumont, hierarchy's absence – total equality – is less an ideal than a dangerous denial of any differences in condition or capacity between individuals.[39] Hierarchy is inevitable in human society because our species has consistently made or embraced assessments of value. And proffering values entails asking who embodies them and to what degree. The question before us is therefore not 'whether value' but rather what values should be embraced and how relationships should be structured to promote them. The values around which the Quran and the Prophet's teachings structure hierarchy and obligation recognize universals in the human condition, such as family, moral sensibility, the need for material sustenance, and some structure of communal authority. Individuals exist in webs and on rungs of kinship, wealth, authority, talent, and character. It is not a betrayal of Quranic egalitarianism to affirm this. Betrayal comes in insisting, like Baranī, that value and capacity are bound inseparably to lineage or the body.

As with Mālikī dissenters, with caste in South Asia not all scholars endorsed the main Ḥanafī rules on *kafā'a* or saw accommodating caste as appropriate. Numerous, influential critics have emerged since the nineteenth century. In Bengal, the Sufi scholar Munshī Samīr al-Dīn penned and distributed his *The Full Moon of the Heedless* (*Badr al-ghāfilīn*) in the mid 1800s. This booklet was aimed at the common folk and inspiring them to Islamic piety and practice, and it became extremely popular. Among other matters, it criticized the rural *ashrāf* for their Hindu caste customs, such as not praying the Friday communal prayer alongside lower castes.[40]

Standing up against caste gained much greater momentum with the rise of the Indian anti-colonial struggle and its alternating calls for, at times, transnational Muslim unity and, at other times, Muslim–Hindu solidarity. Two leading scholars in British India who rejected the Ḥanafī school's standard position on *kafā'a* were known for their prolific knowledge as well as their activism for Muslim education and Indian solidarity. They saw caste as a betrayal of Islam's true message, a message that their drive to resist colonial rule and Western cultural hegemony made them keen to appreciate. In a famous series of lectures delivered in Madras in 1925, Sayyid Sulaymān Nadwī (d. 1373/1953) totally rejected discrimination by race, descent, caste, or color. He writes that Islam "wiped all this away," "making all children of Adam equal," and citing the same major egalitarian Hadiths and Quranic verses we have already seen. Mosques are open to all, the Quran read by all, "the door of knowledge open to all" and all people equal in rights, Nadwī exclaimed. This is in contrast to Hindu caste and ancient Persian hierarchy as well as Western colonial White supremacism and segregation in the U.S. and South Africa.[41] Muftī Kifāyat Allāh of Deoband (d. 1372/1952) also gave a fatwa that discrimination on the basis of vocation is baseless. While a student, he had supported himself by making and selling skullcaps before spending a successful career as the head of a major madrasa in Delhi. He was also very active in the Jamiat Ulama-i Hind (Union of Indian Scholars), organizing Muslims on political issues and promoting Muslim solidarity in British India and internationally.[42]

The anti-caste message resonated as well within the mid-twentieth-century Islamist movement of the Jama'at-e Islami (though there was internal dissent on this), partially amid competition with Christian and Communist groups all lobbying for converts among the Hindu *dalit* communities.[43] One example is Mawlānā Anīs Aḥmad Falāḥī, a teacher at the Jamiat ul-Falah madrasa, a center of learning in northern India linked to the Jama'at-e Islami. Although Falāḥī himself is of noble descent, he has spoken out against the construct of caste in his classes, arguing it is an import from Hinduism.[44] More recently, Mawlānā ʿAbd al-Ḥamīd Nuʿmānī, a leader of the Union of Indian Scholars, has called for a reinterpretation of the Ḥanafī rules on suitability, abandoning a reliance on the weak Hadiths justifying them and returning to Quranic egalitarianism.[45] A similar argument has been made by Khālid Sayfallāh Raḥmānī, the general secretary of India's Islamic Fiqh Academy and the All India Muslim Personal Law Board. He argues that, though many of the details of Ḥanafī rules on *kafā'a* are anachronistic and rest on contingent legal reasoning, the aims of past and present jurists remain laudable: to help Muslims contract harmonious and lasting marriages.[46] The respected Indian Ḥanafī scholar Ḥabīb al-Raḥmān al-Aʿẓamī (d. 1412/1992), who devoted his scholarly career to the study of Hadiths, wrote a treatise in which he argued against what he saw as Arab supremacism that had crept into Ḥanafī law on marriage in contrast to the strongest evidence from the Quran and Hadiths.[47] Even the most prominent Muslim scholar in Pakistan today, Muftī Taqī ʿUthmānī, though he feels that the Prophet's teachings encourage those of noble birth to marry one another, concludes that a pious bride of lowly birth is better than an impious one of noble birth.[48]

Suitability in marriage and other issues in which hierarchy manifested itself, like suitability to testify in court, have been perennial loci of disagreement in Islamic law. It has not been uncommon for more egalitarian or idealistic principles to find expression even within a school of law that upholds extensive criteria on marriage suitability. Scholars have pushed back when inspired to return to the original ethos of the Quran and Prophetic teaching. The esteem for knowledge of God's religion, for example, was so strong that two prominent Ḥanafī jurists, the Transoxianans al-Bazdawī (d. 482/1089) and Qāḍīkhān (d. 592/1196), had asserted that a lowborn scholar was suitable for a bride from the People of the House because the virtue of knowledge trumped that of lineage.[49]

It is not surprising, however, that the strongest and most sustained call to revive the original spirit of the Quran and the prophetic impulse has rung out from the Muslim revival and reform movements of the eighteenth century. We find this with the Sufi devotion to the 'Muhammadan Way' (*al-ṭarīqa al-muḥammadiyya*) in this period, as is evident in the dynamic Tijānī Sufi community founded by Ibrāhīm Niasse in West Africa. His movement crossed over the rigid lines of caste in Senegambia, with Niasse encouraging marriage between Muslims of all nationalities and backgrounds.[50]

And, of course, we find a swelling of egalitarian spirit among those eighteenth-century Sunni revivalists who sought to preempt the Sunni schools of law, with their centuries of accreted legal reasoning and acculturation, in favor of a direct recourse to the primary sources of the Quran, Hadiths, and the pure ways of the early Muslim community (*salaf*). Although Salafism by that name emerged only in the early twentieth century, the ethos was undoubtably present and active in the eighteenth century, with its epicenter in Mecca and Medina. Indeed, Salafism's inspiration rested at least partially on the much earlier writings of Ibn Taymiyya (d. 728/1328). This Ḥanbalī polymath explained that establishing the significance of lineage, wealth, or vocation can only be done authoritatively by God or the Prophet, and that "there is no explicit, sound scriptural text (*naṣṣ*) on these matters." What reliable Hadiths there are praising Arabs or their virtues are general and do not apply to every single person in that group, he added.[51] Ibn Abī al-ʿIzz (d. 792/1390), an interesting figure who belonged to the Ḥanafī school but was inspired by Ibn Taymiyya, also concludes that the scriptural mandate for egalitarianism clearly shows that one cannot consider lineage in marriage suitability.[52]

The eighteenth-century revival movements revolutionized the practice of Islam in several regions, in particular in South Asia. Munshī Samīr al-Dīn's *Full Moon of the Heedless* was an expression of how scholarly and preaching networks emanating from the Hejaz carried the mission of purifying faith and practice to British India. Caste, often addressed by its proxy of *kafāʾa*, emerged as a target. Pan-Islamist movements like the Jama'at-e Islami were also influenced by Muslim revivalist scholars. And the close engagement with the Prophet's immediate teachings in the form of intensive Hadith scholarship is what pulled South Asian scholars like al-Aʿẓamī away from the gravity of caste and its accommodation in mainstream Islamic law in India.

The Hadith-focused Salafi revivalism that shook Islamic thought from the eighteenth to the twentieth centuries promoted an egalitarian spirit in another society that was riven with an entrenched hierarchy of birth and descent. While in South Asia the looming social obstacle was caste, in central Arabia it was the dominant role of tribal affiliation and hierarchy. In Saudi Arabia, leading Ḥanbalī jurists who subscribed to Ibn Taymiyya's emphasis on the Quran and Hadiths above their school's legacy followed him in their approach to suitability. Among the most famous were three giants of twentieth-century Salafism, ʿAbd al-ʿAzīz Bin Bāz (d. 1420/1999), Ibn ʿUthaymīn (d. 1421/2001), and Nāṣir al-Dīn al-Albānī (d. 1419/1999).[53] Ibn

ʿUthaymīn acknowledges the main Ḥanbalī position: that suitability in character, slave/free status, lineage, and vocation is not required for marriage but that the bride or one of her male relatives can trigger an annulment if any of these is absent. He then objects that it makes no sense to accept a marriage as valid despite the absence of certain features of suitability but then allow its annulment for the absence of those same features. Ibn ʿUthaymīn then grounds this in an example from his own Najdi context, where the division between noble Arab tribes and non-tribal Arabs was a nearly irresistible social barrier, particularly in marriage (Ibn ʿUthaymīn hailed from the prominent tribe of Tamīm, while Bin Bāz's family was non-tribal). "All this is from the Jahiliyya; pride in family merit is an affair of the Jahiliyya," Ibn ʿUthaymīn wrote. No male relative can object to a marriage between a noble tribal person and a non-tribal spouse. Such a marriage is valid, he declared.[54]

An even stronger condemnation of considering anything other than piety in determining suitability came from a purist Salafī scholar so devoted to returning to the Quran and Hadiths directly that he did not even identify with a school of law: the Syrian Hadith scholar and sometime professor at the Islamic University in Medina, Muḥammad Nāṣir al-Dīn al-Albānī (d. 1429/1999). He argued that the Hadith of accepting the pious groom and the absence of sound Hadiths to its contrary show that the only aspects that matter for suitability are religion and character.[55]

Whether from South Asia or Saudi Arabia, these scholars had little patience for custom as they knew it. Or perhaps we could say that the call to heed context had brought the wheel of custom full circle. They might have agreed with Abū al-Walīd, the Cordoban judge who had dismissed the Prophet's example of marrying tribal and non-tribal, Arab and non-Arab to one another as something that had to be done at that time to break the back of Jahiliyya tribal pride. They might also have felt that recent times called for smashing idols too. For Ibn Taymiyya, the threats that decadence, heretical practices, and the pagan Mongols presented to the Muslims of Syria and Egypt were tantamount to Jahiliyya returned. For activist scholars like Nadwī, the existential threats that colonialism and Westernization posed to Muslims from Morocco to Malaysia called for a revival of the early spirit that had allowed Muslims to unify and remake their world. From their perches in the revivalist Ḥanbalī mosques of central Arabia, Bin Bāz, and Ibn ʿUthaymīn saw in Saudi tribalism the very same idol of chauvinism that the Prophet had smashed a millennium and a half earlier.

## WHAT IS THE PURPOSE OF THE LAW?

Like his namesake in the Sous valley of Morocco over a century earlier, whom we met in the previous chapter, the Saudi ʿAbd al-ʿAzīz Bin Bāz knew well the daily realities of domestic disputes in the dry hamlets of Najd. In a society in which family was everything, and tribal solidarity meant so much to the family, custom could not be ignored in pursuit of ideals without great cost. Despite his contempt for tribal chauvinism, Bin Bāz thus nevertheless advised those for whom transgressing the boundaries of tribe and family would come at too high a price to marry within them.[56] Similarly, South Asian Muslim scholars who defended what was, in effect, the caste dimension of *kafāʾa* often did so out of practical concern for the promotion of harmony in the lives of couples and families. In a society in which family was everything, and the social structure of caste meant so much to the family, breaking these strictures came at a great cost. Scholars like Bin Bāz emphasized the Quranic ideal that nobility was defined by piety and decried custom attenuating this. But, in the end, how much did they differ from scholars who endorsed caste sensibilities in South Asia or who accommodated the social stigma of blackness in the Sous valley? If blackness was socially correlative to slave origins, as it was in Morocco, a marriage between the daughter of a respected family and a black man would likely cause severe family unrest. In such a situation, what should a pious Muslim father do?

Love and the ideal of transcending social boundaries often have practical limits. Though a lesser film than *Coming to America*, the TV movie *The Princess and the Marine* (2001) tells the real-life story of the Bahraini princess who eloped with a lowly American Marine in

2000 and settled down to a married life of Las Vegas Americana. Instead of happily ever after, the princess returned to her family in Bahrain a year later and the couple soon divorced due to "incompatibility."[57]

Few would deny the importance of a couple sharing compatible lifestyles and expectations. Though social scientists today are divided on whether individuals' attainment of education and professional level wipes out class background, there is little debate that class remains a significant factor in who marries who and who stays married to who.[58] As a major Ḥanafī scholar of Delhi, ʿAbd al-Ghanī Mujaddidī Dihlawī (d. 1296/1879), explained regarding *kafāʾa*, coming from the same social background helps a couple get along, spend time together, and converse with each another.[59]

Desirable or not, just as blackness in North Africa was a correlate marking class and status, caste in South Asia can be seen as a proxy for class and regional culture. Shaykh Yūnus Jawnpūrī (d. 1438/2017), the senior master of Hadith at the famous Indian Jāmiʿat Maẓāhir ʿUlūm madrasa in Saharanpur, felt strongly that not respecting the customs of caste (phrased as *kafāʾa*) would make marriage a source of constant discord instead of the institution of peace and refuge ordained by God. Experience had made Jawnpūrī very skeptical of 'love marriages' done outside of family and caste. Too often he had seen them fail. For him, the differences in people's lifestyles, expectations, and even dispositions made relationships too difficult. He held this to be true even for people of the same caste but from neighboring regions (Jaunpur and Saharanpur, for example).[60] Even ʿAbd al-Ḥamīd Nuʿmānī, a severe critic of caste, admits that it is imprudent and unwise for a rich family to allow their daughter to marry a poor man. He stops short, however, of prohibiting this as a rule.[61]

A famous Hadith dubs Muslim scholars (*ʿulamāʾ*) "the heirs of the prophets."[62] If even those scholars who oppose caste and tribalism nonetheless counsel surrender to their strictures if discord would ensue, and if many scholars who stand by the legitimacy of *kafāʾa* do so because they see it as a means to promote harmony, then where is the prophetic voice these heirs are supposed to carry? Where is the call for Muslims to confront social reality, transform it, and transcend race or tribe before God? Why have Muslim scholars, in their capacity as the articulators and enforcers of norms, not worked more aggressively to bend society to them?

The charge given to Muslim scholars has never been enviable. They are the guardians of the Shariah, which subsumes those disputes that see the inside of a courtroom and the much wider realms of worship, ritual, ethics, and etiquette that make up daily life. Muslim scholars define God's law as they understand it from the Quran and the Prophet's legacy, and they apply it in society as preachers and moral guides in mosques and judges in courtrooms. Muslim jurists must operate the Shariah as the medium for disputes to be resolved in society as it is, and also hold it up as an ideal for shaping individuals and communities to better conform to what God desires.

These two responsibilities are in tension. Even in scholars' roles as experts answering questions about what can or should be done or not done, we see this divergence expressed in the distinction between *fatwā* (i.e., what they think the Shariah's general expectation or ruling is on a particular question) and *taqwā* (i.e., what should be done by a person striving to go above and beyond the law's basic expectations).[63] Marriage suitability is an issue that straddles moral guidance in private life and the adjudication of disputes in court. *Kafā'a* lays out guidelines for how Muslim families *should* think about selecting spouses. But, as with marriages in many legal systems today, issues of marriage suitability or capacity go unexamined by the law unless later disputes within the family draw a court's attention to them.[64]

The answer to why Muslim scholars deferred so much to the custom of families in issues of marriage lies in how Shariah judges operated in the resolution of disputes in premodern Islamic civilization. As Lawrence Rosen observed in his study of courts in the hinterland of Fez, the functioning of the law was intimately situated in the context of social relations, class, regional culture, and differing customs. The Shariah has always recognized that individuals have rights and obligations *qua* individuals before God and each other, but the judge who applies the law also construes them as embedded in relationships and a social fabric. As Rosen explains, the class, gender, local culture, and expectations that framed litigants' lives shaped how the Moroccan judge addressed cases that came before him. He did not impose the law from on high in a Jupiterian act of shaping the society at his feet but rather guided negotiations within it. The aim of law in Morocco was not to manifest state or religious power or bend society to its image – indeed, its image was profoundly shaped by society. The judge's aim was, as Rosen observed, "to put people back in the position of being able to negotiate their own permissible relationships."[65]

This unambitious approach to adjudication reflected the limited legal and administrative infrastructure that Muslim jurists had at their disposal in the premodern period. In areas like marriage, divorce, contract, and property, Muslim judges and jurists deferred as much as possible to custom because struggling against it was logistically daunting. The technological and administrative capacities that allow the law to comprehensively shape society only came with the all-encompassing modern nation state. Since the emergence of 'Progressive' politics (in the early-twentieth-century American political sense, not the contemporary sense of a social-justice-orientation), philosophers and agents of the state have seen the law as a tool for shaping society at every level. Whether in more traditional modes of legal moralism aimed at 'promoting virtue,' in following the dictates of 'good conscience,' or in the American habit of advancing 'public policy,' modern courts have been agents of change, not mere passive resources for citizens to seek dispute resolution.[66]

In the modern state, with its vast salaried bureaucracy, reams of record keeping, and the enforcing muscle of newly created police forces, courts have had the capacity to play such a role. The premodern infrastructure of justice and governance, by contrast, did not. As Wael Hallaq discusses, the premodern Shariah judiciary labored under the ubiquitous constraints of small governments with diminutive reach, institutions that could make themselves felt only in cities and large towns, and extremely limited capabilities. In a place like the hinterland of Fez or Algiers in 1700 CE, marriage or commercial disputes would necessarily mostly have been resolved at the level of family, village elders, or communal arbitration.[67] For example, we know that even in the early Islamic period, some Muslim judges regularly signed off on marriage agreements. But surviving documents from the 700s and 800s CE from Egypt and Khurasan show that sometimes they were not involved.[68] Marriage agreements were seemingly drawn up and witnessed by a large communal presence without any indication of a judge's approval.

Muslim scholars might issue fatwas or preach equality before God in mosques, but Muslim judges simply did not have the capacity to use courts as vehicles for ambitious social change. In fact, they relied on the social fabric to resolve most disputes before they could enter the courtroom. As one judge in sixteenth-century Lahore would always beg litigants before him, "For God's sake, compromise the matter between you . . . you both know all about the case."[69] A reminder of the limitations of judicial capacity is, ironically, evident in what has happened when the 'Progressive,' modern state ran into massive population growth and an explosion of litigiousness. The U.S. legal system today, which groans under gargantuan case-loads, has increasingly had to surrender its prized mission of advancing 'public policy' to private arbitration and alternative dispute resolution (ADR), even in family law issues like divorce and child custody.[70]

Of course, Muslim scholars have not been impotent. They were, in many ways, the architects of Islamic civilization and its societies. When an issue emerged that they thought merited forceful action, even in a short time frame, they could and did mount pronounced opposition. In late-nineteenth-century Morocco, the scholars heading two major Sufi orders had their devotees boycott sugar and tea – European imports – in order to resist colonial economic and political encroachment.[71] In 1698, when the Moroccan sultan violated the clear dictates of the Shariah by ordering the enslavement of free black Muslims to serve in his army, prominent scholars objected vehemently. Many of them paid with their jobs, their freedom or their lives.[72] Customs of marriage and attraction, however, rarely manifest with such suddenness. In the realm of the mundane, the teaching, preaching, guidance, and legal oversight of Muslim scholars effected immense change in custom, but this occurred over decades or centuries.

Whatever the limitations of means or technology, when and on what matters Muslim scholars have committed themselves to changing their societies is ultimately a matter of priority. Are Muslim scholars excused from combatting antiblack racism in marriage and family life because too much discord would result or because, like the Lahore judge, they could not manage or did not want the responsibility? If they chose to devote themselves more to fighting antiblackness, what means could they pursue? Could they, or anyone, change who falls in love with whom?

# 10

## Conclusion

> White people, black people, brown people, yellow people, get rid of 'em all. All we need is a voluntary, free-spirited, open-ended program of procreative racial deconstruction. Everybody just gotta keep f—in' everybody till they're all the same color.
>
> Senator Jay Billington Bulworth, *Bulworth* (1998)

### MISCEGENATING OUR WAY OUT

One way to discourage antiblack racism would be to blend phenotypes until all humans are the same color. In a movie that was supposed to be edgy, this line by the fictional, truth-speaking Senator Bulworth was one of the edgiest.[1] In his landmark article on the freedom to associate and exclude in a liberal society, Stuart White posits as axiomatic that our beds belong to that "sphere of intimate association in which it is permissible for people to practice whatever pattern of exclusion they like." White's test for when excluding others is legitimate hinges on whether our exclusion would infringe unduly on their right to a sense of shared community, violate their 'opportunity right' to the goods that associating with us offers, or deny them the dignity that comes with inclusion. For White, it is intuitive that our intimate associations are so basic to our identity and expression that we enjoy a presumed right to exclude anyone from them, even on racial grounds and even if that infringes on the opportunity rights of others.[2] White's liberal understanding accords with Appiah's distinction between personal preference regarding race and projecting our race preferences beyond the private sphere. "In our private lives,"

Appiah sets out, "we are morally free to have aesthetic preferences between people, but once our treatment of people raises moral issues, we may not make arbitrary distinctions."[3]

In his provocatively titled and meticulously argued dissertation, "The Duty to Miscegenate," Nathaniel Adam Tobias ~~Coleman~~ [sic] takes White to task for what he sees as arbitrariness. White considers it an undue violation of the dignity interests of black people for a dating agency to refuse to accept black clients. Why, Nathaniel asks, is it any less dignity-denying to refuse a black person the chance to be one's own romantic partner?[4]

White's rules for association and exclusion are premised on the liberal presumption that individuals are all equal, autonomous entities in social space, each free to believe, speak, act, and associate unless it can be reasoned that their conduct unduly harms or burdens others or deprives them of their rights. Nathaniel Adam Tobias ~~Coleman~~, by contrast, aspires to a progressive and just society. He sees White's presumption as naïve.[5] For Nathaniel, equality is not a reality that can be premised. It is a goal not yet realized. And it can only be achieved by a commitment to rectifying the imbalances of power and access to resources that have been brought on by a history of inequality and are sure to prolong it.

Accomplishing this requires conceiving of harm more expansively than the classical Millian view common to Anglo-Saxon civil liberties discourse. To an audience enjoying social privilege and security, for example, a speaker's offensive words might seem no more than the expression of a noxious opinion. But because such a speech act helps perpetuate a system of inequality, it could actually constitute *harm* to an audience of disenfranchised or historically marginalized groups. The harm that otherwise merely offensive speech can cause individuals in such groups can go beyond just sustaining unjust systems. Since those systems have often maintained themselves through violence, speech acts supporting them can also directly cause the apprehension of that violence. And they can, indirectly, facilitate physical violence itself.[6] A byproduct of adopting an expanded notion of harm would thus be the curtailing of the rights assumed as normal in the status quo, since what those culturally and politically empowered consider normal likely harms the equality aims of the marginalized.

For Nathaniel, our predilections and personal associations are thus not truly ours. They have a public dimension. Firstly, what we desire and find appealing is not some authentic expression of an abstract self, standing equal to all other selves. Rather, it has been shaped by the same socio-economic forces and cultural hegemonies that have spawned injustices such as racism. As Amia Srinivasan argues, the liberal move of making consent and desire the sole arbiters of who can and cannot enjoy our intimate company ignores any structure of power, aesthetics, attractiveness and discrimination that "makes its way into the bedroom through the seemingly innocuous mechanism of 'personal preference.'"[7] Second, our desires and preferences involve others, affecting them and assuming reciprocity. We are not actually morally 'free' to choose with whom we associate because our choices form part of a system imbued with racism and injustice. If, Nathaniel asks, Black American women are consistently deemed the race/gender least sexually attractive and least desirable for marriage, and if this fact stems from the systemic antiblack racism of Western society, then choosing not to associate with Black Americans in our intimate sphere is a continuation of that oppression. It continues to render them invisible.[8]

Stuart's and Appiah's arguments for the right of an individual not to associate intimately with another person because of their race rest on pillars of classical liberalism: the primacy of rights, a relatively restrained vision of harm, and the crucial division of private and public. Where these two scholars and Nathaniel diverge is the same place where advocates for free speech on Western college campuses diverge from more progressive voices seeking to prevent speakers who 'harm' certain students by expressing views deemed hateful. It is where progressive critics of the popular comedian Dave Chappelle's jokes about transgenderism diverge from Netflix, the service that has aired his performances. While Netflix replied that the promotion of creative freedom means that Netflix would always feature content that "some people believe is harmful," its critics argue that there is nothing worthwhile about the freedom to harm a community "who needs safety and protection."[9]

Calls for a Bulworthian voluntary program of "racial deconstruction" may not yet be common, but the last decade has seen a slew of essays on whether or not it's 'okay' to have or express racial preferences in online dating, or indeed to have any physical preferences at all.[10] There seems to be a strong consensus against *expressing* categorical preferences on one's dating profiles (e.g., 'No Asian men'). And the major dating platforms have taken steps to prevent language that openly excludes or discriminates against groups.[11] But few voices have ventured to say that it is wrong for an individual to have romantic preferences that exclude certain phenotypes. Explaining the racist and colonial origins of the dominant economy of desire and aesthetic preference is one thing. Telling people that they have to desire someone they don't to help rectify the power imbalances of that economy is another.

Nathaniel does not actually argue that we have a duty to sexually miscegenate. He argues that we have a duty to seek out socialization with the marginalized and those racialized as below us. Others skate close to demanding intimate inclusion, if only through the stick of suggesting the reader is prejudiced otherwise and the carrot of assuming that understanding the oppressive origins of desire will somehow change it. Srinivasan suggests we take on the "duty to transfigure, as best we can, our desires."[12] A widely read 2019 article entitled "Is Refusing to Date Trans People Transphobic?" admits that no one "owes" transgender individuals a date. But it then asserts that a "flat rejection" of any possibility of dating transgender people can only be the result of an "irrational bias" against them.[13] A similar article on not finding overweight people desirable sees this issue as a structural problem like racism as well. In fact, some scholars see revulsion at corpulence as rooted in antiblackness. Sabrina Strings has recently argued that the valorization of the slim male or female figure and a phobia of fatness coalesced in Britain and the U.S. in the late nineteenth and early twentieth centuries as embodiments of the ideals of White civilization and Protestant abstemiousness. These ideals formed in opposition to what Anglo-Saxon culture imagined to be the corpulent and appetitive Black African as well as the non-Anglo-Saxon (e.g., Italian, Irish) White.[14] 'Fatphobia,' one activist declares, should be approached "the same way that we would understand any other type of body-based oppression."[15]

But what is 'being open' to dating someone other than considering the possibility of being attracted to them? What if one feels strongly that one could not feel such attraction? What if one, consciously or subconsciously, approaches dating with the aim of eventual reproduction? Is a conscious or subconscious exclusion of individuals who either have one's same genitalia and/or reproductive system really an 'irrational' bias? There seems to be a unifying argument behind all these objections to the status quo in the power-politics of attraction: if one does not find black people attractive, one is racist; if one does not find transgender people attractive, one is transphobic; if one does not find fat people attractive, one is fatphobic. Srinivasan summarizes this chain of reasoning succinctly, arguing that transcending these 'phobias' requires recognizing that "the very idea of fixed sexual preference is political, not metaphysical."[16]

The problem with this argument, however, is not that attraction is metaphysical but that it is immanently and essentially *physical*. It is not that attraction is *not* political (it is) but that politics and economics are inseparable. A study of thirty-seven countries concluded that females valued 'good earning potential' in mates more than males did, while males valued good looks more than females did. Females favored somewhat older mates, while males valued females under twenty-five – the years of peak reproductive capacity.[17] One of the main theories regarding physical attraction in evolutionary psychology is that it has always had strong economic elements. One argument for why fatness became considered unattractive is based not in antiblackness but in the evolutionary value placed on health in a mate and its bodily indicators. Until the late eighteenth and nineteenth centuries in the West (and much later in some other regions and subcultures in the West), the plumper, Rubenesque female figure was much more attractive than the contemporary, thin Hollywood leading lady. Simply put, for most of human history, accumulated fat was a sign of access to resources. Only in the last century and a half, as the previous default of food shortage and active lifestyles morphed into one of sedentary plenty, has fatness become a health liability.[18]

This is not to say that finding fatness unattractive is an unchangeable reality. Humans might be evolutionarily conditioned to find fit partners attractive, but what constitutes fitness in a society is at least partially socially constructed. One could imagine that, were Hollywood and the media more broadly to fill print, film, and the airwaves with only plus-sized models, heaviness might soon be greatly sought after.

Other common or even universal indicators of attractiveness, however, seem to be tied more closely to biological, not social, advantage. They reflect either outright control of resources or multigenerational access to advantageous genes. Women are attracted to taller men. And the more symmetrical the features of one's face the more attractive it is, possibly because this indicates less defective genes and developmental years free of trauma and stress.[19] This evolutionary-psychology-based theory that human attraction follows cues to more successful reproduction certainly has its critics. One famous study showed that chickens, who presumably gain no evolutionary advantage by their selection of human faces, favor them in the same way people do. This suggests that preferring facial symmetry proceeds from a level even more basic than the human. It is a property of animal nervous systems.[20] This only makes the problem deeper, however. The aim of engineering a society in which attraction is freed from "body-based oppression" would thus seem to be a society in which foundational features of human nature had been successfully altered.

## CAN DISCRIMINATION BE LEGITIMATE?

Voices weighing in on debates over discrimination in online dating are not uniformly aligned against it. There is little objection to services limited to committed Christians or Muslims who want to meet others who share their faith and values. Race- or culture-specific dating apps like Black People Meet and Dil Mil for South Asians also seem to have raised few objections, as they cater to people for whom preserving shared cultural, religious, and marital customs are important.[21]

But why, then, would a White-only dating app be objectionable? One objection would be practical: the majority status of Whites in the West and the domination by White facial and hair features as global standards of beauty make all non-minority-specific dating apps *de facto* White dating apps. A second objection would be prudential: the history of White-only discrimination in justifying indefensible acts of brutality and oppression from the Holocaust to Apartheid have rendered this type of exclusion too nefarious and suspect to tolerate. A third would be principled: allowing a White-only space would be to indulge a culture that, arguably, has always defined itself by the exclusion, often violent and exploitative, of the non-White.

None of these objections apply to minorities or groups that have suffered under majority discrimination, like Blacks in America or Jews globally. It would be acceptable for such groups to formally and openly discriminate in intimacy and marriage because this aims to promote the survival of marginalized communities and their cultures, not to perpetuate the risk of marginalization.[22]

But what about a high-caste Hindu Gujrati family that immigrates to the U.K., or a high-caste Muslim family from Pakistan that immigrates to the U.S.? Though their position in their countries of origin may have been among the elite, their position in their new home societies is that of extreme minorities who will struggle to preserve their religious, linguistic, and cultural heritage. Whatever objection might have been raised about discrimination along caste or communal lines in South Asia would seem substantially reduced as they sought to survive as minorities. It might not be objectionable for them to intentionally exclude those outside their caste. Conceivably, this would extend even to them discriminating against Black American Muslims or Black British, since these would simply be two exogamous groups among a plethora.

It would, however, clearly not be acceptable for this high-caste Pakistani family to exclude a non-high-caste Muslim *simply because he or she was black*, correct? Differences in what blackness can signify and also what can signify blackness make this difficult to answer categorically. As we have seen with the 'social distance' that can exist between African immigrants to the U.S. and Black Americans, African immigrant communities can prefer not to associate with Black Americans due to differences in culture. As we have seen with blackness standing as a correlate to low social status in North Africa, antiblackness can be an expression of class. If the daughter of our high-caste Pakistani Muslim family were to 'swipe left' on any Black American Muslim man that appeared on her Muslim dating app, this would no doubt be seen as antiblack racism. But if she is rejecting *anyone* outside her range of class and cultural comfort, and she saw Black American identity as correlating to a dramatically different class or cultural background, then it is really class or culture that is at play in her decision. A Black American Muslim imam in the U.S. Midwest recalls numerous instances of having to counsel couples made up of second-generation South Asian Muslim immigrants married to Black American Muslims. In these cases, blackness is not a racialized stereotype but rather a specific subset of American culture. The imam was counseling on how to deal with contrasting cultural expectations, not the bodily realities of race.

Here, however, the rules of marriage suitability in Islamic law and the phenomenon of cultural racism should raise alarms about how far discrimination can be allowed. Generally, the rules of suitability in the Shariah are *guidelines* designed to promote harmonious marriage or block an unconventional marriage that had not otherwise been approved by important members of the families. These rules are not designed to prevent marriage when all relevant parties agree that the marriage is in everyone's best interest. The Prophet's guidance that what men should seek in wives is beauty, merit, and wealth but, most of all, piety reiterates that it is the absence of piety alone that is the unresolvable deal-breaker.[23] As scholars of Muslim caste in South Asia have observed, ultimately the only firm bar to Muslim marriage is religion.

Whatever its myopia or overstatement on this point, Mālikī law in North Africa saw somatic blackness as a *correlate* to low social status, not synonymous with it or its equivalent. Exceptions to this correlation could be noble men whose mothers were Black Africans, like Mawlāy Ismāʿīl, or Black African women of exceptional charisma, like Ittifāq. What is racist about cultural racism is that it takes a perceived correlation between culture and race and turns it into an equivalence, defining every member of that race by a cultural stereotype and either denying them acceptance or allowing it only tenuously. Cultural racism denies the individuals of certain races or ethnicities the opportunity that members of the discriminating group grant each other, namely the chance to be treated as individuals. A Pakistani Muslim woman or an Arab Muslim man 'swiping left' on Black Muslims is engaged in the same sort of dismissal. I myself have met pious and accomplished Black African Muslims who speak fluent Urdu.

Such is the insidiousness of antiblackness in the modern world, however, that even antiblack cultural racism, with its denial of 'scientific' racist justifications and its hewing to culture instead of biology, cannot be disassociated from the body. Like Baranī's Muslim casteism, modern antiblackness suffuses value into the body and makes the two inseparable, projecting the stigma of debasement back onto past ancestry and forward onto progeny to come. An important insight of Afropessimism is that, in the modern world at least, the body racialized as black is unappealingly inhuman. This imposed worthlessness then seeps into adjacent features, devaluing curly or coiled hair and darker-toned skin even in bodies not racialized as black. Arab women are all too familiar with the appeal of 'good' or 'soft' (*nāʿim*) hair and the liability of coiled, 'harsh' (*khishin*) hair.

But what if the Pakistani woman or the Arab man are simply not attracted to any of the Black Africans they see? How can anyone be blamed or criticized for their sexual preferences? It might be too late for blame, but it is not too late to influence future responses. Race preference seems like the aspect of attraction most easily alterable by cultural conditioning. Weight is likely acculturated as attractive or not based on how a certain culture assesses access to resources. Sex is determined chromosomally at birth and tied basically to the possibility of reproduction. Facial symmetry may simply be more easily processed by a nervous system. Race, by contrast, is entirely a social construct. It is unconnected with the function of our bodies or their interaction with the natural world around us (with the very limited exception of Hardimon's minimalist race).

Then how can socially constructed aspects of attraction be refashioned or, as Srinivasan puts it, transfigured? Is it transgressive to try? The Shariah tradition of the law's deference to society was less 'liberal' than it was a byproduct of a limited capacity to steer society. The Prophet clearly imposed a duty to trample his society's firmest barriers. In Medina, he paired natives of the city with immigrant Muslims in fictive fraternity, seeking to replace tribal loyalties with common faith. And he literally imposed a duty to miscegenate, obliging a number of noble Arab women and their families to marry low-born or non-tribal Muslims whose faith and character had proven their merit.

Yet I am not sure that the Prophet's limited efforts to arrange examples of miscegenation would manifest today as a state-enforced campaign. The Prophet's precedent certainly makes clear his mission to shape the personalities and moral order of his followers. As his arranging marriages shows, this was not bounded by a Western liberal sense that no state or moral authority can impose on our "sphere of intimate association." But it was limited by a conviction, found in the Quran and Hadiths alike, that the moral order of God's public law should not impose itself into people's homes or demand to know their hearts. The contents of the heart, as the Prophet said, could not be glimpsed.[24] And conduct in the home, were it opened up and subjected to the expectations of public morality, would drive a community to despair and, as the Prophet warned, "ruin it."[25] The Prophet ordered taboo-breaking marriages in specific cases, with specific individuals he knew could bear the burden of exemplification. This species of authority is a world removed from the overwhelming compulsion of the modern state. The same ubiquitous power and reach that have enabled the modern state to engineer social change through the law was viewed with deserved suspicion by the Prophet's community. The caliph ʿUmar bin al-Khaṭṭāb turned a blind eye to bacchanalias held within walled courtyards, exemplifying the Quran's warnings against prying into people's lives and invading their homes to root out sin

(49:12, 2:189). These outweighed and constrained enforcing the Shariah's social vision in all spaces.[26]

Today, the solution lies in the hands of individuals, communities, and communal leadership, who must commit themselves to crossing boundaries of race, class, and culture. In the U.S., for example, one step could be mosque leadership pairing immigrant-founded mosques with predominantly Black Muslim mosques for social events and fund-sharing. Repurposing J.S. Mill's assertion of the freedom not to associate, Nathaniel argues that those racialized as non-black have an obligation to "seek the society" of those racialized as black. Simply allowing association or making interracial marriage legal has not sufficed. The barriers to intimate connection and appreciation must be intentionally breached because it is the maintenance of these barriers that has perpetuated antiblack racism.[27] Similarly, Mohammad Harith Aslam Khawaja has argued that, while it is not strictly racist for someone to say, honestly and with no malice, that they are not attracted to black people, it does perpetuate racial injustice. He advocates what he calls the 'fair chance' rule, namely that we give anyone and everyone a fair chance to appeal to us. Though he does not raise this to the level of a moral duty, he sees it as the way to break down the longstanding racial barriers to attraction and intimate socialization.[28]

The precedent of the Prophet Muhammad was to break idols, whether venerated images or the false gods of sentiment and desire (Quran 45:23). He smashed the idols of tribal chauvinism by, among other acts, arranging the marriage of Muslim women of noble Arab ancestry to pious and talented black-skinned former slaves. Not even those Muslim scholars who, over the centuries, deemed it suitable or pragmatic to indulge the prejudices of custom or recognize custom in prejudicial ways, could deny that Islam had come to, in the words of the Prophet, "drive from you the arrogance of the Age of Ignorance and its pride in descent."[29] They could only suggest that such a mission was not appropriate for their times. For other Muslim scholars, however, the urgency of their eras stood out in clear relief. During the last century, for example, leading scholars in South Asia and Arabia saw caste or tribalism as idols of the Age of Ignorance reemerged.

Our day too has its unmistakable idols. Worldwide, awesome sums are paid to bleach skin, straighten hair, thin noses, or add a crease to an upper eyelid, all money spent and pain endured in the pursuit of an idolized phenotype. Bodies in which the idol of Whiteness inheres are valued over non-White lives in the deployment of military and police violence. Not content with blood and treasure, this idol of the modern era must debase utterly its other, the blackness by which, as Morrison says, the White self "knows itself as . . . not repulsive, but desirable . . ."[30] There is little doubt that, today, the diseases of White supremacy and antiblackness are as vile afflictions as Arab tribal chauvinism was in the seventh century and much more rampant. What excuse could Muslims today give not to respond, as courageous Muslim scholars have always done, to the particular problems of the time? As the great Urdu poet Muhammad Iqbal (d. 1357/1938) wrote, "This age is seeking its Abraham, for this world's house of idols."[31]

# Appendix I

## Antiblack Statements Attributed to Imam al-Shāfiʿī

There are two antiblack reports attributed to al-Shāfiʿī (d. 204/820). I argue that the first is a forgery and that the second is likely too unreliable to be cited with any degree of confidence.

The first report is an anecdote in which al-Shāfiʿī is in the Ḥaram Mosque in Mecca with his students. A man enters, looking around, and al-Shāfiʿī deduces from his actions that he is looking for a black slave (*ʿabd aswad*). He tells the man that his slave is in police custody. The man goes to the police, finds his slave there, and comes back to al-Shāfiʿī asking how he had known this. Al-Shāfiʿī replies that he was only extrapolating from the Prophet's (alleged) Hadith that Black Africans, when they are hungry, they steal, and when they are sated, they fornicate. The slave would thus either have been arrested for theft or fornication. We have already shown that leading Muslim Hadith scholars declared this alleged Hadith to be a forgery. Here I argue that the anecdote about al-Shāfiʿī is also a fabrication, since the sole *isnād* for the report relies on a liar who narrated uncorroborated material.

The first source in which the report appears is Abū Bakr al-Bayhaqī's (d. 458/1066) book on the virtues of al-Shāfiʿī, *Manāqib al-Shāfiʿī*, where it presumably illustrates his insight and prescience.[1] This version of the report is reproduced in similar later works, such as the *Manāqib al-Shāfiʿī* by Fakhr al-Dīn al-Rāzī (d. 606/1209) and a similar work by Ibn Ḥajar al-ʿAsqalānī (d. 852/1449), neither of whom offer any comments about its reliability.[2] The *isnād* from al-Bayhaqī back to al-Shāfiʿī is: the famous Sufi al-Sulamī ← Manṣūr b. ʿAbdallāh al-Harawī ← al-Maghāzilī, in Aleppo ← al-Muzanī, one of al-Shāfiʿī's close disciples (all claiming *samāʿ*). In this *isnād*, al-Harawī was regarded as a liar who narrated unknown material.[3] This renders the chain of transmission too weak to be relied on.

In the second antiblack report al-Shāfiʿī allegedly states that the only reason that the price of Black African slaves is lower than that of others is because of their deficiency in intellect. Otherwise, they would just be another color of human beings, desirable to some and not others. This report also appears in al-Bayhaqī's *Manāqib al-Shāfiʿī* as well as in the contemporaneous *Ḥilyat al-awliyāʾ* of Abū Nuʿaym al-Iṣbahānī (d. 430/1038).[4]

Dealing with the narration in Abū Nuʿaym's *Ḥilya* first, its chain of transmission connecting Abū Nuʿaym to al-Shāfiʿī is totally unreliable, since it includes at least one unknown transmitter (*majhūl al-ḥāl*). Abū Nuʿaym cites this report via an *isnād* that he uses several times for information about al-Shāfiʿī: Muḥammad b. Ibrāhīm ← ʿAbd al-ʿAzīz Ibn Abī al-Rajāʾ ← al-Rabīʿ b. Sulaymān al-Murādī (a senior student of al-Shāfiʿī) (all alleging *samāʿ*). This Muḥammad b. Ibrāhīm has other *isnād*s to al-Rabīʿ, and he also transmits one report allegedly from al-Shāfiʿī via Ibn Abī al-Rajāʾ ← Yūnus b. ʿAbd al-Aʿlā ← al-Shāfiʿī.[5] It is not at all clear who this Muḥammad b. Ibrāhīm is who transmits the offensive report to Abū Nuʿaym, but that is not even the main problem. He may be Muḥammad b. Ibrāhīm al-Farwī (d. 356/966–7), whom Abū Nuʿaym considered reliable (*thiqa*).[6] On one occasion, Abū al-Nuʿaym transmits reports about al-Shāfiʿī via a variation of this *isnād*: Abū al-Shaykh Abū Muḥammad b. Ḥayyān ← Ibrāhīm b. Muḥammad ←Ibn Abī al-Rajāʾ ← al-Rabīʿ.[7] For this variation, it is not clear at all who the Ibrāhīm b. Muḥammad was who served as Abū al-Shaykh's source. But, again, this is not the main problem with this antiblack narration.

The main problem is that [Abū al-Najm] ʿAbd al-ʿAẓīz [b. Aḥmad] Ibn Abī [al-]Rajāʾ (his name varies in narrations) is common to all these *isnād*s but is totally unknown. He appears only once in Abū Nuʿaym's works outside the author's entry on al-Shāfiʿī in the *Ḥilya*: Abū Nuʿaym reports an opinion of the early Kufan scholar Sufyān al-Thawrī via an *isnād* of one Muḥammad b. ʿAlī ← Ibn Abī al-Rajāʾ ← ʿAmr b. Thawr . . . (ʿAmr b. Thawr is also unknown except that al-Ṭabarānī narrated several Hadiths from him).[8] ʿAbd al-ʿAzīz Ibn Abī al-Rajā' does not appear as a source in any known biographical dictionary of the Shāfiʿī school or in the major biographical dictionaries compiled by Isfahani or Baghdadi scholars of the era (he is not to be confused with a well-known Hadith forger of the same name who lived much earlier).[9] He does not appear as a source in al-Khaṭīb al-Baghdādī's (d. 463/1071) entry on al-Shāfiʿī in the *Tārīkh Baghdād*, although al-Khaṭīb includes several reports from Abū Nuʿaym in the entry through other *isnāds* to al-Shāfiʿī's acolyte al-Rabīʿ b. Sulaymān. Ibn Abī al-Rajā' does appear twice in al-Bayhaqī's *Manāqib al-Shāfiʿī*, narrating quotations from Shāfiʿī's disciple al-Muzanī, once with no *isnād* from al-Bayhaqī and once from al-Bayhaqī to al-Muzanī via: al-Ḥākim ← Saʿīd b. Aḥmad b. ʿAbd al-Raḥīm ← Yūsuf b. Aḥmad b. Yūsuf al-Makkī ← ʿAbdallāh b. al-Ḥusayn ← Ibn Abī al-Rajā' (all *samāʿ*). The first report is al-Shāfiʿī saying he does not mind calling God's blessings down on the Prophet when slaughtering an animal (this is also reported from al-Shāfiʿī by al-Rabīʿ in al-Bayhaqī's *Sunan al-kubrā*).[10] The second report is al-Shāfiʿī commenting on a Hadith on predestination (*qadar*) (*sitta laʿanahum Allāh . . .*).[11]

Moving to the narration in al-Bayhaqī's *Manāqib al-Shāfiʿī*, he narrates via his famous teacher al-Ḥākim ←Abū Turāb Aḥmad b. Muḥammad b. al-Ḥusayn al-Musāfirī al-Nawqānī of Tus (d. 341/951) ← Muḥammad b. al-Mundhir Shakkar ← Rabīʿ ← al-Shāfiʿī (all *samāʿ*). Al-Ḥākim heard Hadiths from Abū Turāb in the latter's native Tus and also says that he transmitted Hadiths in Naysābūr more than once. Al-Ḥākim even narrates one Hadith through Abū Turāb in the *Mustadrak* (al-Dhahabī approves of this Hadith). Yet Abū Turāb's reliability is far from clear. Al-Ḥākim was notoriously lax in his approval of transmitters, as pointed out by al-Dhahabī, Kawtharī and others (see Appendix VI).[12] Another, more important problem with this chain of transmission is that Shakkar is not noted as a source of any significance (or at all) for information about al-Shāfiʿī from Rabīʿ. Nor does Abū Turāb stand out anywhere as a source from Shakkar. Neither Abū Turāb nor Shakkar appears in chains for information about al-Shāfiʿī in books of Shāfiʿī law or biographical dictionaries of the school. The only location I have found them used is two instances of al-Bayhaqī citing the *isnād* Ḥākim ← Musāfirī ← Shakkar ← Rabīʿ in his *Manāqib al-Shāfiʿī*. The first is a story about the contrasting opinions of early Ḥanafī scholars and Mālik, the reliability of which al-Bayhaqī doubts. The second is two reports about al-Shāfiʿī's death.[13] The narration of the antiblack report in al-Bayhaqī's work is thus made up of a chain with unremarkable narrators whose only record of corroboration for transmitting information about al-Shāfiʿī outside of al-Bayhaqī's book is the very antiblack report being investigated here.

In summary, the report attributed to al-Shāfiʿī about the weak intellects of Black Africans relies on chains that pass either through unidentified narrators or through narrators simply not established enough to bear the weight of attributing such a dismissive comment to a scholar of al-Shāfiʿī's standing. Two books on al-Shāfiʿī's virtues written by scholars earlier than Abū Nuʿaym and al-Bayhaqī, those of Ibn Abī Ḥātim al-Rāzī (d. 327/938) and Muḥammad b. al-Ḥusayn al-Āburī (d. 363/974), do not include these antiblack reports. In fact, Ibn Abī Ḥātim's book includes several reports from Rabīʿ in which al-Shāfiʿī comes across as 'antiwhite': he wants to return a gift from a seller who is "ruddy and blue" (*ashqar azraq*) because he has never seen any good come from such folk.[14] In early Islamic Arabic, 'blue-eyed' was understood as 'shiny-eyed' and was often seen as a mark of untrustworthiness (pre-Islamic/early Islamic Arabic had only one color for blue/green, *akhḍar*). By the late Abbasid period, Arabic lexicographers listed more meanings of 'blue-eyed': showing blindness or some serious eye malady, having cat-like eyes, or having blue or green eyes in the modern sense.[15]

# Appendix II

## African Languages and Blackness – General

*In the following three appendices, I have tried to gather what information on the relevant languages is available in published studies. I have also asked 1–3 native speakers in each case to answer the following questions: 1) What is the color of a piano? 2) What is the word for the average skin tone of speakers of your language? 3) Can the word for piano and/or for average skin tone be used in negative figures of speech? This is, sadly, nowhere near the type of rigorous research that needs to be done for such an issue. I hope others better equipped will do so.*

The four main language families in Africa are Afro-Asiatic, Nilo-Saharan, Khoisan and the largest, Niger-Congo. The latter stretches from Senegal to South Africa. Niger-Congo languages have only three underived colors: black, white, and red. All other colors are derived from things, like 'leaf-colored' for green, 'sky' for blue, etc.

In Yoruba, *dudu* means 'black.' A piano is *dudu* colored and people's skin tone can also be described as *dudu* without any negative connotation. But *dudu* is also used negatively to describe someone's heart or intentions.

In Jola (Djola, spoken in southern Senegal, Gambia, and Guinea-Bissau), the word for the color black (*-layen*) is also used to indicate the average skin tone of a West African without any negative connotation. But it can also be used in phrases for 'mean/nasty.'

In Wolof, a black person (i.e., 'black' skin color) is *nit ku ñuul*, the same adjective used to describe the color of a piano. This word can also be used negatively for black hearted (*ñuul khol*). In Wolof, *xonq* (red) can be used for a lighter African skin tone or for shiny and well-cared-for skin.

In Pulaar (the Fulani language dialect spoken in Senegal), the word for black (*ɓalawol*) is used to describe the color of an object, e.g., 'black dog' (*rawaandu ɓaleeru*), and locals' typical skin tone, hence 'black people' (sing. *ɓaleejo*, pl. *ɓaleeɓe*) (the color descriptor changes depending on what kind of word it is modifying). There is no negativity associated with this. European Whites are *tuubaako/tuubakooɓe*, which is unrelated to the Pulaar word for the color white. More specific color descriptors are used to specify within 'black' skin tones, and here we see some reflection of the dynamics of color and power in the Sahel (see Appendix III). *Ɓaleejo kurum* means 'very dark,' while the word for red (*boɗeejo*) means a lighter skin tone, with *naawo* meaning a tone in between those two. In rural areas of Senegal (like Bundu), 'dark' (*kurum*) is associated with a lower social status and manual labor. In many dialects of the Fulani language (Fulfulde), *maccube* was the word for non-Fulani slaves and is still used for their descendants. Although not directly derived from a word for blackness or darkness, it is still associated with darker skin tones, with *maccube* people often thought of as black, unrefined and unclean.[1] It is not pejorative to describe skin tone as 'black' (*ɓaleejo*), but the word 'black' is used in phrases with meanings like black-hearted. In Pulaar, there are longstanding traditions of 'white knowledge/lore' (*gandal danewal*), which consists of Islamic learning, as opposed to 'black knowledge/lore' (*gandal balewal*), which includes skills, crafts, or knowledge outside Islamic learning, including specialized crafts but with an association with magic. Such 'black magic,' however, need not be bad and can include such valued skills as healing.[2]

The overall pattern seen so far in Sahel languages is similar in at least three Bantu languages (a different subset of Niger-Congo), the Shona language of southern African (*ane moyo mutema*), Zulu (*mnyama*), where we find 'to have a black heart' (*ukuba nenhliziyo emnyama*), i.e., to be irritable; and Sotho (a person with an average skin tone would be described as *motsho*, lit. 'black,' with the same suffix adjusted for things like a black shirt, *setsho*; *pelo entsho* is a person having a black heart). We find the disconnect between phenotype and the metaphorical use of color in Zulu's use of red in phrases meaning angry, which result not from the face literally becoming ruddy but from the semantic overlap of blood, red, heat, and anger.[3]

In Zarma (a.k.a. Djerma, a Songhay language, spoken in Niger and Mali, from the larger Nilo-Saharan language family), the color black is *borobi* or *bi*. In Zarma one uses *bi* ('black') for the classical Black African phenotype with no negative association, while *daara* is used for lighter African skin tones. In Zarma, *koirey* is 'white' for objects and was used for Berbers, while *gakwaray* (lit., 'white bodies') and *annassara* (derived from the Arabic for Christians) denote European Whites (note: *almasiifu* is the word for Christian). The word for black in Zarma is also used in common pejorative expressions like someone being evil (*a bina gua bi*, lit., 'his heart is black'). It is not negative when used to describe skin tone. In old Songhay, *gabibi* (lit., 'very dark bodies') was used to denote a group of farmers who were sometimes serfs.

In Hausa, a Chadic language (from the larger Afro-Asiatic language family) spoken in northern Nigeria, Niger, etc., the color black is *baƙi*, and *baƙin mutum* denotes a person with a typical Black African skin tone. *Mai haske* (luminous) or *ja* (reddish) are used for a lighter skinned person, such as a more typical Arab complexion (European Whites are called *nasara* or *turawa*, the former derived from the Arabic for Christian and the latter a word with no color component). In Hausa 'black' can be used in pejorative expressions like *baƙin ciki* (lit., 'inner blackness,' meaning sadness; while *farin ciki*, lit., 'inner whiteness,' means happiness) and *baƙin rai* (lit., 'black soul,' meaning resentful). But black is not negative when used to describe someone's skin tone. The color white (*fari*) can be used in negative expressions as well, such as *farar ƙafa* (lit., 'white feet,' someone who brings bad luck).

In Mooré (from the Niger-Congo family and the main language spoken in Burkina Faso, also spoken in Côte d'Ivoire, Ghana, and Mali) 'black' (*sablaga*) is used to describe a black thing like a piano as well as the average person's complexion in Burkina Faso (dark complexion). 'Brown' or 'light-red' (*zêêga*) are used for a lighter complexion. There is no negative valence for using 'black' (*sablaga*) to describe appearance, though the word is *not* used in phrases like the English 'black-hearted.' The word for the color white (*pèèlga*) is used to describe things with the color of snow or cotton, while European White people are called *nassara*, as in Hausa and Zarma.

In Luo (a Nilo-Saharan language spoken in Kenya and Tanzania), the word for the color black is *rateng'*, which is also used to describe a normal skin tone (dark brown or black), with *lando* (light brown) used for a lighter complexion among Luo speakers. There is no negative connotation when *rateng'* is used to describe someone's appearance (there are even people named *Rateng'* because of their appearance). The word appears in songs praising a man or woman's gleaming 'black' skin. *Rateng'* is not really used in negative expressions like 'black-hearted.' Instead, the Luo word for 'darkness' (*mudho*) is used in the same way English speakers use black/dark to connote badness.

# Appendix III

## Race, Blackness, and Language in the Sahel

In the western and central Sahel region (from Senegal to the Lake Chad region), since at least the 1300s CE there has been a distinction between 'whites' (*bīḍān*), usually meaning those seen as coming from the north, often with actual or claimed Arab or Berber origins, and linked to pastoral nomadism; and 'blacks' (*sūdān*), or those peoples seen as indigenous to the Sahel and further to the south, and linked to agriculture. This distinction is complicated because it is shaped by how one group perceives itself, how it perceives others and how that group is perceived by others. Although many *bīḍān* are clearly lighter in skin tone than many *sūdān*, phenomena like concubinage, intermarriage, and affiliation mean that how the term has been deployed and claimed has no necessary relationship to phenotype or skin color. Since identity in the region is generally traced patrilineally and not by skin color, and since taking slave-concubines from other groups was common, being from a *bīḍān* or *sūdān* group might have no correspondence to one's skin tone.

This complexity is exemplified by the case of modern Mauritania. At the scale of the entire Western trans-Sahara/Sahel region, *bīḍān* and *sūdān* has long generally been used for 'those claiming Arab/Berber ancestry and seen as phenotypically lighter' (*bīḍān*) and 'those with ethnic origins from peoples in the Sahel and south and seen as phenotypically darker' (*sūdān*). But *within* Mauritania, *sūdān* is used to mean those people who either are or whose forefathers were once slaves of the *bīḍān*. Because of slave concubinage, however, phenotype is not actually a reliable indicator of *bīḍān* or *sūdān* status. Moreover, around one third of Mauritania's population consists of Black African ethnic groups such as Fulani (called Halpulaar) and

Wolof. These 'ethnic Africans' are not called *sūdān* but rather *kwār* (sing. *kūrī*; this Ḥassāniyya Arabic term may be derived from a Berber word for 'black' or a North African Arabic dialect word for 'unbeliever').[1] To further complicate the situation, in order to contrast themselves from these ethnic Africans, both *bīḍān* and *sūdān* refer to their shared Ḥassāniyya-Arabic-speaking community as *bīḍān*.[2]

The danger of indulging the Western racial assumption that phenotype counts for everything is evident in Dominique Champault's ethnography of the Algerian oasis of Tabelbala in the north-west Sahara in the 1960s. She noted the strength of the class distinctions between the categories of *murābiṭ*, *bin sayyid* (both from Berber and Arab ancestry and thus *bīḍān*), *ḥarāṭīn* (descendants of slaves), and slaves (both considered *sūdān*). The groups were generally endogamous in their marriages, though intermarriage did occur.[3] Champault observed two general phenotypes in and around Tabelbala, which seem to correspond to *sūdān*/*bīḍān* archetypes. The first was "somewhat frail, with long limbs, an elongated skull (*dolicocéphale*), often with a straight face, not very hairy, with hair [with the texture] of a peppercorn, with very black skin, and fine and mobile features." The second type was "nearly the opposite: an extremely robust appearance, with strong musculature, large hips and shoulders, short limbs, less elongated skulls (more medium in proportions), a large face with broad and pronounced cheekbones, and less pronounced pigmentation."[4] But, though she suggests that these phenotypes probably originated from two groups (*bīḍān* and *sūdān*), they are nowhere close to consistent with those *social categories*. Her pictures show a man with pure patrilineal Arab ancestry but who looks like one of the *ḥarāṭīn* (see Pictures 1, 5), and a young woman from an Arab family whose voluminous braids are considered a feature of the *bīḍān* but who looks like the daughter of the *sūdān ḥarāṭīn* (see Pictures 6, 8).

Another common, false assumption about phenotype and identity in the trans-Sahara region is that Berbers are necessarily light skinned. The majority likely are, but there are also Berbers whose features approach the classical Black African phenotype. William B. Hodgson's mid-nineteenth-century, very scholarly work on North African ethnology and language describes some Berbers as "Negros" (e.g., Ouarglis), with wooly hair, thick lips, and brown or bronze skin. Others are "white" (e.g., Mozabbies and the Tuareg).[5] This accords with al-Idrīsī's (d. *circa* 560/1165) testimony eight centuries earlier that there were some Berbers (*Baghāma*) who were black (*sūdān*).[6]

One aspect of the *bīḍān/sūdān* distinction in the Sahel has been power, the balance of which has shifted over time. Some evidence suggests that, in the twelfth century, the phenotypically "deep black" Zāfūn were at least equals in military might to the Berber Almoravid state. The powerful *sūdān* states like Mali and Songhay emerged later, after the thirteenth century. But the *bīḍān* gained an upper hand over *sūdān*-dominated states like Songhay after 1600 CE, with Morocco invading and establishing control over Timbuktu.[7]

The eighteenth and nineteenth centuries were dominated by the Fulani jihad states in what is now Senegal, Mali, Nigeria, and adjoining areas. The pastoralist Fulani often claimed to be *bīḍān* or 'red.' The Sokoto caliph (and ethnic Fulani) Muḥammad Bello echoed his uncle's claim that the Fulani were descended from the union of the Prophet's companion who had led a raid into the Sahara and a local princess (though Bello later rejected this argument, concluding that the ancestors of the Fulani were "Bambara from the people of the *sūdān*").[8] Aḥmad Lobbo (d. 1845 CE), a contemporary of Bello and founder of the Hamdullahi caliphate in the Niger bend, seems to have claimed Arab Quraysh ancestry.[9] Indeed, in 1730 the British explorer Francis Moore (d. 1756) observed that in the Senegambia region the "Pholeys" (presumably, Fulani) were a "People of a tawny Colour," as opposed to what he saw as the beautiful features and unmatched "Blackness" of the Wolof.[10] William Hodgson's 1844 work makes the same insistence – the Fulani "are *not* negroes" but rather a complexion between Arabs and blacks.[11] A Hausa chief in the mid nineteenth century also referred to the Fulani as reddish, and a Hausa history from that time refers to the Fulani Sokoto movement as white.[12] More recently, Coleman Donaldson has observed that some Bambara/Jula/Manding speakers in West Africa do not consider Fulani to be *farafin* (lit. 'black skin,' used to mean 'Black African'). Donaldson notes that the use of *farafin* by people in Senegambia to describe their own phenotype can be traced back at least to the late 1790s, when Mungo Park recorded his friend Karfa saying what the Scotsman heard as '*fato fing*' for 'black people.'[13]

Yet many Fulani are indistinguishable in skin tone from other *sūdān* groups. We also know that, on at least some occasions, Fulani villages were raided by Tuareg slavers in the nineteenth century.[14] In such instances, the *bīḍān* Tuareg were judging those Fulani to be unbelieving *sūdān*. Furthermore, Arab or Middle Eastern ancestry has not been a unique claim of the allegedly lighter-skinned Fulani. Bello also traces the origins of several peoples he describes as Black Africans (*sūdāniyyūn*) back to the Copts of Egypt, and there are also legends among other peoples from the Sahel and south of it that they migrated from the Middle East. A Yoruba legend, for example, claims they originated from Arabia or Iraq.[15]

The liminal status of the Fulani in West Africa has been evident in recent turmoil and violence in the Sahel, with Fulani communities targeted as not indigenous to countries like Nigeria. Ironically, since the late 1980s Fulani in Mauritania have been subjected to sometimes brutal oppression and expulsion as *kwār* interlopers in 'Arab' Mauritania.[16]

The relationship between power perceptions of race differed significantly among the Fulani states. The nineteenth-century pseudo-*Tārīkh al-Fattāsh* sometimes uses *zanj* or *ar-bi* (black people) for slaves, but, as Bruce Hall has pointed out, such usage was not known prior to the 1800s.[17] And, as Zachary Wright has pointed out, the jihad movements had divergent views on caste and trying to preserve certain ethnic groups as permanently enslaved. The Hamdullahi state was invested in preserving and justifying this caste structure, while ʿUmar Tal's contemporaneous Fulani movement opposed it and granted leadership positions to some who had previously been slaves.[18]

One aspect of confusion regarding the possible neutral or negative valence of the term *sūdān* comes from its use as both a toponym and an ethnonym. From the fourteenth century onward, scholars in Timbuktu and elsewhere in the area refer to the region, either the Niger bend area or the wider western Sahel, as *bilād al-sūdān* ('the land of the blacks'). But works like al-Saʿdī's (d. after 1065/1655–6)

*History of the Sudan* or those of Aḥmad Bābā do not feature the authors, who claimed Berber or Arab ancestry, referring to *themselves* as among the *sūdān*. Aḥmad Bābā was called *sūdānī* by his Moroccan students, but he referred to himself as Berber. Later scholars like the Fulani ʿUthmān bin Fūdī (Usman dan Fodio) (d. 1232/1817) and Bello used the word *sūdān/sūdāniyyūn* as an ethnonym only when they were speaking about non-Muslim African tribes, including referring to some of their languages (including Hausa) as *lugha sūdāniyya*. They referred to their own people not as *sūdān* but as Fulani.[19] Ali Mazrui pointed out that citizens of the nation state of Sudan refer to themselves by that term (*sūdānī*), but this seems not to be the result of some longstanding equanimity towards the ethnonym but rather of early-twentieth-century Sudanese nationalism that succeeded *despite* the negative valence of the ethnonym.[20] One instance I have found of a community applying the term *sūdān* to themselves (indeed, without any negative aspect) is a Hausa-speaking source in Kano in the nineteenth century.[21] Although it is not clear when this convention emerged, another instance is the *ḥarāṭīn* segment of Ḥassāniyya Arab society in Mauritania referring to themselves not as *ḥarāṭīn* but as *sūdān*.[22]

The *bīḍān/sūdān* dichotomy continued through the colonial period, both shaping and shaped by French policies. In the Niger bend region, there remains a common classification of Arab, Tuareg, and Fulani/Fulbe as 'white' or 'red' and groups like the Songhay and Bambara as 'blacks.' This distinction has no reliable link to phenotype as categorized by French colonial authorities, even within groups they classified as 'black,' such as the Bambara. In fact, as a class and power marker, the white/black distinction could be replicated within a group that was considered obviously black by outsiders (as with the Fulani above). Bambara elite often claimed Arab or Berber origins and referred to lower status people as 'black.'[23]

Another occasional aspect of the *bīḍān/sūdān* construct in the western and central Sahel is an assumption on the part of some *bīḍān* that they had a stronger connection to Islam. Bruce Hall and Ghislaine Lydon describe tensions in the nineteenth century among some Berber *bīḍān* about acknowledging the standing of the 'black'

Fulani-led Hamdullahi Islamic state. Within the Fulani-led Sokoto Caliphate, meanwhile, its Fulani leaders had replicated the bipartite power dynamic of *bīḍān/sūdān* by referring to themselves as the ruling half of a *fulān/sūdān* binary.[24] Ironically, celebrations of 'African' Islamic scholarship regularly emphasize the Timbuktu tradition of Aḥmad Bābā and the Sankore Mosque. Aḥmad Bābā, however, identified as a Sanhaja Berber, and Sankore literally means 'white noble' in Songhay.[25] As Zachary Wright has demonstrated, however, this in no way undermines the impressive scholarly heritage of non-Berber, West-African scholarship in the premodern period. The Jakhanke and other Soninke and Mande-speaking scholarly lineages flourished in the Western Sahel. Among them was Muḥammad al-Kābarī, a fifteenth-century scholar from west of Timbuktu who became the city's first scholar of renown and authored the earliest surviving text from Islamic West Africa.[26] Even earlier, in the fourteenth century, the Hejazi scholar ʿAbd al-Raḥmān al-Tamīmī had accompanied Mansa Mūsā back from his famous pilgrimage to Mecca and settled in Timbuktu, which he was surprised to find "full of Black African jurists" (*al-fuqahā' al-sūdāniyyīn*) who surpassed him in knowledge of Islamic law.[27] This stereotype of a shallow or ignorant African Islam blossomed among French colonialists (who called it 'Black Islam') and survives in the Mediterranean Middle East. When the Senegalese Sufi scholar Shaykh Ibrāhīm Niasse visited Cairo in 1961 he expressed his disapproval for how Arabs seemed to labor under some sense of obligation to educate their Black African brethren in the basics of Islam. For Niasse, the Islamic movements of the Sahel had a claim to the mantle of the faith that matched or even surpassed that of the modern Arab world.[28]

The nexus of color and power in the Sahel has found fascinating expression in literature from the region. In his brutal novel *Le dernier survivant de la caravane* (The Last Survivor of the Caravan), a story-within-a-story of a Banda village enslaved by Tuareg Muslim raiders, the Central African Republic author Étienne Goyémidé (d. 1997) appropriates the *bīḍān/sūdān*-Muslim/pagan dichotomies and inverts them. Where one might expect a Négritude-inspired celebration of black skin, the world of the villagers is one of light and color.

It is the slavers who dwell in blackness. The novel strictly limits the explicit language of white/black imagery. It appears briefly as the narrator sets the scene of the colonial town in which the story of the raid is recounted. The White (French) colonizers are distant, recalled only as impeccably dressed and benevolent ciphers. Even if the novel's protagonist, the old patriarch and storyteller, is a figure of anti-colonial potential, the Whites are appreciated for their schools, hospitals, and roads. In contrast to the Whites, the narrator speaks on behalf of "the natives (*autochtones*) . . . the true blacks (*nègres*) that we were" with a hint of sarcasm.[29]

Otherwise, the Banda world is full of colors, like the "multicolor" halo of the moon.[30] Ngala, the aged patriarch who survived to tell the tale of enslavement and escape to this new colonized generation, who resisted the French and still refuses to use their soap, who knows that freedom will come once again, had "seen all the colors," alluding perhaps to the Whites and the "vibrant colored canvas tents" of the Tuareg slavers who had taken him as a youth.[31]

Blackness, on the other hand, permeates the novel. But it is not the skin of the Banda villagers that is described as black, not even in reclaimed Négritude. The narrator's people are only referred to as black (*négres*) in facetious contrast to the French. The villagers recounted in the tale of enslavement are the norm; their appearance needs no description. We are accustomed to reading accounts of Black African features written in the Mediterranean world or Europe, exoticizing and often recoiling at them. Here Goyémidé makes the Tuareg the objects of gaze. They are alien and incomprehensible in their cruelty and their language. To the Banda, their prayer is a gymnastic absurdity.[32] Dressed, they are phantoms, turbaned and with their faces covered, except for their eyes and "hooked noses." They are "copper colored," "copper men" (*hommes cuivrés*). When they unveil themselves to pray, they are "copper-toned, with black hair, smooth or curly, with pronounced cheekbones, with black and bushy eyebrows, deep-set eyes, and noses hooked like the beaks of owls."[33]

Though their skin is copper-tone, blackness stands out clearly as the central motif in the descriptions of the Tuareg raiders. They are contrasted with the color range of the natural and normal world. They are, over and over, the men "robed in black" and "with black hearts" (*aux coeurs noirs*).[34] They are like the black crows that alight on a tree as a bad omen, their blackness and sinisterness mentioned over and over.[35] They are "warriors of the shadows," while the Banda villagers are "the warriors of the radiant sun."[36]

Goyémidé's deployment of color imagery stands in contrast to a Muslim author's treatment of slavery's fraught moral and communal legacy in the Sahel. *Shaihu Umar* (1934), a famous Hausa-language novel by the Nigerian intellectual and martyred prime minister, Alhaji Sir Abubakar Tafawa Balewa (d. 1966), is set in the late 1800s and tells the tale of a revered Hausa religious scholar's account of his life between Hausaland and Egypt, of enslavement, kidnapping, kindness, and cruelty. Where Goyémidé all but declares that Muslims are synonymous with the suffering of slavery, *Shaihu Umar* suggests that slavery's engine is powered by lawlessness and the unscrupulous individuals who thrive in it, churning out cruelty and injustice. Like *The Last Survivor*, the characters' color is the undescribed norm. Their blackness is remarked on only when they come into contact with the other. Otherwise, the only times people's skin color is noted is when two people are described as being light skinned. Tellingly, they are the protagonist's father and then his surrogate father figure, a kind and honorable Egyptian (interestingly, in the influential 1976 Nigerian film version of *Shaihu Umar*, the actor portraying the Egyptian looks no different from the rest of the cast).[37]

In the eastern Sahel, usually dealt with in the context of Sudan, the relationship between language, phenotype, notions of race, and power has become increasingly fraught over the last half century. In Sudan (and, after 2011, South Sudan), one can certainly find different phenotypes, from lighter-skinned Arabs to 'blue' (as they are often described in Sudanese Arabic) Dinka. But phenotype is not in any way a consistent guide to whether someone is Arab, non-Arab, Muslim, or non-Muslim. Indeed, the Arab versus African/Black dichotomy in Sudan/South Sudan was solidified *by* the conflict between the Sudanese government in the north and southern separatists during the 1980s and '90s and later by the conflict in Darfur.[38]

There have, of course, always been ethnic identities in the eastern Sudan. Some there have identified as Arab for at least three centuries and have often expressed contempt for animists to their south. After 1920, British colonial policies in Sudan took this vague cultural dichotomy and made it into the administrative reality of the 'Arab' north and the 'indigenous, African' south. This trend continued after Sudan's independence from Britain in 1956. Representatives of the dominant northern Arab constituency openly touted the superiority of their Arab-Islamic civilization and began policies of Arabization throughout Sudan through government organs like the education system. Southern representatives like Dunstan Wai (d. 2005), by contrast, portrayed Sudan as innately in conflict with itself. The country was torn between "the northern Sudanese[, who] view themselves as Arabs," and "the southern Sudanese[, who] feel themselves to be authentically Negroid Africans in every way."[39]

In recent decades, these lines of identity have been reified and tied to phenotypes that had never been reliable indicators of ethnic identity or religion.[40] This new notion of phenotype-as-clear-ethnic-identifier has been caulked onto the African/Arab dichotomy. This was due in part to the Arabization policies of the Sudanese government and in part to an international audience that was eager to view the conflict in Sudan as the latest episode of evil, enslaving Arabs oppressing good and innocent Black Africans (see Chapter 4). This process entered a second phase in the Darfur conflict, where 'Black' and 'Arab' actually gained real meaning for the parties involved as their resonance with international supporters became clear. As the conflict went on, tribes supporting the Darfur rebels were seen as 'African' and those pro government as 'Arab.' Pro-government groups demeaned their foes as 'slaves,' 'blacks,' or 'Nuba,' while rebels cast their opponents as mounted Arab fighters.[41] All the while, at least according to some observers, there was no reliable phenotypical distinction between the sides in the conflict.[42] As Alex de Waal explains, essentially everyone in Darfur is Muslim, and "it is rarely possible" to tell on basis of skin color what group a person belongs to.[43]

# Appendix IV

## Race and Blackness in the Horn of Africa

In Horn-of-Africa languages like Amharic, Tigrinya, and Somali (all Afro-Asiatic) there is a trend of those linguistic communities identifying themselves as lighter than the color 'black.' They tend to view themselves as distinct from (and often above) those they describe as black, namely ethnic groups they see as having more classically African phenotypes. In Amharic, the adjectives that Ethiopians use to describe their average complexion is *kederay/kedereyti* (Professor Hamza Zafar suggests that *kederay* may originate with the Greek word *kédrinos*, meaning 'cedar'), while *qeyih/qeyah* literally means 'red' and is used for Ethiopians of a lighter complexion. The Amharic word for dark skinned/black, *tselim* (masc.)/*tselam* (fem.), is used to describe the typical Black African phenotype, and it has historical associations with populations from which Ethiopians drew slaves (*tsalim barya*, 'dark slaves,' though 'red' Ethiopians were also enslaved). The word for black can also be used in the phrase *tselim libu* ('black-hearted').[1]

In Harari (formally called Gey Senan), a language spoken by a small community in northeast Ethiopia, *dama* (tanned) and *qëh* (red) are used by Hararis to describe their own average skin tone. The Harari word for the color black is *täy*, and this is the word used to describe the typical Black African skin tone (*täy-ach* is 'black people'). Harari can refer to the *täy* complexion to speak derogatively about non-Hararis, with phrases like "His heart is as black as his face" (*qalbizo feyt-so kut täy-inta*).

In Somali, the word for the color black is *madoow*. It is used to describe the average skin tone of Africans south of the Sahara (also called *Bantu* in Somali). If asked to describe their own appearance, some Somalis would also use 'black' (*madoow*) as a color descriptor, while others would use *maarin* (lighter than *madoow*) for the average skin tone of Somalis, with words like *casaan* ('red') and *axmar* ('ruddy') for light skin tones considered attractive in women. Somalis usually do not identify themselves by color. 'Black' (*madoow*) can also be used in pejorative phrases, e.g., to describe someone who lacks understanding (*qalbi madoow*) or to mark an eclipse (*qorrax madoobaad* or *dayax madoobaad*).

# Appendix V

## Arab/Muslim Slavers in Film

The following list is based on the late Jack Shaheen's menhiric tome *Reel Bad Arabs*, rev. ed. (Northampton, MA: Olive Branch Press, 2015) and my own excessive viewing history. I have been fairly restrictive, sticking to films that clearly depict enslavement/captivity carried out by Muslims/Arabs. This list thus excludes films about Arabs seducing/sleazing White women, Middle East hostage dramas, and para-Biblical epics that do not specifically portray Arabs. The list thus excludes *Protocol* (1984), for example, because Goldie Hawn's character is traded, not captured, by the Sheik. Many films fit into more than one of the categories below (e.g., White men and women both enslaved; Black Africans and White people enslaved, etc.), so I have chosen the category that seems most appropriate for each film. All films were produced by U.S. or U.K. studios unless otherwise noted.

### FILMS IN WHICH ARABS/MUSLIMS ENSLAVE/CAPTURE WHITES

1. *Robinson Crusoe* (1916)
2. *The Road to Love* (1916)
3. *The White Sister* (1923)
4. *Old Ironsides* (1926)
5. *Desert Bride* (1928)
6. *King Cowboy* (1928)
7. *Love in the Desert* (1929)
8. *The Pure Hell of St. Trinian's* (1960)

9. *Maciste contro lo Sceicco* (1962) (Italian)
10. *Lionheart* (1987) (NB: not the classic Van Damme film)
11. *Beyond Justice* (1992) (with Omar Sharif)
12. *Don Juan Demarco* (1995)

## FILMS IN WHICH WHITE WOMEN ARE CAPTURED/ENSLAVED/SOLD, SOMETIMES WITH SEDUCTION AND/OR RAPE

1. *Fire and the Sword* (1914)
2. *Imar the Servitor* (1914)
3. *Aladdin from Broadway* (1917)
4. *The Sultan's Wife* (1917)
5. *Bound in Morocco* (1918)
6. *The Demon* (1918)
7. *Male and Female* (1919)
8. *The Man Who Turned White* (1919)
9. *Son of Tarzan* (1920)
10. *The Sheik* (1921)
11. *Tom Mix in Arabia* (1922)
12. *One Stolen Night* (1923)
13. *The Tents of Allah* (1923)
14. *The Shriek of Araby* (1923) (parody of 'The Sheik' genre)
15. *A Son of the Sahara* (1924)
16. *The Sea Hawk* (1924)
17. *Maid in Morocco* (1925)
18. *Made for Love* (1926)
19. *So This is Paris* (1926) (parody of 'The Sheik' genre)
20. *The Lady of the Harem* (1926)
21. *Die Weisse Sklavin* (1927) (German)
22. *One Stolen Night* (1929)
23. *The Crusades* (1935)
24. *The Rest Cure/We're in the Legion Now* (1936)
25. *The Jungle Princess* (1937)
26. *The Lion Man* (1937)

27. *Tarzan's Revenge* (1938)
28. *Man about Town* (1939)
29. *Road to Zanzibar* (1941)
30. *Slave Girl* (1947)
31. *The White Sheik* (1951) (parody of 'The Sheik' genre)
32. *Pirates of Tripoli* (1955)
33. *Drums of Africa* (1963)
34. *Oggi, Domani, Dopodomani* (1965) (Italian)
35. *Mozambique* (1965)
36. *Indomptable Angélique* (1967) (French)
37. *Angélique et le Sultan* (1968) (French)
38. *Deserto di Fuoco* (1971) (Italian)
39. *The Wind and the Lion* (1975)
40. *Ilsa: Harem Keeper of the Oil Sheiks* (1976) (X-rated)
41. *The Seven Percent Solution* (1977)
42. *Emmanuelle Around the World* (1977)
43. *The Happy Hooker Goes to Washington* (1977)
44. *Paradise* (1982)
45. *Sahara* (1983) (made in Israel)
46. *Never Say Never Again* (1983)
47. *Bolero* (1984)
48. *Harem* (1985)
49. *The Lone Runner* (1986)
50. *Allan Quartermain and the Lost City of Gold* (1987)
51. *Intimate Power* (1989)
52. *The Sheltering Sky* (1990)
53. *Operation Condor* (1991) (Hong Kong)
54. *Night Terrors* (1993) (Israel)
55. *Prison Heat* (1993) (filmed in Israel)
56. *Ernest in the Army* (1997)
57. *Taken* (2008)

## FILMS IN WHICH ARABS/MUSLIMS ENSLAVE BLACK AFRICANS

1. *Tarzan of the Apes* (1918)
2. *The Adventures of Tarzan* (1921)
3. *Tarzan the Tiger* (1929)
4. *A Daughter of the Congo* (1930)
5. *Tarzan the Fearless* (1933)
6. *The Lost City* (1935)
7. *Anthony Adverse* (1936)
8. *The Four Feathers* (1939)
9. *Stanley & Livingstone* (1939)
10. *The Desert Hawk* (1944)
11. *The Golden Idol* (1954)
12. *West of Zanzibar* (1954)
13. *Adventures of Captain Africa* (1955)
14. *Storm over the Nile* (1955)
15. *Liane: Die Weisse Sklavin* (titled in English: *Nature Girl and the Slaver*) (1957) (German)
16. *Five Weeks in a Balloon* (1962)
17. *East of Sudan* (1964)
18. *The Naked Prey* (1965)
19. *Slavers* (1978) (German production in English)
20. *Ashanti* (1979) (produced in Israel)
21. *King Solomon's Mines* (1985)
22. *American Ninja 4: The Annihilation* (1991)
23. *Gladiator* (2000)

## FILMS IN WHICH ARABS/MUSLIMS ARE PORTRAYED AS PROMINENTLY INVOLVED IN SLAVE TRADE

1. *Sumurun* (1920) (titled in English: *One Arabian Night*) (German)
2. *Soft Cushions* (1927)
3. *Fleetwing* (1928)

4. *Arabian Nights* (1942)
5. *The Desert Hawk* (1950)
6. *Aladdin and His Lamp* (1952)
7. *The Saracen Blade* (1954)
8. *Yankee Pasha* (1954)
9. *The Prodigal* (1955)
10. *I Only Asked* (1958)
11. *Goliath e la Schiava Ribelle* (1963) (Italian)
12. *La Valle dell'Eco Tonante* (1964) (Italian)
13. *The Long Ships* (1964)

### FILMS IN WHICH ARABS/MUSLIMS ARE PORTRAYED AS AGAINST CAPTIVITY/SLAVERY

1. *The Corsair* (1914)
2. *Barbary Sheep* (1917)
3. *Arabian Love* (1922)
4. *Bitter Victory* (1958)
5. *The Brides of Fu Manchu* (1966)

# Appendix VI

## The Curse of Ham in Islamic Sources

Stories about the Curse of Ham fall into two broad groups: those in which the curse is to slavery and those in which the curse is to blackness. Some versions include both elements. In this section, we will refer to the Curse of Ham: Slavery and the Curse of Ham: Blackness to distinguish between these two motifs.

As a prelude to discussing the Curse of Ham myth, there is the question of what the Islamic tradition in its broadest sense has to say about humans' appearance before Noah's time. There is widely divergent material on Adam's appearance, mostly linked to the etymology of his name. Al-Nawawī and Ibn al-Jawzī list several etymologies, including the explanation that it was simply a foreign loan word like most prophets' names. The most prominent explanation, attributed to Ibn ʿAbbās and also upheld by the linguist al-Zajjāj (d. 311/923), is that Adam was named after the surface of the earth (*adīm al-arḍ*) from which he was created. This was what al-Ṭabarī and Ibn Qutayba (d. 276/889) found most compelling.[1] Abū al-Baqā' al-ʿUkbarī (d. 616/1219) held that Adam could be from darkness (*udma*), presumably of earth. The early scholar al-Naḍr b. Shumayl (d. 204/820) suggested Adam was not from *udma* but rather from *adma*, meaning the lighter underside of skin or hide. Adam was thus named "due to his whiteness."[2] Beyond these opinions, I have not found material explicitly discussing Adam's skin tone. The emphasis on his creation from mud, clay, and mixed earth, however, suggests a dark tone, especially since the Quran states that God created Adam from *ḥama'*, which exegetes almost all gloss as black or blackish, stinky clay (Quran 15:26). Interestingly, in his stories of the prophets, the shadowy figure al-Kisā'ī (d. unknown) gives a report with no source describing Eve as "tender and white" and purer in color than Adam.[3] One Hadith of questionable authenticity aligns the appearance of Adam and Abraham with that of the Prophet: "I am the most similar in appearance to my father Adam. And my father Abraham was the most similar of people to me in body and character" (*ana ashbah al-nās bi-abī ādam ṣ wa kāna abī Ibrāhīm ṣ ashbah al-nās bī khalqan wa khuluqan*).[4] As for Noah, Ibn Qutayba cites Wahb bin Munabbih (d. 114/732) that he had a darkish complexion (*ilā al-udma mā huwa*) but that Ham was originally "white, with a beautiful face."[5]

The Curse of Ham story is often referenced vaguely and without citation in Islamic sources, as in the case of al-Dīnawarī (d. 282/894–5), who mentions that the bizarre forms of distant Africans, who have their eyes and mouths in their chests, had been altered by God due to Noah's anger.[6] Ibn ʿAbd al-Barr's (d. 463/1070) discussion of human descent is representative and drawn on by later scholars. He presents Ham's descendants as having been cursed with blackness and enslavement as well established but provides no evidence. He does offer evidence for African descent from Ham: two reports, one from Wahb bin Munabbih and one from Ibn al-Musayyab (d. 94/713). But neither makes any mention of blackness or slavery.[7] Ibn Qutayba and al-Masʿūdī (d. 345/956) cite the Curse of Ham: Slavery story directly from the Biblical tradition. The only version they cite from earlier Muslim scholars (Curse of Ham: Blackness) comes from Wahb bin Munabbih.[8] Al-Ṭabarī cites the story of Ham's descendants being cursed to slavery on the authority of the prominent Medinan (then Baghdadi) Hadith transmitter, judge and *sīra* author Ibn Isḥāq (d. 150/767), who explicitly quotes "the people of the Torah" for the story. Al-Ṭabarī provides another report recounting both the elements of Curse of Ham: Slavery and the Curse of Ham: Blackness. This does not actually mention the curse but states that Ham's descendants were all born black and with curly hair (while Shem's were "beautiful of face and hair") and were regularly enslaved by Shem's descendants. This report is allegedly the testimony of the Persian Successor ʿAṭā' al-Khurāsānī (d. 135/752–3), but al-Ṭabarī's *isnād* for the report hinges on ʿAṭā's son, ʿUthmān, who was criticized severely for narrating forged Hadiths from his father. Al-Ṭabarī includes another Curse of Ham: Blackness version via an *isnād* to the respected early historian and jurist Ibn Jurayj (d. 150/767), who does not name his source. This version mentions how Ham had slept with his wife while on the Ark, a sin for which Noah "prayed that Ham's progeny would be changed, so from him came the blacks (*al-sūdān*)." This seems to be a clear reference to the pre-Islamic story of Ham being cursed with dark skin for having sex with his wife on the Ark, against Noah's wishes, which appeared in the Palestinian and Babylonian Talmuds in the fourth and fifth centuries CE.[9] Finally, al-Ṭabarī also notes a version of the Curse of Ham: Blackness from an unnamed source.[10]

None of these reports claim to be citing the Prophet or even a Companion of the Prophet as their authority. Some are cited explicitly from Biblical lore. This was probably also the source drawn on by Wahb bin Munabbih, who was a major source of Biblical lore in the Islamic tradition, as well as by Ibn Isḥāq, who was also criticized for passing on such material.[11]

Two versions of the Curse of Ham have been attributed to Companions of the Prophet, but neither is reliable in any way. They are:

**Ibn Masʿūd's Bathing Version: Blackness**: one version of the Curse of Ham: Blackness is found in the *Mustadrak* of the famous Hadith scholar al-Ḥākim al-Naysābūrī (d. 405/1014), with an *isnād* not to the Prophet but to the Companion Ibn Masʿūd (*anna nūḥan ightasala fa-ra'ā ibnahu yanẓuru ilayhi fa-qāla: tanẓuru ilayya wa anā aghtasilu khārra Allāh lawnaka, qāl: fa'swadda fa-huwa abū al-sūdān*) (the wording *ḥāra* in some books is a copyist error).[12] This report was assessed as weak by al-Dhahabī and Ibn al-Mulaqqin (d. 804/1401) and as forged (in the sense that it was not prophetic) by al-Amīr al-Kabīr al-Mālikī (d. 1232/1817). It hinges on one Ibn Abī Labība, who, as al-Dhahabī explains, was a liar and whose chain of narration al-Ṭaḥāwī (d. 321/933) states was no basis for confidence.[13] Although al-Ḥākim regarded it as sound (*ṣaḥīḥ*), his laxity in rating Hadiths has been well established. Al-Dhahabī concluded that only about one third of the

*Mustadrak* met the standards of al-Bukhārī, Muslim or both; about a quarter of the book reaches the level of *ḥasan*, and the rest is weak, uncorroborated, or outright bizarre (*manākīr wa ʿajāʾib*), with around 100 Hadiths total forgeries.[14] Ibn al-Amīr al-Ṣanʿānī confirmed this.[15] Al-Dhahabī and al-Zaylaʿī (d. 762/1361) concluded that al-Ḥākim would declare a Hadith *ṣaḥīḥ* according to the standards of al-Bukhārī and Muslim if it used their transmitters, but he would not verify the contiguity of the *isnād* or check for corroboration.[16] The Meccan scholar Ibn Ḥajar Haytamī is outright dismissive of al-Ḥākim's ruling a Hadith *ṣaḥīḥ*, rejecting it repeatedly as errant.[17]

**Ibn ʿAbbās' Summoning Version: Slavery**: one version of the Curse of Ham to slavery is found in the *Futūḥ Miṣr* of Ibn ʿAbd al-Ḥakam (d. 257/871), with an *isnād* back to the Companion Ibn ʿAbbās, not the Prophet.[18] In this version, Noah calls his sons to him, but Ham does not respond. As a punishment, Noah prays that God debase his descendants and make them slaves to Shem's. This version also includes Noah cursing the descendants of Japheth to be "the worst of mankind" (*shirār al-khalq*). The *isnād* of this report hinges on the Egyptian transmitter Ibn Lahīʿa, who is well known as problematic and whose material, if it can be relied on at all, cannot be relied on in isolation and without corroboration. Al-Masʿūdī seems to refer to something similar to this story briefly and without citation when he recounts how Noah also cursed Japheth for not condemning Ham's laughing at him, making his children also slaves of Shem and making them "the worst of mankind."[19]

# Appendix VII

## Islam and Caste in South Asia

According to received opinion among social scientists, a society with a caste system (derived from the Portuguese word *casta*) is one divided hereditarily into a hierarchy, with its component classes generally falling along lines of vocation and kept separated by rules and rituals of endogamy, purity, and pollution.[1] In South Asia, the theoretical roots of the caste system can be traced back to the *Rig Veda*, with its story of a primal being whose head, arms, thighs, and feet become the four levels (*varna*) of society: scholar-priests (Brahmins), warriors, farmer-merchants, and laborers. Weaving through and alongside the four *varnas* is a much more complicated hierarchy of *jats*, or solidarity groups, organized along regional, tribal, or, most often, occupational lines. Beneath the *varnas* are the *dalits*, or untouchables.

When the famous Muslim polymath al-Bīrūnī (d. *circa* 442/1050) wrote his expertly researched description of Indian cultures and religions, he noted how intense the caste system in India was, "to the point that our differing with them [on this] and our considering the generality of people equal except in piety is the greatest barrier between them and Islam."[2] Whether he was right or not remains a topic of heated debate. That Muslim society in South Asia has long been organized along markedly hierarchical lines is not debated. But scholarship is still divided on whether this constitutes caste or not, whether caste among Muslims replicates caste among Hindus or is only comparable, or if caste-like division among Muslims needs to be approached on its own terms. Social scientists have debated whether caste can be talked about independent of the Hindu heritage or only in comparison with it. But this is irrelevant for the question of

Muslims in South Asia, since they either converted to Islam from Hinduism or have lived in intimate proximity with Hindus for centuries.

An influential study on north India by Mayer (1966) concluded simply that, yes, Muslims in India lived within the caste system, either in the caste-space carved out for Muslims or by communities maintaining aspects of their families' prior caste identity and practices even after converting to Islam.[3] A vocal critic and prolific writer on Muslim caste, Yoginder Sikand, has argued that there is a Muslim caste system but that it is less intense than the Hindu one, lacking true untouchability.[4] All Muslims, for example, can enter any mosque. Dumont (d. 1998) was more skeptical. He concluded that Hindu origins, influence, and proximity meant that Muslims acquired "something of caste," despite their differences and modifications. But, although Muslim society in South Asia was replete with deep group divisions, in marriage, the essential point of caste control, it was much less rigidly divided than its Hindu counterpart. The only group that Islamic law strictly prohibited marrying was Hindus, and massive social opprobrium only resulted from marriage between two drastically different Muslim classes.[5] The Pakistani sociologist Hamza Alavi (d. 2003) argued that, in the Punjab at least, the absence of anxiety around pollution and diet meant Muslim society was structured into kinship groups, not castes.[6] An Indian Muslim anthropologist, Imtiaz Ahmad, replied that kinship groups and caste could and did coexist among Muslims. Though rules of endogamy and concerns about purity vary by region and caste, he argued, they are present enough among Muslims in the region to constitute a comparable phenomenon to Hindu castes.[7] Sylvia Vatuk has pointed out that the question of whether Muslims have caste or not is misplaced; Muslims in India clearly view themselves as organized into kin groups in some sort of hierarchy, but they perceive and justify these identities through means drawn from their Islamic heritage. While some Muslim castes fit into the corresponding Hindu hierarchy of vocationally based castes, others find their standing assessed by a more complex but ultimately Islamically oriented valuation of Arabian blood, Islamic knowledge, and fair skin.[8] One crucial aspect pointed to as a clear divergence between Muslim hierarchy and Hindu caste is that the latter originated in scripture while the former seems to militate against Quranic egalitarianism. As we saw in Chapter 9, however, Muslims who uphold the Islamic legitimacy of caste-like distinction perceive it as the Shariah concept of *kafā'a* (suitability) in marriage.

Though caste is imagined as fixed and timeless, the caste categories within Muslim society were often contested and fluid. During the Mughal period (roughly 1500s–1850 CE), communities that had converted to Islam from indigenous Indian religions often claimed or sought access to higher caste Muslim society, sometimes successfully, sometimes unsuccessfully.[9] The late nineteenth and early twentieth centuries saw increased contestation and fluidity in caste and caste relations among Hindus and Muslims under British rule and in the era of the budding Indian independence movement.[10]

Debate over the existence or absence of caste among Muslims has been political even at an academic level, and it is distinctly so in the public square in South Asia. Many Muslims deny there is a Muslim caste system because they consider it an insult to Islam's egalitarian ethos and an insinuation that Muslims in South Asia are really Hindus covered in an Islamic patina.[11] Many Hindu critics of the Muslim presence in India try to knock Muslims off their egalitarian pedestal by pointing to Muslim caste, while others accept the Muslim denial of caste identity because it keeps Muslims out of the system of affirmative action that the Indian state has erected to assist subordinated castes. Some low-caste (*dalit*) Muslims or other Muslims advocating for them insist that Muslim society is, in fact, riven with caste discrimination. Sometimes both Muslim apologists and anti-Muslim, Hindu activists find themselves united in rebutting complaints about caste discrimination, since in the last century these have played a part in efforts by low-caste Muslims and low-caste Hindus to conjure trans-religious caste solidarity against the system that discriminates against both.[12]

A common response from Muslims opposed to caste discrimination is to dismiss it as the result of centuries of Hindu influence on the Muslim community. Sikand has pointed to the millennium-old heritage of hierarchy and elitism in Islamic civilization, arguing that

Muslims fell under the influence of Persian hierarchicalism at the cost of the Quran's original message of equality before God.[13] The reality falls between the two camps. Muslim views and practices of caste in South Asia are a composite of lingering Hindu cultural sensibilities, extended influence by the South Asian milieu, and Shariah distinctions like *kafāʾa*. The latter provided an Islamic basis for the legitimacy of requiring endogamy along lines of ancestry and vocation, both in the specific rules of the Ḥanafī school (those of Arab descent were only suitable for marriage to others of Arab descent; those of lowly vocation were not suitable for families of loftier vocations) and in the school's legal approach to marriage in new cultural milieus. It seems to have been coincidence that the Prophet's (allegedly) specifying cuppers/barber-surgeons (*ḥajjām*) and weavers (*ḥāʾik*) as lowly vocations not suitable for marriage to others corresponded to weavers (*tanti*) being a despised caste in the Hindu caste tradition. But the Ḥanafī position that other vocations could be added to these two on the basis of how they were viewed by prevalent custom allowed Muslims in South Asia to adopt the Hindu *jat* system essentially in its entirety.

Whatever the case, the nature and intensity of hierarchy and division among Muslims in South Asia (we refer to this as caste for the sake of convenience) has varied a great deal over time and geography. Muslims refer to castes either with a term similar to other Indians, *jati/zat*, or with the Arabic word *qawm* (people, tribe) or the Persianate terms *birādarī* (brotherhood) or *khāndān* (*family*).[14] Caste, of course, affects marriage, but it can also strongly influence who is seen as suitable leaders in a Muslim locality and which mosques are attended. There are even reports that, in northern India, some upper caste Muslims view low caste Muslims as hardly Muslim at all. Studies suggest that caste among South Asian Muslims is most prominent in a band across the northern region, from the Punjab to Bengal. But it exists further south into the Deccan plateau, as far as Tamilnadu.

As with Hindu castes, some Muslim castes are trans-regional while others are regional, either because a certain ethnic group embraced Islam at one point or because of some (real or imagined) instance of migration or contact from Arab, Persian, or Turkic lands.[15] Addressing these less common regional phenomena first, an example is the Meo caste, who live on the borders of the Rajasthan and Haryana states. This Muslim caste claims Rajput descent and is fairly wealthy.[16] An example of the second is the Chawsh caste in Hyderabad, who identify as the descendants of Yemeni Arabs who came to the region to fight for the armies of the Nizam of Hyderabad.[17]

By far the most predominant structures of Muslim caste, however, are based on claims of descent and on vocation. The descent-based castes are specific to Muslims, while there is significant overlap with Hindu caste in vocational ones. While both descent-based and vocational castes tend to transcend region, they can take on specific features in one region or another, sometimes going by different names. A broad generalization divides Muslims into three classes: the *ashrāf*, the *ajlāf* (also, *atrāp*), and the *arzāl* (also, *arjāl*). The *ashrāf* are the noble castes, all claiming foreign origin. The noble castes include those claiming descent from the Prophet (*sayyid*), major Companions (*shaykh*) like Abū Bakr (*ṣiddīqī*), ʿUmar (*fārūqī*), ʿUthmān (*ʿuthmānī*), and ʿAlī (*ʿalawī*); Mughal nobility, and Afghans/Pathans. The middle tier, the *ajlāf*, is vocational and often thought to have originated with Hindus who converted to Islam, including: *anṣārī* (weavers), *kalaal* (liquor sellers), *raeen* (vegetable sellers), *qurayshī* (butchers), etc. The low caste *arzāls* include *lalbegi* (scavengers), *dafali* (drum makers), *hawari* (cleaners), *dhobi* (washers), *halalkhor* (sweepers), and *bhatiara* (inn keepers), etc.[18] Depending on region, the number of vocational castes can be enormous. The 1911 Census in British India found 102 caste groups among Muslims in the Uttar Pradesh region of the Ganges plain, of which only five were *ashrāf*.[19]

# Select Bibliography

*This bibliography includes those items cited in the notes, with the exception of less substantial online pieces or news items.*


Abbasi, Iskander. "Muslims, and the Coloniality of Being: Reframing the Debate on Race and Religion in Modernity." *Journal for the Study of Religion* 33, n. 2 (2020).

ʿAbd al-Majd, Muḥammad Muḥammad. *Imām al-bu'asā' Muḥammad Imām al-ʿAbd*. Cairo: Maṭbaʿat al-Taraqqī, n.d.

Abdul-Khabeer, Su'ad. *Muslim Cool: Race, Religion and Hip Hop*. New York: New York University Press, 2016.

Abdullah, Zain. *Black Mecca*. Oxford: Oxford University Press, 2010.

Abu-Lughod, Lila. "Authorizing Moral Crusades to Save Muslim Women." Farhat Ziadeh Annual Lecture. Seattle: University of Washington, 2012.

Adu-Boahen, Kwabena. "Abolition, Economic Transition, Gender and Slavery: The Expansion of Women's Slaveholding in Ghana, 1807–1874." *Slavery and Abolition* 31, n. 1 (2010): 117–36.

Adams, Francis M. and Charles E. Osgood. "A Cross-Cultural Study of the Affective Meanings of Color." *Journal of Cross-Cultural Psychology* 4, n. 2 (1973): 135–56.

ʿAdawī, ʿAlī b. Aḥmad al-Ṣaʿīdī. *Ḥāshiyat al-ʿAdawī ʿalā Kifāyat al-ṭālib*. Ed. Yūsuf Muḥammad al-Biqāʿī. 2 vols. Beirut: Dār al-Fikr, 1414/1994.

_____ and Muḥammad b. ʿArafa al-Dasūqī et al. *Ḥāshiyat al-Dasūqī ʿalā al-Sharḥ al-kabīr*. 4 vols. Cairo: Dār Iḥyā' al-Kutub al-ʿArabiyya, n.d.

Afigbo, A.E. *The Abolition of the Slave Trade in Southeastern Nigeria, 1885–1950*. Rochester, NY: University of Rochester Press, 2006.

Ahmad, Aisha. "'We Have Captured Your Women': Explaining Jihadist Norm Change." *International Security* 44, n. 1 (2019): 80–116.

Ahmad, Imtiaz, ed. *Caste and Social Stratification among Muslims in India*. Columbia, MO: South Asia Books, 1978.

_____. *Family, Marriage and Kinship among Muslims in India*. New Delhi: Manchar Books, 1976.

Ahmed, Chanfi. *AfroMecca in History: African Societies, Anti-Black Racism, and Teaching in the Haram Mosque in Mecca*. Newcastle: Cambridge Scholars Publishing, 2019.

_____. *West African* ʿulamāʾ *and Salafism in Mecca and Medina*. Leiden: Brill, 2015.

Ahmed, Rafiuddin. *The Bengal Muslims 1871–1906: A Quest for Identity*. 2nd edn. Delhi: Oxford University Press, 1988.

Aïdi, Hisham. "Slavery, Genocide and the Politics of Outrage: Understanding the New Racial Olympics." *Middle East Report* 234 (Spring 2005), https://web.archive.org/web/20210621214723/https://merip.org/2005/03/slavery-genocide-and-the-politics-of-outrage

ʿAjlūnī, Ismāʿīl. *Kashf al-khafā*. Ed. Aḥmad al-Qalāsh. 2 vols. Cairo: Dār al-Turāth, n.d.

Ajuok, Albino Deng. "Response of Southern Sudanese Intellectuals to African Nationalism." *Journal of Pan African Studies* 2, n. 5 (2008): 130–41.

Ājurrī, Abū Bakr. *Al-Sharīʿa*. Ed. ʿAbdallāh ʿUmar al-Dumayjī. 5 vols. Riyadh: Dār al-Waṭan, 1420/1999.

Akande, Habeeb. *Illuminating the Darkness: Blacks and North Africans in Islam*. London: Ta-Ha Pub., 2012.

_____. *Illuminating the Blackness: Blacks and African Muslims in Brazil*. London: Rabaah, 2016.

_____. *A Taste of Honey: Sexuality and Erotology in Islam*. London: Rabaah, 2015.

Akıncı, İdil. "Language, Nation, Difference: Everyday Language Tactics of Young Emiratis." In *Gulf Cooperation Council Culture and Identities in the New Millennium*. Ed. Magdalena Karolak and Nermin Allam, 201–20. Singapore: Palgrave Macmillan, 2020.

Alam, Arshad. "Challenging the Ashrafs: The Politics of Pasmanda Muslim Mahaz." *Journal of Muslim Minority Affairs* 29, n. 2 (2009): 171–81.

_____. "Contextualising Muslim Identity: Ansaris, Deobandis, Barelwis." *Economic and Political Weekly* 44, n. 24 (2009): 86–92.

Alarcón, Odette et al. "The Color of My Skin: A Measure to Assess Children's Perceptions of Their Skin Color." *Applied Development Science* 4, n. 4 (2000): 208–21.

Alavi, Hamza. "Kinship in West Punjab Villages." *Contributions to Indian Sociology* 6 (1972): 1–27.

Albānī, Muḥammad Nāṣir al-Dīn. *Fatāwā al-Shaykh al-Albānī*. Ed. ʿUkāsha ʿAbd al-Mannān al-Ṭayyibī. Cairo: Maktabat al-Turāth al-Islāmī, 1994.

_____. *Silsilat al-aḥādīth al-ḍaʿīfa wa'l-mawḍūʿa*. Riyadh: Maktabat al-Maʿārif, 1420/2000–1425/2005.

_____. *Silsilat al-aḥādīth al-ṣaḥīḥa*. 7 vols. Riyadh: Maktabat al-Maʿārif, 1995–2002.

_____. *Ṣaḥīḥ al-Targhīb wa'l-tarhīb*. 3 vols. Riyadh: Maktabat al-Maʿārif, 1421/2000.

Alexander, Jack. "The culture of race in middle-class Kingston, Jamaica." *American Ethnologist* 4, n. 3 (1977): 413–35.

Ali, Abdullah bin Hamid. *The 'Negro' in Arab-Muslim Consciousness*. Swansea, UK: Claritas, 2018.

Ali, Syed. "Collective and Elective Ethnicity: Caste among Urban Muslims in India." *Sociological Forum* 17, n. 4 (2002): 593–620.

Ālūsī, Abū al-Thanā'. *Rūḥ al-maʿānī*. Ed. ʿAlī ʿAbd al-Bārī ʿAṭiyya. 16 vols. Beirut: Dār al-Kutub al-ʿIlmiyya, 1415/1995.

Amīr al-Kabīr, Muḥammad al-Mālikī. *Al-Nukhba al-bahiyya fī al-aḥādīth al-makdhūba ʿalā khayr al-bariyya*. Ed. Zuhayr al-Shāwīsh. Beirut: al-Maktab al-Islāmī, 1988/1409.

ʿĀmirī, Abū al-Ḥasan. *Kitāb al-Iʿlām bi-manāqib al-islām*. Ed. Aḥmad ʿAbd al-Ḥamīd Gharāb. Riyadh: Dār al-Aṣāla, 1408/1988.

Anderson, Patrick. "Pan-Africanism and Economic Nationalism: W.E.B. Du Bois's Black Reconstruction and the Failings of the 'Black Marxism' Thesis." *Journal of Black Studies* 48, n. 8 (2017): 732–57.

Ansary, A.R. *Qaryat al-Fau: A Portrait of Pre-Islamic Civilisation in Saudi Arabia*. Toledo: Artes Graficas, [1982].

Anṣārī, Shaykh al-Islām Zakariyyā'. *Minḥat al-bārī bi-sharḥ Ṣaḥīḥ al-Bukhārī*. Ed. Sulaymān Durayʿ al-ʿĀzimī. 10 vols. Riyadh: Maktabat al-Rushd, 1426/2005.

Appiah, Kwame Anthony. "But Would That Still Be Me? Notes on Gender, 'Race,' Ethnicity, as Sources of 'Identity'." *Journal of Philosophy* 87 (1990): 493–99.

_____. "Racisms." In *Anatomy of Racism*. Ed. David Theo Goldberg, 3–17. Minneapolis: University of Minnesota Press, 1990.

_____ and Amy Gutmann, eds. *Color Conscious: The Political Morality of Race*. Princeton: Princeton University Press, 1996.

Arjana, Sophia Rose. *Muslims in the Western Imagination*. Oxford: Oxford University Press, 2015.

Asante, Molefi. *The Afrocentric Idea*. Rev. edn. Philadelphia: Temple University Press, 1998.

_____. *Kemet, Afrocentricity, and Knowledge*. Trenton, N.J.: Africa World Press, 1990.

Ashanti, AbdulHaq. *Defining Legends: An Analysis of Afrocentric Writings against Islam*. Birmingham, UK: Dar al-Arqam, 2019.

ʿAthamina, Khalil. "Non-Arab Regiments and Private Militias during the Umayyād Period." *Arabica* 45, n. 3 (1998): 347–78.

Austen, Ralph A. "The 19th Century [sic] Islamic Slave Trade from East Africa (Swahili and Red Sea Coasts): A Tentative Census." *Slavery and Abolition* 9, n. 3 (1988): 21–44.

Ayana, Daniel. "Re-Mapping Africa: The Northern *Zanj, Damadim, Yamyam, Yam/Yamjam, Habasha/Ahabish, Zanj-Ahabish* and *Zanj ed-Damadam* – The Horn of Africa between the Ninth and Fifteenth Centuries." *History in Africa* 46 (2019): 57–104.

ʿAyyāshī, ʿAbdallāh b. Muḥammad. *Al-Riḥla al-ʿAyyāshiyya li'l-baqāʿ al-ḥijāziyya*. Ed. Aḥmad Farīd al-Mazīdī. 2 vols. Beirut: Dār al-Kutub al-ʿIlmiyya, 2011.

Aʿẓamī, Ḥabīb al-Raḥmān. *Ansāb wa kifāyat kī sharʿī ḥaythiyyat*. Azamgar: Markaz Taḥqīqāt wa Khadamāt ʿIlmiyya, n.d.

Badāyūnī, ʿAbd al-Qādir. *Muntakhab-t-Tawarikh*. Trans. T. Wolseley Haig. Delhi: Idarah-i-Adabiyat-i-Delli, 1899.

Baepler, Paul M. "The Barbary Captivity Narrative in American Culture." *Early American Literature* 39, n. 2 (2004): 217–46.

_____, ed. *White Slaves, African Masters: An Anthology of American Barbary Captivity Narratives*. Chicago: University of Chicago Press, 1999.

Baghawī, al-Ḥusayn b. Masʿūd. *Maʿālim al-tanzīl*. Ed. Muḥammad ʿAbdallāh al-Nimr et al. 8 vols. Riyadh: Dār al-Ṭība, 1417/1997.

_____. *Sharḥ al-sunna*. Ed. Shuʿayb al-Arnāʾūṭ and Muḥammad Zuhayr al-Shāwīsh. 15 vols. Beirut: al-Maktab al-Islāmī, 1403/1983.

_____. *Al-Tahdhīb fī fiqh al-imām al-Shāfiʿī*. Ed. ʿĀdil Aḥmad ʿAbd al-Mawjūd and ʿAlī Muḥammad Muʿawwaḍ. 8 vols. Beirut: Dār al-Kutub al-ʿIlmiyya, 1418/1997.

Baghdādī, al-Khaṭīb. *Tārīkh Baghdād*. Ed. Muṣṭafā ʿAbd al-Qādir ʿAṭā. 24 vols. Beirut: Dār al-Kutub al-ʿIlmiyya, 1417/1998.

Bail, Christopher. *Terrified: How Anti-Muslim Fringe Organizations Became Mainstream*. Princeton: Princeton University Press, 2014.

Baines, John. "Color Terminology and Color Classification: Ancient Egyptian Color Terminology and Polychromy." *American Anthropologist* 87, n. 2 (1985): 282–97.

Balādhurī, Aḥmad b. Yaḥyā. *Kitāb jumal min Ansāb al-ashrāf*. Ed. Suhayl Zakkār and Riyāḍ al-Ziriklī. 13 vols. Beirut: Dār al-Fikr, 1417/1996.

Balewa, Abubakar Tafawa. *Shaihu Umar*. Trans. Mervin Hiskett. Princeton: Markus Wiener, 1989.

Balibar, Étienne. "Is there a Neo-Racism?" In *Race, Nation, Class: Ambiguous Identities*. Ed. Étienne Balibar and Immanuel Wallerstein, 17–28. London: Verso, 1991.

Baranī, Ḍiyāʾ al-Dīn. *Fatāvāy-i Jahāndārī*. Ed. Afsar Saleem Khan. Lahore: Research Society of Pakistan, 1972.

Bartels, Emily C. "Making more of the Moor: Aaron, Othello, and Renaissance Refashionings of Race." *Shakespeare Quarterly* 41, n. 4 (1990): 433–54.

_____. "Too Many Blackamoors: Deportations, Discrimination, and Elizabeth I." *Studies in English Literature* 46, n. 2 (2006): 305–22.

Barth, Fredrik. *Sohar: Culture and Society in an Omani Town*. Baltimore: Johns Hopkins University Press, 1983.

Bartilī, Muḥammad b. Abī Bakr al-Walātī. *Fatḥ al-shukūr fī maʿrifat aʿyān ʿulamāʾ al-Takrūr*. Ed. ʿAbd al-Wadūd Wuld ʿAbdallāh and Aḥmad Jamāl Wuld al-Ḥasan. Cairo: Dār Najībawayh, 2010.

Barzanjī, Jaʿfar b. Ḥasan et al. *Majmūʿ mushtamil ʿalā mawlid al-Nabī (s) li'l-Barzanjī wa'l-Daybaʿ wa'l-ʿAzab*. Cairo: Maṭbaʿat Muṣṭafā al-Bābī al-Ḥalabī, 1342/1923.

Bayḍāwī, ʿAbdallāh b. ʿUmar. *Anwār al-tanzīl wa asrār al-taʾwīl*. Ed. Muḥammad ʿAbd al-Raḥmān al-Marʿashlī. 5 vols. Beirut: Dār Iḥyāʾ al-Turāth al-ʿArabī, 1418/1998.

Bayhaqī, Abū Bakr Aḥmad. *Manāqib al-Shāfiʿī*. Ed. al-Sayyid Aḥmad Ṣaqr. 2 vols. Cairo: Dār al-Turāth, 1970.

_____. *Shuʿab al-īmān*. Ed. Muḥammad Saʿīd Zaghlūl. 7 vols. Beirut: Dār al-Kutub al-ʿIlmiyya, 1990.

_____. *Al-Sunan al-kubrā*. Ed. Muḥammad ʿAbd al-Qādir ʿAṭā. 11 vols. Beirut: Dār al-Kutub al-ʿIlmiyya, 1999.

Bazzaz, Sahar. *Forgotten Saints: History, Power, and Politics in the Making of Modern Morocco*. Cambridge, MA: Harvard University Press, 2010.

Behnstedt, Peter and Manfred Woidich. *Wortatlas der arabischen Dialekte*. Leiden: Brill, 2010.

Bell, Melina Constantine. "John Stuart Mill's Harm Principle and Free Speech: Expanding the Notion of Harm." *Utilitas* 33 (2021): 162–79.

Bello, Muḥammad. *Infāq al-maysūr fī tārīkh bilād al-Takrūr*. Ed. Sulaymān Mūsā. Gusau, Nigeria: Iqra' Publishing, 2013, published in two-volume set *Mukhtārāt min mu'allafāt amīr al-mu'minīn Muḥammad Billū*.

_____. *Jalā' al-ṣudūr ʿammā yakhtaliju fīhā min ṣadā al-gharūr*. Ed. Thānī Yūsuf Birnin Tudu. Gusau, Nigeria: Iqra' Publishing, 2013, published in two-volume set *Mukhtārāt min mu'allafāt amīr al-mu'minīn Muḥammad Billū*.

_____. *Risalat li 'l-Amraad as-Shafiyya: A Letter of Healing*. Trans. Abu Alfa Umar Muhammad Shareef bin Farid. Sennar, Sudan: Sankore' Institute of Islamic-African Studies International, 1415/1995.

Bender, M. Lionel. "Color Term Encoding in a Special Lexical Domain: Sudanese Arabic Skin Colors." *Anthropological Linguistics* 25, n. 1 (1983): 19–27.

Berlin, Brent and Paul Kay. *Basic Color Terms*. Berkeley: University of California Press, 1969.

Bernasconi, Robert, ed. *Race*. Oxford: Wiley-Blackwell, 2001.

Béteille, André. "Race and Descent as Social Categories in India." In *Color and Race*. Ed. John H. Franklin, 166–85. Boston: Houghton Mifflin, 1968.

Bhardwaj, Maya. "Political Blackness and the search for multiracial solidarity." *Roar*, 4 May 2021, https://web.archive.org/web/20210820231304/https://roarmag.org/essays/political-blackness-multiracial-solidarity

Bhopal, Raj. "Glossary of terms relating to ethnicity and race: for reflection and debate." *Journal of Epidemiology and Community Health* 58 (2004): 441–45.

Bin Bāz, ʿAbd al-ʿAzīz. *Al-Ḥulal al-ibrīziyya min al-taʿlīqāt al-bāziyya*. Ed. ʿAbdallāh Māniʿ al-Rūqī. 4 vols. Riyadh: Dār al-Tadmuriyya, 1428/2007.

Bīrūnī, Abū al-Rayḥān Muḥammad. *Taḥqīq mā li'l-Hind*. Hyderabad: Dā'irat al-Maʿārif al-ʿUthmāniyya, 1377/1958.

Bishku, Michael B. "Israel and South Sudan: A Convergence of Interests." *Middle East Policy* 26, n. 4 (2019): 40–52.

Blassingame, John. *The Slave Community: Plantation Life in the Antebellum South*. Rev. edn. New York: Oxford University Press, 1979.

Blum, Lawrence. *"I'm Not Racist But . . .": The Moral Quandary of Race*. Ithaca, NY: Cornell University Press, 2002.

Bourke, Joanna. "Bestiality, Zoophilia and Human–Animal Sexual Interactions." *Paragraph* 42, n. 1 (2019): 91–115.

Boxill, Bernard, ed. *Race and Racism*. New York: Oxford University Press, 2001.

Boyd, Jean and Beverley B. Mack. *Collected Works of Nana Asma'u, Daughter of Usman 'dan Fodiyo*. East Lansing: Michigan State University Press, 1997.

Braudel, Fernand. *The Mediterranean: Vol. 2*. Berkeley: University of California Press, 1995.

Brenner, Athalya. *Colour Terms in the Old Testament*. Sheffield: Journal of the Study of the Old Testament, 1982.

Brockopp, Jonathan. "Islamic Origins and Incidental Normativity." *Journal of the American Academy of Religion* 84, n. 1 (2016): 28–43.

Brooks, Francis. *Barbarian Cruelty*. London: Edmund Bohun, 1692–3.

Brown, Jonathan A.C. *Slavery & Islam*. London: Oneworld, 2019.

_____. "Slavery and Sufism: The *Ḥilyat al-Awliyā'* of Abū Nu'aym al-Iṣbahānī (d. 430/1038) as a Source on Slavery in Medieval Islamic Civilization." *Annals of the Japanese Association for Middle East Studies* 36, n. 2 (2020): 29–44.

Bruce, James. *Travels to Discover the Source of the Nile*. Edinburgh: J. Ruthven, 1790.

Brulin, Remi. "Le discours américain sur le terrorisme: Constitution, evolution et contextes d'enonciation (1972–1992)." PhD dissertation, Université de la Sorbonne Nouvelle, 2011.

Brunschvig, Robert. "Métiers vils en Islam." *Studia Islamica* 16 (1962): 41–60.

Bryon, Gay L. *Symbolic Blackness and Ethnic Difference in Early Christian Literature*. London: Routledge, 2002.

Bujayrimī, Sulaymān b. Muḥammad. *Tuḥfat al-ḥabīb ʿalā sharḥ al-khaṭīb*. 4 vols. Beirut: Dār al-Fikr, 1410/1995.

Bukhārī, Muḥammad b. Ismāʿīl. *Al-Tārīkh al-kabīr*. Ed. Muṣṭafā ʿAbd al-Qādir ʿAṭā. 9 vols. Beirut: Dār al-Kutub al-ʿIlmiyya, 1422/2001.

Burckhardt, Titus. *Mystical Astrology According to Ibn 'Arabi*. Trans. Bulent Rauf. Louisville, KY: Fons Vitae, 2001.

Būsnīna, Munjī, ed. *Mawsūʿat aʿlām al-ʿulamā' wa'l-udabā' al-ʿarab wa'l-muslimīn*. 8 vols. Beirut: Dār al-Jīl, 1425/2005.

Buss, David M. "Sex differences in human mate preferences: Evolutionary hypotheses tested in 37 cultures." *Behavioral and Brain Sciences* 12 (1989): 1–49.

Caine, Michael. *Elephant to Hollywood*. New York: Henry Holt, 2010.

Carroll, Scott T. "Wrestling in Ancient Nubia." *Journal of Sport History* 15, n. 2 (1988): 121–37.

Champault, Dominique. *Une Oasis du Sahara Nord-Occidental – Tabelbala*. Paris: Éditions du Centre National de la Recherche Scientifique, 1969.

Chapdelaine, Robin Phylisia. *The Persistence of Slavery*. Amherst: University of Massachusetts Press, 2021.

Chelebī, Evliyā'. *An Ottoman Traveler: Selections from the Book of Travels by Evliya Çelebi*. Trans. Robert Dankoff and Sooyong Kim. London: Eland, 2010.

Chelebī, Kātib. *The Balance of Truth*. Trans. G.L. Lewis. London: George Allen & Unwin, 1957.

Clarence-Smith, William Gervase and David Eltis. "White Servitude." In *The Cambridge World History of Slavery, Volume 3: AD 1420–1804*. Ed. David Eltis and Stanley Engerman, 132–59. Cambridge: Cambridge University Press, 2011.

Clark, Andrew F. "'The Ties that Bind': Servility and Dependency among the Fulbe of Bundu (Senegambia), c. 1930s – 1980s." *Slavery & Abolition* 19, n. 2 (1998): 91–108.

Clark, Kenneth B. and Mamie P. Clark. "Emotional Factors in Racial Identification and Preference in Negro Children." *Journal of Negro Education* 19, n. 3 (1950): 341–50.

Cleaveland, Timothy. "Ahmad Baba al-Timbukti and his Islamic critique of racial slavery in the Maghrib." *Journal of North African Studies* 20, n. 1 (2015): 42–64.

_____. *Becoming Walata: A History of Saharan Social Formation and Transformation*. Portsmouth, NH: Heinemann, 2002.

Cleveland, William L. *Islam against West: Shakib Arslan and the Campaign for Islamic Nationalism*. Austin: University of Texas Press, 1985.

Coard, Stephanie Irby; Breland, Alfiee M.; and Patricia Raskin. "Perceptions of and Preferences for Skin Color, Black Racial Identity, and Self-Esteem among African Americans." *Journal of Applied Social Psychology* 31, n. 11 (2001): 2256–74.

~~Coleman~~ [sic], Nathaniel Adam Tobias. "The Duty to Miscegenate." PhD dissertation, University of Michigan, 2013.

Colley, Linda. *Captives*. New York: Pantheon Books, 2002.

Condorcet, Nicolas de Caritat. "On Slavery. Rules for the Society of the Friends of Negroes (1788)." In *Condorcet: Political Writings*. Ed. Steven Lukes and Nadia Urbinati. Cambridge: Cambridge University Press, 2012.

_____. *Réflexions sur l'esclavage des nègres*. Neufchatel: la Société Typographique, 1781.

Conrad, David and Humphrey Fisher. "The Conquest that Never Was: Ghana and the Almoravids, 1076. I. The External Arabic Sources." *History in Africa* 9 (1982): 21–59.

Corlett, J. Angelo. *Race, Racism and Reparations*. Ithaca, NY: Cornell University Press, 2003.

van Dalen, Dorrit. *Doubt, Scholarship and Society in 17th-Century Central Sudanic Africa*. Leiden: Brill, 2016.

Damīrī, Kamāl al-Dīn Muḥammad b. Mūsā. *Al-Najm al-wahhāj fī sharḥ al-Minhāj*. 10 vols. Jeddah: Dār al-Minhāj, 1425/2004.

Daniel, Norman. *Islam and the West*. Edinburgh: Edinburgh University Press, 1960.

Daulatzai, Sohail. *Black Star, Crescent Moon*. Minneapolis: University of Minnesota Press, 2012.

Davis, David Brion. *Slavery and Human Progress*. Oxford: Oxford University Press, 1984.

Davis, Robert C. *Christian Slaves, Muslim Masters: White Slavery in the*

*Mediterranean, the Barbary Coast, and Italy, 1500–1800*. New York: Palgrave Macmillan, 2003.

Dāwūdī, Shams al-Dīn Muḥammad. *Tarjamat al-ʿallāma al-Suyūṭī*. Ms. Wetzstein I.20, Berlin Staatsbibliothek.

Dearden, Seton, ed. *Tully's Letters written during a Ten Years' Residence at the Court of Tripoli*. London: Darf, 2002, first published 1846.

Delgado, Richard and Jean Stefancic. "Critical Race Theory: An Annotated Bibliography." *Virginia Law Review* 79, n. 2 (1993): 461–516.

Dell, Jeremy. "Unbraiding the Qur'an: Wolofal and the *Tafsīr* Tradition of Senegambia." *Islamic Africa* 9 (2018): 55–76.

Desai, Ashwin. "Indian South Africans and the Black Consciousness Movement under apartheid." *Diaspora Studies* 8, n. 1 (2015): 37–50.

Deutsch, Nathaniel. "The 'Asiatic Black Man': An African American Orientalism?" *Journal of Asian American Studies* 4, n. 3 (2001): 193–208.

Dhahabī, Shams al-Dīn. *Siyar aʿlām al-nubalāʾ*. Ed. Shuʿayb al-Arnāʾūṭ et al. 3rd edn. 25 vols. Beirut: Muʾassasat al-Risāla, 1992–98.

_____. *Tadhkirat al-ḥuffāẓ*. Ed. Zakariyyā ʿUmayrāt. 4 vols. in 2. Beirut: Dār al-Kutub al-ʿIlmiyya, 1419/1998.

Diagne, Souleymane Bachir. *The Ink of the Scholars: Reflections on Philosophy in Africa*. Trans. Jonathan Adjemian. Dakar: Council for the Development of Social Science Research in Africa, 2016.

Dihlawī, ʿAbd al-Ghanī Mujaddadī. *Injāḥ al-ḥāja sharḥ Sunan Ibn Mājah*. Delhi: Maṭbaʿat Ḥusayn Muḥammad, 1273/1856–7.

Dihlawī, Shāh Walī Allāh. *Ḥujjat Allāh al-bāligha*. Ed. Saʿīd Aḥmad Palanpūrī. 2 vols. Deoband: Maktabat Ḥijāz, 2010.

Dijk, Wil O. *Seventeenth-century Burma and the Dutch East India Company, 1634–1680*. Singapore: NIAS Press, 2006.

Dilley, Roy. "Specialist Knowledge Practices of Craftsmen and Clerics in Senegal." *Africa: J. of the International African Institute* 79, n. 1 (2009): 53–70.

Dīnawarī, Aḥmad b. Dāwūd. *Al-Akhbār al-ṭiwāl*. Ed. ʿAbd al-Munʿim ʿĀmir and Jamāl al-Dīn al-Shayyāl. Beirut: Dār Iḥyāʾ al-Turāth al-ʿArabī, 1960.

Diop, Cheikh Anta. *Precolonial Black Africa*. Trans. Harold Salemson. Chicago: Lawrence Hill Books, 1987.

Diouf, Sylviane A. *Servants of Allah: African Muslims Enslaved in the Americas*. New York: New York University Press, 1998.

Donaldson, Coleman. "Clear Language: Script, Register and the N'ko Movement of Manding-Speaking West Africa." PhD dissertation, University of Pennsylvania, 2017.

Doniger, Wendy. *The Laws of Manu*. London: Penguin, 1991.

Du Bois, W.E.B. *Black Reconstruction in America*. New York: Harcourt, Brace & Co., 1935.

Dugast, Fabienne and Iwona Gajda. "Reconsidering contacts between southern Arabia and the highlands of Tigrai in the 1st millennium BC." Paper presented to the 18th International Conference of Ethiopian Studies, Dire Dawa, Ethiopia, 2012.

Dunn, Ross E. *The Adventures of Ibn Battuta*. Berkeley: University of California Press, 2012, originally published 1989.

Dutt, R.C. "Art. IV: The Social Life of the Hindus in the Rig-Veda Period." *Calcutta Review* 85 (1887): 49–97.

Duyvendak, J.J.L. *China's Discovery of Africa*. London: Authur Probsthain, 1949.

Edelstein, Dan. *On the Spirit of Rights*. Chicago: University of Chicago Press, 2019.

Egilsson, Ólafur. *The Travels of Reverend Ólafur Egilsson*. Ed. and trans. Karl Smári Hreinsson and Adam Nichols. Washington DC: Catholic University Press, 2008.

Eknoyan, Garabed. "A History of Obesity, or How What Was Good Became Ugly and Then Bad." *Advances in Chronic Kidney Disease* 13, n. 4 (2006): 421–27.

El-Nagar, Omar Abdel Raziq. "West Africa and the Muslim Pilgrimage: An Historical Study with Special Reference to the Nineteenth Century." PhD dissertation, SOAS, 1969.

Essien-Udom, E.U. *Black Nationalism: A Search for an Identity in America*. Chicago: University of Chicago Press, 1962.

Fanselow, Frank S. "The Disinvention of Caste among Tamil Muslims." In *Caste Today*. Ed. C.J. Fuller, 202–26. Oxford: Oxford University Press, 1996.

Fāzāzī, Abū Zayd ʿAbd al-Raḥmān et al. *Dīwān al-Wasāʾil al-mutaqabbila fī madḥ al-Nabī (s)*. Cairo: al-Maṭbaʿa al-Maymaniyya, 1322/1904.

Federspiel, Howard. *Sultans, Shamans and Saints: Islam and Muslims in Southeast Asia*. Honolulu: University of Hawaii Press, 2007.

Fernyhough, Timothy. "Women, Gender History, and Slavery in Nineteenth-Century Ethiopia." In *Women and Slavery*. Ed. Gwyn Campbell, Suzanne Miers and Joseph C. Miller, 1:216–17. Athens, OH: Ohio University Press, 2007.

Fischbach, Michael R. *Black Power and Palestine*. Palo Alto: Stanford University Press, 2019.

Fischer, Henry G. "Varia Aegyptiaca." *Journal of the American Research Center in Egypt* 2 (1963): 15–51.

Fletcher, Catherine. *The Black Prince of Florence*. New York: Oxford University Press, 2016.

Fodio, Usman dan. *Al-Ajwiba al-muḥarrara ʿan asʾila muqarrara*. In *Mukhtārāt al-Shaykh ʿUthmān bin Fūdī*. Gusau, Nigeria: Iqraʾ, 2013.

_____. *Ḍiyāʾ al-ḥukkām fīmā lahum wa ʿalayhim min al-aḥkām*. Ed. Sulaymān Mūsā Atthāʾī. In *Mukhtārāt al-Shaykh ʿUthmān bin Fūdī*. Gusau, Nigeria: Iqraʾ, 2013.

_____. *Ḍiyāʾ al-siyāsāt*. Ed. Muḥammad Mūdī Shūnī. In *Mukhtārāt al-Shaykh ʿUthmān bin Fūdī*. Gusau, Nigeria: Iqraʾ, 2013.

Francione, Gary and Robert Garner, eds. *The Animal Rights Debate: Abolition or Regulation*? New York: Columbia University Press, 2010.

Fredrickson, George M. *Racism: A Short History*. Princeton: Princeton University Press, 2015.

Frost, Peter. "Fair Women, Dark Men: The Forgotten Roots of Colour Prejudice." *History of European Ideas* 12, n. 5 (1990): 669–79.

Fry, Peter. "The politics of 'racial' classification in Brazil." *Journal de la Société des Américanistes* 95, n. 2 (2009): 261–82.

Fūdī, ʿUthmān bin, see Fodio, Usman dan.

Gallonnier, Juliette. "When 'White Devils' Join the Deen: White American Converts to Islam and the Experience of Non-Normative Whiteness." *Notes & Documents – CNRS* (2015): 1–44.

Gangūhī, ʿAbd al-Nabī. *Sunan al-hudā fī mutābaʿat al-muṣṭafā*. Ms. 132, National Library of India, Kolkata.

Garcia, J. L. A. "The Heart of Racism." *Journal of Social Philosophy* 27 (1996): 5–45.

García-García, Marcos et al. "The zooarchaeological identification of a 'Morisco' community after the Christian conquest of Granada (Spain, early 16th century): sociocultural continuities and economic innovations." *Archaeological and Anthropological Sciences* 13, n. 3 (2021).

Geiss, Imanuel. *Geschichte der Rassismus*. Berlin: Suhrkamp, 1988.

George, Michele. "Images of Black Slaves in the Roman Empire." *Syllecta Classica* 14 (2003): 161–85.

Ghanea Bassiri, Kambiz. *A History of Islam in America*. Cambridge: Cambridge University Press, 2010.

Gharnāṭī, Abū Ḥāmid. *Riḥlat al-Gharnāṭī: Tuḥfat al-albāb wa nukhbat al-ʿujāb*. Ed. Qāsim Wahb. Abu Dhabi: Dār al-Suwaydī, 2003.

Ghazālī, Abū Ḥāmid. *The Fatāwā of al-Ghazzālī*. Ed. Mustafa Mahmoud Abu Sway. Kuala Lumpur: International Institute of Islamic Thought, 1996.

_____. *Iḥyāʾ ʿulūm al-dīn*. Ed. Muḥammad Wahbī Sulaymān and Usāma ʿAmmūra. 5 vols. Damascus: Dār al-Fikr, 1426/2006.

_____. *Al-Wasīṭ*. Ed. Aḥmad Maḥmūd Ibrāhīm and Muḥammad Muḥammad Tāmir. 7 vols. Cairo: Dār al-Salām, 1417/1997.

Ghirlanda, Stefano; Jansson, Liselotte; and Magnus Enquist. "Chickens Prefer Beautiful Humans." *Human Nature* 13, n. 3 (2002): 383–89.

Gilli-Elewy, Hend. "On the Provenance of Slaves in Mecca during the Time of the Prophet Muhammad." *International Journal of Middle East Studies* 49, n. 1 (2017): 164–68.

Gilmore, Ruth Wilson. *Golden Gulag: Prisons, Surplus, Crisis, and Opposition in Globalizing California*. Berkeley: University of California Press, 2007.

Goldberg, David T. "The Social Formation of Racist Discourse." In *Anatomy of Racism*. Ed. David Theo Goldberg, 295–318. Minneapolis: University of Minnesota Press, 1990.

Goldenberg, David. *Black and Slave: The Origins and History of the Curse of Ham*. Berlin: De Gruyter, 2017.

_____. *The Curse of Ham*. Princeton: Princeton University Press, 2009.

Gomez, Michael. *African Dominion: A New History of Empire in Early and Medieval West Africa*. Princeton: Princeton University Press, 2018.
Goyémidé, Étienne. *Le dernier survivant de la caravane*. Paris: Hatier, 1985.
Gruber, Christiane. *The Praiseworthy One*. Bloomington, IN: Indiana University Press, 2019.
Gubara, Dahlia. "Revisiting Race and Slavery through ʿAbd al-Rahman al-Jabarti's *ʿAja'ib al-athar*." *Comparative Studies of South Asia, Africa and the Middle East* 38, n. 2 (2018): 230–45.
Guo, Li. "Tales of a Medieval Cairene Harem: Domestic Life in al-Biqāʿī's Autobiographical Chronicle." *Mamluk Studies Review* 9, n. 1 (2005): 101–21.
Gupta, Charu. *Sexuality, Obscenity, Community: Women, Muslims, and the Hindu Public in Colonial India*. New York: Palgrave, 2002.
Ḥaddādī, Abū Bakr b. ʿAlī. *Al-Jawhara al-nayyira ʿalā Mukhtaṣar al-Qudūrī*. Cairo: al-Maṭbaʿa al-Khayriyya, 1322/1904.
Hagedorn, Jan Hinrich. "Domestic Slavery in Syria and Egypt, 1200–1500." PhD dissertation, University of St. Andrews, 2019.
Hall, Bruce. "Bellah Histories of Decolonization, Iklan Paths to Freedom: The Meanings of Race and Slavery in the Late-Colonial Niger Bend (Mali), 1944–1960." *International Journal of African Historical Studies* 44, n. 1 (2011): 61–87.
_____. *A History of Race in Muslim West Africa, 1600–1960*. Cambridge: Cambridge University Press, 2011.
Hall, Kim F. *Things of Darkness: Economies of Race and Gender in Early Modern England*. Ithaca, NY: Cornell University Press, 1995.
Hallaq, Wael B. *Sharīʿa*. Cambridge: Cambridge University Press, 2009.
El Hamel, Chouki. *Black Morocco*. Cambridge: Cambridge University Press, 2013.
Ḥanafī, Aḥmad al-Qināʾī. *Kitāb Jawāhir al-ḥisān fī tārīkh al-ḥubshān*. Bulaq: al-Maṭbaʿa al-Amīriyya, 1321/1903.
Hanna, Nelly. *In Praise of Books: A Cultural History of Cairo's Middle Class, Sixteenth to the Eighteenth Century*. Syracuse: Syracuse University Press, 2003.
Hannaford, Ivan. *Race: The History of an Idea in the West*. Baltimore: Johns Hopkins University Press, 1996.
Hararī, Muḥammad Amīn. *Al-Kawkab al-wahhāj wa'l-rawḍ al-bahhāj fī sharḥ Ṣaḥīḥ Muslim b. al-Ḥajjāj*. Ed. Hāshim ʿAlī Muḥammad Mahdī. 26 vols. Jedda: Dār al-Minhāj, 1430/2009.
_____. *Murshid dhawī al-ḥijā wa'l-ḥāja ilā Sunan Ibn Mājah*. Ed. Hāshim Muḥammad Mahdī. 26 vols. Jedda: Dār al-Minhāj, 1439/2018.
Hardimon, Michael O. *Rethinking Race*. Cambridge, MA: Harvard University Press, 2017.
Hardy, Paul A. "Medieval Muslim Philosophers on Race." In *Philosophers on Race*. Ed. Julie K. Ward and Tommy L. Lott, 38–62. Oxford: Blackwell, 2002.
Harris, Leonard, ed. *Racism*. Amherst: Humanity Books, 1999.

Harris, Sam and Maajid Nawaz. *Islam and the Future of Tolerance*. Cambridge, MA: Harvard University Press, 2015.

Hartman, Saidiya. *Scenes of Subjugation: Terror, Slavery, and Self-Making in Nineteenth-Century America*. New York: Oxford University Press, 1997.

Haytamī, Ibn Ḥajar. *Ashraf al-wasā'il ilā fahm al-Shamā'il*. Ed. Aḥmad Farīd al-Mazīdī. Beirut: Dār al-Kutub al-ʿIlmiyya, 1419/1998.

_____ and ʿAbd al-Ḥamīd al-Shirwānī. *Ḥawāshī Tuḥfat al-muḥtāj bi-sharḥ al-Minhāj*. 10 vols. Cairo: Maṭbaʿat Muṣṭafā Muḥammad, 1357/1938.

_____. *Mablagh al-arab fī fakhr al-ʿarab*. Ed. Yusrī ʿAbd al-Ghanī ʿAbdallāh. Beirut: Dār al-Kutub al-ʿIlmiyya, 1410/1990.

_____. *Al-Ṣawāʿiq al-muḥriqa fī al-radd ʿalā ahl al-bidaʿ wa'l-zandaqa*. Ed. ʿĀdil Shūsha et al. Mansoura: Maṭbaʿat Fayāḍ, 1429/2008.

_____. *Al-ʿUmda fī sharḥ al-Burda*. Ed. Bassām Muḥammad Bārūd. Abu Dhabi: Dār al-Faqīh, 2005.

Hedghammer, Thomas. *The Caravan: Abdallah Azzam and the Rise of Global Jihad*. Cambridge: Cambridge University Press, 2020.

Heikal, Mohamed. *Autumn of Fury*. New York: Random House, 1983.

Henige, David. "Measuring the Immeasurable: The Atlantic Slave Trade, West African Population and the Pyrrhonian Critic." *Journal of African History* 27 (1986): 295–313.

Hentati, Nejmeddine. "Rôle de la coutume dans la formation du droit malikite." *Der Islam* 93, n. 1 (2016): 65–84.

Hertz, Friedrich. *Race and Civilization*. Trans. A.S. Levetus and W. Entz. London: Kegan Paul, 1928.

Hickman, Christine B. "The Devil and the One Drop Rule: Racial Categories, African Americans, and the U.S. Census." *Michigan Law Review* 95, n. 5 (1997): 1161–1265.

Hochman, Adam. "Is 'Race' Modern? Disambiguating the Question." *Du Bois Review* 16, n. 2 (2019): 647–65.

Hodgson, William B. *Notes on Northern Africa, the Sahara and Soudan*. New York: Wiley & Putnam, 1844.

Hoetink, Hermannus. *The Two Variants in Caribbean Race Relations*. Trans. Eva M. Hooykaas. London: Oxford University Press, 1967.

Holes, Clive. *Dialect, Culture, & Society in Eastern Arabia Vol. 2: Ethnographic Texts*. Leiden: Brill, 2005.

Hopkins, J.F.P., trans. *Corpus of early Arabic sources for West African history*. Ed. Nehemiah Levtzion. Cambridge: Cambridge University Press, 1981.

Hopper, Matthew S. "The African Presence in Eastern Arabia." In *The Persian Gulf in Modern Times*. Ed. Lawrence Potter, 327–50. New York: Palgrave Macmillan, 2014.

Hoyland, Robert G. *Seeing Islam as Others Saw It*. Princeton: Darwin Press, 1997.

Hugo, Victor. *Victor Hugo, Actes et Paroles. Pendant l'exil, 1852–1870 (vol. 2)*. Paris: Michel Lévy Frères, 1875.

Hunting, Claudine. "The Philosophes and Black Slavery: 1748–1765." *Journal of the History of Ideas* 69, n. 3 (1978): 405–18.

Hunwick, John O. "Back to West African Zanj Again: A Document of Sale from Timbuktu." *Sudanic Africa* 7 (1996): 53–60.

_____., trans. *Sharīʿa in Songhay: The Replies of al-Maghīlī to the Questions of Askia al-Ḥajj Muḥammad.* London: Oxford University Press, 1985.

_____. *Timbuktu and the Songhay Empire: al-Saʿdī's* Ta'rīkh al-sūdān *down to 1613 and other Contemporary Documents.* Leiden: Brill, 1999.

_____ and Eve Troutt Powell. *The African Diaspora in the Mediterranean Lands of Islam.* Princeton: Markus Wiener, 2002.

Hurgronje, C. Snouck. *Mekka in the Latter Part of the Nineteenth Century.* Leiden: Brill, 2014.

Ḥuṣnī, Taqī al-Dīn al-Dimashqī. *Kifāyat al-akhyār.* Ed. ʿAbd al-Qādir al-Arnā'ūṭ. Damascus: Dār al-Basha'ir, 1422/2001.

Ibn ʿAbd al-Bāqī, Muḥammad. *Al-Ṭirāz al-manqūsh fī maḥāsin al-ḥubūsh.* Ed. ʿAbdallāh Muḥammad al-Ghazālī. Kuwait: Mu'assasat Fahd al-Marzūq al-Ṣaḥafiyya, 1995.

Ibn ʿAbd al-Barr, Yūsuf b. ʿAbdallāh. *Al-Istīʿāb fī maʿrifat al-aṣḥāb.* Ed. ʿAlī Muḥammad al-Bijāwī. 4 vols. Beirut: Dār al-Jīl, 1412/1992.

_____. *Al-Qaṣd wa'l-amam bi-taʿrīf uṣūl ansāb al-ʿarab wa'l-ʿajam.* Cairo: Maktabat al-Quds, 1350/1932.

Ibn ʿAbd al-Ḥakam, ʿAbd al-Raḥmān. *Futūḥ Miṣr wa'l-maghrib.* Ed. Charles Torrey. Cairo: al-Hay'a al-ʿĀmma li'l-Thaqāfa, 1999, reprint of Yale edition.

Ibn ʿAbd Rabbih, Aḥmad b. Muḥammad. *Al-ʿIqd al-farīd.* Ed. Mufīd Muḥammad Qumayḥa. 8 vols. Beirut: Dār al-Kutub al-ʿIlmiyya, 1404/1983.

Ibn Abī al-ʿIzz al-Ḥanafī. *Al-Tanbīh ʿalā mushkilāt al-Hidāya.* Ed. ʿAbd al-Ḥakīm Muḥammad Shākir and Anwar Ṣāliḥ Abū Zayd. 5 vols. Riyadh: Maktabat al-Rushd, 1424/2003.

Ibn Abī Shayba, Abū Bakr. *Muṣannaf.* Ed. Kamāl Yūsuf al-Ḥūt. 7 vols. Riyadh: Maktabat al-Rushd, 1409/1999.

Ibn Abī Zayd al-Qayrawānī. *Kitāb al-Nawādir wa'l-ziyādāt.* Ed. Muḥammad ʿAbd al-ʿAzīz al-Dabbāgh et al. 15 vols. Beirut: Dār al-Gharb al-Islāmī, 1999.

Ibn ʿĀbidīn, Muḥammad Amīn. "Nashr al-ʿarf fī banā' baʿḍ al-aḥkām ʿalā al-ʿurf." In *Majmūʿat Rasā'il Ibn ʿĀbidīn.* 2 vols. Damascus: [Muḥammad Ḥāshim al-Kutubī], 1907.

Ibn al-ʿAdhārī, Aḥmad b. Muḥammad. *Al-Bayān al-mughrib fī akhbār al-andalus wa'l-maghrib.* Ed. Bashshār ʿAwwād Maʿrūf. 4 vols. Beirut: Dār al-Gharb al-Islāmī, 1434/2013.

Ibn al-ʿArabī, Abū Bakr. *Aḥkām al-Qur'ān.* Ed. Muḥammad ʿAbd al-Qādir ʿAṭā. 4 vols. Beirut: Dār al-Kutub al-ʿIlmiyya, 1424/2003.

_____. *ʿĀriḍat al-aḥwadhī.* 13 vols. Beirut: Dār al-Kutub al-ʿIlmiyya, n.d.

Ibn ʿArabī, Muḥyī al-Dīn. *Al-Futūḥāt al-makkiyya.* Ed. Aḥmad Shams al-Dīn. 9 vols. Beirut: Dār al-Kutub al-ʿIlmiyya, 1420/1999.

Ibn ʿAsākir, Abū al-Qāsim ʿAlī. *Tārīkh madīnat Dimashq.* Ed. ʿUmar ʿAmrawī. 80 vols. Beirut: Dār al-Fikr, 1995–1997.

Ibn al-Barādha'ī, Abū al-Sa'īd Khalaf. *Kitāb al-Tahdhīb fī ikhtiṣār al-Mudawwana*. Ed. Muḥammad Amīn Wuld Muḥammad Sālim. Dubai: Dār al-Buḥūth li'l-Dirāsāt al-Islāmiyya, 1423/2002.

Ibn Baṭṭāl, 'Alī b. Khalaf. *Sharḥ Ṣaḥīḥ al-Bukhārī*. Ed. Abū Tamīm Yāsir Ibrāhīm. 10 vols. Riyadh: Maktabat al-Rushd, 1423/2003.

Ibn Baṭṭūṭa, Muḥammad b. 'Abdallāh. *Ibn Battuta in Black Africa*. Ed. and trans. Said Hamdun and Noël King. London: Rex Collings, 1975.

Ibn Buṭlān, al-Mukhtār b. al-Ḥasan. "Risāla jāmi'a li-funūn nāfi'a fī shirā al-raqīq wa taqlīb al-'abīd." In *Nawādir al-makhṭūṭāt*. Ed. 'Abd al-Salām Hārūn. 2 vols., 1:351–89. Cairo: Muṣṭafā al-Bābī al-Ḥalabī, n.d.

Ibn Ḍuwayyān, Ibrāhīm b. Muḥammad. *Manār al-sabīl fī sharḥ al-Dalīl*. Ed. Zuhayr al-Shāwīsh. 7th edn. 2 vols. Damascus: al-Maktab al-Islāmī, 1989.

Ibn Ḥajar al-'Asqalānī, Shihāb al-Dīn Aḥmad. *Fatḥ al-bārī sharḥ Ṣaḥīḥ al-Bukhārī*. Ed. Ayman Fu'ād 'Abd al-Bāqī and 'Abd al-'Azīz bin Bāz. 15 vols. Beirut: Dār al-Kutub al-'Ilmiyya, 1418/1997.

_____. *Al-Iṣāba fī tamyīz al-ṣaḥāba*. Ed. 'Ādil Aḥmad 'Abd al-Mawjūd and 'Alī Aḥmad Mu'awwaḍ. 8 vols. Beirut: Dār al-Kutub al-'Ilmiyya, 1415/1994.

_____. *Tahdhīb al-tahdhīb*. Ed. Muṣṭafā 'Abd al-Qādir 'Aṭā. 12 vols. Beirut: Dār al-Kutub al-'Ilmiyya, 1415/1994.

_____. *Talkhīṣ al-ḥabīr*. Ed. Ḥasan 'Abbās Quṭb. 4 vols. Cairo: Mu'assasat Qurṭuba, 1416/1995.

_____. *Tawālī al-ta'sīs li-ma'ālī Muḥammad b. al-Idrīs*. Ed. Abū al-Fidā' 'Abdallāh al-Qāḍī. Beirut: Dār al-Kutub al-'Ilmiyya, 1406/1986.

Ibn Faḍlān, Aḥmad. *Kitāb Risālat Ibn Faḍlān*. Abu Dhabi: Dār al-Suwaydī, 2003.

Ibn al-Faqīh, Aḥmad b. Muḥammad. *Kitāb al-Buldān*. Ed. Yūsuf al-Hādī. Beirut: 'Ālam al-Kutub, 1416/1996.

Ibn Ḥanbal, Aḥmad. *Kitāb al-Zuhd*. Ed. 'Abd al-Salām Shāhīn. Beirut: Dār al-Kutub al-'Ilmiyya, 1999/1420.

Ibn Ḥawqal, 'Alī. *Kitāb Ṣūrat al-arḍ*. 2 vols. Beirut: Dār Ṣādir, 1938.

Ibn Ḥibbān al-Bustī, Muḥammad. *Kitāb al-Majrūḥīn*. Ed. Muḥammad Ibrāhīm Zāyid. 3 vols. Aleppo: Dār al-Wa'ī, 1396/1976.

_____. *Al-Sīra al-nabawiyya wa akhbār al-khulafā'*. Ed. al-Sayyid 'Azīz Bik et als. 2 vols. Beirut: al-Kutub al-Thaqāfiyya, 1417/1997.

Ibn Hubayra, Yaḥyā b. Muḥammad. *Kitāb al-Ifṣāḥ 'an ma'ānī al-ṣiḥāḥ*. Ed. Fu'ād 'Abd al-Mun'im Aḥmad. 8 vols. Riyadh: Dār al-Waṭan, 1417/1997.

Ibn al-Humām, Kamāl al-Dīn Muḥammad b. 'Abd al-Wāḥid. *Fatḥ al-qadīr*. 10 vols. Beirut: Dār al-Fikr, n.d.

Ibn al-Jawzī, 'Abd al-Raḥmān b. 'Alī. *Kashf al-mushkil min ḥadīth al-ṣaḥīḥayn*. Ed. 'Alī Ḥusayn al-Bawwāb. 4 vols. Riyadh: Dār al-Waṭan, 1418/1997.

_____. *Kitāb al-Mawḍū'āt*. Ed. 'Abd al-Raḥmān Muḥammad 'Uthmān. 3 vols. Medina: al-Maktaba al-Salafiyya, 1386–88/1966–68.

_____. *Kitāb al-Tabṣira*. 2 vols. Beirut: Dār al-Kutub al-'Ilmiyya, 1406/1986.

_____. *Al-Muntaẓam fī tārīkh al-mulūk wa'l-umam*. Ed. Muḥammad 'Abd al-Qādir 'Aṭā and Muṣṭafā 'Abd al-Qādir 'Aṭā. 18 vols. Beirut: Dār al-Kutub al-'Ilmiyya, 1999.

_____. *Ṣifat al-ṣafwa*. Ed. Khālid Muṣṭafā al-Ṭarṭūsī. Beirut: Dār al-Kitāb al-ʿArabī. 1433/2012.

_____. *Tanwīr al-ghabash fī faḍl al-sūdān wa'l-ḥabash*. Ed. Marzūq ʿAlī Ibrāhīm. Riyadh: Dār al-Sharīf, 1419/1998.

Ibn al-Kalbī, Hishām. *Jamharat al-nasab*. Ed. Nājī Ḥasan. Beirut: ʿĀlam al-Kutub, 1407/1986.

Ibn Khaldūn, ʿAbd al-Raḥmān b. Muḥammad. *The Muqaddimah*. Trans. Franz Rosenthal. Ed. N.J. Dawood. Princeton: Princeton University Press, 1967.

Ibn Maryam, Muḥammad al-Malītī. *Al-Bustān fī dhikr al-ʿulamā' wa'l-awliyā' bi-Tilimsān*. Ed. ʿAbd al-Qādir al-Būbāya. Beirut: Dār al-Kutub al-ʿIlmiyya, 2014.

Ibn al-Mulaqqin, Sirāj al-Dīn ʿUmar. *Mukhtaṣar al-Mustadrak li'l-ḥāfiẓ al-Dhahabī*. Ed. Saʿd ʿAbdallāh Āl Ḥumayyid and ʿAbdallāh Ḥamad al-Luḥaydān. 8 vols. Riyadh: Dār al-ʿĀṣima, 1991.

Ibn al-Munayyir, Aḥmad b. Muḥammad. *Al-Mutawārī ʿalā abwāb al-Bukhārī*. Ed. Ṣalāḥ al-Dīn Maqbūl Aḥmad. Kuwait: Maktabat al-Muʿallā, 1407/1987.

Ibn al-Mundhir, Abū Bakr. *Kitāb al-Ishrāf*. Ed. Ṣaghīr Aḥmad al-Anṣārī Abū Ḥammād. Ras al-Khayma: Maktabat Makka al-Thaqāfiyya, 1425/2004.

Ibn Nāṣir al-Dīn, Muḥammad al-Dimashqī. *Jāmiʿ al-āthār fī al-siyar wa mawlid al-mukhtār*. Ed. Abū Yaʿqūb Nash'at Kamāl. 8 vols. Qatar: Awqāf; and Fayyoum: Dār al-Falāḥ, 1431/2010.

Ibn Nujaym, Zayn al-Dīn Ibrāhīm. *Al-Baḥr al-rā'iq sharḥ Kanz al-daqā'iq*. 2nd edn. 8 vols. Beirut: Dār al-Kitāb al-Islāmī, n.d.

Ibn Qayyim al-Jawziyya, Muḥammad b. Abī Bakr. *Iʿlām al-muwaqqiʿīn*. Ed. Muḥammad ʿIzz al-Dīn Khaṭṭāb. 5 vols. Beirut: Dār Iḥyā' al-Turāth al-ʿArabī, 2001

Ibn Qudāma, Muwaffaq al-Dīn. *Al-Mughnī*. Ed. ʿAbdallāh al-Turkī and ʿAbd al-Fattāḥ al-Ḥuluw. 12 vols. Cairo: Hujr, 1986.

Ibn Qutayba, ʿAbdallāh b. Muslim. *Al-Maʿārif*. Ed. Tharwat ʿUkāsha. 4th edn. Cairo: Dār al-Maʿārif, 1981.

_____. *Al-Shiʿr wa'l-shuʿarā'*. 2 vols. Cairo: Dār al-Ḥadīth, 1423/2002.

Ibn Rajab, Zayn al-Dīn ʿAbd al-Raḥmān. *Sharḥ ʿIlal al-Tirmidhī*. 2 vols. n.p.: Dār al-Mallāḥ, 1398/1978.

Ibn Saʿd, Muḥammad. *Al-Juz' al-mutammam li-ṭabaqāt Ibn Saʿd al-ṭabaqa al-rābiʿa min al-ṣaḥāba*. Ed. ʿAbd al-ʿAzīz ʿAbdallāh al-Sullūmī. Taif: Maktabat al-Ṣiddīq, 1416/1996.

_____. *Al-Ṭabaqāt al-kubrā*. Ed. Iḥsān ʿAbbās. 8 vols. Beirut: Dār Ṣādir, 1968.

Ibn Sallām al-Jumaḥī, Muḥammad. *Ṭabaqāt fuḥūl al-shuʿarā'*. Ed. Maḥmūd Shākir. [Cairo]: Dār al-Madanī, n.d.

Ibn Shahrāshūb, Muḥammad b. ʿAlī. *Manāqib āl Abī Ṭālib*. Beirut: Dār al-Aḍwā', 1412/1991.

Ibn Taymiyya, Taqī al-Dīn Aḥmad. *Majmūʿat al-fatāwā*. Ed. Sayyid Ḥusayn al-ʿAffānī and Khayrī Saʿīd. 35 vols. Cairo: al-Maktaba al-Tawfīqiyya, n.d.

_____. *Al-Ṣārim al-maslūl ʿalā shātim al-rasūl*. Ed. Muḥammad Muḥyī al-Dīn ʿAbd al-Ḥamīd. N.p.: al-Ḥaras al-Waṭanī al-Suʿūdī, 1403/1983.

Ibn ʿUthaymīn, Muḥammad Ṣāliḥ. *Al-Sharḥ al-mumtiʿ ʿalā Zād al-mustaqniʿ*. 15 vols. Riyadh: Dār Ibn al-Jawzī, 1427/2006.

Idris, Amir. "Historicizing Race, Ethnicity, and the Crisis of Citizenship in Sudan and South Sudan." *Middle East Journal* 73, n. 4 (2019): 591–606.

Idrīsī, Muḥammad b. Muḥammad. *Nuzhat al-mushtāq fī ikhtirāq al-āfāq*. 2 vols. Beirut: ʿĀlam al-Kutub, 1409/1989.

Ignatiev, Noel. *How the Irish Became White*. New York: Routledge, 1995.

Iqbāl, Muḥammad. *Ḍarb-i kalīm*. Lahore: n.p., [1934].

Isaac, Benjamin. *The Invention of Racism in Classical Antiquity*. Princeton: Princeton University Press, 2004.

Iṣbahānī, Abū Nuʿaym. *Ḥilyat al-awliyā'*. 10 vols. Beirut: Dār al-Fikr, and Cairo: Maktabat al-Khānjī, 1416/1996.

Iṣfahānī, al-Rāghib al-Ḥusayn. *Muʿjam mufradāt alfāẓ al-Qur'ān*. Ed. Ibrāhīm Shams al-Dīn. Beirut: Dār al-Kutub al-ʿIlmiyya, 1418/1997.

Iṣṭakhrī, Ibrāhīm b. Muḥammad. *Kitāb Masālik al-mamālik*. Beirut: Dār Ṣādir, [1990], reprint of 1927 Brill edition.

ʿIyāḍ, al-Qāḍī b. Mūsā. *Ikmāl al-muʿlim bi-fawā'id Muslim*. Ed. Yaḥyā Ismāʿīl. 9 vols. Cairo: Dār al-Wafā', 1419/1998.

_____. *Al-Shifā' bi-taʿrīf ḥuqūq al-muṣṭafā*. Ed. ʿAbduh ʿAlī Kūshak. Manama: Maktabat Niẓām Yaʿqūbī, 1436/2015.

_____. *Mashāriq al-anwār*. 2 vols. Cairo: Dār al-Turāth, 1978.

Jackson, Peter. *The Delhi Sultanate*. Cambridge: Cambridge University Press, 1999.

Jackson, Sherman. *Islam and the Blackamerican*. Oxford: Oxford University Press, 2005.

Jacobson, Matthew Frye. *Whiteness of a Different Color: European Immigrants and the Alchemy of Race*. Cambridge, MA: Harvard University Press, 1999.

Jāḥiẓ, ʿAmr b. Baḥr. *Al-Ḥayawān*. Ed. ʿAbd al-Salām Hārūn. Beirut: Dār al-Jīl, 1996.

_____. *Rasā'il al-Jāḥiẓ*. Ed. ʿAbd al-Salām Hārūn. 4 vols. Cairo: Maktabat al-Khānjī, 1384/1964.

James, Michael Rabinder. "The Political Ontology of Race." *Polity* 44, n. 1 (2012): 106–34.

Jārimī, Muḥammad al-Sanūsī [al-Ghānī al-Sūdānī?]. *Tanbīh ahl al-ṭughyān ʿalā ḥurriyyat al-sūdān*. Ahmed Baba Institute of Higher Learning and Islamic Research (IHERI-AB), Ms. 1575.

Al-Jaṣṣāṣ, Abū Bakr. *Sharḥ Mukhtaṣar al-Ṭaḥāwī*. Ed. Sā'id Bakdāsh et al. 8 vols. Beirut: Dār al-Bashā'ir al-Islāmiyya, 1431/2010.

Jazūlī, Abū Bakr. *Guide to Goodness: Dalā'il al-khayrāt*. Trans. Andrey Hassan Rosowsky. 2nd edn. Chicago: Qazi, 2006.

"Thomas Jefferson's Thoughts on the Negro – I." *Journal of Negro History* 3, n. 1 (1918): 55–89.

Jeffery, Arthur. "Ghevond's Text of the Correspondence between ʿUmar II and Leo III." *Harvard Theological Review* 37, n. 4 (1944): 269–332.

Johannet, René. *Le Principe des Nationalités*. Paris: Nouvelle Librarie Nationale, 1918.

Jok, Jok Madut. "Appendix: 'They Call Us Animals,' Testimonies of Abductees and Slaves in Sudan." In *Buying Freedom: The Ethics and Economics of Slave Redemption*. Ed. Kwame Anthony Appiah and Martin Bunzl, 259–67. Princeton: Princeton University Press, 2007.

_____. "Slavery and Slave Redemption in the Sudan." In *Buying Freedom: The Ethics and Economics of Slave Redemption*, 143–57.

Jones, B. C.; Little, A.C.; and D.I. Perrett. "Why are symmetrical faces attractive?" *Advances in Psychology Research* 19 (2003): 145–66.

Jordan, Phillip E. and Maria Hernandez-Reif. "Re-Examination of Young Children's Racial Attitudes and Skin Tone Preferences." *Journal of Black Psychology* 35, n. 3 (2009): 388–403.

Jordan, Winthrop D. *White over Black: American Attitudes toward the Negro, 1550–1812*. 2nd edn. Chapel Hill, NC: University of North Carolina Press, 2012.

Jung, Moon-Kie and João H. Costa Vargas, ed. *Antiblackness*. Durham: Duke University Press, 2021.

Juwaynī, Imām al-Ḥaramayn ʿAbd al-Malik. *Al-Burhān fī uṣūl al-fiqh*. Ed. Ṣalāḥ Muḥammad ʿUwayḍa. 2 vols. Beirut: Dār al-Kutub al-ʿIlmiyya, 1418/1997.

_____. *Nihāyat al-maṭlab fī dirāyat al-madhhab*. Ed. ʿAbd al-ʿAẓīm Maḥmūd al-Dīb. 20 vols. Jeddah: Dār al-Minhāj, 1428/2007.

Kane, Ousmane. *Beyond Timbuktu*. Cambridge, MA: Harvard University Press, 2016.

Karras, Ruth. *Slavery and Society in Medieval Scandinavia*. New Haven: Yale University Press, 1988.

Kāsānī, ʿAlāʾ al-Dīn. *Badāʾiʿ al-ṣanāʾiʿ*. 7 vols. Beirut: Dār al-Kutub al-ʿIlmiyya, 1406/1986.

Kattānī, Muḥammad b. Jaʿfar. *Al-Yumn wa'l-isʿād bi-mawlid khayr al-ʿibād*. Rabat: al-Maṭbaʿa al-Ahliyya, 1345/1926.

_____. *Salwat al-anfās wa muḥādathat al-akyās mimman uqbira min al-ʿulamāʾ wa'l-ṣulaḥāʾ bi-fās*. Ed. ʿAbdallāh al-Kāmil al-Kattānī et al. 3 vols. Casablanca: Dār al-Thaqāfa, 2004.

Kawtharī, Muḥammad Zāhid. *Maqālāt*. 2nd edn. Cairo: Dār al-Salām, 1428/2007.

Kay, Paul et al. *World Color Survey*. Stanford: CSLI Publications, 2009.

Key, Andre E. "Toward a Typology of Black Hebrew Religious Thought and Practice." *Journal of Africana Religions* 2, n. 1 (2014): 31–66.

Khān, Aḥmad Riḍā. *Jadd al-mumtār ʿalā Radd al-muḥtār*. 4 vols. Karachi: Maktabat al-Madīna, 1426/2006.

Khannous, Touria. "Race in pre-Islamic poetry: The work of Antara Ibn Shaddad." *African and Black Diaspora* 6, n. 1 (2016): 66–80.

Khaṭṭābī, Abū Sulaymān Ḥamd. *Aʿlām al-ḥadīth*. Ed. Muḥammad Saʿd Āl Suʿūd. 4 vols. Riyadh: Markaz al-Buḥūth al-ʿIlmiyya, 1409/1988.

_____. *Gharīb al-ḥadīth*. Ed. ʿAbd al-Karīm Ibrāhīm al-Gharbāwī. 3 vols. Damascus: Dār al-Fikr, 1402/1982.

_____. *Ma'ālim al-sunan*. 2nd edn. 4 vols. Beirut: al-Maktaba al-'Ilmiyya, 1981.

Khawaja, Mohammad Harith Aslam. "Are Racial Preferences in Dating Morally Defensible?" *Episteme* 30, n. 2 (2019): 35–46.

Khuḍarī, Muḥammad. *Nūr al-yaqīn fī sīrat sayyid al-mursalīn*. Manama: Maktabat Niẓām al-Ya'qūbī, 1434/2013.

Kidd, Thomas S. "'Is It Worse to Follow Mahomet than the Devil?' Early American Uses of Islam." *Church History* 72, n. 4 (2003): 766–90.

Kirmānī, Shams al-Dīn Muḥammad b. Yūsuf. *Al-Bukhārī bi-sharḥ al-Kirmānī*. 2nd edn. 25 vols. Beirut: Dār Iḥyā' al-Turāth al-'Arabī, 1401/1981.

Kisā'ī, Muḥammad b. 'Abdallāh. *Tales of the Prophets*. Trans. Wheeler M. Thackston. Chicago: Kazi, 1997.

Knappert, Jan. *Swahili Islamic Poetry: Volume II The Two Burdas*. Leiden: Brill, 1971.

Knight, Michael Muhammad. *Metaphysical Africa: Truth and Blackness in the Ansaru Allah Community*. University Park, PA: Penn State University Press, 2020.

Kopytoff, Igor and Suzanne Miers. "African 'Slavery' as an Institution of Marginality." In *Slavery in Africa*. Ed. Miers and Kopytoff, 8–84. Madison: University of Wisconsin Press, 1977.

Kundnani, Arun. *The Muslims are Coming! Islamophobia, Extremism, and the Domestic War on Terror*. New York: Verso, 2015.

Kuykendall, Ronald. "Hegel and Africa: An Evaluation of the Treatment of Africa in The Philosophy of History." *Journal of Black Studies* 23, n. 4 (1993): 571–81.

Lakhmī, 'Alī b. Muḥammad. *Al-Tabṣira*. Ed. Aḥmad 'Abd al-Karīm Najīb. 14 vols. Doha: Wizārat al-Awqāf, n.d.

Laknawī, 'Abd al-Ḥayy. *'Umdat al-ri'āya 'alā sharḥ al-Wiqāya*. Ed. Ṣalāḥ Muḥammad Abū al-Ḥājj. 7 vols. Beirut: Dār al-Kutub al-'Ilmiyya, 2009.

Lange, Christian. "'On That Day When Faces Will Be White or Black' (Q3:106): Towards a Semiology of the Face in the Arabo-Islamic Tradition." *Journal of the American Oriental Society* 127, n. 4 (2007): 429–45.

Lape, Peter. "Focus on Islam IV: Archaeological approaches to the study of Islam in Island Southeast Asia." *Antiquity* 79, n. 306 (2005): 829–36.

Larkin, Margaret. *Al-Mutanabbi: Voice of the 'Abbasid Poetic Ideal*. Oxford: Oneworld, 2008.

Lean, Nathan. *The Islamophobia Industry*. 2nd edn. London: Pluto Press, 2017.

Lenski, Noel. "Captivity and Slavery among the Saracens in Late Antiquity (Ca. 250–630 CE)." *AnTard* 19 (2011): 237–66.

Leroy, Justin. "Black History in Occupied Territory: On the Entanglements of Slavery and Settler Colonialism." *Theory & Event* 19, n. 4 (2016): n.a.

Lewis, Bernard. "The Crows of the Arabs." *Critical Inquiry* 12, n. 1 (1985): 88–97.

_____. *Race and Slavery in the Middle East*. Oxford: Oxford University Press, 1990.

Lumbley, Coral. "The 'dark Welsh': Color, race, and alterity in the matter of medieval Wales." *Literature Compass* 16, n. 9–10 (2019): 1–19.

Lydon, Ghislaine. *On Trans-Saharan Trails: Islamic Law, Trade Networks, and Cross-Cultural Exchange in Nineteenth-Century Western Africa*. Cambridge: Cambridge University Press, 2009.

MacLaury, Robert E.; Paramel, Galina V.; and Don Dedrick, eds. *Anthropology of Color*. Philadelphia: John Benjamins, 2007.

MacMichael, H.A. *The Tribes of Northern and Central Kordofán*. Cambridge: Cambridge University Press, 1912.

Majlisī, Muḥammad b. Muḥammad Sālim. *Minaḥ al-ʿalī fī sharḥ kitāb al-Akhḍarī*. Ed. Abbāhu Muḥammad ʿAlī al-Majlisī al-Shinqīṭī and Muḥammad Maḥfūẓ Aḥmad. [Nouakchott]: Taṣwīr al-ʿĀṣimiyya, 1426/2005.

Maoqing, Chen. "Incest, Zoophilia, and Lust for Power in Tang Xianzu and Shakespeare." *Partial Answers* 14, n. 2 (2016): 217–36.

Maqdisī, Muḥammad b. Ṭāhir. *Tadhkirat al-mawḍūʿāt*. Ed. Muḥammad Muṣṭafā al-Ḥadarī al-Ḥabṭī. Mecca: al-Maktabat al-Salafiyya, 1401/1981.

Marcus, Steven. *The Other Victorians: A Study of Sexuality and Pornography in Mid-Nineteenth-Century England*. New York: Norton, 1974.

Marghīnānī, Burhān al-Dīn ʿAlī. *Al-Hidāya*. 4 vols. Lahore: Maktaba Raḥmāniyya, n.d.

Maribel, Manning and Hisham Aidi, eds. *Black Routes to Islam*. New York: Palgrave Macmillan, 2009.

Martin, Esmond Bradley. *Zanzibar: Tradition and Revolution*. North Pomfret, VT: Hamish Hamilton, 1978.

_____ and T.C.I. Ryan. "A Quantitative Assessment of the Arab Slave Trade of East Africa, 1770–1896." *Kenya Historical Review* 5, n. 1 (1977): 71–91.

Massing, Jean Michel. "From Greek Proverb to Soap Advert: Washing the Ethiopian." *Journal of the Warburg and Courtauld Institutes* 58 (1995): 180–201.

Masʿūdī, ʿAlī b. al-Ḥusayn. *Akhbār al-zamān*. Beirut: Dār al-Andalus, 1416/1996.

_____. *Kitāb al-Tanbīh wa'l-ashrāf*. Ed. ʿAbdallāh Ismāʿīl al-Ṣāwī. Cairo: Dār al-Ṣāwī, 1357/1938.

_____. *Murūj al-dhahab*. Ed. Kamāl Ḥasan Marʿī. 4 vols. Beirut: al-Maktaba al-ʿAṣriyya, 2005.

Matar, Nabil. *British Captives from the Mediterranean to the Atlantic, 1563–1760*. Leiden: Brill, 2014.

_____. *Turks, Moors, and Englishmen in the Age of Discovery*. New York: Columbia University Press, 1999.

Mathee, Mohamed Shahed. "Muftis and the Women of Timbuktu: History through Timbuktu's Fatwas, 1907–1960." PhD dissertation, University of Cape Town, 2011.

Mathews, Nathaniel. "Arab-Islamic slavery: a problematic term for a complex reality." *Research Africa Reviews* 4, n. 2 (2020): 6–11.

Matory, J. Lorand. *The Fetish Revisited*. Durham, N.C.: Duke University Press, 2018.

Mauny, Raymond. *Les siècles obscurs de l'Afrique noire*. Paris: Fayard, 1971.

Māwardī, Abū al-Ḥasan. *Al-Nukat wa'l-ʿuyūn/Tafsīr al-Māwardī*. Ed. Al-Sayyid ʿAbd al-Maqṣūd ʿAbd al-Raḥīm. 6 vols. Beirut: Dār al-Kutub al-ʿIlmiyya, n.d.

Maydānī, Aḥmad b. Muḥammad. *Majmaʿ al-amthāl*. Ed. Muḥammad Muḥyī al-Dīn ʿAbd al-Ḥamīd. 2 vols. Cairo: Maṭbaʿat al-Sunna al-Muḥammadiyya, 1374/1955.
Mayer, Adrien C. *Caste and Kinship in Central India*. Berkeley: University of California Press, 1966.
Mazrui, Ali. "The Black Arabs in Comparative Perspective: The Political Sociology of Race Mixture." In *The Southern Sudan*. Ed. Dunston Wai, 47–81. London: Frank Cass, 1973.
_____. "Black Orientalism? Further Reflections on 'Wonders of the African World'." *The Black Scholar* 30, n. 1 (2000): 15–18.
_____. "The Re-invention of Africa: Edward Said, V.Y. Mudimbe, and Beyond." *Research in African Literatures* 36, n. 3 (2005): 68–82.
Mbabuike, Michael C. "Wonders Shall Never Cease: Decoding Henry Louis Gates's Ambiguous Adventure." *Journal of Black Studies* 31, n. 2 (2000): 232–46.
McAlister, Melani. *The Kingdom of God Has No Borders: A Global History of American Evangelicals*. Oxford: Oxford University Press, 2018.
McCants, William. *The ISIS Apocalypse*. New York: St. Martin's Press, 2015.
McCarthy, Jesse. "On Afropessism." *LA Review of Books*, 20 July 2020, https://web.archive.org/web/20210802012436/https://lareviewofbooks.org/article/on-afropessimism
McGrath, Elizabeth. "The Black Andromeda." *Journal of the Warburg and Courtauld Institutes* 55 (1992): 1–18.
Meer, Nasar and Tariq Modood. "The Racialisation of Muslims." In *Thinking Through Islamophobia*. Ed. Salman Sayyid and AbdoolKarim Vakil, 69–84. New York: Columbia University Press, 2010.
Meier, Brian P.; Robinson, Michael D.; and Gerald L. Clore. "Why Good Guys Wear White: Automatic Inferences About Stimulus Valence Based on Brightness." *Psychological Science* 15, n. 2 (2004): 82 87.
Meshal, Reem. "Antagonistic *Sharīʿa*s and the Construction of Orthodoxy in Sixteenth-Century Cairo." *Journal of Islamic Studies* 21, no. 2 (2010): 183–212.
Metcalf, Barbara. *Islamic Revival in British India*. Princeton: Princeton University Press, 1982.
_____. *Perfecting Women: Mawlana Ashraf ʿAli Thanawi's* Bihishti Zewar. Berkeley: University of California Press, 1990.
Miers, Suzanne. "Britain and the Suppression of Slavery in Ethiopia." *Slavery and Abolition* 18, n. 3 (1997): 257–88.
Miles, Robert and Malcolm Brown. *Racism*. 2nd edn. New York: Routledge, 2003.
Miller, Michael T. "Black Judaism(s) and the Hebrew Israelites." *Religion Compass* 13, n. 11 (2019): 1–10.
Mills, Charles W. "'Heart' Attack: A Critique of Jorge Garcia's Volitional Conception of Racism." *Journal of Ethics* 7, n. 3 (2003): 29–62.
_____. *The Racial Contract*. Ithaca, NY: Cornell University Press, 1997.

Mīr Ghulām ʿAlī Āzād, Ḥassān al-Hind. *Maʾāthir al-kirām*. Ed. ʿAbdallāh Khān. 2 vols. Hyderabad: Maṭbaʿa Mufīd ʿĀlim Āgra, 1910.

Mirdāsī, ʿAbd al-Laṭīf b. al-Musabbiḥ. *ʿUmdat al-bayān*. Ed. Aḥmad Farīd al-Mazīdī. Beirut: Dār al-Kutub al-ʿIlmiyya, 2010.

Mishra, Neha. "India and Colorism: The Finer Nuances." *Washington University Global Studies Law Review* 14, n. 4 (2015): 725–50.

Miskawayh, Aḥmad b. Muḥammad. *Tahdhīb al-akhlāq*. Ed. ʿImād al-Hilālī. Beirut: Manshūrāt al-Jamal, 2011.

Montesquieu, Charles-Lois de Secondat. *l'Esprit des lois*. Ed. Laurent Versini. 2 vols. Paris: Gallimard, 1995.

Mottahedeh, Roy P. "The Shuʿûbîyah Controversy and the Social History of Early Islamic Iran." *International Journal of Middle East Studies* 7 (1976): 161–82.

Motzki, Harald. "The Role of Non-Arab Converts in the Development of Early Islamic Law." *Islamic Law and Society* 6, n. 3 (1999): 293–317.

Mubarak, Ahmad and Dawud Walid. *Centering Black Narrative: Black Muslim Nobles among the Early Pious Muslims*. USA: Itrah Press, 2016.

Mubarrad, Muḥammad b. Yazīd. *Al-Kāmil*. Ed. Muḥammad Abū al-Faḍl Ibrāhīm. 4 vols. Cairo: Dār al-Fikr al-ʿArabī, 1417/1997.

Munāwī, ʿAbd al-Raʾūf. *Fayḍ al-qadīr sharḥ al-Jāmiʿ al-ṣaghīr*. Ed. Ḥamdī al-Damardāsh Muḥammad. 13 vols. Mecca: Maktabat Nizār Muṣṭafā al-Bāz, 1998.

Mundhirī, ʿAbd al-ʿAẓīm. *Al-Takmila li-wafayāt al-naqala*. Ed. Bashshār ʿAwwād Maʿrūf. 4 vols. Beirut: Muʾassasat al-Risāla, 1405/1984.

Muqātil b. Sulaymān. *Tafsīr Muqātil b. Sulaymān*. Ed. ʿAbdallāh Maḥmūd Shaḥḥāta. 5 vols. Beirut: Dār Iḥyāʾ al-Turāth al-ʿArabī, 1423/2002.

Mutanabbī, Aḥmad. *Sharḥ al-Wāḥidī li-dīwān al-Mutanabbī*. Ed. Yāsīn Ayyūbī and Quṣayy al-Ḥusayn. Beirut: Dār al-Rāʾid al-ʿArabī, 1419/1999.

Muṭīʿī, Muḥammad Bakhīt. *Majmūʿat rasāʾil al-ʿallāma Muḥammad Bakhīt al-Muṭīʿī*. 2nd edn. Cairo: Maktabat al-Qāhira, 1932.

Nabhānī, Yūsuf. *Saʿādat al-dārayn fī al-ṣalāt ʿalā sayyid al-kawnayn*. Ed. ʿAbd al-Wārith Muḥammad ʿAlī. Beirut: Dār al-Kutub al-ʿIlmiyya, 1417/1997.

Nadwī, Abū al-Ḥasan. *Plain Speaking to Muslims*. Indore: Board of Islamic Studies, 1987.

Nadwī, Muḥammad Zayd Maẓāhirī, ed. *Dictums of al-Muḥaddith Shaykh Yūnus Jaunpūrī Collection 1*. Trans. Muhammad Talha. Leicester, UK: Qurtuba Books, 1440/2019.

Nadwī, Sayyid Sulaymān. *Khuṭubāt-i Madrās*. Karachi: Majlis-i Nashriyyāt-i Islām, n.d.

Nagar, Itisha. "The Unfair Selection: A Study on Skin-Color Bias in Arranged Indian Marriages." *Sage Open* 8, n. 2 (2018): 1–8.

Nawawī, Muḥyī al-Dīn Yaḥyā. *Rawḍat al-ṭālibīn*. Ed. Zuhayr al-Shāwīsh. 12 vols. Beirut: al-Maktab al-Islāmī, 1412/1991.

_____. *Sharḥ Ṣaḥīḥ Muslim*. 15 vols. Beirut: Dār al-Qalam, 1987.

_____. *Tahdhīb al-asmā' wa'l-lughāt*. Ed. ʿAbduh ʿAlī Kūshak. 4 vols. Manama: Maktabat Niẓām Yaʿqūbī, 1434/2013.

Naylor, Paul. *From Rebels to Rulers: Writing Legitimacy in the Early Sokoto State*. Suffolk, UK: James Currey, 2021.

Naysābūrī, al-Ḥākim Muḥammad. *Al-Mustadrak*. Hyderabad: Dā'irat al-Maʿārif al-ʿUthmāniyya, n.d.

Neill, Michael. "'Mulattos,' 'Blacks,' and 'Indian Moors': *Othello* in Early Modern Constructions of Human Difference." *Shakespeare Quarterly* 49, n. 4 (1998): 361–74.

Niasse, Ibrāhīm. *Al-Dawāwīn al-sitt*. Dakar: Muḥammad Ma'mūn Niasse, 1988.

_____. *Fī riyāḍ al-tafsīr*. Ed. Muḥammad b. al-Shaykh ʿAbdallāh al-Tijānī et al. 2nd edn. Cairo: al-Sharika al-Dawliyya li'l-Ṭibāʿa, 1433/2011.

_____. *The Removal of Confusion*. Trans. Zachary Wright et al. Louisville, KY: Fons Vitae, 2010.

Nobili, Mauro. *Sultan, Caliph, and the Renewer of the Faith*. Cambridge: Cambridge University Press, 2020.

Van Norden, Linda. *The Black Feet of the Peacock: The Color Concept of 'Black' from the Greeks through the Renaissance*. Lanham, MD: University Press of America, 1985.

Norris, H.T. *Ṣūfī Mystics of the Niger Desert*. Oxford: Clarendon Press, 1990.

Nubāhī, Abū al-Ḥasan ʿAlī. *Tārīkh quḍāt al-andalus*. Ed. Maryam Qāsim Ṭawīl. Beirut: Dār al-Kutub al-ʿIlmiyya, 1415/1995.

Nunn, Nathan. "The Long-Term Effects of Africa's Slave Trades." *Quarterly Journal of Economics* 123, n. 1 (2008): 139–76.

Ochonu, Moses E. "Slavery, Theology and Anti-Blackness in the Arab World." *Research Africa Reviews* 5, n. 1 (2021): 10–19.

Ogunnaike, Oludamini. *Poetry in Praise of Prophetic Perfection*. Cambridge: Islamic Text Society, 2020.

Okoth, Kevin Ochieng. "The Flatness of Blackness: Afro-Pessimism and the Erasure of Anti-Colonial Thought." *Salvage*, 16 January 2020, https://web.archive.org/web/20210803133012/https://salvage.zone/issue-seven/the-flatness-of-blackness-afro-pessimism-and-the-erasure-of-anti-colonial-thought

Olaloku-Teriba, Annie. "Afro-Pessimism and the (Un)logic of Anti-Blackness." *Historical Materialism*, 26, n. 2 (2018): 96–122, https://web.archive.org/web/20210804135211/https://www.historicalmaterialism.org/articles/afro-pessimism-and-unlogic-anti-blackness

_____. "Political blackness and Palestinian solidarity." *Red Pepper*, 22 September 2020, https://web.archive.org/web/20210804143102/https://www.redpepper.org.uk/political-blackness-and-palestinian-solidarity

Olsavsky, Jesse. "The Abolitionist Tradition in the Making of W.E.B. Du Bois's Marxism and Anti-Imperialism." *Socialism and Democracy* 32, n. 3 (2018): 14–35.

Olsson, J.T. "The world in Arab eyes: a reassessment of the climes in medieval Islamic scholarship." *Bulletin of the School of Oriental and African Studies* 77, n. 3 (2014): 487–508.

Park, Mungo. *Travels in the Interior of Africa*. Edinburgh: Adam and Charles Black, 1858.

Patterson, Orlando. *Slavery and Social Death*. Cambridge, MA: Harvard University Press, 1982.

Peled, Ilan. "Gender and Sex Crimes in the Ancient Near East: Law and Custom." In *Structures of Power: Law and Gender across the Ancient Near East and Beyond*. Ed. Ilan Peled, 27–40. Chicago: Oriental Institute of the University of Chicago, 2018.

Pelliot, Paul. *Notes on Marco Polo I*. Paris: Imprimerie Nationale, 1959.

Pelteret, David. *Slavery in Early Mediaeval England*. Suffolk: Boydell Press, 1995.

Postman, Neil. *Amusing Ourselves to Death*. New York: Penguin, 1985.

Prasad Sahai, Nandita. "The 'Other' Culture: Craft Societies and Widow Remarriage in Early Modern India." *Journal of Women's History* 19, n. 2 (2007): 36–58.

Prasanna, L.C. et al. "Facial Indices of North and South Indian Adults: Reliability in Stature Estimation and Sexual Dimorphism." *Journal of Clinical and Diagnostic Research* 7, n. 8 (2013): 1540–42.

de la Puente, Cristina. "The Ethnic Origins of Female Slaves in al-Andalus." In *Concubines and Courtesans*. Ed. Matthew S. Gordon and Kathryn A. Hain, 124–36. New York: Oxford University Press, 2017.

Qāḍīkhān, al-Ḥasan b. Manṣūr. *Fatāwā Qāḍīkhān*. Ed. Sālim Muṣṭafā al-Badrī. 3 vols. Beirut: Dār al-Kutub al-ʿIlmiyya, 1988.

Qādirī, Muḥammad b. al-Ṭayyib. *Nashr al-mathānī li-ahl al-qarn al-ḥādī ʿashar wa'l-thānī*. Ed. Muḥammad Ḥajjī and Aḥmad al-Tawfīq. 4 vols. Rabat: Dār al-Maghrib, 1397/1977.

Qāri', Mullā ʿAlī. *Asrār al-marfūʿa fī al-akhbār al-mawḍūʿa*. Ed. Muḥammad Luṭfī Ṣabbāgh. Beirut: al-Maktab al-Islāmī, 1986.

_____. *Majmūʿ rasā'il al-ʿallāmā al-Mullā ʿAlī al-Qārī'*. Ed. Māhir Adīb Ḥabbūsh et al. 8 vols. Istanbul: Dār al-Lubāb, 2016.

_____. *Sharḥ al-Shifā'*, printed on the margins of al-Khifājī, Aḥmad Shihāb al-Dīn. *Nasīm al-riyāḍ fī sharḥ Shifā' al-Qāḍī ʿIyāḍ*. 4 vols. Beirut: Dār al-Kitāb al-ʿArabī, reprint of Cairo: al-Maṭbaʿa al-Azhariyya, 1909.

_____ and ʿAbd al-Ra'ūf al-Munāwī. *Kitāb al-Wasā'il fī sharḥ al-Shamā'il*. 2 vols. Cairo: Muṣṭafā al-Bābī al-Ḥalabī, 1318/1901.

Qasṭallānī, Shihāb al-Dīn. *Al-Mawāhib al-ladunniyya*. 3 vols. Cairo: al-Maktaba al-Tawfīqiyya, n.d.

Quadri, Junaid. *Transformations of Tradition*. Oxford: Oxford University Press, 2021.

Qudūrī, Aḥmad b. Muḥammad. *Mukhtaṣar*. Trans. Ṭāhir Maḥmood Kiānī. London: Ta-Ha Publishers, 2010.

Qurṭubī, Abū al-Walīd Hishām b. ʿAbdallāh. *Al-Mufīd li'l-ḥukkām fīmā yuʿraḍu lahum min nawāzil al-aḥkām*. Ed. Aḥmad ʿAbd al-Karīm Najīb. Dublin: Markaz Najībawayh, 1433/2012.

Qurṭubī, ʿArīb b. Saʿd. *Ṣilat Tārīkh al-Ṭabarī*. Ed. M.J. De Goeje. Leiden: Brill, 1897.

Qurṭubī, Muḥammad b. Aḥmad. *Al-Jāmiʿ li-aḥkām al-Qur'ān*. Ed. Muḥammad Ibrāhīm al-Ḥifnāwī and Maḥmūd Ḥamīd ʿUthmān. 20 vols. in 10. Cairo: Dār al-Ḥadīth, 1994.

Raffaelli, Ida et al. ed. *Lexicalization Patterns in Color Naming: A Cross-Linguistic Perspective*. Amsterdam: John Benjamins, 2019.

Rāfiʿī, ʿAbd al-Karīm. *Al-Tadwīn fī akhbār Qazvīn*. Ed. ʿAzīz Allāh al-ʿUṭāridī. 4 vols. Beirut: Dār al-Kutub al-ʿIlmiyya, 1987.

Raḥmānī, Khālid Sayf Allāh. *Jadīd fiqhī masā'il*. Karachi: Zamzam Publishers, 2010.

Rai, Santosh Kumar. "Social histories of exclusion and moments of resistance: The case of Muslim Julaha weavers in colonial United Provinces." *Indian Economic and Social History Review* 55, n. 4 (2018): 549–74.

Raser, Timothy. "Victor Hugo's Politics and Aesthetics of Race in *Bug-Jargal*." *The Romantic Review* 89, n. 3 (1998): 307–19.

Rāzī, Fakhr al-Dīn. *Al-Firāsa*. Ed. Muṣṭafā ʿĀshūr. Cairo: Dār al-Qur'ān, n.d.

_____. *Mafātīḥ al-ghayb*. 32 vols. Beirut: Dār Iḥyā' al-Turāth al-ʿArabī, 1420/2000.

_____. *Manāqib al-imām al-Shāfiʿī*. Ed. Aḥmad Ḥijāzī al-Saqqā. Cairo: Maktabat al-Kulliyyāt al-Azhariyya, 1406/1986.

Rāzī, Ibn Abī Ḥātim. *Ādāb al-Shāfiʿī wa manāqibuhu*. Ed. ʿAbd al-Ghanī ʿAbd al-Khāliq. Beirut: Dār al-Kutub al-ʿIlmiyya, 1424/2003.

Richardson, Kristina. "Blue and Green Eyes in the Islamicate Middle Ages." *Annales islamologiques* 48, n. 1 (2014): 13–29.

Roberts, Allen F. and Mary Nooter Roberts. *A Saint in the City: Sufi Arts of Urban Senegal*. Los Angeles: UCLA Fowler Museum of Cultural History, 2003.

Robinson, Cedric. *Black Marxism: The Making of the Black Radical Tradition*. 3rd edn. Chapel Hill, NC: University of North Carolina Press, 2020, original published 1983.

Robinson, David. *The Holy War of Umar Tall*. Oxford: Clarendon Press, 1985.

_____. *Paths of Accommodation*. Athens, OH: Ohio University Press, 2000.

Rodd, Francis. *People of the Veil*. Oosterhout, Netherlands: Anthropological Books, 1966.

Rosen, Lawrence. *The Anthropology of Justice: Law as Culture in Islamic Society*. Cambridge: Cambridge University Press, 1989.

Rosen, Marjorie. "The Man Who Would Be Caine." *Film Comment* 16, n. 4 (1980): 18–23.

Ross, W.D., ed. *The Works of Aristotle Vol. VI*. Oxford: Clarendon Press, 1913.

Roth, Martha T. *Law Collections from Mesopotamia and Asia Minor*. Ed. Piotr Michalowski. Atlanta: Scholars Press, 1995.

Rotter, Gernot. "Die Stellung des Negers in der islamisch-arabischen Gesellschaft bis zum XVI Jahrhundert." PhD dissertation, University of Bonn, 1967.

La Rue, George Michael. "African Slave Women in Egypt, ca. 1820 to the Plague of 1834–35." In *Women and Slavery*. Ed. Gwyn Campbell, Suzanne

Miers and Joseph C. Miller, 169–89. Athens, OH: Ohio University Press, 2007.

Ruf, Urs Peter. *Ending Slavery: Hierarchy, Dependency and Gender in Central Mauritania*. Bielefeld: Transcript Verlag, 1999.

Ruffle, Karen. *Gender, Sainthood, and Everyday Practice in South Asian Shi'ism*. Chapel Hill: University of North Carolina Press, 2011.

Rūmī, Jālāl al-Dīn. *Tales from the Masnavi*. Trans. A.J. Arberry. London: George Allen & Unwin, 1961.

Saad, Elias N. *Social History of Timbuktu*. Cambridge: Cambridge University Press, 1983.

Ṣabbāgh, ʿAbd al-Raḥmān. *Sharḥ ʿAbd al-Raḥmān al-Ṣabbāgh ʿalā Matn al-Waghlīsiyya*. [No ms. number], Bibliotheque de Manuscits Lmuḥub Ulahbib, Bijaïa.

Ṣabbān, Muḥammad b. ʿAlī. *Itḥāf ahl al-islām bi-mā yataʿallaqu bi'l-muṣṭafā wa ahl baytihi al-kirām*. Ms. 1444, Maktabat Jāmiʿat Riyāḍ.

Sabban, Rima. "Encountering Domestic Slavery: A Narrative from the Arabian Gulf." In *Slavery in the Islamic World*. Ed. Mary Ann Fay, 125–53. New York: Palgrave Macmillan, 2019.

Ṣābi', Hilāl b. al-Ḥasan. *Rusūm dār al-khilāfa*. Ed. Mikhā'īl ʿAwwād. Beirut: Dār al-Rā'id al-ʿArabī, n.d.

Sadler, Rodney S., Jr. "Can a Cushite Change His Skin? Cushites, 'Racial Othering,' and the Hebrew Bible." *Interpretation* 60, n. 4 (2006): 386–403.

Safi, Omid. "'The Real Intention Was My Beloved': The Moon in Persian Sufi Poetry." In *The Moon: a Voyage through Time*. Ed. Christiane Gruber. Toronto: Aga Khan Museum, 2019.

Sahai, Nandita Prasad. "The 'Other' Culture: Craft Societies and Widow Remarriage in Early Modern India." *Journal of Women's History* 19, n. 2 (2007): 36–58.

Saḥnūn b. Saʿīd. *Al-Mudawwana*. 16 vols. Riyadh: Wizārat al-Shu'ūn al-Islāmiyya, [1424/2004], reprint of the 1324/1906 Cairo Maṭbaʿat al-Saʿāda edition.

Ṣāʿid al-Andalusī. *Science in the Medieval World: Book of the Categories of Nations*. Trans. and ed. Semaʿan I. Salem and Alok Kumar. Austin: University of Texas Press, 1991.

Sakhāwī, Shams al-Dīn Muḥammad. *Al-Maqāṣid al-ḥasana*. Ed. Muḥammad ʿUthman al-Khisht. Beirut: Dār al-Kitāb al-ʿArabī, 2004

Salamon, Hagar. "Slavery among the 'Beta-Israel' in Ethiopia: Religious Dimensions of Inter-group Perceptions." *Slavery & Abolition* 15, n. 1 (1994): 72–88.

Samʿānī, ʿAbd al-Karīm. *Al-Ansāb*. Ed. ʿAbd al-Raḥmān b. Yaḥyā al-Muʿallimī. Hyderabad: Dā'irat al-Maʿārif al-ʿUthmāniyya, 1382/1962.

Samʿānī, Abū al-Muẓaffar Manṣūr b. Muḥammad. *Tafsīr*. Ed. Yāsīn Ibrāhīm and Ghunaym ʿAbbās. 6 vols. Riyadh: Dār al-Waṭan, 1418/1997.

Ṣanʿānī, ʿAbd al-Razzāq. *Muṣannaf*. Ed. Ḥabīb al-Raḥmān al-Aʿẓamī. 11 vols. Beirut: al-Maktab al-Islāmī, 1403/1983.

Ṣanʿānī, Muḥammad b. Ismāʿīl. *Irshād al-nuqqād ilā taysīr al-ijtihād.* Ed. Muḥammad Ṣubḥī Ḥasan Ḥallāq. Beirut: Mu'assasat al-Rayyān, 1413/1992.

_____. *Al-Masā'il al-muhimma fīmā taʿummu bihi al-balwā.* Ed. Muḥammad al-Aṣghar al-Muqaṭṭirī. Beirut: Dār Ibn Ḥazm, 2004.

Sanneh, Lamin. *The Jakhanke Muslim Clerics.* Lanham, MD: University Press of America, 1989.

Sarakhsī, Muḥammad b. Aḥmad. *Al-Mabsūṭ.* 30 vols. Beirut: Dār al-Maʿrifa, 1409/1989.

_____. *Sharḥ al-siyar al-kabīr.* 5 vols. Beirut: Dār al-Kutub al-ʿIlmiyya, 1417/1997.

Savage, Elizabeth. *A Gateway to Hell, a Gateway to Paradise: The North African Response to the Arab Conquest.* Princeton: Darwin Press, 1997.

Schafer, Edward H. *The Golden Peaches of Samarkand: A Study of T'ang Exotics.* N.p.: Pickle Partners, 2016.

Schenkel, Wolfgang. "Color terms in ancient Egyptian and Coptic." In *Anthropology of Color.* Ed. Robert E. MacLaury, Galina V. Paramel and Don Dedrick, 211–28. Philadelphia: John Benjamins, 2007.

Schiefenhövel, Wulf. "Biased Semantics for Right and Left in 50 Indo-European and non-Indo-European Languages." *Annals of the New York Academy of Sciences* 1288 (2013): 135–52.

Schine, Rachel. "Conceiving the Pre-Modern Black-Arab Hero." *Journal of Arabic Literature* 48, n. 3 (2017): 298–326.

Schwartzman, Luisa Farah. "Who are the Blacks? The Question of Racial Classification in Brazilian Affirmative Action Policies in Higher Education." *Cahiers de la Recherche sur l'Éducation et les Saviors* 7 (2008): 27–47.

Scott, James M. *Geography in Early Judaism and Christianity.* Cambridge: Cambridge University Press, 2002.

Seesemann, Rüdiger. "The *Shurafā'* and the 'Blacksmith': The Role of the Idaw ʿAlī of Mauritania in the Career of the Senegalese Shaykh Ibrāhīm Niasse (1900–1975)." In *The Transmission of Learning in Islamic Africa.* Ed. Scott S. Reese, 72–98. Leiden: Brill, 2004.

Seif, Huda. "The Accursed Minority: The Ethno-Cultural Persecution of Al-Akhdam in the Republic of Yemen: A Documentary & Advocacy Project." *Muslim World Journal of Human Rights* 2, n. 1 (2005): 1–39.

Serjeant, R.B. "South Arabia." In *Commoners, Climbers and Notables.* Ed. C.A.O. van Nieuwenhuijze, 226–47. Leiden: Brill, 1977.

Shaheen, Jack. "'*Ashanti*': The Arab as Black-Slaver." *Middle East Perspective* 12, n. 8 (1979): 4–5.

_____. *Reel Bad Arabs.* Rev. edn. Northampton, MA: Olive Branch Press, 2015.

Shakir, Zaid. *Scattered Pictures: Reflections of an American Muslim.* Hayward, CA: Zaytuna, 2005.

Sharkey, Heather J. "Arab Identity and Ideology in Sudan: The Politics of Language, Ethnicity, and Race." *African Affairs* 107, n. 426 (2008): 21–43.

Shawkānī, Muḥammad b. ʿAlī. *Al-Fawā'id al-majmūʿa fī al-aḥādīth al-mawḍūʿa.* Ed. ʿAbd al-Raḥmān al-Muʿallimī. Beirut: al-Maktab al-Islāmī, 1392/1972.

Sheriff, Abdul. *Slaves, Spices and Ivory in Zanzibar*. Athens, OH: Ohio University Press, 1987.

_____. "*Suria*: Concubines or Secondary Slave Wife." In *Sex, Power and Slavery*. Ed. Gwyn Campbell and Elizabeth Elbourne. Athens, GA: Ohio University Press, 2014.

Shillī, Muḥammad b. Abī Bakr Bāʿalawī. *Al-Mushriʿ al-rawī fī manāqib al-sāda al-kirām Āl Abī ʿAlawī*. 2 vols. Cairo: al-Maṭbaʿa al-ʿĀmira, 1319/1901–2.

Shinqīṭī, Aḥmad b. Aḥmad. *Mawāhib al-jalīl min adillat Khalīl*. Ed. ʿAbdallāh Ibrāhīm al-Anṣārī. Doha: Idārat Iḥyā' al-Turāth al-Islāmī, 1407/1986.

Shinqīṭī, Aḥmad Amīn. *Al-Wasīṭ fī tarājim udabā' Shinqīṭ*. Cairo: al-Sharika al-Dawliyya li'l-Ṭibāʿa, 1422/2002.

Shinqīṭī, Muḥammad Amīn. *Riḥlat al-ḥajj ilā bayt Allāh al-ḥarām*. Mecca: Dār al-ʿĀlam al-Fawā'id, 1426/2006.

Shinqīṭī, Muḥammad al-Khaḍir. *Kawthar al-maʿānī al-darārī fī kashf khabāyā Ṣaḥīḥ al-Bukhārī*. 14 vols. Beirut: Mu'assasat al-Risālā, 1415/1995.

Shīrāzī, Abū Isḥāq. *Al-Muhadhdhab fī fiqh al-imām al-Shāfiʿī*. Ed. Muḥammad al-Zuḥaylī. 6 vols. Beirut: al-Dār al-Shāmiyya and Damascus: Dār al-Qalam, Dār al-Kutub al-ʿIlmiyya, 1416/1997.

Sifry, Micah L. "Jesse and the Jews: Palestine and the Struggle for the Democratic Party." *Middle East Report* 155 (1988): 4–11.

Sikand, Yoginder. *Islam, Caste and Dalit-Muslim Relations in India*. New Delhi: Global Media Productions, 2004.

Simonsohn, Uriel. *A Common Justice: The Legal Allegiances of Christians and Jews under Early Islam*. Philadelphia: University of Pennsylvania Press, 2011.

Sinai, Nicolai. "When did the consonantal skeleton of the Quran reach closure? Part II." *Bulletin of the School of Oriental and African Studies* 77, n. 3 (2014): 509–21.

Sindī, Abū al-Ḥasan Muḥammad b. ʿAbd al-Hādī. *Ḥāshiyat al-Sindī ʿalā Sunan Ibn Mājah*. 2 vols. Beirut: Dār al-Jīl, n.d.

Singh, Sabita. *The Politics of Marriage in Medieval India: Gender and Alliance in Rajasthan*. New Delhi: Oxford University Press, 2019.

Snowden, Frank M., Jr. *Blacks in Antiquity: Ethiopians in the Greco-Roman Experience*. Cambridge, MA: Belknap Press, 1970.

Society for the Extinction of the Slave Trade and for the Civilization of Africa. *Abridgement of Sir T. Fowell Buxton's Work on the African Slave Trade and its Remedy*. London: John Murray, 1840.

Soyinka, Wole. *The Burden of Memory, the Muse of Forgiveness*. New York: Oxford University Press, 1999.

Srinivasan, Amia. "Does anyone have the right to sex?" *London Review of Books*, 40, n. 6 (22 March 2018).

_____. *The Right to Sex*. New York: Farrar, Straus and Giroux, 2021.

Starratt, Priscilla. "Tuareg Slavery and Slave Trade." *Slavery & Abolition* 2, n. 2 (1981): 83–113.

Stetkevych, Suzanne P. *The Poetics of Islamic Legitimacy*. Bloomington, IN: Indiana University Press, 2002.

Streib, Jessi. *The Power of the Past: Understanding Cross-Class Marriages.* Oxford: Oxford University Press, 2015.

Strickland, Debra Higgs. *Saracens, Demons, and Jews: Making Monsters in Medieval Art.* Princeton: Princeton University Press, 2003.

Strings, Sabrina. *Fearing the Black Body: The Racial Origins of Fat Phobia.* New York: New York University Press, 2019.

Stulp, Gert; Buunk, Abraham P.; and Thomas V. Pollet. "Women want taller men more than men want shorter women." *Personality and Individual Differences* 54 (2013): 877–83

Stuurdman, Siep. *The Invention of Humanity.* Cambridge, MA: Harvard University Press, 2017.

Subkī, Taqī al-Dīn. *Al-Sayf al-maslūl ʿalā man sabba al-Rasūl.* Ed. Iyyād Aḥmad al-Ghawj. Amman: Dār al-Fatḥ, 1421/2000.

Sulamī, Muḥammad b. al-Ḥusayn. *Ṭabaqāt al-ṣūfiyya.* Ed. Nūr al-Dīn Sudayba. 3rd edn. Cairo: Maktabat al-Khānjī, 1418/1997.

Sun, Vincent C. and Chien-Chung Chen. "Basic color categories and Mandarin Chinese color terms." *PLOS One* 13, n. 11 (2018).

Suyūṭī, Jalāl al-Dīn. *Al-Ashbāh wa'l-naẓā'ir.* Ed. Muḥammad al-Muʿtaṣim al-Baghdādī. Beirut: Dār al-Kitāb al-ʿArabī, 1414/1993.

_____. *Azhār al-ʿurūsh fī akhbār al-ḥubūsh.* Ed. ʿAbdallāh Muḥammad al-Ghazālī. Kuwait: Markaz al-Makhṭūṭāt wa'l-Turāth wa'l-Wathā'iq, 1416/1995.

_____. *Al-Durar al-muntathira fī al-aḥādīth al-mushtahira.* Ed. Maḥmūd al-Arnā'ūṭ and Muḥammad Badr al-Dīn Qahwajī. Kuwait: Maktabat Dār al-ʿUrūba, 1408/1988.

_____. *Al-Durr al-manthūr.* 6 vols. Cairo: Maṭbaʿat al-Anwār al-Muḥammadiyya, 1990.

_____. *Al-Ḥāwī li'l-fatāwī.* 2 vols. Beirut: Dār al-Kitāb al-ʿArabī, n.d.

____. *Al-Khaṣā'iṣ al-kubrā.* 2 vols. Beirut: Dār al-Kitāb al-ʿArabī, reprint of the 1320/1902 Hyderabad Dā'irat al-Maʿārif al-ʿUthmāniyya edition.

_____. *Al-La'ālī' al-maṣnūʿa fī al-aḥādīth al-mawḍūʿa.* Ed. Ṣāliḥ Muḥammad ʿUwayda. 3 vols. Beirut: Dār al-Kutub al-ʿIlmiyya, 1996.

______. *Nuzhat al-ʿumr fī al-tafḍīl bayn al-bīḍ wa'l-sūd wa'l-sumr.* Damascus: al-Maktaba al-ʿArabiyya, 1346/1927.

_____. *Rafʿ sha'n al-ḥubshān.* Ed. Muḥammad ʿAbd al-Wahhāb Faḍl. Cairo: self-published, 1411/1991.

_____. *Al-Tawshīḥ sharḥ al-Jāmiʿ al-ṣaḥīḥ.* Ed. Riḍwān Jāmiʿ Riḍwān. Riyadh: Maktabat al-Rushd, 1419/1998.

Al-Ṭabarānī, Abū al-Qāsim. *Al-Muʿjam al-awsaṭ.* Ed. Ṭāriq ʿAwaḍ Allāh and ʿAbd al-Muḥsin Ibrāhīm. 10 vols. Cairo: Dār al-Ḥaramayn, 1995.

_____. *Al-Muʿjam al-kabīr.* Ed. Ḥamdī ʿAbd al-Majīd al-Salafī. 25 vols. Beirut: Dār Iḥyā' al-Turāth al-ʿArabī, n.d.

Ṭabarī, Muḥammad b. Jarīr. *Jāmiʿ al-bayān li-āy al-Qur'ān/ Tafsīr al-Ṭabarī.* Ed. Aḥmad Shākir. 24 vols. Beirut: Mu'assasat al-Risāla, 1420/2000.

_____. *Tārīkh al-rusul wa'l-mulūk.* 6 vols. Beirut: Dār al-Kutub al-ʿIlmiyya, 2003/1424.

Ṭahṭāwī, Rifāʿat. *An Imam in Paris*. Trans. Daniel L. Newman. London: Saqi, 2004.

_____. *Kitāb Takhlīṣ al-ibrīz fī talkhīṣ bārīz*. Cairo: Dār al-Taqdima, 1323/1905.

Ṭarābulusī, ʿAlāʾ al-Dīn ʿAlī. *Muʿīn al-ḥukkām fīmā yataraddadu bayn al-khaṣmayn min al-aḥkām*. Cairo: al-Maṭbaʿa al-Maymaniyya, 1310/1892.

Tareen, SherAli. *Defending Muḥammad in Modernity*. Notre Dame, IN: Notre Dame University Press, 2020.

Taylor, John R. and Thandi G. Mbense. "Red dogs and rotten mealies: How Zulus talk about anger." In *Speaking of Emotions*. Ed. Angeliki Athanasiadou and Elzbieta Tabakowska, 191–226. Berlin: De Gruyter, 1998.

Tewolde, Amanuel Isak. "Encounters with Race: Eritrean Refugees and Asylum-Seekers' Self-identification Practices in Relation to the Experience of Racialisation in Post-Apartheid South Africa." PhD dissertation, University of Pretoria, 2018.

Thaʿālabī, Abū Zayd. *Tafsīr al-Thaʿālabī / al-Jawāhir al-ḥisān fī tafsīr al-Qurʾān*. Ed. Muḥammad ʿAlī Muʿawwaḍ and ʿĀdil Aḥmad ʿAbd al-Mawjūd. 5 vols. Beirut: Dār Iḥyāʾ al-Turāth al-ʿArabī, 1418/1998.

Thaʿlabī, Abū Isḥāq. *al-Kashf waʾl-bayān ʿan tafsīr al-Qurʾān*. Ed. Muḥammad Ibn ʿĀshūr and Naẓīr al-Sāʿidī. 10 vols. Beirut: Dār Iḥyāʾ al-Turāth al-ʿArabī, 1422/2002.

Thanawi, Ashraf ʿAlī. *Heavenly Ornaments*. Trans. Molana Muhammad Mahomedy. Karachi: Zam Zam, 2016.

Thavapalan, Shiyanthi. *The Meaning of Color in Ancient Mesopotamia*. Leiden: Brill, 2020.

_____. "Speaking of Colours." In *Mesopotamian Sculpture in Colour*. Ed. Astrid Nunn and Heinrich Piening, 194–99. Gladbeck: PeWe Verlag, 2020.

Thompson, Lloyd A. *Romans and Blacks*. Norman, OK: University of Oklahoma Press, 1989.

Ṭībī, al-Ḥusayn b. ʿAbdallāh. *Al-Kāshif ʿan ḥaqāʾiq al-sunan (sharḥ Mishkāt al-maṣābīḥ)*. Ed. ʿAbd al-Ḥamīd Hindāwī. 13 vols. Mecca: Maktabat Nizār Muṣṭafā al-Bāz, 1417/1997.

Tolmacheva, Marina. "Toward a Definition of the Term Zanj." *Azania* 26, n. 1 (1986): 105–13.

Toure, Saadou Oumar. *Ḥall al-masāʾil fī sharḥ Mukhtaṣar al-Akhḍarī biʾl-dalāʾil*. n.p: n.p, [1971].

Troughton, Thomas. *Barbarian Cruelty*. London: R. Walker, 1751.

Tsri, Kewsi. *Africans Are Not Black*. London: Routledge, 2016.

Ugochukwu, Françoise. "Goyemide on Slavery: The Liberating Power of The Word." *Nordic Journal of African Studies* 15, n. 1 (2006): 27–41.

ʿUkbarī, Abū al-Baqāʾ. *Sharḥ Dīwān al-Mutanabbī*. Ed. Muṣṭafā al-Saqqā, Ibrāhīm al-Abyārī and ʿAbd al-Ḥafīẓ Shalabī. 4 vols. Beirut: Dār al-Maʿrifa, n.d.

Ullmann, Manfred. *Der Neger in der Bildersprache der arabischen Dichter*. Wiesbaden: Harrossowitz Verlag, 1998.

ʿUmarī, Aḥmad Ibn Faḍlallāh. *Masālik al-abṣār fī mamālik al-amṣār*. Ed. Kāmil Salmān al-Jubūrī. Beirut: Dār al-Kutub al-ʿIlmiyya, 2010.
Ustinov, Peter. *Dear Me*. Boston: Little, Brown & Co., 1977.
ʿUthmānī, Muftī Taqī. *Takmilat Fatḥ al-mulhim*. 3 vols. Karachi: Maktabat Dār al-ʿUlūm Karātshī, 2004.
Vartija, Devin J. *The Color of Equality*. Philadelphia: University of Pennsylvania Press, 2021.
Vatuk, Sylvia. "Identity and Difference or Equality and Inequality in South Asian Muslim Society." In *Caste Today*. Ed. C.J. Fuller, 227–62. Oxford: Oxford University Press, 1996.
Vink, Markus. "'The World's Oldest Trade': Dutch Slavery and Slave Trade in the Indian Ocean in the Seventeenth Century." *Journal of World History* 14, n. 2 (2003): 131–77.
Wagatsuma, Hiroshi. "The Social Perception of Skin Color in Japan." In *Color and Race*. Ed. John Hope Franklin, 129–65. Boston: Houghton Mifflin, 1968.
Van Wagenen, Aimee. "The Promise and Impossibility of Representing Anti-Essentialism: Reading *Bulworth* through Critical Race Theory." *Race, Gender & Class* 14, n. 1–2 (2007): 157–77.
Waghlīsī, ʿAbd al-Raḥmān b. Aḥmad. *Al-Muqaddima al-Waghlīsiyya ʿalā madhhab al-sāda al-mālikiyya*. Ed. Amal Muḥammad Najīb. Dublin: al-Markaz al-Najībawayh, 1428/2007.
Walid, Dawud. *Blackness and Islam*. Wembley, UK: Algorithm, 2021.
Walters, Dolores M. "Perceptions of Social Inequality in the Yemen Arab Republic." PhD dissertation, New York University, 1987.
Wāqidī, Muḥammad b. ʿUmar. *Maghāzī*. Ed. Marsden Jones. Beirut: Dār al-Aʿlamī, 1409/1989.
Wazzānī, Abū ʿĪsā Sīdī al-Mahdī b. Muḥammad. *Al-Nawāzil al-jadīda al-kubrā fī-mā li-ahl Fās wa ghayrihim min al-badū wa'l-qurā*. Ed. ʿUmar ʿImād. 12 vols. Casablanca: Maṭbaʿat al Faḍāla, 1997.
_____. *Al-Nawāzil al-ṣughrā*. Ed. Muḥammad al-Sayyid ʿUthmān. 4 vols. Beirut: Dār al-Kutub al-ʿIlmiyya, 1435/2014.
Weiss, Gillian. *Captives and Corsairs: France and Slavery in the Early Modern Mediterranean*. Palo Alto: Stanford University Press, 2011.
Welchman, Jennifer. "Locke and Slavery and Inalienable Rights." *Canadian Journal of Philosophy* 25, n. 1 (1995): 67–81.
Westermann, William L. *The Slave Systems of Greek and Roman Antiquity*. Philadelphia: American Philosophical Society, 1955.
de Wet, Chris L. *The Unbound God: Slavery and the Formation of Early Christian Thought*. London: Routledge, 2018.
Wheatcroft, Andrew. *The Ottomans: Dissolving Images*. London: Penguin, 1995.
Wheatley, Paul. "Geographical Notes on some Commodities involved in Sung Maritime Trade." *Journal of the Malayan Branch, Royal Asiatic Society* 32, n. 2 (1959): 5–149.
Wheeler, J. Talboys. *Early Records of British India: A History of the English Settlements in India*. London: Trüber, 1848.

Whitaker, Cord J. "Black Metaphors in the *King of Tars*." *Journal of English and Germanic Philology* 112, n. 2 (2013): 169–93.

White, Stuart. "Freedom of Association and the Right to Exclude." *Journal of Political Philosophy* 5, n. 4 (1997): 373–91.

Whitford, David M. *The Curse of Ham in the Early Modern Era*. Burlington, VT: Ashgate, 2009.

Wilderson, Frank B. III. " 'We're Trying to Destroy the World': Anti-Blackness and Police Violence after Ferguson: An Interview with Frank B. Wilderson III." Ill Will Editions, Nov. 2014, https://illwilleditions.noblogs.org/files/2015/09/Wilderson-We-Are-Trying-to-Destroy-the-World-READ.pdf

Wilkerson, Isabel. *Caste*. New York: Random House, 2020.

Wilks, Ivor. *Wa and the Wala*. Cambridge: Cambridge University Press, 1989.

Williams, Chancellor. *The Destruction of Black Civilization*. Rev. edn. Chicago: Third World Press, 1974.

Wolf, Kenneth Baxter. "The 'Moors' of West Africa and the Beginnings of the Portuguese Slave Trade." *Journal of Medieval and Renaissance Studies* 24, n. 3 (1994): 449–69.

Wright, John. *The Trans-Saharan Slave Trade*. London: Routledge, 2007.

Wright, Zachary V. "The African Roots of a Global Eighteenth-Century Islamic Scholarly Renewal." In *Islamic Scholarship in Africa*. Ed. Ousmane Kane, 22–40. Suffolk, UK: James Currey, 2021.

_____. "The Islamic Intellectual Tradition of Sudanic Africa, with Analysis of a Fifteenth-Century Timbuktu Manuscript." *The Palgrave Handbook of Islam in Africa*. Ed. F. Ngom et al., 55–76. London: Palgrave, 2020.

_____. *Living Knowledge in West African Islam*. Leiden: Brill, 2015.

_____. *Realizing Islam: The Tijaniyya in North Africa and the Eighteenth-Century Muslim World*. Chapel Hill: University of North Carolina Press, 2020.

Wyatt, Don J. *The Blacks of Premodern China*. Philadelphia: University of Pennsylvania Press, 2019.

Yesufe, Endris Mohammed. "The *Ramsa* of *šayḫ* Aḥmad Ādam, *al-Danī al-Awwal* (d. 1903)." *Aethiopica* 19 (2016): 102–12.

Yin, Rong and Haosheng Ye. "The Black and White Metaphor Representation of Moral Concepts and Its Influence on Moral Cognition." *Acta Psychologica Sinica* 46, n. 9 (2014): 1331–46.

Zabīdī, Muḥammad Murtaḍā. *Itḥāf al-sāda al-muttaqīn sharḥ Iḥyāʾ ʿulūm al-dīn*. 10 vols. Beirut: Mu'assasat al-Tārīkh al-ʿArabī, 1994.

Zahan, Dominique. "White, Red, and Black: Colour Symbolism in Black Africa." In *The Realms of Colour*. Ed. Adolf Portmann and Rudolf Ritsema, 365–96. Leiden: Brill, 1974.

Zarkashī, Badr al-Dīn Muḥammad. *Al-La'ālī al-manthūra fī al-aḥādīth al-mashhūra*. Ed. Muḥammad Luṭfī al-Ṣabbāgh. Beirut: al-Maktab al-Islāmī, 1417/1996.

Zarrūq, Aḥmad. *Sharḥ al-ʿallāma Zarrūq ʿalā al-Muqaddima al-Waghlīsiyya*. Ed. Maḥfūẓ Bū Kirāʿ and ʿAmmār Basṭa. Beirut: Dār Ibn Ḥazm, 2010.

Zaylaʿī, Jamāl al-Dīn. *Naṣb al-rāya li-aḥādīth al-Hidāya.* Ed. Muḥammad ʿAwwāma. Jeddah: Mu'assasat al-Rayyān, 1997.

Zeltner, Jean-Claude. "Histoire des Arabes sur les rives du lac Tchad." *Annales de l'Université d'Abidjan* F, n. 2 (1970): 110–236.

Zurqānī, ʿAbd al-Bāqī. *Sharḥ al-Zurqānī ʿalā Mukhtaṣar Sīdī Khalīl.* Ed. ʿAbd al-Salām Muḥammad Amīn. 8 vols. Beirut: Dār al-Kutub al-ʿIlmiyya, 1422/2002.

# Notes

## 1. INTRODUCTION: READING AND MISREADING

1. *Wa lam yubāli Ibn ʿImrān bi-udmatihi, ḥattā iṣṭafāhu kalīman khayr maʿbūd*; Ibn al-Abbār, *Tuḥfat al-qādim*, ed. Iḥsān ʿAbbās (Beirut: Dār al-Gharb al-Islāmī, 1406/1986), 157. I am indebted to Andrea Brigaglia for alerting me to al-Kānimī, see Brigaglia, "Note di Viaggio dela Qaṣīda nel Sudan Centrale (Greater Lake Chad Basin)," forthcoming.
2. Shams al-Dīn al-Dhahabī, *Siyar aʿlām al-nubalāʾ*, ed. Shuʿayb al-Arnāʾūṭ et al., 25 vols. (Beirut: Muʾassasat al-Risāla, 1992–98), 5:363–4.
3. Abū Nuʿaym al-Iṣbahānī, *Ḥilyat al-awliyāʾ*, 10 vols. (Beirut: Dār al-Fikr, and Cairo: Maktabat al-Khānjī, 1996), 2:365, 10:173–4.
4. The Companion quoted is Abū ʿUbayda b. al-Jarrāḥ; Ibn Ḥanbal, *Kitāb al-Zuhd*, ed. ʿAbd al-Salām Shāhīn (Beirut: Dār al-Kutub al-ʿIlmiyya, 1999/1420), 151.
5. *Ṣaḥīḥ Muslim*: *kitāb al-birr waʾl-ṣila, bāb naṣr al-akh ẓāliman aw maẓlūman.*
6. Rudolph Ware, Zachary Wright and Amir Syed, *Jihad of the Pen* (Cairo: American University in Cairo Press, 2018), 140. See also Cheikh Anta Babou, *Fighting the Greater Jihad: Amadu Bamba and the Founding of the Muridiyya of Senegal* (Athens, OH: Ohio University Press, 2007), 61–2. The Senegalese Tijānī Sufi master Ibrāhīm Niasse references Bamba's line in his own expression of similar concerns; Zachary Wright, "Islam, Blackness, and African Cultural Distinction: The Islamic Negritude of Shaykh Ibrāhīm Niasse," *Journal of Africana Religions*, forthcoming.
7. Zachary Wright, *Living Knowledge in West African Islam* (Leiden: Brill, 2015), 98.
8. French officials, as well as one of Niasse's sons, reported mumblings among the Idaw ʿAlī that Niasse was black as well as from the blacksmith caste in West Africa, which was seen as the lowest rung on the social ladder. This caste objection was also trotted out by competitors among the followers of other Senegalese Sufi masters; Rüdiger Seesemann, "The *Shurafāʾ* and the 'Blacksmith': The Role of the Idaw ʿAlī of Mauritania in the Career of the Senegalese Shaykh Ibrāhīm Niasse (1900–1975)," in *The Transmission of Learning in Islamic Africa*, ed. Scott S. Reese, 72–98 (Leiden: Brill, 2004), 89–93, 95–96.
9. This was reported to me by Saad Bouh's great grandson, Saad Bouh Cheikh, November 2021. Saad Bouh and Ahmadu Bamba were both masters in the Qādirī Sufi order.
10. *Sunan* of Abū Dāwūd: *kitāb al-adab, bāb fī al-tafākhur biʾl-aḥsāb.*
11. See, for example, Layla Abdullah-Poulos, "Colorism Dehumanizes," YouTube.com, 11 November 2016, https://www.youtube.com/watch?v=92IaJLHki2c;

"When Islamic Scholarship is Anti Black," YouTube.com, 29 June 2019, https://www.youtube.com/watch?v=7LmZ2p0VF08&t=113s. Thanks to Habeeb Akande for drawing my attention to this.

12. For these books, see Bibliography; Zaid Shakir, *Scattered Pictures* (Hayward, CA: Zaytuna, 2005), 63–82; and Iskander Abbasi, "Anti-Blackness in the Muslim World: Beyond Apologetics and Orientalism," *Maydan*, 14 October 2020, https://web.archive.org/web/20220107210159/https://themaydan.com/2020/10/anti-blackness-in-the-muslim-world-beyond-apologetics-and-orientalism/; Rasul Miller, "Is Islam an Anti-Black Religion?" *Sapelo Square*, 25 April 2017, https://web.archive.org/web/20210917142135/https://sapelosquare.com/2017/04/25/is-islam-an-anti-black-religion/.
13. Kātib Chelebī, *Kashf al-ẓunūn*, ed. Muḥammad ʿAbd al-Qādir ʿAṭā, 7 vols. (Beirut: Dār al-Kutub al-ʿIlmiyya, 1429/2008), 2:256; Jalāl al-Dīn al-Suyūṭī, *Nuzhat al-ʿumr fī al-tafḍīl bayn al-bīḍ wa'l-sūd wa'l-sumr* (Damascus: al-Maktaba al-ʿArabiyya, 1346/1927), 2; Khayr al-Dīn al-Ziriklī, *Aʿlām*, 16th ed. (Beirut: Dār al-ʿIlm li'l-Malāyīn, 2005), 2:312; 6:211, 266. I had not come across the *Rawnaq al-ḥisān* of al-Zamzamī until Habeeb Akande drew my attention to it.
14. Muḥammad al-Sanūsī al-Jārimī al-Ghānī, *Tanbīh ahl al-ṭughyān ʿalā ḥurriyyat al-sūdān*, Ahmed Baba Institute of Higher Learning and Islamic Research (IHERI-AB), Ms. 1575, 9.
15. See Marina Tolmacheva, "Toward a Definition of the Term Zanj," *Azania* 26, n. 1 (1986): 105–113.
16. For example, in the 1400s a female slave brought to Cairo from present-day Libya is called *al-zanjiyya*; Li Guo, "Tales of a Medieval Cairene Harem: Domestic Life in al-Biqāʿī's Autobiographical Chronicle," *Mamluk Studies Review* 9, n. 1 (2005): 110. See also John O. Hunwick, "Back to West African Zanj Again: A Document of Sale from Timbuktu," *Sudanic Africa* 7 (1996): 53–60.
17. See Daniel Ayana, "Re-Mapping Africa: The Northern *Zanj, Damadim, Yamyam, Yam/Yamjam, Habasha/Ahabish, Zanj-Ahabish* and *Zanj ed-Damadam* – The Horn of Africa between the Ninth and Fifteenth Centuries," *History in Africa* 46 (2019): 57–104.
18. For useful references on this contested issue, see R. Bhopal, "Glossary of terms relating to ethnicity and race: for reflection and debate," *Journal of Epidemiology and Community Health* 58 (2004): 441–45; Merrill Perlman, "Black and white: why capitalization matters," *Columbia Journalism Review*, 23 June 2015, https://www.cjr.org/analysis/language_corner_1.php. The convention adopted by J. Lorand Matory, whereby Black is for self-identification and black is for third-party identification, is consistent and useful. It also admits up front the subjective view of authors in deciding what looks 'black'; J. Lorand Matory, *The Fetish Revisited* (Durham, N.C.: Duke University Press, 2018), x. Thanks to Nathaniel Mathews for alerting me to this source.
19. John Hunwick and Eve Troutt Powell, ed., *The African Diaspora in the Mediterranean Lands of Islam* (Princeton: Markus Wiener, 2002), xii.
20. Afifa Ltifi, "Black Tunisians and the Pitfalls of Bourguiba's Homogenization Project," *Project on Middle East Political Science* (POMEPS), https://web.archive.org/web/20220205041546/https://pomeps.org/black-tunisians-and-the-pitfalls-of-bourguibas-homogenization-project.
21. Chouki El Hamel, *Black Morocco* (Cambridge: Cambridge University Press, 2013), 246, 270–73.

22. See Aisha Yusuff, "Missing in Plain Sight: Who are the Afro-Arabs and Where are They in the World?" *Amaliah*, 22 September 2020, https://web.archive.org/web/20211117175303/https://www.amaliah.com/post/60270/afro-arab-history-afro-palestinians-afro-iraqis-anti-black-racism-in-the-world-amaliah-identity; Jaclynn Ashly, "Afro-Palestinians talk heritage and resistance," *Al-Jazeera*, 5 August 2017, https://web.archive.org/web/20220110173954/https://www.aljazeera.com/features/2017/8/5/afro-palestinians-talk-heritage-and-resistance; Fayida Jailler, "The History of Afro-Palestinians, Past and Present," *Travel Noire*, 26 May 2021, https://web.archive.org/web/20220110174235/https://travelnoire.com/history-afro-palestinians-past-and-present.
23. Iman Sultan, "What It Means to Be Black and South Asian," *Zora*, 19 October 2020, https://web.archive.org/web/20211118011312/https://zora.medium.com/what-it-means-to-be-black-and-south-asian-838d748bb05d.
24. How could one verify the claim of Minority Rights Group International that there may be as many as 1.5–2 million Black Iraqis? See https://web.archive.org/web/20220110184101/https://minorityrights.org/minorities/black-iraqis/; For a view of the complexities involved, see Paul Tiyambe Zeleza, *In Search of African Diasporas*, 540, cf. 452, 463, 498, 502–3, 505, 545.
25. See, for example, https://www.academia.edu/61622742/Western_Views_on_Muslim_Slavery.
26. Joseph Massad discusses the "Western internationalization of [homosexuality and] homophobia into areas of the world where neither homosexual identities nor homophobic identities existed"; Félix Boggio Éwanjé-Épée and Stella Magliani-Belkacem, "The Empire of Sexuality: An Interview with Joseph Massad," *Jadaliyya*, 5 March 2013, https://web.archive.org/web/20211124190928/https://www.jadaliyya.com/Details/28167.
27. Jonathon [sic] Glassman, "Sorting Out the Tribes: The Creation of Racial Identities in Colonial Zanzibar's Newspaper Wars," *Journal of African History* 41 (2000): 395–428.
28. Sunni M. Khalid, "The Root: Race and Racism Divide Egypt," NPR, 7 February 2011, https://www.npr.org/2011/02/07/133562448/the-root-egypts-race-problem.
29. See Su'ad Abdul-Khabeer, *Muslim Cool: Race, Religion and Hip Hop* (New York: New York University Press, 2016), 126–27; Shyla González-Doğan, " 'You're Black. You're from Africa. You can't be the Principal': Limited Leadership in Islamic Institutions," *Journal of Muslim Minority Affairs* 41, n. 4 (2021): 576–89. For Arabocentrism in American Islam, African Muslims and Black American Muslims, see Zain Abdullah, *Black Mecca* (Oxford: Oxford University Press, 2010), 74.
30. Edward Westermark and Shareef 'Abd-es-Salam El-Baqqali, *Wit and Wisdom in Morocco* (London: George Routledge & Sons, 1930), 131–32.
31. Peter Behnstedt and Manfred Woidich, *Wortatlas der arabischen Dialekte* (Leiden: Brill, 2010), 56–58 (thanks to Lameen Souag for pointing me to this source); Clive Holes, *Dialect, Culture, & Society in Eastern Arabia 2: Ethnographic Texts* (Leiden: Brill, 2005), 41, 170, 307; Catherine Taine-Cheikh, "La Mauritanie en noir et blanc. Petite promenade linguistique en Hassâniyya," *Revue du monde musulman et de la Méditerranée* 54 (1989): 97.
32. Palestinian: *ḥubb ḥabībak law kān ʿabd iswid/ḥabībak illī tiḥibb law kān ʿabd iswid*; Egyptian: *ḥabībak illī tiḥibbu wa law kān ʿabd nūbī*; Ismāʿīl al-Yūsuf, *al-Jāmiʿ fī al-amthāl al-ʿāmmiyya al-filasṭīniyya* (Amman: al-Ahliyya, 2003), 139–140; Aḥmad Taymūr Bāshā, *al-Amthāl al-ʿāmmiyya* (Cairo: Dār al-Shurūq, 2010), 224.

33. We see Persian phrases like "I was stricken with shame" (lit. "my face became blackened," *rūsiyāh shudam*); Sayf Ghiffārī, *Farhang-i iṣṭilāḥāt*, 7th edn. (Tehran: Nashr-i Paykān, 2002), 244. See also ʿAlī Akbar Dikhudā, *Amthāl ū ḥikam*, 4 vols. (Tehran: Chāpkhāni-yi Sipahr, 1992), 2:998–99.
34. In Palestinian: *ilhum yawm iswid mithl al-faḥm* and *al-dayn sawād al-khaddayn*; see al-Yūsuf, *al-Jāmiʿ*, 15, 46, 176, 182, 392. For Egyptian, see Taymūr Bāshā, 25, 34, 113, 137, 155, 265, 272, 575. There are exceptions, of course, such as the Egyptian usage of *aswad al-rās* to mean human being; ibid., 280
35. İdil Akıncı, "Language, Nation, Difference: Everyday Language Tactics of Young Emiratis," in *Gulf Cooperation Council Culture and Identities in the New Millennium*, ed. Magdalena Karolak and Nermin Allam (Singapore: Palgrave Macmillan, 2020), 213.
36. For Kuwait, I am relying on my own extensive anecdotal experience and also testimony of native speakers. For clear awareness of what *khāl* means and its relation to mother's family, see Rima Sabban, "Encountering Domestic Slavery: A Narrative from the Arabian Gulf," in *Slavery in the Islamic World*, ed. Mary Ann Fay (New York: Palgrave Macmillan, 2019), 143; Aḥmad Amīn al-Shinqīṭī, *al-Wasīṭ fī tarājim udabāʾ Shinqīṭ* (Cairo: al-Sharika al-Dawliyya li'l-Ṭibāʿa, 1422/2002), 484.
37. Jonathan Brown, *Slavery & Islam* (London: Oneworld, 2019), 78. This is the phenomenon that the late Ali Mazrui called "ascending miscegenation"; Ali Mazrui, "The Black Arabs in Comparative Perspective: The Political Sociology of Race Mixture," in *The Southern Sudan*, ed. Dunstan Wai (London: Frank Cass, 1973), 54–55.
38. Another word, *khawal*, from the same root appears as 'servant' in famous Hadiths, but this is not likely the root since this was already the plural form of the word.
39. Matthew S. Hopper, "The African Presence in Eastern Arabia," in *The Persian Gulf in Modern Times*, ed. Lawrence Potter (New York: Palgrave Macmillan, 2014), 329, 343. This collapse was brought about by the advents of Japanese cultured pearls and American date production.
40. Rifʿat al-Ṭahṭāwī, *Kitāb Takhlīṣ al-ibrīz fī talkhīṣ bārīz* (Cairo: Dār al-Taqdima, 1323/1905), 7. For similar expressions from the late nineteenth and early twentieth centuries, see ʿAlī Bāshā Mubārak, *ʿAlam al-dīn*, 4 vols. (Alexandria: Maṭbaʿat al-Jazīra, 1882), 2:713–14; Ḥusayn al-Jisr, *al-Risāla al-ḥamīdiyya*, ed. Muḥammad al-Muʿtaṣim bi'llāh al-Baghdādī (Tripoli, Lebanon: Dār al-Īmān, 1998), 427–28.
41. William Cleveland, *Islam against West: Shakib Arslan and the Campaign for Islamic Nationalism* (Austin: University of Texas Press, 1985), 59.
42. Leon Carl Brown, "Color in Northern Africa," in *Color and Race*, ed. John Hope Franklin, 186–204 (Boston: Houghton Mifflin, 1968), 198.
43. Dolores M. Walters, *Perceptions of Social Inequality in the Yemen Arab Republic* (PhD dissertation, New York University, 1987), 115; Urs Peter Ruf, *Ending Slavery: Hierarchy, Dependency and Gender in Central Mauritania* (Bielefeld: Transcript Verlag, 1999), 39; Fredrik Barth, *Sohar: Culture and Society in an Omani Town* (Baltimore: Johns Hopkins University Press, 1983), 98, 228.
44. See, for example, Jan H. Hagedorn, *Domestic Slavery in Syria and Egypt, 1200–1500* (PhD dissertation, University of St. Andrews, 2019), 130.
45. Bruce Hall, *A History of Race in Muslim West Africa, 1600–1960* (Cambridge: Cambridge University Press, 2011), 288, 290, 299–301, 307.
46. For the proposed etymology of *ḥarāṭīn*, see Ruf, *Ending Slavery*, 39.
47. The sultan, Mawlāy Ismāʿīl, eventually collected about 81 signatures from scholars supporting his proposal, either because of threats or because they were toadies of the ruler; El Hamel, *Black Morocco*, 103, 160, 163–74.

48. The Global Slavery Index, which measures forced labor and forced marriage, estimates that there are 90,000 living in "modern slavery" in Mauritania, or 2.4 percent of the population; https://www.hrw.org/world-report/2020/country-chapters/mauritania#.
49. Ruf, *Ending Slavery*, 40, 126.
50. Ruf, 39, 255; *Mauritania's Campaign of Terror* (Human Rights Watch, 1994), 93.
51. Walters, *Perceptions of Social Inequality in the Yemen Arab Republic*, 24, 222, 229; Huda Seif, "The Accursed Minority: The Ethno-Cultural Persecution of Al-Akhdam in the Republic of Yemen: A Documentary & Advocacy Project," *Muslim World Journal of Human Rights* 2, n. 1 (2005): 1, 13. Walters' dissertation is dated, her fieldwork having been carried out in Yemen in the early 1980s, but it is the most in-depth and comprehensive treatment of the Akhdam, and there is little to suggest that her observations and conclusions are not still relevant.
52. Travelers record the term Akhdam being used as far back as 1873; Walters, 18, 59, 91, 103, 115, 185; Seif, 15. Depending on regions, in Yemen other professions are also considered lowly (*nāqiṣ*), including barbers/circumcizers (*muzayyin*), cuppers (*ḥajjām*), butchers, and café proprietors; Walters, 29, 112, 117–18; R.B. Serjeant, "South Arabia," in *Commoners, Climbers and Notables*, ed. C.A.O. van Nieuwenhuijze, 226–47 (Leiden: Brill, 1977), 233. Interestingly, at various points in early-modern Yemeni history, Yemeni Jews were ordered to clear latrines (waste was used as fuel and fertilizer). Leading ulama rejected this as unacceptable, since it altered the established *dhimmī* agreements. See Joseph Sadan, "The 'Latrines Decree' in the Yemen Versus the Dhimma Principles," in *Pluralism and Identity: Studies in Ritual Behavior*, ed. Jan Platvoet and Karel van der Toorn, 167–85 (Leiden: Brill, 1995), 179; and Jane Hathaway "The Mawzaʿ Exile at the Juncture of Zaydi and Ottoman Messianism," *AJS Review* 29, No. 1 (2005): 111–28.
53. *ighsil baʿd al-kalb wa iksir baʿd al-khādim; lā taghurrak ḥusn al-akhdām, al-najāsa fī al-ʿaẓām*; Walters, 205–6; Seif, 4.
54. Walters, 103, 185, 203.
55. Walters, 58, 20, 25, 121; Ruf, *Ending Slavery*, 39.
56. Walters, 60, 110, 111–12.
57. Walters, 65, 113.
58. Walters, 44, 121.
59. Ruf, *Ending Slavery*, 40, 281–82.
60. See Human Rights Watch, *Mauritania's Campaign of Terror*, 13–14, 18, 62, 72.
61. Human Rights Watch, *Mauritania's Campaign of Terror*, 95.
62. Ruf, *Ending Slavery*, 43, 157, 280. Thanks to Khaled Esseissah for discussing this with me. The instance of human-rights activism in Mauritania that caused the most controversy in the Arabic media both inside and outside the country did not involve the Haratin or Black Africans but rather a shocking 2014 article by Muḥammad Wuld Imkhayṭīr, a member of the country's subordinated artisan caste (*muʿallimīn*), which led to the author's conviction for apostasy. His article criticized the Quran and accused the Prophet of, in effect, nepotism, arguing that unjust, family-based corruption was present even in Islam's revealed scripture. Imkhayṭīr later moved to France, where he has devoted himself to advocating for social justice and rights for the *muʿallimīn*. For the original article, see https://web.archive.org/web/20211120041033/http://www.yennayri.com/news.php?extend.2211.7. For Imkhayṭīr's public recantation, see https://www.youtube.com/watch?v=77kQM3d1vZE in 2017.

63. Francis Rodd, *People of the Veil* (Oosterhout, Netherlands: Anthropological Books, 1966), 150–1; Priscilla Starratt, "Tuareg Slavery and Slave Trade," *Slavery & Abolition* 2, n. 2 (1981): 95.
64. I have seen a claim, made without citation or evidence, that the Omani Sultan Said bin Taimur (r. 1932–70) ordered all Black Africans in his realm classified as slaves, but I have found no corroboration for this, nor do experts on Oman that I have spoken to believe this to be true; "The Struggle for Liberation in Oman," *MERIP Reports* 36 (1975): 11.
65. Thomas S. Kidd, "'Is It Worse to Follow Mahomet than the Devil?' Early American Uses of Islam," *Church History* 72, n. 4 (2003): 770. Thanks to Mohamed Fadel for this.
66. Mohamed Heikal, *Autumn of Fury* (New York: Random House, 1983), 8–9, 13, 25.
67. Louis A. DeCaro, Jr., *On the Side of My People: A Religious Life of Malcolm X* (New York: New York University Press, 1996), 241.
68. Hānī Mājid Fayrūzī, *Ma'ālī al-shaykh Muḥammad Surūr al-Ṣabbān* (Mecca: Jāmi'at Umm al-Qurā, n.d.), 32–36 (thanks to Hasan Alsulami for getting this book for me). Thanks to Omar Suleiman for informing me about the middle names of Malcolm's daughters.
69. *Lā yakrahu al-dhamm illā kull dhī anaf, wa laysa lu'm li'ām al-khalq minhājī*; Ibn al-Abbār, 157.
70. Adham al-Jundī, *Tuḥfat al-zaman fī tartīb tarājim a'lām al-adab wa'l-fann* (Beirut: Dār al-Muqtabis, 1426/2015), 4:203–9; Muḥammad Muḥammad 'Abd al-Majd, *Imām al-bu'asā' Muḥammad Imām al-'Abd* (Cairo: Maṭba'at al-Taraqqī, n.d.), 3.
71. First: *anta 'abd wa'l-hawā akhbaranī anna waṣl al-'abd fī al-ḥubb ḥarām, qultu: yā hādhī anā 'abd al-hawā wa'l-hawā yaḥkumu mā bayn al-anām, wa idhā mā kuntu 'abdan aswadan* [sic] *fa''lamī annī fatā ḥurr al-kalām*; Second: *nasabūnī ilā al-'abīd majāzan ba'd faḍlī wa'stashhadū bi-sawādī, ḍā'a qadarī fa-qumtu andubu ḥaẓẓī fa-sawādī 'alayhi thawb ḥidād*; 'Abd al-Majd, *Imām al-bu'asā'*, 12.
72. 'Abd al-Majd, *Imām al-bu'asā'*, 31.
73. Dave Calvert, "Jokes as performance text: a close reading of Rat Pack banter," *Comedy Studies* 7, n. 1 (2016): 38–47; Wil Haygood, *In Black and White: The Life of Sammy Davis, Jr.* (New York: Alfred Knopf, 2003), 301, 314.
74. Francis Moore, *Travels to the inland parts of Africa* (London: E. Cave, 1738), 29.
75. *Wonders of the African World with Henry Louis Gates, Jr.*, "The Swahili Coast," PBS, 1999.
76. For criticism of Gates' series, see Michael C. Mbabuike, "Wonders Shall Never Cease: Decoding Henry Louis Gates's Ambiguous Adventure," *Journal of Black Studies* 31, n. 2 (2000): 234.
77. Muḥammad al-Sanūsī al-Jārimī al-Ghānī, *Tanbīh ahl al-ṭughyān*, 6.
78. See Timothy Cleaveland, "Ahmad Baba al-Timbukti and his Islamic critique of racial slavery in the Maghrib," *Journal of North African Studies* 20, n. 1 (2015): 55; Muḥammad b. al-Ṭayyib al-Qādirī, *Nashr al-mathānī li-ahl al-qarn al-ḥādī 'ashar wa'l-thānī*, ed. Muḥammad Ḥajjī and Aḥmad al-Tawfīq, 4 vols. (Rabat: Dār al-Maghrib, 1397/1977), 1:274.
79. Cleaveland, "Ahmad Baba al-Timbukti," 46.
80. Mohamed Mathee, "Muftis and the Women of Timbuktu: History through Timbuktu's Fatwas, 1907–1960" (PhD dissertation, University of Cape Town, 2011), 224–237; Hunwick, *Timbuktu and the Songhay Empire: al-Sa'dī's* Ta'rīkh al-sūdān *down to 1613 and other Contemporary Documents* (Leiden: Brill, 1999), 44, 50.

81. Elias N. Saad, *Social History of Timbuktu* (Cambridge: Cambridge University Press, 1983), 5, 8–9.
82. Saad, *Social History of Timbuktu*, 50.
83. See, for example, Margaret Larkin's fine book, *Al-Mutanabbi: Voice of the 'Abbasid Poetic Ideal* (Oxford: Oneworld, 2008), 76.
84. *Gharsihi* would mean 'his planting,' and *ghirsihi* the caul membrane, usually part of the amniotic sack, that on occasion covers up parts of a newborn baby. Al-ʿUkbarī favors the latter; Abū al-Baqā' al-ʿUkbarī, *Sharḥ Dīwān al-Mutanabbī*, ed. Muṣṭafā al-Saqqā, Ibrāhīm al-Abyārī and ʿAbd al-Ḥafīẓ Shalabī, 4 vols. (Beirut: Dār al-Maʿrifa, n.d.), 2:205.
85. Al-Mutanabbī, *Sharḥ al-Wāḥidī li-dīwān al-Mutanabbī*, ed. Yāsīn Ayyūbī and Quṣayy al-Ḥusayn (Beirut: Dār al-Rā'id al-ʿArabī, 1419/1999), 1765–66.
86. Al-Mutanabbī, *Sharḥ al-Wāḥidī*, 1858–59. Translation taken from Suzanne P. Stetkevych, *The Poetics of Islamic Legitimacy* (Bloomington, IN: Indiana University Press, 2002), 228.
87. Al-ʿUkbarī, *Sharḥ*, 2:46.
88. Al-Mutanabbī, *Sharḥ al-Wāḥidī*, 1766, 1840, 1854–55.
89. Hagedorn, 77, 94.
90. Al-Mukhtār b. al-Ḥasan Ibn Buṭlān, "Risāla jāmiʿa li-funūn nāfiʿa fī shirā al-raqīq wa taqlīb al-ʿabīd," in *Nawādir al-makhṭūṭāt*, ed. ʿAbd al-Salām Hārūn, 2 vols. (Cairo: Muṣṭafā al-Bābī al-Ḥalabī, n.d.), 1: 371.
91. Chanfi Ahmed, *West African* ʿulamā' *and Salafism in Mecca and Medina* (Leiden: Brill, 2015), 130–31.
92. Muḥammad Amīn al-Shinqīṭī, *Riḥlat al-ḥajj ilā bayt Allāh al-ḥarām* (Mecca: Dār ʿĀlam al-Fawā'id, 1426/2006), 72, 86.
93. Al-Shinqīṭī, *Riḥla*, 72, 75, 83, 86.
94. Muḥammad Ibn ʿAbd al-Bāqī, *al-Ṭirāz al-manqūsh fī maḥāsin al-ḥubūsh*, ed. ʿAbdallāh Muḥammad al-Ghazālī (Kuwait: Mu'assasat Fahd al-Marzūq al-Ṣaḥafiyya, 1995), 107–9.

## 2. THE BACKGROUND OF RACE AND RACISM

1. Fear of a Brown Person, "Aamer Rahman (Fear of a Brown Planet) – Reverse Racism," Youtube.com, 28 November 2013, https://www.youtube.com/watch?v=dw_mRaIHb-M. Also available at http://genius.com/Aamer-rahman-reverse-racism-annotated.
2. 'Race' as a word entered European languages after the 1200s and soon came to refer to lineage. Only in the late 1700s did it take on the sense we understand today. 'Racism' was a word coined in the 1930s to describe Nazi views on race; Ivan Hannaford, *Race: The History of an Idea in the West* (Baltimore: Johns Hopkins University Press, 1996), 5–6. For philosophical and legal discussions of race and racism, see Robert Bernasconi, ed., *Race* (Oxford: Wiley-Blackwell, 2001); Bernard Boxill, "Introduction," in *Race and Racism*, ed. Bernard Boxill (New York: Oxford University Press, 2001), 1–42; J.L.A. Garcia, "The Heart of Racism," *Journal of Social Philosophy* 27 (1996): 5–45; Kwame Anthony Appiah, "Racisms," in *Anatomy of Racism*, ed. David Theo Goldberg (Minneapolis: University of

Minnesota Press, 1990), 3–17; Robert Miles and Malcolm Brown, *Racism*, 2nd ed. (New York: Routledge, 2003); Lawrence Blum, *"I'm Not Racist But . . .": The Moral Quandary of Race* (Ithaca, NY: Cornell University Press, 2002); Richard Delgado and Jean Stefancic, "Critical Race Theory: An Annotated Bibliography," *Virginia Law Review* 79, n. 2 (1993): 461–516; Charles W. Mills, *The Racial Contract* (Ithaca, NY: Cornell University Press, 1997); J. Angelo Corlett, *Race, Racism and Reparations* (Ithaca, NY: Cornell University Press, 2003). For a historical discussion, see Hannaford, *Race: The History of an Idea in the West*; Adam Hochman, "Is 'Race' Modern? Disambiguating the Question," *Du Bois Review* 16, n. 2 (2019): 647–65. For sociological discussions, see Gordon Allport, *The Nature of Prejudice* (Boston: Addison-Wesley, 1954); Kwame Ture and Charles Hamilton, *Black Power* (New York: Random House, 1967). For a comprehensive collection on race in a global setting, see Leonard Harris, ed., *Racism* (Amherst: Humanity Books, 1999).

3. For foundational work on this, see Kwame Anthony Appiah and Amy Gutmann, eds., *Color Conscious: The Political Morality of Race* (Princeton: Princeton University Press, 1996), 67–74.
4. For the construction of Whiteness, see Nell Irvin Painter, *The History of White People* (New York: W.W. Norton, 2010); Ian F. Haney López, *White by Law: The Legal Construction of Race* (New York: New York University Press, 2006) (in the law, White was constructed as what was not not-White); Cheryl I. Harris, "Whiteness as Property," *Harvard Law Review* 106, n. 8 (1993): 1710–91; Matthew F. Jacobson, *Whiteness of a Different Color* (Cambridge, MA: Harvard University Press, 1998), 8 (". . . in the 1920s and after . . . partly in response to a new racial alchemy generated by African-American migrations to the North and West, whiteness was reconsolidated: the late nineteenth century's probationary white groups were now remade and granted the scientific stamp of authenticity as the unitary Caucasian race – an earlier era's Celts, Slavs, Hebrews, Iberics, and Saracens, among others, had become the Caucasians so familiar to our own visual economy and racial lexicon"). Toni Morrison famously wrote that White America conceived of African Blackness as "the vehicle by which the American self knows itself as not enslaved, but free; not repulsive, but desirable . . ."; Toni Morrison, *Playing in the Dark* (New York: Vintage Books, 1993), 52. For White ethnicity in the U.S. as the flexible and open-ended 'working-class' identity claim and population roughly equivalent to Hillary Clinton's "deplorables," see Yiorgos Anagnostou, "'White Ethnicity': A Reappraisal," *Italian American Review* 3, n. 2 (2013): 102.
5. See Michael O. Hardimon, *Rethinking Race* (Cambridge, MA: Harvard University Press, 2017).
6. See Hardimon, *Rethinking Race*, 31 ff. James calls this the popular acceptance of "a milder, egalitarian" version of biological race; Michael Rabinder James, "The Political Ontology of Race," *Polity* 44, n. 1 (2012): 107 (thanks to Iskander Abbasi for this source). See also Michael Yudell et al., "Taking race out of human genetics," *Science* 351, n. 6273 (2016): 564–65.
7. My discussion here is guided significantly by James, "The Political Ontology of Race." See also Corlett, *Race, Racism, and Reparations*, 9. See also Gary Gutting's interview with Elizabeth Anderson, "What's Wrong with Inequality?," *New York Times*, 23 April 2015, https://web.archive.org/web/20210703131926/https://opinionator.blogs.nytimes.com/author/elizabeth-anderson/.
8. Hardimon, *Rethinking Race*, 31 ff.

9. This issue continues to be hotly debated. See Ewen Callaway, "Evidence mounts for interbreeding bonanza in ancient human species," *Nature* (2016), https://www.nature.com/articles/nature.2016.19394.
10. The Minotaur of Greek myth was born of the unnatural union of Queen Pasiphae and a white bull sent by the gods. For Biblical laws against bestiality, see Leviticus 20:15–16. For the Hittite laws, see Martha T. Roth, *Law Collections from Mesopotamia and Asia Minor,* ed. Piotr Michalowski (Atlanta: Scholars Press, 1995), laws 187, 188, 199 and 200a. For laws regarding and tension over the comingling of human and animal sexuality in cultural imagery, see Ilan Peled, "Gender and Sex Crimes in the Ancient Near East: Law and Custom," in *Structures of Power: Law and Gender across the Ancient Near East and Beyond,* ed. Ilan Peled (Chicago: Oriental Institute of the University of Chicago, 2018), 27–40; Chen Maoqing, "Incest, Zoophilia, and Lust for Power in Tang Xianzu and Shakespeare," *Partial Answers* 14, n. 2 (2016): 217–36. For the Indian Laws of Manu, see Wendy Doniger, *The Laws of Manu* (London: Penguin, 1991), 267–68. Kinsey's mid-twentieth-century surveys in rural America showed that, depending on the region, between 17% and 65% of males had reached orgasm through sexual contact with an animal. In a 1972 survey of a more urban American population, Hunt found that 5% of men and 2% of women reported at least one sexual encounter with an animal; Joanna Bourke, "Bestiality, Zoophilia and Human–Animal Sexual Interactions," *Paragraph* 42, n. 1 (2019): 95–96. The title of the U.K. Home Office's 2000 report *Setting the Boundaries: Reforming the Laws of Sex Offenses* is telling. It is also revealing that strict animal rights objections to caging animals, using their labor, and eating their meat is often phrased in the language of abolition, that much contemporary objection to permitting bestiality comes from animal rights advocates who see it as denying animals the right of consent (usually considered a monopoly of humans), and that animal rights advocates often dismiss objections to the preceding arguments as speciesism (analogical to racism). See Bourke above and Gary Francione and Robert Garner, ed., *The Animal Rights Debate: Abolition or Regulation*? (New York: Columbia University Press, 2010).
11. See Hannaford, *Race: The History of an Idea in the West*; Imanuel Geiss, *Geschichte der Rassismus* (Berlin: Suhrkamp, 1988); Thomas F. Gossett, *Race: The History of an Idea in America,* rev. ed. (Oxford: Oxford University Press, 1997), 3–8; Painter, *A History of White People,* 1–5. For arguments that classical and medieval representations of Jew, Muslims, Africans, etc., prefigured racism, see Geraldine Heng, *The Invention of Race in the European Middle Ages* (Cambridge: Cambridge University Press, 2018). For the argument that racism can be traced back to Aristotle, see Benjamin Isaac, *The Invention of Racism in Classical Antiquity* (Princeton: Princeton University Press, 2004).
12. See George M. Fredrickson, *Racism: A Short History* (Princeton: Princeton University Press, 2015); Hannaford, *Race,* 122–26; Gil Anidjar, *Blood* (New York: Columbia University Press, 2014).
13. See, for example, Martin Barker, *The New Racism* (London: Junction Books, 1981); Étienne Balibar, "Is there a Neo-Racism?" in *Race, Nation, Class: Ambiguous Identities,* ed. Étienne Balibar and Immanuel Wallerstein (London: Verso, 1991), 17–28.
14. See Tariq Modood, "'Difference,' Cultural Racism and Anti-Racism," in *Race and Racism,* ed. Bernard Boxill (Oxford: Oxford University Press, 2001), 238–56.

15. Bruce Hall, *A History of Race in Muslim West Africa*, 11. Miles and Brown see as key the way that racialization attributes "meaning to somatic characteristics," but they insist that such characteristics are constructed through "signifying processes"; Miles and Brown, *Racism*, 88–92.
16. For an excellent review of the knot of questions around academic definitions of race, see Adam Hochman, "Is 'Race' Modern? Disambiguating the Question," 647–65. I would side with Geraldine Heng, who defines race as "one of the primary names we have – a name we retain for the strategic, epistemological, and political commitments it recognizes – that is attached to a repeating tendency, of the gravest import, to demarcate human beings through differences among humans that are selectively essentialized as absolute and fundamental, in order to distribute positions and powers differentially to human groups"; Heng, *The Invention of Race in the European Middle Ages*, cited from Hochman, 655. Thanks to Saadia Yacoob for alerting me to this source.
17. Fredrickson, *Racism*, 5–6. He explains that racism is "what happens when ethnicity is deemed essential or indelible and made hierarchical;" ibid., 155. See also Miles and Brown, *Racism*, 101.
18. Fredrickson defines the *sine qua nons* of racism as "difference and power"; Fredrickson, 9. Viewing the issue from a critical theory approach focused on state power and institutions, Ruth Gilmore defines racism as, "specifically . . . the state-sanctioned or extralegal production and exploitation of group-differentiated vulnerability to premature death." Ruth Wilson Gilmore, *Golden Gulag: Prisons, Surplus, Crisis, and Opposition in Globalizing California* (Berkeley: University of California Press, 2007), 28.
19. Appiah, "Racisms," 4–5, 10–11, 15–16. See also Corlett, *Race, Racism and Reparations*, 7–8.
20. George MacDonald Fraser, *The Light's on at Signpost* (London: HarperCollins, 2002), 215–16, 232.
21. For more on this, see Arun Kundnani's excellent *The Muslims are Coming! Islamophobia, Extremism, and the Domestic War on Terror* (New York: Verso, 2015); Nasar Meer and Tariq Modood, "The Racialisation of Muslims," in *Thinking Through Islamophobia*, ed. Salman Sayyid and AbdoolKarim Vakil (New York: Columbia University Press, 2010), 78–9. Iskander Abbasi sees medieval/early-modern European perceptions of Islam/Muslims and their relationship to it/them as laying the groundwork for early-modern conceptions of race and the power structures built on them; Iskander Abbasi, "Muslims, and the Coloniality of Being: Reframing the Debate on Race and Religion in Modernity," *Journal for the Study of Religion* 33, n. 2 (2020).
22. Meer and Modood, 77.
23. See Appiah, "But Would That Still Be Me? Notes on Gender, 'Race,' Ethnicity, as Sources of 'Identity,' " *Journal of Philosophy* 87 (1990): 493–99.
24. Ida Raffaelli et al., "Introduction," in *Lexicalization Patterns in Color Naming: A Cross-Linguistic Perspective*, ed. Ida Raffaelli et al. (Amsterdam: John Benjamins, 2019), 1–19.
25. In the 1600s, in the Chesapeake world of Virginia and Maryland, a large mixed-raced population termed mulattos was moved from an ambiguous, liminal legal and social status to one clearly below free Whites (e.g., a 1691 law in Virginia stated that a child born of a White [hence, free] woman and a 'Negro' father was to be sold as a servant until the age of 30). By the 1720s mulattos' legal status in the

region had been fixed and, socially, the One Drop rule dominated; Joel Williamson, *New People: Miscegenation and Mulattos in the United States* (London: Free Press, 1980), 7–8, 13, 73.

26. Christine B. Hickman, "The Devil and the One Drop Rule: Racial Categories, African Americans, and the U.S. Census," *Michigan Law Review* 95, n. 5 (1997): 1174.
27. From the late 1600s to the 1920s, individuals of mixed-race parentage were classified as 'Negro,' just as slave was collapsed into African. Although the notion that visible or known African ancestry made one Black was socially dominant by the 1720s (particularly in the Chesapeake colonies), legal definitions of blackness did not embrace the One Drop Rule until the 1920s and '30s. Blackness had been defined as ¼ parentage in Virginia (1785), ⅛ in South Carolina (1895), North Carolina, Maryland, Florida, Tennessee, Mississippi, and Missouri; Williamson, 13, 93, 98.
28. Habeeb Akande, *Illuminating the Blackness: Blacks and African Muslims in Brazil* (London: Rabaah, 2016), 22–28; Luisa Farah Schwartzman, "Who are the Blacks? The Question of Racial Classification in Brazilian Affirmative Action Policies in Higher Education," *Cahiers de la Recherche sur l'Éducation et les Saviors* 7 (2008): 27–47; Peter Fry, "The politics of 'racial' classification in Brazil," *Journal de la Société des Américanistes* 95, n. 2 (2009): 261–82.
29. Lloyd A. Thompson, *Romans and Blacks* (Norman, OK: University of Oklahoma Press, 1989), 131–32; Hiroshi Wagatsuma, "The Social Perception of Skin Color in Japan," in *Color and Race*, ed. John Hope Franklin (Boston: Houghton Mifflin, 1968), 129–131; André Béteille, "Race and Descent as Social Categories in India," in *Color and Race*, ed. John H. Franklin, 172–75.
30. Itisha Nagar, "The Unfair Selection: A Study on Skin-Color Bias in Arranged Indian Marriages," *Sage Open* 8, n. 2 (2018): 1–8.
31. R.C. Dutt, "Art. IV: The Social Life of the Hindus in the Rig-Veda Period," *Calcutta Review* 85 (1887): 65–66.
32. Béteille, "Race and Descent as Social Categories in India," 172, 174.
33. Neha Mishra, "India and Colorism: The Finer Nuances," *Washington University Global Studies Law Review* 14, n. 4 (2015): 729.
34. Mishra, "India and Colorism," 732, 736. For variations in facial structure and stature between north and south India, see L.C. Prasanna et al., "Facial Indices of North and South Indian Adults: Reliability in Stature Estimation and Sexual Dimorphism," *Journal of Clinical and Diagnostic Research* 7, n. 8 (2013): 1540–42.
35. Mishra, 732–35; "Passing for White: Merle Oberon," *You Must Remember This*, 10 February 2020, http://www.youmustrememberthispodcast.com/episodes/2020/2/3/passing-for-white-merle-oberon-make-me-over-episode-4.
36. Emma Graham-Harrison, "Black man is washed whiter in China's racist detergent advert," *The Guardian*, 28 May 2016, https://www.theguardian.com/world/2016/may/28/china-racist-detergent-advert-outrage.
37. As David Goldberg observed, "there is considerable historical variation both in the conception of races and the kinds of social expressions we characterize as racist"; David T. Goldberg, "The Social Formation of Racist Discourse," *Anatomy of Racism*, 295. For a belief-centered definition, see Sami Zubaida, "Racism," in *The Blackwell Dictionary of Modern Social Thought*, ed. William Outhwaite (Chichester: Blackwell, 2006), 549–51.
38. Painter, xii.

39. Miles and Brown, *Racism*, 101–109.
40. Blum, *"I'm Not Racist But . . .": The Moral Quandary of Racism*, 10–15.
41. J.L.A. Garcia, "The Heart of Racism," in *Race and Racism*, ed. Bernard Boxill (Oxford: Oxford University Press, 2001), 259, 284, 291. For a criticism of Garcia's theory, including the idea that beliefs often entail ill will, see Charles W. Mills, " 'Heart' Attack: A Critique of Jorge Garcia's Volitional Conception of Racism," *Journal of Ethics* 7, n. 3 (2003): 29–62.
42. Corlett, *Race, Racism and Reparations*, 64–81.
43. For a defense of U.S. progress since the era of open racist beliefs and laws, see Ward Connerly, "America isn't a racist country," *Wall Street Journal*, 24 July 2020, https://web.archive.org/web/20210713162943/https://www.wsj.com/articles/america-isnt-a-racist-country-11595628914.
44. See, for example, John McWhorter's tweet regarding Kendi's definition of racism at the 2021 Aspen Ideas Festival, https://twitter.com/JohnHMcWhorter/status/1399670923221946372?ref_src=twsrc%5Etfw%7Ctwcamp%5Etweetembed%7Ctwterm%5E1399670923221946372%7Ctwgr%5E%7Ctwcon%5Es1_&ref_url=https%3A%2F%2Fnotthebee.com%2Farticle%2Fsit-back-and-bask-in-the-genius-of-critical-race-theory-scholar-ibram-x-kendi-as-he-defines-racism-in-the-manner-of-a-7th-grader-who-forgot-to-study-for-his-vocabulary-test; Anthony Monteiro, "The Invention of Ibram X Kendi and the Ideological Crisis of Our Time," *Black Agenda Report*, 2 September 2020, https://web.archive.org/web/20210713154716/https://blackagendareport.com/invention-ibram-x-kendi-and-ideological-crises-our-time.
45. For example, @DrSuad, "Don't buy it! The convenient anti-blackness of it all!" Twitter, 31 December 2021, 7:02am, https://twitter.com/DrSuad/status/1476886492291211269; idem, "All that to say, there is a reason why Africa proper was missing and we need to be honest about that," Twitter, 31 December 2021, 6:59pm, https://twitter.com/drsuad/status/1477066980142338060?s=11.
46. Some scholars have offered arguments for antiblack racism being present in medieval Islamic civilization; Touria Khannous, "Race in pre-Islamic poetry: The work of Antara Ibn Shaddad," *African and Black Diaspora* 6, n. 1 (2016): 66–80; Bernard Lewis, *Race and Slavery in the Middle East* (New York: Oxford University Press, 1990). A more common view is that applying racism (as opposed to racialism) to medieval Islamic civilization is anachronistic. See Rachel Schine, "Conceiving the Pre-Modern Black-Arab Hero," *Journal of Arabic Literature* 48, n. 3 (2017): 301.
47. For a similar, contemporaneous expression in Western Europe, see Claire Weed, *Ethnicity in Medieval Europe, 950–1250* (Suffolk: Boydell & Brewer, 2021).
48. See, for example, Timothy Cleaveland, *Becoming Walata: A History of Saharan Social Formation and Transformation* (Portsmouth, NH: Heinemann, 2002).
49. El Hamel, *Black Morocco*, 103. For a contrast with the situation before this, see Bruce Hall, *A History of Race in Muslim West Africa*, 73.
50. Jurists from the Persianate world, for example, regularly noted that Arabs considered family lineage meaningful in matters such as marriage while Persians and Turks (*ʿajam*) did not; Ibn al-Rifʿa, *Kifāyat al-nabīh fī sharḥ al-Tanbīh*, ed. Majdī Muḥammad Surūr BāSullūm, 21 vols. (Beirut: Dār al-Kutub al-ʿIlmiyya, 2009), 13:64; ʿAbd al-Ḥayy al-Laknawī, *ʿUmdat al-riʿāya ʿalā sharḥ al-Wiqāya*, ed. Ṣalāḥ Muḥammad Abū al-Ḥājj, 7 vols. (Beirut: Dār al-Kutub al-ʿIlmiyya, 2009), 3:91; Muwaffaq al-Dīn Ibn Qudāma, *al-Mughnī*, ed. ʿAbdallāh al-Turkī and ʿAbd al-Fattāḥ al-Ḥuluw, 12 vols. (Cairo: Hujr, 1986), 7:378.

51. Abū Bakr Ibn al-ʿArabī, *Aḥkām al-Qurʾān*, ed. Muḥammad ʿAbd al-Qādir ʿAṭā, 4 vols. (Beirut: Dār al-Kutub al-ʿIlmiyya, 1424/2003), 1:536. As a tenth-century judge's manual from Iraq puts it, a debtor claiming bankruptcy can be imprisoned for up to four months to determine if he has any assets, since a rich person could not put up with that much time behind bars. If one could, then that would be "anomalous and rare, not something one is accustomed to see in people's customary conduct." See Abū Bakr al-Khaṣṣāf, *Adab al-qāḍī*, ed. Farhat Ziadeh (Cairo: Maṭbaʿat Jablāwī, 1979), 256–58.
52. This scholar was Muslim b. Khālid al-Zanjī; al-Dhahabī, *Siyar aʿlām al-nubalāʾ*, 8:178. A collection of sayings from the eleventh century CE includes, "Blacks can be caught using dates" (*al-sūdān bi'l-tamr yuṣṭādūn*); Aḥmad b. Muḥammad al-Maydānī, *Majmaʿ al-amthāl*, ed. Muḥammad Muḥyī al-Dīn ʿAbd al-Ḥamīd, 2 vols. (Cairo: Maṭbaʿat al-Sunna al-Muḥammadiyya, 1374/1955), 1:357.

## 3. BLACKNESS CONTESTED

1. Léopold Sédar Senghor, *Poèmes* (Paris: Éditions du Seuil, 1964), 83.
2. Noel Ignatiev, *How the Irish Became White* (New York: Routledge, 1995), 13, 40–41; Charles W. Mills, "The Illumination of Blackness," in *Antiblackness*, ed. Moon-Kie Jung and João H. Costa Vargas (Durham: Duke University Press, 2021), 33.
3. Ronan McGreevy, "Village rejoices in presidential status with more verses of 'Barack Obama,'" *Irish Times*, 6 November 2018," https://web.archive.org/web/20210816041836/https://www.irishtimes.com/news/village-rejoices-in-presidential-status-with-more-verses-of-barack-obama-1.906049?via=mr.
4. See Cornel West's interview, Jonathan Capehart, "Ben Carson and Cornel West actually agree: Obama's 'not black enough'," *Washington Post*, 23 February 2016, https://web.archive.org/web/20210905042752/https://www.washingtonpost.com/blogs/post-partisan/wp/2016/02/23/ben-carson-and-cornel-west-actually-agree-obamas-not-black-enough/. For an in-depth analysis of this question, see Michelle M. Wright, *Physics of Blackness* (Minneapolis: University of Minnesota Press, 2015), 62–72. Thanks to Sana Jamal for alerting me to this source.
5. "The Other African Americans," *Economist*, 19 October 2019, https://www.economist.com/united-states/2019/10/19/the-other-african-americans; Valerie Russ, "Who is black in America? Tensions flare between black Americans and black immigrants," *Philadelphia Inquirer*, 19 October 2018, https://web.archive.org/web/20210816044635/https://www.inquirer.com/philly/news/cynthia-erivo-harriet-tubman-movie-luvvie-ajayi-american-descendants-of-slaves-20181018.html.
6. Coleman Donaldson, "Clear Language: Script, Register and the N'ko Movement of Manding-Speaking West Africa" (PhD dissertation, University of Pennsylvania, 2017), 175. See also second-generation American youth of Ethiopian and Eritrean descent debating whether they are Black or not, Miskeen Central, "I'm Not Black?!? MC Podcast #010," 11 November 2019, https://www.youtube.com/watch?v=6elpqKTjovY&t=1297s.

7. For a recent and controversial comic probe into this matter, see Marcus Jones, "Saturday Night Live host Dave Chappelle asks America to 'look at Pete Davidson's lips'," *Entertainment Weekly*, n.d., https://ew.com/tv/saturday-night-live-dave-chappelle-look-at-pete-davidsons-lips/.
8. https://www.lawinsider.com/dictionary/black-or-african-american, among other sources, Illinois statutes. Although the notion that visible or known African ancestry made one Black was socially dominant by the 1720s (particularly in the Chesapeake colonies), legal definitions of blackness did not embrace the One Drop Rule until the 1920s and '30s. Blackness had been defined as ¼ parentage in Virginia (1785), ⅛ in South Carolina (1895), North Carolina, Maryland, Florida, Tennessee, Mississippi, and Missouri; Williamson, 13, 93, 98.
9. http://web.archive.org/web/20200109004008/https:/policy.m4bl.org/glossary/.
10. See Andrea Abrams, *God and Blackness* (New York: New York University Press, 2014), 5–9; Marcus B. Montague-Mfuni, "Unpacking Our Definition of 'Black'," *The Harvard Crimson*, 4 March 2020, https://web.archive.org/web/20210830151820/https://www.thecrimson.com/column/african-american/article/2020/3/4/montague-mfuni-unpacking-definition-of-black/.
11. Wright, *Physics of Blackness*, 1.
12. Lewis R. Gordon, *Existentia Africana: Understanding Africana Existential Thought* (London: Taylor & Francis, 2000), 63. Thanks to Jared Sexton for alerting me to this source.
13. https://www.metmuseum.org/art/collection/search/318622. See also statues and masks from the Lower Congo (with an otherwise fairly mimetic mask with skin colored white as part of an ancestor cult); Joseph Cornet, *Art of Africa: Treasures from the Congo* (London: Phaidon, 1971), 24–25, 35. Of course, depictions could also be fantastic. Medieval European depictions of 'Ethiopians' (i.e., Black Africans) range from a very realistic twelfth-century French one to a fantastic, bizarre one from fifteenth-century France; Debra Higgs Strickland, *Saracens, Demons, and Jews: Making Monsters in Medieval Art* (Princeton: Princeton University Press, 2003), 10, 45.
14. See https://web.archive.org/save/https://oi.uchicago.edu/museum-exhibits/nubia/head-nubian.
15. "Egyptians see Nubians as subjects," Oriental Institute, University of Chicago, https://web.archive.org/web/20210812134128/https://oi.uchicago.edu/museum-exhibits/nubia/egyptians-see-nubians-subjects. See also the image of two foreign captives, one clearly African, produced in the Ptolemaic period at the Museo Egizio (Cat. 2327), https://collezioni.museoegizio.it/en-GB/material/Cat_2327; and the illustration from the Valley of the Kings in David Goldenberg, *Black and Slave: The Origins and History of the Curse of Ham* (Berlin: De Gruyter, 2017), 170.
16. Scott T. Carroll, "Wrestling in Ancient Nubia," *Journal of Sport History* 15, n. 2 (1988): 127–32. Keith W. Crawford, "Critique of the 'Black Pharaohs' Theme: Racist Perspectives of Egyptian and Kushite/Nubian Interactions in Popular Media," *African Archaeological Review* 38 (2021): 695–712.
17. Rodney S. Sadler, Jr., "Can a Cushite Change His Skin? Cushites, 'Racial Othering,' and the Hebrew Bible," *Interpretation* 60, n. 4 (2006): 389–90.
18. Shiyanthi Thavapalan, "Speaking of Colours," in *Mesopotamian Sculpture in Colour*, ed. Astrid Nunn and Heinrich Piening (Gladbeck: PeWe Verlag, 2020), 198–99.

19. Sadler, "Can a Cushite Change His Skin?," 398–400. See also Thompson, *Romans and Blacks*, 57. It is interesting that the Old Testament does not use the color descriptor black explicitly for human skin color, but rather to convey their grief.
20. Sadler, 399.
21. For a succinct review of the range of Greek conceptions of Ethiopia, see Thompson, 59.
22. Kenneth Baxter Wolf, "The 'Moors' of West Africa and the Beginnings of the Portuguese Slave Trade," *Journal of Medieval and Renaissance Studies* 24, n. 3 (1994): 458.
23. In a scene in the film *True Romance* (1993), a police officer taunts a Mafioso by telling him that he was, in fact, the spawn of miscegenation, since "the Moors conquered Sicily. And the Moors are n_____s." (Ironically, this same notion of the non-Whiteness of Sicilians was alluded to by the Circuit Court in Alabama in the 1922 Rollins v. State case). Characters in TV and movies announced as Moors or Moorish are often played by Black actors. The character of Azeem the Moor in *Robin Hood: Prince of Thieves* (1991) is played by Morgan Freeman. The same occurs in two episodes of *Highlander: The Series*: the Moor Kassim in 'Promises' (1996) is played by Ricco Ross, and the Moor Xavier St. Cloud in 'The Finale: Part 1' (1995) et al. is played by Roland Gift, whose father is Afro-Caribbean and mother is British. For insights into whether Gift was Black or biracial and according to whom, see Dave Simpson, "Interview: Fine Young Cannibal Roland Gift: 'I went back to where being pretty didn't matter,'" *The Guardian*, 3 December 2020, https://web.archive.org/web/20210429192150/https://www.theguardian.com/music/2020/dec/03/fine-young-cannibal-roland-gift-i-went-back-to-where-being-pretty-didnt-matter.
24. See Thompson, 59–61, 97–98.
25. Herodotus, *Histories*, 3.101.
26. Frank M. Snowden, Jr., *Blacks in Antiquity: Ethiopians in the Greco-Roman Experience* (Cambridge, MA: Belknap Press, 1970), 1–14, 171; Elizabeth McGrath, "The Black Andromeda," *Journal of the Warburg and Courtauld Institutes* 55 (1992): 2–3.
27. See also David Brion Davis, *Slavery and Human Progress* (Oxford: Oxford University Press, 1984), 33. There has been some argument that the image of two horses that Plato conjures to describe the challenge of disciplining the self is inherently antiblack. In his *Phaedrus* dialogue, Plato gives the simile of a charioteer driving two horses, one good and one bad. The good one is white with black eyes, needs no whip, seeks glory but with temperance and modesty, is straight and of good form (elsewhere he describes it as being of good stock). The bad one is crooked, massive, has black (*malanchros*) skin and grey eyes, is hot blooded (or blood-red in complexion, depending on the translation), wanton, and hard to control. Plato uses this image to describe the challenge of taming and controlling one's desire when one sees one's beloved, with the dark horse wanting to lunge at her and needing to be controlled, until, at last, the charioteer can break it; *Phaedrus*, 253c-e, 246a-b. It has also been argued that Plato associates whiteness with goodness. In the *Philebus* dialogue, Plato uses the contemplation of spectrums of purity/impurity and intensity/dilution to talk about the value, purpose, and desirability of pleasure and the good. He uses whiteness as an example of a spectrum to ponder, from pure to attenuated; *Philebus*, 53, 58c-d. But there is no indication in this discussion that there is something about whiteness that merits

this use as an example other than it being something that one can easily talk about being muddied or altered on a spectrum. Similarly, the bad, carnal horse is not black because it's bad (it is bad in the sense of not being pure and godlike) but because it is bodily, expressing human bodily desires. Hence it is described as blood red in complexion or hot-blooded, returning to the association of blackness and heat seen in explanations of the color of Ethiopians. NB: for Plato black and white were the first two primary colors; *Timeus*, 67e-68.

28. Herodotus, *Histories*, 3:20.
29. For various ancient theories about the cause of blackness and 'woolly' hair (heat, sun, humidity, water, ancestral traits), see Strabo, *Geography*, Book 15, Section 1, 23–4. Herodotus suggests that it is either due to black semen (at least there is a correlation, he says) or heat; *Histories*, 3:101, 2:22. The heat argument is followed by Isidore of Seville, the nearness of the sun argument by humanists like Leo le Roy and Leo Africanus. Francis Bacon argued it was due to the environment overall; Linda Van Norden, *The Black Feet of the Peacock: The Color Concept of 'Black' from the Greeks through the Renaissance* (Lanham, MD: University Press of America, 1985), 219–24.
30. Ovid, *Metamorphosis*, 2.235.
31. For a good summary of the climatic, astrological, and humoral theories, see Strickland, *Saracens, Demons, and Jews*, 30–38.
32. Thompson, *Romans and Blacks*, 131; H. Hoetink, *The Two Variants in Caribbean Race Relations*, trans. Eva M. Hooykaas (London: Oxford University Press, 1967), 120. Interestingly, even before the nineteenth century, Japanese used the word white (*shiroi*) to refer to the lighter (more desirable) shades of their own skin tone; Wagatsuma, "The Social Perception of Skin Color in Japan," 129. The same applies to India; Béteille, 172–75. Peter Frost has made the fascinating (but controversial) argument that women have been depicted with lighter skin globally due to having generally less melanin than men in their same populations. See Peter Frost, "Fair Women, Dark Men: The Forgotten Roots of Colour Prejudice," *History of European Ideas* 12, n. 5 (1990): 672; idem, "White Skin Privilege: Modern Myth, Forgotten Past," *Evolutionary Studies in Imaginative Culture* 4, n. 2 (2020): 63–81.
33. Crawford, "Critique of the 'Black Pharaohs' Theme," 706, 710.
34. Thompson, *Romans and Blacks*, 35, 105, 107; Pseudo-Aristotle, *Physiognomonica*, 812a, in W.D. Ross, ed., *The Works of Aristotle Vol. VI* (Oxford: Clarendon Press, 1913).
35. Snowden, 169, 176, 179.
36. Petronius, *Satyricon*, trans. Michael Heseltine, section 102.
37. Thompson, *Romans and Blacks*, 48, 109.
38. Thompson, 27.
39. Isaac does not really discuss Africans or blackness, nor does he really address Snowden's evidence. He mounts a short rebuttal in a footnote; Benjamin Isaac, *The Invention of Racism in Classical Antiquity*, 356.
40. Thompson, 131–32. For the association of Ethiopia with innocence and philosophy, see Thompson, 99.
41. Don J. Wyatt, *The Blacks of Premodern China* (Philadelphia: University of Pennsylvania Press, 2019), 20.
42. J.J.L. Duyvendak, *China's Discovery of Africa* (London: Authur Probsthain, 1949), 14, 15, 22–24.
43. Mildred Europa Taylor, "The fascinating history of Melanesians, the world's only black blondes," *Face2Face Africa*, 28 September 2018, https://web.archive.org/

web/20210904163055/https://face2faceafrica.com/article/the-fascinating-history-of-melanesians-the-worlds-only-black-blondes. Thanks to Kristina Richardson for pointing this out.

44. Edward H. Schafer, *The Golden Peaches of Samarkand: A Study of T'ang Exotics* (n.p.: Pickle Partners, 2016), 75; Paul Wheatley, "Geographical Notes on some Commodities involved in Sung Maritime Trade," *Journal of the Malayan Branch, Royal Asiatic Society* 32, n. 2 (1959): 54–55; Duyvendak, *China's Discovery of Africa*, 22. Chinese scholars often grouped slaves brought from Southeast Asia, India, and East Africa under the term originally used for people from the Mekong region, *K'un-lun*, which came to mean people with dark skin and curly hair; Paul Pelliot, *Notes on Marco Polo I* (Paris: Imprimerie Nationale, 1959), 600.
45. Robert G. Hoyland, *Seeing Islam as Others Saw It* (Princeton: Darwin Press, 1997), 250.
46. For an argument that the historical use of the word black to denigrate means that the word should be abandoned (as opposed to reclaimed), see Kewsi Tsri, *Africans Are Not Black* (London: Routledge, 2016).
47. Wagatsuma, 137.
48. Ibn Khaldūn observed that, unlike Africans, northern Europeans and Slavs were not referred to by their color because the Arab/Persian authors of ethnologies already referred to themselves as white; Ibn Khaldūn, *The Muqaddimah*, trans. Franz Rosenthal, ed. N.J. Dawood (Princeton: Princeton University Press, 1969), 60–61.
49. Odette Alarcón et al., "The Color of My Skin: A Measure to Assess Children's Perceptions of Their Skin Color," *Applied Development Science* 4, n. 4 (2000): 208–21. In this study, Puerto Rican children, some of them with Black African features, were asked to pick one of several cards that they felt best matched their skin tone. None picked the black card. Interestingly, the authors even admit, "the 'white' card chosen by the children was a pink-cream-white card and that the 'black' card was a brown–black color." See also Melinda Fakuade, "How do children of color learn to draw themselves?" *The Outline*, 10 July 2018, https://web.archive.org/web/20210819015040/https://theoutline.com/post/5291/children-of-color-self-portraits. In one of the famous studies performed by Kenneth and Mamie Clark, in which children were asked to color an outline of a child identified as themselves, it is unfortunately not specified whether the children used black or brown crayons. See Kenneth B. Clark and Mamie P. Clark, "Emotional Factors in Racial Identification and Preference in Negro Children," *Journal of Negro Education* 19, n. 3 (1950): 344.
50. Brent Berlin and Paul Kay, *Basic Color Terms* (Berkeley: University of California Press, 1969); Kay et al., *World Color Survey* (Stanford: CSLI Publications, 2009). Chinese seems to have had an unusually robust set of color names for brown (like 'tea-colored'). I have not found any clarifications for when such descriptors appeared, however. See Vincent C. Sun and Chien-Chung Chen, "Basic color categories and Mandarin Chinese color terms," *PLOS One* 13, n. 11 (2018).
51. Dominique Zahan, "White, Red, and Black: Colour Symbolism in Black Africa," in *The Realms of Colour*, ed. Adolf Portmann and Rudolf Ritsema, 365–396 (Leiden: Brill, 1974), 365–66.
52. Henry G. Fischer, "Varia Aegyptiaca," *Journal of the American Research Center in Egypt* 2 (1963): 19–20; John Baines, "Color Terminology and Color Classification: Ancient Egyptian Color Terminology and Polychromy," *American Anthropologist*

87, n. 2 (1985): 283, 285–86. Egyptians used their color term for white in descriptions of milk, teeth, and the white of the eye. Their word for black was used for, among other things, the pupil of the eye; Wolfgang Schenkel, "Color terms in ancient Egyptian and Coptic," in *Anthropology of Color*, ed. Robert E. MacLaury, Galina V. Paramel and Don Dedrick (Philadelphia: John Benjamins, 2007), 222.

53. Zahan, 366.
54. Wagatsuma, "The Social Perception of Skin Color in Japan," 133.
55. Thompson, 40–42, 112; Strickland, *Saracens, Demons, and Jews*, 69–86. For more on this issue, see Gay L. Bryon, *Symbolic Blackness and Ethnic Difference in Early Christian Literature* (London: Routledge, 2002).
56. Snowden, 198, 205. Incredibly, Snowden does not see these expressions as negative but rather as a continuity of the Greco-Roman idea of the Ethiopian as an extreme of difference; Snowden, 197–215.
57. Snowden, 204.
58. Augustine, *City of God*, Book XVI, Chapter 2; Chris L. de Wet, *The Unbound God: Slavery and the Formation of Early Christian Thought* (London: Routledge, 2018), 120–123.
59. Compare this with the New Revised Standard Version. Surprisingly, Snowden sees this Christian discourse as a continuity of the Greco-Roman trope of Ethiopia as the paradigmatic 'distant other' and registers no shift into negativity; Snowden, 197–215; McGrath, 6–7.
60. Medieval European depictions of the crucifixion show Jesus and those around him looking no different from how local Europeans were depicted, which is not surprising considering that these depictions were often strikingly anachronistic. See https://www.medievalists.net/2015/04/the-crucifixion-of-jesus-in-medieval-art/.
61. *The Song of Roland*, trans. Dorothy L. Sayers (Baltimore: Penguin, 1957), sections 113, 144.
62. Strickland, *Saracens, Demons, and Jews*, 168–72, 179. See also Sophia Rose Arjana, *Muslims in the Western Imagination* (Oxford: Oxford University Press, 2015), 23, 25, 38–42, 49, 67.
63. Cord Whitaker, "Black Metaphors in the *King of Tars*," *Journal of English and Germanic Philology* 112, n. 2 (2013): 169–93.
64. See Jean Michel Massing, "From Greek Proverb to Soap Advert: Washing the Ethiopian," *Journal of the Warburg and Courtauld Institutes* 58 (1995): 182.
65. Massing, "From Greek Proverb to Soap Advert: Washing the Ethiopian," 190–91.
66. Siep Stuurdman, *The Invention of Humanity* (Cambridge, MA: Harvard University Press, 2017), 305.
67. Van Norden, *The Black Feet of the Peacock*, 78–79.
68. Kim F. Hall, *Things of Darkness: Economies of Race and Gender in Early Modern England* (Ithaca, NY: Cornell University Press, 1995).
69. It seems that, while moor, blackamoor, etc., could mean any of the inhabitants of the southern shore of the Mediterranean, 'Negars' was used only for people from Sub-Sahelian West Africa; Emily C. Bartels, "Too Many Blackamoors: Deportations, Discrimination, and Elizabeth I," *Studies in English Literature* 46, n. 2 (2006): 307–8.
70. *Othello* Act 1 Scene 1; Massing, "From Greek Proverb to Soap Advert," 181, 186; Van Norden, *The Black Feet of the Peacock*, 67–97.
71. Nabil Matar, *Turks, Moors, and Englishmen in the Age of Discovery* (New York: Columbia University Press, 1999), 4, 12–13.

72. Devin J. Vartija, *The Color of Equality* (Philadelphia: University of Pennsylvania Press, 2021), 63.
73. Cedric Robinson, *Black Marxism: The Making of the Black Radical Tradition*, 3rd ed. (Chapel Hill, NC: University of North Carolina Press, 2020, original published 1983), 81–2, 100; Matar, *Turks, Moors, and Englishmen*, 12–13.
74. Charles-Lois de Secondat de Montesquieu, *l'Esprit des lois*, ed. Laurent Versini, 2 vols. (Paris: Gallimard, 1995), 1:443–49, 473–75 (books 14:ii, 15:v–vi); Claudine Hunting, "The Philosophes and Black Slavery: 1748–1765," *Journal of the History of Ideas* 69, n. 3 (1978): 417; Dan Edelstein, *On the Spirit of Rights* (Chicago: University of Chicago Press, 2019), 132.
75. Jennifer Welchman, "Locke and Slavery and Inalienable Rights," *Canadian Journal of Philosophy* 25, n. 1 (1995): 79.
76. "Thomas Jefferson's Thoughts on the Negro – I," *Journal of Negro History* 3, n. 1 (1918): 57, 65–68.
77. Winthrop D. Jordan, *White over Black: American Attitudes toward the Negro, 1550–1812*, 2nd ed. (Chapel Hill, NC: University of North Carolina Press, 2012), 235–38.
78. Nicolas de Caritat de Condorcet, *Réflexions sur l'esclavage des nègres* (Neufchatel: la Société Typographique, 1781); idem, "On Slavery. Rules for the Society of the Friends of Negroes (1788)," in *Condorcet: Political Writings*, ed. Steven Lukes and Nadia Urbinati (Cambridge: Cambridge University Press, 2012), 150, 154.
79. Clark and Clark, "Emotional Factors in Racial Identification and Preference in Negro Children," 341–50; Phillip E. Jordan and Maria Hernandez-Reif, "Re-Examination of Young Children's Racial Attitudes and Skin Tone Preferences," *Journal of Black Psychology* 35, n. 3 (2009): 388–403; Stephanie Irby Coard, Alfiee M. Breland and Patricia Raskin, "Perceptions of and Preferences for Skin Color, Black Racial Identity, and Self-Esteem among African Americans," *Journal of Applied Social Psychology* 31, n. 11 (2001): 2256–74, etc.
80. Massing, "From Greek Proverb to Soap Advert: Washing the Ethiopian," 190–1.
81. The influential 1969 study on color in world languages by Berlin and Kay concluded that a black/white distinction was the most basic stage of color description in a language, while a follow-up study, the 2009 World Color Survey, concluded it was a more nuanced dark-cool/warm-light instead of black/white; Brent Berlin and Paul Kay, *Basic Color Terms* (Berkeley: University of California Press, 1969); Kay et al., *World Color Survey* (Stanford: CSLI Publications, 2009).
82. Andrew F. Clark, "'The Ties that Bind': Servility and Dependency among the Fulbe of Bundu (Senegambia), c. 1930s – 1980s," *Slavery & Abolition* 19, n. 2 (1998): 98–9.
83. Francis M. Adams and Charles E. Osgood, "A Cross-Cultural Study of the Affective Meanings of Color," *Journal of Cross-Cultural Psychology* 4, n. 2 (1973): 135–56. This study examined 23 languages, but none is African. But a study of color naming in 350 African languages found, among other things: 1) salient association of white with positive traits like kindness, honesty, innocence, as well as with positive judgments like good or true (these languages are Afar, Bambara, Buli, Cebaara, Kikongo, Mambay, Minyanka, Nugunu, Nyakyusa, Swahili, and Tupuri). 2) noteworthy colexification (e.g., in French, wife and woman are colexified under *femme*; in Arabic breathe and soul are colexified under *nafs*) of white with pure/clean and black with dirty. This study found that there was not much that stood out as "specifically African" in color naming; Guillaume Segerer and Martine Vanhove,

"Color naming in Africa," in *Lexicalization Patterns in Color Naming*, 306–8, 317; Maria Bulakh, "Basic color terms from Proto-Semitic to Old Ethiopic," in *Anthropology of Color*, ed. Robert E. MacLaury, Galina V. Paramel and Don Dedrick (Philadelphia: John Benjamins, 2007), 250. See also Zahan, "White, Red, and Black: Colour Symbolism in Black Africa," 375–77 (though Zahan's chapter seems to contain a glaring contradiction, cf. 376, 385). Zahan also brings up the fascinating case of how albinos are viewed in many parts of Africa south of the Sahara, namely that their bodies are connected to the supernatural or heaven (hence, the tragic demand for their body parts); ibid., 393. See also http://albinism-in-africa.com/. There seems to be a similar, near-universal phenomenon of the association of the right hand with good, the left with bad; Wulf Schiefenhövel, "Biased Semantics for Right and Left in 50 Indo-European and non-Indo-European Languages," *Annals of the New York Academy of Sciences* 1288 (2013): 135–52. Interestingly, early Biblical Hebrew seems to have developed a white/red contrast before a white/black one; Athalya Brenner, *Colour Terms in the Old Testament* (Sheffield: Journal of the Study of the Old Testament, 1982), 56–57. Ancient Akkadian writings show an association of black with death and misery (e.g., a black dog as a bad omen), sometimes in a binary contrast with red associated with health and prosperity; Thavapalan, "Speaking of Colours," 197, 199.

84. A psychology study showed an association between brightness and positive response and vice versa, though the authors acknowledge that 95% of the participant pool was White; Brian P. Meier, Michael D. Robinson, and Gerald L. Clore, "Why Good Guys Wear White: Automatic Inferences About Stimulus Valence Based on Brightness," *Psychological Science* 15, n. 2 (2004): 82–87. See a Chinese-language study suggesting a metaphorical association of white with moral, black with immoral; Rong YIN and Haosheng YE, "The Black and White Metaphor Representation of Moral Concepts and Its Influence on Moral Cognition," *Acta Psychologica Sinica* 46, n. 9 (2014): 1331–46.
85. Ruth Karras, *Slavery and Society in Medieval Scandinavia* (New Haven: Yale University Press, 1988), 56, 59, 63–4. See the *Rigsthula*, verses 7–34 (here from *The Poetic Edda*, trans. Henry Adams Bellows). See also David Pelteret, *Slavery in Early Mediaeval England* (Suffolk: Boydell Press, 1995), 52.
86. Coral Lumbley, "The 'dark Welsh': Color, race, and alterity in the matter of medieval Wales," *Literature Compass* 16, n. 9–10 (2019): 5.
87. Karras, *Slavery and Society in Medieval Scandinavia*, 56, 59, 63–4; Pelteret, *Slavery in Early Mediaeval England*, 52. In the high medieval period in Western Europe, some among the nobility held that the peasants were descended from Ham and thus condemned to serfdom, while the nobles believed themselves to be descended from the Trojans. There is probably no link between the Curse of Ham and the *Rigsthula*'s hierarchy, however, since at that time in Europe the Curse was not understood as relating mainly to darkness/black skin color; David M. Whitford, *The Curse of Ham in the Early Modern Era* (Burlington, VT: Ashgate, 2009), 41; Friedrich Hertz, *Race and Civilization*, trans. A.S. Levetus and W. Entz (London: Kegan Paul, 1928), 4; René Johannet, *Le Principe des Nationalités* (Paris: Nouvelle Librarie Nationale, 1918), 28. In an interesting passage describing his captivity in Morocco in 1745–6, the Englishman Thomas Troughton says, with all their time out in the hot sun, "our Hides were all perfectly tann'd; and had it been possible for our most intimate Acquaintance to have seen us, they would never have known us, but took us rather for *Negroe* Slaves than *European* Captives." See Thomas

Troughton, *Barbarian Cruelty* (London: R. Walker, 1751), 63. Interestingly, in her study of blackness in Elizabethan literature, Kim Hall notes how sunburn is a "liminal space" between black and white; Hall, *Things of Darkness*, 118.

88. W.E.B. Du Bois, *Black Reconstruction in America* (New York: Harcourt, Brace & Co., 1935), 15–16.
89. Sohail Daulatzai, *Black Star, Crescent Moon* (Minneapolis: University of Minnesota Press, 2012), 31; Nathaniel Deutsch, "The 'Asiatic Black Man': An African American Orientalism?," *Journal of Asian American Studies* 4, n. 3 (2001): 196.
90. See Deutsch, 202.
91. Ashwin Desai, "Indian South Africans and the Black Consciousness Movement under apartheid," *Diaspora Studies* 8, n. 1 (2015): 37, 40. Thanks to Maya Bhardwaj for alerting me to this source.
92. Maya Bhardwaj, "Political Blackness and the search for multiracial solidarity," *Roar*, 4 May 2021, https://roarmag.org/essays/political-blackness-multiracial-solidarity/.
93. Mungo Park, *Travels in the Interior of Africa* (Edinburgh: Adam and Charles Black, 1858), 217; Rudyard Kipling, *Gunga Din*; J. Talboys Wheeler, *Early Records of British India: A History of the English Settlements in India* (London: Trüber, 1848), 49; William Dalrymple, *The Last Mughal* (London: Bloomsbury, 2006), 246, 311, 314.
94. Sarah Ihmoud, "Born Palestinian, Born Black: Antiblackness and the Womb of Zionist Settler Colonialisms," in *Antiblackness*, ed. Jung and Costa Vargas, 299. See also Justin Leroy, "Black History in Occupied Territory: On the Entanglements of Slavery and Settler Colonialism," *Theory & Event* 19, n. 4 (2016): 7; Susan Abulhawa, "The Palestinian struggle is a black struggle," *The Electronic Intifada*, 11 June 2013, https://web.archive.org/web/20210830174942/https://electronicintifada.net/content/palestinian-struggle-black-struggle/12530 (NB: it seems that Abulhawa did not actually favor this title for her essay). For a roundtable on the question of Black–Palestinian solidarity from a variety of perspectives, see Noura Erakat, moderator, "Roundtable on Anti-Blackness and Black-Palestinian Solidarity," *Jadaliyya*, 3 June 2015, https://web.archive.org/web/20210830180306/https://www.jadaliyya.com/Details/32145.
95. Satanico Pandemonium, "Huey P. Newton Speaks at a 1970 News Conference," 24 July 2014, https://www.youtube.com/watch?v=NplrUhW79b8, last accessed 3 August 2021. Thanks to Annie Olaloku-Teriba for pointing me to this source.
96. C. Robinson, *Black Marxism*, 310–13, 316; Robin D.G. Kelley, "Forward: Why *Black Marxism*? Why Now?," forward to *Black Marxism*, by C. Robinson, xxvii.
97. Annie Olaloku-Teriba, "Political blackness and Palestinian solidarity," *Red Pepper*, 22 September 2020, https://web.archive.org/web/20210804143102/https://www.redpepper.org.uk/political-blackness-and-palestinian-solidarity/.
98. Micah L. Sifry, "Jesse and the Jews: Palestine and the Struggle for the Democratic Party," *Middle East Report* 155 (1988): 4–11. For more on this tension and its history, see Michael R. Fischbach, *Black Power and Palestine* (Palo Alto: Stanford University Press, 2019).
99. Kwame Anthony Appiah, "What We Can Learn from the Rise and Fall of 'Political Blackness'," *New York Times*, 7 October 2020 https://www.nytimes.com/2020/10/07/opinion/political-blackness-race.html.
100. For the challenges and pitfalls faced by political blackness, see Appiah, "What We Can Learn from the Rise and Fall of 'Political Blackness'."

101. Hisham Aïdi, "Slavery, Genocide and the Politics of Outrage: Understanding the New Racial Olympics," 234 *Middle East Report* (Spring 2005), https://web.archive.org/web/20210621214723/https://merip.org/2005/03/slavery-genocide-and-the-politics-of-outrage/, last accessed 21 June 2021. Aïdi also observes that part of the Black Nationalist turn against Islamic solidarity in the U.S. has been the Arab chauvinism of many Islamic organizations in North America coupled with, since 9/11, a desire to distance themselves from the bugbear of 'Islamic terrorism.' He makes the excellent point that, today in the West, assimilation and belonging is achieved by the ideological exclusion of the Arab/Muslim. Regarding the history of Muslim 'passing,' there are several accounts from the 1700s and 1800s in the southern U.S. of Muslim slaves insisting they were 'Moorish' and not Negro, considering themselves above other slaves or petitioning for release. Some plantation owners valued them for their literacy or put them in management roles. But Muslims were also the driving force of several major slave rebellions in the Caribbean and South America; Kambiz Ghanea Bassiri, *A History of Islam in America* (Cambridge: Cambridge University Press, 2010), 22–24; William B. Hodgson, *Notes on Northern Africa, the Sahara and Soudan* (New York: Wiley & Putnam, 1844), 68; Margarita Rosa, "Du'as of the Enslaved: The Malê Slave Rebellion in Bahía, Brazil," *Yaqeen*, 5 April 2018, https://yaqeeninstitute.org/margarita-rosa/duas-of-the-enslaved-the-male-slave-rebellion-in-bahia-brazil.
102. E.U. Essien-Udom, *Black Nationalism: A Search for an Identity in America* (Chicago: University of Chicago Press, 1962), 34, 262, 275.
103. The Movement for Black Lives, for example, defines a Black person as one "who identifies as Black AND has African indigenous ancestry that predates colonization . . ."; http://web.archive.org/web/20200109004008/https:/policy.m4bl.org/glossary/.
104. See Maya Bhardwaj, "Political Blackness and the search for multiracial solidarity," *Roar*, 4 May 2021, https://web.archive.org/web/20210820231304/https://roarmag.org/essays/political-blackness-multiracial-solidarity/.
105. Olaloku-Teriba, "Political blackness and Palestinian solidarity."
106. Jesse McCarthy, "On Afropessism," *LA Review of Books*, 20 July 2020, https://web.archive.org/web/20210802012436/https://lareviewofbooks.org/article/on-afropessimism/.
107. Fanon is looked to as a founding articulator of political blackness and Afropessimism. Du Bois is even more hotly contested as a proponent of Marxism, anti-imperialism, pan-Africanism, Black Radicalism, or Afropessimism. See C. Robinson, *Black Marxism*; Jesse Olsavsky, "The Abolitionist Tradition in the Making of W.E.B. Du Bois's Marxism and Anti-Imperialism," *Socialism and Democracy* 32, n. 3 (2018): 14–35; Patrick Anderson, "Pan-Africanism and Economic Nationalism: W.E.B. Du Bois's Black Reconstruction and the Failings of the 'Black Marxism' Thesis," *Journal of Black Studies* 48, n. 8 (2017): 732–57.
108. Orlando Patterson, *Slavery and Social Death* (Cambridge, MA: Harvard University Press, 1982), 7–8, 13.
109. See Saidiya Hartman, *Scenes of Subjugation: Terror, Slavery, and Self-Making in Nineteenth-Century America* (New York: Oxford University Press, 1997), 116.
110. As Olaloku-Teriba explains, "Were 'black' meant as a metaphor for the condition of total alienation from self, this might make sense. However, because the Afropessimist imaginary ties itself to a morphological account of blackness, this leads us to a theoretical dead end." Annie Olaloku-Teriba, "Afro-Pessimism and the

(Un)logic of Anti-Blackness," *Historical Materialism*, 26, n. 2 (2018): 96–122, https://web.archive.org/web/20210804135211/https://www.historicalmaterialism.org/articles/afro-pessimism-and-unlogic-anti-blackness.

111. João H. Costa Vargas and Moon-Kie Jung, "Introduction: Antiblackness of the Social and the Human," in *Antiblackness*, ed. Jung and Costa Vargas, 7.
112. Frank B. Wilderson III, "Afropessimism and the Ruse of Analogy: Violence, Freedom Struggles, and the Death of Black Desire," in *Antiblackness*, ed. Jung and Costa Vargas, 39–40, 42, 50.
113. Ibid., 40.
114. Ibid., 39, 42.
115. Costa Vargas and Jung, "Introduction," 9.
116. Jesse McCarthy, "On Afropessimism."
117. Kevin Ochieng Okoth, "The Flatness of Blackness: Afro-Pessimism and the Erasure of Anti-Colonial Thought," *Salvage*, 16 January 2020, https://web.archive.org/web/20210803133012/https://salvage.zone/issue-seven/the-flatness-of-blackness-afro-pessimism-and-the-erasure-of-anti-colonial-thought/; Olaloku-Teriba, "Afro-Pessimism and the (Un)logic of Anti-Blackness."
118. Leroy, "Black History in Occupied Territory."
119. Wilderson: "the Arabs and the Jews are as much a part of the Black slave trade – the creation of Blackness as social death – as anyone else. As I told a friend of mine, 'yeah we're going to help you get rid of Israel, but the moment that you set up your shit we're going to be right there to jack you up, because anti-Blackness is as important and necessary to the formation of Arab psychic life as it is to the formation of Jewish psychic life.'" Wilderson, "'We're Trying to Destroy the World': Anti-Blackness and Police Violence after Ferguson: An Interview with Frank B. Wilderson III," 13 (available from Ill Will Editions, November 2014, https://illwilleditions.noblogs.org/files/2015/09/Wilderson-We-Are-Trying-to-Destroy-the-World-READ.pdf).
120. For example, see Mills, "The Illumination of Blackness," 23, 31, and the next chapter in this book.
121. According to Behnstedt and Woidich, this usage is prevalent in all Arab speaking areas east of Egypt, though instances of *aswad* (black) and *zinjī* (Zanj) are also attested, and the study does not note dialects like those in Kuwait and the U.A.E. where *khāl/akhwāl* (maternal uncle) is used; Behnstedt and Woidich, *Wortatlas der arabischen Dialekte*, 56–58.
122. Wilderson, "Afropessimism and the Ruse of Analogy," 55.
123. Wilderson, "'We're Trying to Destroy the World'," 8.
124. Okoth, "The Flatness of Blackness: Afro-Pessimism and the Erasure of Anti-Colonial Thought." https://data.worldbank.org/indicator/SP.POP.TOTL?end=2020&locations=ZG&start=2020.
125. Okoth, "The Flatness of Blackness: Afro-Pessimism and the Erasure of Anti-Colonial Thought."
126. Markus Vink, "'The World's Oldest Trade': Dutch Slavery and Slave Trade in the Indian Ocean in the Seventeenth Century," *Journal of World History* 14, n. 2 (2003): 136, 143–45, 169, 171; Wil O. Dijk, *Seventeenth-century Burma and the Dutch East India Company, 1634–1680* (Singapore: NIAS Press, 2006), 64, 141. See also Ananya Chakravarti, *The Konkan: Space, Mobility and Society on an Indian Ocean Coast, 1498–2019*, forthcoming, Chapter 1.
127. https://www.rijksmuseum.nl/en/stories/slavery/story/paulus-story.

128. See Wolf, "The 'Moors' of West Africa and the Beginnings of the Portuguese Slave Trade," 449.
129. Christina Bush, "Anti-Blackness," https://web.archive.org/web/20210830150204/https://subjectguides.library.american.edu/c.php?g=1025915&p=7749761; Movement for Black Lives, "Glossary," http://web.archive.org/web/20200109004008/https:/policy.m4bl.org/glossary/.
130. See how the clear black/white distinction in the U.S. differs from how 'white' and 'fair' are applied in Jamaica; Jack Alexander, "The culture of race in middle-class Kingston, Jamaica," *American Ethnologist* 4, n. 3 (1977): 417–19. And contrast with opinions about the 'race' of the Alessandro de' Medici Duke of Florence (d. 1537 CE); Catherine Fletcher, *The Black Prince of Florence* (New York: Oxford University Press, 2016), 251–60.
131. For the metaphor as opposed to the actualities of blackness, see Mark Tseng Putterman, "Against Antiblackness as Metaphor," *Reappropriate,* 19 December 2016, https://web.archive.org/web/20210830191332/https://dyv1bugovvq1g.cloudfront.net/21/reappropriate.co/2016/12/against-antiblackness-as-metaphor/.js.
132. As Jacobson succinctly describes, ". . . in the 1920s and after . . . partly in response to a new racial alchemy generated by African-American migrations to the North and West, whiteness was reconsolidated: the late nineteenth century's probationary white groups were now remade and granted the scientific stamp of authenticity as the unitary Caucasian race – an earlier era's Celts, Slavs, Hebrews, Iberics, and Saracens, among others, had become the Caucasians so familiar to our own visual economy and racial lexicon." Jacobson, *Whiteness of a Different Color,* 8.
133. Brown, *Slavery & Islam,* 387.
134. Muḥammad b. Jarīr al-Ṭabarī, *Tārīkh al-rusul wa'l-mulūk,* 6 vols. (Beirut: Dār al-Kutub al-ʿIlmiyya, 2003/1424), 5:322–324.

## 4. THE WESTERN NARRATIVE OF ISLAM, SLAVERY, AND ANTIBLACKNESS

1. Stefan Molyneux (@StefanMolyneux), "The Muslim slave trade was 200 times the American slave trade. Muslims castrated slave boys. White Christians fought to end slavery worldwide. Muslims as a whole have yet to apologize for slavery. Some Muslims still practice slavery. White guilt? Frack right off. We're done," Twitter, 30 December 2018, account removed; [Anonymous] (@TruthfulBitch6), "But what about that shadowy place?" Twitter, 19 June 2021, 4:45am, https://twitter.com/TruthfulBitch6/status/1406171254550405120.
2. Hesham Shehab and Benjamin Baird, "Islamists appropriate Black Lives Matter movement, despite history of anti-black bigotry," *Israel National News,* 20 July 2020, https://web.archive.org/web/20210706104302/https://www.israelnationalnews.com/News/News.aspx/282937.
3. https://web.archive.org/save/https://watchclub.house/detail/179368.
4. Moses E. Ochonu, "Slavery, Theology and Anti-Blackness in the Arab World," *Research Africa Reviews* 5, n. 1 (2021): 17.

5. For an Israeli public affairs officer using the term *Hasbara* unapologetically and explaining it, see Ambassador Gideon Meir, "What 'Hasbara' Is Really All About," *Israeli Ministry of Foreign Affairs*, 24 May 2005, Ihttps://web.archive.org/web/20210729194111/https://www.mfa.gov.il/mfa/abouttheministry/pages/what%20hasbara%20is%20really%20all%20about%20-%20may%202005.aspx.
6. Kwame Zulu Shabazz (@kzshabazz), "Christianity and Islam have done a thorough job of brainwashing many of our people. Its [sic] sad to see African people who cannot see spirituality outside the foreign, imperial, belligerent, intolerant Abrahamic box.," Twitter, 10 December 2020, 12:46pm, https://twitter.com/kzshabazz/status/1337091453193949184.
7. Graham Daseler, "Slavery Is Not Our Original Sin," *The American Conservative*, 10 September 2020, https://web.archive.org/web/20210728142254/https://www.theamericanconservative.com/articles/slavery-is-not-our-original-sin/.
8. The Nigerian writer Wole Soyinka implies that Islam cannot be African and that Muslim areas cannot be part of Africa. Africa is what was invaded and enslaved by both Christians and Muslims; Wole Soyinka, *The Burden of Memory, the Muse of Forgiveness* (New York: Oxford University Press, 1999), 48–9, 54.
9. Cheikh Anta Diop, *Precolonial Black Africa*, trans. Harold Salemson (Chicago: Lawrence Hill Books, 1987), 102, Chapter 8.
10. Chancellor Williams, *The Destruction of Black Civilization*, rev. ed. (Chicago: Third World Press, 1974), 23–24, 35–36, 149, 261, 355–400. See also Wole Soyinka, *The Burden of Memory*, 42, 52–54; Hisham Aïdi, "Slavery, Genocide and the Politics of Outrage: Understanding the New Racial Olympics," *Middle East Report* 234 (Spring, 2005), https://web.archive.org/web/20210621214723/https://merip.org/2005/03/slavery-genocide-and-the-politics-of-outrage/; Rasul Miller, "Is Islam an Anti-Black Religion?" *Sapelo Square*, 25 April 2017, https://web.archive.org/web/20210917142135/https://sapelosquare.com/2017/04/25/is-islam-an-anti-black-religion/. For an American conservative adopting this point, see Edward N Luttwak (@ELuttwak), "Given that the enslavement of Africans is of some contemporary interest, it is strange that Arab names are taken up by Americans with African roots, given that Arab slave-raiding was underway in Muhammad's time a millennium before North American slavery & that it lingers even now" Twitter, 6 December 2021, 2:35pm, https://twitter.com/ELuttwak/status/1467940747827716103.
11. See Goraw Z, "Dr. Clarke – Islamic_Arab Destruction of Black People Pt1[/Pt1/Pt3]," https://www.youtube.com/watch?v=akQXXDteUqg, https://www.youtube.com/watch?v=KDi38MTFaXQ, 6 June 2011, accessed 8 June 2021.
12. Molefi Asante, *The Afrocentric Idea*, rev. ed. (Philadelphia, PA: Temple University Press, 1998), 198; idem, *Kemet, Afrocentricity, and Knowledge* (Trenton, N.J.: Africa World Press, 1990).
13. https://web.archive.org/web/20210618214817/https://patch.com/new-jersey/newarknj/black-holocaust.
14. Nathaniel Mathews, personal communication and idem, "Responding to 'Hoteps': Three Points on 'Islamic' Slavery," *Sapelo Square*, 18 April 2017, https://web.archive.org/web/20210901143854/https://sapelosquare.com/2017/04/18/responding-to-hoteps-three-points-on-islamic-slavery/.
15. "Khufu Interviews Olatunji Mwamba 'Afrikan Origins of Islam'," http://raisingawarenessgroup.com/recent-articles/olatunjioriginsofislam/, 1 October 2017, accessed 8 June 2021.

16. Compare Andre Key's heuristic definition of Black Judaism as foregrounding ethnic suffering with Michael T. Miller, "Black Judaism(s) and the Hebrew Israelites," *Religion Compass* 13, n. 11 (2019): 1–10. Interestingly, one strain of Black Judaism identified Islam and Judaism as jointly Abrahamic. See Michael Muhammad Knight, *Metaphysical Africa: Truth and Blackness in the Ansaru Allah Community* (University Park, PA: Penn State University Press, 2020).
17. Andre E. Key, "Toward a Typology of Black Hebrew Religious Thought and Practice," *Journal of Africana Religions* 2, n. 1 (2014): 31–66. For examples of the beliefs and expressions, see https://mrhebrew1.com/.
18. Ali Mazrui, "Black Orientalism? Further Reflections on 'Wonders of the African World'," *The Black Scholar* 30, n. 1 (2000): 15–18.
19. Michele George, "Images of Black Slaves in the Roman Empire," *Syllecta Classica* 14 (2003): 161–85. Thanks to Ali Al-Arian for this insight.
20. https://www.slavevoyages.org/voyage/database#statistics.
21. I think this number is a ceiling for the number of people enslaved and exported. It builds on various estimates done by scholars, which are difficult to combine because they either focus on one particular vector of trade or are limited to specific time periods. Nathan Nunn has estimated that the total number for the 'Islamic' trade was 5.4 million people between 1400 and 1900. There are scholarly estimates for the Trans-Saharan trade for the whole Islamic period: between Wright's 6–7 million, Ralph Austen's 9.4 million and Raymond Mauny's 14 million people in twelve centuries (not considering Tadeusz Lewicki's absurd and baseless estimate of 12–19 million people passing through Egypt's slave markets in the sixteenth century alone). Estimates for the Indian Ocean and Red Sea trades are limited to the eighteenth–nineteenth-century window. The estimates for the slave trade out of East Africa by Ryan and Martin – about 1.3 million people between 1770 and 1896, with around 424,000 exported onward to Arabia, the Persian Gulf and India – is exaggerated according to Austen and Abdul Sheriff. Sheriff demonstrated the errors in several of Ryan's and Martin's assumptions and reports that, in the early 1800s, the annual East African slave trade consisted of between 6,000 and 12,000 people per year, rising to 13,000 in the 1840s and then to 20,000 in the 1860s as demand peaked. Austen extrapolates Sheriff's study to arrive at a total of 237,500 for the nineteenth century. Austen's own estimate, based on available data, is an export of 313,000 slaves from the Swahili coast in the nineteenth century, along with 492,000 from the Red Sea slave trade (departing from the northern Horn up to Port Sudan, then across to Arabia). Austen thus estimates a total of 805,000 for the whole East African slave trade in the nineteenth century. Though it seems irresponsible to speculate so freely, if we assume the annual number of 6,000 from the early 1800s for every year back to 700 CE onward, that extremely dubious calculus would give a total 6.2 million total slaves removed from all of East Africa during the Islamic period. Combined with the lower and higher estimates for the Trans-Saharan routes, that puts the entire Muslim slave trade from Africa (excluding slaves who remained in North Africa) at between 12.2 million and 15.6 million people; Nathan Nunn, "The Long-Term Effects of Africa's Slave Trades," *Quarterly Journal of Economics* 123, n. 1 (2008): 152; John Wright, *The Trans-Saharan Slave Trade* (London: Routledge, 2007), 22–24, 39, 167; Esmond Bradley Martin and T.C.I. Ryan, "A Quantitative Assessment of the Arab Slave Trade of East Africa, 1770–1896," *Kenya Historical Review* 5, n. 1 (1977): 71–91; Abdul Sheriff, *Slaves, Spices and Ivory in Zanzibar* (Athens, OH: Ohio University Press, 1987), 60; Ralph

A. Austen, "The 19th Century [sic] Islamic Slave Trade from East Africa (Swahili and Red Sea Coasts): A Tentative Census," *Slavery and Abolition* 9, n. 3 (1988): 29, 31, 33; Raymond Mauny, *Les siècles obscurs de l'Afrique noire* (Paris: Fayard, 1971), 240–1, 279; David Henige, "Measuring the Immeasurable: The Atlantic Slave Trade, West African Population and the Pyrrhonian Critic," *Journal of African History* 27 (1986): 301–2.

22. Cedric Robinson, *Black Marxism*, 309–10.
23. Goldenberg, *Black and Slave*, 83; William L. Westermann, *The Slave Systems of Greek and Roman Antiquity* (Philadelphia: American Philosophical Society, 1955), 135.
24. Dahlia Gubara, "Revisiting Race and Slavery through ʿAbd al-Rahman al-Jabarti's *ʿAja'ib al-athar*," *Comparative Studies of South Asia, Africa and the Middle East* 38, n. 2 (2018): 230–245.
25. See "The World's Muslims: Unity in Diversity," Pew Research Center, 9 August 2012, https://www.pewforum.org/2012/08/09/the-worlds-muslims-unity-and-diversity-executive-summary/.
26. Nathaniel Mathews, "Arab-Islamic slavery: a problematic term for a complex reality," *Research Africa Reviews* 4, n. 2 (2020): 6. Western conservatives, always eager to talk about Arab-Islamic Slavery, are equally eager to be vindicated against accusations of Orientalism. I saw this clearly in one review of my *Slavery & Islam* (2019), a book in which I argued that one could accurately speak in a limited sense of an 'Islamic Slavery,' because wherever Muslims lived the Shariah shaped the legal norms and practices of slavery to one extent or another. The reviewer, a fellow at the conservative U.S. Hoover Institution, dismisses the book's discussions of slavery in the West but seizes on the affirmation of 'Islamic slavery,' seeing this as exculpatory evidence against the accusation that AIS is merely an Orientalist invention. See Barnaby Crowcroft, "Sanctioned by Sharia?: Slavery & Islam," *Literary Review*, 28 July 2021, https://web.archive.org/web/20210728140917/https://literaryreview.co.uk/sanctioned-by-sharia. See also John J. Miller, "The Unknown Slavery: In the Muslim world, that is – and it's not over," *National Review* (20 May 2002): 41–43; Raymond Ibrahim, "Islam's Hidden Role in the Atlantic Slave Trade," *Middle East Forum*, 6 February 2020, https://web.archive.org/web/20210708222716/https://www.meforum.org/60383/islam-hidden-role-in-the-transatlantic-slave-trade.
27. Sherman Jackson, *Islam and the Blackamerican* (Oxford: Oxford University Press, 2005), 99–129.
28. Soyinka, *The Burden of Memory*, 48.
29. Souleymane Bachir Diagne, *L'encre des savants* (Dakar: CODESRIA, 2013), 16; idem, *The Ink of the Scholars: Reflections on Philosophy in Africa*, trans. Jonathan Adjemian (Dakar: Council for the Development of Social Science Research in Africa, 2016), 4–6.
30. Ousmane Kane, *Beyond Timbuktu* (Cambridge, MA: Harvard University Press, 2016), 208.
31. Mazrui, "The Re-invention of Africa," 75. Mazrui notes the linguistic and cultural proximity between Ethiopia and Arabia. I have added the other elements of comparison here. The South Arabian presence, attested by numerous epigraphic inscriptions from the first half of the first millennium BCE, may have been political, commercial, or migratory. See Fabienne Dugast and Iwona Gajda, "Reconsidering contacts between southern Arabia and the highlands of Tigrai in

the 1st millennium BC," paper presented to the 18th International Conference of Ethiopian Studies, Dire Dawa, Ethiopia, 2012.

32. Ronald Kuykendall, "Hegel and Africa: An Evaluation of the Treatment of Africa in the Philosophy of History," *Journal of Black Studies* 23, n. 4 (1993): 571–81. See also AbdulHaq al-Ashanti, *Defining Legends* (Birmingham, UK: Dar al-Arqam, 2019), 25–47.
33. Ochonu, "Slavery, Theology and Anti-Blackness in the Arab World," 17.
34. Brown, *Slavery & Islam*, 163–4.
35. David Goldenberg, *The Curse of Ham* (Princeton: Princeton University Press, 2009), 172–74, 197; idem, *Black and Slave*, 76–77; David M. Whitford, *The Curse of Ham in the Early Modern Era* (Burlington, VT: Ashgate, 2009), 25–27. De Wet shows that it was the Syriac *Cave of Treasures* (dating from between the fourth and early seventh centuries CE) that generalized the Curse to all Ham's descendants, not just to Canaan's; de Wet, *The Unbound God*, 131. See also Appendix VI.
36. Ochonu, "Slavery, Theology and Anti-Blackness in the Arab World," 12–13.
37. David Goldenberg's exhaustive research (two monographs) on the Curse of Ham leaves little doubt that the neatly comprehensive 'Curse-of-Ham-to-Slavery-and-Blackness-and-that-explains-the-African-phenotype' was refined and packaged in Islamic civilization, beginning in the Abbasid period. But his contention that Western Europe learned of this content from Islamic civilization is highly tendentious and relies on circumstantial evidence. More importantly, the components of the complete Curse of Ham package (Ham, Africa, slavery, blackness) were all manifestly known and available in Latin and Mediterranean Christendom prior to Islam. Of course, the Curse of Ham to Slavery version was present explicitly in the Old Testament, which Western Christians clearly read. The notion that Ham's descendants had populated Africa was known to Josephus (d. *circa* 100 CE), though Josephus specifically states that it was only Canaan's offspring who were cursed. The Book of Jubilees has Ham's descendants populate the hot, southern portions of the earth, while his two brothers receive the temperate middle zone and the cold north respectively. And Ham's realm aligned with what some Greco-Roman geographers, like Posidonius (d. *circa* 150 BCE), had labelled "the Ethiopic zone." Augustine seems to have combined the Greco-Roman etiology for African features (climate, heat) with descent from Ham. Indeed, Augustine claims that the name Ham derives from a word for heat. He describes Ham's descendants in highly critical terms as apart, hot, and blazing with impatience and heresy due to the curse. Gregory of Nyssa associated the Ethiopian's color with the state of sin and loss prior to baptism, and the Christian philosopher John Philoponus (d. *circa* 570 CE) of Alexandria identified Ethiopians as slaves to more northern masters. A version of Ham being punished with dark skin appears in the fourth- and fifth-century CE Talmuds, but this material does not seem to have entered the Latin Christian tradition. See Josephus, *Antiquities of the Jews*, I.6.2–3; James M. Scott, *Geography in Early Judaism and Christianity* (Cambridge: Cambridge University Press, 2002), 33; Augustine, *City of God*, Book XVI, Chapter 2; de Wet, *The Unbound God*, 129–30; Snowden, 198, 205; David Goldenberg, *Black and Slave*, 76–77, 84, 87; Whitford, *The Curse of Ham in the Early Modern Era*, 25–27.
38. Arthur Jeffery, "Ghevond's Text of the Correspondence between ʿUmar II and Leo III," *Harvard Theological Review* 37, n. 4 (1944): 325–26; Norman Daniel, *Islam and the West* (Edinburgh: Edinburgh University Press, 1960), 135–44.

39. Nabil Matar, *Turks, Moors, and Englishmen in the Age of Discovery* (New York: Columbia University Press, 1999), 181–83; Gillian Weiss, *Captives and Corsairs: France and Slavery in the Early Modern Mediterranean* (Palo Alto: Stanford University Press, 2011), 53, 131.
40. See Weiss, *Captives and Corsairs*, 139 and Appendix 1 in the book.
41. Matar, *British Captives from the Mediterranean to the Atlantic, 1563–1760* (Leiden: Brill, 2014), 193; William Gervase Clarence-Smith and David Eltis, "White Servitude," in *The Cambridge World History of Slavery, Volume 3: AD 1420–1804*, ed. David Eltis and Stanley Engerman, 132–59 (Cambridge: Cambridge University Press, 2011), 139, 144; Linda Colley, *Captives* (New York: Pantheon Books, 2002), 56–65, 99–134.
42. Paul M. Baepler, ed., *White Slaves, African Masters: An Anthology of American Barbary Captivity Narratives* (Chicago: University of Chicago Press, 1999), 147–57, 247–84.
43. Robert C. Davis, *Christian Slaves, Muslim Masters: White Slavery in the Mediterranean, the Barbary Coast, and Italy, 1500–1800* (New York: Palgrave Macmillan, 2003), 23; Sam Harris and Maajid Nawaz, *Islam and the Future of Tolerance* (Cambridge, MA: Harvard University Press, 2015), 101. John Blassingame's summary is cautious in his *The Slave Community: Plantation Life in the Antebellum South*, rev. ed. (New York: Oxford University Press, 1979), 49–50.
44. Matar, *British Captives from the Mediterranean to the Atlantic*, 9–12.
45. I based this estimate on Weiss, Appendix 1 (pp. 179–211). I rounded to the nearest thousand or to the center of the range given for every year, then I picked the mode from those years - Tunis (1535–1817): 2k in any given year; Morocco (1512–1815): 2k in any given year; Algiers (1530–1690): 20k, and Algiers (1690–1830): 1–2 k.
46. See Kim Hall, *Things of Darkness*.
47. Baepler, "The Barbary Captivity Narrative in American Culture," *Early American Literature* 39, n. 2 (2004): 219–20; Cotton Mather, "The Glory of Goodness," in *White Slaves, African Masters*, ed. Paul Baepler, 62, 66.
48. Here building on Baepler, "The Barbary Captivity Narrative," 224, 232–33. See also Francis Brooks, *Barbarian Cruelty* (London: Edmund Bohun, 1692–3), 8, 12; Troughton, *Barbarian Cruelty*, 16, 65.
49. See Weiss, *Captives and Corsairs*, 62; Fernand Braudel, *The Mediterranean: Vol. 2* (Berkeley: University of California Press, 1995, rev. ed., first published 1966), 872–86.
50. Ólafur Egilsson, *The Travels of Reverend Ólafur Egilsson*, ed. and trans. Karl Smári Hreinsson and Adam Nichols (Washington DC: Catholic University Press, 2008), xxiii–xxv. Thanks to Mohamad Ballan for this source.
51. Braudel, *The Mediterranean*, 2:867.
52. Lila Abu-Lughod, "Authorizing Moral Crusades to Save Muslim Women," Farhat Ziadeh Annual Lecture (Seattle: University of Washington, 2012), 11, 20–21; Andrew Wheatcroft, *The Ottomans: Dissolving Images* (London: Penguin, 1995), 208–30.
53. See *Lustful Turk*, letters 4, 6, 18; Weiss, *Captives and Corsairs*, 46–7, 53, 136; Matar, *Turks, Moors and Englishmen*, 118–23, 193–94. See also Steven Marcus, *The Other Victorians: A Study of Sexuality and Pornography in Mid-Nineteenth-Century England* (New York: Norton, 1974), 197–216.
54. Baepler, "The Barbary Captivity Narrative," 221–26.

55. See Appendix V.
56. Wright, *The Trans-Saharan Slave Trade*, 59–62. For growing awareness on the part of Europeans of increased slave trade into Egypt in the 1830s after Muḥammad ʿAlī's 1820 invasion of the Sudan and his state-led expansion of the slave trade to acquire military recruits, see George Michael la Rue, "African Slave Women in Egypt, ca. 1820 to the Plague of 1834–35," in *Women and Slavery*, ed. Gwyn Campbell, Suzanne Miers and Joseph C. Miller, 169–189 (Athens, OH: Ohio University Press, 2007).
57. Society for the Extinction of the Slave Trade and for the Civilization of Africa, *Abridgement of Sir T. Fowell Buxton's Work on the African Slave Trade and its Remedy* (London: John Murray, 1840), 11. Effectively reducing the place of Islam in early-modern Africa to the 'Arab' slave trade is something that even a classic tome that can hardly be called Afrocentric, Valentine Mudimbe's *The Invention of Africa*, falls into. Like Said's Orientalism, *The Invention of Africa* explores how European – and later African and European – imaginings of 'Africa' created it. Mudimbe dismisses what he considers to be an overly positive assessment of Islam by concluding that "[t]hroughout the nineteenth century in Central Africa, Islamic factions represented an objective evil and practiced a shameful slave-trade." V.Y. Mudimbe, *The Invention of Africa* (Bloomington, IN: Indiana University Press, 1988), 115. See Ali Mazrui, "The Re-invention of Africa: Edward Said, V.Y. Mudimbe, and Beyond," *Research in African Literatures* 36, n. 3 (2005): 71.
58. Ivor Wilks, *Wa and the Wala* (Cambridge: Cambridge University Press, 1989), 114.
59. Kwabena Adu-Boahen, "Abolition, Economic Transition, Gender and Slavery: The Expansion of Women's Slaveholding in Ghana, 1807–1874," *Slavery and Abolition* 31, n. 1 (2010): 117–36, especially pp. 125, 129.
60. Robin Phylisia Chapdelaine, *The Persistence of Slavery* (Amherst: University of Massachusetts Press, 2021), 17, 37; A.E. Afigbo, *The Abolition of the Slave Trade in Southeastern Nigeria*, 1885–1950 (Rochester, NY: University of Rochester Press, 2006), 115.
61. Suzanne Miers, "Britain and the Suppression of Slavery in Ethiopia," *Slavery and Abolition* 18, n. 3 (1997): 257–88.
62. Esmond B. Martin, *Zanzibar: Tradition and Revolution* (North Pomfret, VT: Hamish Hamilton, 1978), 32–33; S. von Sicard, "al-Murdjībī, Ḥamīd b. Muḥammad," *Encyclopaedia of Islam II* (Leiden: Brill, 2012); Hopper, "The African Presence in Eastern Arabia," 334–35.
63. The film is lost, sadly; https://web.archive.org/web/20210621185607/https://www.daaracarchive.org/2018/03/a-daughter-of-congo-1930–lost-film.html?m=1.
64. Jack Shaheen, *Reel Bad Arabs*, rev. ed. (Northampton, MA: Olive Branch Press, 2015), 199. See Appendix V.
65. "Is There Slavery in the Sudan?," Anti-Slavery International, March 2001, http://www.antislavery.org/wp-content/uploads/2017/01/isthereslaveryinsudanreport.pdf.
66. Amir Idris, "Historicizing Race, Ethnicity, and the Crisis of Citizenship in Sudan and South Sudan," *Middle East Journal* 73, n. 4 (2019): 595; Jok Madut Jok, "Appendix: 'They Call Us Animals,' Testimonies of Abductees and Slaves in Sudan," in *Buying Freedom: The Ethics and Economics of Slave Redemption*, ed. Kwame Anthony Appiah and Martin Bunzl (Princeton: Princeton University Press, 2007), 259–67.

67. See, for example, H.A. MacMichael, *The Tribes of Northern and Central Kordofán* (Cambridge: Cambridge University Press, 1912), 235; Mazrui, "The Black Arabs in Comparative Perspective," 72.
68. Chapdelaine, *The Persistence of Slavery*, 168–69.
69. Alex de Waal, "Counter-Insurgency on the Cheap," *London Review of Books* 16, n. 5 (5 August 2004), https://web.archive.org/web/20210622191836/https://www.lrb.co.uk/the-paper/v26/n15/alex-de-waal/counter-insurgency-on-the-cheap, last accessed 22 June 2021.
70. Declan Walsh, "The great slave scam," *The Irish Times*, 23 February 2002, https://web.archive.org/web/20210621213644/https://www.irishtimes.com/news/the-great-slave-scam-1.1051560, last seen 21 June 2021; Melani McAlister, *The Kingdom of God Has No Borders: A Global History of American Evangelicals* (Oxford: Oxford University Press, 2018), 187–88. See also Jok, *War and Slavery in Sudan* (Philadelphia: University of Pennsylvania Press, 2001), 173–76.
71. See, for example, Bulama Bukarti, "Nigeria's school kidnapping crisis is even worse than you think," *Washington Post*, 9 June 2021, https://www.washingtonpost.com/opinions/2021/06/09/nigerias-school-kidnapping-crisis-is-even-worse-than-you-think/.
72. Marjorie Rosen, "The Man Who Would Be Caine," *Film Comment* 16, n. 4 (1980): 20; Jack Shaheen, "'*Ashanti*': The Arab as Black-Slaver," *Middle East Perspective* 12, n. 8 (1979): 4–5; Michael Caine, *Elephant to Hollywood* (New York: Henry Holt, 2010), 161. This star-studded cast seems to have been arranged mostly by the Swiss producer George-Alain Vuille's cajoling. See Fraser, *Light's on at Signpost*, 198, 205.
73. Oddly, Ustinov's 1977 memoir, which predates *Ashanti*, displays an admirable concern for the Palestinian cause. The actor, despite being of Jewish ancestry, was evidently accused of antisemitism for this. See Peter Ustinov, *Dear Me* (Boston: Little, Brown & Co., 1977), 349–51.
74. In 2003, for example, the American Jewish Committee issued an announcement that Steven Emerson's book *Jihad in America* was "a must read" and publicly supported the nomination of Daniel Pipes to the U.S. Institute of Peace Board of Directors. See https://web.archive.org/web/20210809214816/https://www.splcenter.org/fighting-hate/extremist-files/group/center-security-policy; https://web.archive.org/web/20210809215337/https://hwpi.harvard.edu/pluralism archive/news/update-american-jewish-committee-urges-approval-daniel-pipes. See Nathan Lean, *The Islamophobia Industry*, 2nd ed. (London: Pluto Press, 2017), 140–162; Christopher Bail, *Terrified: How Anti-Muslim Fringe Organizations Became Mainstream* (Princeton: Princeton University Press, 2014), 69; Elly Bulkin and Donna Nevel, "Follow the Money: From Islamophobia to Israel Right or Wrong," *Alternet*, 3 October 2012, https://web.archive.org/web/20210705214100/https://www.alternet.org/2012/10/follow-money-islamophobia-israel-right-or-wrong/; M.J. Rosenberg, "Inside Story: Why ADL is Opposing Ground Zero Mosque," *Huffington Post*, 31 July 2010, https://web.archive.org/web/20210705214626/https://www.huffpost.com/entry/inside-story-why-adl-is-o_b_666281; Richard Silverstein, "Jewish Foundations Support Islamophobia at Home, Settler Triumphalism Abroad," *Tikun Olam*, 5 January 2013, https://web.archive.org/web/20210705215618/https://www.richardsilverstein.com/2013/01/05/jewish-foundations-support-islamophobia-at-home-settler-extremism-abroad/; Max Blumenthal, "The Sugar Mama of Anti-Muslim Hate," *The Nation*,

14 June 2012, https://web.archive.org/web/20210706191219/https://www.thenation.com/article/archive/sugar-mama-anti-muslim-hate/; Matthew Duss, "Some Zionist Groups Stoke Fear Of Islam for Political Profit," *Forward*, 22 September 2010, https://web.archive.org/web/20210706190322/https://forward.com/articles/131502/some-zionist-groups-stoke-fear-of-islam-for-politi/; Wajahat Ali et al., *Fear Inc.: The Roots of the Islamophobia Network in America* (Washington DC: Center for American Progress, 2011). Examples of the funding nexus between the Pro-Israel universe and Islamophobia in the U.S. are legion, as documented by the Center for American Progress's Fear Inc. report and by Alternet. One is the Newton D. & Rochelle F. Becker Foundation, a philanthropic organization founded to "combat media bias against Israel" but which has donated to the most pernicious Islamophobic organizations, including the Investigative Project on Terrorism, the Counterterrorism & Security Education and Research Foundation, Middle East Forum, the Center for Security Policy, the Clarion Fund, the David Horowitz Freedom Center, and Act! For America (see *Fear Inc.*, 19–20). Examples of the nexus of people and activities are similarly numerous. One identified by Nathan Lean shows Islamophobia and vehement support for Israel comingling so gratuitously that a political strategy linking the two is the only conceivable explanation. David Yerushalmi, an Islamophobic American-Israeli dual national who has devoted himself to passing laws against 'Shariah' in the U.S., produced a report entitled "Shariah: The Threat to America" for a pro-Israel organization. At a 2011 event at the National Press Club, titled "Israel: You are Not Alone," Frank Gaffney, a leading Islamophobe and committed supporter of Israel, and Jerry Boykin, a former U.S. general and extreme Christian Zionist, held up Yerushalmi's report while emphasizing the importance of the integrity of Israel's borders. What relation does 'Shariah' in the U.S. have to Israel's security? Similarly, in 2008, after leading Zionist organizations had funded the production and mass distribution of an intensely Islamophobic 'documentary' entitled *Obsession: Radical Islam's War against the West* (2007), a screening of the film in New York required attendees to register at Israeliactivism.com; Lean, *The Islamophobia Industry*, 140–162.

75. See Remi Brulin, "Le discours américain sur le terrorisme: Constitution, evolution et contextes d'enonciation (1972–1992)," (PhD dissertation, Université de la Sorbonne Nouvelle, 2011), 80–91, 151–160; Lean, 144.
76. Lean, 144.
77. The report (#1064), written by Shoshana Bryen, has since been removed but is partially available at https://web.archive.org/web/20210705201957/https://calevbenyefuneh.blogspot.com/2011/02/disconnect-part-iii-west.html.
78. James A. Michener, "*Roots*," *New York Times*, 27 February 1977, https://www.nytimes.com/1977/02/27/archives/roots-unique-in-its-time-the-guest-word.html; idem, "Israel and the Arabs," *New York Review*, 28 September 1967, https://web.archive.org/web/20210705071136/https://www.nybooks.com/articles/1967/09/28/israel-and-the-arabs-1/. My attention was drawn to Michener's review by Manning Maribel and Hisham Aidi, eds., *Black Routes to Islam* (New York: Palgrave Macmillan, 2009).
79. See https://bridge.georgetown.edu/research/factsheet-middle-east-forum/.
80. Daniel Pipes and Khaled Duran, "Muslims in the West: Can Conflict be Averted?," *danielpipes.org*, August 1993, https://web.archive.org/web/20210706194540/http://www.danielpipes.org/232/muslims-in-the-west-can-conflict-be-averted.

81. See John J. Miller, "The Unknown Slavery: In the Muslim world, that is – and it's not over," *National Review* (20 May 2002): 41–43; Raymond Ibrahim, "Islam's Hidden Role in the Atlantic Slave Trade," *Middle East Forum*, 6 February 2020, https://web.archive.org/web/20210708222716/https://www.meforum.org/60383/islam-hidden-role-in-the-transatlantic-slave-trade.
82. https://www.jns.org/the-david-project-becomes-hillel-us-center-for-community-outreach/, http://www.iabolish.com/aasg/history.html, https://www.camera.org/.
83. International Labour Organization and Walk Free Foundation, *Global Estimates of Modern Slavery* (Geneva: International Labour Organization, 2017), 26–27.
84. "Modern slavery: Everywhere in (supply) chains," *Economist*, 14 March 2015, https://www.economist.com/international/2015/03/12/everywhere-in-supply-chains.
85. Yotam Gidron, *Israel in Africa* (London: Zed Books, 2020), 35 (thanks to Alden Young for alerting me to this source). The issue of opposition to versus relations with Israel had already emerged as a point of disagreement between the Egyptian president Abd al-Nasser and some sub-Saharan African leaders, for example, of Cameroon, in 1963; Harry B. Ellis, "The Arab-Israeli Conflict Today," in *The United States and the Middle East*, ed. Georgiana Stevens (Englewood Cliffs, NJ: Prentice-Hall, 1964), 113–14.
86. Michael B. Bishku, "Israel and South Sudan: A Convergence of Interests," *Middle East Policy* 26, n. 4 (2019): 41–43.
87. Jok, "Slavery and Slave Redemption in the Sudan," in *Buying Freedom: The Ethics and Economics of Slave Redemption*, ed. Appiah and Bunzl, 143, 146.
88. McAlister, *The Kingdom of God Has No Borders*, 185–86; "Simon Deng, Former Sudanese Slave, Human Rights Advocate," International Humanist and Ethical Union, 21 June 2005, https://web.archive.org/web/20071027094709/http://www.iheu.org/node/1539.
89. Some other points made by Jacobs: his main concern has been "jihad slavery"; in Mauretania slaves are tortured for "breaking a dish," while in the American South slaves were just "called uppity"; in Mauretania, Arabs/Berbers forcibly converted Black Africans to Islam. It is interesting that Jacobs seems to suggest that another large African country with a huge Muslim plurality, Nigeria, could face a fate similar to Sudan's. He stresses that the Fulani tribes in Nigeria are raiding and enslaving blacks in what he believes is becoming a new Sudan situation; "IBSI Online featuring Charles Jacobs," FacebookLive, 7 July 2021, https://web.archive.org/web/20210708225925/https://www.facebook.com/login/?next=https%3A%2F%2Fwww.facebook.com%2FIBSInow%2Fvideos%2F891021165091067%2F%3Fextid%3DNS-UNK-UNK-UNK-IOS_GK0T-GK1C.
90. McAlister, *The Kingdom of God Has No Borders*, 175–94.
91. Armin Rosen, "Birth of a Nation: with American Evangelicals on the ground in South Sudan," *The Weekly Standard* 17, n. 24 (21 May 2012).
92. Dunstan Wai, *The African-Arab Conflict in the Sudan* (New York: Africana Publishing, 1981), 1, 16–20; idem, "Introduction," in *The Southern Sudan: The Problem of National Integration*, ed. Dunston M. Wai (London: Frank Cass, 1973), 1.
93. Albino Deng Ajuok, "Response of Southern Sudanese Intellectuals to African Nationalism," *Journal of Pan African Studies* 2, n. 5 (2008): 131.
94. Sam Kestenbaum, "Watch: Black Zionist Slams Pro-Palestinian Group – Cites Arab Slave Trade," *Forward*, 14 July 2016, https://web.archive.org/web/

20210708223303/https://forward.com/news/344932/watch-black-zionist-slams-pro-palestinian-group-cites-arab-slave-trade/. See also Chloe Valdary, "To the Students for Justice in Palestine, a Letter from an Angry Black Woman," *Tablet*, 28 July 2014, https://web.archive.org/web/20210830175432/https://www.tabletmag.com/sections/news/articles/students-justice-palestine.

95. Clyde Zemir, "Marc Lamont Hill's one-sided view on racism in the Middle East," *Jerusalem Post*, 17 March 2017, https://web.archive.org/web/20210708220219/https://www.jpost.com/blogs/israel-palestine-my-thoughts/-483236; idem, "Marc Lamont Hill's Curious Hypocrisy on racism in the Middle East," *Times of Israel*, 4 March 2017, https://web.archive.org/web/20210708222013/https://blogs.timesofisrael.com/marc-lamont-hills-curious-hypocrisy-on-racism-in-the-middle-east/.
96. Raymond Ibrahim, "Islam's Hidden Role in the Atlantic Slave Trade," *Middle East Forum*, 6 February 2020, https://web.archive.org/web/20210708222716/https://www.meforum.org/60383/islam-hidden-role-in-the-transatlantic-slave-trade.
97. Baepler, "The Barbary Captivity Narrative in American Culture," 240.
98. Aisha Ahmad, "'We Have Captured Your Women': Explaining Jihadist Norm Change," *International Security* 44, n. 1 (2019): 80.
99. Thomas Hedghammer, *The Caravan: Abdallah Azzam and the Rise of Global Jihad* (Cambridge: Cambridge University Press, 2020), 307.
100. Ahmad, "'We Have Captured Your Women': Explaining Jihadist Norm Change," 105–7.
101. The conclusion in this sentence is my own, extrapolating from the source cited here. See Bulama Bukarti, "Nigeria's school kidnapping crisis is even worse than you think," *Washington Post*, 9 June 2021, https://www.washingtonpost.com/opinions/2021/06/09/nigerias-school-kidnapping-crisis-is-even-worse-than-you-think/.
102. William McCants, *The ISIS Apocalypse* (New York: St. Martin's Press, 2015), 111–15.
103. See Hassan Hassan, "Isis has reached new depths of depravity. But there is a brutal logic behind it," *The Guardian*, 7 February 2015, https://web.archive.org/web/20210621213444/https://www.theguardian.com/world/2015/feb/08/isis-islamic-state-ideology-sharia-syria-iraq-jordan-pilot, last accessed 21 June 2021.

## 5. THE PROPHET, ARABIA, AND THE RISE OF ANTIBLACKNESS

1. Ibn ʿAbd al-Ḥakam, *Futūḥ Miṣr wa'l-maghrib*, ed. Charles Torrey (Cairo: al-Hay'a al-ʿĀmma li'l-Thaqāfa, [1999], reprint of Yale edition), 66.
2. Muḥammad b. Aḥmad al-Qurṭubī, *al-Jāmiʿ li-aḥkām al-Qur'ān*, ed. Muḥammad Ibrāhīm al-Ḥifnāwī and Maḥmūd Ḥamīd ʿUthmān, 20 vols. (Cairo: Dār al-Ḥadīth, 1994), 8:605. For an early report about Bilāl being called a black crow, see *Tafsīr Muqātil b. Sulaymān*, ed. ʿAbdallāh Maḥmūd Shaḥḥāta, 5 vols. (Beirut: Dār Iḥyā' al-Turāth al-ʿArabī, 1423/2002), 4:97. For the report about the Prophet stating that Adam was created from dust, see *Jāmiʿ al-Tirmidhī: kitāb tafsīr al-Qur'ān, bāb min sūrat al-ḥujurāt.*

3. *Sunan* of Abū Dāwūd: *kitāb al-sunna, bāb fī al-qadar*; *Jāmiʿ al-Tirmidhī*: *kitāb al-tafsīr, bāb min sūrat al-baqara*. Al-Tirmidhī rates the Hadith *ḥasan ṣaḥīḥ*. Al-Albānī and Shuʿayb al-Arnā'ūṭ judge it *ṣaḥīḥ*. Al-Suyūṭī judges it *ṣaḥīḥ* and sees it as the basis for understanding variations in human phenotypes; Jalāl al-Dīn al-Suyūṭī, *Rafʿ sha'n al-ḥubshān*, ed. Muḥammad ʿAbd al-Wahhāb Faḍl (Cairo: self-published, 1411/1991), 371. See also Muḥammad Nāṣir al-Dīn al-Albānī, *Silsilat al-aḥādīth al-ṣaḥīḥa*, 7 vols. (Riyadh: Maktabat al-Maʿārif, 1995–2002), 4:172 (#1630); Shuʿayb al-Arnā'ūṭ et al., ed., *Musnad al-imām Aḥmad Ibn Ḥanbal*, 50 vols. (Beirut: Mu'assasat al-Risāla, 1416/1995–1421/2001), 32:353–54, 413.
4. *Ṣaḥīḥ Muslim*: *kitāb al-dhikr wa'l-duʿā' wa'l-tawba . . .*; *bāb faḍl al-ijtimāʿ ʿalā tilāwat al-Qur'ān . . .*
5. *Ṣaḥīḥ al-Bukhārī*: *kitāb al-janā'iz, bāb al-ṣalāt ʿalā al-qabr baʿd mā dufina*; *Ṣaḥīḥ Muslim*: *kitāb al-janā'iz, bāb al-ṣalāt ʿalā al-qabr*.
6. Abū Bakr Ibn al-ʿArabī, *ʿĀriḍat al-aḥwadhī*, 13 vols. (Beirut: Dār al-Kutub al-ʿIlmiyya, n.d.), 12:158–9. The *isnād* given by Ibn al-ʿArabī for this report goes from Ibn Wahb ← Mālik ←(*ʿan*) Dāwūd b. Qays ← (*ʿan*) Zayd b. Aslam.
7. Abū Bakr al-Bayhaqī, *Shuʿab al-īmān*, ed. Muḥammad Saʿīd Zaghlūl, 7 vols. (Beirut: Dār al-Kutub al-ʿIlmiyya, 1990), 4:288; Ibn ʿAsākir, *Tārīkh madīnat Dimashq*, ed. ʿUmar ʿAmrawī, 80 vols. (Beirut: Dār al-Fikr, 1995–1997), 10:464.
8. *Musnad* of Aḥmad Ibn Ḥanbal (Maymaniyya printing), 5:411. In another Hadith, the Prophet rebukes a man for insulting someone's lineage by saying, "By Him who holds my soul in His hand, you are no better than anyone you see among the red or black unless you best them in piety"; Ibn Ḥanbal, *Kitāb al-Zuhd*, 322.
9. *Ṣaḥīḥ al-Bukhārī*: *kitāb al-adab, bāb mā yunhā min al-sibāb wa'l-laʿn*. Though some scholars, including Ibn Ḥajar, have suggested that the person whom Abū Dharr insulted was Bilāl, this is not actually mentioned in any narration of this particular Hadith. There is a unique narration provided by the Andalusian scholar Ibn Baṭṭāl (d. 449/1057) that does identify the person as Bilāl and that Abū Dharr had denigrated his mother's blackness (*sawād*). Another, different and much weaker Hadith also mentions an occasion on which Bilāl was insulted and includes the Prophet's remarks about how race has no meaning when compared to faith and merit. It appears in the works of al-Bayhaqī and Ibn ʿAsākir; Ibn Baṭṭāl, *Sharḥ Ṣaḥīḥ al-Bukhārī*, ed. Abū Tamīm Yāsir Ibrāhīm, 10 vols. (Riyadh: Maktabat al-Rushd, 1423/2003), 1:87; al-Bayhaqī, *Shuʿab al-īmān*, 4:288; Ibn ʿAsākir, *Tārīkh madīnat Dimashq*, 10:464. It is interesting that Abū Dharr was described as being "black" or "of a dark-brown tone"; al-Ṭabarī, *The History of al-Ṭabarī: Vol. 39: Biographies of the Prophet's Companions and their Successors*, trans. Ella Landau-Tasseron (Albany: State University of New York Press, 1998), 69–70.
10. University of Leeds, "Black Lives Matter: Bilal and the Formation of the Early Islamicate," 12 April 2017, https://www.youtube.com/watch?v=wIlQ8AdB9wM, last accessed 4 August 2021.
11. See, for example, U.S. companies debating language that draws on the black-bad/white-good metaphor "'Whitelist,' 'Blacklist': The New Debate Over Security Terminology," *Dice*, 17 July 2020, https://web.archive.org/web/20210911165248/https://insights.dice.com/2020/07/17/whitelist-blacklist-the-new-debate-over-security-terminology/.
12. Hishām Ibn al-Kalbī, *Jamharat al-nasab*, ed. Nājī Ḥasan (Beirut: ʿĀlam al-Kutub, 1407/1986), 52, 94; Ibn Saʿd, *al-Juz' al-mutammam li-ṭabaqāt Ibn Saʿd al-ṭabaqa al-rābiʿa min al-ṣaḥāba*, ed. ʿAbd al-ʿAzīz ʿAbdallāh al-Sullūmī (Taif: Maktabat al-

Ṣiddīq, 1416/1996), 282, 423; ʿAbd al-Razzāq al-Ṣanʿānī, *Muṣannaf*, ed. Ḥabīb al-Raḥmān al-Aʿẓamī, 11 vols. (Beirut: al-Maktab al-Islāmī, 1403/1983), 7:72, 133. According to Ibn Saʿd, the mother of Muḥammad b. al-Ḥanafiyya (d. 81/701) was either an Arab woman captured from the enemy Ḥanīf tribe at the Battle of Yamāma or a "black, Sindī woman" who was a slave of that tribe taken as a prize; Ibn Saʿd, *al-Ṭabaqāt al-kubrā*, ed. Iḥsān ʿAbbās, 8 vols. (Beirut: Dār Ṣādir, 1968), 5:91.

13. Al-Ṣanʿānī, *Muṣannaf*, 4:57; Muḥammad b. ʿUmar al-Wāqidī, *Maghāzī*, ed. Marsden Jones (Beirut: Dār al-Aʿlamī, 1409/1989), 2:681.
14. *Muwaṭṭa'*: *kitāb al-ʿitq wa'l-walā', bāb mā yajūzu min al-ʿitq fī al-riqāb al-wājiba.*
15. Al-Ṭabarī, *Tārīkh*, 2:384.
16. Al-Dhahabī, *Siyar*, 3:56; al-Masʿūdī, *Murūj al-dhahab*, ed. Kamāl Ḥasan Marʿī, 4 vols. (Beirut: al-Maktaba al-ʿAṣriyya, 1425/2005), 2:241; Ibn ʿAbd al-Barr, *al-Istīʿāb fī maʿrifat al-aṣḥāb*, ed. ʿAlī Muḥammad al-Bijāwī, 4 vols. (Beirut: Dār al-Jīl, 1412/1992), 3:1184; al-Suyūṭī, *Rafʿ sha'n al-ḥubshān*, 373. A report in al-Ṭabarī's *History* describes ʿUmar as *ādam* ('dark'), another as "an unhealthy white" (*abyaḍ amhaq*), another as white with a reddish hue; al-Ṭabarī, *Tārīkh*, 2:562.
17. *Ṣaḥīḥ al-Bukhārī*: *kitāb al-ṭalāq, bāb al-talāʿun fī al-masjid*; al-Ṣanʿānī, *Muṣannaf*, 7:136, 166; *Sunan* of Abū Dāwūd: *kitāb al-ṭalāq, bāb al-walad li'l-firāsh.* The freeman literally describes his wife's child as white "as a leper" (*al-wazagha*). I have rendered it as vitiligo here because 1) no one has been able to communicate exactly what this sort of leprosy (*baraṣ*) looks like; 2) it has often been rendered as vitiligo; and 3) present-day readers would see no link to whiteness in a mention of leprosy. See Matthew L. Long, "Leprosy in Islam," in *Disability in Judaism, Christianity, and Islam*, ed., Darla Schumm and Michael Stoltzfus (London: Palgrave Macmillan, 2011), 43–61. Thanks to Tesneem Alkiek for this source.
18. See, for example, Igor Kopytoff and Suzanne Miers, "African 'Slavery' as an Institution of Marginality," in *Slavery in Africa*, ed. Miers and Kopytoff (Madison: University of Wisconsin Press, 1977), 8–84.
19. Hend Gilli-Elewy, "On the Provenance of Slaves in Mecca during the Time of the Prophet Muhammad," *Intl. Journal of Middle East Studies* 49, n. 1 (2017): 164–67; Noel Lenski, "Captivity and Slavery among the Saracens in Late Antiquity (Ca. 250–630 CE)," *AnTard* 19 (2011): 248, 259.
20. See al-Ṭabarī, *Tārīkh*, 2:216–18; Ibn Saʿd, *Ṭabaqāt*, 1:496–98.
21. Al-Ṭabarī, *Jāmiʿ al-bayān li-āy al-Qur'ān*, ed. Aḥmad Shākir, 24 vols. (Beirut: Mu'assasat al-Risāla, 1420/2000), 9:59; Muqātil b. Sulaymān, *Tafsīr Muqātil b. Sulaymān*, 2:583.
22. Ṣuhayb (d. 38–9/658–9), a slave from northern Syria who was later freed, was "very red." Khabbāb b. al-Aratt (d. 37/657–8) was an Arab of the Tamīm tribe who was a sword maker and had been captured and enslaved; Ibn Ḥajar, *al-Iṣāba fī tamyīz al-ṣaḥāba*, ed. ʿĀdil Aḥmad ʿAbd al-Mawjūd and ʿAlī Aḥmad Muʿawwaḍ, 8 vols. (Beirut: Dār al-Kutub al-ʿIlmiyya, 1415/1994), 3:65, 2:221–2. Slaves made up the bulk of the first converts to Islam. As ʿAmmār recalled, "I saw the Messenger of God, and there was no one with him except five slaves, two women and Abū Bakr"; *Ṣaḥīḥ al-Bukhārī*: *kitāb faḍā'il aṣḥāb al-nabī, bāb* 6.
23. Abū Nuʿaym al-Iṣbahānī, *Ḥilyat al-awliyā'*, 1:186–7, 200.
24. Ibn ʿAbd al-Barr, *al-Istīʿāb fī maʿrifat al-aṣḥāb*, 2:134.
25. Ibn Qutayba, *al-Shiʿr wa'l-shuʿarā'*, 2 vols. (Cairo: Dār al-Ḥadīth, 1423/2002), 1:243.

26. Al-Dhahabī, *Siyar*, 3:56; al-Masʿūdī, *Murūj al-dhahab*, 2:241; Ibn ʿAbd al-Barr, *al-Istīʿāb fī maʿrifat al-aṣḥāb*, 3:1184; al-Suyūṭī, *Rafʿ sha'n al-ḥubshān*, 373. A report in al-Ṭabarī's *History* describes ʿUmar as *ādam* (dark), another as "white and unhealthy" (*abyaḍ amhaq*), another as white with a reddish hue; al-Ṭabarī, *Tārīkh*, 2:562.
27. Ibn Sallām al-Jumaḥī, *Ṭabaqāt fuḥūl al-shuʿarā'*, ed. Maḥmūd Shākir ([Cairo]: Dār al-Madanī, [n.d.]), 1:199–200.
28. Ibn Saʿd, *Ṭabaqāt*, 4:64. Al-Bukhārī notes a version in which ʿUrwa (d. 93/711–2) provides the explanation; al-Bukhārī, *al-Tārīkh al-kabīr*, ed. Muṣṭafā ʿAbd al-Qādir ʿAṭā, 9 vols. (Beirut: Dār al-Kutub al-ʿIlmiyya, 1422/2001), 2:17.
29. Al-Dhahabī, *Siyar* 1:228; *Musnad Aḥmad*, 6:281.
30. In one famous Hadith the Prophet doted on the young Usāma and said that, if he were a girl, he would dress her up, ornament her and find her a husband; *Sunan Ibn Mājah: kitāb al-nikāḥ, bāb al-shafāʿa fī al-tazwīj*; *Musnad Aḥmad*, 6:222.
31. In a well-known Hadith, the Prophet expresses his disapproval of people second-guessing his putting Zayd and Usāma in charge of campaigns when more senior Companions were present; *Ṣaḥīḥ al-Bukhārī*: *kitāb al-maghāzī, bāb ghazwat Zayd b. Ḥāritha*; *Ṣaḥīḥ Muslim*: *kitāb faḍā'il al-ṣaḥāba, bāb faḍā'il Zayd b. Ḥāritha . . .*
32. Al-Dhahabī favors the report that Zayd was light colored and his son dark, since there were reliable reports that the two looked nothing alike; al-Dhahabī, *Siyar*, 1:222–3. See also *Sunan* of Abū Dāwūd: *kitāb al-ṭalāq, bāb fī al-qāfa*.
33. There is a unique version of the Hadith mentioned above about the Prophet talking about marrying off Usāma. In this version, a black (*aswad*) son of Usāma enters in upon the Prophet (s), and Umm Salama (allegedly) says that, if he were a girl, he would never get married; al-Wāqidī, *Maghāzī*, 3:125.
34. See Sean Anthony, *The Caliph and the Heretic* (Leiden: Brill, 2011), 65, 73.
35. A.R. al-Ansary, *Qaryat al-Fau: A Portrait of Pre-Islamic Civilisation in Saudi Arabia* (Toledo: Artes Graficas, [1982]), 27, 135–37.
36. Nicolai Sinai, "When did the consonantal skeleton of the Quran reach closure? Part II," *Bulletin of the School of Oriental and African Studies* 77, n. 3 (2014): 509–21; Jonathan Brockopp, "Islamic Origins and Incidental Normativity," *Journal of the American Academy of Religion* 84, n. 1 (2016): 28–43.
37. In the early *Tafsīr* of Muqātil b. Sulaymān, the language of whitening and blackening of faces is passed over as obvious; Muqātil b. Sulaymān, *Tafsīr*, 1:187, 294. Although I cannot provide any clear date for when this story was circulating (prior to 150/767), Muqātil b. Sulaymān and al-Ṭabarī provide a report attributed to the Prophet that the people of Thamūd, after they hamstrung God's camel, were warned of their impending doom by their faces first turning yellow as if they were painted, then red as if they were covered with blood, then black (*muswadda*) as if they were covered with pitch; al-Ṭabarī, *Tārīkh*, 1:140; Muqātil, *Tafsīr*, 4:713.
38. Al-Jāḥiẓ, *Rasā'il al-Jāḥiẓ*, ed. ʿAbd al-Salām Hārūn, 4 vols. (Cairo: Maktabat al-Khānjī, 1384/1964), 1:207.
39. Abdullah bin Hamid Ali, *The 'Negro' in Arab-Muslim Consciousness* (Swansea, UK: Claritas, 2018), 39. Two Hadith narrations are interesting in this regard, showing that 'redness' was not somehow more praiseworthy than a darker tone. Ibn ʿUmar corrected another companion who quoted the Prophet describing Jesus as 'red'; he was actually dark in tone (*ādam*); *Ṣaḥīḥ al-Bukhārī*: *kitāb aḥādīth al-anbiyā', bāb wa'dhkur fī al-kitāb Maryam . . .*

40. Interestingly, the ancient Egyptian and Coptic words for red (*mrš*, etc., Coptic *mroš*) seem to have been understood as the Arabic *ashqar* (fair, ruddy); Wolfgang Schenkel, "Color terms in ancient Egyptian and Coptic," 223.
41. This Iraqi scholar was Ibrāhīm al-Ḥarbī (d. 285/898); al-Dhahabī, *Siyar*, 8:178.
42. Al-Dhahabī adds that, to denote the darker brown "color of Indians," Arabs would use "brown" (*asmar*) and "dark brown" (*ādam*). "Black" (*aswad*) meant the color of sub-Saharan Africans or a similar color; al-Dhahabī, *Siyar a'lām al-nubalā'*, 2:168. As Ahmad Mubarak and Dawud Walid have shown, when early Arabs described someone as black (*aswad*) or very dark (*ādam*), this did not necessarily mean they were Black African or even that they had any African ancestry; Ahmad Mubarak and Dawud Walid, *Centering Black Narrative: Black Muslim Nobles among the Early Pious Muslims* (USA: Itrah Press, 2016), 25–26.
43. *Sunan* of Abū Dāwūd: *kitāb al-ṣalāt, bāb mā yujzi'u al-ummī wa'l-'ajamī min al-qirā'a*. See also Ibn Sa'd, *al-Ṭabaqāt al-kubrā*, 1:41.
44. Mubarrad (d. 286/900) of Baghdad said the *'ajam* were seen as red by Arabs, and the Arabs saw themselves as black; Muḥammad b. Yazīd al-Mubarrad, *al-Kāmil*, ed. Muḥammad Abū al-Faḍl Ibrāhīm, 4 vols. (Cairo: Dār al-Fikr al-'Arabī, 1417/1997), 2:94; Ibn Manẓūr, *Lisān al-'Arab*, 15 vols. (Beirut: Dār Ṣādir, 1414/1994), 13:431. Al-Jāḥiẓ insists that Arabs considered themselves among the 'blacks,' not 'red.' Al-Nawawī seems to favor this as well because "of the preponderance of brownness (*sumra*)" among Arabs, but he also notes opinions to the contrary; al-Jāḥiẓ, *Rasā'il*, 1:216; al-Nawawī, *Sharḥ Ṣaḥīḥ Muslim*, 15 vols. (Beirut: Dār al-Qalam, 1987), 5:7–8.
45. Al-Mas'ūdī, *Kitāb al-Tanbīh wa'l-ashrāf*, ed. 'Abdallāh Ismā'īl al-Ṣāwī (Cairo: Dār al-Ṣāwī, 1357/1938), 22; Ibn Faḍlān, *Kitāb Risālat Ibn Faḍlān* (Abu Dhabi: Dār al-Suwaydī, 2003), 101. It is interesting that, on the other end of the spectrum of human phenotype, in modern Sudanese Arabic, blue (*azraq*) is often used to describe the extremely, perhaps uniquely, dark skin tone of some Nilotic people (Europeans have used the same adjective); M. Lionel Bender, "Color Term Encoding in a Special Lexical Domain: Sudanese Arabic Skin Colors," *Anthropological Linguistics* 25, n. 1 (1983): 24.
46. Quoted in Ibn al-Faqīh (d. *circa* 290/900), *Kitāb al-Buldān*, ed. Yūsuf al-Hādī (Beirut: 'Ālam al-Kutub, 1416/1996), 199.
47. Quoted in Ibn Faḍlallāh al-'Umarī, *Masālik al-abṣār fī mamālik al-amṣār*, ed. Kāmil Salmān al-Jubūrī (Beirut: Dār al-Kutub al-'Ilmiyya, 2010), 3:153.
48. See the number of narrations on the lunar or solar light of the Prophet's face; al-Suyūṭī, *al-Khaṣā'iṣ al-kubrā*, 2 vols. (Beirut: Dār al-Kitāb al-'Arabī, reprint of the 1320/1902 Hyderabad Dā'irat al-Ma'ārif al-'Uthmāniyya edition), 1:71–77.
49. *Ṣaḥīḥ Muslim*: *kitāb al-faḍā'il, bāb kāna al-Nabī abyaḍ*. See also Ibn Sa'd, *Ṭabaqāt*, 1:411–3; al-Ṭabarī, *Tārīkh*, 2:221–22.
50. *Jāmi' al-Tirmidhī*: *kitāb al-manāqib 'an rasūl Allāh, bāb mā jā'a fī ṣifat al-nabī* (s); *kitāb al-libās, bāb mā jā'a fī al-jumma wa ittikhādh al-sha'ar*; al-Ṭabarī, *Tārīkh*, 2:221.
51. *Ṣaḥīḥ al-Bukhārī*: *kitāb al-manāqib, bāb ṣifat al-Nabī* (s); al-Ṭabarī, *Tārīkh*, 2:221. See also al-Khaṭṭābī, *Gharīb al-ḥadīth*, ed. 'Abd al-Karīm Ibrāhīm al-Gharbāwī, 3 vols. (Damascus: Dār al-Fikr, 1402/1982), 1:214. Al-Qasṭallānī concludes that the great majority (*jumhūr*) of the Companions described "his luminous color" as white (*bayāḍ*); Shihāb al-Dīn al-Qasṭallānī, *al-Mawāhib al-ladunniyya*, 3 vols. (Cairo: al-Maktaba al-Tawfīqiyya, n.d.), 2:85. Ibn Nāṣir al-Dīn al-Dimashqī (d. 842

/1438) concludes that his skin that was exposed to the elements was *abyaḍ* with a reddish hue, while his skin under his clothing was *abyaḍ azhar*; Ibn Nāṣir al-Dīn, *Jāmiʿ al-āthār fī al-siyar wa mawlid al-mukhtār*, ed. Abū Yaʿqūb Nash'at Kamāl, 8 vols. (Qatar: Awqāf; and Fayyoum: Dār al-Falāḥ, 1431/2010), 4:394–400, and pp. 360–400 for a more extensive list of reports. This was seconded by Murtaḍā al-Zabīdī (d. 1205/1791); al-Zabīdī, *Itḥāf al-sāda al-muttaqīn sharḥ Iḥyā' ʿulūm al-dīn*, 10 vols. (Beirut: Dār Iḥyā' al-Turāth al-ʿArabī, [1973]), 7:155. The Palestinian traditionalist Yūsuf al-Nabhānī (d. 1932) recounts his numerous dream visions of the Prophet, saying that when he first saw him in human form in 1316/1898, his face was "radiant white" (*abyaḍ azhar*), which al-Nabhānī describes as "pure white" (*ṣāfī al-bayāḍ*), not tinged with ruddiness. He suggests that the varied reports about the Prophet's color can be explained by his delicate countenance changing with his mood, exhaustion, etc. Al-Nabhānī's first dream vision of the Prophet was seeing a beautiful face, which could only have been his, appear in the full moon as it drew close to the sleeper; Yūsuf al-Nabhānī, *Saʿādat al-dārayn fī al-ṣalāt ʿalā sayyid al-kawnayn*, ed. ʿAbd al-Wārith Muḥammad ʿAlī (Beirut: Dār al-Kutub al-ʿIlmiyya, 1417/1997), 437–8.

52. The *hilye* has been excellently described as a " 'verbal icon." See Christiane Gruber, *The Praiseworthy One* (Bloomington, IN: Indiana University Press, 2019), 286, 291–2, 299, 342.
53. Al-Nawawī, *Sharḥ Ṣaḥīḥ Muslim*, 15:110; Ibn Ḥibbān al-Bustī, *al-Sīra al-nabawiyya wa akhbār al-khulafā'*, ed. al-Sayyid ʿAzīz Bik et als., 2 vols. (Beirut: al-Kutub al-Thaqāfiyya, 1417/1997), 1:410; Muḥammad b. ʿAlī al-Ṣabbān (d. 1206/1792), *Itḥāf ahl al-islām bi-mā yataʿallaqu bi'l-muṣṭafā wa ahl baytihi al-kirām*, Ms. 1444, Maktabat Jāmiʿat Riyāḍ, 10a; Muḥammad al-Khuḍarī, *Nūr al-yaqīn fī sīrat sayyid al-mursalīn* (Manama: Maktabat Niẓām al-Yaʿqūbī, 1434/2013), 301; Muḥammad b. Jaʿfar al-Kattānī, *al-Yumn wa'l-isʿād bi-mawlid khayr al-ʿibād* (Rabat: al-Maṭbaʿa al-Ahliyya, 1345/1926), 37.
54. Ali, *The 'Negro' in Arab-Muslim Consciousness*, 42. Ali's book includes a translation of Ibn Ḥajar's discussion of the Prophet's (s) color from his *Fatḥ al-Bārī*. See Ali, *The 'Negro' in Arab-Muslim Consciousness*, 193–7.
55. Bernard Lewis, "The Crows of the Arabs," *Critical Inquiry* 12, n. 1 (1985): 92, 96. Here Lewis differs with Gernot Rotter, who saw this poetry as an historically accurate reflection of Jahiliyya and early Islamic sentiments; Rotter, "Die Stellung des Negers in der islamisch-arabischen Gesellschaft bis zum XVI Jahrhundert," (dissertation, University of Bonn, 1967).
56. Interest in the 'Crows of the Arabs' was part of this aesthetic of exoticizing blackness. This appealed to some Muslim scholars of poetry and not to others. Ibn Sallām al-Jumaḥī (d. 232/846) and Ibn Qutayba (d. 276/889) were both early Sunnis scholars from non-Arab backgrounds who wrote histories of Arab poets. Ibn Qutayba was very interested in the 'Crows of the Arabs' as a phenomenon and in their poetry playing on their color. Ibn Sallām, on the other hand, showed no interest in 'The Crows' or blackness in general. He doesn't even mention ʿAntara's appearance and mentions that Nuṣayb was black only offhand; Ibn Qutayba, *al-Shiʿr wa'l-shuʿarā'*, 1:244, 329, 353, 396; Ibn Sallām al-Jumaḥī, *Ṭabaqāt fuḥūl al-shuʿarā'*, 1:152, 2:675.
57. Al-Jāḥiẓ, 1:197. In his *History*, al-Ṭabarī reports that, when the Sassanid Persians took Yemen from the Ethiopians, the commander ordered that "no black" be left alive in Yemen, nor any child "born of an Arab woman from a black man," nor

anyone left with curly hair who had any black (*sūdān*) ancestry; al-Ṭabarī, *Tārīkh*, 1:449.

58. *Musnad* of Ibn Ḥanbal, 1:203.
59. See the Ethiopian words referenced in *Ṣaḥīḥ al-Bukhārī*: *kitāb al-janā'iz, bāb binā' al-masjid ʿalā al-qabr; kitāb al-fitan, bāb ẓuhūr al-fitan; kitāb al-tafsīr, bāb sūrat al-anbiyā'*; *Ṣaḥīḥ Muslim*: *kitāb al-salām, bāb lā ʿadwā wa lā ṭiyara . . .*; *Sunan* of Abū Dāwūd: *kitāb al-ashriba, bāb al-nahy ʿan al-muskir*.
60. See, for example, Ibn Ḥibbān's narration of the Hadith of the Ethiopians dancing in the mosque; Ibn Ḥajar al-ʿAsqalānī, *Fatḥ al-bārī sharḥ Ṣaḥīḥ al-Bukhārī*, ed. Ayman Fu'ād ʿAbd al-Bāqī and ʿAbd al-ʿAzīz bin Bāz, 15 vols. (Beirut: Dār al-Kutub al-ʿIlmiyya, 1418/1997), 2:564.
61. Khalil ʿAthamina, "Non-Arab Regiments and Private Militias during the Umayyād Period," *Arabica* 45, n. 3 (1998): 358–59, 367, 372–73; al-Balādhurī, *Kitāb jumal min Ansāb al-ashrāf*, ed. Suhayl Zakkār and Riyāḍ al-Ziriklī, 13 vols. (Beirut: Dār al-Fikr, 1417/1996), 5:362.
62. Goldenberg, *Black and Slave*, 83.
63. Thompson, *Romans and Blacks*, 104.
64. Goldenberg, *Black and Slave*, 85.
65. Lewis, "Crows of the Arabs," 92; idem, *Race and Slavery in the Middle East* (Oxford: Oxford University Press, 1990), 50–6. Black African slaves started appearing in the slave markets of newly conquered Muslim north Africa at the end of the 600s CE; Elizabeth Savage, *A Gateway to Hell, a Gateway to Paradise: The North African Response to the Arab Conquest* (Princeton: Darwin Press, 1997), 73–5.
66. Khurāsānī manumission and *mukātaba* deeds dating from between 138–160/ 755–777 note either Persian or Turkic names; Geoffrey Khan, *Arabic Documents from Early Islamic Khurasan* (London: Nour Foundation, 2007), 150–65.
67. Al-Ṭabarī, *Tārīkh*, 3:404.
68. This has also been noted for Islamic Iberia in the Umayyad period, see Cristina de la Puente "The Ethnic Origins of Female Slaves in al-Andalus," in *Concubines and Courtesans*, ed. Matthew S. Gordon and Kathryn A. Hain (New York: Oxford University Press, 2017), 128. One premodern context in which estimations about the make-up of the slave population have been possible is Syria from 1200–1500 CE. Jan Hagedorn estimates, on the basis of documentary evidence, that the majority of slaves there were "Turkic," i.e., hailed from the Pontic steppe or beyond; Hagedorn, *Domestic Slavery in Syria and Egypt, 1200–1500*, 124.
69. See, for example, al-Ṭabarī, *Tārīkh*, 5:557; ʿArīb b. Saʿd al-Qurṭubī, *Ṣilat Tārīkh al-Ṭabarī*, ed. M.J. De Goeje (Leiden: Brill, 1897), 168.
70. The court of the Abbasid caliph al-Muqtadir (d. 320/932) reportedly included 11,000 Slavic, Greek, and Black African eunuchs (al-Ṣābi' [d. 448/1056] divides them into 7,000 Black African and 4,000 Slavic). Celebrations to greet a Byzantine ambassador featured 7,000 male slaves, 4,000 of whom were white (*bīḍ*) and 3,000 black. Another 4,000 black slaves were also present, possibly as guards; Hilāl b. al-Ḥasan al-Ṣābi', *Rusūm dār al-khilāfa*, ed. Mikhā'īl ʿAwwād (Beirut: Dār al-Rā'id al-ʿArabī, n.d.), 8; al-Khaṭīb al-Baghdādī, *Tārīkh Baghdād*, ed. Muṣṭafā ʿAbd al-Qādir ʿAṭā, 24 vols. (Beirut: Dār al-Kutub al-ʿIlmiyya, 1417/1998), 1:116–17, 119; 3:339 (a *jāriya* who helped her owner, a scholar, with dictation and copying); 10:411–13 (al-Aṣmaʿī's encounters with elite slave concubines); 12:450; 13:476.
71. Ibn Abī Zayd al-Qayrawānī, *Kitāb al-Nawādir wa'l-ziyādāt*, ed. Muḥammad ʿAbd al-ʿAzīz al-Dabbāgh et al., 15 vols. (Beirut: Dār al-Gharb al-Islāmī, 1999), 14:331.

72. Al-Sulamī, *Ṭabaqāt al-ṣūfiyya*, ed. Nūr al-Dīn Sudayba, 3rd ed. (Cairo: Maktabat al-Khānjī, 1418/1997), 322.
73. Al-Khaṭīb, *Tārīkh Baghdād*, 9:312.
74. *Ṣaḥīḥ al-Bukhārī: kitāb aḥādīth al-anbiyā', bāb w'udhkur fī al-kitāb Maryam . . .*; *Musnad* of Ibn Ḥanbal, 2:395.
75. I coined the term broadened metonym in order to capture how the phenomenon combines both trope and semantic change. The use of 'black' to indicate slave was not merely a choice of figure. It was a change in language, just as *'abd* would become a primary word for Black African in numerous Arabic dialects. Under the hypernym of 'slave,' there were hyponyms like 'Turkic slave,' 'European slave,' and 'Black African slave,' etc. 'Black' became a metonym for Black African slave, and the word then underwent a process of semantic broadening, like 'coke' coming to mean 'any carbonated drink' in the American South while also surviving as the name of a particular brand of drink. The *'abd*-to-*aswad* semantic change would be analogous to 'greens' denoting 'vegetables'; https://dare.wisc.edu/surveys/survey-results/1965–1970/foods/h78/; https://web.archive.org/web/20211218205105/https://popvssoda.com/countystats/total-county.html.
76. https://ucr.fbi.gov/crime-in-the-u.s/2019/crime-in-the-u.s.-2019/topic-pages/tables/table-43?__cf_chl_managed_tk__=X3LZm277h0nhCtr6Ft5kUzQCjUJ6U-L8yk7oLpYDIVuM-1639862298-0-gaNycGzNCFE
77. *kamā khadamat sūd takhdam bīḍ; ṭul mā tajid aswad lā tusakhkhir abyaḍ*; 'Ubaydallāh b. Aḥmad al-Zajjālī (d. 694/1294), *Amthāl al-'awāmm fī al-andalus*, ed. Muḥammad Bin Sharīfa, 2 vols. (Fez: Maṭba'at Muḥammad al-Khāmis, 1395/1975), 2:266, 246. For a study on the origin of slaves in Muslim Iberia, see Cristina de la Puente "The Ethnic Origins of Female Slaves in al-Andalus," 124–36.
78. Behnstedt and Woidich, *Wortatlas der arabischen Dialekte*, 56–58.
79. George, "Images of Black Slaves in the Roman Empire," 161–85; Hoetink, *The Two Variants in Caribbean Race Relations*, 153.
80. 'Abd al-'Aẓīm al-Mundhirī, al-*Takmila li-wafayāt al-naqala*, ed. Bashshār 'Awwād Ma'rūf, 4 vols. (Beirut: Mu'assasat al-Risāla, 1405/1984), 2:399.
81. This was named after the scholar teaching there, Madrasat Ibn Rashīq; al-Maqrīzī, *Kitāb al-Mawā'iẓ wa'l-i'tibār bi-dhikr al-khiṭaṭ wa'l-āthār*, ed. Khalīl al-Manṣūr, 4 vols. (Beirut: Dār al-Kutub al-'Ilmiyya, 1418/1998), 4:203; al-'Umarī, *Masālik al-abṣār*, 4:46. A dormitory for students from Bornu may also have been set up in Cairo in the mid 1200s. See Kane, *Beyond Timbuktu*, 44. Trimingham says that the *riwāqs* present in his day at al-Azhar for Africans were those for *maghāriba*, *barābra* (Nubians), *sannāriyya* (eastern Sudan), *jabarta* (Ethiopians), *barnawiyya* (Kanuri and Hausa), *ṣulayḥ* (Dar Sila and Waday) and *ardufur* (Darfur); J. Spencer Trimingham, *Islam in West Africa* (Oxford: Clarendon Press, 1959), 85.
82. Place names like Zayla' and Takrūr do not appear in books like Ibn al-Jawzī's *Muntaẓam*, al-Dhahabī's *Siyar a'lām al-nubalā'* or the geographically-assiduous *Takmila* of al-Mundhirī (d. 656/1258), which, on the other hand mentions numerous scholar/merchants who visited India and even a scholar named Muḥammad b. al-Ma'mūn al-Muṭawwi'ī al-Lāhūrī (d. 603/1206–7), who came from Lahore to study in Baghdad and Egypt; al-Mundhirī, al-*Takmila*, 1:457; 2:122, 266, 345, 412; 3:337, 621; Ibn al-Jawzī, *al-Muntaẓam fī tārīkh al-mulūk wa'l-umam*, ed. Muḥammad 'Abd al-Qādir 'Aṭā and Muṣṭafā 'Abd al-Qādir 'Aṭā, 18 vols. (Beirut: Dār al-Kutub al-'Ilmiyya, 1999), 17:152; 18:67. The first pilgrim known to have visited Mecca from the Sahel was Mai Dunama b. Umme of

Kanem, who did Hajj three times between 1098 and 1150. It was only between the eleventh and early fourteenth centuries that the reputation and name of Takrūr became well established in the Middle East; Omar Abdel Raziq El-Nagar, "West Africa and the Muslim Pilgrimage: An Historical Study with Special Reference to the Nineteenth Century," (PhD dissertation, SOAS, 1969), 45, 57, 61; David Conrad and Humphrey Fisher, "The Conquest that Never Was: Ghana and the Almoravids, 1076.I. The External Arabic Sources," *History in Africa* 9 (1982): 23.

83. In 818/1415, a large crowd of mendicants and Sufis (*fuqarā'*) from eastern lands (*'ajam*) and the Horn of Africa (*zayāli'*) had taken up residence in the Azhar Mosque; al-Maqrīzī, 4:57.
84. Al-Maydānī, *Majma' al-amthāl*, 2:62.
85. 'Abd al-Razzāq, *Muṣannaf*, 4:484. This was phrased (inaccurately) as a Prophetic Hadith in the late 700s CE, with the interesting addition of "... in their lands," which suggests a problem with their religious beliefs and slaughter: *nahā 'an dhabā'iḥ al-zanj fī bilādihim*; Ibn Ḥibbān, *Kitāb al-Majrūḥīn*, ed. Muḥammad Ibrāhīm Zāyid, 3 vols. (Aleppo: Dār al-Wa'ī, 1396/1976), 2:19.
86. Ibn Taymiyya, *Majmū'at al-fatāwā*, ed. Sayyid Ḥusayn al-'Affānī and Khayrī Sa'īd, 35 vols. (Cairo: al-Maktaba al-Tawfīqiyya, n.d.), 13:145.
87. De Wet shows that it was the Syriac *Cave of Treasures* (dating from between the fourth and early seventh centuries CE) that generalized the Curse to all Ham's descendants, not just to Canaan's; de Wet, *The Unbound God*, 129–31. See also Appendix VI. A version of Ham being punished with dark skin appears in the fourth- and fifth-century CE Talmuds. See Josephus, *Antiquities of the Jews*, I.6.2–3; James M. Scott, *Geography in Early Judaism and Christianity*, 33; Augustine, *City of God*, Book XVI, Chapter 2; Snowden, 198, 205; Goldenberg, *The Curse of Ham*, 172–74, 197; idem, *Black and Slave*, 76–77, 84, 87; Whitford, *The Curse of Ham in the Early Modern Era*, 25–27.
88. Al-Jāḥiẓ explains that, by Torah, early Muslim scholars meant the Jewish written tradition overall; al-Jāḥiẓ, *al-Ḥayawān*, ed. 'Abd al-Salām Hārūn (Beirut: Dār al-Jīl, 1996), 4:202–3.
89. El Hamel, *Black Morocco*, 61–71.
90. Al-Ṭabarī, *Tārīkh*, 5:619.
91. These include Ethiopians, East Africans (*zanjiyyāt*) and a group of Black Africans from the Sahara (*zaghāwiyyāt*); Ibn Buṭlān, "Risāla jāmi'a," 1:373–78.
92. Aḥmad b. Muḥammad Miskawayh, *Tahdhīb al-akhlāq*, ed. 'Imād al-Hilālī (Beirut: Manshūrāt al-Jamal, 2011), 416–17.
93. From Ibn Sīnā's *Shifā'*, cited from Paul A. Hardy, "Medieval Muslim Philosophers on Race," in *Philosophers on Race*, ed. Julie K. Ward and Tommy L. Lott, 38–62 (Oxford: Blackwell, 2002), 44.
94. The climatic etiology is upheld by al-Idrīsī (d. *circa* 560/1165), Shams al-Dīn al-Dimashqī, Ibn Khaldūn and possibly Ibn Ḥawqal; Shams al-Dīn al-Dimashqī, *Nukhbat al-dahr fī 'ajā'ib al-barr wa'l-baḥr*, ed. M.A.F. Mehren (St. Petersburg: M.M. Eggers et Comp., 1866), 15, 17, 266, 273; al-Idrīsī, *Nuzhat al-mushtāq fī ikhtirāq al-āfāq*, 2 vols. (Beirut: 'Ālam al-Kutub, 1409/1989), 1:18; Ibn Ḥawqal, *Kitāb Ṣūrat al-arḍ*, 2 vols. (Beirut: Dār Ṣādir, 1938), 1:105.
95. Even al-Khaṭīb al-Baghdādī, a Sunni scholar whose main specialization was the very un-philosophically engaged science of Hadith criticism, noted how Baghdad was so centrally located on the earth that its people avoided the extremes in

phenotype and disposition of the surrounding civilizations; al-Khaṭīb, *Tārīkh Baghdād*, 1:51.

96. J.T. Olsson, "The world in Arab eyes: a reassessment of the climes in medieval Islamic scholarship," *Bulletin of the School of Oriental and African Studies* 77, n. 3 (2014): 500–1.
97. Ṣāʿid al-Andalusī, *Science in the Medieval World: Book of the Categories of Nations*, trans. and ed., Semaʿan I. Salem and Alok Kumar (Austin: University of Texas Press, 1991), 7–8.
98. Shams al-Dīn al-Dimashqī, *Nukhbat al-dahr*, 268, 273.
99. Ibn Khaldūn, *Muqaddimah*, 59.
100. J.F.P. Hopkins, trans., *Corpus of early Arabic sources for West African history*, ed. N. Levtzion (Cambridge: Cambridge University Press, 1981), 367.
101. Hagedorn, *Domestic Slavery in Egypt and Syria, 1300–1500*, 69.
102. Hagedorn, 68, 76–77.
103. *Al-qaṭam f'arḍ al-ṣaqāliba*; al-Zajjālī, *Amthāl al-ʿawāmm fī al-andalus*, 2:119–20.
104. This is also sometimes a description given to people in the Sahelian areas, with Muslims sometimes noted as exceptions. For other positive views, see Aḥmad b. ʿAbd al-Mu'min al-Sharīshī, *Sharḥ Maqāmāt al-Ḥarīrī*, ed. Muḥammad Abū al-Faḍl, 5 vols. (Beirut: al-Maktaba al-ʿAṣriyya, 1413/1992), 1:335 (great wealth and comfort); Ibn Ḥawqal, *Ṣūrat al-arḍ* (Ibāḍī sources noting travel to the Sahel for medicine), both apud Hopkins, *Corpus of early Arabic sources for West African History*, 45, 49, 89, 91, 97, 179; al-Idrīsī, *Nuzhat al-mushtāq*, 1:18–19, 110 (where he notes both the justice of the ruler of Ghana and the animalistic and appetitive lifestyle of Africans further to the south); Ibn Baṭṭūṭa, *Ibn Battuta in Black Africa*, ed. and trans. Said Hamdun and Noël King (London: Rex Collings, 1975), 35, 47. One of the most negative assessments of the people inhabiting the clime of Black Africa, their natures conditioned by the climate, is Shams al-Dīn al-Dimashqī, *Nukhbat al-dahr*, 15, 17, 241, 266, 273.
105. Al-Iṣṭakhrī, *Kitāb Masālik al-mamālik* (Beirut: Dār Ṣādir, [1990], reprint of 1927 Brill edition), 40.
106. Ibn Khaldūn, *The Muqaddimah*, 59.
107. ʿAlī b. Mūsā Ibn Saʿīd al-Maghribī, *Kitāb al-Jughrāfiyā*, ed. Ismāʿīl al-ʿArabī (Beirut: al-Maktab al-Tijārī, 1970), 114.
108. Abū Ḥāmid al-Gharnāṭī, *Riḥlat al-Gharnāṭī: Tuḥfat al-albāb wa nukhbat al-ʿujāb*, ed. Qāsim Wahb (Abu Dhabi: Dār al-Suwaydī, 2003), 30. See also Ṣāʿid al-Andalusī, *Science in the Medieval World*, 8. For the similar view held by Muslims in what became southern Mali and the states to the south towards the non-Muslims 'bamana/Bambara' across the frontier of Islam, see Brian Petersen, *Islamization from Below: The Making of Muslim Communities in the Rural French Sudan, 1880–1960* (New Haven: Yale University Press, 2011), 26.
109. H.T. Norris, *Ṣūfī Mystics of the Niger Desert* (Oxford: Clarendon Press, 1990), xxvi–xxvii, 3, 62, 75.
110. Muḥammad Bello (Billū), *Infāq al-maysūr fī tārīkh bilād al-Takrūr*, ed. Sulaymān Mūsā (Gusau, Nigeria: Iqra' Publishing, 2013), 1:134–35, 147, 149–51, 226, 254, 335. See also Paul Naylor, *From Rebels to Rulers: Writing Legitimacy in the Early Sokoto State* (Suffolk, UK: James Currey, 2021), 132–34.
111. Naylor, 130.
112. John O. Hunwick, trans., *Sharīʿa in Songhay: The Replies of al-Maghīlī to the Questions of Askia al-Ḥajj Muḥammad* (London: Oxford University Press, 1985), 73–91.

113. Aḥmad Bābā, *Miʿrāj al-Ṣuʿūd: Aḥmad Bābā's Replies on Slavery*, trans. John Hunwick and Fatima Harrak (Rabat: Imprimerie El-Maarif Al-Jadidi, 2000), 11, 39–40, 46, 50–52. See also Naylor, *From Rebels to Rulers*, 131–32. Naylor quotes Bello as quoting al-Mukhtār al-Kuntī (d. 1226/1811) that most Black Africans to his south were non-Muslim. I have been unable to verify this attribution to al-Kuntī.
114. Hall, *A History of Race in Muslim West Africa*, 85.
115. Van Dalen focuses on the anti-tobacco work of Bagirmi scholar Muḥammad al-Wālī (fl. 1680s); Dorrit van Dalen, *Doubt, Scholarship and Society in 17th-Century Central Sudanic Africa* (Leiden: Brill, 2016), 158. See also Hall, *A History of Race in Muslim West Africa*, 80–81.
116. Seton Dearden, ed., *Tully's Letters written during a Ten Years' Residence at the Court of Tripoli* (London: Darf, 2002, first published 1846), 225. See also Stephanie Zehnle, *A Geography of Jihad: Sokoto Jihadism and the Islamic Frontier in West Africa* (Berlin: Walter de Gruyter, 2020), 146, 150, 471, 473, 562–63.

## 6. ANTIBLACKNESS IN THE QURAN AND SUNNA?

1. Walter Benjamin, *Selected Writings*, eds. Marcus Bullock and Michael Jennings, 4 vols. (Cambridge, MA: Belknap Press, 1996), 4:395.
2. Neil Postman, *Amusing Ourselves to Death* (New York: Penguin, 1985), 146–47.
3. For a Christian discussion of this, see Joelle Kidd, "Rethinking darkness and light," *Anglican Journal*, 10 February 2021, https://web.archive.org/web/20211129161039/https://www.anglicanjournal.com/rethinking-darkness-and-light/.
4. Christian Lange, "'On That Day When Faces Will Be White or Black' (Q3:106): Towards a Semiology of the Face in the Arabo-Islamic Tradition," *Journal of the American Oriental Society* 127, n. 4 (2007): 429.
5. Fakhr al-Dīn al-Rāzī, *Mafātīḥ al-ghayb / Tafsīr al-Rāzī* (Beirut: Dār Iḥyā' al-Turāth al-ʿArabī, 1420/2000), 8:317–18, 27:469, cf. 14:250.
6. Al-Rāzī, *Mafātīḥ*, 29:367. Thanks to Muntasir Zaman for pointing this out.
7. Al-Rāzī, *Mafātīḥ*, 27:469.
8. Al-Qurṭubī, *Jāmiʿ*, 2:524.
9. Al-Ṭabarī, *Tārīkh*, 1:140; Muqātil, *Tafsīr*, 4:713.
10. Al-Rāzī, *Mafātīḥ*, 31:62.
11. Al-Rāghib al-Iṣfahānī, *Muʿjam mufradāt alfāẓ al-Qur'ān*, ed. Ibrāhīm Shams al-Dīn (Beirut: Dār al-Kutub al-ʿIlmiyya, 1418/1997), 277–78; Abū al-Muẓaffar al-Samʿānī, *Tafsīr*, ed. Yāsīn Ibrāhīm and Ghunaym ʿAbbās, 6 vols. (Riyadh: Dār al-Waṭan, 1418/1997), 1:347.
12. Muḥammad Billū, *Jalā' al-ṣudūr ʿammā yakhtaliju fīhā min ṣadā al-gharūr*, ed. Thānī Yūsuf Birnin Tudu (Gusau, Nigeria: Iqra' Publishing, 2013, published in two-volume set *Mukhtārāt min mu'allafāt amīr al-mu'minīn Muḥammad Billū*), 1:52; Ibrāhīm Niasse, *Fī riyāḍ al-tafsīr*, ed. Muḥammad b. al-Shaykh ʿAbdallāh al-Tijānī et al., 2nd ed. (Cairo: al-Sharika al-Dawliyya li'l-Ṭibāʿa, 1433/2011), 1:309–10; 3:282. The Senegalese *tafsīr* scholar Muḥammad Dem (d. 1965 CE) also glosses whitened and blackened with the Wolof words for those two colors. Thanks to

Jeremy Dell for help on this, and see for Dem's commentary, Jeremy Dell, "Unbraiding the Qur'an: Wolofal and the *Tafsīr* Tradition of Senegambia," *Islamic Africa* 9 (2018): 55–76.

13. Al-Qurṭubī, *Jāmiʿ*, 2:523–5; ʿAbd al-Karīm al-Qushayrī, *Tafsīr al-Qushayrī*, ed. ʿAbd al-Laṭīf Ḥasan ʿAbd al-Raḥmān, 3 vols. (Beirut: Dār al-Kutub al-ʿIlmiyya, 1428/2007), 1:166; al-Ḥusayn b. Masʿūd al-Baghawī, *Maʿālim al-tanzīl*, ed. Muḥammad ʿAbdallāh al-Nimr et al., 8 vols. (Riyadh: Dār al-Ṭība, 1417/1997), 2:87; ʿAbdallāh b. ʿUmar al-Bayḍāwī, *Anwār al-tanzīl wa asrār al-taʾwīl*, ed. Muḥammad ʿAbd al-Raḥmān al-Marʿashlī, 5 vols. (Beirut: Dār Iḥyāʾ al-Turāth al-ʿArabī, 1418/1998), 2:32; Abū Isḥāq al-Thaʿlabī, *al-Kashf waʾl-bayān ʿan tafsīr al-Qurʾān*, ed. Muḥammad Ibn ʿĀshūr and Naẓīr al-Sāʿidī, 10 vols. (Beirut: Dār Iḥyāʾ al-Turāth al-ʿArabī, 1422/2002), 3:124–5; Abū Zayd al-Thaʿālabī, *Tafsīr al-Thaʿālabī / al-Jawāhir al-ḥisān fī tafsīr al-Qurʾān*, ed. Muḥammad ʿAlī Muʿawwaḍ and ʿĀdil Aḥmad ʿAbd al-Mawjūd, 5 vols. (Beirut: Dār Iḥyāʾ al-Turāth al-ʿArabī, 1418/1998), 2:90; al-Māwardī, *al-Nukat waʾl-ʿuyūn/Tafsīr al-Māwardī*, ed. al-Sayyid ʿAbd al-Maqṣūd ʿAbd al-Raḥīm, 6 vols. (Beirut: Dār al-Kutub al-ʿIlmiyya, n.d.), 1:415.
14. Abū al-Faḍl Rashīd al-Dīn Maybūdī, *Kashf al-asrār wa ʿuddat al-abrār*, ed. Zahrā Khalūʾī (online pdf), 520.
15. Abū al-Thanāʾ al-Ālūsī, *Rūḥ al-maʿānī*, ed. ʿAlī ʿAbd al-Bārī ʿAṭiyya, 16 vols. (Beirut: Dār al-Kutub al-ʿIlmiyya, 1415/1995), 2:241.
16. Al-Māwardī, *al-Nukat waʾl-ʿuyūn*, 3:194.
17. Al-Ṭabarī, *Jāmiʿ al-bayān*, 15:72; Muqātil, *Tafsīr*, 2:236; al-Qurṭubī, *Jāmiʿ*, 4:635–36.
18. Ibn al-Jawzī, *Kitāb al-Mawḍūʿāt*, ed. ʿAbd al-Raḥmān Muḥammad ʿUthmān, 3 vols. (Medina: al-Maktaba al-Salafiyya, 1386–88/1966–68), 2:232–34.
19. Jonathan A.C. Brown, "The Rules of *Matn* Criticism," *Islamic Law and Society* 19 (2012): 362–4. See also Muḥammad b. ʿAlī al-Shawkānī, *al-Fawāʾid al-majmūʿa fī al-aḥādīth al-mawḍūʿa*, ed. ʿAbd al-Raḥmān al-Muʿallimī (Beirut: al-Maktab al-Islāmī, 1392/1971–72), 414–17.
20. Muḥammad b. Ṭāhir al-Maqdisī, *Tadhkirat al-mawḍūʿāt*, ed. Muḥammad Muṣṭafā al-Ḥadarī al-Ḥabṭī (Mecca: al-Maktabat al-Salafiyya, 1401/1981), 147.
21. Ibn Ḥajar, *Tahdhīb al-tahdhīb*, ed. Muṣṭafā ʿAbd al-Qādir ʿAṭā, 12 vols. (Beirut: Dār al-Kutub al-ʿIlmiyya, 1415/1994), 10:135. See also Ibn ʿAdī, *al-Kāmil fī ḍuʿafāʾ al-rijāl*, 7 vols. (Beirut: Dār al-Fikr, 1985), 5:1903–4.
22. Brown, "Even If It's Not True It's True: Using Unreliable Hadiths in Sunni Islam," *Islamic Law and Society* 18 (2011): 24.
23. Aḥmad bin al-Ṣiddīq al-Ghumārī, *al-Mughīr ʿalā al-aḥādīth al-mawḍūʿa fī al-Jāmiʿ al-ṣaghīr* (Beirut: Dār al-Rāʾid al-ʿArabī, 1402/1982), 39, 59, 71, 73.
24. See al-Suyūṭī, *al-Laʾālīʾ al-maṣnūʿa fī al-aḥādīth al-mawḍūʿa*, ed. Ṣāliḥ Muḥammad ʿUwayda, 3 vols. (Beirut: Dār al-Kutub al-ʿIlmiyya, 1996), 3:405–410.
25. Al-Suyūṭī grades the Hadith describing Zanj as disfigured as weak in his *Jāmiʿ al-ṣaghīr* (#4568). In two of his works on the virtues of Black Africans, al-Suyūṭī follows the alleged Hadith "There is no good in Ethiopians, when they are sated they fornicate (*lā khayr fī al-ḥabasha*) . . ." with unqualified criticism of its *isnād* and none of the qualifying language found in his larger *Laʾālīʾ al-maṣnūʿa*, grading it as weak in his *Jāmiʿ al-ṣaghīr* (#4592); al-Suyūṭī, *Azhār al-ʿurūsh fī akhbār al-ḥubūsh*, ed. ʿAbdallāh Muḥammad al-Ghazālī (Kuwait: Markaz al-Makhṭūṭāt waʾl-Turāth waʾl-Wathāʾiq, 1416/1995), 25; idem, *Rafʿ shaʾn al-ḥubshān*, 86. Incidentally, this forgery was an enduring one. Burckhardt reports "*kull ʿabd in jāʿa saraq wa in shabiʿ fasaq*" as an

Arabic saying, though he notes that it was no longer in usage in Egypt in 1817; John L. Burckhardt, *Arabic Proverbs* (Mineola, USA: Dover, 2004), 203.

26. Al-Ṭabarānī, *al-Muʿjam al-kabīr*, ed. Ḥamdī ʿAbd al-Majīd al-Salafī, 25 vols. (Beirut: Dār Iḥyāʾ al-Turāth al-ʿArabī, [n.d.]), 12:436 (#13595); idem, *al-Muʿjam al-awsaṭ*, ed. Ṭāriq ʿAwaḍ Allāh and ʿAbd al-Muḥsin Ibrāhīm, 10 vols. (Cairo: Dār al-Ḥaramayn, 1995), 2:162 (#1581). For a summary of the flaws in this Hadith, see al-Albānī, *Silsilat al-aḥādīth al-ḍaʿīfa*, 14:1:280–3 (#6618), 11:1:219–20 (#5129).
27. ʿ*Nāzaʿatahu jubba lahu min al-ṣūf tadkhulu baynahu wa bayn jubbatihi*ʾ; al-Ḥākim, *al-Mustadrak* (Hyderabad: Dāʾirat al-Maʿārif al-ʿUthmāniyya, [n.d.]), 2:93–4 (affirmed by al-Dhahabī); al-Albānī, *Ṣaḥīḥ al-Targhīb waʾl-tarhīb*, 3 vols. (Riyadh: Maktabat al-Maʿārif, 1421/2000), 2:143–4.
28. Al-Ṭabarī, *Tārīkh*, 2:616 (year 30). The second version, with references to the connection of this episode to Abū Dharr's disagreements with Muʿāwiya, and ʿUthmān settling Abū Dharr in Rabadha, is from a source decades earlier and via an *isnād* of all reliable transmitters, in contrast to al-Ṭabarī's. See Ibn Saʿd, *Ṭabaqāt*, 4:226–27. Versions of the Hadith that Abū Dharr cites differ in wording. Some read, "an Ethiopian slave," others "a mutilated black slave," or "a mutilated Ethiopian slave." For this Hadith, see *Ṣaḥīḥ al-Bukhārī*: *kitāb al-aḥkām, bāb al-samʿ waʾl-ṭāʿa liʾl-imām mā lam takun maʿṣiya*; *Ṣaḥīḥ Muslim*: *kitāb al-imāra, bāb wujūb ṭāʿat al-umarāʾ fī ghayr maʿṣiya* . . . (from Abū Dharr and Umm al-Ḥuṣayn; the wordings are *ʿabd mujaddaʿ ḥasibtuhā qālat aswad / ʿabdan ḥabashiyyan mujaddaʿ al-aṭrāf*). See also Abū Bakr al-Ājurrī, *al-Sharīʿa*, ed. ʿAbdallāh ʿUmar al-Dumayjī, 5 vols. (Riyadh: Dār al-Waṭan, 1420/1999), 1:380. It appears as part of a report attributed to the caliph ʿUmar in Ibn Abī Shayba, *Muṣannaf*, ed. Kamāl Yūsuf al-Ḥūt, 7 vols. (Riyadh: Maktabat al-Rushd, 1409/1999), 6:544.
29. For the version with the raisin simile, see: *Ṣaḥīḥ al-Bukhārī*: *kitāb al-adhān, bāb imāmat al-ʿabd* . . ., *bāb imāmat al-maftūn waʾl-mubtadiʿ*; *kitāb al-aḥkām, bāb al-samʿ waʾl-ṭāʿa liʾl-imām mā lam takun maʿṣiya*; *Sunan Ibn Mājah*: *kitāb al-jihād, bāb ṭāʿat al-imām*; *Musnad Aḥmad Ibn Ḥanbal*, 3:114, 171; Abū Dāwūd al-Ṭayālisī, *Musnad*, ed. Muḥammad ʿAbd al-Muḥsin al-Turkī et al., 4 vols. (Cairo: Hujr, 1420 /1999), 3:560.
30. Since the famous Hadith scholar of Basra, Shuʿba b. al-Ḥajjāj (d. 160/776), transmits the raisin-simile version (from Abū al-Tayyāḥ, from Anas) as well as the version without the raisin simile (from Abū ʿImrān, from ʿAbdallāh b. al-Ṣāmit, from Abū Dharr), any confusion about the wording occurred in the first two or three generations of the report's transmission, all of which took place in Basra. Moreover, Anas' narration is actually his recollection of what the Prophet said to Abū Dharr, while the non-raisin version is Abū Dharr's own recollection. Finally, the transmitter who passed on Abū Dharr's report to the next generation was Abū Dharr's own nephew, which further strengthens the case that the non-raisin-simile version is more reliable.
31. *Sunan al-Dārimī*: introductory chapters, *bāb al-taswiya fī al-ʿilm*. There is also another Hadith, considered very weak by Muslim scholars, which instructs Muslims to marry for piety rather than beauty or wealth, concluding that "a clipped-eared (*kharmāʾ*), black slave woman who is religious is better." See *Sunan Ibn Mājah*: *kitāb al-nikāḥ, bāb tazwīj dhāt dīn*; al-Bayhaqī, *al-Sunan al-kubrā*, ed. Muḥammad ʿAbd al-Qādir ʿAṭā, 11 vols. (Beirut: Dār al-Kutub al-ʿIlmiyya, 1999), 7:128–29; al-Albānī, *Silsilat al-aḥādīth al-ḍaʿīfa waʾl-mawḍūʿa* (Riyadh: Maktabat al-Maʿārif, 1420/2000–1425/2005), 3:172–73 (#1060).

32. Ibn Taymiyya, *Majmūʿat al-fatāwā*, 28:318–19.
33. *Ṣaḥīḥ al-Bukhārī: kitāb al-aḥkām, bāb al-samʿ wa'l-ṭāʿa li'l-imām mā lam takun maʿṣiya; Jāmiʿ al-Tirmidhī: kitāb al-jihād, bāb mā jā'a lā ṭāʿa li-makhlūq fī maʿṣiyat al-khāliq*.
34. Dominique Champault, *Une Oasis du Sahara Nord-Occidental – Tabelbala* (Paris: Éditions du Centre National de la Recherche Scientifique, 1969), 40. This adjective was used by two contemporaries of Qāḍī ʿIyāḍ in their descriptions of Africans, Abū Ḥāmid al-Gharnāṭī, *Riḥlat al-Gharnāṭī*, 30; and al-Idrīsī, *Nuzhat al-mushtāq*, 1:18. See also Shams al-Dīn al-Dimashqī, *Nukhbat al-dahr*, 273. The imagery of peppercorns appears very occasionally in Arabic poetry. Another interesting verse of poetry by Ibn Billīṭa reads: "Curliness ruled over his locks, which piled on one another as if they were mulberries"; Manfred Ullmann, *Der Neger in der Bildersprache der arabischen Dichter* (Wiesbaden: Harrossowitz Verlag, 1998), 197–98, 213.
35. Ḥamd al-Khaṭṭābī, *Aʿlām al-ḥadīth*, ed. Muḥammad Saʿd Āl Suʿūd, 4 vols. (Markaz al-Buḥūth al-ʿIlmiyya, 1409/1988), 4:334; Ibn Baṭṭāl, *Sharḥ Ṣaḥīḥ al-Bukhārī*, 2:319–20; Qāḍī ʿIyāḍ, *Mashāriq al-anwār*, 2 vols. (Cairo: Dār al-Turāth, 1978), 1:309; Ibn Hubayra, *Kitāb al-Ifṣāḥ ʿan maʿānī al-ṣiḥāḥ*, ed. Fu'ād ʿAbd al-Munʿim Aḥmad, 8 vols. (Riyadh: Dār al-Waṭan, 1417/1997), 5:324.
36. Ibn al-Jawzī, *Kashf al-mushkil min ḥadīth al-ṣaḥīḥayn*, ed. ʿAlī Ḥusayn al-Bawwāb, 4 vols. (Riyadh: Dār al-Waṭan, 1418/1997), 3:292.
37. Ibn al-Munayyir, *al-Mutawārī ʿalā abwāb al-Bukhārī*, ed. Ṣalāḥ al-Dīn Maqbūl Aḥmad (Kuwait: Maktabat al-Muʿallā, 1407/1987), 98.
38. Al-Nawawī, *Sharḥ Ṣaḥīḥ Muslim*, 9/10:52; al-Ḥusayn b. ʿAbdallāh al-Ṭībī, *al-Kāshif ʿan ḥaqā'iq al-sunan (sharḥ Mishkāt al-maṣābīḥ)*, ed. ʿAbd al-Ḥamīd Hindāwī, 13 vols. (Mecca: Maktabat Nizār Muṣṭafā al-Bāz, 1417/1997), 8:2558.
39. Shams al-Dīn Muḥammad b. Yūsuf al-Kirmānī, *al-Bukhārī bi-sharḥ al-Kirmānī*, 2nd ed., 25 vols. (Beirut: Dār Iḥyā' al-Turāth al-ʿArabī, 1401/1981), 5:75.
40. Ibn Ḥajar, *Fatḥ al-bārī*, 2:238; 13:153.
41. Zakariyyā' al-Anṣārī, *Minḥat al-bārī bi-sharḥ Ṣaḥīḥ al-Bukhārī*, ed. Sulaymān Durayʿ al-ʿĀzimī, 10 vols. (Riyadh: Maktabat al-Rushd, 1426/2005), 2:409; Muḥammad al-Khaḍir al-Shinqīṭī, *Kawthar al-maʿānī al-darārī fī kashf khabāyā Ṣaḥīḥ al-Bukhārī*, 14 vols. (Beirut: Mu'assasat al-Risāla, 1415/1995), 9:14.
42. Abū al-Ḥasan Muḥammad b. ʿAbd al-Hādī al-Sindī, *Ḥāshiyat al-Sindī ʿalā Sunan Ibn Mājah*, 2 vols. (Beirut: Dār al-Jīl, n.d.), 2:201.
43. Oliver Pritchard-Jones, "Orwell prize-winning author to rewrite memoir over 'chocolate skin' line," *Express*, 11 August 2021, https://www.express.co.uk/news/uk/1475666/orwell-prize-Kate-Clanchy-Some-Kids-I-Taught-Philip-Pullman-woke-latest, last accessed September 2021. Thanks to Kristina Richardson for alerting me to this incident. For another instance of this, see Trevor Noah, *Born a Crime* (New York: Spiegel & Grau, 2016), 54.
44. Dawud Walid, *Blackness and Islam* (Wembley, UK: Algorithm, 2021), 32–33.
45. Al-Rāzī, *al-Firāsa*, ed. Muṣṭafā ʿĀshūr (Cairo: Dār al-Qur'ān, n.d.), 62.
46. See, for example, https://ourworldindata.org/human-height.
47. See, for example, Anna Funk, "Lost Research Notes Clear Up Racial Bias Debate in Old Skull Size Study," *Discover*, 21 October 2018, https://www.discovermagazine.com/planet-earth/lost-research-notes-clear-up-racial-bias-debate-in-old-skull-size-study, last accessed September 2021. It has already been established that brain size does not correlate to intelligence, but, hypothetically, if a researcher found that

people from the Horn of Africa had smaller average head sizes proportional to their bodies than Arabs, would such a finding actually be engaged with seriously?

48. Jayaprakash Satyamurthy (@flightofsand), "Believe me, nobody likes being described as 'chocolate coloured' or 'almond eyed'. This is basic stuff. I am sure the good intentions and obviously inclusive agenda Clanchy demonstrates made her book sail through a probably white-only vetting process," Twitter, 6 August 2021, 5:57am, https://twitter.com/flightofsand/status/1423583957937889283.
49. Shaykh Saʿīd Fūda, "Lectures on the *Waraqāt* of al-Juwaynī," 2004; Ibn Ḥajar, *Fatḥ*, 2:267. This is on the basis of 1) the maxim that the presumption is that language is interpreted according to its literal/evident meaning (*al-aṣl an naḥmila al-alfāẓ ʿalā al-ḥaqīqa*) and 2) that literal meaning is what is understood as the evident meaning of speech in the context of the original speaker and audience (*mā ustuʿmila fīmā uṣṭuliḥa ʿalayhi min al-mukhāṭaba*). Also relevant here is the maxim noted by al-Suyūṭī and others that "The custom according to which language is interpreted is the contemporaneous and prior not the subsequent (*al-ʿurf alladhī tuḥmalu ʿalayhi al-alfāẓ innamā huwa al-muqārin al-sābiq dūn al-muta'akhkhir*)"; al-Suyūṭī, *al-Ashbāh wa'l-naẓā'ir*, ed. Muḥammad al-Muʿtaṣim al-Baghdādī (Beirut: Dār al-Kitāb al-ʿArabī, 1414/1993), 193. Habeeb Akande points out the excellent example of the Prophet promising his followers that guiding another to Islam will bring them a reward more valuable than red camels (*ḥumr al-naʿam*), which were particularly valuable in the Hejaz at that time; *Ṣaḥīḥ al-Bukhārī: kitāb al-jihād wa'l-siyar, bāb duʿā' al-Nabī (s) ilā al-islām* . . .
50. Al-Ṭabarī, *Tārīkh*, 2:616.
51. Al-Suyūṭī, *al-Tawshīḥ sharḥ al-Jāmiʿ al-ṣaḥīḥ*, ed. Riḍwān Jāmiʿ Riḍwān (Riyadh: Maktabat al-Rushd, 1419/1998), 711. The son, Muḥammad Abū al-Ṭayyib, was born when al-Suyūṭī was twenty-two, in 870 AH; Muḥammad Āl Rihāb, "Maḥḍar samāʿ kitāb al-Mirqāt al-ʿaliyya fī sharḥ al-asmā' al-nabawiyya," *Alukah*, 31 December 2014, https://web.archive.org/web/20210917173524/https://www.alukah.net/culture/1188/80578/.
52. Though the amount of praise poetry and prose (*madḥ*) written about the Prophet is astounding, I found no commentaries on any Hadith collections listed in John Hunwick's *Arabic Literature of Africa, vol. 4: The Writings of Western Sudanic Africa* (Leiden: Brill, 2013). For examples of the *Ṣaḥīḥayn* being read and studied regularly, see John Hunwick, *Timbuktu and the Songhay Empire*, 46, 61, 69–70. I have found three commentaries on *Ṣaḥīḥ al-Bukhārī* by Berber and Mauritanian scholars: a commentary on Ibn Abī Ḥamza's abridgement of *Ṣaḥīḥ al-Bukhārī* by Muḥammad ʿAbdallāh b. Ṭālib al-Maḥjūbī of Walata (d. 1220/805–6) (WAAMD ID#49161); the *Miṣbāḥ kull sār mufattish ʿan Ṣaḥīḥ al-Bukhārī* by Sīdī Muḥammad b. Bāba ʿAynaynā al-Niʿmāwī (d. 1378/1959)(WAAMD ID#48588); and the *Kawthar al-maʿānī al-darārī fī kashf khabāyā Ṣaḥīḥ al-Bukhārī* by Muḥammad al-Khaḍir b. Sīdī ʿAbd Allāh al-Jakanī (Ould al-Bara) (d. 1354/1935–6)(WAAMD ID#44570). See the West African Arabic Manuscript Database https://waamd.lib.berkeley.edu/home.
53. ʿUthmān bin Fūdī, "al-Ajwiba al-muḥarrara ʿan as'ila muqarrara," in *Mukhtārāt al-Shaykh ʿUthmān bin Fūdī* (Gusau, Nigeria: Iqra', 2013), 2:171; idem, *Ḍiyā' al-ḥukkām fīmā lahum wa ʿalayhim min al-aḥkām*, ed. Sulaymān Mūsā Atthā'ī (Gusau, Nigeria: Iqra', 2013), 3:116.
54. Muḥammad Billū, "Risalat li 'l-Amraad as-Shafiyya: A Letter of Healing" [sic], trans. Abu Alfa Umar Muhammad Shareef bin Farid (Sennar, Sudan: Sankore' Institute of Islamic-African Studies International, 1415/1995), [63].

55. Muḥammad Amīn al-Hararī, *al-Kawkab al-wahhāj wa'l-rawḍ al-bahhāj fī sharḥ Ṣaḥīḥ Muslim b. al-Ḥajjāj*, ed. Hāshim ʿAlī Muḥammad Mahdī, 26 vols. (Jedda: Dār al-Minhāj, 1430/2009), 14:298; 20:55; al-Nawawī, *Sharḥ Ṣaḥīḥ Muslim*, 9/10:52.
56. Al-Hararī, *Murshid dhawī al-ḥijā wa'l-ḥāja ilā Sunan Ibn Mājah*, ed. Hāshim Muḥammad Mahdī, 26 vols. (Jedda: Dār al-Minhāj, 1439/2018), 1:161–62.
57. Though this Hadith is rated as *ṣaḥīḥ*, it is narrated by an unusually isolated chain of transmission (only one chain for three generations): Al-Layth ← Abū al-Zubayr al-Makkī ← Jābir ← The Prophet (s). See *Ṣaḥīḥ Muslim*: *kitāb al-musāqāt, bāb jawāz bayʿ al-ḥayawān bi'l-ḥayawān min jinsihi mutafāḍilan*; *Jāmiʿ al-Tirmidhī*: *kitāb al-siyar, bāb mā jā'a fī bayʿat al-ʿabd*; *Sunan Ibn Mājah*: *kitāb al-jihād, bāb al-bayʿa*; *Sunan* of Abū Dāwūd: *kitāb al-buyūʿ, bāb fī dhālika idhā kāna yadan bi-yad*; *Sunan al-Nasā'ī*: *kitāb al-buyūʿ, bāb bayʿ al-ḥayawān bi'l-ḥayawān yadan bi-yad mutafāḍilan*; *Musnad Aḥmad*, 3:349–50, 372; al-Bayhaqī, *al-Sunan al-kubrā*, 5:469.
58. See *Ṣaḥīḥ Muslim*: *kitāb al-musāqāt, bāb al-ṣarf wa bayʿ al-dhahab bi'l-wariq naqdan.*
59. The return of Muslims like Abū Jandal to the unbelievers after the Treaty of Ḥudaybiyya is understood to be abrogated by the Quranic verse 60:10 and it is also understood that this action was an exceptional privilege of the Prophet; al-Sarakhsī, *Sharḥ al-siyar al-kabīr*, 5 vols. (Beirut: Dār al-Kutub al-ʿIlmiyya, 1417/1997), 4:302–3.
60. Al-Sarakhsī, *Sharḥ al-Siyar al-kabīr*, 1:239.
61. Al-Qāḍī ʿIyāḍ, *Ikmāl al-muʿlim bi-fawā'id Muslim*, ed. Yaḥyā Ismāʿīl, 9 vols. (Cairo: Dār al-Wafā', 1419/1998), 5:301–2; Anwar Shāh Kashmīrī, "al-ʿArf al-shadhī," in *Jāmiʿ al-Tirmidhī al-muḥashshā* (Karachi: Qadīmī Kutubkhāne, n.d.), 302–3. Cf., al-Qudūrī, *Mukhtaṣar*, trans. Ṭāhir Maḥmood Kiānī (London: Ta-Ha Publishers, 2010), 665. Al-Shaybānī and al-Sarakhsī discuss how, if non-Muslim enemies come into the Muslim polity with their security guaranteed (*amān*), and they have Muslim captives/slaves with them, then the Muslims should purchase them to free them; al-Sarakhsī, *Sharḥ al-siyar al-kabīr*, 4:318.
62. *Ṣaḥīḥ al-Bukhārī*: *kitāb al-janā'iz, bāb idhā aslama al-ṣaby wa māta hal yuṣallī ʿalayhi . . .*
63. Al-Khaṭṭābī, *Maʿālim al-sunan*, 2nd ed., 4 vols. (Beirut: al-Maktaba al-ʿIlmiyya, 1981), 4:32; Ibn al-Mundhir, *Kitāb al-Ishrāf*, ed. Ṣaghīr Aḥmad al-Anṣārī Abū Ḥammād (Ras al-Khayma: Maktabat Makka al-Thaqāfiyya, 1425/2004), 7:14. For paying the compensation (*ghurra*) for causing a miscarriage, Mālik held that a 'red' slave was preferrable to a 'black' one, but that this was not set in the Sunna of the Prophet and was subject to availability and demand; Saḥnūn b. Saʿīd, *al-Mudawwana*, 16 vols. (Riyadh: Wizārat al-Shu'ūn al-Islāmiyya, [1424/2004]), 16:204–5.
64. *Muwaṭṭa'*: *kitāb al-buyūʿ, bāb mā jā'a fī bayʿ al-ʿurbān*. Here I take the translation from Mohammad Fadel's and Connell Monette's translation of the *Muwaṭṭa'* (Cambridge, MA: Harvard University Press, 2019), 537.
65. *Ṣaḥīḥ Muslim*: *kitāb al-aymān, bāb nadb man ḥalafa yamīnan . . .*
66. *Ṣaḥīḥ al-Bukhārī*: *kitāb al-hiba, bāb man istawhaba min aṣḥābihi shay'a.*
67. Al-Qurṭubī, *Jāmiʿ*, 6:540 (on Quran 24:33).
68. Al-Jāḥiẓ, *Rasā'il*, 1:212.
69. Al-Jāḥiẓ, *Rasā'il*, 1:196.

70. As al-Dhahabī says, "He was among the most esteemed scholars and practitioners, raised up by his piety despite being a black *mawlā*"; al-Dhahabī, *Siyar*, 6:31. See also al-Bukhārī, *al-Tārīkh al-kabīr*, 8:217; al-Dhahabī, *Tadhkirat al-ḥuffāẓ*, ed. Zakariyyā ʿUmayrāt, 4 vols. in 2 (Beirut: Dār al-Kutub al-ʿIlmiyya, 1419/1998), 1:96–97.
71. Harald Motzki, "The Role of Non-Arab Converts in the Development of Early Islamic Law," *Islamic Law and Society* 6, n. 3 (1999): 308–315; Brown, *Slavery & Islam*, 111–2.
72. Ibn Buṭlān, "Risāla jāmiʿa li-funūn nāfiʿa fī shirā al-raqīq wa taqlīb al-ʿabīd," 1:388.
73. Al-Sarakhsī, *al-Mabsūṭ*, 30 vols. (Beirut: Dār al-Maʿrifa, 1409/1989), 5:69; ʿAlā' al-Dīn al-Kāsānī, *Badā'iʿ al-ṣanā'iʿ*, 7 vols. (Beirut: Dār al-Kutub al-ʿIlmiyya, 1406/1986), 2:283–4; Ibn Nujaym, *al-Baḥr al-rā'iq sharḥ kanz al-daqā'iq*, 2nd ed., 8 vols. (Beirut: Dār al-Kitāb al-Islāmī, n.d.), 3:175. Abū Bakr al-Ḥaddādī of Yemen (d. 800 /1398) also interprets Abū Ḥanīfa's phrase *abyaḍ* as Byzantine, but he says that the middle tier of *waṣīf* was Slavic, not Sindi; Abū Bakr b. ʿAlī al-Ḥaddādī, *al-Jawhara al-nayyira ʿalā Mukhtaṣar al-Qudūrī* (Cairo: al-Maṭbaʿa al-Khayriyya, 1322/1904), 2:18. Al-Jāḥiẓ imagines his opponents claiming that the 'whites' are greater in number than 'blacks,' since 'whites' inhabit Iran from its southeast to northeast, Anatolia, Slavic lands and Frankish lands beyond; al-Jāḥiẓ, *Rasā'il*, 1:215.

## 7. ANTIBLACKNESS, SUFISM, AND VENERATION OF THE PROPHET

1. This Hadith appears via an *isnād* in the ninth-century author al-Mufaḍḍal b. Sulaymān al-Ḍabbī's *al-Fākhir fī al-amthāl*, ed. Muḥammad ʿUthmān (Beirut: Dār al-Kutub al-ʿIlmiyya, 2011), 154. I have not found it anywhere else. It is likely highly unreliable.
2. "*Il n'y a sur terre ni blancs, ni noirs, il y a des esprits; vous en êtes un. Devant Dieu, toutes les âmes sont blanches*"; Victor Hugo, "À Monsieur Heurtelou," *Victor Hugo, Actes et Paroles. Pendant l'exil, 1852–1870 (vol. 2)* (Paris: Michel Lévy Frères, 1875), 195–96. For the usage of this quotation, see Thompson, *Romans and Blacks*, 44.
3. Hugo's error is the same as that of present-day liberals who either claim 'not to see color' or endorse color-blindness: denying that the racial reality of Black and White perpetuates White domination by refusing to recognize how society's structures disadvantage blacks. This is a fair criticism, though it is anachronistic to expect a nineteenth-century French novelist to have grasped the systemic racism only identified a century later. See Timothy Raser, "Victor Hugo's Politics and Aesthetics of Race in *Bug-Jargal*," *The Romantic Review* 89, n. 3 (1998): 318.
4. "'Whitelist,' 'Blacklist': The New Debate Over Security Terminology," *Dice*, 17 July 2020, https://web.archive.org/web/20211103024834/https://insights.dice.com/2020/07/17/whitelist-blacklist-the-new-debate-over-security-terminology; Paulina Cachero, "Women of color call out Dictionary.com's 'offensive' definition of 'black': 'This needs to change'," *Yahoo!*, 7 June 2019, https://web.archive.org/web/20211103025229/https://www.yahoo.com/now/women-of-color-call-out-dictionarycoms-offensive-definition-black-000906372.html?guccounter=1.

5. Jālāl al-Dīn Rūmī, *Tales from the Masnavi*, trans. A.J. Arberry (London: George Allen & Unwin, 1961), 255.
6. Ibn al-Jawzī, *Tanwīr al-ghabash fī faḍl al-sūdān wa'l-ḥabash*, ed. Marzūq ʿAlī Ibrāhīm (Riyadh: Dār al-Sharīf, 1419/1998), 179. The mention of the moon is missing from two narrations of this story found in Abū Nuʿaym, *Ḥilya*, 9:368, 391. There the man is simply described as "whitening" (*ibyaḍḍa*). See also Abū al-Ḥasan al-Sirjānī, *Sufism, Black and White*, ed. Bilal Orfali and Nada Saab (Leiden: Brill, 2012), 12–16.
7. Interestingly, this clause is missing from the text of this report in Ibn al-Jawzī's *Tanwīr al-ghabash*, though the author cites it via Abū Nuʿaym al-Iṣbahānī. Ibn al-Jawzī also abridges other sentences here and there in the report. See Ibn al-Jawzī, *Tanwīr al-ghabash*, 216.
8. Ibn al-Jawzī, *Ṣifat al-ṣafwa*, ed. Khālid Muṣṭafā al-Ṭarṭūsī (Beirut: Dār al-Kitāb al-ʿArabī, 1433/2012), 366, 399–401.
9. See Rūmī, *Mathnavī*, line 3476 (Book 1, Story 14). Thanks to Omid Safi for bringing this to my attention. The story of the competition between the Chinese and Greek artists that this verse is part of appears in al-Ghazālī, *Iḥyā' ʿulūm al-dīn*, ed. Muḥammad Wahbī Sulaymān and Usāma ʿAmmūra, 5 vols. (Damascus: Dār al-Fikr, 1426/2006), 3:1637.
10. Titus Burckhardt, *Mystical Astrology According to Ibn ʿArabi*, trans. Bulent Rauf (Louisville, KY: Fons Vitae, 2001), 30–31. For a summary of the moon in Sufi tradition, see Omid Safi, "'The Real Intention Was My Beloved': The Moon in Persian Sufi Poetry," in *The Moon: a Voyage through Time*, ed. Christiane Gruber (Toronto: Aga Khan Museum, 2019), 37–46.
11. Muḥammad b. ʿAlī Ibn Shahrāshūb, *Manāqib āl Abī Ṭālib* (Beirut: Dār al-Aḍwā', 1412/1991), 4:419. Thanks to Rodrigo Adem for this citation.
12. Jonathan Brown, "Slavery and Sufism: The *Ḥilyat al-Awliyā'* of Abū Nuʿaym al-Iṣbahānī (d. 430/1038) as a Source on Slavery in Medieval Islamic Civilization," *Annals of the Japanese Association for Middle East Studies* 36, n. 2 (2020): 36–39.
13. Ibn al-Jawzī, *Ṣifat al-ṣafwa*, 727, 852–53.
14. Though al-Burnāwī appears as an enigmatic muse from al-Dabbāgh's perspective, Zachary Wright has shown how he was actually much better known and his conventional scholarly credentials well established; Wright, "The African Roots of a Global Eighteenth-Century Islamic Scholarly Renewal," in *Islamic Scholarship in Africa*, ed. Ousmane Kane (Suffolk, UK: James Currey, 2021), 34–36.
15. See, for example, the bloated cadaver of a Zanjī reprimanding a Sufi in a dream; Ibn al-Jawzī, *Ṣifat al-ṣafwa*, 623 (bio of Maymūn b. Siyāh).
16. Al-Rāzī, *Mafātīḥ al-ghayb*, 28:114.
17. Al-Ghazālī cites this story as being told by an early Sufi of Basra named ʿAbd al-Wāḥid b. Zayd (d. *circa* 160/775), who had met this man on Hajj. The man would not do anything without calling God's peace and blessings upon the Prophet (s) as a result of this experience; al-Ghazālī, *Iḥyā' ʿulūm al-dīn*, 4:3422.
18. Mullā ʿAlī al-Qārī', *Majmūʿ rasā'il al-ʿallāmā al-Mullā ʿAlī al-Qārī'*, ed. Māhir Adīb Ḥabbūsh et al., 8 vols. (Istanbul: Dār al-Lubāb, 2016), 5:241–2 (verse 101). Here Mullā ʿAlī is following his teacher Ibn Ḥajar al-Haytamī, *al-ʿUmda fī sharḥ al-Burda*, ed. Bassām Muḥammad Bārūd (Abu Dhabi: Dār al-Faqīh, 2005), 476–7.
19. As we discussed earlier, many Muslim scholars held that, on the Day of Judgment, people's whitened/blackened faces would actually be visible to one another. But even this position did not associate this with African or non-African phenotypes

in this world. Mullā ʿAlī al-Qāri' cites Shihāb al-Dīn Aḥmad b. ʿAbd al-Salām al-Manūfī's (d. 931/1525) lost abridgment of his teacher al-Sakhāwī's *al-Maqāṣid al-ḥasana*, titled *al-Durra al-lāmiʿa fī bayan kathīr min al-aḥādīth al-shāʾiʿa*. According to Mullā ʿAlī al-Qāri', who cites al-Manūfī several times in his works (the only book he mentions is his *Mukhtaṣar*), al-Manūfī noted how a Hadith mentioned by al-Sakhāwī (roundly criticized by Hadith scholars) of the Prophet telling an Ethiopian man "the whiteness of a black man will be seen across the distance of a thousand years in the Garden" entailed that "the believers among the Black Africans (*sūdān*) will enter the Garden white." Al-Manūfī adds that Ibn Ḥajar "explicitly states this" in his *Fatḥ al-Bārī*. I have not found any evidence of this in the *Fatḥ* other than Ibn Ḥajar's explanation of the Quranic verse *wujūh yawma'idhin nāḍira* (Quran 75:22) as meaning that the believers' faces will be expressing delight with whiteness and purity (*bi'l-bayāḍ wa'l-ṣafā'*), which in no way suggests any transformation of phenotype; Mullā ʿAlī al-Qāri', *al-Asrār al-marfūʿa fī al-akhbār al-mawḍūʿa*, ed. Muḥammad Luṭfī Ṣabbāgh (Beirut: al-Maktab al-Islāmī, 1986), 202; idem, *Majmūʿ rasā'il*, 4:108; Ismāʿīl al-ʿAjlūnī, *Kashf al-khafā'*, ed. Aḥmad al-Qalāsh, 2 vols. (Cairo: Dār al-Turāth, [n.d.]), 1:473; Ibn Ḥajar, *Fatḥ al-Bārī*, 13:522 (according to almost all glosses of the verse); al-Suyūṭī, *al-Durr al-manthūr*, 6 vols. (Cairo: Maṭbaʿat al-Anwār al-Muḥammadiyya, 1990), 6:321–23.

20. *Ṣaḥīḥ al-Bukhārī: kitāb al-taʿbīr, bāb taʿbīr al-ru'ya baʿd ṣalāt al-ṣubḥ.*
21. *Ṣaḥīḥ al-Bukhārī: kitāb al-īmān, bāb tafāḍul ahl al-īmān fī al-aʿmāl.* The binary juxtaposition of burned/white can also be seen in a story about an early Muslim, Saʿdūn al-Khawlānī, being killed on the North African coast by Berber raiders who then tried to burn his body. No matter how long they burned it, however, "he remained white in color (*abyaḍ al-lawn*)." Someone suggested maybe he had done Hajj three times, since it was reported that the Prophet said that whoever performs Hajj three times, "God forbids his hair and skin from the Fire." See Qāḍī ʿIyāḍ bin Mūsā, *al-Shifā' bi-taʿrīf ḥuqūq al-muṣtafā*, ed. ʿAbduh ʿAlī Kūshak (Manama: Maktabat Niẓām Yaʿqūbī, 1436/2015), 599.
22. Shuʿayb al-Arnā'ūṭ declares this Hadith weak, while al-Albānī rates it *ṣaḥīḥ* and al-Suyūṭī *ḥasan*; al-Arnā'ūṭ, ed., *Musnad al-imām Aḥmad*, 45:481–82; al-Albānī, *Silsilat al-aḥādīth al-ṣaḥīḥa*, #49.
23. Other Hadiths with similar meanings but without the black/white imagery (*inna Allāh qabaḍa qabḍatan bi-yamīnihi . . .; inna Allāh khalaqa Ādam thumma akhadha al-khalq min ẓahrihi . . .*) are rated *ṣaḥīḥ* by al-Arnā'ūṭ, ed. *Musnad*, 29:134–35, 206.
24. Jaʿfar b. Ḥasan al-Barzanjī, *Majmūʿ mushtamil ʿalā mawlid al-Nabī (s) li'l-Barzanjī wa'l-Daybaʿ wa'l-ʿAzab* (Cairo: Maṭbaʿat Muṣṭafā al-Bābī al-Ḥalabī, 1342/1923), 38.
25. Al-Nabhānī, *Saʿādat al-dārayn*, 7, 437–8.
26. Nelly Hanna, *In Praise of Books: A Cultural History of Cairo's Middle Class, Sixteenth to the Eighteenth Century* (Syracuse: Syracuse University Press, 2003), 95.
27. Abū Bakr al-Jazūlī, *Guide to Goodness: Dalā'il al-khayrāt*, trans. Andrey Hassan Rosowsky, 2nd ed. (Chicago: Qazi, 2006), 77, 80, 121, 141.
28. Jan Knappert, *Swahili Islamic Poetry: Volume II The Two Burdas* (Leiden: Brill, 1971), 166, 203.
29. Abū Zayd ʿAbd al-Raḥmān al-Fāzāzī et al., *Dīwān al-Wasā'il al-mutaqabbila fī madḥ al-Nabī (s)* (Cairo: al-Maṭbaʿa al-Maymaniyya, 1322/1904), 22, 26, 38, 57,

118, 135; Oludamini Ogunnaike, *Poetry in Praise of Prophetic Perfection* (Cambridge: Islamic Text Society, 2020), 97.

30. Ogunnaike, *Poetry in Praise of Prophetic Perfection*, 37, 127.
31. Jean Boyd and Beverley B. Mack, *Collected Works of Nana Asma'u, Daughter of Usman 'dan Fodiyo* (East Lansing: Michigan State University Press, 1997), 126, 184, 258, 294.
32. Bamba, "Al-Ḥamdu li'llāh al-jazīl al-niʿma, wajaba ḥamdu Allāh wa'l-ṣalātu," [2] (available at https://almaktabatoulmouridiya.wordpress.com/2016/05/28/%D9%85%D8%AC%D9%85%D9%88%D8%B9%D8%A9-%D9%85%D9%86-%D9%82%D8%B5%D8%A7%D8%A6%D8%AF-%D8%A3%D8%A8%D9%8A-%D8%A7%D9%84%D9%85%D8%AD%D8%A7%D9%85%D8%AF-%D8%A7%D9%84%D8%B4%D9%8A%D8%AE-%D8%A7%D9%84%D8%AE%D8%AF/comment-page-1/); idem, "Kanz al-muhtadīn fī al-ṣalāt ʿalā khayr al-mursalīn," [4] (available at https://almaktabatoulmouridiya.wordpress.com/2016/05/28/%D9%85%D8%AC%D9%85%D9%88%D8%B9%D8%A9-%D9%85%D9%86-%D9%82%D8%B5%D8%A7%D8%A6%D8%AF-%D8%A3%D8%A8%D9%8A-%D8%A7%D9%84%D9%85%D8%AD%D8%A7%D9%85%D8%AF-%D8%A7%D9%84%D8%B4%D9%8A%D8%AE-%D8%A7%D9%84%D8%AE%D8%AF/comment-page-1/).
33. I acquired a hand-copied ms. of this poem in Addis Ababa in 2010. See Endris Mohammed Yesufe, "The *Ramsa* of *šayḫ* Aḥmad Ādam, *al-Danī al-Awwal* (d. 1903)," *Aethiopica* 19 (2016): 102–12.
34. Ogunnaike, *Poetry in Praise of Prophetic Perfection*, 37, 127. Shaykh Niasse's *Taysīr al-wuṣūl* can be found in *al-Dawāwīn al-sitt* (Dakar: Muḥammad Ma'mūn Niasse, 1988), 10, and part is translated by Zachary Wright at https://tijani.org/niasse-poetry.
35. *Wa min ḥubbihi tabyaḍḍu sūd wa bughḍuhu/bihi iswadda aqwām li'ām min al-bīḍ*; Niasse, "Taysīr al-wuṣūl," in *Āfāq al-shiʿr ʿind al-shaykh Ibrāhīm Anyās*, ed. Muḥammad ʿAbdallāh al-Tijānī (Nouakchott: Muḥammad al-Tijānī, 2018), 1:186. Thanks to Oludamini Ogunnaike for alerting me to this and helping me understand it.
36. Hall, *History of Race in Muslim West Africa*, 308. In one place in his history, al-Bartilī (d. 1219/1805) uses the term *bīḍ* instead of *bīḍān*; Muḥammad b. Abī Bakr al-Bartilī al-Walātī (d. 1219/1805), *Fatḥ al-shukūr fī maʿrifat aʿyān ʿulamāʾ al-Takrūr*, ed. ʿAbd al-Wadūd Wuld ʿAbdallāh and Aḥmad Jamāl Wuld al-Ḥasan (Cairo: Dār Najībawayh, 2010), 281.
37. Qāḍī ʿIyāḍ, *al-Shifāʾ*, 769, 850; Taqī al-Dīn al-Subkī, *al-Sayf al-maslūl ʿalā man sabba al-Rasūl*, ed. Iyyād Aḥmad al-Ghawj (Amman: Dār al-Fatḥ, 1421/2000), 407; Ibn Taymiyya, *al-Ṣārim al-maslūl ʿalā shātim al-rasūl*, ed. Muḥammad Muḥyī al-Dīn ʿAbd al-Ḥamīd (n.p.: al-Ḥaras al-Waṭanī al-Suʿūdī, 1403/1983), 526.
38. Qāḍī ʿIyāḍ, *al-Shifāʾ*, 850. See also al-Nawawī, *Rawḍat al-ṭālibīn*, ed. Zuhayr al-Shāwīsh, 12 vols. (Beirut: al-Maktab al-Islāmī, 1412/1991), 10:70; ʿAlī al-Qāriʾ, *Sharḥ al-Shifāʾ*, printed on the margins of Aḥmad Shihāb al-Dīn al-Khifājī, *Nasīm al-riyāḍ fī sharḥ Shifāʾ al-Qāḍī ʿIyāḍ*, 4 vols. (Beirut: Dār al-Kitāb al-ʿArabī, reprint of Cairo: al-Maṭbaʿa al-Azhariyya, 1909), 4:394.
39. ʿAbdallāh b. Muḥammad al-ʿAyyāshī, *al-Riḥla al-ʿAyyāshiyya li'l-baqāʿ al-ḥijāziyya*, ed. Aḥmad Farīd al-Mazīdī, 2 vols. (Beirut: Dār al-Kutub al-ʿIlmiyya, 2011), 1:58.
40. See *al-Fatāwā al-hindiyya*, 2nd ed. (Cairo: al-Maṭbaʿa al-Amīriyya, 1310/1892), 2:263–64.

41. Al-Qārī', *Sharḥ al-Shifā'*, 4:394. Cf. Sir Thomas Browne (d. 1682) noted that blackness could not be considered a curse since it is not insulting to those peoples characterized by it; Hall, *Things of Darkness*, 13.
42. Ibn Ḥajar al-Haytamī, *Ashraf al-wasā'il ilā fahm al-Shamā'il*, ed. Aḥmad Farīd al-Mazīdī (Beirut: Dār al-Kutub al-ʿIlmiyya, 1419/1998), 43–44. Cf. al-Qārī' and ʿAbd al-Ra'ūf al-Munāwī, *Kitāb al-Wasā'il fī sharḥ al-Shamā'il*, 2 vols. (Cairo: Muṣṭafā al-Bābī al-Ḥalabī, 1318/1901), 1:11–12.
43. ʿAbd al-Ḥamīd al-Shirwānī and al-Haytamī, *Ḥawāshī Tuḥfat al-muḥtāj bi-sharḥ al-Minhāj*, 10 vols. (Cairo: Maṭbaʿat Muṣṭafā Muḥammad, 1357/1938), 1:450.
44. ʿAbd al-Ḥamīd al-Shirwānī (d. 1301/1883–4) of Mecca adds his own reflection: how could anyone be declared an unbeliever for contradicting something not established as an axiomatic tenet of the faith (*maʿlūma bi'l-ḍarūra*)?; Sulaymān b. Muḥammad al-Bujayrimī (d. 1221/1806), *Tuḥfat al-ḥabīb ʿalā sharḥ al-khaṭīb*, 4 vols. (Beirut: Dār al-Fikr, 1410/1995), 1:410.
45. Ousmane Kane, personal communication; idem, *Beyond Timbuktu*, 86; Muḥammad b. ʿIyāḍ, *al-Taʿrīf bi'l-qāḍī ʿIyāḍ*, 113.
46. Al-Jāḥiẓ, *Rasā'il*, 1:215. For the changing standards of beauty in Arabic-Islamic civilization, see Habeeb Akande, *A Taste of Honey: Sexuality and Erotology in Islam* (London: Rabaah, 2015), 105–10.
47. Ibn ʿAbd al-Bāqī, *al-Ṭirāz al-manqūsh fī maḥāsin al-ḥubūsh*, 119, 130.
48. Evliyā' Chelebī, *An Ottoman Traveler: Selections from the Book of Travels by Evliya Çelebi*, trans. Robert Dankoff and Sooyong Kim (London: Eland, 2010), 361.
49. James Bruce, *Travels to Discover the Source of the Nile* (Edinburgh: J. Ruthven, 1790), 308.
50. C. Snouck Hurgronje, *Mekka in the Latter Part of the Nineteenth Century* (Leiden: Brill, 2014), 106–9.
51. Charles White, *Three Years in Constantinople*, 3 vols. (London: Henry Colburn, 1846), 2:285–86, 298.
52. Al-Sharīshī, *Sharḥ Maqāmāt al-Ḥarīrī*, 1:335.
53. Hagedorn, *Domestic Slavery in Syria and Egypt*, 30.
54. Rifāʿat al-Ṭahṭāwī, *An Imam in Paris*, trans. Daniel L. Newman (London: Saqi, 2004), 180.
55. Abdul Sheriff, "*Suria*: Concubines or Secondary Slave Wife," in *Sex, Power and Slavery*, ed. Gwyn Campbell and Elizabeth Elbourne (Athens, GA: Ohio University Press, 2014), 113.
56. The Prophet reportedly said, '*dakhaltu al-janna fa-ra'aytu jāriya admā' laʿsā', fa-qultu: mā hādhihi yā Jibrā'īl? Fa-qāla innā Allāh taʿālā ʿarafa shahwat Jaʿfar b. Abī Ṭālib li'l-udm al-laʿas fa-khalaqa lahu hādhā*; ʿAbd al-Karīm al-Rāfiʿī, *al-Tadwīn fī akhbār Qazvīn*, ed. ʿAzīz Allāh al-ʿUṭāridī, 4 vols. (Beirut: Dār al-Kutub al-ʿIlmiyya, 1987), 2:35.
57. Though this book is lost, Ibn al-Jawzī seems to have quoted almost his entire chapter on this from Ibn al-Marzubān; Ibn al-Jawzī, *Tanwīr al-ghabash*, 233–45.
58. Ibid., 233, cf. 243.
59. *ismaʿ maqālat ḥaqq/wa kun bi-ḥaqqika ʿawnī, inna al-malīḥ malīḥ/yuḥabbu fī kull lawn*; al-Suyūṭī, *Nuzhat al-ʿumr*, 16; Shams al-Dīn Muḥammad al-Dāwūdī, *Tarjamat al-ʿallāma al-Suyūṭī* (Ms. Wetzstein I.20, Staatsbibliothek, Berlin), 92a. Ghuṣūn gave birth to a son when al-Suyūṭī was 21. For a summary of an important source on this, see https://www.alukah.net/culture/1188/80578/#_ftnref1.

## 8. ANTIBLACKNESS IN MĀLIKĪ MARRIAGE LAW

1. *Ṣaḥīḥ al-Bukhārī: kitāb al-nikāḥ, bāb al-akfā' fī al-dīn.* The meaning of *ḥasab* here has been debated, with some saying that it means descent (*nasab*) and some that it means character and conduct. The latter is buttressed by the narration of the Hadith via Abū Sa'īd al-Khudrī in the *Mustadrak* of al-Ḥākim and *Ṣaḥīḥ Ibn Ḥibbān*, which has the word 'character' (*khuluq*) instead of *ḥasab*; al-Ḥākim al-Naysābūrī, *al-Mustadrak*, 2:161.
2. Abū 'Īsā Sīdī al-Mahdī b. Muḥammad al-Wazzānī, *al-Nawāzil al-ṣughrā*, ed. Muḥammad al-Sayyid 'Uthmān, 4 vols. (Beirut: Dār al-Kutub al-'Ilmiyya, 1435/2014), 2:189. I have not been able to identify this 'Abd al-'Azīz b. 'Alī beyond al-Wazzānī's reference to him. I have checked sources like al-Kattānī's *Salwat al-anfās*, Muḥammad Mukhtār al-Sūsī's *al-Ma'sūl*, Ibn Zaydān's *Itḥāf a'lām al-nās bi-jamāl akhbār ḥāḍirat Miknās* and al-Shifshāwī's *Dawḥat al-nāshir li-maḥāsin man kāna bi'l-maghrib min mashāyikh al-qarn al-'āshir*, with no luck.
3. Al-Wazzānī, *al-Nawāzil al-ṣughrā*, 2:188. As is often the case in this work, it is unclear who the speaker is in the text cited here. It may be Abū 'Alī al-Ḥusayn al-Simlālī of Sous (d. 899/1494). But it seems more likely it is al-Wazzānī himself. The role of custom in substantially modifying Mālikī law on marriage suitability was first brought to my attention by Razan Idris, for which I thank her.
4. Al-Dhahabī, *Tadhkirat al-ḥuffāẓ*, 4:114–16.
5. The reformist movement in question was known as the Qadizadeli, and the specific prayer was the *ṣalāt al-raghā'ib*; Kātib Chelebī, *The Balance of Truth*, trans. G.L. Lewis (London: George Allen & Unwin, 1957), 48, 95, 97, 99. For the Qadizadeli, see Madeline Zilfi, "The Kadizadelis: Discordant Revivalism in Seventeenth-Century Istanbul," *Journal of Near Eastern Studies* 45, n. 4 (1986): 257.
6. Shams al-Dīn Muḥammad al-Dāwūdī, *Tarjamat al-'allāma al-Suyūṭī*, 37a-38a; al-Suyūṭī, *al-Ḥāwī li'l-fatāwī*, 2 vols. (Beirut: Dār al-Kitāb al-'Arabī, n.d.), 1:151–53.
7. E.g., Quran 2:228–29, 233, 241, and the Prophet's instruction to Hind, wife of Abū Sufyān, to take what she needed for herself and her children "according to what is customary" from her cheap husband; *Ṣaḥīḥ al-Bukhārī: kitāb al-buyū', bāb man ajrā amr al-amṣār . . .*
8. This is also sometimes vowelled as *al-'āda muḥakkama*, which is understood as 'custom has been deemed dispositive.' The phrase *al-'āda muḥakkima* seems to originate, in a slightly different sense, in the work of al-Juwaynī (d. 478/1085); Imām al-Ḥaramayn al-Juwaynī, *al-Burhān fī uṣūl al-fiqh*, ed. Ṣalāḥ Muḥammad 'Uwayḍa, 2 vols. (Beirut: Dār al-Kutub al-'Ilmiyya, 1418/1997), 1:222; idem, *Nihāyat al-maṭlab fī dirāyat al-madhhab*, ed. 'Abd al-'Aẓīm Maḥmūd al-Dīb, 20 vols. (Jeddah: Dār al-Minhāj, 1428/2007), 8:163. The compilation of the five main maxims has been traced to Qāḍī Ḥusayn al-Marwazī (d. 462/1069), a Shāfi'ī scholar of Baghdad.
9. 'Alā' al-Dīn 'Alī al-Ṭarābulusī, *Mu'īn al-ḥukkām fīmā yataraddadu bayn al-khaṣmayn min al-aḥkām* (Cairo: al-Maṭba'a al-Maymaniyya, 1310/1892), 199; al-Ghazālī, *The Fatāwā of al-Ghazzālī*, ed. Mustafa Mahmoud Abu Sway (Kuala Lumpur: International Institute of Islamic Thought, 1996), 109–10; al-Marghīnānī, *al-Hidāya*, 4 vols. (Lahore: Maktaba Raḥmāniyya, n.d.), 4:61; al-Wazzānī, *al-Nawāzil al-ṣughrā*, 2:188–9; Ibn Qudāma, *al-Mughnī*, 7:455.

10. Ibn ʿĀbidīn, "Nashr al-ʿarf fī banāʾ baʿḍ al-aḥkām ʿalā al-ʿurf," in *Majmūʿat Rasāʾil Ibn ʿĀbidīn*, 2 vols. (Damascus: [Muḥammad Hāshim al-Kutubī], [1907]), 2:115. The jurist in question was one Muḥammad b. al-Faḍl al-Kumārī (d. 381/991).
11. Billū, *Rafʿ al-shubha fī al-tashabbuh biʾl-kafara waʾl-ẓalama waʾl-jahala fī al-aqwāl waʾl-afʿāl wa jamīʿ al-aḥwāl*, ed. Yaḥyā Muḥammad (Gusau, Nigeria: Iqraʾ, 2013, published in a 2-volume *Mukhtārāt min muʾallafāt amīr al-muʾminīn Muḥammad Billū*), 2:14–15.
12. Nejmeddine Hentati, "Rôle de la coutume dans la formation du droit malikite," *Der Islam* 93, n. 1 (2016): 75; al-Wazzānī, *al-Nawāzil al-jadīda al-kubrā fī-mā li-ahl Fās wa ghayrihim min al-badū waʾl-qurā*, ed. ʿUmar ʿImād, 12 vols. (Casablanca: Maṭbaʿat al-Faḍāla, 1997), 10:225. Mālikī jurists in North Africa did not treat deviating from the main opinion (*mashhūr*) of their school lightly. Shaykh Sīdī Ibrāhīm Ibn Hilāl of Sijilmasa (d. 903/1497–8) insisted that "it is not permissible to give fatwas except by the *mashhūr* ruling, and there is no acting except by the *mashhūr*." But it was broadly allowed if done by senior scholars or in situations where it was deemed a necessity; al-Wazzānī, *al-Nawāzil al-jadīda*, 4:3–6, 9–10, 16, 40–41, 81; ʿAbd al-Ḥayy al-Kattānī, *Fahris al-fahāris*, ed. Iḥsān ʿAbbās (Beirut: Dār al-Gharb al-Islāmī, 1406/1986), 2:1107. See Ibn Maryam, *al-Bustān fī dhikr al-ʿulamāʾ waʾl-awliyāʾ bi-Tilimsān*, ed. ʿAbd al-Qādir al-Būbāya (Beirut: Dār al-Kutub al-ʿIlmiyya, 2014), 155–56. In one instance in Cairo in 1524 CE, a Mālikī judge fell into conflict with the chief judge (Ḥanafī) overseeing him because the chief judge insisted that his junior rule by the *mashhūr* of his school while the latter insisted on his right as a senior scholar to choose among the Mālikī school's rulings on an issue; Reem Meshal, "Antagonistic *Sharīʿa*s and the Construction of Orthodoxy in Sixteenth-Century Cairo," *Journal of Islamic Studies* 21, no. 2 (2010): 200.
13. Abū al-Ḥasan ʿAlī al-Nubāhī, *Tārīkh quḍāt al-andalus*, ed. Maryam Qāsim Ṭawīl (Beirut: Dār al-Kutub al-ʿIlmiyya, 1415/1995), 44–45. For the first Hadith, see *Sunan* of Abū Dāwūd: *kitāb al-adab, bāb fī qiyām al-rajul biʾl-rajul*. For the second, see *Ṣaḥīḥ al-Bukhārī*: *kitāb al-adab, bāb al-hijra*.
14. The Indic taboo on widowhood has been articulated around the widow's 'failure' to properly protect or serve her husband and for not joining him in death. Widows are also a vector of anxiety over the temptation presented by women and loss of sexual control over them. See Charu Gupta, *Sexuality, Obscenity, Community: Women, Muslims, and the Hindu Public in Colonial India* (New York: Palgrave, 2002), 301–307. The taboo on widow remarriage goes back at least to the Laws of Manu (*circa* 100 CE) and seems to have become very strong among Rajputs in the Mughal era; Sabita Singh, *The Politics of Marriage in Medieval India: Gender and Alliance in Rajasthan* (New Delhi: Oxford University Press, 2019), 185, 197. For the absorption of upper-caste taboos around widowhood into Muslim practice, see Karen Ruffle, *Gender, Sainthood, and Everyday Practice in South Asian Shiʾism* (Chapel Hill: University of North Carolina Press, 2011), 87–88. Widows not remarrying was a function of an even larger socio-legal issue of caste, as one feature that distinguished high-caste Hindus was the taboo on widow remarriage. See Nandita Prasad Sahai, "The 'Other' Culture: Craft Societies and Widow Remarriage in Early Modern India," *Journal of Women's History* 19, n. 2 (2007): 36–58. Widow remarriage was normal among the agricultural castes, such as the Jats, and artisanal castes; Singh, *The Politics of Marriage in Medieval India*, 191.
15. Ḥassān al-Hind Mīr Ghulām ʿAlī Āzād, *Maʾāthir al-kirām*, ed. ʿAbdallāh Khān, 2 vols. (Hyderabad: Maṭbaʿa Mufīd ʿĀlim Āgra, 1910), 1:56–59. There seems to

have been a trend among ulama in India in the mid to late sixteenth century towards combatting 'indigenous' heretical practices, meaning not necessarily elements adopted from Indian religions but rather anything not traceable back to an Arabian source. ʿAbd al-Nabī Gangūhī (d. 991/1583–4), a leading scholar in the Mughal capital until he fell from imperial grace, had studied with al-Haytamī in Mecca and condemned worship practices common in India, like performing two prayer cycles at night while reading *Āyat al-Kursī* and performing a third call to prayer right before the Friday prayer. In fact, anticipating the later approach of Deoband scholars, Gangūhī states that any practice that the ignorant masses mistake as normative is rendered discouraged (*makrūh*) because of that; ʿAbd al-Nabī Gangūhī, *Sunan al-hudā fī mutāba ʿat al-muṣṭafā*, 113a-b, 114b, 155b, 157a-b, 189a. See also ʿAbd al-Ḥayy al-Ḥasanī, *Nuzhat al-khawāṭir fī bahjat al-masāmiʿ wa'l-nawāẓir*, 3rd edn. (Hyderabad: Dā'irat al-Maʿārif al-ʿUthmāniyya, 1989), 5:62 (condemning local marriage customs), 403 (judge in Jaunpur bans extra *adhān* on Friday, prohibits fines as punishment).

16. SherAli Tareen, *Defending Muḥammad in Modernity* (Notre Dame, IN: Notre Dame University Press, 2020), 58.
17. Barbara Metcalf, *Islamic Revival in British India* (Princeton: Princeton University Press, 1982), 74, 144–45. For criticism of Indian dowry traditions influencing Muslim practice, see Abū al-Ḥasan al-Nadwī, *Plain Speaking to Muslims* (Indore: Board of Islamic Studies, 1987), 10–13. Jamāl al-Dīn Dihlawī (d. 1299/1881–2), an acolyte of the reformist tradition of Shāh Walī Allāh who helped build Bhopal into a scholarly center, advocated the remarriage of divorcees; ʿAbd al-Ḥayy al-Ḥasanī, *Nuzhat al-khawāṭir*, 7:149.
18. Peter Lape, "Focus on Islam IV: Archaeological approaches to the study of Islam in Island Southeast Asia," *Antiquity* 79, n. 306 (2005): 829–36; Marcos García-García et al., "The zooarchaeological identification of a 'Morisco' community after the Christian conquest of Granada (Spain, early 16th century): sociocultural continuities and economic innovations," *Archaeological and Anthropological Sciences*, 13, n. 3 (2021).
19. Ross E. Dunn, *The Adventures of Ibn Battuta* (Berkeley: University of California Press, 2012, originally published 1989), 234–35.
20. Howard Federspiel, *Sultans, Shamans and Saints: Islam and Muslims in Southeast Asia* (Honolulu: University of Hawaii Press, 2007), 104–5.
21. Al-Wazzānī, *al-Nawāzil al-ṣughrā*, 4:432.
22. Muḥammad Bakhīt al-Muṭīʿī, "Kitāb Aḥsan al-kalām fī-mā yataʿallaqu bi'l-sunna wa'l-bidʿa min al-aḥkām," in *Majmūʿat rasā'il al-ʿallāma Muḥammad Bakhīt al-Muṭīʿī*, 2nd ed. (Cairo: Maktabat al-Qāhira, 1932), 3, 30. See also Junaid Quadri, *Transformations of Tradition* (Oxford: Oxford University Press, 2021).
23. ʿAbd al-Raḥmān b. Aḥmad al-Waghlīsī, *al-Muqaddima al-Waghlīsiyya ʿalā madhhab al-sāda al-mālikiyya*, ed. Amal Muḥammad Najīb (Dublin: al-Markaz al-Najībawayh, 1428/2007), 60. Compare with the absence of such specifics in the discussion of Ibn Qayyim al-Jawziyya (Ḥanbalī), *Iʿlām al-muwaqqiʿīn*, ed. Muḥammad ʿIzz al-Dīn Khaṭṭāb, 5 vols. (Beirut: Dār Iḥyā' al-Turāth al-ʿArabī, 2001), 2:34. For the Shāfiʿī school, see al-Ghazālī, *al-Wasīṭ*, ed. Aḥmad Maḥmūd Ibrāhīm and Muḥammad Muḥammad Tāmir, 7 vols. (Cairo: Dār al-Salām, 1417/1997), 5:36. Another Shāfiʿī scholar, Taqī al-Dīn al-Ḥuṣnī of Damascus (d. 829/1426) explains that everything depends on whether the specific woman is attractive or not (he notes how beautiful some Turkish slave women are); Taqī al-Dīn al-

Ḥuṣnī, *Kifāyat al-akhyār*, ed. ʿAbd al-Qādir al-Arnāʾūṭ (Damascus: Dār al-Bashāʾir, 1422/2001), 417.

24. Al-Jaṣṣāṣ, *Sharḥ Mukhtaṣar al-Ṭaḥāwī*, ed. Sāʾid Bakdāsh et al., 8 vols. (Beirut: Dār al-Bashāʾir al-Islāmiyya, 1431/2010), 4:251.
25. Ali, *The 'Negro' in Arab-Muslim Consciousness*, 173 ff.
26. See, for example, Layla Abdullah-Poulos, "When Islamic Scholarship is Anti Black," YouTube.com, 29 June 2019, https://www.youtube.com/watch?v=7LmZ2p0VF08&t=113s. Thanks to Habeeb Akande for drawing my attention to this.
27. Some Mālikīs and some Ḥanafīs and one narration from Ibn Ḥanbal (not considered the correct position by Ibn Qudāma) hold that marriages between non-*kaf*'s should be annulled, but the vast majority of scholars accept such marriages as valid if the bride and her guardian choose that man; Ibn Qudāma, *al-Mughnī*, 7:372–3.
28. Ali, *The 'Negro' in Arab-Muslim Consciousness*, 173 ff.
29. ʿAlī b. Muḥammad al-Lakhmī, *al-Tabṣira*, ed. Aḥmad ʿAbd al-Karīm Najīb, 14 vols. (Doha: Wizārat al-Awqāf, n.d.), 4:1891.
30. Al-Wazzānī, *al-Nawāzil al-ṣughrā*, 2:171, 188–89.
31. Abū al-Walīd Hishām al-Qurṭubī, *al-Mufīd li'l-ḥukkām fīmā yuʿraḍu lahum min nawāzil al-aḥkām*, ed. Aḥmad ʿAbd al-Karīm Najīb (Dublin: Markaz Najībawayh, 1433/2012), 2:75. In this case, the author is affirming the affirmation offered by Ibn Abī Zayd al-Qayrawānī (d. 386/996). Thanks to my student Mohamad Ali for this reference. See also al-Lakhmī, 4:1823.
32. Westermark and El-Baqqali, *Wit and Wisdom in Morocco*, 131–32; al-Zajjālī, *Amthāl al-ʿawāmm*, 2:286, 246.
33. Aḥmad al-Tijānī (d. 1815) freed and married two of his slave women, Mubāraka and Mabrūka, both of whom bore him children. They were almost certainly Black African; Zachary Wright, *Realizing Islam: The Tijaniyya in North Africa and the Eighteenth-Century Muslim World* (Chapel Hill: University of North Carolina Press, 2020), 61.
34. Aḥmad b. Muḥammad Ibn al-ʿAdhārī, *al-Bayān al-mughrib fī akhbār al-andalus wa'l-maghrib*, ed. Bashshār ʿAwwād Maʿrūf, 4 vols. (Beirut: Dār al-Gharb al-Islāmī, 1434/2013), 3:14.
35. El Hamel, *Black Morocco*, 95–96.
36. See, for example, Hagedorn, 130. When pilgrims traveling from Marrakesh across North Africa in 1662 CE were harassed by raiders, a black pilgrim was seized because the bandits thought he was a slave; al-ʿAyyāshī, *al-Riḥla*, 157. Gomez alludes to this irony, perhaps with an eye to criticizing some modern scholarship; Michael Gomez, *African Dominion: A New History of Empire in Early and Medieval West Africa* (Princeton: Princeton University Press, 2018), 55.
37. Ali, *The 'Negro' in Arab-Muslim Consciousness*, 174–5.
38. Dearden, *Tully's Letters*, 17, 72, 163.
39. Ali, *The 'Negro' in Arab-Muslim Consciousness*, 176.
40. Al-Wazzānī, *al-Nawāzil al-ṣughrā*, 2:188–89.
41. Abū al-Walīd al-Qurṭubī, *al-Mufīd li'l-ḥukkām*, 2:73–74.
42. ʿAbd al-Laṭīf b. al-Musabbiḥ al-Mirdāsī, *ʿUmdat al-bayān*, ed. Aḥmad Farīd al-Mazīdī (Beirut: Dār al-Kutub al-ʿIlmiyya, 2010), 26 (thanks to David Drennan for locating this for me).
43. This could be read *tushtahā akthar min al-ḥarāʾir* ("is desired more than free women") or *tashtahī akthar min al-ḥarāʾir* ("desires more than free women"). The

first reading would be more consistent with the theme of desirability, and is, in fact, specified as correct by ʿAbd al-Qādir al-Fāsī (d. 1091/1680). The second would be more grammatically standard and fits with the idea of Black Africans being hypersexual; Aḥmad Zarrūq, *Sharḥ al-ʿallāma Zarrūq ʿalā al-Muqaddima al-Waghlīsiyya*, ed. Maḥfūẓ Bū Kirāʿ and ʿAmmār Basṭa (Beirut: Dār Ibn Ḥazm, 2010), 181–83; ʿAbd al-Qādir al-Fāsī, *al-Ajwiba al-ṣughrā*, published with al-Mirdāsī, *ʿUmdat al-bayān*, 206. The commentary of one ʿAbd al-Raḥmān al-Ṣabbāgh, copied in 1191/1776, offers no remarkable discussion on this point, emphasizing that one can look at a person who would not be a cause of temptation; ʿAbd al-Raḥmān al-Ṣabbāgh, *Sharḥ ʿAbd al-Raḥmān al-Ṣabbāgh ʿalā Matn al-Waghlīsiyya*, [97a].

44. Ibn Ḥajar, *al-Durar al-kāmina fī aʿyān al-miʾa al-thāmina*, 4 vols. (Beirut: Dār Iḥyāʾ al-Turāth al-ʿArabī, reprint of 1931 Hyderabad edition), 1:80.
45. ʿAbd al-Bāqī al-Zurqānī, *Sharḥ al-Zurqānī ʿalā Mukhtaṣar Sīdī Khalīl*, ed. ʿAbd al-Salām Muḥammad Amīn, 8 vols. (Beirut: Dār al-Kutub al-ʿIlmiyya, 1422/2002), 3:314–15; ʿAlī b. Aḥmad al-Ṣaʿīdī al-ʿAdawī, *Ḥāshiyat al-ʿAdawī ʿalā Kifāyat al-ṭālib*, ed. Yūsuf Muḥammad al-Biqāʿī, 2 vols. (Beirut: Dār al-Fikr, 1414/1994), 2:46.
46. Muḥammad b. ʿArafa al-Dasūqī et al., *Ḥāshiyat al-Dasūqī ʿalā al-Sharḥ al-kabīr*, 4 vols. (Cairo: Dār Iḥyāʾ al-Kutub al-ʿArabiyya, n.d.), 2:250.
47. Muḥammad b. Muḥammad Sālim al-Majlisī, *Minaḥ al-ʿalī fī sharḥ kitāb al-Akhḍarī*, ed. Abbāhu Muḥammad ʿAlī al-Majlisī al-Shinqīṭī and Muḥammad Maḥfūẓ Aḥmad ([Nouakchott]: Taṣwīr al-ʿĀṣimiyya, 1426/2005), 59–60, 80.
48. See Saʿd b. ʿUmar Jalyā Tūrī al-Fūtī (Saadou Oumar Toure), *Ḥall al-masāʾil fī sharḥ Mukhtaṣar al-Akhḍarī biʾl-dalāʾil* (n.p: n.p, [1971]). For an excellent biography of this figure, see *Mawsūʿat aʿlām al-ʿulamāʾ waʾl-udabāʾ al-ʿarab waʾl-muslimīn*, ed. Munjī Būsnīna, 8 vols. (Beirut: Dār al-Jīl, 1425/2005), 4:691–93.
49. Al-Qurṭubī, *al-Jāmiʿ li-aḥkām al-Qurʾān*, 2:69–70. This Hadith appears both as part of a sermon of the Prophet narrated via a *ṣaḥīfa* from ʿAbdallāh b. ʿAmr b. al-ʿĀṣ and as a discrete Hadith taken from that sermon. See *Sunan* of Abū Dāwūd: *kitāb al-jihād, bāb fī al-sariyya taruddu ʿalā ahl al-ʿaskar*; *Sunan al-Nasāʾī*: *kitāb al-qasāma, bāb suqūṭ al-qawad min al-muslim liʾl-kāfir*; *Sunan Ibn Mājah*: *kitāb al-diyāt, bāb al-muslimūn tatakāfaʾu dimāʾuhum*; al-Bayhaqī, *al-Sunan al-kubrā*, 8:54–55. Al-Albānī grades it *ḥasan*, and Shuʿayb al-Arnāʾūṭ and al-Ḥākim grade it as *ṣaḥīḥ*; al-Albānī, *Ṣaḥīḥ al-Jāmiʿ al-ṣaghīr*, 2:1137; al-Arnāʾūṭ, ed., *Musnad Aḥmad*, 11:403, 587; al-Ḥākim, *al-Mustadrak*, 2:141. It also appears with the initial wording *(w)aʾl-muslimūn yad ʿalā man siwāhum tatakāfaʾu dimāʾuhum* . . .
50. Aḥmad al-Shinqīṭī, *Mawāhib al-jalīl min adillat Khalīl*, ed. ʿAbdallāh Ibrāhīm al-Anṣārī (Doha: Idārat Iḥyāʾ al-Turāth al-Islāmī, 1407/1986), 3:32.
51. Abū Bakr Ibn al-ʿArabī, *Aḥkām al-Qurʾān*, 1:631; al-Qurṭubī, *Jāmiʿ*, 3:344.
52. Ali, *The 'Negro' in Arab-Muslim Consciousness*, 185.
53. Hasan Ali Kettani, "al-Akhīr // Dawrat Sharḥ al-Waghlīsiyya // Aḥkām al-Ṣiyām waʾl-akhlāq waʾl-adab," YouTube, 26 August 2021 (see minutes 41–44), https://www.youtube.com/watch?v=n4TDg0J_7ak&list=PL7Q03ZIW8WAGL2sWJ8R0toUUrV1q6LyN0&index=5.
54. Saḥnūn ʿAbd al-Salām b. Saʿīd, *al-Mudawwana*, 16 vols. (Riyadh: Wizārat al-Shuʾūn al-Islāmiyya waʾl-Awqāf, reprint of the 1324/1906 Cairo Maṭbaʿat al-Saʿāda edition), 16:21, 32.
55. See the West African Arabic Manuscript Database at https://waamd.lib.berkeley.edu/home, WAAMD #7589 (Niamey #1601), WAAMD #13950 (Segou #5675),

WAAMD #14523 (Segou #5709); Timbuktu WAAMDs #32551, #32556, #56308, #56347, #56353, #56359, #57039, #58089, #62904, #67770, #67858, #70491, #70807, #71397, #72024, #78056, #78151, #78912, #78943, #83259, #83561, #83624, #83984, #84177, #88259.

56. This is based on Hunwick's bibliography of literature in the region as well as the West African Arabic Manuscript Database.
57. Ali, *The 'Negro' in Arab-Muslim Consciousness*, 176.
58. See Juliette Gallonnier, "When 'White Devils' Join the Deen: White American Converts to Islam and the Experience of Non-Normative Whiteness," *Notes & Documents – CNRS* (2015): 19; https://www.aljazeera.com/opinions/2020/8/20/the-hidden-racism-of-the-muslim-marriage-market
59. Ibrāhīm Niasse, *The Removal of Confusion*, trans. Zachary Wright et al. (Louisville, KY: Fons Vitae, 2010), 255–56. Shaykh Niasse draws on the famous Ottoman *tafsīr Rūḥ al-bayān* by Bursavi Ismail Hakki (d. 1127/1715), who in turn cites the commentary of Muḥammad Shaykhīzāde (d. *circa* 950/1543).

## 9. WHAT IS THE POINT OF THE LAW? ISLAMIC HIERARCHY OR ISLAMIC EGALITARIANISM

1. For the origins and ubiquity of the Cinderella narrative, see Jack Zipes, ed., *The Great Fairy Tale Tradition* (New York: Norton, 2001), 444; Fay Beauchamp, "Asian Origins of Cinderella: The Zhuang Storyteller of Guangxi," *Oral Tradition* 25, n. 2 (2010): 450–51.
2. See https://www.sfsu.edu/~medieval/romances/freine.html; Beauchamp, "Asian Origins of Cinderella," 482.
3. Eskender A. Yousuf, "A call to address anti-Blackness within African immigrant communities," *Minnpost*, 28 July 2020, https://web.archive.org/web/20211228185606/https://www.minnpost.com/community-voices/2020/07/a-call-to-address-anti-blackness-within-african-immigrant-communities/; Ohimai Amaize, "The 'Social Distance' between Africa and African Americans," *Jstor Daily*, 14 July 2021, https://daily.jstor.org/the-social-distance-between-africa-and-african-americans/.
4. Ali, *The 'Negro' in Arab-Muslim Consciousness*, 177; Abū al-Walīd al-Qurṭubī, *al-Mufīd li'l-ḥukkām*, 2:73; al-Dasūqī, *Ḥāshiyat al-Dasūqī*, 2:250.
5. *Jāmiʿ al-Tirmidhī*: *kitāb al-nikāḥ, bāb idhā jā'akum man tarḍā* . . .; *Sunan Ibn Mājah*: *kitāb al-nikāḥ, bāb al-akfā'*; al-Bayhaqī, *Sunan al-kubrā*, 7:132; al-Ḥākim, *al-Mustadrak*, 2:165. Al-Suyūṭī considers it *ṣaḥīḥ*, al-Albānī considers it *ḥasan*; al-Albānī, *Silsilat al-aḥādīth al-ṣaḥīḥa*, 3:20 (#1022). This Hadith appears in a book, a fragment of which has been found in a manuscript from the late 800s CE, the *Jāmiʿ* of Ibn Wahb (d. 197/813), though it is not in that early fragment. This narration includes the questioner asking the Prophet, "Even if he is Ethiopian?" and the Prophet replying, "Even if he is black (*aswad*)"; ʿAbdallāh b. Wahb, *Jāmiʿ*, ed. Rifʿat Fawzī ʿAbd al-Muṭṭalib (Mansoura: Dār al-Wafā', 1405 /2005), 143.
6. Ibn Qudāma, *Mughnī*, 7:372. The Hadith begins: *takhayyarū li-nuṭafikum fa'nkiḥū al-akfā'* . . . Al-Suyūṭī and al-Albānī consider it *ṣaḥīḥ*, and Ibn Ḥajar suggests it is

*ḥasan*; al-Albānī, *Silsilat al-aḥādīth al-ṣaḥīḥa*, 3:56–7 (#1067); ʿAbd al-Raʾūf al-Munāwī, *Fayḍ al-qadīr sharḥ al-Jāmiʿ al-ṣaghīr*, ed. Ḥamdī al-Damardāsh Muḥammad, 13 vols. (Mecca: Maktabat Nizār Muṣṭafā al-Bāz, 1998), 5:2659–60. Muḥammad Zāhid al-Kawtharī, on the other hand, is highly critical of this Hadith; al-Kawtharī, *Maqālāt*, 2nd ed. (Cairo: Dār al-Salām, 1428/2007), 40–43.

7. *Ṣaḥīḥ Muslim*: *kitāb al-ṭalāq, bāb al-muṭallaqa thalātha lā nafaqa lahā.*
8. *ʿal-ʿarab baʿḍuhum akfāʾ baʿḍ waʾl-mawālī baʿḍuhum akfāʾ baʿḍ illā ḥāʾik aw ḥajjām,*ʾ *ʿal-nās akfāʾ illā al-ḥāʾik waʾl-ḥajjām*ʾ; al-Sarakhsī, *al-Mabsūṭ*, 5:33–36 (in another common edition, p. 25); Ibn Ḥajar, *Talkhīṣ al-ḥabīr*, ed. Ḥasan ʿAbbās Quṭb, 4 vols. (Cairo: Muʾassasat Qurṭuba, 1416/1995), 3:336–37. Al-Bayhaqī admits that the Hadiths instructing Muslims to consider aspects like lineage and profession as part of *kafāʾa* are mostly too weak to be "the basis for proof"; al-Bayhaqī, *al-Sunan al-kubrā*, 7:214.
9. See Ibn Ḥajar al-Haytamī, *Mablagh al-arab fī fakhr al-ʿarab*, ed. Yusrī ʿAbd al-Ghanī ʿAbdallāh (Beirut: Dār al-Kutub al-ʿIlmiyya, 1410/1990), 24–26, 28, 50.
10. For the first Hadith, see *Jāmiʿ al-Tirmidhī*: *kitāb al-tafsīr, bāb min sūrat al-ḥujarāt.* For the second, ʿ*Aqīlū dhawī al-hayʾāt ʿatharātihim illā al-ḥudūd*ʾ, see *Sunan* of Abū Dāwūd: *kitāb al-ḥudūd, bāb fī al-ḥadd yushfaʿu fīhi.* Ibn Ḥajar strongly suggests that this second Hadith is not reliable, while al-Albānī feels it is; Ibn Ḥajar, *Talkhīṣ al-ḥabīr*, 4:149–50; al-Albānī, *Silsilat al-aḥādīth al-ṣaḥīḥa*, #638.
11. Ibn Ḍuwayyān, *Manār al-sabīl fī sharḥ al-Dalīl*, ed. Zuhayr al-Shāwīsh, 7th ed., 2 vols. (Damascus: al-Maktab al-Islāmī, 1989), 2:159; Ibn Qudāma, *Mughnī*, 7:374–77; Ibn Rajab, *Sharḥ ʿIlal al-Tirmidhī*, 2 vols. (n.p.: Dār al-Mallāḥ, 1398/1978), 1:311.
12. Al-Sarakhsī, *Mabsuṭ*, 5:33–36 (in another common edition, p. 25); al-Ḥasan b. Manṣūr Qāḍīkhān, *Fatāwā Qāḍīkhān*, ed. Sālim Muṣṭafā al-Badrī, 3 vols. (Beirut: Dār al-Kutub al-ʿIlmiyya, 1988), 1:309; Ibn Ḍuwayyān, *Manār al-sabīl*, 2:160.
13. Al-Jaṣṣāṣ, *Sharḥ Mukhtaṣar al-Ṭaḥāwī*, ed. Sāʾid Bakdāsh et al., 8 vols. (Beirut: Dār al-Bashāʾir al-Islāmiyya, 1431/2010), 4:250–3; al-Sarakhsī, *Mabsuṭ*, 5:33–36 (in another common edition, p. 25); Qāḍīkhān, *Fatāwā Qāḍīkhān*, 1:309; Ibn Ḍuwayyān, *Manār al-sabīl*, 2:160.
14. Kamāl al-Dīn Muḥammad b. ʿAbd al-Wāḥid Ibn al-Humām, *Fatḥ al-qadīr*, 10 vols. (Beirut: Dār al-Fikr, n.d.), 3:302.
15. *Ṣaḥīḥ Muslim*: *kitāb al-janāʾiz, bāb fīman yuthnā ʿalayhi khayran aw sharran min al-mawtā*; Muḥammad b. Ismāʿīl al-Ṣanʿānī, *al-Masāʾil al-muhimma fīmā taʿummu bihi al-balwā*, ed. Muḥammad al-Aṣghar al-Muqaṭṭirī (Beirut: Dār Ibn Ḥazm, 2004), 48–49.
16. Robert Brunschvig, "Métiers vils en Islam," *Studia Islamica* 16 (1962): 58.
17. Abū Isḥāq al-Shīrāzī, *al-Muhadhdhab fī fiqh al-imām al-Shāfiʿī*, ed. Muḥammad al-Zuḥaylī, 6 vols. (Beirut: al-Dār al-Shāmiyya and Damascus: Dār al-Qalam, 1416/1997), 5:600–1.
18. Al-Ḥusayn b. ʿAbdallāh al-Ṭībī, *al-Kāshif ʿan ḥaqāʾiq al-sunan (sharḥ Mishkāt al-maṣābīḥ)*, ed. ʿAbd al-Ḥamīd Hindāwī, 13 vols. (Mecca: Maktabat Nizār Muṣṭafā al-Bāz, 1417/1997), 7:2263; Muḥammad Anwar Shāh Kashmīrī and Aḥmad ʿAlī al-Sahāranpūrī, *Jāmiʿ al-Tirmidhī al-muḥashshā* (Karachi: Qadīmī Kutubkhāne, n.d.), 1:265; Murtaḍa al-Zabīdī, *Itḥāf al-sāda al-muttaqīn*, 10 vols. (Beirut: Muʾassasat al-Tārīkh al-ʿArabī, 1994), 5:287.
19. Al-Baghawī, *Sharḥ al-sunna*, ed. Shuʿayb al-Arnāʾūṭ and Muḥammad Zuhayr al-Shāwīsh, 15 vols. (Beirut: al-Maktab al-Islāmī, 1403/1983), 9:9; see also idem, *al-*

*Tahdhīb fī fiqh al-imām al-Shāfi'ī*, ed. 'Ādil Aḥmad 'Abd al-Mawjūd and 'Alī Muḥammad Mu'awwaḍ, 8 vols. (Beirut: Dār al-Kutub al-'Ilmiyya, 1418/1997), 5:298. See also al-Munāwī, *Fayḍ al-qadīr*, 1:465–6, 2:629.

20. Kamāl al-Dīn Muḥammad b. Mūsā al-Damīrī, *al-Najm al-wahhāj fī sharḥ al-Minhāj*, 10 vols. (Jedda: Dār al-Minhāj, 1425/2004), 6:396; al-Sarakhsī, *Mabsūṭ*, 5:23; 'Abd al-Ḥayy al-Laknawī, *'Umdat al-ri'āya 'alā sharḥ al-Wiqāya*, ed. Ṣalāḥ Muḥammad Abū al-Ḥājj, 7 vols. (Beirut: Dār al-Kutub al-'Ilmiyya, 2009), 3:89; Roy P. Mottahedeh, "The Shu'ûbîyah Controversy and the Social History of Early Islamic Iran," *International Journal of Middle East Studies* 7 (1976): 177; Louise Marlow, *Hierarchy and Egalitarianism in Islamic Thought* (Cambridge: Cambridge University Press, 1997), 21–22, 98–99.
21. Al-Damīrī, *al-Najm al-wahhāj*, 6:396; al-Sarakhsī, *Mabsūṭ*, 5:23; al-Laknawī, *'Umdat al-ri'āya*, 3:89; Mottahedeh, "The Shu'ûbîyah Controversy," 177; Marlow, *Hierarchy and Egalitarianism in Islamic Thought*, 21–22, 98–99.
22. Shāh Walī Allāh Dihlawī, *Ḥujjat Allāh al-bāligha*, ed. Sa'īd Aḥmad Palanpūrī, 2 vols. (Deoband: Maktabat Ḥijāz, 2010), 2:384, 388.
23. Marlow, 42–87.
24. Marlow, 53.
25. Abū al-Ḥasan al-'Āmirī, *Kitāb al-I'lām bi-manāqib al-islām*, ed. Aḥmad 'Abd al-Ḥamīd Gharāb (Riyadh: Dār al-Aṣāla, 1408/1988), 175–76; Marlow, 88–89.
26. Marlow, 145–46.
27. *Ṣaḥīḥ al-Bukhārī*: *kitāb aḥādīth al-anbiyā', bāb qawl Allāh ta'ālā wa'ttakhadha Allāh ibrāhīm khalīl.*
28. Ibn 'Abd Rabbih, *al-'Iqd al-farīd*, ed. Mufīd Muḥammad Qumayḥa, 8 vols. (Beirut: Dār al-Kutub al-'Ilmiyya, 1404/1983), 2:226.
29. Al-Rāzī, *Mafātīḥ*, 28:114.
30. Ḍiyā' al-Dīn Baranī, *Fatāvāy-i Jahāndārī*, ed. Afsar Saleem Khan (Lahore: Research Society of Pakistan, 1972), 298. Peter Jackson describes Baranī as particularly grumpy and bitter in his old age, having fallen from royal favor and become bitter about those he considered to be low-born replacing him; Peter Jackson, *The Delhi Sultanate* (Cambridge: Cambridge University Press, 1999), 292.
31. Muḥammad b. Abī Bakr al-Shillī Bā'alawī, *al-Mushri' al-rawī fī manāqib al-sāda al-kirām Āl Abī 'Alawī*, 2 vols. (Cairo: al-Maṭba'a al-'Āmira, 1319/1901–2), 1:9–18, 20–21, 117–18.
32. Mīr Ghulām 'Alī Āzād, *Ma'āthir al-kirām*, 1:58–59; Ibn Ḥajar al-Haytamī, *al-Ṣawā'iq al-muḥriqa fī al-radd 'alā ahl al-bida' wa'l-zandaqa*, ed. 'Ādil Shūsha et al. (Mansoura: Maṭba'at Fayāḍ, 1429/2008), 632–33; Shihāb al-Dīn Dawlatābādī, *Manāqib-i sādāt* (Kitābkhāni-yi Majlis-i Shūrāyi Millī, Tehran, Ms. 14124), 11a; Ibn 'Arabī, *al-Futūḥāt al-makkiyya*, ed. Aḥmad Shams al-Dīn, 9 vols. (Beirut: Dār al-Kutub al-'Ilmiyya, 1420/1999), 1:298 (Chapter 29).
33. Barbara Metcalf, *Perfecting Women: Mawlana Ashraf 'Ali Thanawi's* Bihishti Zewar (Berkeley: University of California Press, 1990), 25.
34. Ashraf 'Alī Thanawi, *Heavenly Ornaments*, trans. Molana Muhammad Mahomedy (Karachi: Zam Zam, 2016), 412–14 (thanks to Fareeha Khan for this information).
35. Aḥmad Riḍā Khān, *Jadd al-mumtār 'alā Radd al-muḥtār*, 4 vols. (Karachi: Maktabat al-Madīna, 1426/2006), 3:554–556 (collated by followers from his other writings and placed as commentary).
36. *Ṣaḥīḥ Muslim*: *muqaddima.*

37. For these rights, see Brown, *Slavery & Islam*, 299–301; For example, al-Muzanī, *Mukhtaṣar*, ed. ʿAbd al-Qādir Shāhīn (Beirut: Dār al-Kutub al-ʿIlmiyya, 1998), 133; al-Khaṭṭābī, *Maʿālim al-sunan*, 3:319.
38. Louis Dumont, *Homo Hierarchicus: The Caste System and its Implications*, trans. Mark Sainsbury (Chicago: University of Chicago Press, 1970, French original, 1966), 20.
39. Ibid., 16.
40. Rafiuddin Ahmed, *The Bengal Muslims 1871–1906: A Quest for Identity*, 2nd edn. (Delhi: Oxford University Press, 1988), xxiv–xxv.
41. Sayyid Sulaymān al-Nadwī, *Khuṭubāt-i Madrās* (Karachi: Majlis-i Nashriyyāt-i Islām, n.d.), 192–95.
42. See Yoginder Sikand, *Islam, Caste and Dalit-Muslim Relations in India* (New Delhi: Global Media Productions, 2004), 37; Yūsuf al-Marʿashlī, *Nathr al-jawāhir wa'l-durar fī ʿulamā' al-qarn al-rābiʿ ʿashar*, 2 vols. (Beirut: Dār al-Maʿrifa, 1427/2006), 1:987.
43. For Muslim scholars discussing the obstacle that *kafā'a* rules presented to convincing low-caste Hindus to convert to Islam as well as potential consequences, see Sikand, *Islam, Caste and Dalit-Muslim Relations in India*, 30, 40, 60, 71.
44. Masood Alam Falahi, "Caste and Caste-Based Discrimination among Indian Muslims – Part 1: The domination of 'high' caste Muslims that parallels the Hindu case," *NewageIslam*, 31 October 2010, https://web.archive.org/web/20211008213548/https://www.newageislam.com/books-documents/caste-caste-based-discrimination-among-indian-muslims-part-1-domination-high-caste-muslims-that-parallels-hindu-case/d/3611.
45. Sikand, 29–32.
46. Khalid Saifullah Rahmani (Khālid Sayf Allāh Raḥmānī), *Jadīd fiqhī masā'il* (Karachi: Zamzam Publishers, 2010), 40–69.
47. Ḥabīb al-Raḥmān al-Aʿẓamī, *Ansāb wa kifā'at kī sharʿī ḥaythiyyat* (Azamgar: Markaz Taḥqīqāt wa Khadamāt ʿIlmiyya, 1420/1999).
48. Muftī Taqī ʿUthmānī, *Takmilat Fatḥ al-mulhim*, 3 vols. (Karachi: Maktabat Dār al-ʿUlūm Karātshī, 2004), 1:109. Muftī Taqī's father, the prominent Deoband scholar Muftī Shafīʿ ʿUthmānī, was embroiled in a controversy over a fatwa he issued, published in 1933 as *Nihāyat al-arab fī ghāyat al-nasab*, which laid out the classical Ḥanafī arguments on *kafā'a*. Muftī Shafīʿ quoted medieval speculations on how some professions, such as butchery and weaving, could negatively affect one's character. This had not been controversial in the premodern period, hidden in the pages of voluminous works like al-Ghazālī's *Iḥyā'*. But published without explanation or mitigation in the twentieth century it was an outrage. The late nineteenth and early twentieth centuries had seen Julaha (weaver) communities in north India mobilize and argue along Islamic lines for greater respect from the high caste Muslims who taxed them. The controversy was severe enough that Muftī Shafīʿ had to step down from Deoband's fatwa committee for several years. See editor's introduction to *Nihāyat al-arab* in Muftī Shafīʿ ʿUthmānī, *Jawāhir al-fiqh* (Karachi: Maktabat Dār al-ʿUlūm Karāchī, 2010), 4:319–20.
49. Qāḍīkhān, *Fatāwā Qāḍīkhān*, 1:309. The Fez scholar Muḥammad al-Mahdī al-Ṣakhrāwī, by contrast, wrote a small book entitled *Khulāṣat al-adab fī al-radd ʿalā man zaʿama anna sharaf al-ʿilm afḍal min sharaf al-nasab*; al-Kattānī, *Salwat al-anfās*, 2:40.
50. Wright, *Living Knowledge in West African Islam*, 98. See also Seeseman, "The *Shurafā'* and the 'Blacksmith'."

51. Ibn Taymiyya, *Majmūʿat al-fatāwā*, 19:20–21.
52. Ibn Abī al-ʿIzz al-Ḥanafī, *al-Tanbīh ʿalā mushkilāt al-Hidāya*, ed. ʿAbd al-Ḥakīm Muḥammad Shākir and Anwar Ṣāliḥ Abū Zayd, 5 vols. (Riyadh: Maktabat al-Rushd, 1424/2003), 3:1219–1223.
53. ʿAbd al-ʿAzīz Bin Bāz, *al-Ḥulal al-ibrīziyya min al-taʿlīqāt al-bāziyya*, ed. ʿAbdallāh Mānīʿ al-Rūqī, 4 vols. (Riyadh: Dār al-Tadmuriyya, 1428/2007), 3:68.
54. Ibn ʿUthaymīn, *al-Sharḥ al-mumtiʿ ʿalā Zād al-mustaqniʿ*, 15 vols. (Riyadh: Dār Ibn al-Jawzī, 1427/2006), 12:100–5.
55. Al-Albānī, *Silsilat al-aḥādīth al-ṣaḥīḥa*, 3:56–7 (#1067).
56. https://web.archive.org/web/20211023025836/https://binbaz.org.sa/fatwas/3285/%D9%85%D9%88%D9%82%D9%81-%D8%A7%D9%84%D8%A7%D8%B3%D9%84%D8%A7%D9%85-%D9%85%D9%86-%D8%A7%D9%84%D8%AA%D9%85%D9%8A%D9%8A%D8%B2-%D8%A7%D9%84%D8%B9%D9%86%D8%B5%D8%B1%D9%8A
57. "Fairy tale goes flat for Marine who wed princess," *NBC News*, 2 December 2004, https://web.archive.org/web/20220104161211/https://www.nbcnews.com/news/amp/wbna6628334; "Report: Bahraini Princess Who Wed Marine Goes Home," *Yahoo News*, 29 September 2001, https://web.archive.org/web/20011001233401/http://dailynews.yahoo.com/h/nm/20010929/re/people_princess_dc_1.html.
58. Jessi Streib, *The Power of the Past: Understanding Cross-Class Marriages* (Oxford: Oxford University Press, 2015), 6, 246.
59. ʿAbd al-Ghanī Mujaddidī Dihlawī, *Injāḥ al-ḥāja sharḥ Sunan Ibn Mājah* (Delhi: Maṭbaʿat Ḥusayn Muḥammad, 1273/1856–7), 350; al-Suyūṭī at al., *Sunan Ibn Mājah al-muḥashshā* (Karachi: Qadīmī Kutubkhāne, n.d.), 141.
60. Muḥammad Zayd Maẓāhirī Nadwī, ed., *Dictums of al-Muḥaddith Shaykh Yūnus Jaunpūrī Collection 1*, trans. Muhammad Talha (Leicester, UK: Qurtuba Books, 1440/2019), 47–49.
61. Sikand, 33.
62. *Sunan* of Abū Dāwūd: *kitāb al-ʿilm, bāb al-ḥathth ʿalā ṭalab al-ʿilm*. There has been criticism of the Hadith's *isnād*, but al-Sakhāwī and Ibn Ḥajar summarize that it definitely has some basis (*aṣl*) in Prophetic speech; al-Sakhāwī, *al-Maqāṣid al-ḥasana*, 293.
63. See, for example, al-Albānī, *Fatāwā al-Shaykh al-Albānī*, ed. ʿUkāsha ʿAbd al-Mannān al-Ṭayyibī (Cairo: Maktabat al-Turāth al-Islāmī, 1994), 400; Kawtharī, *Maqālāt*, 101. This is often also expressed as the difference between the main ruling a mufti is giving and what they offer as the *waraʿ*, or more electively pious, demanding, and cautious option.
64. Harry D. Krause and David P. Meyer, *Family Law* ([Eagan, MN]: Thomson West, 2007), 51.
65. Lawrence Rosen, *The Anthropology of Justice: Law as Culture in Islamic Society* (Cambridge: Cambridge University Press, 1989), 11–17.
66. Even when practicality requires barring parties to res judicata cases from availing themselves of changes to the laws involved in those cases (no doubt made for good, public-policy reasons), 'public policy' interest is still allowed as a theoretical exception. See Harrington v. Vandalia-Butler Board of Ed. (1981), 649 F.2d 434.
67. Wael Hallaq, *Sharīʿa* (Cambridge: Cambridge University Press, 2009), 159–63. See also Uriel Simonsohn, *A Common Justice: The Legal Allegiances of Christians and Jews under Early Islam* (Philadelphia: University of Pennsylvania Press, 2011), 34.

68. See Adolf Grohmann, "Arabischen Papyri aus den Staatlichen Museen zu Berlin," *Der Islam* 22, no. 1 (1935), 30–31, 37–40; Khan, *Arabic Documents*, 144–50; Muḥammad b. Yūsuf al-Kindī, *Kitāb al-Wulāt wa Kitāb al-Quḍāt*, ed. Rhuvon Guest (Beirut: al-Ābā, 1908 and Leiden: Brill, 1912), 367; Judith Tucker, *In the House of the Law*, 71.
69. ʿAbd al-Qādir al-Badāyūnī, *Muntakhab-t-Tawarikh*, trans. T. Wolseley Haig (Delhi: Idarah-i-Adabiyat-i-Delli, 1899), 3:147.
70. Though U.S. states have substantially withdrawn from prescribing norms of and for marriage, divorce, etc., leaving them to private individuals, they have not done so for child custody. There, the notion of the state-defined 'best interest of the child' still theoretically prevails. Yet, despite U.S. courts' stated aim of promoting and safe-guarding the best interest of the child, they routinely rubber stamp marital separation and child custody agreements; E. Gary Spitko, "Reclaiming the 'Creatures of the State': Contracting for Child Custody Decision-making in the Best Interests of the Family," *Washington & Lee Law Review* 57, n. 1139 (2000): 1160, n. 65; Jana B. Singer, "The Privatization of Family Law," *Wisconsin Law Review* 1443 (1992): 1475.
71. Sahar Bazzaz, *Forgotten Saints: History, Power, and Politics in the Making of Modern Morocco* (Cambridge, MA: Harvard University Press, 2010), 98.
72. The sultan, Mawlāy Ismāʿīl, eventually collected about 81 signatures from scholars supporting his proposal, either because of threats or because they were toadies of the ruler; El Hamel, *Black Morocco*, 163–74.

## 10. CONCLUSION

1. See Aimee Van Wagenen, "The Promise and Impossibility of Representing Anti-Essentialism: Reading Bulworth through Critical Race Theory," *Race, Gender & Class* 14, n. 1–2 (2007): 157–77.
2. Stuart White, "Freedom of Association and the Right to Exclude," *Journal of Political Philosophy* 5, n. 4 (1997): 386, 390.
3. Kwame Anthony Appiah, "Racisms," 12.
4. Nathaniel Adam Tobias ~~Coleman~~, "The Duty to Miscegenate," (PhD dissertation, University of Michigan, 2013), 119. The line through the last name represents the author's rejection of a name "imposed . . . in an act of attempted ownership."
5. I have grounded Nathaniel Adam Tobias ~~Coleman~~'s reasoning in his progressive sensibility, but it may well simply stem from how severe sexual racism has been in the U.S. Even Garcia, whose definition of racism is the most minimalist and classically liberal, does not support Appiah's notion that racial discrimination in the intimate sphere could be morally acceptable. The dynamics of inter-racial attraction and marriage in the U.S., he explains, cannot be separated from "deep-seated racial antipathy"; Garcia, "The Heart of Racism," 270.
6. Melina Constantine Bell, "John Stuart Mill's Harm Principle and Free Speech: Expanding the Notion of Harm," *Utilitas* 33 (2021): 168 ff. Bell provides a good introduction to the debate over whether racist or sexist speech is harmful enough to merit prohibition or simply offensive, with what she calls the 'civil rights' camp

(including Critical Race Theorists like Mari Matsuda) arguing for forms of prohibition and the 'civil liberties' camp arguing against.

7. Amia Srinivasan, "Does anyone have the right to sex?" *London Review of Books*, 40, n. 6 (22 March 2018), https://www.lrb.co.uk/the-paper/v40/n06/amia-srinivasan/does-anyone-have-the-right-to-sex; idem, *The Right to Sex* (New York: Farrar, Straus and Giroux, 2021), 84.
8. ~~Coleman,~~ "The Duty to Miscegenate," 24–25, 35, 41–46, 55–56, 105–6, 121–25. See also John Johnson, *It Ain't All Good: Why Black Men should not Date White Women* (Gilbert, AZ: African American Images, 2004).
9. Matt Donnelly, "Netflix's Ted Sarandos Defends Dave Chappelle Special in Staff Memo: 'Artistic Freedom' Is Different for Stand-Up," *Variety*, 11 October 2021, https://web.archive.org/web/20211015135640/https://variety.com/2021/film/news/dave-chappelle-stand-up-netflix-controversy-1235086299/; Kylie Cheung, "Dave Chappelle and the warped self-victimhood of transphobes," *Salon*, 9 October 2021, https://web.archive.org/web/20211023033629/https://www.salon.com/2021/10/09/dave-chappelle-terf-transphobia-joyce-carol-oates/.
10. See Reihan Salam, "Is It Racist to Date Only People of Your Own Race?" *Slate*, 22 April 2014, https://web.archive.org/web/20210713143847/https://slate.com/news-and-politics/2014/04/okcupid-and-race-is-it-racist-to-date-only-people-of-your-own-race.html; Iman Amrani, "Is it racist to have a preference in whom you date?," *New Statesman*, 19 July 2017, https://web.archive.org/web/20210713145228/https://www.newstatesman.com/politics/uk/2017/07/it-racist-have-preference-whom-you-date; Hemanth Nalamothu, "The Un-Beddability of Brown Dudes," *Medium*, 25 December 2019, https://web.archive.org/web/20210713143508/https://medium.com/pulpmag/the-un-f-ability-of-brown-dudes-4b782a24bf5c; Chris Stokel-Walker, "Why is it OK for online daters to block whole ethnic groups?," *Guardian*, 29 September 2018, https://web.archive.org/web/20210713144901/https://www.theguardian.com/technology/2018/sep/29/wltm-colour-blind-dating-app-racial-discrimination-grindr-tinder-algorithm-racism; Damona Hoffman, "Date Lab: Daters say they don't tolerate racial bias. Their actions say they do have racial preferences," *Washington Post*, 25 June 2020, https://web.archive.org/web/20210713144303/https://www.washingtonpost.com/lifestyle/magazine/date-labdaters-say-they-dont-tolerate-racial-bias-their-actions-say-they-do-have-racial-preferences/2020/06/18/0d1eace4–a039–11ea-9590–1858a893bd59_story.html; idem, "Dear Damona: IS it racist if I don't want to date outside my own race," *Los Angeles Times*, 19 July 2020, https://web.archive.org/web/20210614210820/https://www.latimes.com/lifestyle/story/2020–07–19/dear-damona-is-it-racist-to-not-do-interracial-dating; Kristen Pizzo, "Can White People Have Racial Dating Preferences?," *An Injustice!*, 19 January 2020, https://web.archive.org/web/20210614211505/https://aninjusticemag.com/can-white-people-have-racial-dating-preferences-3cf1dd5dd528?gi=afc6e2175828.
11. Chris Stokel-Walker, "Why is it OK for online daters to block whole ethnic groups?," *Guardian*, 29 September 2018, https://web.archive.org/web/20210713144901/https://www.theguardian.com/technology/2018/sep/29/wltm-colour-blind-dating-app-racial-discrimination-grindr-tinder-algorithm-racism.
12. Srinivasan, *The Right to Sex*, 90.
13. Brynn Tannehill, "Is Refusing to Date Trans People Transphobic?" *Advocate*, 14 December 2019, https://www.advocate.com/commentary/2019/12/14/refusing-date-trans-people-transphobic.

14. See Sabrina Strings, *Fearing the Black Body: The Racial Origins of Fat Phobia* (New York: New York University Press, 2019), 6–9.
15. Sonalee Rashatwar, "Fatphobia Is Not a Sexual Preference," *Wearyourvoicemag*, 9 October 2019, https://web.archive.org/web/20211012202407/https://www.wearyourvoicemag.com/fatphobia-is-not-a-sexual-preference/.
16. Srinivasan, *The Right to Sex*, 90.
17. David M. Buss, "Sex differences in human mate preferences: Evolutionary hypotheses tested in 37 cultures," *Behavioral and Brain Sciences* 12 (1989): 1–49.
18. Garabed Eknoyan, "A History of Obesity, or How What Was Good Became Ugly and Then Bad," *Advances in Chronic Kidney Disease* 13, n. 4 (2006): 423–24.
19. Gert Stulp, Abraham P. Buunk and Thomas V. Pollet, "Women want taller men more than men want shorter women," *Personality and Individual Differences* 54 (2013): 877–883; B.C. Jones, A.C. Little and D.I. Perrett, "Why are symmetrical faces attractive?" *Advances in Psychology Research* 19 (2003): 145–166.
20. Stefano Ghirlanda, Liselotte Jansson, and Magnus Enquist, "Chickens Prefer Beautiful Humans," *Human Nature* 13, n. 3 (2002): 383–89. Thanks to Chris Haufe for his help on this.
21. Kyndall Cunningham, "Is it Racist to Have a Racial Dating Preference?" *Rewire*, 21 December 2018, https://web.archive.org/web/20210721174622/https://www.rewire.org/racist-racial-dating-preference/?__cf_chl_captcha_tk__=pmd_a42abf04af415d31aacd974e20862283062766d5-1626889495-0-gqNtZGzNAvijcnBszQh6.
22. See Judish Shulevitz, "Racism, Schmacism: Opposing Intermarriage," *Slate*, 1 May 2000, https://slate.com/news-and-politics/2000/05/racism-schmacism-opposing-intermarriage.html, accessed October 2021.
23. *Ṣaḥīḥ al-Bukhārī*: *kitāb al-nikāḥ, bāb al-akfā' fī al-dīn.*
24. *Muwaṭṭa'* of Mālik: *kitāb qaṣr al-ṣalāt fī al-safar, bāb jāmi' al-ṣalāt.*
25. *Sunan* of Abū Dāwūd: *kitāb al-adab, bāb fī al-nahy 'an al-tajassus.*
26. Al-Bayhaqī, *al-Sunan al-kubrā*, 8:578–579; Abū Bakr Muḥammad al-Kharā'ṭī, *Makārim al-akhlāq*, ed. Ayman 'Abd al-Jabbār al-Baḥīrī (Cairo: Dār al-Āfāq al-'Arabiyya, 1419/1999), 152. See also Wael Hallaq, *The Impossible State* (New York: Columbia University Press, 2014).
27. ~~Coleman~~, 102; John S. Mill, *On Liberty*, 4th ed. (London: Longmans, Green, Reader & Dyer, 1869), 139.
28. Mohammad Harith Aslam Khawaja, "Are Racial Preferences in Dating Morally Defensible?" *Episteme* 30, n. 2 (2019): 40–41.
29. *Sunan* of Abū Dāwūd: *kitāb al-adab, bāb fī al-tafākhur bi'l-aḥsāb.*
30. Toni Morrison, *Playing in the Dark*, 52.
31. Muḥammad Iqbāl, *Ḍarb-i kalīm* (Lahore: n.p., [1934]), 7. Thanks to my student Saad Yacoob for telling me about this verse.

## APPENDIX I: ANTIBLACK STATEMENTS ATTRIBUTED TO IMAM AL-SHĀFI'Ī

1. Abū Bakr al-Bayhaqī, *Manāqib al-Shāfi'ī*, ed. al-Sayyid Aḥmad Ṣaqr, 2 vols. (Cairo: Dār al-Turāth, 1970), 2:134–135.

2. Fakhr al-Dīn al-Rāzī, *Manāqib al-imām al-Shāfiʿī*, ed. Aḥmad Ḥijāzī al-Saqqā (Cairo: Maktabat al-Kulliyyāt al-Azhariyya, 1406/1986), 331–332; Ibn Ḥajar, *Tawālī al-taʾsīs li-maʿālī Muḥammad b. al-Idrīs*, ed. Abū al-Fidāʾ ʿAbdallāh al-Qāḍī (Beirut: Dār al-Kutub al-ʿIlmiyya, 1406/1986), 117–8. The editions of al-Bayhaqī's and al-Rāzī's books have the word for prison (*al-ḥabs*) appearing as 'Ethiopians' (*al-ḥabash*), which makes no sense in the meaning of the story. The correct *ḥabs* appears in later works citing the story from al-Bayhaqī, such as the *Tawālī* of Ibn Ḥajar, the *Kashf al-khafā* of al-ʿAjlūnī, and the *Tuḥfat al-aḥwadhī* of al-Mubārakpūrī.
3. Al-Khaṭīb, *Tārīkh Baghdād*, 13:84–85.
4. Al-Bayhaqī, *Manāqib al-Shāfiʿī*, 2:206; Abū Nuʿaym al-Iṣbahānī, *Ḥilyat al-awliyāʾ*, 9:129.
5. Abū Nuʿaym, *Ḥilya*, 9:119, 70.
6. Ibn al-Jawzī, *al-Muntaẓam*, 14:186.
7. Abū Nuʿaym, *Ḥilya*, 9:107.
8. Ibid., 7:54.
9. Ibid., 9:128.
10. Al-Bayhaqī, *Sunan al-kubrā*, 9:480.
11. Al-Bayhaqī, *Manāqib al-Shāfiʿī*, 2:353–4.
12. ʿAbd al-Karīm al-Samʿānī, *al-Ansāb*, ed. ʿAbd al-Raḥmān b. Yaḥyā al-Muʿallimī (Hyderabad: Dāʾirat al-Maʿārif al-ʿUthmāniyya, 1382/1962), 12:35–6; al-Ḥākim al-Naysābūrī, *al-Mustadrak*, 1:307; al-Dhahabī, *Siyar*, 17:175; al-Kawtharī, *Maqālāt*, 40–43.
13. Al-Bayhaqī, *Manāqib al-Shāfiʿī*, 1:146; 2:291.
14. Ibn Abī Ḥātim al-Rāzī, *Ādāb al-Shāfiʿī wa manāqibuhu*, ed. ʿAbd al-Ghanī ʿAbd al-Khāliq (Beirut: Dār al-Kutub al-ʿIlmiyya, 1424/2003), 97.
15. See Kristina Richardson, "Blue and Green Eyes in the Islamicate Middle Ages," *Annales islamologiques* 48, n. 1 (2014): 13–29.

## APPENDIX II: AFRICAN LANGUAGES AND BLACKNESS – GENERAL

1. See Andrew F. Clark, "'The Ties that Bind': Servility and Dependency among the Fulbe of Bundu (Senegambia), c. 1930s – 1980s," *Slavery & Abolition* 19, n. 2 (1998): 98–9.
2. Roy Dilley, "Specialist Knowledge Practices of Craftsmen and Clerics in Senegal," *Africa: J. of the Intl. African Inst.* 79, n. 1 (2009): 55, 66. This may be linked to the usage of 'white talismans' versus 'black talismans' in Mauritanian Ḥassāniyya Arabic, which have a similar valence. See Taine-Cheikh, "La Mauritanie en noir et blanc," 98.
3. John R. Taylor and Thandi G. Mbense, "Red dogs and rotten mealies: How Zulus talk about anger," in *Speaking of Emotions*, ed. Angeliki Athanasiadou and Elzbieta Tabakowska (Berlin: De Gruyter, 1998), 203.

## APPENDIX III: RACE, BLACKNESS, AND LANGUAGE IN THE SAHEL

1. Catherine Taine-Cheikh has proposed that this word might have been adapted from the Tuareg word *ekăwel*, meaning 'to be very dark or black,' which is used similarly in that language. Aguadé and Meouak suggest that *kwār* comes from the Algerian Arabic word *gawrī* (pl. *gwār*) for unbeliever, which in turn is a version of the Turkish *gāvur* gloss of *kāfir*. Other possibilities are that *kwār* might also originate in a sub-Saharan placename such as Kawar in Chad. Or it might come from *kwaara*, the Zarma word for village or town (Lameen Souag, personal communication); Taine-Cheikh, "La Mauritanie en noir et blanc," 101–2; Jorge Agoudé and Mohamed Meouak, "A propos de l'etymologie du mot 'kūri' en arabe dialectal ḥassāniyya," *Al-Qantara*, 14, n. 1 (1993): 217–219; Ruf, *Ending Slavery: Hierarchy, Dependency and Gender in Central Mauritania*, 38–39, 302. Thanks to Lameen Souag for a great deal of help on this.
2. Hall, *A History of Race in Muslim West Africa*, 13, 36 ff., 57–64, 69 ff., 100–3.
3. Champault, *Une Oasis du Sahara Nord-Occidental – Tabelbala*, 282; Ruf, 39.
4. Champault, *Une Oasis du Sahara Nord-Occidental*, 40.
5. William B. Hodgson, *Notes on Northern Africa, the Sahara and Soudan* (New York: Wiley & Putnam, 1844), 22, 27, 29.
6. Al-Idrīsī, *Nuzhat al-mushtāq fī ikhtirāq al-āfāq*, 1:27.
7. See Conrad and Fisher, "The Conquest that Never Was," 31. See also Cleaveland, *Becoming Walata*, 79, 130.
8. Bello, *Infāq al-maysūr*, 1:335–36; Naylor, *From Rebels to Rulers*, 72, 130.
9. Mauro Nobili, *Sultan Caliph, and the Renewer of the Faith* (Cambridge: Cambridge University Press, 2020), 104, 109, 223; William B. Hodgson, *Notes on Northern Africa, the Sahara and Soudan*, 50. For Fulani claims about their Islamic manifest destiny, see David Robinson, *The Holy War of Umar Tall* (Oxford: Clarendon Press, 1985), 82.
10. Moore, *Travels to the inland parts of Africa*, 30. See also Zehnle, *A Geography of Jihad*, 23.
11. Hodgson, *Notes on Northern Africa*, 49.
12. Zehnle, *A Geography of Jihad*, 230, 470.
13. Donaldson, "Clear Language: Script, Register and the N'ko Movement of Manding-Speaking West Africa," 175, and personal communication; Park, *Travels in the Interior of Africa*, 298.
14. Hunwick and Powell, *The African Diaspora in the Mediterranean Lands of Islam*, 56 (a selection from F.J.G. Mercadier, *L'Esclave de Timimoun*).
15. Bello, *Infāq al-maysūr*, 1:147, 335 (regarding the people of Ghobir and Mali); Thomas Hodgkin, *Nigerian Perspectives*, 2nd ed. (London: Oxford University Press, 1975), 78–81.
16. *Mauritania's Campaign of Terror: State-Sponsored Repression of Black Africans* (Human Rights Watch, 1994), 18, 72.
17. Hall, *History of Race*,73–74.
18. Wright, *Living Knowledge in West African Islam*, 68–9.
19. Usman dan Fodio, *al-Ajwiba al-muḥarrara ʿan as'ila muqarrara*, ed. ʿAbdallāh Muḥammad Sīfāw (Gusau, Nigeria: Iqra', 2013, in in *Mukhtārāt al-Shaykh ʿUthmān bin Fūdī*), 2:173–74; idem, *Ḍiyā' al-siyāsāt*, ed. Muḥammad Mūdī Shūnī (Gusau,

Nigeria: Iqra', 2013), 64; Bello, *Infāq al-maysūr*, 1:134–35, 147, 149–51, 226, 254, 335.

20. Mazrui, "The Re-invention of Africa," 70. See Muddathir 'Abd al-Rahim, "Arabism, Africanism, and Self-Identification in the Sudan," in *The Southern Sudan*, ed. Dunstan Wai (London: Frank Cass, 1973), 33; Heather J. Sharkey, "Arab Identity and Ideology in Sudan: The Politics of Language, Ethnicity, and Race," *African Affairs* 107, n. 426 (2008): 31.
21. Zehnle, *A Geography of Jihad*, 470.
22. Ruf, *Ending Slavery*, 40.
23. See Bruce Hall, "Bellah Histories of Decolonialization . . .," *Intl. J. of African Hist. Studies* 44, n. 1 (2011): 63; Jean-Claude Zeltner, "Histoire des Arabes sur les rives du lac Tchad," *Annales de l'Université d'Abidjan* F, n. 2 (1970): 163–4; Starratt, "Tuareg Slavery and Slave Trade," 88–9.
24. David Robinson, *Paths of Accommodation* (Athens, OH: Ohio University Press, 2000), 78, 304; Bruce Hall, *A History of Race in Muslim West Africa*, 13, 36 ff., 57–64, 69 ff., 100–3; Ghislaine Lydon, *On Trans-Saharan Trails: Islamic Law, Trade Networks, and Cross-Cultural Exchange in Nineteenth-Century Western Africa* (Cambridge: Cambridge University Press, 2009), 309–310.
25. Specifically, this is in the Koyra Chiini variant of Songhay; Hunwick, ed., *Timbuktu and the Songhay Empire*, lviii. Thanks to Lameen Souag for help on this.
26. Z. Wright, "The Islamic Intellectual Tradition of Sudanic Africa, with Analysis of a Fifteenth-Century Timbuktu Manuscript," *The Palgrave Handbook of Islam in Africa*, ed. F. Ngom et al. (London: Palgrave, 2020), 60–61, 65–66; Lamin Sanneh, *The Jakhanke Muslim Clerics* (Lanham, MD: University Press of America, 1989).
27. Al-Bartilī, *Fatḥ al-shukūr*, 313; Hunwick, *Timbuktu*, 73–74.
28. Zachary Wright, *Living Knowledge in West African Islam*, 276–78. For another expression of this, see Abubakar Tafawa Balewa, *Shaihu Umar*, trans. Mervin Hiskett (Princeton: Markus Wiener, 1989), 19.
29. Étienne Goyémidé, *Le dernier survivant de la caravane* (Paris: Hatier, 1985), 17. For awareness of this novel I am grateful to Françoise Ugochukwu's article, "Goyemide on Slavery: The Liberating Power of The Word," *Nordic Journal of African Studies* 15, n. 1 (2006): 27–41. Elsewhere in the novel one only finds white/black imagery in the coloring of the villagers' loyal dog, who tracks the enslaved villagers along with the village's most skilled hunter and ultimately portends their freedom; Goyémidé, *Le dernier survivant de la caravane*, 77.
30. Ibid., 117.
31. Ibid., 22–23, 47.
32. Ibid., 43, 47.
33. Ibid., 32, 43, 47, 75.
34. Ibid., 32, 36, 52, 45, 47.
35. Ibid., 46.
36. Ibid., 35, 37.
37. Abubakar Tafawa Balewa, *Shaihu Umar*, 19, 53, 64.
38. See John Ryle, "Disaster in Darfur," *New York Review of Books*, 12 August 2004, https://web.archive.org/web/20210618164808/https://www.nybooks.com/articles/2004/08/12/disaster-in-darfur/.
39. Dunstan Wai, *The African-Arab Conflict in the Sudan* (New York: Africana Publishing, 1981), 1.

40. Amir Idris, "Historicizing Race, Ethnicity, and the Crisis of Citizenship in Sudan and South Sudan," *Middle East Journal* 73, n. 4 (2019): 591–606. The variability in phenotype, between 'black' and 'Arab,' even in one family was noted by James Bruce in 1772; H.A. MacMichael, *The Tribes of Northern and Central Kordofán* (Cambridge: Cambridge University Press, 1912), 226, see also v.
41. "Report of the International Commission of Inquiry on Darfur to the United Nations Secretary-General," 25 January 2005, 129.
42. "Peace Under Fire: Sudan's Darfur Crisis," *The New Humanitarian*, 8 May 2004, https://web.archive.org/web/20210511175856/https://www.thenewhumanitarian.org/fr/node/227853. See also Alex de Waal, "Darfur's deep grievances defy all hopes for an easy solution," *The Guardian*, 25 July 2004, https://www.theguardian.com/society/2004/jul/25/internationalaidanddevelopment.voluntarysector.
43. Alex de Waal, "Counter-Insurgency on the Cheap," *London Review of Books* 16, n. 5 (5 August 2004), https://www.lrb.co.uk/the-paper/v26/n15/alex-de-waal/counter-insurgency-on-the-cheap.

## APPENDIX IV: RACE AND BLACKNESS IN THE HORN OF AFRICA

1. See Timothy Fernyhough, "Women, Gender History, and Slavery in Nineteenth-Century Ethiopia," in *Women and Slavery*, ed. Miers et al., 216–17; Cf. Amanuel Isak Tewolde, "Encounters with Race: Eritrean Refugees and Asylum-Seekers' Self-identification Practices in Relation to the Experience of Racialisation in Post-Apartheid South Africa," (PhD dissertation, University of Pretoria, 2018), 43; Hagar Salamon, "Slavery among the 'Beta-Israel' in Ethiopia: Religious Dimensions of Inter-group Perceptions," *Slavery & Abolition* 15, n. 1 (1994): 72–88.

## APPENDIX VI: THE CURSE OF HAM IN ISLAMIC SOURCES

1. Al-Ṭabarī, *Jāmiʿ al-bayān*, 1:480–82; Ibn Qutayba, *al-Maʿārif*, ed. Tharwat ʿUkāsha, 4th ed. (Cairo: Dār al-Maʿārif, 1981), 11.
2. Al-Nawawī, *Tahdhīb al-asmāʾ waʾl-lughāt*, ed. ʿAbduh ʿAlī Kūshak, 4 vols. (Manama: Maktabat Niẓām Yaʿqūbī, 1434/2013), 1:264; Ibn al-Jawzī, *Kitāb al-Tabṣira*, 2 vols. (Beirut: Dār al-Kutub al-ʿIlmiyya, 1406/1986), 1:25; Muḥammad b. ʿAbdallāh al-Kisāʾī, *Tales of the Prophets*, trans. Wheeler M. Thackston (Chicago: Kazi Publications, 1997), 23, 31.
3. Al-Kisāʾī, *Tales of the Prophets*, 31.
4. Abū Nuʿaym, *Dalāʾil al-nubuwwa*, ed. Muḥammad Rawwās Qalʿajī, 2 vols. (Beirut: Dār al-Nafāʾis, 1406/1986), 2:640; al-Nawawī, *Tahdhīb al-asmāʾ*, 1:264.
5. Ibn Qutayba, *al-Maʿārif*, 21, 26.

6. Al-Dīnawarī, *al-Akhbār al-ṭiwāl*, ed. ʿAbd al-Munʿim ʿĀmir and Jamāl al-Dīn al-Shayyāl (Beirut: Dār Iḥyā' al-Turāth al-ʿArabī, 1960), 12.
7. Ibn ʿAbd al-Barr, *al-Qaṣd wa'l-amam bi-taʿrīf uṣūl ansāb al-ʿarab wa'l-ʿajam* (Cairo: Maktabat al-Quds, 1350/1932), 10, 23, 26 (Ibn ʿAbd al-Barr is the authority later drawn on by Ibn Khaldūn, see Hopkins, *Corpus of early Arabic source for West African history*, 332).
8. Ibn Qutayba, *al-Maʿārif*, 25–26; al-Masʿūdī, *Murūj al-dhahab*, 1:27, 33; idem, *Akhbār al-zamān* (Beirut: Dār al-Andalus, 1416/1996), 107. For an unusual account of Ham and his wife begetting black children, attributed to Kaʿb al-Aḥbār, see al-Kisā'ī, *Tales of the Prophets*, 105, 107–8.
9. Whitford, *The Curse of Ham in the Early Modern Era*, 25–27.
10. Al-Ṭabarī, *Tārīkh*, 1:117, 125–26, 129; idem, *Tafsīr al-Ṭabarī*, ed. Aḥmad Shākir, 24 vols. (Beirut: Mu'assasat al-Risāla, 1420/2000), 15:325 (on Quran 11:40); Ibn Ḥajar, *Tahdhīb al-tahdhīb*, 7:123. The report via ʿAṭā' is also found in al-Thaʿlabī, *ʿArā'is al-majālis* ([Bulaq]: n.p., 1335/1916), 36. I am embarrassed to say that in my book *Slavery & Islam* I misidentified the early figure quoted in one of al-Ṭabarī's *isnād*s as the Successor al-Sā'ib b. Mālik al-Thaqafī – a stupid instance of not seeing an *ibn*. But the *isnād* to ʿAṭā' al-Khurāsānī is even less reliable than the one I had mistaken it for, so my point stands *a fortiori*.
11. Ibn Ḥajar, *Tahdhīb al-tahdhīb*, 9:37.
12. Ibn al-Mulaqqin, *Mukhtaṣar al-Mustadrak li'l-ḥāfiẓ al-Dhahabī*, ed. Saʿd ʿAbdallāh Āl Ḥumayyid and ʿAbdallāh Ḥamad al-Luḥaydān, 8 vols. (Riyadh: Dār al-ʿĀṣima, 1991), 2:999.
13. Badr al-Dīn al-Zarkashī, *al-La'ālī al-manthūra fī al-aḥādīth al-mashhūra*, ed. Muḥammad Luṭfī al-Ṣabbāgh (Beirut: al-Maktab al-Islāmī, 1417/1996), 172 (no comment but noting al-Ḥākim's *taṣḥīḥ*); al-Sakhāwī, *al-Maqāṣid al-ḥasana*, 137 (no comment but noting al-Ḥākim's *taṣḥīḥ*); al-Suyūṭī, *al-Durar al-muntathira fī al-aḥādīth al-mushtahira*, ed. Maḥmūd al-Arnā'ūṭ and Muḥammad Badr al-Dīn Qahwajī (Kuwait: Maktabat Dār al-ʿUrūba, 1408/1988), 152 (no comment but noting al-Ḥākim's *taṣḥīḥ*); al-ʿAjlūnī, *Kashf al-khafā*, 1:299; Muḥammad al-Amīr al-Kabīr al-Mālikī, *al-Nukhba al-bahiyya fī al-aḥādīth al-makdhūba ʿalā khayr al-bariyya*, ed. Zuhayr al-Shāwīsh (Beirut: al-Maktab al-Islāmī, 1988/1409), 41 (forgery); al-Dhahabī, *Mīzān*, 4:595; al-Albānī, *Silsilat al-aḥādīth al-ḍaʿīfa*, #4543; Ibn ʿAsākir, *Tārīkh madīnat Dimashq*, 62:278. Thanks to Muntasir Zaman for his help with this.
14. Al-Dhahabī, *Siyar aʿlām al-nubalā'*, 17:175.
15. Muḥammad b. Ismāʿīl al-Ṣanʿānī, *Irshād al-nuqqād*, ed. Muḥammad Ṣubḥī Ḥasan Ḥallāq (Beirut: Mu'assasat al-Rayyān, 1413/1992), 52. See also Nuʿmān b. Maḥmūd al-Ālūsī, *al-Āyāt al-bayyināt fī ʿadam samāʿ al-amwāt ʿind al-ḥanafiyya al-sādāt*, ed. Muḥammad Nāṣir al-Dīn al-Albānī (Beirut: al-Maktab al-Islāmī, 1405 /1985), 69.
16. Jamāl al-Dīn al-Zaylaʿī, *Naṣb al-rāya li-aḥādīth al-Hidāya*, ed. Muḥammad ʿAwwāma (Jeddah: Mu'assasat al-Rayyān, 1997), 1:342.
17. Haytamī, *Mablagh al-arab fī fakhr al-ʿarab*, 24, 94–95.
18. Ibn ʿAbd al-Ḥakam, *Futūḥ Miṣr wa'l-maghrib*, 7–8.
19. Al-Masʿūdī, *Akhbār al-zamān*, 107.

## APPENDIX VII: ISLAM AND CASTE IN SOUTH ASIA

1. C. Bouglé's definition of caste is the division of people into a hierarchy that is hereditary and distinguished by separation in matters of marriage and contact, with this division falling along labor and occupation. See C. Bouglé, *Essais sur le régime des castes*, *apud* Dumont, *Homo Hierarchicus*, 21. For a review of efforts to define caste, see ibid., 267–68. More recently, Isabel Wilkerson has listed the essential elements of a caste system as 1) this system being rooted in divine will or order; 2) heritability; 3) endogamy and marriage control; 4) purity and pollution; 5) occupation; 6) dehumanization and stigma; 7) the use of cruelty and violence to enforce it; and 8) a system imbued with clear values of inherent superiority and inferiority; Isabel Wilkerson, *Caste* (New York: Random House, 2020).
2. Al-Bīrūnī says that Indians called their system colors or lineage, *jātaku*; al-Bīrūnū, *Taḥqīq mā li'l-Hind* (Hyderabad: Dā'irat al-Maʿārif al-ʿUthmāniyya, 1377/1958), 76.
3. Adrien C. Mayer, *Caste and Kinship in Central India* (Berkeley: University of California Press, 1966), 34–35, 40; Yoginder Sikand, *Islam, Caste and Dalit-Muslim Relations in India*, 22.
4. Sikand, "Islam and Caste Inequality among Indian Muslims," *Countercurrents*, 15 February 200[?], https://web.archive.org/web/20211010043807/https://roundtableindia.co.in/index.php?option=com_content&view=article&id=5379%3Acaste-and-caste-based-discrimination-among-indian-muslims-part-1&catid=124%3Aresearch&Itemid=140. See also Ahmed, *The Bengal Muslims*, 13, 20.
5. Dumont, *Homo Hierarchicus*, 207, 210.
6. Hamza Alavi "Kinship in West Punjab Villages," *Contributions to Indian Sociology* 6 (1972): 1–27.
7. Imtiaz Ahmad, "Caste and Kinship in a Muslim Village of Eastern Uttar Pradesh," in *Family, Marriage and Kinship among Muslims in India*, 342; ibid., 5–17.
8. Sylvia Vatuk, "Identity and Difference or Equality and Inequality in South Asian Muslim Society," in *Caste Today*, ed. C.J. Fuller (Oxford: Oxford University Press, 1996), 232–33.
9. Arthur F. Buehler, "Trends of ashrāfization in India," in *Sayyids and Sharifs in Muslim Societies*, ed. Morimoto Kazuo (Abingdon, UK: Routledge, 2012), 231–46.
10. See Santosh Kumar Rai, "Social histories of exclusion and moments of resistance: The case of Muslim Julaha weavers in colonial United Provinces," *Indian Economic and Social History Review* 55, n. 4 (2018): 549–74.
11. For a discussion of Muslim denial of the existence of caste, see Abdul Malik Mujahid, *Conversion to Islam: Untouchables' Strategy for Protest in India* (Chambersburg, PA: Anima Books, 1989), 109–12.
12. Prashant K. Trivedi, Fahimuddin, et al., "Does Untouchability Exist among Muslims? Evidence from Uttar Pradesh," *Economic & Political Weekly* 51, n. 15 (9 April 2016), https://web.archive.org/web/20211006224044/https://www.epw.in/journal/2016/15/insight/does-untouchability-exist-among-muslims.html. See also Frank S. Fanselow, "The Disinvention of Caste among Tamil Muslims," in *Caste Today*, ed. C.J. Fuller (Oxford: Oxford University Press, 1996), 202–26. See also Sikand, *Islam, Caste and Dalit-Muslim Relations in India*, 71–72, 82, 85–88.
13. Sikand, *Islam, Caste and Dalit-Muslim Relations in India*, 21 ff.

14. Hasan Ali, "Elements of Caste among the Muslims in a District in Southern Bihar," in *Caste and Social Stratification among Muslims in India*, ed. Imtiaz Ahmad, 24; Arshad Alam, "Contextualising Muslim Identity: Ansaris, Deobandis, Barelwis," *Economic and Political Weekly* 44, n. 24 (2009): 86–92.
15. Fanselow, "The Disinvention of Caste among Tamil Muslims," 216.
16. Partap C. Aggarwal, "Kinship and Marriage among the Meos of Rajestan," in *Family, Marriage and Kinship among Muslims in India*, ed. Imtiaz Ahmad, 265–96.
17. Syed Ali, "Collective and Elective Ethnicity: Caste among Urban Muslims in India," *Sociological Forum* 17, n. 4 (2002): 604.
18. Arshad Alam, "Challenging the Ashrafs: The Politics of Pasmanda Muslim Mahaz," *Journal of Muslim Minority Affairs* 29, n. 2 (2009): 173; Ahmed, *The Bengal Muslims*, 13–15, 18.
19. https://thewire.in/caste/caste-among-indian-muslims-real-why-deny-reservation

# Index